Calling This Place Home

With best wishes

Joan Jensen

MINNESOTA HISTORICAL SOCIETY PRESS

Calling This Place Home

Women on the Wisconsin Frontier,
1850–1925

JOAN M. JENSEN

Joan M. Jensen

Publication of this book was supported in part with funds provided by the Ken and Nina Rothchild Endowed Fund for Women's History

www.mhspress.org

The Minnesota Historical Society Press is a member of the Association of American University Presses.

Manufactured in the United States of America

10 9 8 7 6 5 4 3 2 1

∞ The paper used in this publication meets the minimum requirements of the American National Standard for Information Sciences—Permanence for Printed Library Materials, ANSI Z39.48-1984.

International Standard Book Number 13:
    978-0-87351-563-4 (cloth)
International Standard Book Number 10:
    0-87351-563-3 (cloth)

Library of Congress
Cataloging-in-Publication Data

Jensen, Joan M.
Calling this place home : women on the
    Wisconsin frontier, 1850–1925 /
    Joan M. Jensen.
        p.   cm.
Includes bibliographical references and index.
ISBN-13: 978-0-87351-563-4 (cloth : alk. paper)
ISBN-10: 0-87351-563-3 (cloth : alk. paper)
    1. Women—Wisconsin—History.
    2. Women—Wisconsin—Social conditions.
    3. Wisconsin—History—19th century.
    4. Wisconsin—History—20th century.
    I. Title.
HQ1438.W5J46 2006
305.409775'09034—dc22   2006002282

Sections of various chapters have appeared in different form in the following publications:
    "Out of Wisconsin: Country Daughters in the City," *Minnesota History* 59.2 (Summer 2004): 48–61.
    " 'I'd Rather be Dancing': Wisconsin Women Moving On," *Frontiers* 22.1 (2001): 1–20.
    "Sexuality on a Northern Frontier: The Gendering and Disciplining of Rural Wisconsin Women, 1850–1920," *Agricultural History* 73.2 (Spring 1999): 136–67.
    "The Death of Rosa: Sexuality in Rural America," *Agricultural History* 67.4 (Fall 1993): 1–12.

For Mary Ann Reynolds
Family Archivist and Storyteller

Table of Contents

Preface

Many people have helped with this long project. Any list would be only a partial recognition of those who offered support, encouragement, and bits of information to add to the mosaic. Relatives, friends, archivists, librarians, strangers who responded to e-mail and letter all made this a richer and fuller account than I could have composed alone.

I also thank the institutions that partially funded this project over the years. New Mexico State University gave me much-needed time away from teaching with sabbaticals and summer grants. In spring 1988 I received a Senior Fulbright Fellowship that allowed me to teach and to study immigrant history with Dirk Hoerder and Christiane Harzig at the University of Bremen. The National Endowment for the Humanities offered me early support with a Summer Grant in 1989 and a Travel to Collections Grant in 1990. The New Mexico Endowment for the Humanities helped with a Summer Grant in 1994. In 1995, when I realized that Native women had to play a larger part in my story, Peter Iverson generously invited me to sit in on his Native History graduate seminar at Arizona State University, and the Newberry Library offered me a fellowship to catch up on recent Native American history. Finally, a research grant in 2001 from the Minnesota Historical Society allowed me to trace the lives of some of these Wisconsin women in the Twin Cities.

A few people were key in helping me finish this long project. Monica Torres, who fifteen years ago helped me conceptualize *Loosening the Bonds: Mid-Atlantic Farm Women, 1850–1950,* moved back to Las Cruces just in time to assist me in organizing the final draft of this second regional study of rural women. With amazing patience, Karen Lerner helped me sort out fifteen years of footnotes. My partner John Gustinis read the manuscript, offered me a first edit, cooked, cleaned, and took me on afternoon bird-watching walks to lift my flagging spirits. At the Minnesota Historical Society, Debbie Miller, Ann Regan, and Anne Kaplan continued to encourage my work on rural women as they have over the years. The enthusiasm of my editor, Wisconsin-born Shannon Pennefeather, carried me through the last trying months of revision. Members of the Rural Women's Studies Association (RWSA) were a constant source of inspiration for the larger task of writing rural women into history. Most importantly, my cousin Mary Ann Reynolds never wavered in her conviction that the history of the people of this region was important and that trying to understand it was a worthwhile task. This book is dedicated to her. I hope that this study will open the landscape of north-central Wisconsin to continued study by those whose lives it has touched.

Introduction

Most of the events in this book take place in northern central Wisconsin. Described in the early nineteenth century by eastern Euro-Americans as a part of the "Old Northwest" or even the "Far West," it became in the late nineteenth century the "West" and then part of the "Midwest." Euro-Americans spread westward from eastern states and south from what is now Canada. So too did a number of Native groups. Europeans immigrated from all directions. By 1850, the people of many cultures called this place home. To Native peoples already there, it was their homeland.

Settler families there participated actively in the Civil War: husbands and sons went off to the battlefront; women and older men farmed and supported the Union cause from the home front. After the war, farm families settled the southeastern area of the state rapidly. In north-central Wisconsin in 1860, however, only a sprinkling of non-Native settlements existed. Much of the land was only marginal for farming. On this northern frontier, Natives and settlers still jostled for space to live. They experienced the transition from a fur-trading to a lumbering economy, and as that latter economy waned at the turn of the century, all people scrambled for economic alternatives. This northern Wisconsin frontier was similar to that west of the Mississippi during the late nineteenth and early twentieth centuries. Both frontiers shared common characteristics: a swift and ruthless exploitation and destruction of natural resources, settlement by non-Native peoples, enclosure and containment of Native communities in circumscribed areas which the national government attempted to control.

Wisconsin has long been the locale of a search for theories about the settlement process. When in the early twentieth century Frederick Jackson Turner imagined the frontier as a process of settlement that influenced national character, he was living in and looking back at his youth in Wisconsin. To some extent, his theories inscribed the early peopling of southern Wisconsin by Euro-Americans. He envisioned a frontier moving west across the country under the impetus of white men while white women were subsumed under the term "family." In his theory, indigenous Native peoples were quickly replaced by "pioneers."

Turner's vision of the West and the frontier process has been challenged during the last thirty years by many historians attempting to restore a more diverse and complex history to the region. This book is a part of that revisioning of the West and the frontier. The multicultural heartland was the scene of great rural population change. The filling by European and American settlers of northern and western space, of a land already settled by people native to this area, is still the defining story of the Midwest. Non-Native settlers filled up this northern frontier as they did the western frontier in the late nineteenth century, like a great wave moving through the land. The wave flooded this land and then receded as economies and cultures could no longer sustain the large numbers of people. To stay in place settlers developed tourism and dairying, while experts offered them advice on modernizing their farms and cultures. Through this great wave, buffeted by settlers and their governments, Native communities survived at great cost to themselves and to their cultures.

This book covers the years from 1850 to 1925, a time during which the lumbering economy grew, attracting new immigrants. Once most of the profitable forests were gone, the settlers turned to food production and recreation for a growing industrial and urban nation. This book spans a period during which reformers and communities tried to come to terms with the quick industrialization and settlement of the hinterland. It explores three aspects of rural women's lives: building economies, protecting families and communities, and making new homes. It ends with the exodus of settler daughters to early-twentieth-century cities and includes a final chapter on how we may remember the histories of the women absent in most accounts of this era, the women who formed the bedrock of the families and communities that occupied this area.

Native and settler women lived through dramatic changes in the time covered by this book. During this period, immigrants from Europe and Americans from the East arrived on this northern frontier to claim parts of these Native homelands as their own. Through these changes, Native women preserved their cultures, adapted to new circumstances, and created new cultures; settler women did the same. Both groups played a crucial social and economic role as the fur trade declined in importance, the timbering industry grew, and tourism and dairying came to dominate the economy.

As in fur trading, women played an essential role in the timber economy. They worked in the forests and in the small villages that formed around the new enterprises. Mostly they tended the subsistence farms that produced the labor and food supplies for the developing lumber economy. They raised children and managed small log homes, made clothing, cleared and planted fields, harvested wild and domestic crops, created communities, nurtured traditional cultures, and blended old and new. They were not alone. Their children worked with them; men and older boys joined them when not at work in forest industries. Women sold surplus food, clothing, handwork, and household items to local stores.

The Native women in this study are part of three northern Wisconsin nations: the Lac du Flambeau Band of Chippewa (part of the Ojibwe or Anishinaabe), the Menominee, and the Ho-Chunk. The Lac du Flambeau Chippewa and the Menominee occupied territories retained by them under nineteenth-century treaties. The Wisconsin Ho-Chunk, those who refused to leave for Nebraska when the government forcibly attempted to resettle them, eventually occupied and homesteaded small, scattered parcels of land. The women of these three Native nations shared a common economic history in the fur trade and a larger culture that developed in the western Great Lakes area south of Lake Superior and west of Lake Michigan. Native people did not disappear after signing treaties with the American government. Some did move west, but many remained, refusing to leave their homelands and by various strategies managing to build new communities. These women are part of three nations that persisted into the lumbering economy and fashioned new ways to live within the encircling wave of outsiders who settled in their midst. Each nation had its own history, its own culture, and its own differences within those cultures. Individual women chose their own paths as well.

Natives and settlers shared this regional culture but faced different conditions. Chippewa and Menominee communities, now assigned to specific areas of their homelands called "reserves" or "reservations," faced colonial efforts to control them and their families as well as their freedom of movement. Their task was to adopt new crops and to make the remaining timberlands sustainable, which the Menominee did well by developing new lumbering techniques and sawmills. The Ho-Chunk, who had taken up scattered farmlands, were in a more isolated and precarious position. They increased their skill in making and selling handmade objects to tourists who found the remaining islands of forest more attractive to visit now that they opened onto lakes and scenic wonders. Above all, women had the primary task of preserving their families and adapting and passing on as much of their cultural traditions as possible. North-central Wisconsin was the homeland of women from these three quite different Native nations. Out of necessity, they had to share their lands with others.

The settler women who were arriving in large numbers by the mid-nineteenth century were equally diverse. I have selected women from four counties—Lincoln, Taylor, Clark, and Marathon—to represent these settlers. By the turn of the century the natural forest bounty of north-central Wisconsin was almost all harvested. What remained was sometimes called the "cutover," literally, land left after the trees were removed. It consisted of stumps, brush, trees not profitable to harvest, and huge quantities of stones. The two northernmost counties, Lincoln and Taylor, were part of a heavily wooded and then logged-over section that agricultural experts judged unsuitable for modern farming methods. In these areas communities developed economies based on tourism.

The two more southerly counties, Clark and Marathon, although once heavily timbered and then cut over, were suited to the development of modern dairying and cheese making. Well into the twentieth century, men continued to travel into the woods during the winter to cut timber from the remaining forests. That work brought cash to sustain families while they established themselves on small farms. As lumbering disappeared, farm families looked for new ways to create income on the farms that now had to sustain them year-round and produce the cash that men had previously brought from cutting down the forest. Dairying seemed the best way to use men's labor to bring in cash. And so in the first two decades of the twentieth century, the cows that women had kept for family use and to sell surplus milk, butter, and cheese locally were transformed into small efficient herds cared for by women and men, with local cheese factories where families turned surplus milk into cheese and marketed it to the growing cities of Milwaukee, Chicago, St. Paul, and Minneapolis. The transition to dairying was slow, however, and created far fewer jobs for young women than young men. Thus, during the first decades of the twentieth century many daughters left for the cities to work in the growing urban economies.

The rise of tourism, the flourishing dairy business, and the new ways women sustained the economy and families of north-central Wisconsin are at the core of this book. My task was to trace the working lives of women of different traditions—Native American and Euro-American—as the older fur trading culture gave way to the new lumbering culture and it, in turn, gave way to the dairying and tourism cultures. I have tried to return women to this landscape, to place them in these northern forests where they worked, and to show how they moved from one economy to the other as lumbering, farming, and tourism succeeded fur trading. I have collected stories about their lives and exploits, their memories, and subsequent memories about them.

Over the last fifteen years, I have studied both written texts and visual images in this attempt to uncover and recreate the lives of women who left few written records of their own. By piecing together bits of information gleaned from many sources, I have been able to reveal and illuminate the lives of some of the most silent, forgotten people in our history: female, rural, mostly immigrant or Native American individuals who settled on what became a northern frontier, a place where communities developed side by side with some shared and some very different constraints on their daily lives.

A number of my most interesting discoveries resulted from noticing a photograph and then trying to find out about the woman it portrayed. At other times, a photograph graphically explained the landscape in ways that words could hardly convey. A photograph of a white steepled church rising out of a clearing surrounded by huge tree stumps eloquently explained what the "cutover" meant to early settler families. These images became an essential part of my research as I looked for ways to "read" their content and interpret them.

I found thousands of documents that yielded up pieces with which to recreate the patterns of communities. More than one hundred collections in the Wisconsin Historical Society gave me many early clues, but sometimes important pieces rested far from Wisconsin. Such was the case with the records of the Sisters of the Sorrowful Mother, the women who in this region of Wisconsin established most of the early hospitals, a number of which survive to the present. Their records reside at Our Lady of Sorrow Convent in Broken Arrow, Oklahoma.

Stories about women's lives are a big part of this book, and I use them to illuminate the past in various ways. Each chapter begins with the story of an individual woman who experienced the broader themes related in that section. Some are stories I recreated after searching many sources, such as the story of Rosalie and her daughters Jane and Kate, women of mixed Native and French heritage who taught Menominee children for more than three decades. Another story belongs to Isabella, a young Cherokee who arrived at Lac du Flambeau as a government nurse, later resigned to marry a Chippewa man, and then stayed on to serve as community nurse and midwife for the next sixty years. The story of my grandmother Matilda Rauscher, who lived in our home for a decade in the 1950s, threads through this larger story and is expanded in the section that discusses the ways in which women provided for their old age. My mother Theresa's story helped me tell of poor farm girls who badly wanted education but who often had to drop out of school to help their families.

In this study, I combine individual family histories with an account of the surrounding region and peoples. Some are family stories, shared with me by my own family and by others who still remember their grandmothers and great-grandmothers. Family histories are the legacy of the poor, the foreign born, and the disfranchised; as such they are important to the story of any region. I want these women to be a part of our shared vision of the past and their descendants to share in the shaping of the future. What they make of this history is, of course, up to them. I hope those who read this book become more conscious of how many stories make up our past. Landscape, as Keith Basso recently wrote, is rich in memory. Each place should remind us of the layers of culture associated with it. I wrote this book to help me reach this layered understanding. I hope it will help others to do the same.

This book is a scholarly history, but I have chosen to include autobiographical information as well, mainly in the form of comments about my research experiences. These experiences range from clambering up a narrow wooden stairway in the log cabin where my mother grew up and finding her seventh-grade textbooks from the 1910s to standing alone in the cemetery of a huge Polish church now boarded up and abandoned in a Wisconsin cornfield. These moments were memorable for me, and I hope they will make history more immediate for readers as well.

I originally began this study with settler women, one of whom was my grandmother. Midway through the research, I realized that it could not be a story of settler women alone: Native women were constantly present in the written and visual sources I located. It became evident that although the story would take longer for me to write, it could best be told with many grand-mothers, both settler and Native. I expanded my work in four contiguous settler communities with predominantly immigrant populations to include the three Native communities.

The core of this story remains rooted in four counties of north-central Wisconsin and the three Native communities pushed to their periphery as Euro-American settlers moved in. The three Native nations form a triangle surrounding the four settler counties, the Chippewa to the north, the Menomi-nee to the southeast, and the Ho-Chunk to the southwest. In 1850, these three Native communities, together with peoples of the Potawatomi, Oneida, and Stockbridge-Munsee Band of the Mohican Nation, controlled most of northern Wisconsin.

Native people did not disappear from the historical records after 1850, as most Euro-American accounts assured me they had. They continuously crossed these lands individually and in groups during the late nineteenth century. Moreover, as they developed their own economies and cultures in the early twentieth century, they provided important examples of the ways women lived within the lumbering and tourist economies, especially in the case of the Menominee and Lac du Flambeau peoples. The Ho-Chunk community was affected by its dispersal throughout the area, although its center remained Black River Falls in Jackson County, where today the Ho-Chunk Nation main-tains its headquarters. Families live scattered, with some clusters near Marshfield and in other predominantly settler communities.

If their presence first induced me to study the history of these groups of Native rural women, several intellectual reasons also dictated their inclusion. Women absent from Euro-American settlement narratives were very present in the minds of the people in northern Wisconsin when I began this research. The land had been Native, rights had been retained by treaty, and in the 1980s conflict flared up over those rights. Land issues have been reopened, and the narratives that historians create to describe the past are being challenged. No story of this region can be created from settler experiences alone. Although it disrupted what had been a tidy research plan, I could not ignore contempo-rary as well as historical Native activities and claims. They have been a contin-uing part of the settler story. Native people were displaced—not replaced.

A NOTE ON NOMENCLATURE

As times change, terms change. Many people of the Lac du Flambeau community, although part of the larger Anishinaabe or Ojibwe culture, still call themselves Chippewa. The Menominee have retained the Menominee name. The people once called Winnebago prefer to be called Ho-Chunk. I use the terms *Native, Indigenous,* or *Indian* to refer to the people of the Menominee, Chippewa, and Ho-Chunk nations. Women from these three communities had very different histories, as I have tried to make clear, but they were subject to the same federal policies and shared important experiences as Euro-Americans took possession of their ancestral lands and encroached on lands reserved for them by the federal government. Whenever referring to specific communities, I use the name that community seems to prefer. For people of mixed French and Native heritage, I use the term *Métis.* Usually I reserve this term for women who chose to remain within Native cultures. For those who lived outside their home community, I simply use the term *mixed heritage.*

Settler or *Euro-American* refers to those who immigrated into and settled this area, displacing Native peoples in the process. While Native women were the first "settlers," I have found it more convenient to use this term to refer to the newcomers, both those who settled in the eastern part of the United States and then migrated to the Wisconsin area and those who immigrated directly from Europe.[1]

Scholars still wrangle over the term *frontier.* I have retained it here to emphasize the process of settlement by Euro-Americans. Parts of northern Michigan, Wisconsin, and Minnesota retained many of the characteristics of an early settlement phase long after the southern parts of these states had been well settled and were major agricultural producers. In this sense, these northern areas shared much with territories west of the Mississippi during the late nineteenth and early twentieth centuries, when Native and settler communities still contested the boundaries of land and culture.

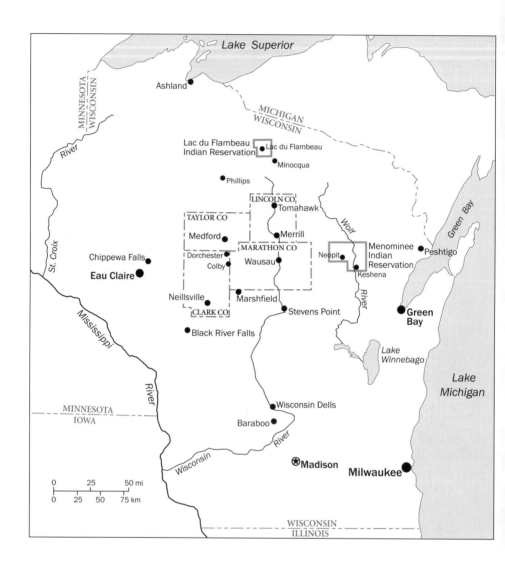

Calling This Place Home

I

Building Economies

1

Moving In, Staying Put

Matilda Rauscher, my maternal grandmother, arrived in northern Wisconsin in 1892. She brought few possessions with her as she traveled from her small Bohemian village of Christianburg north to Hamburg, then by boat to New York and by train to Wisconsin. Although she was accompanied by a sister and brother-in-law and planned to join her future husband, Karl Schopper, who was already in northern Wisconsin, she came as a single woman who expected first to work in the lumber economy, then to marry and own a farm with her husband. Matilda was part of a larger German migration from the Austro-Hungarian Empire late in the nineteenth century. She had moved from a land that could not sustain its agricultural population as the region industrialized.

The land to which she moved was still occupied by Indigenous people, a population recently diminished through forced relocation to lands west of the Mississippi. The federal government failed in its effort to clear the area of its Indigenous inhabitants during the early nineteenth century. Resistance to removal by a number of tribes made that policy impossible to implement, and the government had signed treaties reserving parts of their homelands to the Ojibwe, Menominee, and other tribes. Despite attempts by the government to keep Ho-Chunk people in Nebraska, many returned to their homelands as well. Thus, when Euro-American settlers began to arrive in large numbers after 1850, they settled among Native people.

Early settlers commented on the presence of Indigenous people who still had villages nearby or who moved seasonally through the land to hunt and gather food and to visit old burial sites. Mixed-heritage families sometimes settled on land near trading posts. Many Catholics traced their lineage to these prominent fur-trade families in which Native women had important economic and social positions. Other families rejoined communities that maternal ancestors had left to marry incoming French men, moving back to land tribes had retained. Still others simply lived on the margins of the growing and more numerous settler communities. By the late nineteenth century a few had passed into the settler population and kept their family histories to themselves.

Between 1850 and 1892, when my grandmother arrived, settlers had gradually labeled the remaining Native people as outsiders and moved their own stories to the center of their historical memory. Euro-Americans now called this place their home and told their histories beginning with the arrival of early settlers. This chapter begins with the story of Anna, the daughter of one of these early outsider families.

The Settlers
Anna's Story [Lansworth Stanley, born in Wisconsin, 1870–1964]

In 1993, the Dorchester librarian received an undated handwritten manuscript titled "The Autobiography of Anna Leona Lansworth Stanley." In the autobiography, Anna recalled her childhood in Dorchester, carrying on an old Yankee female tradition of reviewing her life and memorializing the place she once called home by writing about it.

Anna explained that in 1876, when she was six years old, she arrived in Dorchester, Clark County, with her family. Anna Lansworth was born in 1870 on the family farm in Dane County, about twenty miles from Madison, in southern Wisconsin. Anna's father, John, then a thirty-year-old Civil War veteran, went north in 1872 to locate land and to build a log cabin for the family. Four years later, John, Anna's mother, Susan, and their daughters moved to this northern frontier. Dorchester was not yet a town when Anna arrived, just a clearing around a sawmill next to the railroad station, the rails a slash through the forest.[1]

Stump land. When settlers reached north-central Wisconsin, they faced roads that were little more than trails through the forest. Muddy in spring, washboarded in summer, roads were easiest traveled in winter, when families could use horse-drawn sleighs.

Anna's father had already built a log cabin two miles south of Dorchester, and Susan and her daughters made their way through the forest to it. The nearest trading post was at the town of Colby, and John had to blaze his own trail there to pack groceries to the family cabin six miles away. When the road was passable with oxen it still required a full day to get to Colby for supplies. Ho-Chunk and Chippewa bands hunted and gathered all around the family. Anna remembered her family and theirs gathering great quantities of wild blackberries, raspberries, strawberries, blueberries, cranberries, cowslip greens, and watercress. Settlers and Natives seemed to coexist peacefully.

But the naming of the town Dorchester, after a village in southwest England near the coast in Dorset County, signaled the beginning of Euro-American outposts in this land of the Ho-Chunk and Chippewa. By 1873, the government had extinguished all Native claims to land formerly reserved to them under the treaty of 1825, opening that land to settlement. Dorchester grew quickly. By 1880, it had at least two hotels: Central House and Donnelly's House. It had a number of general merchandise stores, including Miltmore Brothers (which housed the U.S. post office), Benson's, and La Boussier's. It had a boot and shoe shop, a gristmill, a number of saloons, and a Catholic church to which a missionary from Medford came each Sunday to preach. The Baptists had no church, nor did any of the Lutherans or Methodists, but the streets were busy with activity, for four hundred people lived in Dorchester by 1881. The town had already outgrown its one-room schoolhouse, and more than a hundred students crowded the two-story frame school building.

As Dorchester grew, the Lansworth family moved from their farm into town, and Anna's mother, Susan, opened a boarding house. At one time, with the help of a maid, the boarding house accommodated seventeen lumbermen. Susan also made all the clothes for herself and her seven children—all girls—on her Howe sewing machine. When she sewed, the younger children played with her scrap bag and button box, building families of dolls, while the older ones went to school with well-supplied lunch boxes and cared for their siblings when they returned. Both Susan and her husband, who had obtained medical training while in the army, were practical nurses. They were also temperance supporters. When Susan had a chance, she cornered lumbermen, urging them to take the temperance pledge. "My mother was very busy," Anna concluded. She remembered a youth filled with contentment and happiness for the simple things of life. The people were kindhearted, the little mill town like a family. Or so it seemed to Anna as she wrote of these early days.

In Dorchester the Baptist church congregation, which Anna's grandfather served as pastor, became an important part of her life. She remembered attending Sunday school and church service. On Sunday afternoons, her mother gathered the family around her Loring and Blake organ, the only one in town, to sing hymns. Then they attended evening service. Anna belonged to the

Baptist Young People's Union, and while her parents were members of the Good Templar temperance organization, she joined the Juvenile Temple, which drew kids with its formal ritual, regalia, and secret passwords. The Sunday school had a library from which Anna could borrow books and her mother ordered the *Youth Companion*. She read the Alger books, the "Oliver Optics" series. *Oliver Twist, The Mill on the Floss, The Bushbangers of Australia* were some of the titles she remembered. And she "adored" the trashy romances she managed to find and read.

Anna completed the eighth grade, took her examination for the certificate, and began high school in nearby Colby. In 1887, at seventeen, she graduated and then taught school for two years in Clintonville, a small town in Waupaca County, east of Stevens Point. She rotated among three county schools there, staggering three-month terms. She lived frugally and saved her earnings, hoping to enter Weyland Academy, a Baptist-supported institution established northeast of Madison at Beaver Dam in 1855. Anna was typically Yankee in her desire to move up and out of the small village that she had found so comforting in childhood.

From its origin, Weyland had accepted women, and when Anna arrived in 1890, thirty young women were housed at a dormitory called Warren Cottage. Anna was the only woman in the class of eight that graduated in 1894, but undergraduate women were prominent in the ceremonies that beautiful June day. Young women competed for prizes for instrumental music and "declamation." Anna played her guitar and sang a song she wrote especially for the occasion. Her talk, "The Victories of Defeat," was one of the featured declamations. In the following years, women took an even more prominent place at the academy. By 1896, half the graduating class was female.[2]

After graduation Anna easily found teaching jobs in the city schools. Eight years later, she married a fellow Weyland graduate who was then a high school principal. In Clintonville, where the family settled and her husband became superintendent of schools, Anna raised four daughters. In the 1920s and 1930s, she become active on the library board, served as president of the Woman's Club, wrote poetry, and worked for the local newspaper. Fifty years after graduating from Weyland, she still kept in touch, sending word of her activities for the alumni newsletter. Sometime during these years she wrote down her early experiences growing up in Dorchester.[3]

WAVES OF SETTLEMENT

Anna's autobiography was almost a classic story of American-born settlers' migration into northern Wisconsin. Her family's move was part of a second wave of settlement that occurred after the lower third of the state had been occupied. Settlers spread northward in the 1850s as the Indigenous Nations negotiated for land and rights with an impatient U.S. government. Composed mainly of American-born and European immigrants, the settlers pushed agricultural development northwest along river valleys and old pathways to the heavily forested and less fertile areas approaching Stevens Point, an outpost and stepping-off place for the northern and western forests.

This agricultural salient within the timber economy opened the way for two more periods of settlement. In the late 1860s and 1870s, new settlers moved north of Stevens Point into the upper Wisconsin River Valley, where a new outpost named Wausau claimed a place on the river, and they moved westward along the upper Black River, where Marshfield formed another outpost. From Wausau and Marshfield, newer immigrants moved onto the logged-over land that lumber companies disposed of cheaply. A fourth settlement wave of the 1880s to the 1920s scattered would-be farmers across the stumpy land in the counties that form the core of this study—Clark and Marathon to the south, Lincoln and Taylor in the heart of the cutover. Frequently referred to as Wisconsin's "last frontier," this area has been described by geographer Robert Ostergren as "never exclusively agricultural or totally successful." Environmental conditions, Ostergren wrote, could only be "exploited" through "special adaptations, endless hard work, and a certain amount of good fortune."[4]

American-born women were among the first wave to reach northern Wisconsin. During the Civil War these women took over most of the farm work. A visitor to southern Wisconsin in 1863 noted the presence of women in the fields. She expected to see German women but not an American-born middle-aged woman from Cattaraugus, New York. There was no help to be hired, the New Yorker explained, for all the young men, including her sons, had gone to war. She and her daughters, like their neighbors, were working in the wheat harvest, even though her man did not like it. It was an unusual sight, the visitor noted: "women were in the field everywhere, driving the reapers, bending and shocking and loading grain.... How skillfully they drove the horses round and round the wheat field.... Each hard-handed, brown toiling woman was a heroine."[5]

The hard-handed, sun-tanned, toiling women did their work neatly and precisely and were glad to do it for the war effort, despite the displeasure of some men. Southern Wisconsin agriculture gradually evolved from field crops to dairying as better wheat-growing land to the west opened for settlement in the 1870s. Many farmers sold out and followed the wheat fields to Minnesota and the Dakotas. Others replaced wheat fields with meadows and dairy cows. Dairying provided a new cash income as southern Wisconsin became the milk shed for Chicago and Milwaukee. Women now processed milk, made butter, and raised pigs, chickens, and calves for replenishing dairy stock and for sale. The farms in this area were known for numerous outbuildings that gave evidence of family industry—chicken coops, pigpens, granaries, grain bins, corncribs, tool and machine sheds, windmills, and after the 1880s a few silos, along with root cellars, smokehouses, and summer kitchens. These were developing farms.[6]

Others headed north to the Wisconsin frontier. There they created farms similar to those in the southern part of the state if they could afford land along the rivers and streams. Most, however, purchased cheaper land back from the rivers, where they farmed like the Lansworth family in small clearings hewed out of the woods, with a log house and perhaps a log shed. Some sold their surplus to nearby lumber mills and camps. Others moved into town like the Lansworths, opening small businesses, running boarding houses and hotels.

Of the three types of farms in the north, only a few were "developed" commercial enterprises. Some were truck farms clustered near mills and camps. The rest were subsistence farms, newly settled as the timber was logged and the land sold off to settlers. As logging proceeded, on the Native reservations similar subsistence farms evolved from an older agricultural tradition that combined cultivation with hunting and harvesting of wild rice and maple syrup. Most north-central farms at this time produced only subsistence with small sales of surplus.

Women of European heritage also came to this difficult frontier with their husbands and children. To Marathon County came Germans, Czechs, Poles, Norwegians, Dutch. To Clark County came German, Swedish, Danish, and Slovenian immigrants. To Taylor County came Germans and Poles, Norwegians and Finns. To Lincoln County came Germans and Swedes. By 1900, some twenty-five thousand Germans, Poles, Scandinavians, and French and English Canadian townspeople serviced the rural settlers and provided a market for their goods. Stevens Point, Marshfield, Merrill, and Neenah—each with five thousand predominantly immigrant people—and a scattering of smaller towns served as markets and distribution points.

The published 1910 census reflected the ethnic diversity of immigrants to these four counties. Census returns showed that most were from Germany and Austria, with others from Norway, Sweden, and Denmark. The unpublished population census revealed an even more complex mix, for among the immigrants from Germany, Austria, and Russia were large numbers of Poles, whose country had been occupied and carved up by these three nations. More than three thousand Polish households existed, more than half in Marathon County and almost a third in Clark County.[7]

While a sprinkling of black households was recorded in the published census, only the manuscript census hints at the diversity of these households and the women within them. Most families labeled as black were, in fact, mixed racially. Hattie Moon, a white woman born in Pennsylvania, was married to black Alabama-born trapper Jackson Moon. Jane Mitchell, a white Wisconsin-born woman, was married to Kentucky farmer John Mitchell. Mary Huron, born in North Carolina, lived with her Pennsylvania-born daughter Luze Crawford, her white son-in-law John Crawford, who was from Tennessee, Luze's three Wisconsin-born children from a previous marriage, and a grandson. Juley Prebbels of Louisiana and Jennie Netter of Kentucky, both black, lived next door to each other in the town of Medford, with their black husbands who were from Arkansas and Kentucky.

GERMANS

Each group of new settlers contributed to the ethnic mix in northern Wisconsin, but the late nineteenth century brought the group that was to leave the largest imprint on these four counties—Germans. Their numbers swelled in the 1870s and 1880s. Earlier, the revolution of 1848 had driven a number of German intellectuals and artisans from northern Germany to Wisconsin. The later immigration brought poorer immigrants from diverse rural areas farther south and from the Austro-Hungarian Empire.

German farmers were in the north-central counties by the 1850s. Most came from northern provinces, those affected by the potato famine and plummeting wool prices. A number were carpenters and artisans or small tradesmen, and many were laborers. These groups arrived with near parity of the sexes. Heavy taxes and licensing costs burdened them at home; in Wisconsin they hoped to find cheap lands and high wages, at least in relation to the cost of living. Although some came from industrial areas, the majority were farmers or rural laborers. This migration from northern Germany gradually decreased as a result of the country's new industrial wealth, and migration from the less-developed southern German and Austrian countryside increased. My grandmother arrived as the stream of northern German immigrants was declining. She came from the poor agricultural laboring class of Germans in Bohemia, then part of the Austro-Hungarian Empire. These German Bohemians (*Böhmish*) are sometimes called "border people" because they lived in villages close to Bavaria, in mixed Czech-German communities. While a few settled together in south-central Minnesota near New Ulm and in northeast Wisconsin near Green Bay, others like my grandmother scattered to northern Wisconsin wherever they could find cheap farmland. I knew my grandmother was from Bohemia, but she never told me what that meant or anything about her early life there. To me *bohemian* meant being an artist or living marginally in society. Perhaps my interpretation was not so far from the truth. But more importantly, these families brought an ethic of intense self-reliance and a pride in their family's well-being as well as a strong sense of community.[8]

There are few collected letters for these early German immigrants to northern Wisconsin. Surviving letters from southern Wisconsin describe German women well pleased with their new surroundings and eager to plant their gardens. German pioneer letters from the late 1840s describe community building and the arrival of many immigrants to areas north of Milwaukee. With their gardens of vegetables and flowers, stock of ducks, geese, chickens, and cows, and neighborhood dances, they lived very prosperously in Wisconsin.

Between 1852 and 1905, the state of Wisconsin encouraged immigration from Germany to the northern counties. In 1852, it stationed in New York a commissioner of immigration who distributed passes donated by the railroad so the newly arrived could travel directly from New York to Wisconsin. The agent gave the immigrants pamphlets touting the fertility of the soil and the cheapness of land. Agents competed to attract and exploit the immigrants: one wrote in 1853 that the immigrant was "but an article of trade which they try to buy as cheap, and to sell as high, as they possibly can do." The immigrant's usual route was through New York, but by 1854, as war unsettled large portions of Germany, middle-class families thronged in through Quebec as well. Wisconsin closed its New York immigrant office in 1855. By 1871, the state had established a board of immigration with county representation on it and a commissioner of immigration to encourage relocation into northern Wisconsin specifically. State officials, who considered the northern areas "nonproductive," urged counties with unoccupied land to establish auxiliary immigration boards. They distributed pamphlets in English, German, and Norwegian and asked established farmers to encourage their former neighbors in Europe to join them. Clark, Marathon, and Taylor were among the counties recruiting immigrants.[9]

As lumbering declined, railroads actively promoted immigration as well. Companies wanted to sell their lands and to spur economic development that would produce commodities to be transported by rail. Agents of the Wisconsin Central Railway expanded efforts in Germany to promote immigration between 1880 and 1891. Ministers organized entire communities to emigrate. The Wisconsin Central Railway established an immigrant house in Medford to provide free lodging for new immigrants for two weeks after their arrival. By 1900 the railroad was also recruiting in Chicago with free stereopticon-illustrated lectures.[10]

In addition to heavy immigration directly from Europe, German immigrants from other parts of the United States were always a part of the settlers streaming into northern Wisconsin. In the 1850s, German-born families arrived in Marathon County from Ohio and Pennsylvania. One colony from Pittsburgh took up land along the Wisconsin River in 1856. Farmers' children, seeking land of their own, were already moving northwest from the Milwaukee area in the 1870s when a Milwaukee law firm that owned a large tract in western Marathon County established the community of Black Creek Falls, later known as Athens. With settlers moving north from Iowa, southern Minnesota,

Home Restaurant, 1910s. Family-owned and -staffed restaurants, such as this one in Taylor County, offered meals for travelers and working people as well as rare treats for visiting farm families. Some families supplemented inadequate farm income by taking in boarders or opening small shops, or they moved into town permanently.

and southern Wisconsin, land values skyrocketed, making it worthwhile for earlier settlers to sell out and move farther north or west. As more people came, they found especially good land in Clark County.[11]

An account written by John S. Roeseler in 1899, "A Few Isolated Facts Relating to the History of My Life," reviewed the ethnic composition in the north-central counties. Roeseler was born in 1859 and grew up in a German family in Dodge County, but he lived in Neillsville in Clark County by the time he wrote his account. He gathered information on ethnicity from teachers and county clerks, who reported that Marathon, Taylor, Lincoln, and Clark counties were now predominantly German.

A detailed analysis of the change in Taylor County's population came from one of Roeseler's informants. In the townships of Deer Creek and Little Black, French Canadians and native-born Americans at first had made up half the population of 160, another quarter was Irish and Scandinavian, and the rest were of mixed origin. German immigration exploded after the Wisconsin Central Railway hired local agents in Medford to help attract settlers. Deer Creek and Little Black townships then grew from 160 to 650 immigrants, most of German ethnicity from all parts of the German Empire, from Switzerland, and from Bohemia. Now six of the eleven townships were predominantly German, and in another three townships they were equal in number to native-born

Americans. Of the remaining three townships, two were predominantly Scandinavian and native-born American. They came, one informant explained, "to escape the oppressive military regulations of their native countries which require the service of the able male population and place all the heavy burdens of labor to support life and taxes to meet the heavy expenses of standing armies upon the shoulders of the old and infirm men, women, and children."[12]

This same informant explained that immigrants came with suitable work clothing and a few tools, eager to find wage work and cheap land. Wages in Wisconsin lumber camps were 50 to 75 percent higher than in Europe, and with these cash wages immigrants purchased land cheaply from companies that had logged out the most profitable timber. Then the settlers logged off the less desirable timber on this stumpy land and used their profits to buy farm implements. The new immigrants melded their customs, quickly adopting American public institutions of education and government but maintaining their own church and social traditions. The older people tended to retain European habits, the middle-aged learned the American language and customs of labor, and the young acquired the language and adopted American habits. This informant was not favorably impressed with these new German immigrants. According to him they had too many church holidays, were intemperate, managed town governments inefficiently, and were "uncongenial." It resulted, he said, in "a serious depreciation of the value of real estate, which will require time to overcome."[13]

Few of the informants from other counties were quite so pessimistic about German immigrants, but they all agreed, some even writing their assessment in German, that during this wave of immigration the German population had soared. These German immigrants were much poorer than those who had come to America earlier in the century. The new majority were looking for good wages, low taxes, and a peaceful land. The cultural pattern was the same in all the counties: Germans supported the English school and maintained their own church schools. They spoke German to children at home but expected them to learn English in school. Like Taylor County, Lincoln County was now predominantly German, although the county seat of Merrill still had a large French Canadian population. Clark County had a German majority, a sprinkling of Scandinavian, Polish, and Slovenian settlers, and only a few townships dominated by native-born Americans. The editor of the *Deutscher-Amerikaner* reported that in densely German western Marathon County, farmers conformed to general laws but kept church and family life as they would in Germany, except for young people who worked and lived in English-speaking families. The largest city in Marathon County, Wausau, was now two-thirds German. At different times between 1861 and 1920, thirteen German-language newspapers served the German-reading population of these four counties.[14]

If other Germans were like my German Bohemian grandmother Matilda Rauscher, they came with very little. Matilda brought a trunk, but as a single woman she probably packed only personal possessions—her work permit document, samplers she had embroidered at school in the 1880s, her German breviary, some sewing tools, what few clothes she had accumulated, perhaps a few seeds for the garden she planned. According to a family story, the man she was to marry came with his possessions wrapped in a kerchief tied to a pole. Migration to work elsewhere was already common in Germany. These young, single people came as they might to work at a harvest or in a neighboring town.

GERMANS AT DORCHESTER

Anna Jantsch left her home in Marschendorf, Bohemia, in 1881 and settled with her husband, Johann, a carpenter by trade, near Dorchester, Wisconsin. Children sometimes asked Anna whether she missed their old home. "No," she always replied. Marschendorf was an industrializing area; the village offered only poverty, not opportunities for the young couple. After their second son died in infancy, Johann and Anna decided to follow other young people out of their village. Anna was not interested in returning to the land of her birth. She loved northern Wisconsin, especially the way the sun set behind the pines.

Anna and Johann settled first in the village of Stevens Point, where she safely birthed her first daughter, Mary. Johann had a good job. Anna had a fancy new hat to wear in town. Johann knew nothing about farming or about picking out good farmland, but Wenzel Rohl, a German friend who had settled east of Dorchester, urged Johann to buy the forty acres north of his farm. Land was going fast, he warned, and Johann could buy this farm with a log house already on the land for only $250. Wenzel did not tell the young couple that one-third of the parcel was a swamp fed by a creek that frequently overflowed, that the land was full of stones, that except for a small clearing around the house they would have to chop down trees and clear undergrowth before even a garden could be started. The couple bought the forty acres. Anna sold her hat.[15]

After settling near Dorchester, Anna birthed three more children. The couple cleared the land and planted crops. Anna hoed, raked hay, cut and shocked rye. Anna later told her daughter-in-law that while working in the fields she always wore an apron to wrap up the baby in case she gave birth. Anna would eventually birth ten children with similar lack of fuss. She also helped neighbor women birth their children and was often paid in kind. She took in boarders— loggers and families without a place to stay. In winter, Johann logged to bring in cash. In summer, when he could get carpentry work he did that. At the end of seven years, the couple could afford to build a larger log house, send passage money to Johann's sixty-seven-year-old mother, and buy a cow. Anna could now make butter to pay for groceries. The family walked everywhere because they had no horse. When the weather was good, they walked more than four miles to the Catholic church in Dorchester.[16]

Mary Jantsch, who was born in Stevens Point in 1882, moved with her parents to the farm in Marathon County a few months later. When Mary died in 1972, she was living near the village of Athens, fewer than twenty miles from the original Jantsch farm. Mary left to earn money elsewhere in her youth, but she returned every summer to work on the farm, chose to marry a man who had grown up on a nearby farm, and lived out her life close to her own family. There never was another place she called home.

Mary learned to care for herself and to help Anna as soon as she was able. She worked beside her mother: milking and making butter, haying and hoeing, clearing fields of stones, helping cook for the neighbor men when they came to help log or build the barn. Mary grew up eating rye bread and lard, and when she attended school she walked the mile to the Bruckerville school carrying rye bread and syrup in her tin pail. She mothered the younger children as needed. By 1897, at fifteen, with school days past and younger children at home to help with chores and child care, Mary also worked out on neighboring farms. She was a healthy, lively young woman. On summer evenings, when neighbors had assembled to help with the building and logging, Mary would join in the dancing after her chores were done. She twirled and sashayed across splintery granary floors to the accordion's two-step, square dance, waltz, and schottische tunes.[17]

Although Mary was already attracting young men's attention with her witty conversation and good humor, she had no intention of marrying young. During the next twenty years she continued to work for others, first on neighboring farms, then, after a girlfriend wrote to her about the money to be made doing housework fifty miles west in Chippewa Falls, she traveled there by train. The friend arranged for a job so she could begin work as soon as she arrived. Mary wrote cheerful letters home, and each summer, her trunk full of gifts for younger children, she returned to work on the farm. She helped each sister in turn get jobs in Chippewa Falls. German families expected eldest daughters to care for parents, and perhaps she did not plan to marry at all. None of the older children seemed anxious to marry. Henry, the eldest son, finally did so in 1912 at age thirty-three. Two younger sisters married before Mary, in 1917 and early 1920. Anna and Johann were talking of moving into Dorchester and letting the sons take over the farm.

Now thirty-eight, Mary finally felt free to think of her own life. She had met thirty-five-year-old Joseph Gierl, a farmer from Colby, through a cousin years earlier. When Mary's brother Joe attended high school in Colby, the Gierl and Jantsch families frequently visited each other. Mary and Joe began to court, but each still had family duties. Then it was 1917 and there was a war on. Everyone not involved in war work was needed on his or her own farm. Finally, in 1920, nothing could further delay the marriage of the middle-aged couple. The Jantsch family held a big wedding in Dorchester at the Catholic church and a reception for neighbors on the farm. Mary left the farm that day, but she moved only a few miles away, to nearby Abbotsford, where the Gierls had a house built for them. It was close enough to Dorchester for Mary to keep an eye on her parents and visit them frequently. After the birth of their first child, they settled near and then took over the family farm. When, at last, they felt able to buy a better farm of their own, they moved to nearby Athens. Mary was still on that farm when Joe died in 1947. She farmed with unmarried brother John and son Edward until he married in 1950. Then Mary and John moved to a small farm near the newly-weds, where she continued to garden and raise chickens until she died there twenty-two years later.

My grandmother Matilda lived across the road from the Jantsch family. Anna Jantsch would have hurried over that March day in 1894 to help Matilda bear her first daughter, also named Mary. Matilda was robust and healthy from her outdoor work; there were no complications. Matilda bore four more children in quick succession before her husband, Karl, died in 1901. Facing the prospect of raising five young children alone, Matilda married Leo Schopp less than a year after Karl died. Leo, a musician and seasonal lumberjack, did not like farming and refused to do it. He was well liked by his neighbors, but what Matilda needed was someone to help her farm and to add a little cash to the meager farm income. Leo did little of either. As Matilda bore Leo's three children, the relationship became one of acrimonious shouting. Mary endured the painful disintegration of this second marriage. She and her brother Frank, one year younger, helped Matilda with the farm and housework. They took care of the younger children, supervised their daily chores. By the age of twelve Mary was helping everywhere. Matilda saw that Mary went to school through the seventh grade. After that, her farm work expanded to full time.

Mary was fourteen when Matilda birthed her last child in 1908. The next five years were the hardest for the family. Still, there was time for fun, at neighborhood and church picnics. As Mary reached sixteen, there were dances at weddings and at a nearby dance hall. A family photograph taken around that time shows her dressed carefully in a dark skirt, a white high-necked and long-sleeved blouse, and a straw hat with flowers and bows. Within a few years, Mary had met Frank Sacher, a German Bohemian immigrant. Mary could have met Frank at one of the many dances farmers still held in their granaries, where Mary's stepfather played his accordion, or at a wedding in Dorchester. Now eighteen, she would have been looking for a suitable partner with whom to farm. Frank offered her a way out of the cramped log house and the endless struggle to feed and clothe the family of nine.

Frank Sacher was five when his family arrived in the United States in 1899. They settled in Stetsonville, just ten miles north of Dorchester. After less than a decade in Marathon County—the Sacher family did not stay long enough to appear on the federal census—they moved north to Canada. Between 1905 and 1910, years when land prices were rising in Marathon County but prices for farm products were not, there was a "Canada craze" in northern Wisconsin. The Canadian government, looking for settlers for the western prairies, distributed enticing brochures advertising "The Last Best West." Under the Dominion Lands Act of 1908, prairie land, 160 acres of it, was available for a ten-dollar filing fee. The two older Jantsch sons were interested in moving north permanently, too, and even sold a cow to get money to pay the filing fee for a homestead in Saskatchewan. Cautious neighbors went to scout the land; one's returning words cooled the Jantsch sons' desire to move north: "It is a lonesome land, and in winter it is colder than it is even here." That ended the craze for most, although Leo and others from Marathon County traveled north each fall to work in the wheat harvest.

Despite the discouraging reports, Frank's parents decided to move to Saskatchewan. The Sachers were badly in need of more land. They had arrived in northern Wisconsin when prices had already increased, and they had four sons who wanted to farm. Canada seemed a more promising place to establish their children on farms. The pioneer conditions did not worry them, but they found little land left to homestead by 1910. Near Browning, in southern Saskatchewan, some of the early homesteaders were ready to sell their wheat farms and move on. Browning seemed on the brink of an agricultural boom. The Canadian Northern Railway had a depot there. Plans were already under way for a cooperative grain elevator, and settlers had applied to establish a post office in the general store. The tiny hamlet had a hardware store, a poolroom-barbershop, a lumberyard, a blacksmith, and a sturdy five-year-old schoolhouse. The community was mainly composed of German, Danish, and Norwegian Lutherans. There were not enough Catholics to have their own parish, but they were served by missionaries in nearby Lampman, which had been settled by Catholics of Irish, French, and Belgian descent who were working hard to establish a parish. They planned to raise funds for a new church.[18]

In 1910, the Sacher parents and their four sons and two daughters moved to a quarter section of land with an unfinished house near Browning. If Frank did not already know Mary, he met her on his frequent winter trips back to visit friends and neighbors. By 1914, the family was well established in Browning. Frank Sr., a carpenter, built furniture and a large granary where they could hold dances. The sons were working at good jobs and buying land. Frank was twenty-four and ready to marry.[19]

By 1914 Mary was working in Minneapolis. She had probably moved there in the fall of 1913, for she shows up in the early 1914 city register as a maid. The other children were now old enough to take care of the farm. Although the family would have welcomed any money she chose to send home, they did not expect her to share her earnings, only to support herself. As a live-in maid Mary had few expenses and could save her earnings to buy new clothes and a few items with which to start her own household. In late July 1914, Frank arrived in Minneapolis from Canada to marry twenty-year-old Mary. Her eighteen-year-old sister Anna came from Dorchester to witness the simple ceremony conducted by the Catholic priest, and the couple returned by train to Dorchester to visit with family and friends. Then they headed for their farm in Canada. Mary was Matilda's only daughter to farm.[20]

I only learned later how poor she was, how hard a life she had on her Canadian farm. During the 1940s, finally, a good crop of soybeans and high wartime crop prices helped ease the hardship. In the 1950s Mary and her husband moved off the farm into the nearby village of Arcola. They played bingo and visited friends; she was a member of the Altar Society. Then, in November 1960, Mary contracted meningitis, and, after frantic efforts to save her, the hospital staff ordered a quick burial, fearful of the disease spreading. I found Mary's grave in a small cemetery on a hill outside Arcola. Today the nearby farmlands are dotted with oil wells. The British American Oil Company began to drill for oil near Lampman in 1954; soon after Mary's death, oil beneath their farm made her husband a rich man.[21]

I have a photograph of myself sitting atop a giant workhorse at the Browning farm, where we visited Mary and Frank in the summer of 1938 when I was four. Mary never had children, apparently due to poor health. The Saskatchewan farms were hard hit by the drought and the Depression of the 1930s, and the farm never prospered. Times were hard and crops were poor, but she was able to save enough money to visit her sister Theresa in St. Paul, so I came to know her growing up there in the 1930s. She would take her little niece to see the Christmas window decorations in the big downtown stores. I loved the visits of this cheerful and good-humored woman. She joked and played with me, teasing me about my asthma. When the mechanically animated big brown bear in the Christmas display window breathed with a raspy sound, I called it "the big brown thing." "The little brown thing," she affectionately dubbed me when I wheezed. She made my disability something special and part of our fun with each other. And so I remember her, the aunt who had to leave the farm to stay on a farm, who left me a small happy legacy in her visits.

POLES AND SCANDINAVIANS

A few Polish immigrants came to Wisconsin after the revolution of 1848, but, like the Germans, Poles came to northern Wisconsin in much larger numbers in the 1870s and 1880s. One group of settlers named their village Poniatowski, after the Polish revolutionary. Another group established farms near Thorp in Clark County. Others who settled in southeastern Marathon County maintained close ties to the larger Polish population of Portage County and saw Stevens Point as their urban center.

Polish settlers came mainly from areas controlled by Prussia. These immigrants remembered a ruthless economic and cultural occupation by Germans and especially resented suppression of the Polish language, for all school subjects had to be taught in German. They also detested the control these invaders had over their economy. Polish farmers performed all their work by hand, and, after seemingly endless toil, the Prussian officials confiscated part of the grain crop for food storage and paid in return a price far below what farmers could get on the open market. In the 1890s, Prussian authorities attempted to "Germanize" the Polish countryside, buying out small landholders to replace them with German farmers. In response, the Poles established underground schools for their children and mutual aid societies to help Polish landowners hold on to their land. The Polish Catholic Church became the center of community resistance to the Germans and the champion of Polish nationalism. Most immigrants to Wisconsin became day laborers or small landowners who worked in industry. After the Russian revolution of 1905, a second group arrived from the part of Poland ruled by Russia. Later still, Poles came from Austrian-controlled areas of their country. Polish communities were bound together by the Polish language, by the Roman Catholic faith, and by unwritten family traditions. The desire to own land led urban immigrant families to save from hard-earned factory wages so that, as workers aged and found factory work difficult, they could buy farmland.

The few Polish immigrants who settled in Portage County in the early nineteenth century had brought wealth with them and developed prosperous farms. By the time the poorer newcomers arrived in the early twentieth century, the best land was already claimed and sellers were demanding high prices. These Polish families had to settle on less fertile land. They found sandy patches along the Plover River in Marathon County to be inexpensive and suitable for raising potatoes. Savings went to purchase land, build a log house, buy a cow and a horse and plow. Like German subsistence settlers, Polish men took wage jobs to support farm ventures. They usually sought year-round employment in the many wood-processing mills close to home, seeking stable cash incomes and the convenience of living at home. Women found domestic jobs with wealthier farm families. Some picked in the cranberry bogs during harvest season, and a few earned income from midwifery. All of them worked hard in the fields to make their small farms successful. By the late nineteenth century, the public square at Stevens Point had become a central focus for the marketing of produce raised by Polish settlers in the Plover River area.[22]

Scandinavian immigrants were scattered among this predominantly German and Polish population. Unlike other areas of Wisconsin and neighboring Minnesota, only a few Scandinavian communities are identifiable. One predominately Danish community, discussed in greater detail later in this section, existed at Withee in Clark County. A number of Swedish families migrated to Marinette County in the nineteenth century, primarily to work in the lumber camps. A few drifted down to the four north-central counties to work building the railroads. The census of 1880 shows large numbers of Scandinavian men, most of them boarding with Scandinavian families, working on the railroads in Clark County. Maggie and August Lindahl, for example, were boarding sixty-four men in 1880. Maggie, then age eighteen, was born in Wisconsin of Norwegian/Swedish parents; August was a Swedish immigrant. More than 70 percent of their boarders were Swedish. Emma Lungreen and her husband, Charles, cared for twenty-four boarders, most of whom were also Swedish. These families ran farms to feed their boarders. Some stayed as railroad construction moved on, but others moved with railroad crews. These were not centers of Swedish concentration, but by 1910 perhaps six hundred families had settled in the four-county region, two-thirds of them in Lincoln County. Because of the continuing importance of lumbering there, single women no doubt found household work in private homes or the boarding houses that Swedish families ran near the mills. Married couples carved out small farms nearby. Their enterprises remained closely linked to the lumber/railroad economy.[23]

Norwegian women also made north-central Wisconsin their home. In 1890, 20 percent of all Norwegian immigrants in the United States lived in Wisconsin, and by 1930 Norwegians were the state's third-largest immigrant group (after Germans and Poles), but most moved farther west to Minnesota and the Dakotas. Those who remained in Wisconsin tended to settle in the southern or western parts of the state. After 1860 some scattered north to work in the lumbering industry, and some purchased land and remained in north-central Wisconsin. Like the Swedes, Norwegian women also often worked as servants before marrying and then helped run boarding houses after marriage. When families were able to buy land, women helped clear and plant it, tended animals, and usually milked and made butter. Most families lived in Marathon and Clark counties. A number started dairies in Pine Valley.[24]

One group of Finnish immigrants settled near Owen in Clark County after the turn of the century. Ninety-six Finnish families were still there in 1941. They kept to themselves and did not mix with their non-Finnish neighbors. Their experiences were not far different from other farmers, however: clearing land, burning brush, raising a garden and potatoes for cash, developing small milk herds. Herman Crego of Saxon remembered that his wife—after putting their eight children to bed—would bring coffee and join him in the fields where he was burning brush. They worked together until after midnight. They also dug potatoes together by lantern light. Both father and mother, he said, had to be unafraid of hard work in order to survive. A second community of Finns existed in Lincoln County, most of them migrating there in the early 1900s from jobs in urban areas. Many worked as laborers after their arrival in the north, few had any help from parents in setting up farms, and about 40 percent did not stay in agriculture. Two-thirds of the women married other Finns, and more than 60 percent became cooperative members and attended meetings.[25]

Thus north-central Wisconsin became known for its mixed ethnic heritage, primarily Germans and Poles but some Scandinavians as well. Before the mid-1920s a few Czech families settled in these counties, and at least one Slovenian community existed at Willard. Each left descendants and a small imprint on the land. Their family histories reveal the rich diversity that would contribute to the midwestern heritage.

POLES AND DANES AT THORP AND WITHEE

Today the towns of Thorp and Withee look like typical Wisconsin communities. They lie just off Highway 29, the main east-west thoroughfare that stretches from Wausau to Eau Claire. The towns both have residential communities spreading back from short main streets. Schools and libraries are places of activity, as are churches on Sundays. There are general stores, gas stations, motels.

Thorp and Withee look very similar to the outsider, but their cultural histories are very different. Just east of Thorp was a Polish farming community, and north of Withee was a Danish one, each united by religion and nationality. For their first thirty years, the two communities stood a few miles apart with little interaction. That changed in the 1920s. When rural sociologist H. R. Pedersen arrived to do field work for his doctoral thesis in the late 1940s, intermarriage was common. Most of the things that had made the communities dissimilar were disappearing. Old timers still remembered the differences.

In some ways, the farming communities had similar beginnings. The Spaulding Land Company offered parcels to urban ethnic communities in the 1890s and promoted colonization schemes. Settlers could buy inexpensive farms on adjoining acreage, and the company promised to donate land for their churches. The first Polish settlers from Milwaukee arrived east of Thorp in 1891. The first Danes came the following year from Chicago and settled farther east, just north of the village of Withee, in the township of Hixon. Both communities soon attracted others who wished to settle with those of similar ethnicity and religion. Both reached their peak in population from 1900 to 1910, and then their distinct delineations gradually faded when children intermarried and left

St. Hedwig's Catholic Church. Built in 1904 by the Polish community near Thorp in Clark County, this brick church accommodated 1,500 parishioners, many of whom lie nearby in the church cemetery. The community maintained the boarded-up church after the congregation ceased using it around 1970.

in the 1920s. Although both developed dairy farms, the Danish group accul-
turated in two generations while the Polish community remained distinct
much longer.

Today, not much remains physically of either ethnic farming community.
East of Thorp the Polish church, now abandoned, still rises solidly on the
horizon. The cemetery behind the church is well maintained, and there is a
small museum in the old parish house cared for by volunteers. The area is
called Poznan, after the Polish city. North of Withee, the old Danish cemetery
still remains, the headstones proclaiming the earlier presence of the Hansens,
Neilsons, and Jensens, reminders of the Danish community that once flourished there. The towns of Thorp and Withee both thrived on the dairy economy of the surrounding farms.

The Polish community of Poznan was a few miles east of Thorp. By the
time the railroad reached the small clearing in 1880, the earlier Chippewa villages
were gone but families still hunted in the area and visited the nearby burial
sites of their ancestors. Merchants and artisans settled in the new village to
serve the early logging industry. When logging declined at the end of the
1890s, so too did the town's population. The establishment of a creamery in
1897 brought the farm families into town and money into the community. By
1917 Thorp had five cheese factories in addition to the creamery. The farmers
delivered more than 5 million pounds of milk and 315,000 pounds of cream to
the factories that year. In 1916, the creamery produced almost 400,000 pounds
of butter and almost 2 million pounds of cheese. The following year, butter
production declined to less than 100,000 pounds, and cheese increased to
more than 3 million pounds. Dairying seemed to be the stable activity that
allowed the community to thrive.[26]

Thorp was never a Polish town. As the hinterland filled with Polish families,
Thorp remained a typical northern Wisconsin village with a diverse group of
families—German, Swedish, Norwegian, Irish, and Dutch immigrants, along
with migrants from New England and the Mid-Atlantic states. The settlers
brought their skills into the small village as seamstresses, clerks, and carpenters
and as boarding house, store, and hotel keepers. As the Polish community
grew, so too did the village, but it retained its separate identity as an ethnically
mixed community, with an overlay of Yankee elite—the banker, the doctor, the
teacher. Unlike Stevens Point, which had its own Polish community, the village
of Thorp was primarily a place where Polish farm families came not to live but
to buy and sell.

The heart of the Polish community remained at Poznan, around St. Hedwig's
Catholic Church. There was never much more than the church at Poznan—
perhaps a blacksmith, but no business community. Though boarded up when
I visited in 2002, St. Hedwig's still dominated the countryside. The huge brick
church stood empty, but the Thorp Historical Society had converted the

rectory into a small museum. Don Regalski, who had worked at the Blue Moon Cheese Company in Thorp, showed me around. The rooms were thoughtfully arranged by topic, even to a small bedroom for a single man in what had once been the furnace room.

Like other Polish settlers, many were refugees from American cities, where men had worked at hard manual labor. Paul Polnaszek, who arrived with the first group in 1891, worked in a stone quarry outside of Chicago. Many of the first settlers came from Poznan, a region of Poland under Prussian control, hence the village's name. Of the 180 households in this community censused by the government in 1900, 86 percent had parents from Poland, almost all from Prussian-controlled areas. A few German, Danish, and Yankee families were interspersed with the Polish families.

The Polish immigrants came to the United States to escape what descendant Linda Osowski Daines called "national slavery." Occupation by foreign countries had destroyed their national state, but the Polish people had forged a culture of resistance centered on language, the Catholic Church, and family traditions. The Polish immigrants used these traditions to create urban communities in Milwaukee and Chicago, but they responded eagerly when land agents offered the weary city dwellers cheap land in Clark County and promised to donate ten acres for a church. Men had worked an average of twelve years in heavy industry, and although they found farm work difficult, they were as committed to it as were the Polish women.[27]

We can plot the history of the Polish community through the history of St. Hedwig's Catholic Church. The first settlers built a wood church in 1891. By 1897 they had built a rectory and settled in their first resident Polish priest, Father Korczyk. In 1904 the community obtained a loan for $18,900 and built a huge new brick structure modeled on a thirteenth-century Polish church southeast of Poznan. Named in honor of St. Hedwig, the church was large enough to accommodate 1,500 people. In December 1907, after three years of construction, the congregation celebrated its first Mass. For sixty-three years Mass was offered in the church. When I visited in 2002, none had been offered for thirty years. The building still stood, my guide Regalski explained, because it was too expensive to tear down. It remained a monument to the faith that kept the community together.[28]

In the cemetery just back of St. Hedwig's church, Paulina Detmer Osowski lies buried. Paulina never wrote about her life, but her granddaughter did, and that family history tells us much about the Polish farm women who came to Poznan. Twenty-one-year-old Paulina arrived in the United States in 1887 with Joseph, her husband of two years, and their young son. Joseph had been born in Prussian-controlled Gdansk and was ten years older than Paulina. Soon after their arrival, Paulina bore her first daughter, and two years later they moved to Milwaukee. By 1905, when the family resettled in Thorp to join

Polish friends, Paulina had already borne ten children; she would bear two more in the next five years. Unlike many Polish settlers, the Osowskis were rather well-off. Joseph was only a laborer and Paulina took in boarders for a while, but they had prospered in Milwaukee and were able to sell a lot they owned there for $4,000, money they used to buy their eighty-acre Poznan farm in 1905. Five years later they bought a second eighty acres for $4,500.

Paulina's children remember her appearance. A stocky woman, she always wore a cotton triangle as scarf tied under her chin, ankle-length skirts, wool socks, and low rubber boots for outdoor work. They remembered her as "strong, but gentle . . . [someone who] managed well and worked hard . . . doing farm work until the day before she died." Eventually the family had twenty-nine cows along with cattle, hogs, sheep, chickens, and geese as well as fields for growing vegetables and fodder.

Paulina tried to farm as she had in Poland. In practice, Wisconsin farm life could never be exactly like that of European Polish women who lived in villages with fields laid out some distance away. Early Milwaukee land agents may have had this type of structure in mind when they first began to survey for Poznan, for they promised settlers a village lot if they purchased forty acres of land. A fire in May 1891 apparently forced the agent to move the community's location farther south and abandon the idea of providing free village lots. Thus the settlers had to live on their land and travel into the village for most of their needs. The women had no close village life. Nor did they cut wheat with a sickle as they had in Poland or raise and process flax into linen. They did continue to perform hard outdoor work, which they seemed to enjoy, both working in the fields and caring for animals.[29]

Paulina always reserved the milking for herself. After milking on Sunday morning, she would walk two miles to St. Hedwig's, where she was a member of the Rosary Society. In winter, her wire-rimmed glasses froze to her cheeks as she made her way over the frozen land. In the evenings Paulina read to Joseph and her family. She spoke Polish, German, and English and read and wrote Polish and German. With Paulina as the compass, the Osowski family thrived. Milk and cream money allowed them a steady income for the farm. She organized the work of the children, and when most had grown and scattered to Milwaukee and Chicago, she asked them to send grandchildren to the farm for the summer so they could help with the haying, harvesting of peas, and shocking of grain. Paulina and Joseph stayed on the farm for the rest of their lives, always keeping some children with them to help farm and never moving into town. Joseph died in 1938. Paulina continued milking until her death in 1939.

Most families arrived with fewer resources than the Osowskis and instead worked for other farmers. Young women worked off the family farm for at least two years before marriage, usually from age seventeen to nineteen. This system followed the European rural custom practiced even by wealthier families. The apprenticeship at neighboring farms gave young people a chance to see how others worked and to scout marriage prospects.

Unlike Paulina, most of the first-generation immigrants were not well educated because they had resisted the Prussian system, preferring underground Polish schooling, which was sporadic and frequently interrupted. The Wisconsin-born attended local common schools with other Polish children rather than the parochial school in Thorp. Like other farm children, they spoke their parents' native tongue at home and seldom finished grammar school. Informal training was most important.

Native-born daughters did not stay in agriculture. All but 15 percent of daughters left their family farms, while half the sons remained to farm. Parents wanted their daughters to marry Poles, but most married out, leaving Polish sons to marry non-Polish women. Elders made arrangements for their own care by having children farm with them, a practice that also might have discouraged young women. Only one son, or a daughter and her husband, was taken in to help with the farm, so the daughter or daughter-in-law would have to share a house and farm owned and controlled by the parents. The two women who shared the house would develop skills for working together. Children who did not take over the farm still had to give bond to support their parents as long as they lived. This "pension mortgage" system insured that parents would not be dependent upon the state or on the decisions of their children. The first generation had practiced farming longest and felt they knew best. The master farmer was usually father and patriarch, the son or son-in-law the apprentice as long as the father lived.

Farm women, despite their heavy outdoor work, managed to keep daughters in school a few years longer than sons. Then most daughters went off to the city to work, mainly as waitresses and domestic servants. To stay in agriculture, a daughter had to find a man willing to submit to her father's control. Security and family responsibility were important to Poles. In return, children could always return home to live, and they could send their own children home for the summers. They retained their family's cultural values even if, like the Osowski daughter who wrote her family history, they left the farm. They moved on but remembered and valued the older patriarchal Polish farm family and women's crucial role in it.[30]

Like the Polish community near Thorp, the Danish community near Withee also began with urban neighborhoods negotiating with agents to buy parcels of adjoining land for settlement. Earlier, Danish families had bought farmsteads south of Withee in Longwood township, but their farms were interspersed with Norwegian, German, and Yankee settlers. This settlement, north of Withee in Hixon township, began as an attempt to obtain contiguous farmland and establish a distinct Danish settlement pattern.

The leader of the Danish settlers at Withee was the Reverend Andreas Sextus Nielsen, a Chicago follower of the teachings of Grundtvig, founder of a reform movement within the Danish Lutheran Church. Nielsen was anxious to get his parishioners settled somewhere in the country where they could develop a model community that embodied Grundtvigian social and religious beliefs. When Spaulding, the lumberman who owned the Withee land, visited the Lutheran synod at Waupaca to invite the settlers north, some were skeptical. One man who had traveled to Withee declared it too hard to farm there and refused to move. The Sterling lumber company promised to donate eighty acres to Nielsen and another forty for a church and to offer reduced rates on 320-acre parcels for church members. Before the group arrived, however, Sterling went bankrupt, and new owner John S. Owen told Nielsen they would have to pay for the church land. The Danes drew up a petition and threatened to walk away from their contracts, but Owen backed down and fulfilled his predecessor's promises. Nielsen and his wife, Johane, led the settlers north to Withee in April 1893. They officially organized their congregation, and families set to work on the unpromising land.[31]

Nielsen seems to have been a popular minister in Chicago, but he could find only two families to join him the first years—the Frosts and the Jorgensens. Alfred Frost, who was born near Withee in 1894, told his family's story. The Frosts had moved often after arriving in the United States from Denmark: Iowa, Minnesota, Chicago. Alfred's father was the man who refused to join the venture after seeing the land, but he finally agreed to move with Nielsen. When they arrived, Frost's mother asked, "What have you gotten us into?" But later, each time his father threatened to leave, she would urge him to stay. They had moved so much. That first year they maneuvered between the stumps with a walking plow and planted potatoes, and in the winter they hauled lumber. They bought a cow and chickens. His mother skimmed milk in the basement and sold butter as well as surplus eggs in town. They got by. A few more families joined them.[32]

As word of the community taking form in Withee spread, Danish families began to come from Superior, Green Bay, and other cities. The Rasmussens, Hansens, Pedersens, Jensens, and more Nielsens joined. Soon there were so many families with the same last names that they were known by where they came from (Superior Pedersens) or the man's occupation (Blacksmith Hansens). At first they met in homes, but by 1896 there were already thirty families in the congregation and 110 baptized members, enough to raise funds for a brick building to be used as a combination church and school. They started a Danish summer bible school and formed a Danish Brotherhood and a Sisterhood.[33]

The groups were to provide the Grundtvigians with a social life in keeping with their religious life. By 1909, however, the congregation was quarreling

over what that social fellowship should include. There was too much dancing and card playing for some members. To keep the congregation intact, the
community agreed to build Dana Hall, not next to the church but south of it,
closer to town.

Dana Hall was an attempt to pass on the old values to the next generation. It became the center for a separate young people's society, the Trillium
(*Skovlien*). By 1913, the Trillium hired a teacher of folk dancing and gymnas-
tics, created Danish folk costumes, and gave public performances for Fourth
of July picnics and ball games. A photograph from 1913 shows the children
of the first settlers—the Sorensens, Frosts, Hansens, Stockholms, Jacobsens,
Andreasens. The young women wear laced vests, white blouses, aprons, dark
skirts and stockings, peaked caps. The young men wear white stockings and
knee britches, vests, white shirts. By now the Danish Lutheran activities had
become part of the town's activities.

A stroll through Withee in 1912 would have shown Danes to be well integrated there. The Danish language was heard not only in the streets when farmers came into town but in the many shops that Danes operated. While most
Danes were farmers, the community also included a good many merchants
and professionals. Charles Larsen had a blacksmith shop, Christensen a feed
mill, Petersen a creamery. Alva Hack Nielsen would soon manage the Farmers'
Cooperative Store, where Danish farmers bought their groceries. Danes were
active in the cooperative livestock association. Hans Nielsen had a cheese factory just west of Withee. Pete Hansen operated a photography and art studio
where his sister-in-law Katherine Stockholm Hansen worked, and Ed Nielsen
ran a jewelry shop. There was a Danish doctor and a Danish pharmacist. Danish women acted as midwives. Katherine Stockholm's mother served as a community nurse, going out at all hours to deliver children.

The Danes were well integrated into the town because of an ethnic pattern
they practiced. Farm daughters worked in town as domestic servants, married
in their mid-twenties, often to village Danes, and had few children. When
farm children came of age, most Danish parents sold their farms to them and
moved into Withee. During the 1920s, as fewer Danish-born families joined
the community and more immigrant children married outside of it, the
Grundtvigians moved toward the more traditional Lutheran doctrines. The
Danish Lutheran Church north of Withee became the center of a Lutheran
rather than just a Danish community. The better-educated children left farms
and married non-Danish professionals and artisans. Thus both Danish parents and children left the farms in greater numbers than did the Poles.

Some women stayed on the farms. We have from sociologist Harold Pedersen an account of one woman who continued farming after her husband died.
Mrs. A. M. Nielsen's first name is not on the schedule that Pedersen filled out
in 1948, so I refer to her simply as "AM." She was then sixty-two, running the

Home sewing, 1910s. Settlers and Native women sewed on treadle machines and darned, patched, and ironed with care. Clothing was important for rural families, and its care enabled family members to present themselves in public with dignity. Native girls learned to sew by hand and by machine in boarding schools, creating most of the clothing worn in school and later at home. Catalog and newspaper pictures often served as models for homemade patterns, and country stores sold inexpensive, mass-produced patterns.

farm with her fourth son, Howard, who was thirty-five, and expecting to pass the farm on to him. AM was born in Denmark in 1886, left home to work out at fourteen, and probably came to the United States soon after. When she married in 1905, at nineteen, her husband had already been farming a 160-acre farm for eleven years, and he belonged to the dairy and feed store co-operatives. Between 1905 and 1922, she birthed nine children, four daughters and five sons, and farmed with her husband. After he died, she stayed on to farm with Howard.[34]

We know AM stayed on the farm for more than forty years with two of her daughters nearby: Alma, who began working at thirteen for a Danish farmer and later married and lived on a farm, and Dora, who left home at nineteen, married a Swede, and lived on the "next farm." The two younger daughters, however, left the farm at fifteen. One married a Norwegian at eighteen and farmed in Polk County; the other married a Dane and moved to California. Three of AM's four sons left farming, two to work in St. Paul. In 1948, AM listed herself as a member of St. Paul's Lutheran Church Ladies' Aid Society and gave her occupation as "housework."[35]

By the 1920s, native-born Polish and Danish daughters were venturing farther and farther from home. The Nielsen and Osowski children were not much different. Few daughters married men from their ethnic or religious birth groups. They formed part of what came to be known in the 1950s as the "melting pot." They retained many ethnic traditions but were not self-conscious about them. Withee and Thorp remained trading centers for farmers, their residents linked to cities by the many who left. Families continued to be the basis for relationships, but now they were ethnically mixed. They carried the value of family relationships and community with them as they moved together into a common culture.

Native Nations
INDIAN HOMELANDS

Wherever Euro-Americans came from, they settled among Indian nations long established in Wisconsin. Settlers often did not know the tribal affiliations of the Indian people they encountered as they settled among them. By the 1850s, most Wisconsin Indian nations had signed treaties regulating their relations with the U.S. government. Interpretation of those international treaties is still under dispute, but the practical result was that Indian nations lost control over much of their land and many of their people were forced to move west of the Mississippi River. In north-central Wisconsin, settlers were most likely to encounter people from the Ho-Chunk, Menominee, or Lac du Flambeau Chippewa bands. The Ho-Chunk, old residents of the Great Lakes region, had returned to Wisconsin after being forcibly moved west by the U.S. government. They had no land guaranteed to them in Wisconsin, yet they refused to leave. The Menominee, who also consider themselves indigenous to Wisconsin, likewise refused to move westward. They retained 236,000 acres of land under an 1854 treaty. The Lac du Flambeau Chippewa, who have an oral tradition of migration from the Great Lakes region to the East Coast and then back west to Madeline Island, settled inland and had control of seventy thousand acres through an 1854 treaty. Because treaties confirmed the rights of these people to hunt, fish, and gather throughout their original homelands, they often traveled outside these reserves.[36]

The Ho-Chunk had a difficult time maintaining access to their traditional homelands. According to Ho-Chunk accounts, they had lived for thousands of years in the western Great Lakes region, south and west of present-day Green Bay. In the 1820s, the U.S. government recognized that the Ho-Chunk held title to more than 7 million acres of land in Wisconsin alone as well as a large area in northern Illinois. They cultivated large fields of corn, beans, and squash along the river ways. As American miners moved northwest into the lead fields of southern Wisconsin, the government forced the Ho-Chunk first to Iowa, then to northern Minnesota, then to South Dakota, and finally in 1865 to Nebraska. Despite official removal, groups constantly returned to their homelands. As settlers now occupied the choicest lands, some Ho-Chunk purchased remaining parcels and others simply occupied unclaimed land held by the federal government.

Ho-Chunk studio portrait. Although Ho-Chunk did not permit photographers to enter their villages or encampments, individuals might commission a family portrait or allow photographs to be taken of their performances while in town or at fairs. Ho-Chunk women can usually be identified by their many strings of beads, which they wore for formal occasions.

The injustice of the situation finally came to a climax near Reedsburg in 1873, when soldiers arrested and removed Ho-Chunk leader Yellow Thunder and his family from their land. Settlers, who sided with Yellow Thunder, forced soldiers to free him and then joined in pressuring Congress to allow Ho-Chunk families to homestead forty-acre parcels of land. A statute allowing them to do so became law in 1875.

Families then scattered to take up land wherever it remained available. They found parcels in the counties of Adams, Clark, Jackson, Juneau, Marathon, Shawano, Trempealeau, and Wood. These homesteads provided a base and a living for about half of the Ho-Chunk, who built log houses and farmed much as did the settlers. Others continued to rely on yearly rounds of trapping, hunting, sugaring, ricing, and berry picking. During July, August, and September, people gathered near Black River Falls, where the wild blueberry marshes were the most extensive in the state. They traveled north to gather raspberries and blackberries and south to work in the cultivated cranberry marshes settlers had established. Some hired out to husk corn and pick potatoes, using canvas tents for their migratory work. By the turn of the century, the Ho-Chunk had established what anthropologist Nancy Oestreich Lurie calls a "systematic itinerant economy." With this independent and self-sufficient lifestyle, they could maintain their customs and language. Women continued to weave baskets, cutting ash splints on the land of kin and friends, and to make elaborately beaded arm bands, belts, bandoliers, garters, and hair bindings.[37]

In 1902, when ethnologist A. E. Jenks tried to locate the Wisconsin Ho-Chunk through letters to postal officials, he found they were scattered in various parts of the state. About twelve families wintered from November to March near Fountain City. One family and a single man wintered eighteen miles north of Fountain City near Alma. In Marquette and Jefferson counties, many families moved to winter locations on Green Lake. Eight or ten people stayed near the popular summer resort of Ripon. Several hundred lived in the eastern part of Marathon County in Pike Lake township. A few wintered in northwest Dane County. Indian agents at the Menominee and Lac Courte Oreilles reservations reported that Ho-Chunk families came to participate in summer dances but that most lived near Wittenberg and Black River Falls.[38]

Regardless of where they lived, Ho-Chunk people gathered annually near Kilbourn City, later known as the Dells. Nearby, Yellow Thunder had a forty-acre homestead, where soldiers had arrested him in 1873 and where he died the following year. He was buried near the road that led south from Kilbourn City to Baraboo, a spot the Historical Society of Sauk County later commemorated with a historical marker. Ho-Chunk elders remembered they would dance at the site where he died and camp at the Dells to renew themselves spiritually. Photographer Henry H. Bennett noted that when he arrived at Kilbourn City in 1857, Ho-Chunk, Ojibwe, and Menominee people regularly visited there, but by 1894 only Ho-Chunk came to fish and hunt. "They seem more loth to leave this region than either of the other tribes," he wrote to a friend.[39]

The Menominee had a different experience. They managed to resist removal and were able to retain some of their homelands. In the early 1800s, as settlers moved into the present-day Green Bay area, the Menominee moved from their villages to the Little Chute on the lower Fox River. Then, in 1837, as that area also became settled by Euro-Americans, they moved southwest of what is now Appleton to Lake Poygan. In 1852 the American government also threatened to remove them from their homelands to the west. The Menominee Nation negotiated a treaty in which they agreed to move once more, but only to a location chosen by the people, on the Wolf River, away from lakeshores where they had previously settled. The spot chosen was one where the women had often camped to gather cranberries and rushes for their woven mats, near a falls where the sturgeon spawned. There were clearings for dwellings and gardens, maple groves for sugaring, and abundant wild rice beds nearby. They hoped it would be a good place to raise their children and avoid the terrible troubles of the previous decades. A devastating smallpox epidemic carried off one in four of the population in 1834; a cholera epidemic in 1847 killed many more. Those who survived appeared healthy to the Quakers who visited them in 1847, but the government argued the isolation of the new area would keep them safer. Settlers proved both helpful—signing petitions for the Menominee to stay in Wisconsin—and hostile—burning and looting their homes.

After the fall harvest in 1852, more than two thousand Menominee people prepared to travel to their new home on the Wolf River. Of this group, women probably made up more than half the adults and children more than half the entire population. The women gathered together household goods—essential pots, spoons, pails, and baskets for spring sugaring—hand axes for chopping wood, and mats for shelters. They readied important sewing implements: steel awls set into bone handles, metal spangles, some ribbons, wool cloth. The fur-trading system had allowed women to perfect tanning skills, to purchase new tools for domestic use, and to acquire European sewing skills which they had blended with Native techniques and designs to create new objects of great beauty. They were already known for their geometrical ribbonwork sewing and their floral appliqué pouches, bands, and sashes. Their moccasins were in great demand by Native and non-Native alike. The women would have taken these prized objects with them to their new home. Most dressed simply in blue frocks over long leggings with embroidered edges and a short upper top.[40]

Decades later, survivors remembered that trip well. The government delayed their departure until November and then forced them to leave some implements and all their stock behind. High waters made the trip extremely dangerous; canoes tipped and many elders and children drowned. As the harsh winter closed in, ice began to form and they had to make camp along the way and resume their travel in the spring. The group that finally assembled along the shores of the Wolf River included many Menominee of mixed heritage who had intermarried with French and Scotch-English. Métis families from Green Bay joined them, as did some four hundred individuals who had lived and farmed at Lake Poygan and identified with the Menominee community. Families settled in clan groupings around separate chiefs. The government recognized Oshkosh, of the Bear Clan, as the principal chief in negotiations, but the other chiefs considered themselves autonomous on most matters.

The first two winters at the new settlement were difficult. It was cold, and there was a lack of wildlife for food. The government had promised farm equipment, goods, and rations but failed to deliver them to the struggling community. When the government did send provisions, they were meager, sometimes even rotten. The bands had to make their own decisions on how best to survive. Some settled near Keshena Falls; others on the banks of Lake Oconto. There was also conflict with Father Florimond Bonduel, the Capuchin priest who had helped broker the agreement with the government that allowed the Menominee to remain in Wisconsin and who accompanied them to their new home. In the midst of these privations, Bonduel asked for compensation for his services in negotiating the treaty and title to land for a church. When the chiefs refused his claims, Bonduel chopped down the cross he had raised over the new community, declared the Menominee an ungrateful people who did not deserve a missionary, and departed. Chief Oshkosh wrote in 1854 to the subagent at Butte des Morts, John Suydam, that the priest "has already created some hard feeling amongst us." Moreover, white settlers were building mills along the Oconto, on land clearly belonging to the Menominee. Oshkosh asked the government for help in repulsing the depredations on their land.[41]

The tribe signed two treaties defining the boundaries of their new homeland, each time under renewed governmental threats that they might still be forcibly removed west. The government claimed the right to apportion despite the chiefs' protests that they had control over such decisions. The agent threatened the leaders that if they did not submit, "the Strong Arm, that rules over this country" would arrest and put them in prison.[42]

The relocated community on the Wolf River survived the first years primarily on its own, clearing the land, planting gardens, constructing shelters. By 1861 its members had built 75 log houses and 112 frame houses, had accumulated stock, and were cultivating 400 acres of land. The women planted gardens, and families processed large quantities of maple sugar to sell to traders. The community suffered crushing losses of crops and stock due to severe winter weather followed by drought. The government had appointed a blacksmith but replaced him in 1861 and added a foreman for the repair shop, a farmer, a miller, an interpreter, and several Native strikers to scout for lumber possibilities. More than one hundred Menominee men left to serve in the Union army that year, some as young as fourteen. The women took much of the responsibility for the community's survival during the war years.[43]

The end of the war coincided with an outbreak of smallpox. The non-Christians scattered to live in the forests. The Christians who stayed suffered enormous losses before they, too, left their villages. Great winds and fires swept through the standing timber in 1868. Yet the Menominee refused to leave their homelands. That same year Mary Weso, a young Métis of Scotch-English-French and Menominee heritage, married one of the young Civil War veterans, Henry Lookaround of the Eagle Clan. Mary was born in the 1840s during the first difficult days of the relocation and survived the hard times of the early 1860s. Descendants remembered her as a robust woman, noted for her buckskin and beadwork, cooking skills, hospitality, and work for the Catholic church. Mary and Henry built a log cabin on the shore of the Wolf River, leased farm teams, and operated their own lumber camp. She lived to age seventy-four. What stories she must have told her grandchildren.[44]

These hardy Menominee women developed subsistence farming during the next decades as the lumbering economy took hold. In 1890, almost forty years after settlement along the Wolf, a group of Menominee women feasted visiting ethnologist Walter Hoffman. He reported that they served him roast beef, pound cake, raspberry pie, and coffee. Most were bilingual and Catholic. They lived in comfortable log houses that differed little from settlers' except for the beautiful hand-woven rush mats that often covered the wood floors. They used modern stoves and had mosquito netting to fend off the worst summer insects.[45]

The Chippewa people at Lac du Flambeau had yet a different history during the late nineteenth century. By the 1840s, the Chippewa Band of the Lake Superior Ojibwe had established a permanent village at what was later known as Lac du Flambeau, but they continued their seasonal travel to harvest resources. The band ceded a large tract of land in treaties but refused to give up members' rights to harvest natural resources everywhere in their homelands. The women produced items that trading posts and settlers were eager to obtain: tanned hides, woven mats and birch-bark baskets, sewn moccasins and snowshoes. They sold food surpluses from their gardens at the trading posts and in the nearest settler communities. This informal economy was well established in the nineteenth century.[46]

Anishinaabe sugaring camp, 1840s. Women organized spring sugaring trips, maintained the needed equipment, and supervised the processing in this essential family enterprise. Lac du Flambeau elders remembered processing 10,000 pounds of maple sugar and several hundred gallons of syrup in 1920. The Anishinaabe considered maple sugar a sacred food given by the creator for their use. Feasts, singing, and dancing preceded the annual maple sugar harvest. Leaders maintained that the privilege of making sugar from maple trees throughout their historical lands was reserved to them by treaty.

In 1850, when President Zachary Taylor attempted to revoke the Chippewas' harvesting rights, the chiefs immediately opposed the claim, forming alliances with missionaries, news editors, and local whites who benefited from business with the Native community. In 1851 the government issued an order to remove the entire band to Minnesota, but united opposition forced it to withdraw this command as well. Although the government encouraged the band to make a living within the reserved lands, it did not rescind members' rights to hunt and gather on their traditional homelands. Thus the band continued to practice their old economy through much of the nineteenth century. They hunted, fished, gathered, and gardened.[47]

There was no way for the government to know just what kind of enterprise was going on at Lac du Flambeau for most of the nineteenth century. For many years, the government's main contact with the band was through an agent who brought annuities by train to Phillips, about seventy-five miles from his post at Ashland and some forty miles from the Lac du Flambeau village. The agent dispensed annuities in Phillips rather than bringing them overland because the forest was dense and the roads impassable. Inaccessibility was one reason the government tried to consolidate the band at Bad River in 1872, but again the Chippewa refused to leave their homelands. By 1886 the government had increased contact with Lac du Flambeau by assigning a farmer and a teacher to the village. Both reported that the yearly rounds of hunting and gathering continued. The school, for example, would empty as families prepared to leave the village for hunting in fall. Children returned in December or January, left again for sugaring in April, and returned in summer when the women planted their gardens.[48]

By the 1890s women had developed extensive gardens and alternative sources of food. They were also producing large quantities of handcrafts for sale. Families had cut lumber from their allotments and some men were working in sawmills. But women and men were steadily losing access to off-reservation resources. At the end of the 1870s, the state of Wisconsin claimed control of the wildlife over the entire area, not only for commercial and sport hunters and fishers but also on land reserved to the band. Federal district courts held that Congress alone could control the rights to hunt, fish, and gather on reservations, but in 1896 the Wisconsin attorney general held that when Wisconsin became a state it abrogated any previous exemptions and that when off their reservations Native people came under state laws. In 1908 the Wisconsin Supreme Court supported this claim, and the state maintained its right for seventy-five years, until the U.S. Supreme Court held it unconstitutional in 1983.[49]

Despite growing efforts to keep Native peoples confined to reservations in Wisconsin, a few created communities on abandoned cut-over land. In these villages, outside government agents' control, Indians formed separate communities. Best known are those created by groups of Potawatomi, Ojibwe, and a few Ho-Chunk near Rozellville in Marathon County during the 1870s to 1890s, near Perkinstown in Taylor County from 1896 to 1906, and at McCord in Oneida County from 1905 to 1930. Usually known to settlers simply as "Indian farms," these communities established subsistence economies—they gardened, planted, hunted, processed maple sugar, and created and sold beadwork and baskets to settler neighbors. Rozellville became a trade center, "Indian-oriented," as one account put it, for the nearby village hosted dances and feasts that attracted hundreds of Indian people annually. As settlers claimed the surrounding land, these families moved northwest to Perkinstown and, after a smallpox epidemic there in 1901, northeast to McCord.[50]

Through all these economic struggles during the late nineteenth and early twentieth centuries, Indian women mostly stayed put. Their unwillingness to leave their homeland encouraged experimentation with new methods of surviving on the land: lumbering, farming, and creating handcrafted products to sell. They persuaded their families to continue hunting, fishing, sugaring, and ricing and passed on older processing methods even as they acquired new skills. Homelands meant just that to Indian women: places you called home, places where you stayed despite hard times, places to which you could always return.

2

Woodlands

My grandmother Matilda Rauscher went straight to Phillips, a lumbering town, when she arrived in the United States from Bohemia in 1892. With her she brought a small document about the size of today's passport, her *Dienstbuch*, or Domestic Servant Book. She must have felt for this document often as she traveled to Hamburg, then to New York by ship, then to Wisconsin by train, and on north to Phillips. There were jobs in Phillips, and she came with her recommendation in that booklet. Each member of the Austro-Hungarian Empire had to register for this work permit on reaching the age of fourteen, and each employer entered in a space reserved for comments opinions of the worker's job performance. Matilda kept this document all her life, and I inherited it when she died. The single entry in it testified that Matilda had been employed in Bohemia and had completed her work service well. In northern Wisconsin, where many boarding house–keepers were of German heritage, it would have ensured Matilda's prompt hiring as an experienced worker.

Twenty-one years before Matilda arrived, another immigrant domestic worker had similarly come seeking work. This story of women in the woodlands economy begins with Emina, a young woman from Sweden who worked southeast of Phillips at Peshtigo Village. It was 1871 and the lumbering economy was in full swing there. During the next twenty years it would move west, creating lumbering towns such as Phillips—and a demand for women's work.

Forest and Fire
Emina's Story [Johnson, born in Sweden, 1854]

Emina went to church that October evening in 1871 with her sweetheart. Her mistress, Margaret Sheppard, and the youngest son had gone to New York State to visit family. An older son was in Racine visiting his grandparents. Her boss, William Sheppard, assistant manager of the lumber mill, and eight-year-old Fred stayed at home. The family home stood on a bluff along the Peshtigo River. Emina's job was to care for the household and to look after young Fred.[1]

Emina came from Sweden to the small logging village on the Peshtigo River because of the job opportunities. Like other young Swedish immigrant women, she took a job as a domestic servant. It was easy for these enterprising young women to find work in the booming Peshtigo Village. William Ogden, a Chicago developer, declared the site perfect for establishing what he boasted was the country's largest woodware factory. Peshtigo Village lay seven miles up the river from its mouth at Peshtigo Harbor on Lake Michigan's Green Bay. The Peshtigo Company built a dam, and by 1867 a wooden railroad with steel straps spiked to its surface joined Peshtigo Village to the harbor. Within three years, the Peshtigo Company had built docks, a steam-powered mill, and a woodware factory. Sheppard was second-in-command at the lumber mill that stood on the east side of the river just below the dam and provided wood for the gigantic factory that lay farther south of the mill on the same bank. The mill had 97 saws that cut 150,000 feet of timber each day. Workers at the woodware factory daily turned out 50 boxes of clothespins, 200 wooden keelers (small tubs used as baby bathtubs), 600 common pails, 5,000 broom handles, plus hundreds of fish kits and paint and tobacco pails and thousands of shingles.[2]

Between the mill and the factory a single bridge linked the village settlements that lined both banks. Streets spread in rectangles east and west of the river. To the east, just across the road from the mill, stood a three-storied company boarding house for unmarried workers. Nearby were company houses for workers with families and a company store. Fred's school and a Congregational church, probably the one Emina attended, stood near the workers' housing.

Across the bridge to the west, outside company land, a second community flourished. Liquor was not prohibited there, and enterprising businessmen had established saloons. There, too, Catholics were building a church. The Catholic community shared its priest with Marinette, the nearest village, about seven miles northeast of Peshtigo Village. Farther to the west lay three settlements, called simply Upper, Middle, and Lower Sugar Bush. *Sugar bush* was the name given to areas where maple trees flourished. These settler communities lay away from the river. There families were clearing small areas to farm, and some women were already selling eggs, butter, and vegetables to the companies for their logging and milling employees.

Around the small settler villages rose the hardwood trees that fed the mill that fed the factory. The resident Catholic priest, Reverend Peter Pernin, wrote, "Trees, trees everywhere, nothing else but trees as far as you can travel from the bay, either towards the north or west." Today experts describe the forest as mixed coniferous-deciduous: to the north boreal, to the south deciduous. To lumber companies, trees signified great profits; to the settlers, a chance to own a home and a farm. It was a logging frontier.[3]

Lake Michigan joined two economies, one rooted in the forest villages of Wisconsin, the other in Chicago, where workers sorted the Peshtigo broom handles, clothespins, and keelers as well as thousands of board feet of white pine lumber for markets in the East and the West. Capitalists raised money for logging and milling ventures. Railroads took the finished lumber and broom handles to the timberless prairies for settler houses and households.[4]

The lumber industry was part of a vast enterprise—the harvesting of timber in broad swaths that reached from lake to river and back from the river into the heart of the land. Each October thousands of lumbermen arrived. Single women came to work in the many boarding houses and to provide services for the single men or to work in the homes of wealthier mill supervisors like Sheppard. Married women who accompanied their husbands either cared for their own families on nearby farms in the sugar bush or in the small workers' houses at Peshtigo Village or lived with them at scattered logging camps. Cutting, transporting, milling, and manufacturing in this forest world was hard and dangerous work, and many women tended to the needs of men involved in it.

But this is Emina's story. By the time Emina and her sweetheart returned home from church that October evening, they could see red spots rising and falling on the horizon. The air was deadly still—almost ominous. They heard a low rumble from the southwest. Villagers soon crowded into the home to rouse Sheppard, who had gone to bed early, exhausted from fighting forest fires the week before.

It had been an extremely dry fall, and forest fires had become common. For the past few weeks the fires gave all the villagers concern. Every man joined in keeping the fires from the village, and boys helped pass buckets of water from the river. Sheppard was in charge of the firefighters, and the villagers came to him for advice.

The red spots on the horizon quickly lengthened into tongues of flame borne on what seemed to be a tornado. Great balls of fire shot through the air, followed by huge burning logs. Villagers had approached the earlier fires with grim determination to save the village, but fighting this fire seemed impossible. They ran for the river.

From the bluff, Emina and Fred watched the villagers below as they attempted to escape the firestorm. People from both sides of town ran for the bridge, which collapsed under their weight. People clung to logs and booms in the water as tongues of flame and burning logs showered down on them. The big boarding house shook on its foundation. That was all Emina saw, for Sheppard ordered her to take Fred to shelter under the river bluff. After burying a gun, a violin, and silverware, the two men joined them.

A woman whose father had a water mill about five miles from Menominee described the fire's progress from survivors' accounts. One sawmill survivor told her that he, too, first heard a distant rumbling. It sounded like the roar of breakers or of a railway train passing through hilly country, at times dying away and again increasing to such violence that the windows shook. Then fine cinders began to fall. He roused the camp—five men, two women, a boy six years old, and an infant—and checked with another crew located near a river where sixteen men and boys and two women were in camp. This crew told him the town of Peshtigo was probably burning, judging by the glare and the awful fire raging in that direction. They planned to take a wagon to the village of Menominee, another five miles away, but just then the tornado that preceded the fire crossed the river and swept toward them, breaking down the forest, twisting off huge trees by the roots and laying them flat in all directions. Instead of fleeing in the wagon, all took refuge under a high stream bank. In about two minutes the tornado swept over without harm. They went back to the camp to collect valuables and then returned to the pond. Balls of fire as large as a person's head began to shoot like bombs from the coming fire. Soon the balls were falling all around, and a hundred fires blazed in the clearing. The balls did not fall directly from the sky but shot over from the woods in a parabola, like a shell fired at short range. They dashed pails of water over each other. Then, the survivor wrote, "a wave of fire over a hundred feet high came rolling through the woods, lit up everything with a fearful glare, reared its awful crest for a moment towards heaven and then swept like lightning in huge tongues of flame across the clearing." From below the ten-foot bank they watched the amphitheater of flame. Everything blazed at once for half a mile up and down the stream as far as they could see, the flames reaching to twice the height of the trees. As the flame passed over their heads, they ducked into the water and stayed under as long as possible.[5]

From below the bank in Peshtigo, Emina saw the same fearful spectacle. By keeping their clothes constantly damp, Emina, her young man, Fred, and Sheppard survived the next hour while Peshtigo Village burned. When the quartet emerged from the river they saw dazed survivors searching for their families among the burned bodies strewn about the streets. No boats, wagons, or animals survived. At first light a man began the eight-mile walk to Peshtigo Harbor to get help. A few hours later a wagon and team arrived, following the charred railroad tracks. Another wagon from Marinette brought bread and coffee, and a tent was set up for women, children, and the badly injured.

In four hours, a ten-mile swath of fire cut through forty miles, killing an estimated twelve hundred people. Several hundred bodies were found in Peshtigo, most of them unidentified immigrant workers in the boarding house, others in the Congregational and Catholic churches, where people had sought refuge. One young survivor later recounted that seven women gave birth that night in the mud and ooze of the riverbank while men poured water over them. Several of the women died. Only three of the babies lived.[6]

The heaviest casualties were in the Sugar Bush communities, where there was no river for refuge. There crews found 241 burned bodies, almost half of them children. Women who worked at some sixty logging camps scattered around Peshtigo also died. About five miles from Menominee at a small mill, a family kept a boarding house for a crew of ten, the woman serving as cook. The family with their infant stayed behind with a few men while the rest of the crew, including the bookkeeper, went into town that Sunday. The bookkeeper returned to camp just as the fierce, hot gusts of wind were fanning the smoldering logs into flame. He grabbed the account books, scooped up the baby, and ran to the riverbank. The woman and the others also managed to get to the river. Later someone found them there alive, blinded from the smoke and heat and badly blistered. The bookkeeper roped them together and guided them out over burnt logs and ashes to the nearby village of Frenchtown. The woman and her baby died several months later.[7]

Near Marinette at Birch Creek, a settlement of about forty families, every building burned and twenty-two bodies were later identified. As in other places, families that tried to outrun the flames died. Two girls there, aged ten and eleven, were the only survivors of a family of nine simply because they could not run. When the two youngsters began to stumble and fall, their father threw them into the water and mud under the roots of an overturned tree and told them to crouch down and stay until he came for them. They survived while the rest of the fleeing family died. One woman recalled that the great forests lay row after row, as though cut with a scythe, their tops pointing north. Near Birch Creek, she said, the fire burned so deeply into the peat bogs near the river that smoke came up through the snow that winter and the bogs were still smoking the following summer.[8]

The refugees were taken to Peshtigo Harbor settlement and then by steamboat to Green Bay. Emina probably left with young Fred for Peshtigo Harbor. Although this story is hers, it was not written by her but by Fred Sheppard, who recounted her story as he told his own many years later. After the fire, he went with other refugees to Peshtigo Harbor, then to Green Bay, and on to Racine, where he joined his brother and grandparents. Emina probably saw Fred safely into his grandmother's arms, for the men insisted that all women and children leave the devastated area while they organized relief efforts. William Sheppard stayed to supervise the rescue operation as crews of men arrived to bury the dead. Emina later returned to Peshtigo to resume her household duties, for she appears on the Sheppard family census in 1880.

That is all of Emina's life I could locate. With the fragments of other women's stories, it reminds us that settler women were an important part of both the woodlands story and what is often called the deadliest fire in American history.

VICTIMS AND REFUGEES OF THE GREAT FIRES

Most descriptions of the Peshtigo Fire focus on the settlers who died and the harrowing accounts left by survivors of those terrifying days. The five thousand people who survived had lost their homes and needed immediate relief. While the men banished from Peshtigo the women and children who survived the fire, women were quite visible in organizing relief efforts. Those efforts began within hours as the surrounding villages received refugees and sent aid. Larger state efforts started the next day. A telegram from Green Bay arrived at the capitol in Madison on the evening of Monday, October 9, but no one was there to open it until the following morning. The elderly clerk ran to the governor's house on Lake Monona, where he found only the governor's twenty-five-year-old wife, Frances Bull Fairchild. Governor Lucius Fairchild and the chief state officials were all on their way to Chicago with relief supplies for victims of a disastrous fire there.

As the clerk excitedly finished reading the telegram, Frances grabbed her cloak and headed for the capitol to take charge of the Wisconsin disaster relief. After calling the governor back to Wisconsin, she quickly issued orders and made requisitions. She commandeered a carload of food and clothing awaiting shipment to Chicago, called on the women of Madison to bring blankets, which they stuffed into the boxcar, and ordered railroad officials to give the rescue car precedence over all other traffic. Then she called the Madison populace together to fill another boxcar with more food and clothing. Mary Fairchild Morris later recalled that on this Tuesday her mother had "acted as Governor of Wisconsin." Lucius Fairchild returned the following day to resume his duties.[9]

Women in major cities like Green Bay and Milwaukee quickly joined relief committees. They contacted women in other parts of the state and country to

Harper's Weekly *view of the Peshtigo fire. With no photographs to depict the fire, this popular magazine commissioned artists to imagine scenes of families and animals fleeing as flames engulfed their farms.*

send aid. The Civil War had ended just six years earlier, and many women's groups were accustomed to responding to national calls for relief for soldiers, veterans, and their families. During the war, almost every town in Wisconsin had its own women's aid society, which organized oyster dinners and strawberry festivals to raise funds for relief. They made and filled thousands of "comfort bags" for soldiers, providing them with pins, needles, thread, and darning yarn. They knit wool socks, sewed hundreds of flannel shirts, and made jellies, blackberry juice, cakes, and pastries. They sent hundreds of barrels of "anti-scorbutic" food to soldiers to prevent scurvy: sauerkraut, horseradish, onions, potatoes. Wisconsin women sent food and clothing via Chicago and the U.S. Sanitary Commission and through soldiers' aid societies that carried stores, private boxes, and letters directly to hospitals and camps. At home they assisted families by finding employment for wives, daughters, and disabled veterans, and they helped widows and orphans by obtaining contracts to sew uniforms. They saw to it that families received soldiers' savings, state family allotments, and county funds when needed. At the city and town level, most relief work was done by women.[10]

After the Peshtigo fire, the governor and relief committees sent out letters and press releases. Ladies Relief Societies, some as far east as New Jersey and as far north as Quebec, responded with aid for "the Suffering West." Most gathered and sent clothing and provisions. Miss M. Brodish of Decorah, Iowa, wrote to ask if a carload of potatoes would be useful. The Milwaukee relief committee also bought household items, everything from cook stoves and irons to yokes of oxen. It even built houses. It arranged for Mrs. McDole, who had been almost blinded by the fire, to receive free railway passage, and for orphan Charlotte King to be trained as a milliner so she could be self-supporting. Women asked for assistance in purchasing tools to sustain themselves economically. Widow Lydia Russell wrote from Maine, where she had taken refuge to recover her health, to ask if the committee could also help her replace a sewing machine burned in the fire. "If I have that or the means to get on it would be a very great help to me," she wrote. "I am left entirely destitute dependent upon my own labour for my support and am very poorly in health."[11]

At Green Bay a relief committee was quickly organized, and Elizabeth Therese Fisher Baird distributed donations from women's groups. Nellie and Annie Rice wrote to Baird in March 1872 to thank her for the two dollars she had sent. "We lost our house and barn and all the fences," they wrote, "and we had to run to one of the neighbors. We have had to live in a house all Winter that is not sided or plastered and it has been so cold that we couldn't keep warm with two stoves in one room." One person wrote to Baird from Philadelphia, noting that the *New York Tribune* had mentioned her as a suitable person to distribute money to orphans. Thus, with the help of relief by women and men, the homeless refugees gradually resumed their lives.[12]

The danger from fire was far from over. Fires continued long into the twentieth century, less widespread but terrifying nonetheless. Fire followed settlers into their forest homesteads. A nun left an account of a harrowing fire that almost destroyed a hospital near Marshfield in 1893. Sister Alphonsa remembered that the people of Marshfield had just helped the nuns build their hospital and living quarters when the fire began. For six weeks, no one saw the sun because of the smoke. People could hardly open their eyes. Many fled the surrounding farms as the fire consumed houses, barns, and other structures. The farmers dug large ditches: the flames simply jumped across. The fire crawled along the grass and up into the trees. "No one could stop it," Sister Alphonsa recalled. The people of Marshfield brought out one hundred buckets to carry water from the pump to save the hospital. The fire approached their little cemetery and attacked the crosses. The nuns prayed; the priests blessed the air. And then, said Sister Alphonsa, "The dear Lord heard our prayer; a great storm arose and put out the fire."[13]

Only slightly less dramatic was Margaret Gruener's account of a fire she experienced twenty-four years later, in 1917. She was taking care of a small child at a home in a wooded area near Medford when a fire swept through. She grabbed the child, wrapped it in a coat, and headed blindly down the road. Her father, who came looking for her, guided her to safety by calling to her through the smoke.[14]

Such were the stories told by survivors of the lumbering era. They formed a background chorus as the skinning of the land went on. By 1895, although the area around Peshtigo had been logged over and the Peshtigo Harbor settlement abandoned, the town survived, as did the memories of what became known as the Great Peshtigo Fire. Nearly fifty years later, Peshtigo inhabitants formed a historical society and began to collect relics of their famous fire. The fire left little beyond the mass grave where the charred remains of hundreds of villagers lay. But the townspeople collected what household items they could and retold the story from survivors' accounts. The logging frontier had already become a remembered place of great logjams and gigantic loggers, a male frontier. But the fires and the small museum at Peshtigo remind us of the women's frontier, where they worked as maids, cooks, housekeepers, homemakers, and farmers.[15]

SKINNING THE LAND

The fires that destroyed Chicago and Peshtigo in October 1871 created a demand for lumber. The Peshtigo Company began to rebuild immediately. The new Peshtigo mill was ready when high waters came in the spring of 1872, and the crew milled the lumber as usual. The men worked day and night to keep the mills at Peshtigo and the harbor sawing at top speed. The harbor mill reached an output of 250,000 board feet of lumber per day. During the next twenty years logging on a grand scale continued around Peshtigo, the logging crews moving north each season. The need for lumber on the prairies never slackened.

Menominee people had once lived nearby, and Native women still visited in the fall to harvest maple sugar. Hunting groups crossed the area during the winter. Although Native people had been logging in some areas around Peshtigo, newspapers reported only one Native person burned that summer, near Oconto. No Native villages remained within the areas that burned so brutally in October 1871. Fires and tornados had preceded the logging era. The Menominee remembered a site about two miles east of the Wolf River, near the present Menominee Nation, a prairie seven to eight miles long. They talked about the prairie amid the forest as a reminder of the power of their sacred animal, the thunderbird, to bring destruction. One grandmother related how before the white men came a hunting party had visited this area three times. On the first visit it was completely wooded; on the second they found a tornado had destroyed all the animals and trees; on the third it had burned over completely. The thunderbird, she said, had caused destruction in the area so nothing would grow.[16]

Similar winds and fire destroyed many trees in 1868. This time Natives knew that lumber companies were cutting timber illegally on the reservation, increasing the fire danger in the slash-covered areas. Natives, whether Menominee or others the accounts do not say, visited the areas of the fires, some as separate crews and some as part of mixed logging teams. A few Euro-American accounts claim that fires set by Native hunters and the slash of railroad clearings, logging camps, and settlements contributed to the hundreds of individual fires that burned through the forests that dry summer. More often, Natives warned settlers to leave as the fires intensified or showed them methods for surviving forest fires. According to one account, a Sugar Bush farm and trading family survived because the wife was Menominee. She told her husband and sons to plow great circles of land around the house, and her relatives came and helped save the house and trading post by putting wet blankets on the roof. Other accounts grudgingly acknowledged that Native people knew how to survive forest fires. If forewarned, they might clear a wide space around houses. In emergencies they made a clearing, scraped a hole in the ground, and buried themselves under the earth. Or they sought shelter in creeks and rivers. Mainly, Native people chose to leave when fire threatened.[17]

Once the fur trading economy declined, Indigenous people also had to depend upon logging. In 1871, the Menominee Council unanimously rejected the sale of their land to timber companies and ten years later organized their own tribal lumber company. Menominee logged 12 million feet of pine and floated it downriver to mills. Menominee never logged out their timber as did companies that controlled timberlands. Both they and government agents wanted timber to be a sustainable resource. Here, too, women had to maintain small farms while men worked more than half the year at lumbering. Joint management of resources allowed the Menominee community greater flexibility, but women had to supplement the income men made from lumbering with farming and sales of maple sugar, berries, mats, and baskets. All women in these areas worked hard and creatively to support their families.[18]

For most of the men, once the logs were in the water their job was done. Specialized crews took the logs downstream, a dangerous job that required both skill and daring. The rest returned to their homes to do some summer farming. The transition from woodland to farmland was not always easy. The male subculture gave men a lifestyle both difficult and exciting. Some looked forward to being with their families and to farming. For settlers, at least, that was why they had worked for those long hard months.

My grandmother Matilda and her future husband, Karl Schopper, expected to work in the lumber economy only long enough to establish their farm. With his brother Frank, Karl built a small log house on his cut-over land in 1887, then built an identical house a short distance away on land that Frank had purchased. Together they felled the trees for Karl's house with ax and adz, dovetailed the ends, and raised the roof timbers, carefully placing a scrap of lumber with the date "August 1887" in the roof boards. Karl's great-grandson Douglas Elliott found the marker in 1984 when he moved the house to the Colby Rural Arts Museum. It placed Karl on the land six years before Matilda arrived in Wisconsin in 1892. Karl brought Matilda to this log house in 1893 when they married. Each winter until 1901, Karl left to log. Each summer he added to the farm buildings, purchased farm animals, and cleared and planted. Matilda helped him with clearing and planting, and soon she could watch their children run barefoot in the meadows and by the stream that cut through their land. She birthed five children as they built up the farm. She loved working with the horses, planting, harvesting, laboring side by side with Karl in the fields.

Not all men employed in the lumber economy could make that work mesh with farming. My grandfather Leo Schopp, who would become Matilda's second husband after Karl died in 1901, never shared her love of farming. Leo fit as poorly into the migratory lumbering-farming pattern as Karl had fit well. Like Karl, Leo went into the lumber camps each winter. He came home each spring, bringing gifts for the children and carrying his precious accordion, but he could not settle into seasonal farming. Leo was popular as a musician and in demand to play for country dances in the evening. During the day, however, he would lounge about, watching Matilda and the children farm. He worked well in the forest, in logging teams, under a boss's supervision, but he just did not like farm work and refused to do it. Matilda used all her skills to try to involve Leo in the farm enterprise—expecting, asking, urging, finally angrily shouting. She could never make her second man into the farm partner she needed. Despite her growing family, she had to do most of the work with the help of her eight children. The oldest son, Frank, quickly learned to handle the farm work, and when he could do a man's job, Matilda told Leo to leave.

Certainly other farm wives had problems like Matilda's. Men did not always regard their lumbering money as part of a family wage. The money went to the men, usually at the end of the season, and the first claim on that money came as they ran the gauntlet of saloons and brothels set up along the roads leading out of the forests. If they managed to avoid these—and the nearby towns holding similar snares—they might bring some money back to their families, along with special treats. My mother remembered receiving a cap from Leo, a gift she treasured. Lumbering provided necessary cash, but if a man did not bring back his earnings, the farm enterprise could not go forward.

Summer fairs with their many enticements could also part men from their money. Red Cloud Woman complained of her husband spending money at the fair after it was set up in 1910. The Menominee lumber mill paid part of the men's wages in store credit for the family, but other wages belonged to the earner, and women's wages were usually less than those of men. The new Euro-American culture accepted and encouraged men to spend what they

Logging men at Laberges Mill, 1892. Itinerant photographers plied their trade in the logging camps, offering images that were finished as postcards for easy mailing home. Workers pooled their earnings to pay the photographer, and each received one or more copies in return. Matilda's brother Frank Rauscher, who cut logs while she cleaned rooms in a loggers' boarding house, is one of the loggers on this sled photographed near Stetsonville.

had worked so hard to earn. Public entertainment was mainly for men. Even the Keshena fair's merry-go-round seemed the province of men, not children as one might expect today.

There were also saloons closer to home, places that catered to both Native and settler men. The government kept saloons off the reservations, but nearby towns paid their municipal expenses in great part from saloon licenses. Saloons were male preserves, places to drink, swap stories, escape the cramped log houses full of squalling infants and tense wives. Jerkwater, an old saloon close to Matilda's home, was a place where men met. At first women could go there, too, but gradually it became all male—women had to wait outside. Later, inhabitants remembered a nearby brothel, supposedly erected for railroad men but available to others. Women attempted to keep up community dances, places where men, women, and children could meet. The women provided food, and the diligent farmers policed these dances. The community dances, the barn raisings, and the neighborly sharing all existed, as they do in our idealized image of rural life, but they existed in competition with the rough lumberjack culture and male entertainment, the saloons, brothels, and dance halls that competed for men's money, time, and affection. Fortunately for Matilda, she inherited the farm when her first husband died and managed to keep title to it. Competing commercial entertainment cultures posed threats for rural women, however, unless they worked in and profited from them.

Religious and secular reformers all addressed these problems. The issue was not so much what men did as how it affected women and children who had no

Camp village, ca. 1900. Although seldom mentioned in lumbering accounts, women cooked, cleaned, and produced food for logging camps, sometimes laboring alongside men at the end of a cross-saw.

direct access to the economy except through the work of their husbands and fathers. Germans, both Catholic and Protestant, refused to oppose the use of liquor, but other religions, including the Peyote religion (later called the Native American Church) and the Dream Dance, offered ways to help men resist alcohol and support their families. A family needed the work of each individual and support from the community to survive in this difficult economy. Commercial lumbering enterprises could help liberate families by providing cash, but what they gave, commercial entertainment enterprises could destroy.

SERVING THE LUMBERING ECONOMY

While many women ran the small farms from which lumber companies drew large numbers of male workers with enticements of cash, other women created the service infrastructures without which the lumber economy would falter. Women directly served the lumber economy by cooking, cleaning, laundering, running boarding houses and small shops, and providing sexual services for the males who dominated the work force. Women kept both the homes for middle-class families of men who managed the industry and the boarding houses in which lumber workers ate and slept. Families or older women ran boarding homes and hotels, hiring for short periods the young women who did the hardest work of cleaning, washing, cooking, and serving.

Women established this service economy quite early. In 1855, Margaret Swankle appears among a list of six women in the village of Jenny, later renamed Merrill. She ran a sawmill boarding house and in the 1860s and '70s operated the Eagle House Hotel with her husband. In the 1880s, Mrs. Rouleau ran a boarding house in Merrill and was known for her lemon pies, fish, and bread. At Wausau, women similarly operated hotels and boarding houses and also worked for the families of lumber barons who established their mansions there. While only a small number of women worked directly for lumber companies—one account estimated 1.5 percent of employees were women—they formed a crucial part of the overall service sector. At camps, women shared with men the tasks of cooking, but in sawmill towns, women dominated the serving work force. River ballads and chantey songs glorified the male who carried the ax and usually had women grieving for drowned raftmen. In reality, women were more likely the ones who fed the men at their boarding houses. Later, women also helped form office staffs. One floating office and supply store with a staff of eleven, caught on film by a local photographer near Eagle Rapids around 1900, showed six of them to be women.[19]

Athens and Phillips are examples of boarding house towns that sprang up in the 1880s. These boarding houses, huge by comparison with the small log houses of the settlers, were the engine of development. If a lumberjack had a place to live during the week, he could work at the sawmill, and if he could

Women servants at logging town boarding house, 1892. Working women frequently purchased group pictures at nearby studios. Matilda Rauscher is in the center of this group photographed in Phillips.

work, he and his family could get by until the farm could support them. On weekends he went home or to the nearby town. To supply these early boarding houses with food, companies set up farms or large gardens, where women worked raising vegetables.

Athens was established by Fred Rietbrock, a Milwaukee attorney who in the 1880s bought large tracts of land in Marathon County and built a sawmill and a series of two-storied log boarding houses. Rietbrock built his first boarding house in what he called Black Creek Falls (later renamed Athens) and installed the Albrecht family to operate it. Mariana Albrecht ran the boarding house and cooked for lumberjacks. Venison, salt pork, ox meat, potatoes, prunes, and dried apples were her staples. Mariana's husband built log houses for the lumbermen. To one newcomer immigrant who had been promised a city, a settler pointed to the boarding house and said, "*Dett ist die Stadt* (There is the city)."

The promised village soon emerged, with a flour mill, a general store, blacksmith and carpenter shops, another boarding house, a hotel, a saloon, even a village square. By 1882 it had a post office and plat map and Catholic and Lutheran churches. The village grew from 21 settlers in 1883, to 87 people in 1885—almost half of them from Germany or Switzerland—to 750 people in 1900. Despite the name change, Athens remained a company town well into the twentieth century. In 1900, one-third of the population was still employed by Rietbrock.[20]

Phillips, now in Price County, was also a lumbering town when my grandmother Matilda arrived to work in a boarding house in 1892. Sometimes called "the child of the Wisconsin Central Railroad," Phillips by its appearance marked the railroad's 1876 push through the dense pine forests toward Lake Superior. That year, railway officials laid out a town site on the banks of Elk River and named it after E. B. Phillips, the railway's general manager. The first settlers were loggers and tradesmen. Within months town boosters were claiming eight hundred inhabitants, no doubt an exaggeration, but by 1877 the town already had a post office, two hotels, four saloons, a contractor-builder, a painter, a photographer, two physicians, and three general stores. That year a child died, a couple married, and Miss Dunn opened the first school. In 1877 Phillips also had its first fire, which swept away many frame stores and hotels. The townspeople rebuilt, and the railroad continued to advertise with enticing pictures. Lumber companies operating camps on the Flambeau River and its branches established headquarters there and built sawmills to manufacture timber products.

Phillips was prospering when Matilda arrived in 1892. A photograph taken a few years earlier shows piles of lumber along millponds in the foreground, a wooden church off to the left, a few brick stores lining the main street. Behind the piles of lumber, several wooden hotels and two-story boarding houses rise above a welter of workers' homes.[21]

Phillips's dependence on the lumbering economy was evident everywhere when Matilda arrived. Saw logs, boards, and hemlock bark for tanning were stacked around the town. Each winter the camps near Phillips filled with men from Minnesota and Wisconsin. No one was sure how many men came to the camps: estimates ranged from 2,000 to 4,000, enough to outnumber the 2,500 people who had settled along the west bank of the Elk River by 1892. Neat boardwalks now lined sides of the streets and crossed at the corners, allowing people easy access to the stores that served the lumbering community. Along Lake Avenue were the courthouse, a bank, hotels, saloons, and general stores. If Matilda arrived before the end of September, she might have been in time for the Price County Fair, where there were bicycle races, trotting competitions with farm horses, and baseball games. She would have needed twenty-five cents admission, however, and probably she would have had to miss that fair. Perhaps she attended the fair at St. Patrick's Church. Most likely, however, she was more interested in work than in entertainment. She was already engaged to Karl Schopper, who was lumbering that winter to save money for their marriage. Matilda was also working so they could start their married life and family with a little surplus cash.

The family has no stories of where Matilda worked in Phillips. She might have been employed by one of the many hotels or boarding houses along Lake Avenue. These hotels were small, each run by a family with two or three women servants, often German immigrants. The boarders, usually numbering seven or eight in these small hotels, were almost all immigrant men who worked in the tannery or the sawmill—German, Danish, Norwegian, Irish, Canadian.

Or Matilda might have worked for the John R. Davis Company, the principal employer around Phillips. The company owned logging camps, a sawmill, a planing mill, a box factory, a department store, and a large boarding house. About one hundred employees stayed at the boarding house, and it was probably easiest to find work there. It is possible that Karl was working at one of the Davis camps that winter and suggested she first seek employment at the Davis boarding house. We do not know about that, but we do know that during the winter and following spring Matilda had her photograph taken twice by a local studio. Those two photographs have been passed down in the family. Both show Matilda with her fellow workers: one of the women in light summer dresses, the other in dark winter attire. Nothing explicitly identifies these women as serving women, but their role is suggested by the fact that they had their photograph taken as a group rather than in a family unit. It is the first photograph we have of Matilda, her dark hair pulled tightly back from her ears in the fashion of the day, the long-sleeved, high-necked dress, the brooch at her neck. These group photographs provide a rare glimpse of serving women in their best attire. Matilda and her coworkers were part of a vast army of young working women who staffed the service economy. By the fall of 1893, Matilda had left Phillips. On September 10, 1893, in Dorchester, she married Karl Schopper and moved into the log house that she would call home for almost fifty years.

Soon after Matilda left Phillips, a fire destroyed the town. Townspeople rebuilt, this time mostly with brick: some of those buildings along Main Street have survived for more than a century. The population continued to increase: by 1900, some 1,820 people lived there. But by then the lumbering economy was declining. During the next fifteen years, most of the large boarding houses for lumber workers closed. With this skinning of the last useable timber, the economy that serviced it disappeared as well. Women, young and old, would have to seek employment in the growing tourist economy.

NORTH-WOODS TOURISM

Between 1904 and 1913, the lumber industry declined in the north woods. In 1904, the Lake Shore Lumber Company shut down its sawmill at Lake Tomahawk. In 1906, Williams, Salsich and Company closed its sawmill at Star Lake. In 1911, the Yawkey-Bissell Lumber Company shut its mill at Hazelhurst. As each sawmill closed, the surrounding population dropped. Companies moved operations westward, and workers followed or moved elsewhere to farm. From 1,000 residents the population of Hazelhurst dropped to 150 people. Those who wished to remain on their land sought alternatives in the fledgling tourist economy.[22]

Although the provisioning of lumber workers had promoted some farming in the north woods, the poor soil and short growing season meant farming alone was not an option for either settlers or Native people. Small truck farms

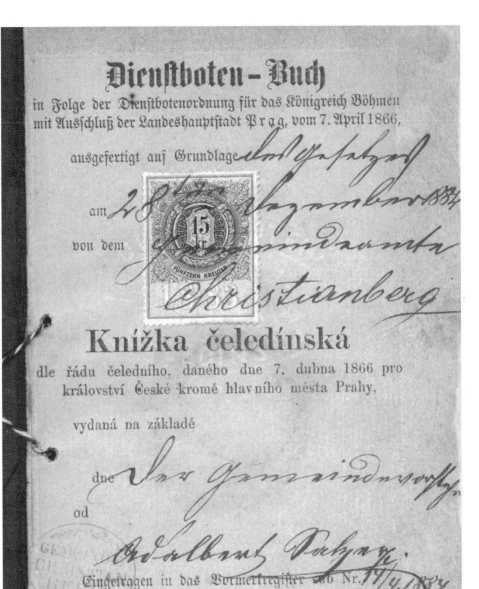

Dienstboten-Buch

in Folge der Dienstbotenordnung für das Königreich Böhmen mit Ausschluß der Landeshauptstadt P r a g, vom 7. April 1866,

ausgefertigt auf Grundlage

am

von dem

15

Christianberg

Knížka čeledínská

dle řádu čeledního, daného dne 7. dubna 1866 pro království České kromě hlavního města Prahy,

vydaná na základě

dne

od

Eingetragen in das Vormerkregister sub Nr.

Matilda's book, 1884. A "servant's book" similar to this one was issued to all workers in the Austro-Hungarian Empire when they reached the age of fourteen and were eligible to work on other families' farms. Employers' remarks reported on how well or poorly the holder of the book performed his or her work.

had offered garden produce, hogs and chickens, milk and butter to boarding houses that lodged thousands of workers during the winter lumbering season. Commercial farming had not proved very successful, except for potatoes, and most agricultural experts did not see a promising future in that crop. Farming did develop in the cutover, especially in southern Lincoln and Taylor counties, those adjacent to what were sometimes called the Wisconsin highlands or lakelands. These areas were also drastically affected by the end of logging and milling and had to cultivate alternative sources of income. A number of towns developed paper pulp processing mills along the rivers. For those farther north, however, tourism seemed to offer the best prospect for a new economy.

Tourism was relatively new to the north woods. In the late nineteenth century, a few settlers established small tourist businesses near new railroad lines cut through the region. One was the village of Minocqua, located on an old fur-trade route abandoned by Ojibwe people in the 1870s. By 1877, the Wisconsin Central Railway arrived west of Minocqua, linking Stevens Point to Ashland, 187 miles north. In 1883, the Milwaukee, Lake Shore, and Western Railroad passed about thirty miles east of Minocqua at Eagle River, which became a popular destination for fishermen. Meanwhile, the Chicago, Milwaukee, and St. Paul Railway, which pioneered excursion fares to the Dells in the 1870s, built an extension from Merrill north to Lake Minocqua. Passenger service began in 1888, and a tourist town was born.

Minocqua developed a dual economy in lumbering and tourism during the early 1890s. It was a commercial center and a supply point for lumbering in winter, and it served summer tourists. By the late 1890s, city newspapers were reporting immense catches of muskellunge and walleye pike in northern Wisconsin lakes. When logging ended, with a tourist base already established and with the north woods gaining a reputation as a fishing mecca, Minocqua had little difficulty making the transition.[23]

A few other towns evolved from logging camps to resorts as lumber men left. A core group of families began to look to tourism as their major income source. Boulder Junction, north of Minocqua, already had resorts by the late 1880s and early 1890s. A major growth spurt occurred between 1897 and 1919, when the thirteen resorts in Vilas County's lakeland region grew to 106. An estimated 5,000 tourists could be accommodated for stays of several weeks, yielding a total of 30,000 people in the three-month summer season, about six times the county's population. In summer, children as well as adults served the visitors.[24]

Geographer Timothy Bawden refers to this growth of resorts as the formation of a "recreation landscape." On Trout Lake steamship launches appeared together with hotels, boathouses, and dance halls. Primitive fishing and hunting camps, like Camp Franklin, transformed themselves from enclaves for wealthy Chicago men into family resorts for the middle class. A few women already insisted on going after the "big game fish," but their numbers increased after railroads promoted fishing for women. By 1898 women were more than 40 percent of the guests; by 1915 they came in numbers equal to men. Guidebooks stressed that women liked to "rough it a bit." They rowed, shot, and tramped through the woods.[25]

Tourism tended to flourish in rural areas peripheral to major economic systems, growing where alternative work was unavailable, especially for women, who usually performed the majority of the service work in developing tourism industries. Resorts were a way for small-scale, family-centered enterprises to diversify farming or other seasonal work. Labor was usually gendered: men acted as guides for fishing and hunting; women rented and cleaned rooms, cooked and served food. Women also produced and preserved much of the food served at the resorts—chickens, garden vegetables, milk, and butter. Men sometimes sought seasonal work elsewhere in the winter while women kept farms going. One early resort owner, Ruth Voss, remembered that after 1918 her husband worked winters in Minneapolis and returned to help her run the resort in the summer. She had a cow, chickens, hogs, and a root cellar and gathered blueberries and cranberries. They charged $100 for a cabin for the season and $1.50 per day. In 1919 they were able to build a new five-bedroom main hotel, where they served meals on a veranda facing Spider Lake.[26]

Voss's resort was one of many that catered to the less wealthy. At Minocqua, small lodges and boarding houses rented camping outfits, boats, and launches and offered rented rooms for $4 to $5 and cottages for $10 to $25 per week. Resorts went up quickly on other lakes: Darrow's Camp at Lake Shishebogama, Hanson's Squirrel Lake Resort, Lost Lake Resort, Ferncroft Inn, and Risman's Resort on Ballard Lake.

Musky Inn on Big St. Germain Lake was one of the early resorts that catered to a wealthier clientele than the small lodges and resorts around Minocqua. It became a model for upscale north-woods tourists. Amandee and Mary Chabrison owned and managed Musky Inn, employing a small group of guides, chambermaids, kitchen help, and waitresses. Marion Stoeckmann, who lived there for many years, working first in the kitchen and then as a waitress, left an account of the resort. French-born Amandee was a noted Chicago and Hot Springs, Arkansas, chef when he and Mary opened their resort hotel in 1904. He cooked; Mary made the pastries; Marion ran the dining room. They catered to an exclusive and wealthy clientele, many of whom returned year after year. The men came first, alone, on Memorial Day, the opening of fishing season. The men returned with their families in the summer for vacations. Sixty to seventy-five guests paid $28.50 per person per week American plan and could take picnic lunches on hikes or fishing outings. The inn furnished boats. Guests had to dress formally for dinner. This new "strenuous life" was replacing the leisurely late-nineteenth-century activities that had preoccupied "the idle rich." The new life still had many conveniences—daily mail, telephone service, special food brought in from the cities, and, more importantly, screened porches. Some wealthy Chicago families brought nannies, maids, and pets. It was, as Bawden says, a "paradoxical frontier," a "cosmetic rusticity." A series of golf courses completed the image: the first was put in at Plum Lake in 1910; Minocqua Heights Golf Club opened in 1916; others soon followed. By the 1920s motorboats and other pleasure craft had become popular.[27]

Recreation in the north woods was more than just a vacation in the woods. Bawden showed in his study of tourism that recreation became a reenactment, carefully controlled and defined to be sure, of what city folk considered to be their heritage—that of explorer, pioneer, lumberjack, trapper, and for some, would-be Indian. Guidebooks showed members of the Lac du Flambeau Chippewa band, often in family groups and usually wearing at least some identifiable Native regalia, within a landscape that featured fishing and hunting, natural scenery, and recreational activities. In the woodlands, urban people could frame their play with the appropriate class amenities, hence the main lodge with formal dress and dining. They could retain the social life of the city along with some well-equipped nights with guides in the wilderness. It was the beginning of the upper-class midwestern American family's long romance with woods and water.[28]

At the turn of the century, the upper class was creating a new culture, still gendered but more united spatially than the earlier "sporting" male culture of the 1870s. Railroad advertising put "cultivated women and natural woods together," touting a "tame wilderness" for men and women alike, with appropriate lodge and cottage architecture based on logs, woodwork, and stone. For example, although an early photograph of the lake country shows women decked out in white dresses and elaborate hats in rowboats primly gathering lily pads, the favorite pastime of women at Musky Inn soon became hiking about in knickers and boots.[29]

Camps featuring preparation for "the strenuous life" soon appeared for the children of the wealthy. Boys were the first to get their own training camps. In 1914, former Chicago Latin School teacher Dr. John P. Sprague and his wife ran the Pottawattomie Lodge, composed of two separate units, his for boys and men, hers for girls and women. They shared canoe trips down the Tomahawk River. By 1924, at Camp Minocqua on Lake Tomahawk, boys had to endure long hikes, handle canoes, and pass a Boy Scout lifesaving test. College prep men had the Tomahawk Club nearby.[30]

Girls' camps were not as numerous as those for boys early in the century, but there were plenty of them. By 1910, nearly a third of the nation's private summer camps catered to young girls; a decade later fully half were for girls. The popularity of summer camps for girls was, in part, a reaction against modernization. The tradition that emphasized "primitivism" seemed especially

Camp Fire Girls canoeing, 1920s. Believing the outdoor life was healthy and appropriate, wealthy midwesterners sent their daughters off to the Wisconsin woods. Formed in 1912, the Camp Fire Girls spread rapidly, establishing camps that often boasted pseudo-Indian names and offered instruction in Indian "woodcrafts." The Tomahawk Leader *reported in 1919 that the "bronzed" camp girls "live a typical Indian life."*

popular among girls and their parents. While girl "scouts" and the so-called "pioneer" tradition later overtook and surpassed the earlier Camp Fire movement, these first camps were often accompanied by the trappings of pseudo-Indian ritual and what was then called "woodcraft." The Camp Fire Girls, formed in 1912 in New England, had almost eight thousand members within two years; by 1924 nearly 220 chapters existed nationwide. Ernest Thompson Seton, who wrote of "woodcraft Indians" regularly for the *Ladies' Home Journal,* emphasized a romanticized communal living, a shared use of resources, and respect for the environment that made northern Wisconsin an ideal site for girls' camps.[31]

In 1912, five sisters started Camp Minne-WaWa, an exclusive girls' camp on Big Carr Lake near the village of Lake Tomahawk. Eight years later Camp Sherwood Forest opened, and then a cluster of girls' camps sprang up, including Camp Agawak, Warwock Woods, Minne-Wanka Lodge, and Camp Osoha, where Helen and Robert Snaddam particularly emphasized Seton's camp philosophy. Camp Minne-WaWa on Carr Lake remained the prototypical girls' camp. Campers took overnight canoe trips down the Tomahawk River and participated in rugged outdoor activities. The *Tomahawk Leader* reported in 1919 of fifteen camp girls from wealthy Chicago and Milwaukee families: "they are bronzed to a deep brown from their outdoor life and it's real outdoor life too as they sleep in pup tents, fry their meals over campfires, and live a typical

Indian life." Girls always had a trip into Minocqua by special launch to purchase curios and sweets. In the early 1920s, a staff of twenty-six included horseback riding and paddling instructors as well as a French and Latin tutor and a camp bugler. Girls had to be from "good families" and "furnish satisfactory references" or be known personally by a counselor or the director. In camp each cabin boasted an Indian name. In middies and bloomers, the girls did exercises in a clearing that also served as a basketball court. Parents paid $200 for eight weeks in 1915; more than $300 by the 1920s.[32]

As the camping craze spread to the middle classes, new lodges and camps sprang up along Minocqua and Trout lakes. Owners formed the Fish and Game Protective Association to attract less affluent tourists for "sport and outings." Major resorts advertised for "the office worker or city dweller," able to stay only a week or ten days. This "pristine wilderness" became increasingly attractive as southern parts of the state were fished out and hatcheries had to be established. Fishing enthusiasts flocked north to lakes still teeming with fish. Anglers who could afford to reach remote lakes looked forward to abundant and easy catches.[33]

These easy catches soon disappeared in the north, and hatcheries had to be established there as well. By 1901, the Minocqua–Eagle River area was already hosting 1,200 visitors who, while still finding some thirty-pound muskellunge, must have started complaining to lodge owners that it was no longer quite so easy to land them. That year the city of Minocqua established its own hatchery, and two years later the state purchased it. The hatchery was meant to supply surrounding lakes specifically for recreational as opposed to commercial fishing, but propagating and stocking northern fish was not easy. Millions of muskellunge eggs taken from fish in Lake Tomahawk died before they could reach hatching jars, and muskie hatchlings did not do well either. Ichthyologists did not discover until later that small fry lie dormant for six to seven days after hatching. Predators and the change in environment finished them off before they could become active. Hatchery officials learned from experience, built a new facility in 1906, and kept trying. As propagation attempts went on, the commission increased restrictions on angling, requiring permits and limiting the catch. By 1917, it dictated a daily maximum of two fish, each no longer than twenty-four inches, and established a closed season when no fishing at all was allowed. Soon "fish stories" were replacing the photographs of thirty-pound muskellunge, but there were now enough smaller fish to keep the average visitor satisfied with fishing in the Minocqua–Eagle River area.[34]

Tourism fit uncomfortably into agriculturists' plans. Except for a few early dissenters, most policymakers and university experts expected lumbering to be followed by farming. As lumbering declined, however, two groups of Wisconsin policymakers envisioned very different futures. One group sought a new agricultural mix that would provide incomes for settlers. They saw a future for northern Wisconsin similar to that of southern Wisconsin. The other group envisioned a reforested north, its dream to restore to whatever extent possible the forests that now lay slashed and cut over as the lumber industry departed. The state board of forestry formulated a plan to create a 1.5-million-acre forest reserve in the five northernmost counties. Experts who studied the situation determined that the lands to be purchased by the state were the least likely to become agricultural areas. Forests would bring tourists, campers, hunters, fishermen, and millions of dollars into the state. By 1912 the board had reserved a bit less than a third of the projected amount and had accumulated a host of enemies across these counties, people who believed the plan would lower tax revenues and slow development of the north country.[35]

Native Survival
Kate's Story [Eastman, born in Wisconsin, 1854– ca. 1925]

Kate Eastman, dressmaker, arrived with her five-year-old daughter, Margaret, at Lac du Flambeau in September 1895. The new boarding school was about to open, and the government had hired her to be the sewing teacher. A sad confluence of events had brought Kate from Ashland to the Lac du Flambeau community. Born on a farm in Fond du Lac County to Bavarian and Prussian immigrants, Kate learned her trade by apprenticing as a girl in an Eau Claire dressmaking shop. At thirty-eight she married and, with her parents close by, bore a daughter and settled into a comfortable life. Then, in 1894 a typhoid epidemic swept Ashland. In quick succession her father, mother, sister, and husband died. Kate's four-year-old daughter caught the fever but recovered. Left with a daughter to raise by herself, Kate heard the government was building a new boarding school at Lac du Flambeau eighty miles southeast of Ashland and was looking for a seamstress to instruct the Native girls. The reservation's agent was still based in Ashland, making application easy. She got the job and on August 28, 1895, entered government service.[36]

We know about Kate's experiences from a memoir about life at Lac du Flambeau between 1895 and 1904 written by her daughter. Although Margaret left the reservation to attend school in Ashland in 1901, she returned during the summer to live with her mother until she, too, moved to Ashland. Kate spent the rest of her life there as a dressmaker, dying of a stroke in 1925 at age seventy-one. Kate never liked her life in Ashland as well as her life at Lac du Flambeau, teaching sewing to the Native girls.[37]

Margaret described the classes at the government school where her mother, Kate, taught. The government school was modeled on a typical trades school, with a student's day divided into two shifts. Each student spent half a day

Sewing students at Lac du Flambeau boarding school, 1895. Kate Eastman, who taught Lac du Flambeau girls plain and fancy sewing from 1895 to 1904, believed they enjoyed learning new sewing skills. Jenny LaCass, Annie Cedarroot, and Annie Corn sit left to right in the front row; in the back row from left to right are Mary Bluesky, Mary Devine, Jessie Chapman, Rose Chapman, unknown, Mable Nagonabeniece, teacher Kate Eastman, and another unknown student.

studying and half a day working at gender-specific tasks. The oldest girls—about forty on each shift—worked in the kitchen, sewing room, laundry, and hospital, while the boys—about forty-five on each shift—worked in the farm, blacksmith shop, carpenter shop, and fields. Boys also performed on ball teams and in a band. Girls learned how to play the piano. In the sewing room, Kate taught the younger girls how to sew and supervised the making of all the children's clothing as well as all the linens for the school. The new superintendent had ordered a supply of sewing materials before Kate arrived: thimbles, needles and pins, linen thread, buttons, hooks and eyes, plus yards and yards of fabric—gingham, calico, shirting, flannel, jean, and crash (a coarse fabric used for draperies and toweling). A dozen new sewing machines stood waiting for Kate and her pupils.[38]

Kate instructed each girl in basic sewing skills, mending, and darning for two years. She also gave advanced dressmaking instruction to young women who wanted to become proficient in the trade. Dressmakers were highly skilled professionals, well paid, and in demand. By 1898, eighteen girls were sufficiently advanced in sewing to learn the skilled task of cutting and fitting dresses using a complicated system to make proportional estimates for patterns.[39]

Margaret described the sewing room, the objects the young women made, and the joy of both teacher and students in the task of learning sewing. Twelve sewing machines sat near the window; a long cutting table occupied the middle of the room. Each girl created three dresses for herself. Her school dress was a sailor suit of dark blue with white dots, trimmed with white braid. Play or work dresses were made of a small blue-and-white gingham check. Sunday dresses were gray flannel with red braid and wool flannel petticoats. Together teacher and students produced prodigious amounts of clothing and linen. "Mother enjoyed teaching them sewing," Margaret recalled, "and the children loved it." Especially appreciated were the Saturday classes where Kate taught "fancy" work. Margaret said these classes made the girls "very happy, and they did very beautiful work." Such beautiful work, in fact, that the school sent samples of their fancy work to the St. Louis Exposition in 1905. Margaret believed theirs was the only government school to teach fancy work.[40]

Kate found ways to share the new skills with the girls' mothers. She saved all the sewing scraps, gave them to the mothers, and helped them make quilts. At their request, she helped grieving parents by covering and lining children's caskets, trimming them with ribbons and silk pillows. "She never asked for pay or refused to do it," Margaret wrote. In turn, Native women taught Kate how to do beadwork. She made beaded moccasins for Margaret. Kate had her daughter join in all the games and ceremonies with the other children, including dancing. On one visit, when asked to point out the white girl playing with Native girls, a visitor picked out a Native girl with light hair and blue eyes. Margaret had dark hair and eyes. Her mother could recognize her at a distance only by the clothing she had put on that morning.[41]

Despite Kate's and the students' enjoyment of sewing, other conditions at the school were not as welcoming to the Native girls. They had to perform all weekly tasks speaking only English. Finally on Friday, when mothers came to visit, bringing fruit and candy, the children could speak Ojibwe. Coerced into being there, threatened with punishment and haircuts for refusing to obey rules, faced with poor health conditions, children struggled to confront the less pleasant aspects of boarding school life. The school at Lac du Flambeau had most of the problems of other government boarding schools during this time, but the assistant matron and the school farmer were Ho-Chunk sister and brother who loved the children and tried to make the enforced education as palatable as possible. The school offered important skills to the girls that they and their mothers valued. The women had previously beaded and sewn, but Kate's sewing classes offered daughters new skills while meeting their mothers' high standards for working with thread and decoration. They applied these new skills to everyday clothing, ceremonial regalia, household embellishment, and items for sale. The nearly ten years Kate spent teaching were important, not only to her and daughter Margaret but also to the Native girls and their mothers.

Kate's years of teaching at Lac du Flambeau contributed to the expansion and perfection of Native women's skills between the 1890s and the 1920s. Handcrafts were not exclusively traditional or contemporary, but a blend of both. Women learned to use new materials and tools for traditional tasks and adapted old skills to new materials and objects: clothing, rugs, quilts, and new forms of beadwork. Handwork of all types flourished. Women proved their skills through the items they brought for competition, through sales at tourist lodges, and at the fairs that began in 1915. When the matron visited their homes in 1925 to conduct an industrial survey, women told her in great detail of the handwork they created employing both Native and settler methods.

LAC DU FLAMBEAU TOURISM

Tourism at Lac du Flambeau offered women an uncertain future. Untried and, for many, unwanted, the decision to bring strangers into their homelands was not taken lightly. Yet the lumbering economy was declining at the same time that the old subsistence base was steadily being eroded by settlers' reluctance to honor Native rights to hunt, fish, and gather and by state laws that violated treaty rights. As in previous times of transition, Native women looked for ways to increase their income using traditional skills. Native women had long depended on handcrafts and surplus foodstuffs as a source of income through both cash and barter. Most of that trade was invisible to the U.S. government, and for most of the nineteenth century the enterprise was reported only through large generalizations about production. In 1879, for example, the government agent reported that the Ojibwe bands in Wisconsin and Minnesota had made 12,000 moccasins, manufactured 94 tons of maple sugar and 274 gallons of syrup, gathered more than 64 tons of wild rice, and raised pumpkins, potatoes, turnips, corn, and other products. While he did not say how much of this production was being traded, some clearly was, if not to settlers then to other Native tribes.[42]

After the Wisconsin attorney general's 1896 opinion that Natives had no claim to rights the federal government had reserved to them by treaty, it became more difficult to depend on the older subsistence patterns. Wardens fanned out across the state to enforce the new game law. In July 1897, an Iron County game warden charged two Lac du Flambeau elders—one eighty-eight and blind, the other seventy-two—for violating game laws when he found the men with venison. The men explained the meat had been given to them by younger men. Nonetheless, the warden handcuffed the elders and, without an interpreter or any attempt to locate their families, imprisoned them for four months. The elderly wife of one of the men, who was with him but not arrested, was put on the street to find her way home as best she could. When the government farmer at Lac du Flambeau heard about the outrage, he wrote to the acting Indian agent at Ashland: "I believe in enforcing the game law on white men as well as Indians. But to be so harsh on these old men who were told when the treaties were made with them that the game belonged to them and they should have the privilege of hunting anywhere they pleased the punishment seems to me to be out of proportion to the offence." He asked the agent to have the district attorney for Iron County send the old men home.[43]

The agent supported the de facto abrogation of treaty rights and insisted the Native men get licenses to hunt off the reservation. For the most part, men grudgingly complied with the law to avoid arrest. They carried licenses and hunted during the prescribed seasons. In October 1898, the Lac du Flambeau farmer wrote that the men were taking out hunting licenses. "It would be impossible to keep them from their annual hunt and I try to teach them to respect the law," he concluded. As was their custom, entire families went on the hunt, and few Native people stayed on the reservation once the hunting season opened. Incidents of harassment and examples of difficulties continued despite Native people's efforts to avoid confrontation. In 1901, state game wardens took a gun from a man who had gone to gather kinnikinnick. He had to appeal to the agent to get his gun returned. The state extended its control: by 1909 it had reduced the hunting season from twenty to ten days and limited each hunter to one deer.[44]

At the same time the subsistence base of Lac du Flambeau people was being restricted, their main source of cash was disappearing as the timber harvest approached completion. The Flambeau Lumber Company began shutting down many logging operations in 1898. As long as the sawmill still operated in the village, it provided jobs for at least some Native men. Native and white mill employees spent their wages year-round in the community. Because it was a company town, much of the revenue went back to the company, but some Native families profited by providing boarding for workers and company officials, opening small stores, and provisioning worker families through truck gardens. It was one of a number of income sources and farming and subsistence activities that helped people survive. The lumber company harvested so aggressively that timber ran out even before the company's contract with the government ended. In 1913 the Flambeau Lumber Company laid off all its employees, closed up the mill and the store, and left for fresh forests in the west. About one hundred non-Native inhabitants left the village. Supervisors, all non-Native, moved with the company or found jobs elsewhere. Workers, facing no cash income and few prospects, followed the company west or tried to get better land for farming. Although as many as 75 percent of adult Native men had worked for the lumber company in 1901, only about twenty-two were employed at the mills at the time it closed. Native men wanted flexible employment to allow time for subsistence and cultural activities, but the company was not willing to accommodate part-time work. Still, Native villagers were hit hard because they had earned cash by providing food and various needs for the company and its employees. The timber economy had lasted fewer than thirty years. School supervisor H. B. Peairs reported he had heard that Flambeau Lumber, in the twenty years it had the lumbering contract, had netted $5 million a year. Now this source of income was gone.[45]

Families scrambled for alternative ways to earn cash, as one government farmer put it, "hustling at some thing or another." A few had already begun to act as guides for tourist parties and to make and sell curios. By the summer of 1901 tourists were so numerous in the area that they were spilling over onto the reservation. The harvest now was not of timber by companies but of fish by individual anglers looking for new fishing spots and by local entrepreneurs who were encouraging tourists to fish on reservation lakes. Tourists brought various documents purportedly allowing them to fish at Lac du Flambeau. The government farmer had no specific instructions on how to treat these interlopers, but he decided not to allow them to fish on the reservation. "I have sent word to the owners of summer resorts to allow none of their guests to fish on reservation," he wrote in August 1901.[46]

Government farmers came and went on the reservation, but the problems persisted. In the summer of 1907, as yet another government farmer had to deal with the summer influx of avid anglers, the problem became acute. The farmer asked for clearer guidelines. "Lac du Flambeau is known as a famous summer resort, and that its lakes abound with gamey fish," he wrote to the agent, complaining that resort owners continued to avoid regulations. Mrs. M. H. Barnum of Minocqua, for example, sent her boarders in a steady stream onto the reservation to fish the "gamey" waters. They claimed Barnum had a "permit" from some government office that entitled "her friends" to fish. They came in "squads," complained the farmer "and fished all over Fence and Crawling Stone lakes and no one could say they weren't her friends." Such blanket permits to "Mr. or Mrs. So and So and friends," as the farmer put it, meant he had no idea who was included under the document. "There appears to be a widespread opinion that permits never wear out, and that a person once gets a permit it is good eternally," he observed dryly. The permits did not make clear how long they were valid, how many fish could be caught, or how they could be disposed of.[47]

The farmer at Lac du Flambeau expected people to obtain a new permit each year, to present their permits to him when they arrived, to hire Native guides, and to follow all regulations. It hardly seemed right, he complained to his superiors,

> that tourists should be allowed to plunder these lakes day after day of fish, and ship out the product of their work by train. It seems that they should be satisfied with the sport and the recreation they get without attempting to satisfy their friends on the outside. As nothing is put back in these waters to replenish the game fish, eventually they will be denuded and the supply exhausted.... If this work of plunder goes on for long, it will be a thing of the past. Unless some protection is given to the fish in its waters.

Regulations had to be enforced for tourists and fishing restricted or there would be no fish.[48]

Commercial agriculture was another alternative to the older lumbering economy. The end of the latter brought a flurry of correspondence among government officials evaluating the prospects for commercial agriculture at Lac du Flambeau. Most Native families continued their traditional subsistence cycle of planting crops and harvesting wild foods. According to a 1912 report by Oscar H. Lipps, all families had good gardens of three to four acres. In summer and early fall, people picked and marketed berries and wild rice for cash income. In fall, they gathered greens and sold them for three or 3.5 cents a pound. They also raised potatoes. Most did their work by hand, for few had teams or plows. About forty families worked larger farms, up to twenty acres. Native families provided all their own food as well as provisions for mill employees and for elders unable to garden. Those families received only a small monthly allowance from timber funds. Lac du Flambeau people had about one hundred horses, which they usually obtained from Plains tribes. It was said that one of the beautifully beaded bandolier bags made by the women would buy a horse. As a whole, families had very few cows; they were not much interested in them and had little experience in keeping them. Cows needed special winter feed and care, and women had no tradition of caring for them or making butter or cheese as a home industry.[49]

Native families had developed a market for their harvest products and for potatoes, which tolerated poor soil. Lipps was not optimistic about introducing commercial agriculture, however, because of the soil and climate. "Most white farmers," he wrote, "would not take this land as a gift and go to the expense of clearing it for farming purposes." Moreover, the people preferred seasonal migration, lived on their scattered farms only in the summer, and moved into the village during the winter. Cattle needed year-round care. The agent added his resistance to farming: "This is not an agricultural country... farming is decidedly unprofitable," he reported, and the people seemed opposed to it. Still, the government continued to encourage farming. Although agents complained about the lack of desire to farm, many people at Lac du Flambeau did farm successfully at a subsistence level and engaged in marketing surplus. But given the wretched conditions that plagued all agricultural development schemes, a mixed economy was a better strategy. The Chippewa attempted to create such an economy, using tourism as well as hunting, gathering, and farming as an economic base. Tourism provided both summer work and winter craft production. By the summer of 1912 about thirty men worked as guides for $2.50 to $5.00 per day. Women provided board and lodging, rented out houses, and sold handcrafts.[50]

Tourism had dangers, however. Tribal leaders had prudently refused to lease campsites, and they closely controlled other sites of religious or historical significance to them, including land around their village. Government officials felt that the chief value of this land was its location on beautiful lakes and that leases would be more profitable than rentals, bringing in "fancy" rates. Agents also proposed that town sites be sold. In other words, they wished to turn much of the land over to non-Native summer residents and entrepreneurs instead of allowing the Native residents to retain the land while profiting from the tourist trade. They envisioned transforming the lumber town into a tourist town. Lipps sketched out his plan in 1912, one of alienating Lac du Flambeau land by leasing or, better yet in his eyes, selling it to wealthy summer tourists. Lipps advised the government to encourage people with inherited land to sell "the choice lake fronts" for summer houses for "well-to-do tourists" who would spend money.[51]

Officials argued that sales of land or long-term leases would benefit the community. Mill families had "squatted" on the land without lease or title; lumber operations had leased the land for only thirty years. The government proposed allotting some village land to Native people who had none but selling the rest to "a good class of summer people." This scheme was a major policy change: it allowed some sales outright and encouraged children to sell as elders died.[52]

Officials made their proposal at a March council meeting in 1914. Council members met alone the night before to discuss the coming proposal and decided to oppose the wholesale leasing schemes as well as town site allotment. They wanted to reserve the land for their children. The next day the superintendent pressured council members to change their decision. He reminded the chief men that most of the land was already allotted and could not be held for their children except through individual inheritance. Some lands were leased at the present time, authorized by the council and the Indian office, but they were used for the care of the needy under informal and revocable agreements.

The new leases would be irrevocable for twenty years. The council members stood firm on not allotting more town sites, but the agent was able to split the vote on leasing.[53]

Although members divided on the question of leasing lands, they united on demanding greater control over tourism. The council members argued that owners and lessees paid no rental fees and purchased nothing. If Native people rented horse teams to the tourists, they could not do their own work. They wanted to be able to appoint their own wardens to prohibit poaching and to make sure that all hunters and fishers employed guides. They wanted an organization to protect, conserve, and propagate fish and impose and collect fines. Anyone leasing could not hunt or fish elsewhere than on the leased land. The superintendent denied the request for Native wardens and argued that if Native men acted as guides it would interfere with full-time farming. It seemed as though he wanted to turn profitable tourism over to the whites and to limit Native people to unprofitable farming on marginal land. On March 25, 1915, at a second meeting, the council reviewed its previous decision. This time the council voted unanimously not to lease to white individuals.[54]

The reassertion of control over the land did not stop sales of already allotted parcels. During the early twentieth century, more than half of Lac du Flambeau land was alienated from the band. The negative vote did, however, keep the village of Lac du Flambeau under the council's control and stop the allotment of tribal lands. An inspector sent by the government in August 1916 urged further allotment of lakeside sites, and much of this land passed into the hands of whites, including Strawberry Island and other sacred sites.[55]

The tribal council did increase its control over tourism. It retained the right of Native men to guide tourists fishing on the reservation and obtained clearer regulations over who could fish, thereby bringing some benefit to the tribe as a whole. By 1917 the Lac du Flambeau council was issuing its own "Fishing and Camping Regulations." Permits had to be obtained by all who wished to fish, and the fees supported a new hatchery that would replenish the stock. Tourism had come to stay. If it did not generate the income that casinos would in the later twentieth century, it became one important seasonal source of cash.[56]

Tourism had cost people in land, but they managed to maintain some control and relatively good relations with the tourists and summer residents. An inspector in 1923 reported that in the summer Indians at Lac du Flambeau sold beadwork, birch canoes, and baskets, danced for tourists, and rented their services as guides for seven dollars a day. While men guided tourists, women made curios to sell and helped with feeding and lodging the visitors. Like white women, Native women cooked, served food, and cleaned tourists' rooms and clothes. A few, like Margaret Gauthier, were able to own family businesses. By combining seasonal service in summer and handcrafts production in winter, women generated income on their own. Many also farmed, gathered large amounts of wild rice in fall, and prepared maple sugar in spring. Tourism had become part of their way of life, one more means toward developing a mixed economy with a subsistence base that would allow them to remain on the land.[57]

MENOMINEE MANAGEMENT

The Menominee Nation is known today for its refusal to allot its land and for managing its forest resources effectively. What role women played in these policies, through their work and influence, is not at all evident to the visitor, as I was when seeing the Menominee homelands for the first time. As I approached the reservation from the west, a tall forest wall loomed at the edge of a cleared field. Then, when it looked as though the road would end, it plunged suddenly through a narrow opening and transported me into a dense forest, into what seemed like a disappeared world. The woods were deceptive, however, for this was not a pristine wilderness but a place where people practiced sustainable forest management. I had heard how the Menominee refused to leave these lands or to allot the 235,000 acres they retained of their original homelands. With careful management, the Menominee people now harvested more timber of better quality than when they began in the mid-1850s. Experts consider the Menominee forest practices of sustainability a model of what might have been in northern Wisconsin.

By the 1890s, women were already combining older skills with new ones in ways that the visiting ethnologists, then and later, seldom described. They searched instead for an "unchanging" Native culture. While the visiting anthropologists enjoyed the hospitality of these Christian bicultural women, most sought out the older, non-Christian women at Zoar, a small community of Menominee that had moved farther into the forests, away from the Christian communities. At Zoar, women wore older style clothing, lived in bark homes, grew large gardens, and told the old stories. Ethnologists wanted to know about these few women rather than how the majority had blended their Native and settler cultures.[58]

The Menominee were well established in the lumbering economy by 1890. The tribe had their first mill by 1867, started major logging in 1880, built a new mill five years later, and were soon managing and controlling the lumber cut. Congress ratified these restrictions on cut, the beginning of a change that would make tribal land different from the surrounding, logged-out land. A 1905 blowdown in the western part of the reserve was the main impetus to careful management. Tribe members could not get wood to the river or to the railroad, so in 1909, on the advice of forester E. A Braniff, they built a large modern mill on the west branch of the Wolf River. The railroad ran a spur to the mill, and a new village, Neopit, soon grew around it. The government invested the milling income, and by 1910 the tribe had $2 million in its logging fund, making it one of the richest tribes in the country. The government did not always manage the funds well, but it supported the practice of sustained yield from the forest. During these years, women joined men in fighting governmental efforts to divide and privatize tribal lands. Because the Menominee did not allot their land and because the mill provided jobs for many Menominee men, the tribe was not as dependent on tourism as was the Lac du Flambeau community.[59]

Tourism and tradition also had an uneasy alliance in Native public performances created to entertain tourists in the early twentieth century. Wild west shows were in their heyday, touring both nationally and internationally. State and county fairs vied for Native groups who could set up encampments, perform mini-pageants of daily life and dance, and join in parades commemorating anniversaries.

For Native people there was a heritage to be preserved and displayed. Such pageantry was a way to affirm their place in history, to use their own cultural identifiers to set themselves off as proudly unique. For generations the Oshkosh family had maintained older religious traditions along with the traditions of leadership. Even though part of the family was now Christian, members made public appearances in traditional dress. Reginald Oshkosh could trace his heritage back to his grandfather Chief Oshkosh and Grandmother Bamboni of the Bear Clan, the largest clan in the tribe. His father, Neopit, became head chief in 1871 and frequently represented the tribe in the white community for ceremonial purposes. Reginald was well educated, highly literate, and economically and politically astute. He advocated the development of agriculture so that the community would not be entirely dependent on lumbering. He was also active in the emerging tourist economy and would later argue in favor of developing tourist camps and fish hatcheries. He already had his own tourist business.[60]

In 1903 Reginald joined his parents' retinue to celebrate the fiftieth anniversary of the town bearing their family name. Reginald and his father led the band on ponies, while his mother and others followed by bus. Reginald's parents posed for an Oshkosh photographer, surrounded by other men and women. Reginald represented the Menominee in March 1913, when thirty-three Indian tribes marched in the inaugural parade for President Woodrow Wilson. On the way, he and others stopped off to help celebrate the laying of the cornerstone at the National Memorial to the American Indian. Oshkosh appeared in buckskin and beads, with blue and red face paint. The *New York Times* called him "a composite picture of all the chiefs whom it took the flower of the Federal Army to subdue." For whites, these pageants satisfied many needs. They reminded them of their own ancient past, allowed them to be part of the emerging art esthetic that praised the "primitive," and confirmed their belief in their own cultural and military superiority.[61]

This mixed economy—lumbering, agriculture, and incipient tourism—helped counter total dependence on a single source of income. Mills employed only some of the Native men and no women. Mills also intermittently closed down, cutting families off from cash income. The government never supported communal agricultural ventures, such as ownership of tribal herds, and individuals who needed capital for teams and equipment had difficulty getting their ventures approved. Maggie Connors complained at a Menominee tribal meeting in September 1915 that her family wanted money to develop cash income for farms. "A person cannot live on vegetables alone," she told the council. Still, the combination of wage work at mills, even if not always offering steady or full-time employment for the men, combined with a saleable surplus from a growing number of farms and some income from tourism gave the Menominee a relatively strong economic base during the early twentieth century.[62]

CURIOS IN THE DELLS

One winter day early in 1904, Emma Pettibone sent a package from her home in Strongs Prairie to Henry H. Bennett, who ran a curio store in his photographic studio in nearby Kilbourn City, a summer tourist site later known as the Wisconsin Dells. In the package was Ho-Chunk beadwork, her own and that of a friend, Susie Prettyman. A few days later Pettibone received a reply. In it, Bennett said he was keeping as much as he could use of the belts, watch fobs, and chains and returning the rest. He asked Pettibone to send more belts, twenty beads wide by twenty-five inches long, for which he promised to pay one dollar each, and some watch fobs twenty beads wide and six inches long, for twenty-five cents each. "Send them before next Saturday," he urged. That day Bennett, a careful businessman, entered in his cashbook "Emma Pettibone, beadwork, $2.75." Later that month, Pettibone and Prettyman received $22 from Bennett for their beadwork.[63]

Kilbourn City, or the Dells, was a popular tourist area about thirty miles south of Pettibone's rural home in Strongs Prairie, about two hundred miles northwest of Chicago, Illinois, and southeast of Minnesota's Twin Cities. The Dells was a particularly wild and scenic area where the Wisconsin River narrowed and plunged through a series of gorges lined with eroded sandstone rocks. Some sixty thousand tourists visited the Dells yearly by 1904. Most took away souvenirs to remember their visit. The beadwork created by Pettibone and Prettyman and the purchase of it by Bennett were part of an elaborate market in beadwork that stretched from Strongs Prairie, through the Dells, and into the hands of thousands of tourists, most from Chicago, the Twin Cities, and Milwaukee but others from eastern states and foreign countries who came each year to wonder at the natural scenery, to visit Bennett's studio, and to buy inexpensive beadwork and other souvenirs crafted by Native people.[64]

Women sold beadwork to Bennett from 1899—when he began to deal in "Indian curios" after his photography business declined with the introduction of hand-held cameras that let tourists take their own photos—until he died in January 1908. They received $0.35 to $1.25 for each piece, and he profited $0.50 to $1.00 on each item. From January to August 1904, Bennett kept lists of the beadwork purchased along with the beadworker's name. He tagged each piece with an Indian name so that tourists would know it had been Native-made. Emma Pettibone

Pete Pettibone's sister, no date. Probably Emma Pettibone. Her skirt and shawl exhibit the fine ribbonwork Ho-Chunk women created. The headwork streamers are ribbons or pendants from the pajgae tied around her hair; the moccasins are typical Ho-Chunk style with flaps.

(Chahememenokga), Susie Prettyman (whose Native name I have not yet been able to identify), and Suzie Red Horn (Weegonheenoogah), whom Bennett considered the most skilled beadworkers, and more than a dozen other women regularly sold their beadwork to Bennett as well as directly to tourists in the summer. The bookkeeping eventually proved too difficult for Bennett, but for that brief period he tried to track the women who produced objects for his store. The names; the notation beadwork, fobs, belts, or moccasins; and the amount of money, usually a few dollars, all indicate that Ho-Chunk women were producing large quantities of beadwork for sale at the Dells during these years.[65]

The Dells first became a destination for "scenic tourism" in the 1860s. By 1875 the railroad was offering inexpensive weekend excursion tickets to entice

Bennett Studio, front room, 1917. Wisconsin Dells photographer H. H. Bennett supplemented his income by selling Ho-Chunk beadwork. His family maintained the photography studio after he died in 1908, continuing to sell curios along with prints of his landscapes. Note the beadwork hanging on the wall in back of the chair. The studio is now a Wisconsin State Historic Site.

middle-class tourists from Chicago, Milwaukee, and St. Paul. Bennett used his photographic views to promote the Dells as an outdoors "wonderland." He hoped to exploit this aesthetic with photographs of Ho-Chunk people as well. Individuals posed for him in the open air or in his studio, but Ho-Chunk leaders never let him photograph their daily life or ceremonies at summer encampments. Tourists increasingly wanted group photographs of the Ho-Chunk, but leaders persistently refused access to these collective activities, even to photographers as well known to them as Bennett. They maintained their right to define the appropriate use and dissemination of information about their cultural activities. With tourists taking their own photographs and Ho-Chunk refusing to allow their images to be sold, Bennett turned to advertising ethnic souvenirs for Dells tourists. During the 1902 tourist season Bennett realized that expanding the sale of beadwork and other Native handwork was the only way to keep his business alive.[66]

Ho-Chunk women were quick to recognize the market potential for souvenirs. By August 1902, they were making Bennett "pretty and salable" beaded watch chains. The chains were flat, about a quarter-inch wide and twenty-four inches long, with about ten inches divided to go around the neck and fasten behind. The watch chains coaxed tourists into his studio. Like other souvenirs, the beadwork carried the burden of representing "Indianness" to tourists. Beadwork was light, inexpensive, easily packed to carry back to the cities, and small enough for personal display. It was evocative of a visit to the Dells and of its Indian past.[67]

Beadworkers did not supply Bennett with enough stock during the summer to meet demand, for they could sell directly to tourists for higher prices. In the winter women had more time to work at their beads but could not sell directly to tourists and needed cash income to subsist until other sources of wage work were available. To accumulate enough stock for the following summer, Bennett began to buy large quantities of beadwork in winter. By January 1903, along with the watch chains women were selling beaded watch fobs, belts, bags, and moccasins to Bennett. Ho-Chunk women also responded to his requests for beadwork by raising prices. In February 1903, Bennett wrote that the Ho-Chunk "handiwork is quite salable" but complained the women "have their prices away up on most all beadwork."[68]

When the women told Bennett they could produce more beadwork if they had better access to beadworking supplies, he began ordering seed beads, needles, and thread. The first supplier sent the wrong size beads and charged more than the beadworkers were willing to pay. He sought another. Bennett explained to Mrs. Patterson, his supplier at Fox Lake, "there are a few Indians hereabouts at times who desire to get beads of me[,] having known and had considerable deal with me in other lines for a number of years, to satisfy that call I must find where I can get beads and sell them at the same price they pay elsewhere, which they say is 15 cents per bunch and I have no reason to doubt, this is my reason for asking for your lowest prices." He also had to return some beads because the women said they were too uneven to use.[69]

Stocking beading supplies thus became crucial for Bennett's business. He wrote to his brother Edd, "I am keeping a small stock of seed beads and selling to the Indians and have got them coming my way." To get the variety, quality, and price the women wanted, he finally had to order from a large supplier in St. Paul. He wrote to Somers & Company in May 1903 that the beadworkers were "getting out of humor and I am looking what might develop into a good trade if I could get the beads."[70]

Coaxed by the beadworkers to provide supplies and an occasional loan, Bennett expected the women to deal only with him. The women preferred to deal with Bennett, whom they had known for many years, but they considered themselves free agents. In addition to selling their work directly to tourists in the summer, they also offered it to a store owner across the street when Bennett would not buy it. That dealer sometimes paid them higher prices, which the women promptly told Bennett about. "It demoralizes them in the matter of prices," Bennett objected in a letter to his brother. In fact, it demoralized him. To keep them from raising prices, he began to buy their work, even when he had more than enough to sell to the summer tourists who visited the Dells.[71]

As his supply increased, Bennett started to job beaded work wholesale to city stores. Gimbel Brothers department store in Milwaukee asked for belts and then for women to demonstrate their art. When Bennett asked one of the best beadworkers to go, she agreed only if she could take a beadworker friend and her brother, who made bows and arrows of hickory wood, and if the store would pay each $2.50 per day. Even though the women had never been to a big city before, they bargained skillfully for their labor. Bennett was soon offering surplus to stores in New York as well, but maintaining a surplus proved difficult. He wrote to one New York company that he did not know if the scarcity of seed beads accounted for the women not bringing in beadwork, but he was finding it impossible to get the colors they wanted and thought that might be the reason.[72]

It was not the reason. The women would not bring their work to him unless he paid more. Bennett felt caught between the women's demands and his competitor across the street. "I would pay them a little more for the sake of giving you as much as possible," he wrote to his New York customer, "but my competitor in that line ... would raise the price above what I could pay and so spoil the trade with them as he has already done." In a letter to his New Mexico supplier, Bennett concluded he could not get enough beadwork, "partly because they, or I[,] could not get the beads for them to work with and partly because there have been parties through this region buying every thing they could get in the way of beadwork." The beads he had been waiting for had just arrived, and he hoped the women would go to work again. To another supplier he wrote that the beadworkers "have learned of the craze for beadwork and are keen for all they can get out of it" and were not willing to learn "white man's methods in business"; thus, he could not count on a steady supply.[73]

The women got what they wanted. When they brought in the belts, Bennett paid a higher price or bought sixteen-bead belts instead of the wider, twenty-bead belts. "The price is steadily advancing," he wrote to his New York buyer. He thought the narrower belts would be "quite as saleable." In a letter to his New Hampshire buyer, he complained that the beadworkers "have gone to selling their work to the tourists here so I am not getting so much as formerly and have to pay more for it." The women were cutting out the middleman as they had learned to do at other resorts or asking Bennett to pay them closer to the street market price.[74]

During the winter of 1904, Bennett increased his services to the Ho-Chunk in an attempt to keep them supplying beadwork. He tried to sell ginseng they had gathered and ordered more beads and German silver ear bobs. By fall, most Ho-Chunk were gone on their regular hunting and gathering rounds. Those who stayed husked corn, dug potatoes, and then went back to beading. Pettibone, Prettyman, and Red Horn, along with the other beadworkers, supplied Bennett with all he needed for the summer as well as for his wholesalers in the East. He estimated that about fifty families traded with him. The beadworkers were now increasing their winter output to meet demand, sending beadwork to him by mail from all over Wisconsin. "They are hard up or unusually industrious," Bennett wrote to Fred Harvey in February 1904. They were both.[75]

As the women increased their production, Bennett kept buying because he was afraid if he did not the beadworkers would sell to other stores. Once they found other buyers, it would be difficult to get them back. The women were producing more, and as they increased their output they also improved the quality and creativity of their work. It was "better and prettier" Bennett thought. They never duplicated a pattern; no two pieces were alike.[76]

Bennett seldom described the beadwork beyond noting the width and length of belts and watch fobs. The belts usually measured nineteen to twenty-one beads wide and twenty-four to twenty-six inches long. The watch fobs were twenty beads wide and six inches long. The women used number twelve needles and many chalk-white beads, which they insisted be absolutely regular or they would not buy them. Bennett described one fob as made of gold-plated wire, with red and yellow beads and a suspended heart-shaped charm.[77]

One type of beadwork that Bennett did describe in detail was what he called a beaded "pa scah da," or what the Ho-Chunk call a *pajgae*. The pajgae is a beaded hair binding unique to Ho-Chunk women, and one they still wear on special occasions. A woman wraps this solid beaded sheathlike piece around a roll of her hair close to the neck. The piece divides into four streamers that reach the floor and sway when she dances. The pieces Bennett described had streamers that measured thirty-two to thirty-six inches long and were four inches wide. The center piece was beaded on a loom like a belt, but the pendants were worked without a loom in a diagonal weaving, sometimes called a side stitch. These were not curios made for the market but cherished heirlooms worn on ceremonial occasions. Bennett recognized that these items were unusual and difficult to make, that each was different, and that he was seldom able to buy them. He sold one to a woman in Pennsylvania for fifteen dollars.[78]

In the 1990s, Jocelyn Riley talked to Ho-Chunk women who as young girls had learned from their mothers the complex beading technique of diagonal weaving for the pajgae. It involved using thread stiffened with beeswax as a needle and manipulating twenty double strands of this thread, each sixty inches long. Rebecca Greendeer remembered that in the 1950s she helped her mother bead and sell medallions at the Dells but that she also learned to make the more complicated pajgae for their own powwow outfits. Learning to weave the pajgae, the women told Riley, taught them patience and endurance. Wearing it, they said, made them proud to be Ho-Chunk and to display their artistic and cultural traditions.[79]

Suzie Red Horn selling beads, 1940s. Suzie's reputation for fine Ho-Chunk beadwork made Bennett eager to purchase her work, but she also sold directly to tourists, as she does in this photograph while a friend looks on.

The market boom for curios that Bennett and the women experienced in 1903–4 soon declined. Bennett wrote to James Standing Water in spring of 1905 that "white folks don't buy it any more and I have got more than I want." To Sam Kettleson he wrote, "The Indian craze is on the wane and I am fully stocked at present with bead belts (ladies), fobs and watch charms, moccasins, bow and arrows, bead purses, birch canoes up to two feet long, medicine charms of weasel, squirrel and muskrat skin, etc." Most of his tourists wanted "cheap stuff," but Bennett bought and sold "Indian relics" to the occasional collector interested in older objects.[80]

For the curio distributor, such as Bennett, the curio trade meant being drawn into Native culture, often through learning language, customs, and the needs of Native producers. Native craftswomen found it advantageous to deal with distributors rather than directly with tourists only if distributors provided services in return. Distributors had to balance supply and demand. Could or would Native beadworkers produce what the merchants needed at a price they could afford? Would the tourist buy what the Native and the merchant had to offer? Beaded belts and watch fobs were popular for a few seasons, but tastes changed, and then tourists preferred postcards.[81]

For the women producers, the market was even more difficult to navigate. Each beadworker operated within a multilayered economic system. All Ho-Chunk women engaged in a subsistence economy, harvesting food as they moved around. In fall, they gathered berries and other foods and sold the surplus. Then the families hunted and trapped. In winter, many families moved back to homesteads, where they processed and stored food. The government annuities and wage work in cranberry fields, husking corn, and digging potatoes, along with selling harvested wild berries, gave them a small cash income, but patching together these endeavors still left them in need.

Women had maintained their beadwork traditions and other handwork skills, including ribbonwork, with which they created regalia to be used by kin in ceremonial and social dances. Providing regalia for children to remind them of their heritage was especially important. Beading for the market was different: items were simpler and more quickly made, and they offered limited opportunities for creativity. Yet the market beadwork allowed women to practice and expand their beadworking skills. They made the items carefully. Each was a small experiment in design and color. When a curio dealer, such as Bennett, ordered materials for them, they had a greater variety and quantity of beads to use for larger ceremonial and social items, allowing them to establish reputations as fine beadworkers within families, communities, and beyond. Bennett often referred to Suzie Red Horn as one of the best beadworkers, along with Pettibone and Prettyman. As women's reputations grew, so did demand for their work. They could bargain for higher prices from distributors or sell directly to tourists. These sales gave women a source of income independent from the government and, in many cases, from family men as well.[82]

As objects pass from one group to another, from producers to consumers, their meaning changes. Native tourist objects were both familiar and exotic, signifying a visit to a special site like the Dells. The Ho-Chunk items—belts and watch fobs—seemed similar to early Euro-American twentieth-century art in their geometric designs, but they were functional in form. At the same time, they symbolized an "exotic" culture and site. Native women who sold their wares dressed much like their white neighbors, perhaps with the addition of a blanket. The women themselves did not appear exotic. The object was the main carrier of cultural difference, and the material, pattern, and cultural aesthetic gave the object its "Indianness."[83]

Attitudes of colonialist romanticism that valued the arts of vanquished Indigenous people mingled with journeys to places of natural wonders like the Dells. Profiting from tourism and producing for subsistence became tied in complicated ways. The result was that the beadwork perpetuated, revived, and created Native art that provided women with a source of income when cash was hard to come by. Anthropologist Terry Reynolds, in looking at the role of pottery in the Pueblo economy, has described it as providing cash income through traditional productive means in a time of transition from an agrarian economy to one integrated into the western market system. Unlike men, Native women seldom entered the market system through regular wage work. Instead, women used what skills and materials they had to provide one part of the cash income needed for families in a market economy. Most importantly, they provided cash income at a time of year when other sources were less readily available. Emphasizing the importance of pottery work to the Acoma women, Reynolds nonetheless argued that producing such handwork integrated Native women into a marginal economy where they would never make a decent wage.[84]

Tuscarora photographer Jolene Rickard looks beyond economics for the significance of Native women's beadwork. For Rickard, beadwork is an object which, whether created for tourists or not, carries a message that reminds us of the spiritual, economic, and cultural survival of Native people. Beadwork is one of the strongest symbols of her people, says Rickard, because it provides a visual connection to the "power of the good mind." It both brings knowledge from the past and helps people survive. The beaded souvenirs women made to sell also carry a message to the consumer. It is more than just exotica purchased by tourists. Rickard calls the beadwork "an island of memory" and the faces of the beadworkers "the face of our survival." Thus we should not look at Suzie Red Horn and the other Ho-Chunk as exploited women producing bead-work only for the money; we should regard their work as symbols or messages of survival.[85]

Ho-Chunk women took great pride in their beadworking skill, whether the work was done to provide beautiful outfits for ceremonial occasions or to produce curios to bring cash income for their families. It offered status within their culture and, to some extent, recognition from the settler culture as well. Curios were perhaps not what they needed or even wanted to make, but Red Horn, Pettibone, and Prettyman, along with the many other women who provided Bennett with fine beadwork, took what their environment had to offer and fashioned it into a trade that gave them satisfaction in performing careful work, passing on traditional skills, and contributing essential income to a rural household.

Many settler families in northern Wisconsin faced similar hard times without sufficient resources. They survived primarily by sending daughters off the land and into the city to work. Tourist art and the skills it helped preserve allowed older Ho-Chunk women and the children to whom they taught their skills an important means of contributing to the ability of their people to stay on their beloved land and to strengthen family and cultural ties at the same time. That "message" was embedded in the belts and watch fobs that the Ho-Chunk beadworkers crafted so carefully and sent to the Dells.

FAIRS AND MARKETS

Fairs, like other programs initiated by the federal government for Native people, meant different things to Native communities than to the government. Fairs started on most reservations in response to a commissioner of Indian Affairs circular to agents suggesting they establish Indian fairs modeled on settlers' agricultural fairs. Indian fairs would encourage improved farming through exhibits and competition for prizes. Reformers could introduce such programs as the "Save the Babies" efforts aimed at improving rural health and other agricultural extension projects. Fairs could replace older festivities with new ones, monitored by agents. In fact, fairs became something more than that, places not only to exhibit newer skills in agriculture and handcrafts but also for proud display of traditional expressive culture and even for Native dancing. Both Menominee and Lac du Flambeau fairs were good examples of the clash and melding of old and new.

Between 1880 and 1920 many Native arts flourished. While Ho-Chunk women expanded their beadwork markets in the Dells early in the twentieth century, at Keshena and Lac du Flambeau markets developed slightly later. These reservations had no special scenic site such as the Dells, but as tourists flooded in for summer retreats, Native women increased their sales to trading posts. Then, between 1905 and 1925, they found that tourists were attracted by the fairs as well as the resorts in northern Wisconsin, providing an additional market for their beadwork, rugs, and other handcrafts.

Like the Lac du Flambeau women, Menominee women welcomed sewing instruction. During the nineteenth century, government teachers had supplied students with materials and training to create pants, shirts, skirts, gowns, dresses, and sunbonnets. There was a real burst of creativity in working with fiber at this time. As dancing for tourists developed at Menominee in the early twentieth century, women produced elaborate regalia. Many older objects were collected by American and European museum agents in the early 1910s and removed from community life, precipitating a tragic loss of religious and ceremonial objects, many of which are still being returned under recent repatriation legislation. The newer regalia used the older designs, and, although much was meant for secular and decorative uses, it was also used in ceremonies.[86]

Menominee women began exhibiting their handwork at the county fair in Shawano in 1909. In preparation for this fair, the superintendent and his wife asked schoolgirls and their mothers to create special handwork. Agent T. B. Wilson arranged for fair officials to offer special premiums for beadwork, and Mrs. Wilson visited older women to gather items for display. These exhibits were well received, and both girls and women won prizes at the fair. Wilson wrote to the commissioner of Indian Affairs that the display of the older women's beadwork "attracted more attention and comment than any other exhibit in the Art Department." The prize winners were mainly older women from the Zoar community: Louise Armour, Red Cloud Woman, and Wausakakomick. They seemed pleased with the attention and the prizes and promised to arrange an even better display at the next fair.[87]

Encouraged by the success of Native participation in the county fair, the superintendent decided that the Menominee should have their own fair the following year, using exhibits of handwork as well as of farm produce to attract Native participants. From that time on, women competed at each annual fair. Although the premiums were small—twenty-five cents to three dollars each—the women actively vied for them and seemed pleased with the recognition the awards brought for their work. A list for the years 1910 to 1916 included forty-two women who won prizes: for embroidery, clothes, quilts, beaded moccasins and gloves, basswood bark bags, beaded shirts and handbags, yarn belts, knitted socks, garters, braided rugs, sofa pillows, and lacework. Exhibits of handcrafts proved to be a magnet for audiences.

The Menominee fair quickly became a special event, attracting hundreds of visitors and providing a place for women to show work, compete, and sell handcrafts as well as visit with people from other communities. In 1913, when industrial teacher Myrtle Marble and Lizzie Cardish Kakak organized the exhibits, they had an entire Women's Building to fill. Marble and Kakak sent some of the best work on to the Wisconsin State Fair in Milwaukee, where women won more prizes.[88]

As the popularity of Native handwork grew, the superintendent received requests to provide sweet grass, ash splints, and other materials for manufac-ture of baskets elsewhere. Such inquiries revealed the community's concerns about involving middlemen both in providing materials and in sales of finished handcrafts. In reply to one inquiry, Nicholson wrote to the commissioner of Indian Affairs that the Menominee feared whites "getting a foothold in here which would not be surrendered." Marble, the assistant supervisor, wrote to one company that the people were unwilling to trust that they would get money for their handcrafts, for they "still look with suspicion upon the white people, especially outside traders, and invariably demand cash for their prod-uct as soon as it is delivered. . . . The Menominees have persistently gone on record against allowing outsiders to come in and purchase, for outside ship-ment, any of the products of the reservation." They had a number of Native and long-time settler traders with whom they preferred to deal: Ida Freden-berg, Jane La Bell, and Polly Davis, as well as Peter Lookaround, Neopit Mer-cantile, Bauer Brothers, and Jerome Lawe. Because of this concern about white exploitation through long-distance trade, the Menominee increased produc-tion for fairs where they could sell directly for cash.[89]

By 1914 the Menominee fair had become an important event for Native and settler alike. Native people came from at least eight other tribes. Non-Native visitors came from nearby Shawano as well as from Appleton, Green Bay, Marshfield, Milwaukee, Oshkosh, and Chicago. Among the visitors from Chicago was businessman Edward E. Ayer, an enthusiastic collector of Indian art and a member of the Board of Indian Commissioners. Ayer told a reporter that the Menominee fair was the most notable fair east of the Albuquerque Navajo fair. Native arts were the highlight of the fair, along with exhibits of wigwams, drumming, singing, and dancing.[90]

Dancing by Native people meant more than just entertainment. For them dancing was a community event, usually with religious and ritual elements. The government had challenged the right of Native groups to perform both traditional and revival dances. At first, it argued that warrior dances promoted resistance to control, then that religious dancing delayed "assimilation," and finally that all dancing wasted time and resources. Native peoples resisted these restrictions, continuing to dance in secret, off reservation, or with the tacit acceptance of agents who knew they could not impose limitations regard-less of orders from Washington. Ho-Chunk, Lac du Flambeau Chippewa, and Menominee continued to dance throughout this period despite sporadic attempts to suppress this right. The Menominee dance group performed before white audiences, with other Native groups, and for themselves. In 1910 they marched in the Keshena fair parade and gave dancing exhibitions.[91]

The interest and support of settlers for Indian performance dance at exhi-bitions and fairs helped encourage the continuance of older dances in new forms and venues. A number of Ho-Chunk and Menominee women regularly

Menominee dance troupe, 1915–16. Settler communities invited Menominee dancers to perform in historical pageants and parades and at county fairs. S. A. Barrett photographed this group for the Milwaukee Public Museum.

performed in these dance groups in the early 1900s. They also continued to participate in private dances and helped organize feasts and giveaways to accompany dances. Communities developed new social dances that incorporated ritual and spiritual aspects of the older dances, and young people quickly adopted settler dances as well. Menominee also maintained their traditions of sacred dance. In the summer of 1914 at Menominee one group held a two-day "medicine dance" to commemorate the passing of Neopit, who had died the year before.[92]

The agent for the Menominee also allowed old-time Native dances at the 1914 fair. He argued that he needed the traditional dances to attract the elders and the modern dances to keep the young people from going to town. Thus traditional settler square dancing and popular modern dances such as the waltz, the tango, and the hesitation as well as traditional dance were a part of the fair. The commissioner ordered the agent to halt *all* traditional Native dances. In greater secrecy than before, the Menominee continued to dance. And the fair continued to grow: in 1921, 2,600 people attended.[93]

After the government had established Indian fairs across the country, Native women increased their production and sales of handcrafts. In July 1914 in Circular 884, "Promotion of Native Industries," commissioner Cato Sells recognized the important rural industry Native women had developed. Sells acknowledged that men sometimes participated in producing Native work, but he recognized that most industries of this type were created by women. He estimated that earnings from blanket weaving, basketry, pottery, beadwork, and lace making earned Native communities approximately $700,000 in 1913. He asked that superintendents and supervisors of schools report to him on the condition of this industry. He asked what objects were being produced and how many, with what value, by whom, at which times of year, and for how long. He asked if local markets were ample and gave full value and if the producers received cash, merchandise, or credit for supplies. He asked if the bureau should attempt to find markets and, if so, what articles should be handled and how long it would take to fill orders. Would Native people send articles to the East through the agent's office, COD or for payment thirty days after delivery? He also wanted to know whether and how agents were encouraging improvement in the articles produced. The circular alerted officials to the importance of women's work and was followed by an increased number of comments on women's industries at Keshena and Lac du Flambeau, but only Myrtle Marble, the industrial teacher at the government boarding school for the Menominee, took the time to make a full report in 1914.[94]

Marble reported that beadwork, buckskin work, basket weaving, and rug braiding were the principal industrial arts practiced by Menominee women. Most of the workers were older women. They did their work during spare time or when especially pressed for funds. "There is good profit in the beadwork and braiding," Marble wrote, "if they can be persuaded to make a business of it." Until the last year, she continued, items were made largely to use about the home, to wear in dances, or to exchange as gifts. Because of these uses, she could not put a value on the objects. Materials for rug weaving came from old garments washed and softened; the beads were procured from traders. As for sales, most of the beadwork, as well as baskets and buckskin work, went to local merchants, who never paid in cash, only in merchandise. A few women sold to recent settlers and to tourists.

Within the last year, Marble had been encouraging women to increase their output. They promised to have handwork on sale at the fair. Marble had also secured a market for the rugs at Marshall Field's in Chicago. Women had few supplies, no surplus cast-off garments, and no cash to buy new materials for braiding. She suggested that remnants or out-of-date clothing could be obtained from large firms if the agency could either advance funds or arrange to pay the costs and deduct them from the price of the rug. Women also expected to be paid as soon as the article was completed and turned over to the local merchant or the agency. They would not make rugs in large numbers if they had to wait several weeks for payment, Marble informed the agent. She thought they might eventually consent to send their work COD, but the best way to promote women's enterprises was to make available a tribal fund upon which they could draw for loans, a practice that had already been used for farmers who wanted to purchase stock and implements.[95]

At Lac du Flambeau, the development of women's handwork can be traced through correspondence about the fairs. Sewing continued to be popular among schoolgirls, who practiced both plain and fancy work. As at Menominee, the demand for handcrafts and the increase in production at Lac du Flambeau preceded establishment of the fairs. As tourist numbers grew, so too did souvenir demand. Women preferred to have local traders such as Margaret Gauthier sell their work and give them credit for household needs. Margaret had developed a considerable trade in women's handwork by 1915, when the first fair was organized. At Lac du Flambeau, Native leaders on committees to organize the fair insisted on offering prizes not only for agricultural skills but also for handcrafts. Women competed with men for the agricultural prizes, exhibiting cows, teams of horses, ponies, pigs, chickens, corn, oats, carrots, tomatoes, pumpkins, butter, home cooking, pickles, jelly, canned fruit, cakes, bread, and rolls, as well as maple sugar and wild rice. Women competed with each other for the handwork prizes.[96]

As at Keshena, the Lac du Flambeau women vied seriously for these prizes because of the prestige the community conferred to the winners. The prizes revealed a wide variety of both Native and non-Native work. Among traditional arts, women entered their beadwork, mats, woven bags, birch-bark work, moccasins, and dance shawls. Several women often show up as winners: Margaret Bison, Tillie Bisonigigig, Nancy Gray, Isabella St. Jermaine, Annie Snow, and Fannie Sun for beadwork; Mary Babidosh, Mary Jackson, and Annie Snow for mats; Agnes Douds, Annie Martin, and Kate Scott for birch-bark work; Isabella St. Jermaine for woven bags. Some of the same women also won for outstanding creations in quilts, fancy work, needlework, comforters, sofa pillows, and rugs. Cecelia Poupart and Maggie Poupart won for needlework and fancy work; Mary Babidosh, Ida Johnson, Isabella St. Jermaine, Kate Shadamo, and Ramona Smith won for quilts and rugs.[97]

The first Lac du Flambeau fair, in October 1915, mainly drew people living on the reservation, but the enthusiastic response led the committee to expand fair offerings. In the following years it fenced the grounds and charged admission. By 1917 the fair was showing moving pictures of Glacier National Park and of tractor engines in farm work, offering a baby show and examinations by a physician, and sponsoring pony, moccasin, canoe, and motorboat races. Students submitted exhibits that, when sent on to Milwaukee for the state fair, won best school exhibit awards. Baseball games were added: in 1917, the Lac du Flambeau team played a team from Odanah; in 1918, a team from Minocqua; and in 1919, a team from Phillips. When Lac du Flambeau invited teams and bands from settler communities, tourists arrived in larger numbers, often in automobiles from some distance. By 1919, Lac du Flambeau Indian exhibits were drawing especial attention. "If we had allowed it," wrote agent James W. Balmer to the commissioner of Indian Affairs, "they would have purchased everything exhibited of Native handwork the first day of the fair."[98]

That year, 1919, a government inspector reported on Lac du Flambeau industries and the fair, reinforcing the impression of success. Practically all Natives attended, he noted. Several hundred tourists had avidly sought Indian products. More than one hundred automobiles parked at the fairgrounds. "Practically everything in Indian Handicraft, such as beadwork, moccasins or buckskin bags, rugs, quilts or other fabrics, and such curios and articles as were made by these Indians—all were sought and fancy prices paid for every product," the inspector reported. Native people were already talking about next year's competition.[99]

The handwork exhibit generated the first detailed description of the displays. "The outlook for the industries of the Indian women on this reservation is excellent due in part to the home market provided by the tourists at this and nearby resorts," field matron Mary E. Spinney wrote enthusiastically. "The braided rugs made by the Chippewa women were much admired and sought for all over the United States," she wrote. Their moccasins were quite popular, as were neck chains, headbands, and sofa pillows. They also crocheted good rag rugs and wove rush mats. They made baskets of all kinds from birch bark and also used it to make large and small canoes, napkin rings, and plant pot covers. "Some of the women make very pretty patch work quilts, the quilting being done in fancy patterns by hand. They also weave a bag which makes good pillows," Spinney reported. She suggested a community center be established where women could visit and exchange ideas.[100]

It is difficult to tell how much income the handcrafts so avidly purchased by tourists brought to Lac du Flambeau women. A 1927 survey estimated sixty-eight people at Lac du Flambeau engaged in making Native art. At that time, there were 260 Native families at Lac du Flambeau, so about a quarter of the families would have been involved in the handcraft trade. That estimate seems low, for the matron's industrial survey taken five years earlier, one in which she especially noted women's handcrafts, showed 135, or approximately half of all households involved in the trade. In order of frequency, women were making the following items: beadwork, moccasins, birch bark, reed mats, rag rugs, hidework, woven bags, crochet, quilts, baskets, knitting, snowshoe parts, dance regalia, embroidery, and clothing. Many women made more than one type of object. Isabella St. Jermaine made five different objects.[101]

Beadworking and moccasin making were the most frequently practiced skills in all age groups. Birch bark, reed mats, rag rugs, and baskets were mainly the work of middle-aged and elder women. Quilts were equally popular, but elders also still made snowshoe parts. Middle-aged women made dance regalia; young women did embroidery and dressmaking. As might be expected, the young and middle-aged women had greatest access to sewing machines, but some elders had sewing and even knitting machines.

Elder handworkers tended to know both Native and settler skills. Mary Ackley taught her daughter Reva how to bead and sew at a young age. By the time she was in high school, Reva sewed suits and a prom dress. Mary was a fine beadworker who also made moccasins despite problems with her eyes. Joe Chosa remembered that his grandmother earned money selling her hand-made moccasins and gloves. His grandmother was probably the forty-nine-year-old woman whom the matron listed making moccasins, reed mats, rag rugs, birch bark, dance regalia, and drums and doing beadwork and hidework. Chosa's mother, Martha Bell, who was twenty-three in 1922, when Chosa was an infant, only crocheted.[102]

That the elders did more handcrafts than the young women did not necessarily mean that skills were declining from generation to generation. Elders usually had more time to devote to handcrafts. The younger women learned the skills as children but did not have time to practice them while raising and caring for their own families. As they completed the tasks of youth and middle age, they practiced their handwork skills—for pleasure, for profit, and to teach the young girls. In this way, skills were passed on and available when women had time for them.

Despite the fairs' success, governmental interest in promoting women's handwork waned in the 1920s. The records do not mention whether the recommended community center was constructed at Lac du Flambeau or whether a systematic effort was made to loan women the money they needed to start small handcraft enterprises. Agents usually knew little about Indian art, and the only indication of an attempt to educate them was Bulletin 4 of 1922. That bulletin simply copied excerpts from an earlier Bureau of Ethnology work that defined Native art as "those elements of the arts which in the higher stages of culture come fully within the realm of taste and culminate in the ornamental and fine arts." Included in this category were beading, basketry, needlework, quillwork, featherwork, and embroidery. Today Native peoples would include this work in the broader category of "expressive culture." The lack of information on Native beadwork was especially evident in the three brief references listed in the 1922 bulletin: one was on Apache beadwork, a second was on bead ornaments of the ancient tribes of Utah and Arizona, and a third was a popular how-to beading book for non-Natives.[103]

The tourist market created by women played an important part in assuring that their handwork skills were practiced and passed on. A ready market made it possible to integrate handwork into the economy. Women were eager to continue traditional skills, adapt them to the market, and acquire new skills.

As with the Ho-Chunk beadwork, women at Lac du Flambeau were able to use their handcrafts to keep their culture alive and to adjust it for new times. The objects carried the message that Native culture was important and deserved to be remembered and transmitted to the next generation. The objects and the skills with which they were made were thus not marginal to the culture or the economy but an essential way of using the economy to preserve the culture.

3

Farmlands

When Matilda arrived at her new log house in 1893 she was leaving the woodlands economy and entering farmlands. Her land did not look much like a farm: a log house surrounded by a small clearing, a small log shed with a cow and a horse. During the next twenty years, she birthed and raised eight children there, buried a first husband, and told a second to leave when he refused to help her farm. These relationships and the burdens and pleasures they brought lay like a grid across the forty acres that was supposed to sustain them all. During those twenty years, Matilda struggled to make her family and her land fit into a pattern of survival. It was a stingy land that did not yield easily a living for eleven people. By 1923, however, a sturdy two-story frame house had replaced the small one of logs, and she had a small herd of Guernsey cows, who warmed the air with their moist breath as she milked. In the house, she processed milk with a complicated mechanical cream separator. Each week she sent milk to the nearby cheese factory and received regular checks in return. Her life work on these forty acres was a microcosm of the economy the settlers imposed on this land and which, in turn, tied them to it. In the end, the small parcel could barely sustain Matilda and her oldest son.

Developers had always maintained that once forests were cleared what remained would make fine farmlands, especially for certain field crops and dairying, for potato culture, and for the raising of swine and sheep. Companies that had purchased and logged lands and hoped to sell the cutover to new immigrants feared state conservation would lessen their profits. The reforestation project challenged these landowners' economic interests, and they revived efforts to develop agriculture in the unpromising land. "Farms not Reforestation" became a rallying cry in Rhinelander and Wausau. When a 1915 decision of the Wisconsin Supreme Court halted the use of state funds for reforestation, state officials refocused their attention on promoting farming for the settler population. This chapter begins with the story of four immigrant women who, like Matilda, shared a dream of living off the land.

Settler Economies
Stories of Mary, Frances, Ursula, and Johanna [Lunka, 1869–1942; Lazar, 1870–1945; Champa, 1870–1952; Francel, 1887–1952; all born in Slovakia or Slovenia]

In April 1910, four women arrived at Gorman railway station in Clark County with their families. Friends and now settlers, the women brought with them eighteen children, aged two months to sixteen years. They had come from Ely, Minnesota. Mary, forty-three, and Frances, forty, had known each other for thirteen years, ever since Mary and her husband arrived in Ely in 1897 after a disastrous attempt to settle in Brazil. Frances had already lived in Ely two years when Mary arrived. Ursula, forty, and Johanna, twenty-nine, reached Ely in the early 1900s. These women's husbands—all named Frank—had come to Clark County the summer before to clear small areas and build log houses on the newly logged land. These settler families came by train, not by oxcart or horse-drawn wagon, yet the land that lay before them looked identical to the land that had faced settler women for the previous sixty years: stumps interspersed with sections of uncleared land.

As the four women looked around, they saw little to mark this small community besides the depot. There was no schoolhouse for their children, no Catholic church in which to worship, no post office to receive mail. The nearest schoolhouse and post office were at Willard, four miles away. Priests came from Greenwood, another eight miles beyond Willard, to say Mass in the Willard schoolhouse each Sunday. A priest who had come during Holy Week

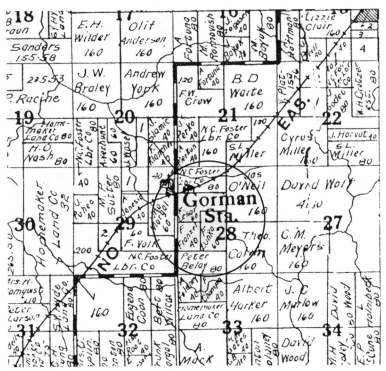

Willard plat map, 1914–15. Plat maps allowed settlers to see exactly where their land was located. This example shows that the four families from Ely, Minnesota, settled close together near Gorman Station so they could easily offer support to one another.

the year before was heard to say, "What is going to happen to your souls, you poor neglected people here in the woods?"[1]

And, others asked, what would happen to their bodies? There were no lodges for men to join to help with medical care or burial expenses should they, heaven forbid, have an accident. There was no doctor close enough to do any good. Gorman had none of the services that had been available to them in Ely. Still, the women were healthy and knew how to help each other in childbirth; they had a rich array of home remedies. There was a store in Willard, they had heard, in an old building that had once served as combination logging camp, store, and school. The owner, Steve Sandburg, was building a new store, due to be finished soon. That was a consolation.

Despite everything, it seemed a godsend that the families had been able to get out of Ely at all. What had brought the four women to—and driven them from—Ely were the iron-ore mines where each of their husbands worked. Mary's husband, Frank Lunka, had worked in the Pennsylvania mines after arriving in the United States as a young man and at Ely since the late 1890s. He was forty-five years old. Frances's husband, Frank Lazar, had worked in the Ely mines since 1893; he was now forty. Ursula's husband, Frank Champa, was forty-five, and Johanna's husband, Frank Francel, was thirty-seven. The mines where the four Franks worked were damp, cold, and dangerous. Each was eager to get out. Frank Lazar had already been injured in a cave-in. He had survived, but others had suffered debilitating injuries or death. The work was hard for men over forty. When the parish priest began to talk about farmland available in north-central Wisconsin, it seemed like a golden opportunity.

The land was relatively inexpensive. It had only to be cleared. The men had little idea of what clearing land entailed, but hard work was not new to them. In their homelands, the immigrants had lived in small agricultural villages centered on parish churches. In the United States, the men found work doing heavy, dangerous tasks. Instead of toiling underground in the damp, cold darkness, in Wisconsin they would be working in the sunshine and fresh air. Clark County was almost two hundred miles south of Ely and dryer than Minnesota. Father Buh, a Slovenian priest who had followed the immigrants to Minnesota, urged them to get out while they could.

The four families were not the first Slovenians to be enticed to Clark County by Father Buh. When he heard the N. C. Foster Company was looking for industrious, hard-working people to buy farms at their Camp No. 9 in north-central Wisconsin, he suggested to Ignac Cesnik, a Slovenian who was selling suburban lots to Slovenians around Joliet, Illinois, that he might help the immigrants get out of Ely. Cesnik bought land and moved north with his wife, Jera, in 1908. The Foster Company made him their land agent and launched an advertising campaign in Slovenian magazines and newspapers. Cesnik met prospective buyers—his countrymen—at the train, put them up at the old bunkhouse on

Cesnik's farm, ca. 1910. The Cesniks were established in Willard at an old logging camp given them by a company that hired the family to sell lots to their fellow Slovenians. They showed their countrywomen and -men property, greeted them and helped them settle, gave them advice on farming their stumpy land, and helped birth their babies. The Cesniks' flourishing farm with outbuildings, stored fodder, teams and wagons, large gardens, and potato fields encouraged settlers to take a chance at farming.

his land, showed them available land, and offered help in getting settled. Jera promised to act as midwife for the women. Ignac and Jera offered similar assistance to the four families from Ely. Families had already been trickling into the area, along with factory workers and miners from other communities. A few Polish workers came from the cities, and a scattering of native-born Americans came for their health. But most, like the four young women, were from Slovenia. Willard and the surrounding countryside would soon become the largest Slovenian community in the country. By the spring of 1912, fifty Slovene families were there and another thirty expected to arrive before fall.[2]

The four women from Ely shared a common Slovenian culture. Each was born either in Hungarian-dominated Slovenia or in Austrian-dominated Slovakia. They were part of the massive 1890–1910 migration that brought to the United States landless peasants who had grown up in the 1870s and 1880s under the control of arrogant Hungarian and Austrian landlords. These landlords despised their hard-working Slovenian agricultural workers. After the immigrants reached the mill and mining towns, it was common for the women to keep animals and raise large gardens while their husbands worked sixteen hours a day in the mill or the mine. They maintained households, took in boarders, and developed skills to make extra income so they could buy land. They spoke Slovenian to their children and to each other, sharing stories of childbirth and farming. All had a vision of what life in Wisconsin would be. They would establish a school where their children could learn English and a church to continue their Catholic faith. All would work in the fields as well as in the home.

Of the four women, only Frances Lazar had learned a trade after arriving in

Ely in 1895. She apprenticed as a seamstress, paying for her instruction by caring for the children and the animals on her employer's farm. For sixteen years in Ely, Frances took in boarders, made wedding dresses for Slovenian brides, kept cows, and sold milk. Frances also birthed eight children in Ely, six of whom had survived to leave for Wisconsin, the eldest son thirteen and the youngest daughter just two months. Frances would bear three more children after arriving in Wisconsin. Her savings helped the Lazars bring her mother from Slovenia in 1903 and buy sixty acres adjacent to the Gorman station.

Mary Klanchor Lunka already had a son and a daughter when she and husband Frank left Slovakia for Pennsylvania. Frank mined there before the family migrated to work on a Brazilian coffee plantation. Of this adventure, they remembered most the pythons and the insects that left maggots in the folds of their skin. After a series of misadventures, on the boat to New York they met a Slovene family who arranged a loan from relatives in Ely, where the Lunkas went to find work. Frank took a job in the iron-ore mines while Mary took in boarders, tended three cows (which she brought along to Wisconsin in a boxcar), raised chickens, and bore three more children. The Lunkas bought sixty acres adjoining the Lazar farm.

Ursula and Johanna were also born in Slovakia, arriving in Ely in 1901 and 1902. Both married there in 1902. In Ely, Ursula Champa bore three and Johanna Francel bore two children. Ursula and Johanna probably took in boarders and raised chickens and cows to accumulate enough money to buy land. The Francels bought forty acres adjoining the Lunkas and Lazars. The Champas got forty acres nearby.

When the census taker came around soon after the families arrived, all told him they were dairy farmers. But that was what they *planned* to be. Wives, husbands, and older children first faced the arduous task of clearing the land of trees, stumps, rocks, and underbrush. The first cash crop was timber harvested from the land and sold to the sawmill and cordwood shipped to the cities in the fall. They cut wood into bolts for box and furniture companies in Menasha and Sheboygan. The Lazar family history recalled that everyone helped with sawing, brushing, burning brush piles, and piling cordwood into boxcars for shipment.[3]

Those first years the families also planted and helped to harvest cucumbers. A pickle station built by Libby, McNeil, and Libby company offered a ready market for cucumbers. Settlers brought them to the station to be graded and put into vats with water and salt. In the winter the pickles were shipped to Chicago. Cucumbers were an ideal truck-garden crop for settler families. Entire families planted and picked. The factory bought crops for a decade before disease invaded the fields and forced the station to close in 1920.[4]

Another source of income, especially from 1911 to 1916, was the abundance of wild blackberries surrounding Willard. When the berries ripened, people

Willard depot, 1910s. The depot linked Willard settlers with the outside world, bringing new settlers, berry pickers for excursions, and needed equipment and catalog orders and shipping pickles and later dairy products to market. Pickle vats are visible under the depot roof.

picked all day and sold them to local stores for seven cents a pound. By shipping them to the nearby town of Fairchild, to the west in Eau Claire County, they could get ten cents per pound. Excursion trains brought people from neighboring small towns, such as Fairchild and Augusta (eleven miles north of Fairchild), to pick their own blackberries. A photograph from this time, captioned *Prehod vlaka v Slovenski farmarski Nasel bini* (Arrival of the train in Slovenian farming settlement), showed the people of Willard greeting the excursionists. All these additional income sources enabled families to buy more cows and dairy equipment.[5]

By 1920 the four families had become what they had envisioned—dairy farmers. Their new cash product was milk. They had brought a few cows, but because in the first years there was no way to market surplus milk, they kept herds for subsistence. The first Willard cheese factory, a cooperative established in 1914, admitted only cooperative members, and few Slovenians seemed to belong, but in 1917 Slovenian farmers at Gorman established their own cheese factory, which accepted milk from all farmers. The Lazars donated the land for a cheese factory, and Slovene farmers built it. With the cheese factory, the Gorman community joined the new regional dairy enterprise already being established elsewhere in Clark County. The subsistence-farming phase ended seven years after the four women arrived in the woods with their husbands and children. The women had what they came for—land of their own, plenty of food, clearings for cash crops, pasture for cows, a place to process milk into cheese. In addition, the settlers had borrowed money, shared work, and scrimped to raise six hundred dollars to build a school; they had organized a

Catholic congregation; and they had formed the Holy Family Society to help members with medical care and funeral expenses. By 1912, they had constructed the Holy Family Church building at Willard and held a First Holy Communion for the children. They now had a school, a church, a post office, roads, choral groups, and stores near their farms. World War I would bring the new nation of Yugoslavia in Europe, but these immigrant women had already made a place of their own in north-central Wisconsin.

SETTLER SUBSISTENCE

I have puzzled over how the predominantly German settler communities of north-central Wisconsin would have seemed to my grandmother when she arrived in 1892 from Bohemia. My grandmother came by ship and then railroad directly to the area around Medford in Taylor County with her sister, brother-in-law, and their small child. Perhaps these Bohemian Germans were recruited by the Wisconsin Central Railroad in the small town of Christianburg, where she had been born twenty-two years before. Perhaps the new immigrants went to live at Medford in the immigrant house for a few weeks while her sister and family picked out land just east of Medford. Matilda went north forty-five miles by rail to Phillips to work in a sawmill boarding house, already planning to marry Karl Schopper. Karl came to the United States from Austria first in 1883 with his brother Frank and their father. Karl and Frank worked lumbering to accumulate cash for down payments on their land. Each brother purchased forty acres, and Frank helped Karl build a log house near Dorchester in 1883. Karl returned to Austria to serve in the military. Perhaps he met Matilda while stationed in Bohemia. He returned permanently in 1887 with his mother, who lived with him in the log house. Matilda had worked in Bohemia since she was fourteen and for one year in Phillips before moving into her log home. Her first dream, having a home of her own, had been realized.

But the home was not yet a farm. Like Matilda and Karl, most immigrants, at least those who came to this cut-over area in the 1880s and 1890s, had little with which to begin their farm enterprise. Most started with only five hundred dollars and a piece of poor, unimproved land. Bankers and land companies that financed land purchases had their own needs. Bankers lent 50 percent of the value of the land, which was worth very little. They charged five to eight percent interest on money lent for three to five years. Most farmers could not repay in that time. Although land companies often granted exemption for a year or two, settlers could seldom pay up even in four or five years. Markets were poor or nonexistent; the clearing of land unexpectedly hard. At least half of the small business ventures were failing as agricultural prices declined in the 1920s. On these farms, the men generally had to devote their time to clearing a few acres every year. The women and children cultivated the small plots of land. Gardens were the basis of these subsistence farms, along with a cow, a pig, and a few chickens.

The first settlers were lucky if they had even one cow for their family needs. The cow was a scruffy thing that weathered the winter without a barn, in a crude shack, or in a shared combination barn and house, the plans for which a few settlers brought with them from Europe. The settlers hewed logs for an 18-by-24-foot log house the first summer and then set up small sheds for the accumulating stock. The men's winter lumbering wages were all the cash a family had. If the husband managed to stay well and avoid accidents and typhus in the camps (never mind the lice) and if the crops went well—and they often did not, as the weather could be brutal—there would be money at least to buy some needed tools and staples for the next year and to pay a bit on the mortgage. Most settlers had to mortgage their land either to subsist or to buy it in the first place.

Matilda and Karl used the log house as their basic farm building, as did other subsistence families. They lived, worked, and processed food there, using the second floor to store seeds and equipment and to provide a place for elders and children to sleep. Karl's mother lived with them until 1896, and then

Matilda in snowscape, 1902. An itinerant photographer stopped by Matilda's log house one snowy April and posed her with three children for a postcard. Matilda's first husband had died in August 1901, and she was about to marry again. She stands in front of the 18-by-24-foot log house in which she raised eight children between 1893 and 1919, when she moved into a new frame house. The log house now stands in the nearby Colby Rural Arts Museum.

Matilda's father came from Germany to join the family. By the time he died in 1902, Matilda and Karl's children were filling this second floor. The family built more outbuildings and moved the farm equipment there. They continued to use the kitchen for processing, separating milk and storing cream, making clabbered milk and cottage cheese on the back of the stove, and churning butter. Matilda made her clothes and those of her children on a treadle sewing machine and knitted socks and mittens by lamplight with bits of wool she gathered from fences. Karl and his brother had built well. The house had a foundation, so technically it was a log house rather than a log cabin. The American log house was modeled on log houses found in Bohemia; those already built in northern Wisconsin would have been familiar to Karl and Matilda.

German-speaking immigrants had brought the model of the log house with them to Pennsylvania in the early eighteenth century, and it had spread across the United States. The Schopper log house was a story-and-a-half tall with side-facing gables and two windows at the gable ends upstairs and one downstairs at the back. It was built of hewn timbers notched and chinked and had a rough wooden floor laid across joists. Matilda and Karl used one downstairs room as a kitchen-bedroom. It contained a double bed for themselves and their youngest children and a wood cooking stove and woodbin, along with storage for food and for implements used to cook and process it. A center brick chimney divided this room from a larger one that had a wood stove for heating, and the family ate and worked there. The house was built so well that it served as the family home until 1919, when Karl's son pulled it back to use as a blacksmith shop and they built a new frame house. As a blacksmith shop and storage space, it stood until the land was sold in 1984. Dismantled and moved to a museum in nearby Colby, it now stands furnished almost as it was. The Schopper log house, one of the few remaining of the thousands that once covered Marathon County, is the symbol of the small subsistence farm, just as the frame house with shingled roof became the symbol of a later development stage of these farms.

Karl had made a down payment on the forty acres, and they had a mortgage to pay off. There was enough to buy a horse, probably one cow, some tools, and supplies for the winter. Matilda was already pregnant when they married, as was the custom among European Germans, and she was pregnant or nursing most of the next seven years as she bore five children. They cleared land, built small outbuildings, paid on their mortgage, had larger gardens, and grew more fodder, but they never went beyond the subsistence stage. They used precious savings to bring Matilda's father, Peter, from Europe. Although Peter was able to help some with the work, his presence increased living costs. When he died in 1902, they could afford no stone to mark his place in the Catholic burial ground in Dorchester.

Matilda and Karl scrimped and labored to buy staples for the growing family. We know little about how subsistence farms like the Schoppers' actually made ends meet. Amazingly, the records of the Dorchester merchant who sold Karl supplies on credit the year during which he built the log house survive. He purchased a few staples and sewing supplies, and a bachelor's indulgence—tobacco.[6]

A list of what a family purchased remains from the Schoppers' neighbors, the Jantsches. When Matilda moved into her log house in 1893, she found the Jantsch family just across the road, already a decade into their farming, still struggling to feed their family. Matilda and Maria Jantsch immediately became close friends. Maria and her husband, Johann, were from the small Bohemian village of Marschendorf and spoke *Plattedeutsch,* the same German dialect Matilda spoke. Maria bore her first son in Bohemia and her first daughter in Stevens Point. Johann was a carpenter, so he was able to save money for land, and in 1883 they moved to Marathon County and purchased, as descendants remembered, "forty acres of stones" for $250. By 1888, there were five children, and the following year John's mother joined them from Bohemia as well. The Jantsch family kept a list of purchases made during a three-month period, from January to March 1888, which indicates the amount spent for supplies for a family of two adults and five children. They went to the store sixteen times during the three months and spent $18.23. About half the money went for rye, white flour, and meal. The remaining purchases were about equally divided among animal feed; sugar, coffee, syrup, and lard; and cloth and sewing supplies. During the three months the family purchased small quantities of crackers, cinnamon, prunes, apples, salt, and vinegar. They would have had their garden products stored away by this time, but they were not yet able to produce enough rye, wheat, or fodder for the entire winter.[7]

It is likely that the Schoppers would have purchased similar store products. As soon as they had cleared sufficient land, they would have planted rye, perhaps some wheat, and fodder crops, the main expense. Expenses for food on their subsistence farm would have been small. Then, ten years into the venture, still unable to move to the second stage that economists so carefully described, a colt kicked Karl Schopper in the stomach. The next day he died.

The economics of death had interrupted the business cycle predicted by Richard T. Ely, a University of Wisconsin economist. Ely termed farms such as the one started by Matilda and Karl "small capitalist businesses," which would go through two stages. The first, which lasted about three years, demanded spending and brought returns only in increased land values. The second, from three to five more years, brought the settlers enough income to establish permanent buildings, accumulate working capital, and develop markets. Ely estimated that a settler would need to invest from one to two thousand dollars in these ventures, as well as the labor of the entire family. Even then, the prospects for moving from the first to the second stage were not good. By the 1920s, in fact, many economists believed the upper tiers of the cutover—including northern Taylor and Lincoln counties—probably should never have been sold to settlers, that it was a mistaken policy to urge the peopling of this forestland. It should have been kept as a timber and recreational resource, they argued, and policymakers must now deal with families already there as a "problem" in need of solution. Tourism did prove a new economic base for Taylor and Lincoln counties, but it was built upon the foundation of subsistence farming.[8]

GARDENING, GATHERING, AND MIXED ECONOMIES

Garden agriculture was central to subsistence farming. Historically, small garden plots or household gardens have been essential to the survival of both landed and landless households. Household gardens, usually women's major responsibility, supply what cannot be obtained through hunting, gathering, or field production. These small-scale home food production systems often include backyard animal production, frequently poultry, which are fed on kitchen and garden waste. Located close to the house, the gardens provide a convenient daily supply of root and leaf vegetables during the growing season as well as surplus for storage, gifts to kin and neighbors, and sale in small quantities at local markets. Sometimes gardens grow to full-time market or truck garden enterprises oriented to supplying urban or nonagricultural rural areas; the truck garden may coexist with commercial field agriculture, especially in the early stages of these economies, when regular income is needed for investment purposes. They continue to be an important part of mixed economies, subsistence combined with wages, cash crops, small-scale cattle raising, and hunting and fishing.[9]

In north-central Wisconsin both men and women worked at clearing fields for gardens. It was hard, dirty, time-consuming work. They felled trees, used teams of horses or mules to pull out stumps, and employed low sleds to gather rocks. The men and women built small outbuildings for stock and fenced gardens.

A yearly cycle of growing and gathering bound families together in work. The major subsistence crops had to be grown, gathered, and processed during a short cycle from the late May thaw to the September frost. It was a busy time for all women, for subsistence was the basis of most Native and settler families during much of the nineteenth century. Gradually, both communities worked to expand their agricultural activities, built larger homes, obtained more tools. Cash incomes from lumbering and, in the case of Native families, some craft production plus these subsistence crops formed the economy upon which most families expected to live. In settler families, as in Native families, women

Stone sled, 1910s. "Stones, stones, stones," settlers complained. Next to clearing brush and clearing land, a family's most onerous task was clearing the stones that appeared each spring after the thaw. Low sleds made the task a bit easier.

controlled most of the subsistence part of this farm cycle—vegetable production, gathering, and processing. Men might plow or help prepare gardens, and both men and children helped plant, hoe, and harvest, but women had the main responsibility for seeing that the family was provided with ample food for its basic subsistence during the following year.

The yearly productive cycle began in late May when women started their vegetable gardens and ended in October when the last of the root crops was harvested. Native women gathered, parched, and stored rice. Settler women threshed rye or wheat but had it ground at a mill. Women gathered garden vegetables and dried or stored them in pits or root cellars to protect them from freezing. They also gathered large quantities of berries to dry. December brought in wild game to be processed and, for settlers, hogs to be butchered.

Seeds were a major concern. Women were the garden seed custodians and usually managed selection, storage, preservation, and exchange. Selection was crucial in new environments and in cross-cultural adaptation. Culinary traditions dictated many choices, but plants also had to be palatable and nutritious and amenable to processing and storage. Settler women negotiated with Native women for domestic seeds, but they also brought seeds from Europe and carefully saved seeds from early crops. They experimented to find the proper varieties for short growing seasons and early frosts. When a plant proved to be frost resistant or fast growing, they saved the seeds and offered them to other new immigrants. For German women, cabbage and kale seeds were particularly important, and they even lured others in Germany with offers of seed. Such long-distance enticements became less important for later immigrants, when German garden crops were well established, but seed trading continued to be a favorite rural practice. Everyone looked over their neighbors' gardens, asked about promising plants, and shared seeds with friends and kin.[10]

The entire garden enterprise took only a small amount of cash but large amounts of planning and managing of family labor. It also took regular attention to cultivating and picking. Women probably started seedlings indoors in late March. As the small seedlings emerged, they watered and nurtured them. Once the seedlings were large enough to plant and the danger of frost seemed past, they dug holes, filled them with water, and transplanted the small plants. They planted the most frost-resistant ones first, then followed with others after carefully evaluating yearly climate conditions, choosing varieties of seeds hardy enough to survive a possible late frost, and finally planted the most fragile.

Careful gardening could give women a variety of vegetables. From the hardy cabbage and the staples of green beans and corn, the women gradually experimented with more diverse types of garden plants. Some successfully grew tomatoes. Experimenting, passing on word of success and failure, visiting gardens and getting advice, bartering abundance—all formed a part of the subsistence cycle. Processing followed the ripening of each type of vegetable. Green beans and corn usually came late in September as women rushed to harvest before the first frost.

For German women, like my grandmother, the main processing equipment remained the cabbage shredder and the sauerkraut crock. Each fall, she packed crocks with shredded cabbage layered in salt, which she checked frequently during the winter as it soured. Her cellar was also well stocked with potatoes. A brother-in-law in Door County once sent her a barrel of apples, and her grateful postcard is the only sample of her writing I have. She also made sausage in winter. These, along with cheese and rye bread, were the early staples that German settler women needed to survive until their next gardens began to produce.

The forest provided many ways for rural families to obtain food and cash. The annual migration and month-long nesting in April and May of passenger pigeons during the 1870s and 1880s provided opportunity to bring in cash for live birds or dead ones, plucked, and packed in ice. Trapshooters practiced on live adult birds sent east by the carload, and eastern restaurants bought barrels of the young squabs. Wisconsin-born Aldo Leopold later wrote about this earlier generation, "less well-housed, well-fed, well-clothed than we are," that had deprived their descendants of the pigeons, now extinct. Native peoples tried to harvest with restraint, but the chance for poor settlers to earn cash made heavy harvesting attractive. Early settlers also handed down stories of how the passenger pigeons stripped their Marathon County orchards bare; thus, slaughtering the birds seemed justified. Gathering wild ginseng provided cash for families, as did making maple syrup; Native people taught settlers how to harvest both foods. Most local markets took ginseng and maple syrup in exchange for supplies. Rivers likewise could provide cash supplements. Young people gathered clams to take home and to sell. Anastasia Furman remembered how clamming on the Wolf and Wisconsin rivers fed a shell button industry in Stevens Point until the 1920s, when the market was killed by cheaper ocean pearl buttons from Japan. Dams and paper mills as well as improved dredging technology destroyed clam beds, removing another source of food and cash. When glass jars and Ball caps became available in the late nineteenth century, canning by the open kettle method became common, allowing greater amounts of gathered and grown food to be preserved.[11]

Settler and Native alike lived off the land's bounty. Homegrown and gathered foods, as well as the foodways of settlers and Indians, mingled in the provisions stored by families. Ida Hewitt, granddaughter of Métis Josephine Gauthier Robert and Gustave Robert, remembered how her grandparents and parents used both wild foods and garden foods during the 1890s through 1910s at home and for sale to bring in cash. She remembered filling wash boilers, which held eight to ten pails, with wild blackberries, each almost an inch long. They canned wild raspberries, gooseberries, currants, cherries, blueberries,

Berry gathering, 1910s. Summer brought settlers and Natives alike into the many wild fields and bogs to gather berries for family eating, canning, and drying and for sales to stores and logging camps. Wild blueberries, blackberries, strawberries, and cranberries were especially plentiful. Ida Hewitt remembered her family made fifty dollars by selling twenty-five bushels of cranberries.

and strawberries, too. They temporarily stored cranberries in dried moss in the woodshed attic and then packed them in water in sealed glass jars. Her mother canned and made jelly of other fruits, which appeared daily on the table along with maple syrup. Her father also made candy with homemade maple sugar or wild honey he gathered. Surplus gathered and processed food earned cash at logging camps and stores. One year the strawberries alone brought in $45, and some years cranberries earned as much as $50. They also sold maple syrup. At one time they made their own butter and cheese at home and sold butter locally. Later they kept eighteen cows and took cream to a creamery.

Almost everything gathered or grown went into storage. Home-cured hams, bacon, and sausage went into the smokehouse. Jars of fruit, kegs of sauerkraut, and large clay-stone jars of salt pork in brine went into the cellar. A third of the cellar was filled with potatoes being held until spring to sell when prices were higher. Pumpkins, squash, parsnips, rutabagas, carrots, onions, and cabbage from the garden kept all year long. Ida recalled that they made their own cheese at home, along with mincemeat from venison and hog's headcheese. To protect the produce from freezing, they packed the outside entrance to the cellar with hay and retrieved stores by a trap door in the kitchen.[12]

Regardless of ethnic culture, women had to produce, gather, and process more than enough food for the coming six months, enough to swap surplus with neighbors or to give away, enough to cushion scarcity in the following season if it was extremely cold or dry. Upon these stores rested the survival of the family and the success of any farming enterprise. To be left without enough food for the winter meant seeking credit at the nearby store or selling precious stock. Not only did women provide for their families, they worked for surplus that they could share at community gatherings and with invited guests. The economy relied upon these stored foods.

On the base of this subsistence farming, families built mixed economies. Mixed economies existed where there were not fully developed markets, making maximum use of family labor for a variety of tasks. Women experimented with poultry, butter making, small livestock, and garden crops with field crop potential. Out of these economies sometimes came viable specialties, especially dairying. Other families chose to maintain their mixed economies because of lack of resources or by preference. In Clark County, many farm families had developed these mixed economies by the 1880s.

Pine Valley, which eventually became a dairying center, offers a fine snapshot of these mixed economies. In 1880, Pine Valley was a newly settled area just north of the county seat of Neillsville. The Black River meandered through this valley north to south, leaving rich bottomland well suited for mixed agricultural farms. When the agriculture census taker visited Pine Valley in June 1880, he stopped at 1,223 farms to ask their owners how much land they owned, its value, how much labor they hired, and what kinds of animals and products they grew. Thus his list gives us a view of what they produced: cereals, root crops, orchards, forest products, maple sugar, butter, eggs. Through the columns left blank, the census also tells us they did not have market gardens, hops, or tobacco. Only three had small nurseries, and eight kept bees. Two of the beekeepers produced 400 and 700 pounds of honey, quantities that indicate more than subsistence, although the census taker did not ask for the value of these products. These were prosperous farms for the time, but few had developed a commercial specialty.

Looking over the census lists, one is struck by the small size of the improved acreage and the mixed crops. Almost 70 percent of the farms had fewer than 40 acres improved, another quarter had 40 to 100, and only seven had more than 100. Visiting these farms, one was likely to see chickens on all, although only eight had flocks of 50 to 100 from which they could have sold eggs in quantity. Almost all were still cutting their trees for profit, but only two sold cords of wood in quantities that brought in $500 or $600. Half the families had apple orchards, but the products of only two were valued over $100. About a third of the farms also produced maple sugar, but only four in quantities of 700 or more pounds. There was a hint of the dairy industry to come: all produced some butter, and 20 percent produced 500 to 2,000 pounds, quantities that were already commercially viable. A few produced large amounts

Women with tools, 1910s. Scythes, rakes, and wagons were familiar tools, especially for German and Polish women, who almost always worked in the fields alongside their men. While women were seldom photographed using farming tools or caring for larger horses, they were often expert at all aspects of farming.

Woman with chickens, 1910s. Chickens became a mainstay of settler and Native farm families. Women and children did most of the work to raise and feed the chickens and to process and sell surplus to neighbors and town stores. Flocks of fifty or sixty hens could keep the family in eggs and poultry as well as provide crucial credit at the local store or bring in much-needed cash.

of cheese. Most, however, still produced little more than the family needed for its own use.

About one-quarter of these farms consumed and sold products valued at one thousand dollars or more. These were the middling farms, with only a few producing large amounts for sale but clearly depending on cash income mainly from their farms rather than from off-farm work and sales of small surpluses. These twenty-nine farms produced a great variety of products. They listed large quantities of field crops: corn, oats, barley, and wheat. In addition to butter, eggs, and maple syrup, a considerable number had flocks of sheep with up to fifty lambs and some sales of animals as well as significant amounts of shear, almost five hundred pounds. Since women no longer wove clothing, most of this wool was sold to factories. In the census taker's notes, there was no direct correlation between the amount these families spent for hired labor and their commercial success as measured by cash value. Those who had the most profit usually also spent the most for labor, but those who spent more for labor made far less than those who had only family labor. A healthy, hard-working family producing a diversity of crops could do quite well in Pine Valley in 1880. In Marathon and Clark counties, many families followed a similar pattern in using subsistence farming as a base for a mixed economy.

Sebold family memories offer a closer view of one of these developing farms. The Sebold farm was closer to town than that of the Schoppers, larger, and more fortunate. Although the family had eleven children, they were a bit better off with their one-hundred-acre farm. Amanda Sebold, who was born the year Karl Schopper died, remembered growing rye and taking it to the mill to be ground. At haying time, her mother took the dark rye bread out to the fields at 3:00 PM together with homemade beer and cheese balls with chives that her father made and aged until moldy. The snack of bread, cheese, and beer allowed the adults to work in the fields until sunset, when they had an evening meal. The Sebolds were soon able to buy a cream separator, which Amanda remembered cranking as a child. Her mother made butter with a dasher churn for home use. They had butter, smoked meat, eggs, and chickens. They gathered wild strawberries that grew along the railroad tracks. Her mother made pies and strawberry *küchen.* The Sebolds had enough surplus to trade eggs for groceries at the Dorchester store and soon had a small herd of dairy cows. In this family, daughters milked and sons strained milk and drove it to the creamery, yielding small but regular creamery checks. Except for eggs and milk, their economic production was similar to that of the earlier stage. They had enough cash to hire threshers for their fields, but the family was so poor that the children had to take turns getting new shoes and owned so few clothes that Amanda's mother had to wash at night so they would all have clean clothes for school the next day. This family made it into the economists' second stage, but only because it carried on old subsistence patterns.[13]

POLISH DREAMS

By the time Polish immigrants settled in northern Wisconsin, late in the nineteenth century and early in the twentieth century, the best land had already been claimed. Earlier Polish settlers had been able to develop prosperous farms in Portage County by the time the newcomers arrived. Those who settled farther north, on less fertile soil, had a more difficult time. Land in Marathon County was more expensive than in northeastern Portage County even though it was rock strewn. Most settled on cheap land, some of it owned by Irish who had moved back to the cities and some of it interspersed with Norwegians and Germans. A few settled in small communities. They found sandy patches along the Plover River inexpensive and suitable for raising potatoes. In Taylor County's Roosevelt township, a group of Polish settlers, mainly from Chicago, started the village of Lublin in 1906.[14]

Savings went to purchase land, to build a log house, to buy a cow and a horse and plow. Like German subsistence settlers, Polish men had to seek off-farm jobs to support the farm ventures. Women found domestic jobs with wealthier farm families. Some picked in the cranberry bogs during harvest season, and a few earned income from midwifery.

In a series of interviews conducted in the 1950s, a group of Polish immigrants described farm lives and women's important role. Martha Liebe, an accomplished knitter, became known for her fine socks and mittens, which she sold for fifty cents a pair, and gloves, which she sold for even more. She worked out, made maple sugar, worked with livestock, and tended and milked cows, giving up her last cow only when she was more than ninety years of age. Members of the Laska family brought $1,100 in gold from Europe, but like other settler families they all worked clearing rocks, brush, and stumps from their land. The children began working out at age twelve to fourteen. Young men went to the lumber camps and returned for summer farm work. Gardens bloomed around their log houses. Michael Lisz remembered his grandmother had thirty rows of crops, each forty to fifty feet long, and many herbs. Grandmothers still made their traditional spiced Polish sausage. The family took chickens, geese, and beef to the market, the *zynek* in Polish. They planted potatoes among the stumps and peeled hemlock bark to sell to tanners.[15]

Other interviewees spoke of Polish mothers doing all kinds of work. Some helped their men build joint houses and barns and thatched them with straw. Michael Lisz remembered "a good strong woman that didn't want to monkey around in the kitchen, she went to help the men." Frances Scuoniewicz put it this way: Polish women were "foolish enough to help. . . . Irish women had more sense." Theodora Koziczkowski, in comparing women's work, believed Polish women worked hardest of all. Theodora worked at everything, except the manure spreader and the binder. She did all the milking and almost all of the pig care. Polish women were anxious to get ahead, so they helped wherever they could, including cutting down trees to sell. "I can saw better than any man," one woman boasted, "got to know how to swing that saw." On smaller farms women also milked and fed pigs. A good horse team was expensive— one man remembered paying $550—everyone had to work to pay for that investment. For Polish couples, marriage was always a close economic partnership. A woman expected to work wherever she was needed, in house, barn, yard, garden, or field. At her wedding feast, the community toasted a bride with a song that wished her married life would be neither rich nor poor.[16]

Polish settlers scattered widely to find cheap and available land, but in each region one place became known for its concentration of Poles. In Marathon and Taylor counties, Polish families lived among other ethnic groups. One third of Portage County's Polish people lived in Stevens Point, which soon became a thriving center of Polish American culture. The town attracted Polish farm families from the entire Plover River Valley.

By the late nineteenth century, the public square at Stevens Point was already a central location for Polish settlers to market their produce. The public square, originally a continuance of the New England town commons, also was a familiar old-world custom. Polish farmers made this market one of the region's biggest and most thriving between 1900 and 1920. By 1914, Polish-owned saloons and shops lined the square and the streets leading to it. Here farmers could sell produce by auction or to shop owners or arrange to sell their entire harvest at the Potato Exchange. They could linger over individual sales to regular customers. One day in 1916, grocer Nick Urbanowski counted

Polish women, 1910s. On Thursdays, Polish farm women put on their distinctive shawls, hitched up their wagons, and brought potatoes, fruit, vegetables, and other farm products to sell at the public market in Stevens Point. At the shops surrounding the public square, they purchased household needs. One day in 1916, grocer Nick Urbanowski counted more than two hundred wagons on a single route into the city.

more than two hundred wagons coming down North Second Street, just one of the routes leading to the market. On traditional Thursday market days, Polish women would hitch up their wagons to take produce into town. Whole families came on Saturdays.

Farm families brought all types of produce: their main commercial crop of potatoes, livestock, grain, vegetables, fruit, berries, maple syrup, firewood, and hay. Photographs show Polish women in their distinctive shawls buying and selling in the square.

The clustering of Polish buyers, sellers, and stores allowed country women to conduct business in Polish, buy from Polish shopkeepers, and perhaps pick up the Polish-language newspaper, *Rolnik* (The Farmer), which was devoted to farm life. Stevens Point was a center for Polish Catholic culture. Families visited the large Polish church and shopped for home devotional goods—a picture of a saint for the wall of the log house or a small religious icon for the bedside table. After 1902, Polish nuns founded their motherhouse for the Sisters of St. Joseph there. At Stevens Point, country daughters could look for city jobs and aspiring teachers could attend the normal school.[17]

Descendants of these Polish pioneers remembered how good Wisconsin seemed to their families despite the hard work. At least they were working for themselves and did not have Germans taxing them and telling them what to do. They could spend their earnings buying farm equipment instead of doing everything by hand as they did in Europe. Frank Beck said his mother was thankful to leave Poland and never wanted to go back. Jan Bohareicz added that Poles had to be tolerant of each other's differences in the United States: although most were Catholic, some Silesians were Protestant; some spoke different Polish dialects, and Polish Ukrainians spoke a separate language altogether. Despite many mixed marriages, when young people found partners among local Germans, Swedes, and, in the 1920s, Norwegians, they still cherished their Polish heritage. North-central Wisconsin is remembered as a place that nourished the dreams of Polish immigrant families—to obtain land, to be independent of government control, and to form a Polish American culture that united all Poles regardless of their regional origins.

Native Economies
Eliza's Story [Fredenberg, born in Menominee Nation, 1844–?]

It was a beautiful day in late May 1922, warm enough to go out in only a light housedress and no jacket. The agency farmer for the Menominee reservation had come to make a survey. Eliza stood just back of the white picket gate while the government farmer took the snapshot. Behind her small figure, the two-story, well-painted frame house rose large and substantial. In the photograph, one can see two fireplaces, an attic, a basement, flowers in the yard. It was Eliza's home. The other buildings, outside the frame of the photograph, were hers, too: an animal barn, a corncrib, a hen house, a garage, a hay barn.[18]

With the aid of a crutch—it was an old injury, Eliza told the agency farmer—she was able to get around. She was seldom sick and got along fairly well despite her injured hip. Nor was it her age, seventy-one, that was causing her to abandon farming after all these years. It was the loss of her good hired man that drove her to quit. She had already sold the improvements and was ready to sell her team and let someone else farm the forty acres. She had a wagon, two ponies, a spike-tooth harrow, a cultivator, and a bobsled. The "well furnished and very neatly kept" house had ten rooms and a player piano, the farmer noted. There was no orchard, but a good well. "The buildings and surroundings are kept in No. 1 shape," he jotted on his census sheet. The year before, Eliza had kept eight and one-half acres in cultivation, raised eight tons of hay and sixty bushels of potatoes, and maintained a large garden and seventy

Eliza Fredenberg, 1922. The agency farmer asked Eliza to pose for a photograph in front of her substantial two-story home. With the help of her hired man, she ran the farm for fifteen years after her husband died. "Has business ability," the farmer noted in his report.

chickens. Eliza had done all this with only a couple years of education at the Catholic school. The farmer noted in the book for the survey, "a good practical education and has business ability."

Born in 1844 at Lake Poygan, Eliza had grown up among Menominee women who were successfully cultivating the land. Menominee were embracing Catholicism at the time, in part, according to one priest, because those who had become converts seemed to be prospering by farming. In the nineteenth century, in many parts of the country, Native peoples had hoped that their Christianity and cultivated crops would allow them to remain on their lands. In Michigan, for example, the Potawatomi had rallied Catholic clergy and neighbors in resisting relocation farther west. The Menominee had argued they should be able to remain in Wisconsin because the land the government wanted them to occupy in the west was not suitable for farming. They, too, asked a Catholic priest to help broker a compromise to allow them to stay on their homelands. By 1847 about five hundred Menominee were farming at Lake Poygan. Accounts of the amount of land the Poygan community cultivated differed: one said they had cleared and fenced two hundred acres of land; a priest's estimate put it closer to one thousand. He may have been padding his missionary balance sheet, but in any event the cultivated acreage was considerable.

Although the school and farm seemed to be flourishing, the agent recommended that the community move west of the Mississippi River. Settlers were pressing to obtain this fertile land for their own farms. Evidence of successful farming did not deter the government from attempting to force relocation farther west so that new settlers could occupy choice farmland. The Menominee delegation sent to inspect the land chosen for them by the government reported that it was not suitable for farming. They preferred to remain in Wisconsin. The government finally agreed that the Menominee could stay but insisted that they move away from the settler communities expanding along the shores of Lake Michigan and Lake Winnebago and resettle on a part of their traditional homelands in a deeply forested area to the northwest along the Wolf River. Eliza was among the more than two thousand women, children, and men who began the trip up the Wolf River from Lake Poygan in November 1852.[19]

Eliza witnessed this struggle to remain farmers and participated in the first attempts to farm the new land in the 1850s. In the 1860s she married Fredenberg, a successful logger, and they farmed together for the next forty years, until 1907 when he died. She went on cultivating and improving her farm for an additional fifteen years.[20]

We know from the agency survey that Eliza was an enrolled member of the Menominee Nation, that her house was near the village of Keshena, and that she had successfully managed the cultivation of a forty-acre farm. Had she not been a widow, however, any farm work she had done would not have been mentioned by the agency farmer. He visited 277 households in conducting his survey. He counted 260 Menominee, none of whom had allotted land, cultivating 3,675 acres. He photographed each family in front of their home. The agency farmer considered Eliza's farm a model one, despite what he called the system of "communistic farming," where tribal members had claims to work land but no title to it. And despite his criticism of that system, families not only subsisted but produced surpluses and ran small truck farms to supply lumber workers and the surrounding white community with food and fodder. Because the agency farmer thought women should mainly "keep house," we do not know what work married women did on the farm, but we know from other reports that many Native people kept extensive farms and, even where land was so poor that white farmers would not try, produced subsistence and beyond. They did many other things, as we have seen—hunted, fished, sugared, riced, gathered berries and ginseng, and produced handcrafts—but they also farmed. On the reservation, like Eliza, and off, where many Native families lived in mixed communities, Native people were successful farmers by both Native and non-Native standards. A woman with a "good practical education and . . . business ability" could make it on her own as well as in partnership with a man.[21]

NATIVE SUBSISTENCE

Between 1907 and 1917, the anthropologist Frances Densmore visited a number of Chippewa communities in Minnesota and Wisconsin. It was a propitious time, for older women still remembered and practiced the old-style industries in which Densmore and other anthropologists of her time were interested. Her descriptions remain the most commonly used to describe "the industrial year" of Chippewa women. "The Chippewa," Densmore wrote, "were a people subsisting chiefly on vegetable products and fish, though they secured deer and other animals by hunting. The making of gardens was an important phase of the industrial year, and a portion of the food thus obtained was stored in caches for winter use." Densmore's most remembered informant was seventy-four-year-old Nodines from the Mille Lacs band in Minnesota, who described the yearly round of economic activity.[22]

"When the ice froze on the lake we started for the game field," Nodines told Densmore. The women carried rice, dried berries, and dried pumpkin flowers along with yarn bags, blankets, and rush mats to winter camps, where they put up wigwams covered with birch bark. The men hunted and gathered wood; the women removed and butchered the kill, chopped the wood, and partially dried the meat over fires. The women also snared rabbits and partridges, repaired the men's leather clothing, tanned hides, and made fishnets. In the evenings, women instructed their children on their obligation to care for elders. In spring, she said, the women wrapped dried meat in tanned deerskins and then moved to the sugar bush, where they tapped the trees while the men and boys ice fished. Grandmothers, with the help of young girls, dried fish and gathered cedar for mats and bags. Meanwhile, the younger women kept the fires going under the large brass kettles in which they boiled down the maple sap and processed and packed the sugar.

After returning to their lakeshore villages, the families made gardens. The women fished while the men cleared the land; then the women planted potatoes, corn, and pumpkins using hoes, grubbing sticks, and crowbar-like implements. After the planting they had a feast. They also caught passenger pigeons using fishnets on poles. They gathered wild potatoes, apples, cranberries, and blueberries, which they dried before storing. Raspberries they often boiled down, then spread the liquid in thin patches like little cakes and dried them leather-hard. The women stored everything in birch-bark *mukuks*.

In fall families camped at the wild rice fields while women harvested there. And after the rice was stored in cedar bags, the women returned to villages to harvest, process, and store the potatoes, corn, pumpkins, and squash from the family gardens. While the men did their fall trapping, the women did the fall fishing, also drying that catch.

In late August or early September the families traveled together to collect treaty annuities, first at Madeline Island, later at Fond du Lac, and later still at Wausau. The women received cloth, blankets, calico or linsey-woolsey, flannel, broadcloth, sewing equipment, and tin dishes. They received flour, pork, and a cash payment of a few dollars, with which they could purchase personal and household needs. An industrial year was then complete. The women had processed enough food to last through the winter, and they were free to sew and do beadwork as they gathered in their winter villages.[23]

The Chippewa were practicing what some scholars call a subsistence economy. Subsistence means different things to different scholars, so I use here a description by Thomas Berger, who studied subsistence in Native Alaskan communities. Subsistence means to live off the land in a particular way, developing special skills and a profound understanding of the local environment that enables people to live directly from the land. It means a complex of human, animal, and environmental relationships—sharing, mutual respect, resourcefulness, understanding. It involves a code of participation, partnership, and obligation in a seasonal cycle of harvesting, processing, and preserving products and careful organization of the labor of men, women, and children. Some products are traded, but this trade is difficult to quantify by the usual means, for it is not controlled by market conditions and commercial profits. More than production, it is also a system for exchange of subsistence products, which are distributed to all households within a community. Cash for equipment needed to sustain the system comes from seasonal employment. Subsistence, then, is an economic base that supports community relationships. The subsistence economy as Berger describes it underlay Native communities in north-central Wisconsin for most of the period here discussed. It allowed people to persist in the early economies. Gardening was at the core of this subsistence economy, a crucial part of a complex system that allowed people to live successfully in a harsh climate.[24]

At Lac du Flambeau, Chippewa women continued their subsistence economy through most of the 1890s and well into the twentieth century. Until 1884, there was no road through the Lac du Flambeau reserve and no government employees lived there. The agents did not even visit the reservation, delivering annuities to Phillips, about seventy-five miles from the agency in Ashland, the nearest point on the Wisconsin Central Railway but still forty miles from the reservation. In his report for 1880, the agent suggested that a road be built so he could take goods to the people and that a farmer be assigned as the people at Lac du Flambeau had "often made demands for assistance." Finally, in 1884 the agent received appropriations to cut a road through the timbered, swampy land to the village, and the government hired a teacher. The first farmer, Daniel Sullivan, did not arrive until 1889, however. The boarding school opened in 1895, but only 15 of the 142 children between ages six and sixteen attended that year. The farmer was so overburdened with other duties that he gave the people little assistance in farming.[25]

Most families at Lac du Flambeau continued their usual subsistence methods throughout the 1890s and into the early twentieth century, but the older hunting, fishing, and gathering practices became more difficult to maintain in the late nineteenth century. Lumber companies dammed rivers. The state introduced new fish species into lakes, causing a decline in native fish. Commercial exploitation of the wild passenger pigeons steadily reduced that food source. Settlers, who had earlier respected the gathering, hunting, and fishing treaty rights of Native people, increasingly restricted these activities on property they now claimed to own exclusively. Ricing, sugaring, and hunting still continued but were much curtailed by declining crops and regulations of various kinds. Adults continued to gather rice and to sugar, though in smaller amounts, as comments from 1918 and 1922 indicate, and without their children, as the government enforced school attendance. The men hunted, especially deer, whose numbers seemed to increase with the clearing of the forests. Most families moved into the village for the winter and used hunting and gathering as part of their food supply despite state and federal government interference.

Women turned increasingly to gathering berries, which still grew in abundance in forests and on land unclaimed by settlers for commercial purposes. They sold surplus berries and learned to can them in the late nineteenth century, when Ball jars and caps became available. Like settler women, they could use the canning kettle to heat the berries and seal them for preserving. Larger gardens supplemented the declining amount of plant food that could be gathered. By the 1880s, Native women were growing rutabagas as well as potatoes among their crops. Root crops grew well, stored easily, and could be harvested late in September, after other crops.

According to the accounts of white traders and travelers, Chippewa women had always been prodigious gardeners, noted for their plantings around larger lakes. Inland temperatures were more extreme. Corn, for example, often froze at Lac du Flambeau and could not be depended upon as a staple. Potatoes did much better. The men were willing to plow, but there were few teams of horses on the reserve. The agent wrote in 1890 that the women "appear to be abundantly able to attend to the work of planting, cultivating, and harvesting the crop [and were] industrious and energetic."[26]

One extended family exemplified the persistence of this subsistence way of life into the early twentieth century. In 1922 this family consisted of a mother, daughter, and granddaughter, her husband and his three children from a first marriage, and the couple's three daughters. One of the husband's sons lived nearby with his wife and their four children. The older women still made moccasins, did bead and birch-bark work, processed maple sugar and syrup, and picked and canned wild berries; the men hunted, fished, and helped with the sugaring. The family lived in two frame houses and one log house, each with ample gardens. Collectively they raised hay and potatoes for sale, picked greens to sell, and sold miniature birch-bark canoes and baskets. One married son worked out part-time as a laborer. The family provided a fine example of the complex lifestyle that could sustain a group of resourceful kin.[27]

Government records reflect a developing federal policy that was chaotic, changing, and discernable primarily through its implementation at the local level. Field reports from hundreds of agents and agency farmers are sometimes tainted by fraud and dishonesty; by racial, religious, and cultural bias; or by sincere error. Agency staff alternately praised Native people for their "progress" in adapting to this farming lifestyle, padding accounts to reflect their success and condemning communities for refusing to adopt these programs. Depending on the official's experience and personal goals, each interpreted differently the vague general policy of encouraging agriculture.

We cannot use these records reliably in isolation, but with careful analysis they can tell us much about government policy and Native resistance to it. Despite their limitations, these records give us glimpses of Native women at work on the land. The customary cultivators of land in most Native cultures, women often had difficulty getting what they wanted and needed from the federal government to improve food production as older food sources declined. At the same time, some Native men resisted demands to assume unaccustomed gender roles in agriculture.

Records show that the federal response to Native needs for agricultural support varied from very helpful at times to absolutely devastating. Native women were not totally dependent upon official policy, but government agents could make life very difficult. Like the settlers, Native families adopted appropriate technology and techniques, adapting what they wanted and needed to survive and rejecting what seemed detrimental to their communities and households. A history of common land ownership and culture made Native communities different but did not remove them from the larger environment within which all rural families worked to create meaningful lives. However enthusiastically embraced or thoughtfully rejected, farming was usually not the sole occupation for rural settler or Native but part of a complicated, carefully balanced way of life.

NATIVE FARMING

Native women were still practicing many aspects of their subsistence farming well into the twentieth century. Seasonal migration had been finely tuned to the availability of wild foods, but as it became more difficult to maintain access on land occupied by settlers, women gradually increased the time devoted to farming, even where the land was very poor, as it was on the Lac du Flambeau reservation.

Early subsistence patterns had seen families leave their home community in fall to hunt and trap. Most families returned early in the year at Lac du Flambeau and remained in camp for several months. Then they moved out to go sugaring at maple groves, which kept them away for about a month, from mid-March to mid-April. By May they were back ready to plant their gardens. In July and early August they picked berries, nearby when local berries were plentiful, farther away when they were not. In late August or early September they packed up again to go ricing, in lakes that were usually some distance from their homes. This normal cycle continued into the late 1880s at Lac du Flambeau. Teachers, in their reports to the agent at Ashland, often commented on the fluctuating attendance of children at the day school as an indication of harvest cycles. Well into January, the children were still gone to hunt and trap with their family. By mid-January most had returned. Until mid-March the children attended school, and then they were away sugaring. By late April they would be back in school. Three months later they would be away berrying with their families, and then they went out gathering rice. By the late 1880s, in September families were also digging potatoes and rutabagas. Although the reservation had a resident farmer, he often shared the duties of agent, and records indicate that little was done in the way of settler-style farming throughout the 1880s.

The first serious efforts to help Native families develop their gardens at Lac du Flambeau came in 1891. That fall, the farmer asked the federal government to send seeds, and he distributed them in May when the women prepared their gardens. By July the gardens were up and the new crops doing well. Each succeeding year, the farmer distributed seeds. In 1893, for example, he ordered seeds for potatoes and rutabagas but also for beets, cucumbers, cabbage, squash, pumpkin, onion sets, field peas, and oats. Beyond seeds, there was not much assistance. What little equipment the farmer furnished was not sturdy enough for the rocky soil and broke easily. He did not arrange for its repair in a timely way, and there was never enough equipment to loan to families who needed it to get started farming. By 1895, the farmer had obtained sturdy tooth harrows, and Native families had purchased horses and equipment to clear land and build log houses and outbuildings. It was impossible to keep the seeds and tools needed for farming without at least a log house. The climate discouraged many of the new farmers. Killing frosts were always possible, affecting even the hardiest vegetable varieties. The weather was exceptionally cold and then dry during 1893 and 1894, just as families were experimenting with farming. Crops failed. The 1895 crop was a bit better, but when the new boarding school opened that year some parents no doubt saw it as a way for their children to be well fed in a difficult time of economic transition. As dairying developed, settlers drained marshes that had produced dependable yearly crops of blueberries and cranberries, turning them into meadows. Or they fenced the swamplands and farmed the berries commercially. Harvesting of wild crops was still possible; it was just harder. Farming seemed necessary but difficult to control as well.[28]

A number of Chippewa families bought farms in established farm communities. Some moved to a small community called Sugar Bush; others scattered throughout the area. Government control of Chippewa income from their timberlands meant they had to request funds to buy farms, teams, and equipment. The allotment of land meant the community as a whole had few ways to manage its resources, either of land or of skills; still, those who remained within the community continued to develop farming on their subsistence base. By 1915 all the families had good gardens, most of them three to four acres; around fifty families, about a third of the community, had planted more than ten acres. Many of these families still sugared and riced, at least enough to provide for their own needs. They continued to fish and to trap. They also gathered and marketed berries and greens. They successfully augmented their older subsistence economy by expanding gardening. They cleared the land necessary for these gardens and built homes, mostly two-room log houses, and some barns. A few families bought or traded for cows; some had teams of horses for plowing and planting. A number of women were raising chickens. Most farms still had gardens of only two to three acres, but crop production doubled between 1914 and 1915.

Families were developing their subsistence base. They continued to harvest and sell wild foods even as they expanded cultivation of crops and built the structures necessary to support this endeavor. Most families now had two houses, one in the village—many bought houses there after the sawmill closed down—and one on their allotments. The village housing allowed them to visit and support each other during the winter and to provide for elders. In addition, they had used part of their community lumber income for stores for the disabled and the elderly. The survey of 1922 showed older women providing large quantities of hand goods for sale. Younger women were farming, gathering, growing, and processing. A few were raising pigs, and a large number—at least 20 percent of all families—were keeping chickens. One family had a flock of sixty. A popular teacher at the school was showing girls how to care for chickens, use incubators, and establish "henneries."

There was a growing interest in adult education. Extension agents held canning demonstrations, and families flocked to the first agricultural programs in 1918. Fairs started in 1915, and prizes for vegetables elicited much competition. Shortage of food from December to March still necessitated supplemental rations for some people, but by any measure the women were doing well with their hybrid economy. The government farmer requested permission to establish a community potato storage and a demonstration garden for hotbeds. The matron asked for a community hall where women could gather to make crafts. Problems still existed, to be sure, but people were successfully adapting their old economy to the community's new economic needs. The new economy the people of Lac du Flambeau built on the base of subsistence provided as good a life as that developed by many of the struggling settler families. Indeed, economic development was impressive for both Native and settler communities during the first two decades of the twentieth century.

The Menominee women have a somewhat different farming history. Land there was always much better than at Lac du Flambeau, but there were also twice as many families to feed, and the first twenty years from 1856 to 1876 were difficult ones because of inadequate supplies and a disinterested government. Many Menominee were farming in the 1870s, as well as selling maple sugar, wild rice, and furs. This mixed economy—sales from harvesting and processing goods, subsistence farming for themselves, and working as loggers—brought relative prosperity in the 1870s. By 1876 most had built permanent homes and were cultivating some ground. The agent reported "a fair harvest" in 1879, the year before annuities ended for the Menominee. Yet, as at Lac du Flambeau, the agent did little to help the people increase their cultivation, even though their access to maple trees and wild rice was declining and income from the fur trade had almost ended. One visitor reported in 1885 that the Christian majority had increased cultivation to 3,500 acres, though this figure must have been an estimate, because six years later the agent was still reporting 3,500 acres under cultivation. By that time farming had developed considerably, and many families had good teams and farming implements. Menominee were also logging. Brian Hosmer, who has studied the timber industry in detail, estimates that between 1882 and 1887 logging alone brought in $320 per man for roughly twelve weeks' work. People had enough surplus to build new houses throughout the 1880s. Agents talked about increasing farming, but there is little evidence of any serious efforts in this direction until after the 1890s.

Beginning in 1909, the Menominee held well-attended agricultural fairs each fall. Each of the three main settlements of Little Oconto (later called South Branch), West Branch, and Keshena had representatives on the fair committee, and their goal was to improve the products from farms. At these fairs, women regularly won prizes for their potatoes, rutabagas, apples, tomatoes, cucumbers, corn, onions, cabbage, beets, and carrots and sometimes for their cows and sheep. In addition to a wide variety of vegetables and cows and sheep, the community was raising horses, rabbits, chickens, ducks, pigs, and geese. They were planting oats, alfalfa, timothy, clover, millet, and wheat. Families invested money in teams, harnesses, wagons, and additional animals. Even though June frosts destroyed most of the corn between 1911 and 1916, almost all families had gardens and some income from selling garden and orchard produce, hay, and ponies. The agent estimated in 1912 that eighteen families at Zoar, about two-thirds of the community, had farms. At West Branch and Little Oconto, every family had a farm, including many with cows, heifers, hogs, and chickens. At the Keshena settlement, which had many other sources of employment, about two-thirds of the 150 families had farms. The agent expected these farms would "gradually drift into dairying and stock raising."[29]

These figures are impressive considering the internal political disputes the agent provoked. He always separated farmers into those who were "progressive" and those who were not. By "progressive," he meant those willing to go into debt to finance more tools and animals and to allot communal land to individual owners. The school supervisors reported in 1913 that most Menominee "do not want to go into debt fearing they cannot make the payments." Almost all elders, and many younger people as well, also consistently opposed allotment of land, an opposition that cut deeply across religious and other differences. Menominee remained one of the few tribes that never allotted their land. This resistance occurred despite the fact that almost all members were Christian and most of them were involved in farming as well as lumbering.[30]

Resistance was fostered by the small community of Zoar, whose members remained uniformly opposed to individual allotment of land and committed to retaining their old religion. During 1915 and 1916 Agent Nicholson constantly complained about the Zoar community for its opposition to allotment and for not adopting Christianity. To a much greater extent than other communities within the Menominee, Zoar also retained older subsistence patterns. Although two-thirds farmed by 1912, a number of the Zoar families continued to combine hunting, trapping, gardening, and allotments (many were married to Potawatomi, who received allotments after they were ended for the Menominee). The Zoarites invited their Christian kin to join them in ritual dancing and feasting, practices Nicholson blamed for their failure to farm. Yet Zoarites participated actively in the annual fairs: women entered vegetables along with traditional handwork. And even Agent Nicholson had to admit they made a "fairly good subsistence."

Elsewhere, by 1914 there was a great deal of enthusiasm for farming. Agents seemed more receptive to working out systems that would accommodate communal land ownership among the Menominee. Active farm extension and fair committees helped increase enthusiasm for farming. Nicholson, however, continued to try to divide the community, using his power to support pro-allotment farmers by giving them permission to buy teams, harnesses, equipment, and animals while refusing those who were not in his favor. It is difficult to determine to what extent he used funding for his own ends. For example, Reginald Oshkosh, admittedly one of the most successful farmers and one who favored allotment, probably was also one of the people to receive loans. Nicholson called him the "natural chief of the tribe" and sent him as one of the tribal representatives to Washington, DC, reminding him to "bring full Indian regalia." He sent no representative from Zoar, the community that opposed allotment.[31]

It appears that Nicholson was less interested in supporting farming than in using it as a way to manipulate the community politically. Other community members complained that the agent was not encouraging farming enough, that the expert farmer seldom visited them. In any event, Nicholson's desire to dominate and to divide apparently led to his replacement.[32]

The enthusiasm for agriculture seemed genuine. When the extension service offered to hold a farm institute at Keshena, *The Wisconsin Agriculturalist* announced that almost the entire adult population signed up. Reginald Oshkosh was quoted as saying that the things "locked in the soil" were "our own gold mine." Many seemed to agree with him at the time. Beginning in 1917, the extension service assigned a special agent, J. F. Wojta, to hold Indian Farmers' Institutes, similar to those organized for settlers. These four-day events usually devoted much time to discussions of clearing land, growing field crops, dairying, and raising poultry. Women attended in large numbers; in some cases almost all family members attended. Wojta met with Menominee farmers in February 1917 and planned a four-day institute at Keshena in late March. He used interpreters to translate the experts' talks into Menominee and offered lantern slides and moving pictures. At Keshena, fifty-eight adults attended the first day and ninety the last—two-thirds of all farm households, if one attended from each. When a second institute was held the following year, 272 attended the final day. The agent noted that quite a few men still worked in the woods in the winter but that they raised fairly good crops of hay, corn, potatoes, and roots.[33]

An outside inspector noted Menominee farming with approval in 1920. He reported that the Menominee had good frame buildings, barns, and outhouses and seemed well equipped to embark on stock raising. He recommended a tribal herd. The people were willing to try, but when a group of sixty-five steers sold in Chicago in 1916 brought three hundred dollars less than they cost to raise, the response was disappointment and, no doubt, distrust of the experts who had advised the venture. An official at Keshena informed the commissioner of Indian Affairs that stock raising could not be pursued because there was no good way to house the livestock in the winter and the snow was too deep to keep them on the range. Officials went back to urging the development of vegetables and dairying.[34]

To sell vegetables and dairy products the farmers needed markets. The Menominee grew fine vegetables, but only a few developed truck gardens because they lacked ready markets. Dairying flourished only on the eastern part of the reservation, where farmers had access to a nearby cheese factory. In 1920, four farmers, each with seven to fifteen cows, were doing well, but there was no factory on the reservation that would have made it possible for others to sell surplus milk. The agent suggested that a cheese factory be established, but this proposal was not pursued. Despite the fact that communal tribal logging was proving to be a success, suggestions for cooperative farming were ignored by agents who continued to argue that nothing could be accomplished without individual allotment of land.[35]

Agency farmers conducted individual surveys in 1922 and 1924, providing the first really detailed information on farming among the Menominee people. Using the criteria of some crops and at least one cow and excluding non-farming families with only gardens, a cow, an orchard, or hay, at least 136 of 239 households, 57 percent, were engaged in farming. Of the nonfarming households, most men worked year-round in the mills while some worked in the mills in winter and farmed part of the summer. They made good money at the mills, three to four dollars a day. Some were also carpenters. Almost everyone had a garden. The 136 households engaged in farming all had teams or horses, and one had a tractor. Most had cultivators and other farm implements, barns and outbuildings. Of these, almost 70 percent had chickens, usually around twenty-five, but more than ten percent had fifty or more. Almost half of the farms also had from one to ten cows. Several of these farms sent cream or milk to creameries and cheese factories. In one case the dairy was providing milk to mill employees. About 25 percent also raised pigs. Farms contracted harvests of beans, corn, and cucumbers to local factories. Women reported large amounts of fruit and vegetables canned. Most of the berries were still being gathered from the plentiful commons, but the combination of settler skills with older customs, gathering and growing, showed the way in which women had adopted and adapted skills. "The Indian women can a great deal of berries and small fruit that are incident to this section," noted one reporter, "also can and dry quite an amount of garden vegetables for winter use."[36]

Some of these farms produced surplus for sale. Josephene and Dave Wilbur sent the cream from their six cows to a creamery and sold three hundred dozen eggs a year, earning $558. In most cases men and women farmed together, but several women, including Madelaine Nowakeshequap, farmed alone. Lottie Wilbur's chickens produced four hundred dozen eggs a year. Eliza Fredenberg, who farmed with the help of her hired man and with whom this section began, was a middling farmer. The agent also described Ida Duquain and her husband as having one of the best small farms; Ida was largely responsible for the farming.

Women thus continued their tradition of gardening, expanding it to include care of animals and processing for home supplies and at least some surplus to sell. They combined working on the land with winter production of great quantities of handwork—for the tourist trade and for cultural continuity. Together, farming and art production reveal Native women as central to the region's developing economy.

Commercial Economies
Edna's Story [Meier, Kelly, born in Wisconsin, 1908–99]

It was the silo that frightened Edna most. The Meiers had one of the early silos, the kind built of wood inside the barn. Her father was a progressive farmer who wanted to experiment with the latest in scientific farming after he moved to Medford in 1900. When Edna told her story to Jean Rannells on February 16, 1985, she was seventy-seven, but she still remembered the terrifying descent into the silo to fill buckets for her dad: "I was always scared because you had to get into the bucket to go down, and I was always afraid that they wouldn't be able to hold the rope steady or let go of it or something, and I would have a fast ride." Edna did not say how old she was then, but being born in 1908, she grew up in a period of intense silo building in the cutover, the decade from 1911 to 1921. During World War I, the agricultural agents from Madison were arguing that anyone who wanted a dairy had to have a silo. Farmers had instigated the use of the silo, but after the university perfected it companies developed so many varieties that it seemed every region of Wisconsin had a different version. By 1924 Wisconsin had more than 100,000 silos, more than twice any other state. Silos meant progress in dairying according to agricultural agents. To farm people, silos also raised the fear of accidents. Edna knew firsthand.[37]

Edna's father was only doing what thousands of other farmers were doing when he built his family's farmhouse and barn in the first decade of the twentieth century. By 1900, when he moved to the Medford area, the economics of dairying were already well worked out, but development was quite slow in Taylor County. Most of the dairies lay along a southern strip just north of Clark County, where dairying developed quickly in the early twentieth century. In 1906, Taylor County had only six creameries and five cheese factories and grew almost no corn. During the next ten years, however, when Edna was growing up, her father was among many farmers who were experimenting with larger herds, more acreage in corn for silage, and increased production of butter. Butter was the main product of the Taylor creameries during these years, with 746,000 pounds being produced in 1910. During 1915, a new extension agent arrived in the county, and he encouraged farmers to build silos. What corn was grown in 1914 failed—it was a cold, wet season. But farmers spent their time improving barns and the care of cream and started two new co-operative creameries. During 1915, farmers erected nineteen silos; no doubt one of them was the one Edna feared. Silos allowed farm families to survive bad years because they could store surplus for more than one year.[38]

And so families like the Meiers intensified their labor, adding cows, feeding them better, and spending more time preparing fields for higher production of corn. With corn, women could also expand their poultry flocks. Gardening was not as successful as elsewhere because the weather was often wet, but production increased during the decade from 1910 to 1920. By 1916, the farms were producing more than 1 million pounds of butter at creameries and another 52,000 pounds on the farm.

Edna grew up learning about the new dairying and being a part of it, including going down into the silo and filling buckets with silage. The family had twenty-two cows and was one of the first dairy families to have stanchions in the barn and a milking machine. Later, when she married, Edna put her early training to good use.

Edna's life paralleled the development of the commercial dairy economy in Taylor County. Unlike most earlier settlers, her father never worked at lumbering when he arrived in 1900. Instead of depending on the declining lumber economy, the family built up a dairy herd and opened a store in Medford. The store was near a cheese factory, and farmers came in on their way home after delivering milk. Store merchandise came in bulk by train, Edna remembered, and the family sold it in small amounts charged to individual family accounts. While part of the family ran the store, the others built the farmhouse and the barn. They went back and forth from farm to store.

The family decided to set up their own cheese factory in the 1920s. Edna was in high school in Medford, and her brother became the cheese maker. As the business grew, he needed help, and so Edna quit school. At the factory, she made cheese, tested milk, kept accounts for each patron, and made out milk payment checks. As she got older and other family members could take over, she left the farm to join her sister and friends who were working in southwestern Wisconsin. She met her future husband there, at a baseball game, and after marrying they farmed on shares, giving 60 percent to the farm owner and keeping 40 percent for themselves. By then it was the 1930s, but they survived as farmers through the Depression. Her work on this second farm was similar to that she had performed on the home farm. She milked and fed cows, used the horse cultivator on the corn crop, helped clean the barn. "I guess I did just about everything on the farm to help," she mused, "Never did any plowing though." And when she had small children, Edna made a place in the barn to keep them safe while she worked nearby. As her son got older, Edna told him fairy tales in the barn. It was, in some ways, even harder while the children were small, when they followed her around the barn. And yet those times were remembered with affection. The daily toil, with the children nearby, was part of a typical dairy farm woman's work. She did it well and skillfully.

DAIRYING

In 1901 the Wisconsin Agricultural Extension Station published a bulletin calling the northern parts of the state "predestined to be a great dairy center."

The author listed as natural resources a profusion of wild and domesticated grasses and a clover crop rarely subject to failure. Such succulent forage crops would allow stock to be grown economically and milk to be produced cheaply. The area had low temperatures as well as springs and flowing streams to keep milk cool. Natural ice, available to be cut and stored for summer use, was cheaper than artificial refrigeration. Cheese would cure slowly in cool temperatures, allowing longer storage. The commentator noted that farmers in the southern counties were already selling valuable lands and moving to the north, where land was cheap. The author was sure the region would become a great dairy center. In the north everything was present to support a dense cow population, which, in turn, could support creameries and cheese factories.[39]

To show the promise of these northern lands, the author described what was already taking place in three different sections. In Lincoln and Taylor counties, farms still sold milk as liquid for direct consumption rather than processing, for these areas were still dominated by lumbering and milling. The two counties had only five creameries and seven cheese factories. The main producers were in Clark County, which already had fifteen creameries and seventeen cheese factories, and Marathon County, which had seventeen creameries and thirty-four cheese factories. These two counties, now only partially interested in lumber, were rapidly being settled and developing dairying. Factories there gave promise of "a new dairy center for the state that may in time rival the lake shore or Green county districts."[40]

Such predictions by university experts were common. The College of Agriculture at the University of Wisconsin in Madison was especially active in promoting agricultural development of the once forested lands in the north. The dean of the College of Agriculture, Professor W. A. Henry, who was investing heavily in northern land, published *Northern Wisconsin, A Handbook for the Homeseeker* in 1895. In it he praised successful farming ventures, assured readers of the ease with which they could farm these stumpy lands, and included photographs of lush crops. By 1897, 50,000 copies of his book had been distributed, along with 60,000 pamphlets in English, German, and Norwegian. He urged farm families in southern Wisconsin who were contemplating leaving the state for land farther west to move north instead.

Henry also encouraged the sons and daughters of farmers in southern Wisconsin, principally children of settlers from the East, to stay in the state but to move north where they could prosper from dairying. The best farmers and citizens, loyal to Wisconsin interests, were already drifting northward, wrote Henry, finding success with a great diversity of crops: clover and bluegrass which seemed indigenous, magnificent potatoes, garden vegetables generally, and field peas, oats, barley, and wheat. Indian corn could also be grown because it was already surviving farther north in Canada. An especially good strategy, Henry advised, was to combine cheese and butter factories, making butter in spring when the price was high and cheese later when butter prices were low. Abundant water and wood, railroads in every portion, settlers who had already tested lands for the best ways to raise animals and crops—the north had everything needed.

Lumber magnate Fred Rietbrock, who owned large areas of cut-over land, likewise touted north-central Wisconsin. In an address to the Dairymen's Association, he lauded this land of gently rolling hills, where the water was clear and the clay loam soil lent itself to dairying. The climate, Rietbrock argued, was similar to that of southern Wisconsin, the people "strong, active and progressive," as they generally were in a country that had "a snug winter in its changes of seasons." Greater snowfall, in fact, kept the ground from freezing as much as in the south, while summers were not so hot and dry. Rails and water provided easy communication to population centers and marketing. Farms were small—80 to 160 acres—but prosperous, and farmers were already winning first prizes for their plants, grain, and fruit. Although a variety of crops could be grown, the land was especially ideal for dairying because it was still inexpensive and could support good fodder crops. Using mixed or single breeds of dairy cows was possible, and pigs could be raised from skim milk. Dairying, he assured his audience, was a family business. Take up a 120-acre farm, cultivate and pasture eighty acres, keep twenty cows and fifty or sixty pigs, and leave the back forty for wood and building, a park, shade for the herd, and maple trees for sugar. Sparkling water, a delightful bracing climate, deep and productive soil—northern Wisconsin was perfect for dairying.

Rietbrock and others suggested that silage could provide food for dairies year-round. "Winter feeding," as the experts called it, was a new process for increasing annual milk production by prolonging it into winter. Dairy farmers had been using a wide variety of crops for feed: clover hay, corn, oatmeal, and chopped roots such as mangel-wurzels. Increasing corn production and cutting it late in September and October, at the roasting stage, could save work, but they needed storage areas. Europeans had already experimented with space-saving upright storage bins in the 1870s, calling them *silos* from the Latin word *sirus* or "cellar," and their contents *silage*, feed that stored compactly and would enable farmers to keep larger herds through the winter cheaply.[41]

The drought of 1886 had proved the benefits of silage. Cows on farms with ample quantities of stored fodder survived; others starved. An 1889 Agricultural Experiment Bulletin carried instructions for building a square wooden silo, and by the following year experts estimated about two thousand had been built. During the next fifteen years, farmers and experts worked out new silo designs and cost analyses. Wood silos, built like wine barrels with tongue-in-groove staves and metal hoops, cost only one hundred dollars. Lumber costs increased in the late nineteenth century, and wooden silos warped and disintegrated after four to six years, so farmers soon switched to concrete silos. By 1911 standard concrete silo instructions had been worked out and circulated by the Agricultural Experiment Station. A farm that grew 3.5 to 6 acres of corn and had a silo with an inside diameter of 14 feet, 26 feet deep, could store 54 to 68 tons of silage and provide 30 pounds of silage a day for each of 20–25 cows for 180 days. To be absolutely secure against long winters or droughts, 6 acres of corn and a silo 34 feet deep to hold 90 tons would feed 30 cows for 240 days. By 1916, the state counted sixty thousand silos, more than 20 percent of all the silos in the United States, and when the agricultural agent arrived in Clark County in 1918 he reported the county was "almost completely covered with silos and silage." In 1923 a county census by Agricultural Experiment agents counted 2,500 silos in Marathon and 2,800 in Clark. Dairying was as well established in these two counties as any in the state.[42]

Farm families struggled to adapt to the new dairy technology. The use of silos posed health hazards. Silos could be fearsome places for young children, as Edna recounted in her story. Dairy women remembered the danger as well when they had to get feed from below in cold weather, and the silage could ice up on the sides and then unexpectedly crash down on whomever had gone through the doors at the bottom to get out the feed. Fresh corn gave off gas that collected in low places, especially at night when the doors were closed; a person going into the pit in the morning could suffocate. Extension bulletins carried warnings to use silos with care. Families were soon telling stories of the dangers of accident or near accident, death or near death.[43]

The general public health problems connected with dairying were less visible to farm families. By 1900, an estimated ten percent of all deaths from tuberculosis in the United States were contracted from infected cattle and swine. Wisconsin officials already knew they had a serious problem. While performing a routine autopsy on a bull from the University of Wisconsin herd in 1894, Professor Harry L. Russell had discovered it had bovine tuberculosis. During the next twenty years, officials worked to eradicate the disease throughout the state. The four north-central Wisconsin counties were a microcosm of these efforts and the role women played in the campaign. The bovine tuberculosis threat did not end in these counties until 1926, when state dairy officials tested the last of the herds and certified them tuberculosis-free. The controversy over bovine tuberculosis was a remarkable example of the intertwining of health and economics. Not many cows had TB, but dairy farmers fiercely resisted testing, thus delaying compliance with public health regulations for more than two decades.

Dairy experts knew that TB could be transmitted from milk to humans, that it was especially dangerous for children from one to five years of age and for elderly adults, and that a bovine tuberculosis test developed in Germany in the late 1880s could detect infected animals. By the 1890s scientists had shown that pasteurization could kill the bacillus, but it was safest for public health to eradicate the disease at its source, from the herds. Many European countries had already taken such precautions. Denmark, for example, had passed regulations for pasteurization and introduced tuberculin tests for cows. It was relatively easy to prohibit diseased cows from entering the United States by requiring tests for imported cattle, and seventeen states including Wisconsin soon required such tests for cattle entering the state. Experts worked to get a similar law passed to test cows being sold within Wisconsin, but lawmakers constantly voted the legislation down, in part because they feared a political backlash in rural areas. When Russell became dean of the College of Agriculture, he supported a TB test of cattle sold within the state and pasteurization of skim milk being returned to farmers by creameries. He gave demonstrations at fairs, told county schools of agriculture to increase testing, and urged farmers to gather data and have veterinarians evaluate it.[44]

As a whole, farmers adamantly refused anything but voluntary testing and self-regulation. One of Russell's biographers called the response to the eradication campaign "apathy and bitter resistance." When Russell invited dairymen and stock breeders to Madison to watch him perform public tests and autopsies in an effort to educate them on the danger of TB, they hissed their disapproval of the testing. Even when autopsies proved the tests accurate, they refused to believe Russell's pronouncement that well-fed, apparently healthy animals were diseased. Russell insisted farmers had an ethical responsibility to voluntarily destroy sick animals. When that argument failed to move owners, he emphasized self-interest: infected cows produced little return. The legislature offered the choice of compensated slaughter or a state-regulated quarantine in 1901, but most dairymen ignored the legislation. A decade later, when the legislature passed a law requiring a TB test, it asked only for voluntary compliance. A U.S. Supreme Court decision upheld the state's right to impose health regulations for bovine tuberculosis in 1913, and Congress appropriated federal funds for states to obtain "tuberculosis-free areas" in 1917, but testing still went slowly. By 1919 officials estimated that about ten percent of all cows in southern Wisconsin still carried the disease and as many as six percent in the entire state remained infected.[45]

By 1920 the state had developed a comprehensive plan for countywide testing. If 57 percent of owners of stock in a county signed a petition to the Wisconsin Livestock Board requesting the test, state and federal testers would examine all the cattle in the county at no charge to the farmers and pay a set price for the destruction of any diseased stock. County boards would then authorize payment of the difference between the amount the state paid the farmer and the appraised value of tuberculin-positive reactors. Once the plan was completed, counties would be declared tuberculin-free. Newly appointed extension agents were to help implement the plan by mobilizing public support for the initial petition.

Now that bovine TB was a question of local initiative, women became involved in the campaign. When the first extension agent arrived in Lincoln County in 1915, he found no support for voluntary testing, but public backing for health measures soon changed. In 1917 women's groups convinced the county to hire its first public nurse, and her work in the public schools testing for tuberculosis proved extremely popular. In 1919 the county board of supervisors agreed to appropriate funds to compensate farms when valuable cows were shown to be infected. Officials and farm families seemed "keen, alert to the danger from tuberculosis," the extension agent soon reported to Madison. By 1920 the majority of farms had signed up to test the county's 21,000 animals. Two hundred animals were killed, farms were compensated where necessary, and the county was declared free of the disease. A women's float at the 1921 county fair boasted that Lincoln County now had TB-free cows.[46]

The same slow progress in eradication occurred in Taylor County between 1915 and 1920. During these years, however, women's groups also worked to raise public awareness about the dangers of tuberculosis. By 1920 the agent reported growing support, and he was soon able to involve town treasurers, assessors, and breeders in the "cleanup campaign." After a booster meeting at Medford where prominent county livestock breeders and state Department of Agriculture officials discussed the economic effects of the disease, local committees obtained the necessary names within ten days, and testing of the county's 29,000 animals began. The campaign was closed in 1922 with a public post-mortem on two cows from an established herd as 1,500 people looked on.[47]

The change in Clark and Marathon counties, which had the largest number of cows, took a bit longer, but there, too, women's groups concerned with public health issues and women within breeders groups helped swell support for testing. In Clark County, the breeders clubs helped the extension agent gain support for testing five thousand herds. The agent later acknowledged that the clubs had been the most important influence in "educating the mass of farmers to the point where they wanted to have their herds tested." By 1923 all tuberculin reactors had been eliminated. In Marathon County, which ranked fourth in the state in its number of herds in 1924, attitudes changed only when breeders clubs supported TB tests. Clubs signed up 2,500 dairy farmers, went to the county board of supervisors for a pledge of $6,500 to pay farmers for any losses, and with this incentive obtained signatures from 60 percent of the herd owners. Those who had not signed argued the petition was illegal because they would be compelled to test their cows, but after a heated public debate in

July 1925 the county commissioners announced the petition was legal and all cattle would be tested. By 1926 Marathon County certified its more than 100,000 dairy cattle TB-free.[48]

The battle over TB testing between 1915 and 1925 marked farm families' and county officials' growing acceptance of dairying as important to the economy of the four north-central counties. Women's support for public health and for county financing, a story developed in greater detail in a later chapter, was a crucial element in the eradication campaign. During this period women in these counties became more actively involved in public health issues, joining breeders clubs, rural women's clubs, anti-TB groups. These movements made tuberculosis a family as well as an economic issue. As one farmer reported to the Dairymen's Association, he and his wife had worried about their own children, finally had their cows tested, and were relieved to find they were TB-free. In the end, it took a wide variety of rural groups to rally others to the cause of protecting families from tuberculosis and making it economically feasible to do so through testing dairy cows. It meant that dairying had become accepted not just as a business but as a way of life.

BUTTER MAKING

In 1880, when Miss Fannie Morley from Wisconsin won the prize for butter making at the International Dairy Fair in New York, the Wisconsin Dairymen's Association printed her engraved portrait as the frontispiece of its annual report. The etching of dairywoman Morley showed her with hair parted neatly in the center and pulled high in a bun, in a plain dark dress with a lace collar and a brooch.[49]

The year before, early in 1879, twenty-year-old Morley had taken over her father's dairy of about seventy cows. She churned 125 pounds of butter at a time, in forty minutes, using a square box churn driven by a horse-powered treadmill, and shipped her butter directly to a Chicago dealer. In 1880 she also sent a sample to the International Dairy Fair, where she won the sweepstakes prize for the best butter made anywhere. The Wisconsin Dairymen's Association asked Morley to speak about butter making at their Waukesha meeting in January 1881. The following year, when the association met in Sheboygan, she spoke on "The Dignity of Buttermaking From a Woman's Standpoint."

Morley was accepted as an expert because women made most of the butter on Wisconsin farms. Agricultural records do not identify the women, but one can trace their responsibilities in butter making through the Wisconsin Dairymen's Association reports. In 1877 one member referred to women making butter under "most adverse circumstances," with no help from their husbands. Speakers at the Wisconsin Dairymen's Association annual meetings assumed the stance of experts and studiously avoided mentioning that their wives were the principal butter makers. Mrs. L. E. Haws of Whitewater chided them in 1878, in one of the few speeches made by a woman, noting dryly as she rose to speak, "Either the speakers, with one exception, who referred to the homework of farmers, the making of butter, etc., were without wives, or else considered them so wholly absorbed in themselves as to be included in the pronoun, I." She went on to say that if women were to be "freed from the responsibility of buttermaking," she would certainly be willing to leave the work to husband and sons, but in her community the first question about butter for sale was "Who made it?" and the answer invariably was "Mrs." and not "Mr." She concluded: "If the farmers of our state consider their wives as helpmeets not servants, they surely have been unfortunate in the manner of expressing their thoughts." She called for a movement to make women's work lighter and more efficient and remarked that it seemed a new era was dawning "for cows as well as women." Few women were early members of the Dairymen's Association— five in 1901—but reports from the 1880s through the early 1900s assumed women were the butter makers. Charles Thorpe mentioned that Mrs. Thorpe "lost her anxious look" when they switched from hand churning to horsepower. C. P. Goodrich noted that his wife, who made the butter, received suggestions on how to improve its quality from the commission man.[50]

In 1881 Morley spoke on the need for "improved apparatus," different methods, and intelligent systematic dairying, citing experts such as Professor X. A. Willard. "The progressive butter maker," she told her mostly male audience, "should be willing to be taught, to be criticized, to study, and to learn from failure.... Let us make the most of our buttermaking, for in so doing we shall make the most of ourselves; and though lesser lights we may be, strive to illume the pathway." She continued, "We know that we, the butter makers of Wisconsin, have nothing to be ashamed of in the way of reputation certainly; and if the work is not dignified enough for us, let us make it so by putting our highest ambition, talent, skill, planning and thinking into the work of raising the standard of our butter." It requires, she concluded, "unceasing vigilance, precision, method." She offered dignity to men as well as women and bridged the debate over homemade butter—which hers was—and factory- or creamery-made butter—as people were predicting all butter would soon be—by pointing out that the fundamental aspect of work was close attention to detail and good discipline for a "young lady or gentleman." Butter making was dignified by the care in curing the cream, the temperature when churned, the coloring, the salting, and many more little things. When a young woman—hired help or daughter—held the position of butter maker it was a good influence and allowed the busy housewife more time to rest and read. Training young people, either female or male, could therefore diminish criticism of butter making as too much work for older women. The ladies of the Congregational Church feted her after the talk.[51]

By common consent, then, older women who had perfected the art of butter making were to be relieved of some of their labor at least. The question was whether daughters would take over or not, and where the butter would be made—on the farm or in factories. At home, with perhaps twenty-five dollars for apparatus, a woman with a churn and a horse could produce as much as 125 pounds of butter at a time, as Morley had done. Selling locally brought only credit at a local store, but, like Morley, dairy farmers were now contacting commission men in Chicago or Milwaukee, and the farm could receive a check instead of credit. There seemed to be no problem in marketing from the farm. Home production continued well into the twentieth century. In 1900, 80 percent of the nation's butter was made on farms, mainly by women. Sixteen years later, in 1916, more than 60 percent was still being processed there.[52]

Members of the Wisconsin Dairymen's Association knew that farm-made butter might still be the finest available, but it could also be of such poor quality that it was sold as "grease grade." Factories, called creameries, had been making butter in the eastern part of the country since 1860, and members often argued that if dairymen in Wisconsin established factories they could make a more consistent product with less labor and sell it for higher prices. Wisconsin soon had more creameries than any other state, or so Wisconsin butter makers stated in 1902 when some members of the Dairymen's Association seceded, proclaiming they needed a separate group to represent them as butter makers and to focus on improving creameries. Kate Pfeffer of Pewaukee was one of the seceding members who attended the second annual meeting in Waukesha—the only woman listed and one of two in a group photograph.

As demand for butter increased in Wisconsin, butter makers expected farmers to expand their herds and bring whole milk to creameries for separating and processing. Factory butter making had been revolutionized when, in 1876, Dr. Carl Gustaf de Laval invented a cream separator powered by a small steam engine that could rapidly process large quantities of milk by centrifugal force. Creameries preferred this new machine separation because cream separated by gravity on the farm and held for several days, especially at peak warm seasons, often arrived at the factory sour. Whole milk stored but a day or two at the farm arrived fresh, so the separator cream was of consistent good quality. But these creameries involved more investment than the few dollars it took for women to produce butter on the farm. A factory had to be built and machinery purchased. Wood and woodenware had to be supplied regularly in large quantities, wages paid for a full-time butter maker and assistants, building and machinery maintained, and accounts kept systematically. To even establish a successful factory a creamery needed at least two hundred cows in a radius of about one and one-half miles. Few farmers could afford to start up their own factories, so they turned to producer cooperatives.

It was not simple to sustain cooperative creameries, as farmers in Lincoln County discovered. In 1895 farmers at Dudley and Gleason built a creamery on the banks of the Prairie River, and farm women carefully separated cream that summer with hopes of regular checks repaying their efforts. Instead, within four months the factory was closed, the operator gone with the proceeds from sales of the butter. Three times during the next fifteen years the families attempted to establish a creamery. Each time they failed. Late in 1914, they tried for a fifth time. They had two hundred cows but needed at least four hundred to maintain the butter-making factory. After canvassing the community in every direction for eight miles, the organizers finally found sufficient cows, ordered the needed machinery, and began building the factory. When it opened in 1915, it was one of only five creameries in the county. The next year, the new agricultural agent helped farmers organize the Tomahawk Cooperative Creamery. More than one hundred farmers put up a total of $1,620 to purchase a privately owned factory, refit it, and hire a butter maker. The cooperative put in a Wizard pasteurizer and electric lights. The Tomahawk Cooperative did not survive. The Prairie River Cooperative Dairy did, along with seven other creameries, which together produced 768,785 pounds of butter in 1922.[53]

One can track the transition to creameries most clearly in Pine Valley, the fertile Clark County area located northwest of Neillsville where mixed farming had proved so successful. According to the Agricultural Census of 1880, twenty-one farms were already producing almost 16,000 pounds of butter annually, each more than 500 pounds, and two were producing more than 1,400 pounds each. Among these top farms were two headed by single women, Maria Mason, who produced almost 800 pounds, and Maribau Reddau, who produced 500. On the other farms, women and men worked together at dairying, probably using horsepower for churning just as Morley had in producing her excellent butter.

By 1895, Clark County farms still produced large quantities of butter by hand, but it had eight creameries where farm families brought milk, usually daily, to be processed in large commercial separators. The creameries made the butter and returned the skim milk to patrons to be used as animal feed. Cooperatively and privately owned factories existed at Granton, Hixon, Loyal, and Thorp. Together these factories were producing 13,000 pounds of butter a year, almost as much as Pine Valley's twenty-one farms in 1880. Pine Valley and Greenwood now each had one small factory producing butter.

During the next decade farmers in Clark County rapidly expanded the number of creameries and the amount of milk and butter production. The few surviving records of these early creameries show a variety of forms, some cooperatives, some associations, some simply arrangements to find a butter maker to move into the community if no local one was available. Sometimes communities vied for trained immigrant butter makers, who were much in demand. Grassland Dairy Products traces its origins to an invitation by a group of Greenwood farmers to Swiss immigrant John Wuethrich to come to Eaton township to equip and operate a creamery. The farmers raised one thousand dollars to build the plant and then enticed the twenty-two-year-old Wuethrich to move from Dodge to Clark County. It is not clear just what the arrangements were to pay for the equipment or the land, but in 1909 Wuethrich married eighteen-year-old Wisconsin-born Vera, and the couple stayed in Clark County, passing on the creamery to their two sons. A hundred years later, the creamery, now a huge modern factory, is still operated by members of the Wuethrich family.[54]

Creameries took over much butter-making activity but left the processing of milk on the farms. Early creameries had installed large De Laval centrifugal cream separators. In the late 1880s, however, the De Laval Company introduced the "Baby," a small, inexpensive, hand-cranked separator that soon slowed the trend toward factory separation. Manufacture of the Baby insured that most cream would be skimmed at home rather than at the creamery. The De Laval Baby hand separator was composed of a complex arrangement of bowls and spouts that allowed the operator to feed whole milk into a spinning bowl, which produced enough centrifugal force to move the heavier skim milk outward while the lighter cream moved inward, thus mechanically separating the milk. The skim milk escaped from an opening in the wall of the spinning bowl near the top as the cream escaped from an opening near the center. The De Laval Company marketed this smaller, hand-powered cream separator at a price affordable to large numbers of farm families. Because of the Baby, women's work increased in importance as butter making grew in volume.

The Baby offered a number of advantages to farm families. Home-separated cream reduced hauling time and expense because cream, the commercially valuable part of milk for butter making, was only a small portion of whole milk. Families could store cream and transport it less frequently than whole milk, keeping the heavy and bulky skim milk to feed animals. Holding the skim milk at home meant it would not be mixed with possibly contaminated milk from diseased herds on other farms. Factory mixing could spread disease to healthy animals, the calves and pigs that were fed skim milk. By separating at home, families could be sure they used skim milk from only their own, presumably healthy animals. Salesmen promised women that the new separators would make their work easier. They assured them that the separator could be kept in the barn where it was handy to milking and that they could rinse it with a little water twice a day and scrub it once or twice a week or not at all. They could deliver cream to the creamery once every two weeks.[55]

The disadvantages were clear soon enough. Farm separating reintroduced the old problem of sour and impure cream. Factories complained of cream

"BABY" NO. I.

DE LAVAL CREAM SEPARATOR.

ACTUAL CAPACITY, 150 LBS. PER HOUR.

(Plain or "hollow" bowl type)

PRICE, - - $75.00

Milk separator, 1894. For settlers who sold cream to butter-making factories, the hand-operated milk separator became a necessity. Women added operating, washing, and scalding the numerous machine parts to their already heavy tasks of milking cows and handling milk.

with strong, rank, or stable odor. Farmers expected their cream to be accepted regardless of condition; creameries needed the cream for their operations and often took whatever the wagons brought. One expert called the salesmen "separator sharks" who were "over-zealous." Wrote another, "[the hand-cranked cream separators] are coming in faster than I would like to see them. . . . Hand separators are getting into [the] country everywhere. Agents in every county and township you can think of. They are forcing those hand separators on the people." The whole-milk creameries were still the most economical where they were well established, but in sparsely settled dairy regions, which north-central Wisconsin surely was, experts reluctantly endorsed the Baby.

Farm women wanted the separators despite the problems that accompanied their use. The challenge, then, was to educate the women who separated the milk, many of whom were newly engaged in dairying and unfamiliar with the requirement that cream arrive properly processed for sanitation and "sweetness." Experts urged creamery owners and managers to tell farmers when their milk was unfit for use, even if a farmer, once rejected, was likely to go elsewhere rather than improve his methods. They urged creameries to wash and steam-clean cans at the factory for patrons to pick up or haulers to deliver. Experts hoped creamery operators would provide a place for patrons to discuss methods and learn about silo building, cow feeding rations, and veterinarians. They envisioned creameries functioning as mini-dairy schools that distributed literature from the agricultural school. A few even suggested that creameries could perform other services for farm families, such as laundry.[56]

Much technical information was exchanged at dairies. Creameries distributed bulletins to aid women in learning to clean cans and to advise farm families on bovine tuberculosis testing. But creameries had to have cream to operate. Competition was strong, and owners could not force farmers to bring in cream often enough. All they could do was inform. Creameries lacked the base to function as the agricultural agents wished. They were too busy to organize clubs for future "dairymen and dairywomen."

Dairy experts urged butter makers to call at patrons' homes to "convince the ladies" that they needed to improve their cream skimming methods. The proper speed in turning the separator, with milk at the right temperature, fresh and warm, would produce excellent results, they promised. Simply running water through the separator to scald the parts unwashed was not enough; doing so would only cook the curd. Women had to disassemble the entire separator immediately after each use—before the curd had dried on the different parts—submerge the parts in warm water, and then, only after the curd was rinsed off, scald them in hot water, dry them with a cloth, and put them in an airy, clean-smelling, and dustless place, exposed to sunlight. Experts assured women that, when accustomed to this work, it need take only fifteen minutes.

As for the creamery owners, house calls presented "a golden opportunity for educating patrons."[57]

Farm women undertook the experts' complicated instructions for processing clean milk. Families moved the separators from the barn, the most convenient location, to a more distant room in the house or built a small milk house where separation, cleaning, and holding could go on. To disassemble the separator after each use, the woman needed only a screwdriver and a wrench, but to clean the machine properly she needed a large quantity of hot water. I asked my cousin how Matilda had managed this process. She had to clean the parts in the house, and her son installed a water tank on the roof that they filled from the pump. She had a wood stove to heat the water. After washing, scalding, and drying, the numerous parts had to be reassembled in the proper order. Each batch of warm, separated cream had to be completely cooled before thoroughly mixing it with cold cream. Women also had to wash and scald milk cans after they were returned from the creamery. Experts recommended two sets of cans, one to take milk and leave at the creamery, another to take home. Milk cans were large, cumbersome, and heavy to handle. Creameries introduced smaller, lighter cans, but still women had to manage increasingly large quantities of whole milk.[58]

Farm families' correct decision to use hand separators was acknowledged by experts in a 1906 Agricultural Extension Station bulletin on "Development of Factory Dairying in Wisconsin." Hand separators had solved the daily hauling problem, improved feed for stock, and reduced the spread of communicable disease, such as tuberculosis. There was still butter production on the farm, but it had been reduced by half between 1900 and 1905, and 50 percent of creamery butter in the state was now made from hand-separator cream. G. H. Benkendorf, instructor in dairying at Madison, admitted "the hand separator is come to stay" and predicted "the hand separator will be regarded as a necessity on every well regulated farm." By 1909, Wisconsin was leading the nation in butter production, with Clark County contributing 2.5 million pounds from thirty-three creameries.

After that year, the amount of milk processing slowly decreased as farm families switched from providing cream to creameries to providing whole milk for cheese making. Making cheese was less work for everyone. By 1910 the state was also producing one-third of the country's cheese. By 1915 the 2 million pounds of butter being produced in Clark County's eighteen butter factories was dwarfed by the almost 11 million pounds of cheese being turned out by 109 cheese factories. The number of creameries continued to decrease until, by 1921, Clark County produced fewer than 900,000 pounds of butter in six creameries while it produced more than 17 million pounds of cheese. To make cheese, no separation of cream was needed. Cheese did not have to be pasteurized because aging made it safe. In 1915 Clark and Marathon counties had both made the transition to cheese production. Even Taylor and Lincoln counties had important cheese-making industries. The decline in butter making and the intensification of cheese making heralded yet another change in women's work.[59]

CHEESE MAKING

My cousin Mary Ann Reynolds arranged for me to interview Alma Parge Lineaweaver by phone. I had seen a 1901 photograph of the Parge family in front of its cheese factory, Henry standing on the porch of the factory in a white jacket, Ida in the foreground near a team and wagon holding their six-month-old son, Parge's sister Anna in the wagon. I knew women were essential to the dairy enterprise and played an important role in butter making, but accounts about cheese making never mentioned women making cheese or working in cheese factories. The Parge cheese factory was just south of Dorchester in Clark County when Alma's mother, Ida Frimund, married Henry Parge. Alma seemed like a perfect person to ask about her mother's role in cheese making.

Ida Frimund lived on a farm in nearby Marathon County when she met the young cheese maker. Born in Milwaukee County in 1882, Henry had moved to Clark County with his family when he was eight. Henry's parents were not cheese makers, but because they wanted Henry to stay near home instead of moving away to work like his seven brothers, they enrolled him as one of the first students in the new dairy school at the University of Wisconsin. After receiving a Master Cheesemaker degree, he returned to the Dorchester area and opened its first cheese factory in 1898. Ida married Henry two years later, and the photo showing them on the factory porch was taken soon after their first child was born. Following the birth of a second child, the couple sold their factory and built a new one about a mile from Ida's family, where Ida's third child, Alma, was born in 1904. Alma told me that her mother was also a cheese maker and worked in the factory with Henry while her younger sister took care of the three children. I learned about Ida's cheese making only because I asked her daughter about it directly. Otherwise, Ida's work would have remained hidden like that of other women employed in family cheese factories.[60]

There are no easily found tracks left by these first cheese makers in Clark County. Local accounts mention that a few individual farms sold milk, butter, and cheese to lumber camps. Early lists of the Dairymen's Association carried no names of cheese factories, creameries, or private dairies for the four northern counties until 1878, when G. and J. Henntzicher of Greenwood are listed as having a cheese factory. George, Jacob, and Henry Henntzicher, French immigrants and probably brothers, appear on the 1880 population census living close together in Greenwood. The three must have cooperated in their dairying ventures, for Henry Henntzicher is mentioned in early accounts as keeping a hotel in the 1860s near Greenwood and listed in the 1880 census as a forty-six-year-old farmer who produced 500 pounds of butter, along with his brother Jacob, who produced 800 pounds. George and Jacob continue to be listed as members in the Dairymen's Association until 1882.[61]

Only George reported a large amount of cheese production in 1880. He told the census taker, local teacher George Slater, that his farm had twenty milk cows and produced four thousand pounds of cheese. That was a major cheese industry in 1880, although Slater recorded him simply as a "farmer." George Henntzicher employed three male workers and one female worker on the farm. There is, of course, no indication of whether he or his German wife, Margaret, or both of them made the cheese, how it was made, or when the Henntzichers quit making cheese. One account mentions a Huntzicker family opening a hotel in Neillsville some time later.[62]

George Henntzicher may have gotten out of the cheese-making business, but other farmers in Clark County were finding profits from cheese making very attractive. A dairy map for 1887 showed Taylor and Lincoln counties producing no cheese at all, while Marathon produced only 5,000 pounds. Clark County, on the other hand, produced more than 78,000 pounds of cheese that year. Thus, even before 1890 Clark was already becoming a major northern cheese-producing area.

Better known than the Henntzicher family for early cheese making in Clark County is the Steinwand family. Ambrose Steinwand reported no cheese making at all on the 1880 agricultural census. Sometime during the next few years Ambrose and his son John developed Colby cheese, mild, soft, moister than Cheddar, and reputedly the only cheese developed in the United States. By 1896 the Steinwands were producing three thousand dollars–worth of cheese a year. The women of the family are never mentioned in these accounts, although early cheese making was usually a family business, with all members cooperating in its production.

While a full history of northern Wisconsin cheese making has yet to be written, the story of the dairy industry in southern Wisconsin probably reflects the general development of cheese making. Until 1873 farms had native cows, usually no barn, and only a well, a cellar, and a farm kitchen for processing milk products. Women made cheese with the help of their children. Their implements were milk pans, skimmers, wooden bowls and ladles, and some sort of cheese press. They let gravity separate milk and cream and made most of their cheese in the summer. Cheese making was not the main enterprise of most early farms until 1873, when the chinch bug destroyed wheat crops and soil exhaustion reduced productivity. High freight prices for field crops made dairying, which combined production and processing to yield a higher-priced product, a good alternative. Marketing was a problem for the few farm families producing large quantities of cheese in the early 1870s. The market was seriously glutted in 1872, when Wisconsin cheese sold for only eight cents per pound. In 1873 dairy operators formed the Wisconsin Dairymen's Association to set up trade boards similar to those already in existence in the East, to establish a uniform value for the product, to encourage standards of production, and to locate a central place where eastern buyers could purchase large lots of uniform grade. By 1875 about three hundred Wisconsin cheese factories were producing thirteen thousand pounds of cheese. Large operations made much of this cheese, but many families owned and staffed smaller factories where women worked alongside men. In 1893 the Wisconsin Cheese Makers' Association organized separately from the Dairymen's Association. They concentrated on cheese making, care and management of factories, sale of products, and "weeding out of incompetency in the business of cheesemaking."[63]

Wisconsin women appear as expert cheese makers in the records of the Dairymen's Association. Mrs. J. A. Smith presented an address on the technical aspects of cheese making at the twelfth annual meeting in Lake Mills in 1884. In 1903 University of Wisconsin professor W. A. Henry noted that several women had enrolled in his Wisconsin Dairy School cheese-making classes. One of his best students was from Sheboygan, "a fine cheesemaker, makes fair wages, and thinks she is going to make higher now she has taken the course." Henry noted that other women were successful cheese makers. He admitted men and women equally to his classes if they had worked one season for at least four months in a cheese factory, had a certified "moral character," and had the $85 to $90 needed for the twelve-week course. Women continued to show up as occasional speakers before the Cheese Makers' Association. Mrs. O. Dix of Auburndale spoke in 1915 on "Managing a Cooperative Cheese Factory," drawing on ten years in cheese making, five in private business, five in the farmer-owned cooperative. She called for cleanliness, orderliness, and better-trained cheese makers, much as had the men.[64]

Cheese making was not as steady and secure as Mrs. Dix's comments might indicate. Disasters overtook families. Factories burned down. Owners suffered accidents that made them unable to continue making cheese. Trained cheese makers were in short supply and frequently left for better offers. For a while cooperatives attempted to run the factories, to spread the risk of the new ventures, but they often failed. The history of the Bruckerville Cheese Factory is a good example.

Fifteen farm families, most of them German, started the Bruckerville Cheese Factory in 1907. An account book for the first two years charts their early enthusiasm. The first entry is a mix of German and English, but the careful accounts for each farmer were kept in English. They found a cheese maker, Christ Marggi, who was willing to run the factory for $464 a year. They moved an old house to land furnished by one of the farmers. Their main expenses, in addition to the cheese maker's wages, were for woodenware, cheese boxes, cheesecloth, firewood, and various costs to refurbish the factory. They counted $143 in expenses the first year. There is no record of other costs for equipment. One of the founders, Wenzel Renner, gave the dedication speech, explaining why they could expect to collect enough milk to keep the factory going. "In Germany only the women did the milking," he began, "Here, even the boys and men are taught to pull and pull; and that is why we are able to dedicate a cheese factory today."[65]

Shipments of cheese began in May 1907 and continued into December. The first year the factory paid its original fifteen patrons an average of $470 each. The other half of the co-op membership received considerably less because they delivered only small amounts of milk to the factory. The Jantsch family, which lived across the road from my grandmother, received checks for $61 from small quantities of milk delivered to the factory from August to November. Another neighbor, Anna Drescher, received $25 for milk brought in October and November. My grandmother Matilda did not have enough cows for any surplus. Still, the prospect of earning milk checks must have made her and other farmers eager to increase their herds.

The second year the cooperative did not do well. Farmers delivered less milk, and the factory processed and sold less cheese. By the third year, deeply in debt, the farmers dissolved the cooperative and sold the factory to Ade Young and a cheese maker named Nutbaum. That partnership lasted only one year. In 1910 Fred Reynolds, a seventeen-year-old who had learned the trade from Nutbaum, bought the factory for $1,100. He moved the Bruckerville Cheese Factory a mile and a half west. For more than forty years the Reynolds family ran the cheese factory there; it closed in 1953. Matilda's granddaughter Mary Ann Schopper would marry into this cheese-making family.

As the history of the Bruckerville Cheese Factory illustrates, families played a central role in the development of cheese making in this area. Mary Ann and her husband, Jerry, supplied the Reynolds and Stetzel family histories, which explain how the business took form. I asked how Fred Reynolds got the money to buy the factory, and Mary Ann explained. When Fred Reynolds and Mary Stetzel decided to marry, they asked her family to loan them the money to buy the cheese factory. Fred's father had died, his mother remarried and had more children, and there was no way that Fred, a stepson, was likely to inherit the family farm. Mary's father, Leopold Stetzel, a member of the original cooperative, was anxious for the cheese factory to survive and to provide a way for the couple to remain nearby. The Stetzels not only loaned their son-in-law the money to buy the factory but also gave the couple an acre of their land facing the county road on which to put the factory. Fred and Mary ran the business as a family farm enterprise. At first, Mary helped in the factory, washing out the milk cans in which farmers brought milk, removing the hoops from the cheese and putting it away, and managing things when Fred went to the railroad station to ship the cheese, to buy cheese boxes, or to purchase other supplies. Mary also birthed and raised twelve children as she helped with the factory.[66]

Fred's son Jerry, also a lifelong cheese maker, remembered the early process. Farmers brought the whole milk in cans, and while Mary scoured the cans, Fred added starter, color, and rennet to the milk and heated it with a wood stove. When it reached 92 degrees and curd formed, he pulled curd knives through it, agitated the curd, and increased the heat. When the whey formed, he ran it off, salted the curd and put it in hoops, pressed it overnight, and then placed it in the drying room for two days. At the end of the first night he turned it, and at the end of the second the cheese was out of the hoops, dipped in paraffin, and ready to ship.

By 1910, when Fred and Mary began their cheese-making business, small towns were able to provide what these corner cheese factories needed. The town of Colby provided cold storage, a cheese box factory, and a marketing cooperative for northern Clark and western Marathon counties. Marshfield performed much the same services for cheese makers in the southern part of Clark County. Marshfield built its first cold storage facility in 1907 and a

Reynold's Cheese Factory, 1918. The parents of Mary Stetzel helped her and new husband Fred Reynolds, shown here at work, purchase and operate their own cheese factory. Family cheese factories depended upon the help of women, who also managed households and their usual farm tasks.

regional cheese box factory in 1911 and formed a cooperative to market cheese and a cheese makers' syndicate to help stabilize prices. Fred took surplus cheese to a factory near Dorchester, which in turn sold the cheese to an agent in Marshfield. Cheese making allowed these farm families to remain on the land after seasonal lumbering jobs disappeared at the end of the nineteenth century.[67]

As with other dairy processes that produced large quantities, cheese making tended to be organized around heavy work, such as emptying milk from large cans into vats. There was no reason, of course, that women could not manage the business and hire strong young men to do the heavy lifting, as older male cheese makers did. Or that the work could not have been organized in smaller units so that women could have done it. Or that, like European women cheese makers, they simply could have done the work. In fact, many women did the regular work in family factories. Immigrant women were accustomed to heavy work, but they usually did not have the funds to be trained as regular cheese makers; American-born families (and the women themselves) often wanted to avoid heavy work. If we knew just what part the women of the Henntzicher, the Steinwand, and other families played in cheese production, or whether like Ida Parge they were also cheese makers, we might be able to say much more about the organization and development of early cheese makers. As it is, the men tend to be remembered as the cheese makers. After all, many families had started cheese factories to provide work for young sons after lumbering declined. Rather than buy land, which was by then too expensive for most families, they helped children buy or establish small family cheese factories.[68]

By 1918, the year young Reynolds posed for a photograph in the family cheese factory, cheese making was well established in Clark County. Growth had been steady since the 1880s. Production in Clark increased from about 78,000 pounds in 1887 to more than 10 million in 1915. Marathon had even greater growth: from 5,000 pounds in 1887 to more than 10 million in 1915. Clark County factories increased from 13 in 1896 to 109 in 1915. In Marathon County the number grew from 9 to 114 during this period.

Men had made the transition from lumbering to dairying and cheese making; women had developed skills needed to run the family cheese-making businesses. Farm women like my grandmother were looking forward to their milk checks. Matilda soon had a small dairy of her own and enough income from sales to the cheese factory to consider replacing her old log house with a new frame one. The photograph, then, stood not only for the solitary Fred Reynolds, a young man working alone as cheese maker, but also for the work that women were doing to make his job possible.[69]

II

Protecting Families and Communities

4

Healing

On an August afternoon in 1901, my grandmother Matilda watched her husband Karl playfully grab the back legs of a colt in the barnyard. When the colt kicked him in the stomach, he crumpled in pain. She helped him into bed and cared for him as best she could. She did not call a doctor. Neither her care nor her home remedies could heal him. He died two days later. Matilda could not save her husband, but according to family tradition she safely birthed seven of her eight children with the help of friend and neighborhood midwife Mary Jantsch. She sought the help of a doctor only for the birth of her sixth child, my mother, in 1902. Family traditions do not say why. Nor do stories describe how she dealt with other health crises. Her youngest daughter, Emma, born in 1908, had a mild case of tuberculosis. We do not know how she was cured. Matilda cared for her father in old age and always worried that she might have to go to the poorhouse herself. She kept her children in school as long as possible before putting them to work full-time at home and on neighboring farms. She sought divine assistance in protecting her children. Each evening they had to kneel before religious pictures to say prayers. When missionaries came to say Sunday Mass and the roads were passable, she took them to church.

Protecting her family was a main task of Matilda's life, as it was of other women in north-central Wisconsin. She performed these activities and, with each of her two husbands, provided food and shelter. This job of protecting continued through early settlement, economic and political change, and migration of children seeking to make their own lives independently. Strange, then, that this fundamental domestic security has been so difficult to document for Matilda and the other women of her time and place.

I knew that women provided protection for their families, but I needed to learn much more about the details of their specific tasks. I looked at the risks of illness to women and their families, how they provided for those who needed healing, whom they asked for assistance. Today most mothers seek trained health-care specialists during the most dangerous times of childbirth and for infants during their first vulnerable years of life, but a century ago most rural women had little outside help. I explored the ways in which they provided special care for the very young, for young women, and the very old; how they ensured that children ages five to fourteen obtained the learning needed to live in their own culturally appropriate ways; and how women provided for spiritual protection and expressed spirituality in their daily lives. My explorations of these crucial family tasks began with the fundamental task of healing and with Rosa, who was not healed.

At Risk
Rosa's Story [Petrusky, born in Slovakia, 1878–96]

A few years ago, while collecting material for this book, I ran across an extraordinary document in the records of the Wisconsin Historical Society in Madison. It was a letter from a farmer in Waushara County to the state attorney dated November 22, 1896. In the letter the farmer, Eugene Caves, told the story of Rosa Petrusky, "a bright girl" who had worked for him before going on to work for another farmer in a nearby county.[1]

Rosa had returned to visit the Caves home and tearfully told the family that she had "been doing wrong," was "in the family way," was "three months along," and had been given "something" to take by the son of a farmer named Pratt, for whom she had worked. The "something" had done no good. The young man then took her "along the road," where a doctor had "done something to her, had probed her womb," then took her back to her former employers, who, he thought, would care for her. The Caves thought Rosa should be with her mother, so they contacted her brother and sent her home. Rosa told her mother about her problem, gave her two dollars, and asked her not to tell her father. The next day Rosa sent for the young man, who took her away. "Next we knew, two weeks later news came to us that she had died," wrote Caves.

Caves's words have stayed with me over the years. I did not want Rosa to die. I wanted her story to end differently. That desire made me want to know more about Rosa and why her story ended this way, with a painful death. I lingered over it. Why did Rosa's story not end with a sexual partner who shared the burdens of childbirth and parenting with her? Why could she not obtain support from friends and family during and after the birth, so that she could either keep her child or arrange a satisfactory adoption? Why could she not have a safe abortion? My desire to find out why none of those options were available to Rosa brought me back to the Caves letter, to a careful examination of his words, to a search for the places and people he mentioned and for the larger community within which the events of Rosa's last days unfolded.[2]

I checked the names and places Caves mentioned in local histories, newspapers, and census data and concluded that Rosa was part of a small community of Austro-Slovakians who migrated to the United States between 1879 and 1899 and settled in Grant township in Portage County, slightly southeast of Wisconsin Rapids and about halfway to Plainfield, where Rosa worked. I could not determine which of the several young Pratt men fathered Rosa's child, but the Pratts were a prominent Protestant Anglo-American family from New

York, with farm and town businesses, long settled in the area. A clerk in the Pratt family drugstore could have provided the pills meant to induce Rosa's abortion. The doctor who performed the improper abortion could have been the town physician. Caves, a recently immigrated Englishman, may have expected a more proactive justice system.[3]

Sharp ethnic, class, and religious differences existed between the two young people who coupled that summer. Caves's words make it quite clear that young Pratt and his family were much wealthier than Rosa and her family. Young Pratt's folks had "considerable money": after Rosa's death they bought her coffin and tried to pay Rosa's father a sum of money. "Her father is poor," Caves wrote. Caves also mentioned what he had heard of the monetary arrangements the Pratts had made with Rosa during the crisis of pregnancy. The Pratts would pay all her expenses for the abortion, continue to pay her wages until she got well, and, when it was over, give her a new silk dress. Caves identified a group of Pratt's young friends who knew about Rosa's pregnancy and helped him obtain the abortion. Caves also accused Pratt's friends of paying off the district attorney so that he would not charge anyone in Rosa's death. The words Caves used—considerable money, poor, a new silk dress, paying off the district attorney—all indicate that he believed Pratt was wealthy enough to obtain secrecy about the abortion and to avoid any criminal charges when Rosa died. For whatever reason, young Pratt refused to assume responsibility for Rosa's child. Instead he paid for the pills and, when they failed, paid a local doctor to physically induce an abortion. After that procedure caused Rosa to develop septic infection, he paid a widow to care for her during the last painful two weeks of her life.

During those last weeks, any chances for Rosa to safely birth her child were dashed. Ideally, Rosa would have had a safe birth with a midwife in attendance and a support network to welcome the child and help her raise it. Because the Slovakian community was small, she probably would have had to find a German or Polish midwife. Had Rosa been able to get to Pike Lake, about forty miles north of the town in which she worked, she might have had Frances Szeesinski deliver her baby. Szeesinski had birthed many babies safely. But if Rosa could buy her mother's silence, then the mother was unlikely to assemble the female network necessary to help her daughter with childbirth. Female kin members, who usually arranged for intra-family support, were conspicuously absent from the Caves narrative.

Ironically, had Rosa been younger and identified by the state as an underage "delinquent," she might have received care in birthing her child and arranging for an adoption. Rosa could then have returned to the community or gone to the city to live and love again. But Rosa had just turned eighteen, the age at which young women were legally emancipated in Wisconsin. Nor could she be labeled *delinquent,* a term applied to young women who engaged too freely in heterosexual relations with different men. Rosa told Caves that she had sexual relations with only her young lover.

Could Rosa have obtained a safe abortion? Certainly many women in the late-nineteenth century had abortions and survived. Abortions after "quickening" (the moment at which the fetus was believed to gain life, usually about three months after conception) were criminalized in Wisconsin in 1849. The state did not generally enforce the law, however, and the number of abortions continued to increase throughout the century. Most Wisconsin inhabitants, especially those in urban areas, could locate health-care practitioners to perform abortions or obtain information on self-abortions. The class of women seeking abortions may have changed, however, as more middle- and upper-class women gained access to birth control. Historians believe poor unwed women, especially immigrants, were most likely to seek abortions by the 1890s.[4]

We do not know how midwives felt about abortion or how many they performed. Catholic Polish midwives might have refused to perform abortions for fear of religious censure as well as state prosecution. States seldom took action against male physicians in the late-nineteenth century, but midwives might have felt more vulnerable because of doctors' growing hostility toward them.[5]

Abortion by instrument was a last resort for Rosa. Caves reported that she had taken pills first, apparently purchased by "young Pratt." When they did not cause Rosa to miscarry, Pratt rented a wagon and provided a male physician to "probe her womb." Rosa did not even know who performed her abortion in that rented wagon on a country road because he kept the collar on his coat turned up to hide his face. As the physician began to probe her womb, Rosa was at great risk of septic infection. Many late-nineteenth-century rural physicians, even in normal practice, did not exercise care to avoid infection. Once she was infected, little could be done to save Rosa. She died in great pain within two weeks of the abortion.

Caves expected the state to obtain justice for Rosa's death. From the care with which he composed his letter, one can tell that Caves assumed the state had some responsibility. Caves called for enforcement of the Wisconsin state law that had criminalized abortion. In reporting Rosa's last painful days—one neighbor told him about her agonized screams—Caves was building a case. Someone should be prosecuted, he insisted to the state attorney. Rosa's parents did obtain an inquest, but the district attorney claimed he had no evidence admissible in court. Caves clearly considered the doctor's actions illegal and did not approve of abortion.[6]

The Wisconsin abortion law, like those in other states, had ostensibly been passed to protect women from the risks of unsafe abortions. Rosa's case seemed a classic one. Pratt was the son of a wealthy, probably Protestant, Anglo-American farmer. The physician was probably well respected in the community. Licensed medical practitioners who acted to help the community's wealthy men were unlikely to be prosecuted. And so none of the alternative scenarios I have mentioned were possible for Rosa. She had no partner to help her birth and raise a child from an unwanted pregnancy, no female kin-centered support network, no safe procedure for termination of her pregnancy, no state to prosecute the people who violated the law and were responsible for her death. Who knows what those few days of love were like for Rosa? What was she thinking when she rode with her lover on those warm summer days? Was she aware of the risks?

Rural women, especially the poor, the immigrant, the young, the ethnically or racially subordinate, did not by and large tell their own stories in the late nineteenth century. And few told their stories for them. Texts such as that created by Caves thus deserve careful scrutiny. They contain, however muted, the voices of the women who lost. They anchor us in the reality of rural women's lives by reminding us of the costs to women who had no right to open and safe health care during the most dangerous periods of their lives.

Rosa's story stayed with me because it described the complex of risks women faced and the difficulties in providing safe health care for themselves and others. Rosa's short, tragic life was only a part of the larger story of healing. She did not have to face the continued health risks that other women did each time they birthed successive children, nursed them through their most vulnerable first year, and defended them from the epidemics that washed through communities unexpectedly and inexplicably. Reflecting on Rosa's story and the other health risks women faced, I realized that had she lived, her health-care responsibilities would have been as central to her later life as they were to my grandmother Matilda.

Rosa's story is at the crossroads of the history of healing in north-central Wisconsin. It links risk, medical practices, and public health policy to the lives of women in important ways. Hers was a maternal mortality, a statistic that showed up nowhere in the official records, that stands for the silence of the records and of the women, part of the shadow life of the system I am about to describe. Her young life ended during her pregnancy, then the single most dangerous time for women of childbearing age, but other health risks affected families as a whole.

FRONTIER RISKS

This story begins before either Rosa or Matilda had arrived in the United States from Europe, in the early and incomplete county records of deaths. Measuring health risks and determining the causes of illness and death still remains an imprecise science. During most of the nineteenth century, as settler and Native populations moved around frequently, reports of health risks are fragmentary or nonexistent. As in other states, the continued outbreak of small-pox moved Wisconsin state agencies to track that disease in the 1880s. By the end of the century, Wisconsin was making a concerted effort to document births and deaths, to calculate health risks through contagious diseases, and to eradicate them. Yet as late as 1915, when Dr. Dorothy Mendenhall began her study of prenatal health care, the medical language of death registrations, if they were even completed, left much doubt about the conditions being described. A highly trained researcher, Mendenhall noted that inspecting death certificates "calls for not only superhuman intuition, but also control of one's temper and sense of humor." [7]

The earliest county death records, those from the 1860s and 1870s, seldom record the cause of death. By the 1880s and 1890s, although often still silent on the causes of death, records are much more complete and begin to point up some important risks. Adult male deaths were apt to be work-related accidents: on railroads, in the woods (killed by falling trees, an adz blow to the head, loading logs), by dynamite explosions, on the farm, falling from wagons, the kick of a horse. Cirrhosis of the liver and alcoholism also show up as causes of death among men, along with a fairly large number of suicides—overdose of morphine, gunshot wounds, poisoning. Women also died violent deaths. Several were shot by their husbands and one slashed her own wrists. By far the largest number of young women, however, died of pregnancy- and birth-related causes. Childbed fever, puerperal fever, septicemia, peritonitis, hemorrhage in confinement, miscarriage, odious labor—whatever term the death certificate used—all reveal that even among young, healthy women, pregnancy and child-birth were dangerous times. [8]

Next to pregnancy and childbirth, the most dangerous age was infancy and youth. When children died, it was usually of contagious diseases or acci-dents. One study of mortalities in 1880 in Clark and Marathon counties found almost 29 percent of deaths were to infants and another 19 percent were to children aged one to five. Thus, almost half of those dying were the very young. And these statistics came from records that under-reported deaths in these age groups. Infant mortality, if recorded at all in the early days, usually had no cause listed or might be simply described as "not well from birth." Of the causes that were recorded, the most common were cholera, diphtheria, whooping cough, dysentery, and meningitis. Young children also died from scarlet fever, measles, and smallpox. [9]

In 1880 the fear of smallpox was still great among settler and Native alike. Malaria had worried the first generation of settlers, but second-generation set-tlers and Native peoples were relatively unaffected by the disease during the period here studied. Smallpox, on the other hand, continued to plague Native peoples and settlers of all ages. While there were fewer cases from the type of smallpox that caused death, a milder variety that caused illness from which most people recovered continued into the 1920s.[10]

Public health programs have eradicated smallpox worldwide, and the characteristics of the disease itself are well known. Smallpox was carried by persons in close contact with others who were overtly ill; symptoms were easily recognized. There was small chance of contracting the viral disease through blankets or clothes, but people in crowds could contract it and then spread it through their households. The disease struck all ages and left people too sick to care for each other. Only vaccination of exposed people could stop its spread.

Among the Native population in the Great Lakes area, smallpox epidemics began during the seventeenth century. Vaccination as a preventative for smallpox was so well known that an 1836 treaty with the Chippewa provided for smallpox vaccinations as well as for medicine and doctors. But early vaccines did not remain effective for long, and the government had only a very primitive medical service in the early nineteenth century. It was difficult for officials to reach isolated Native populations and to convince them that vaccination

Ojibwe smallpox map, 1910s. Memories of smallpox epidemics were still vivid in the early twentieth century when Nawajibigokwe drew this picture map of the Leech Lake, Minnesota, area for anthropologist Frances Densmore. The Ojibwe referred to themselves as "the writing people" because they drew on birch bark, the method used by Nawajibigokwe to tell the story of how her great-grandmother fled a smallpox outbreak by canoe with her mother and four brothers. Only her great-grandmother, Wigubins, survived.

would save their families. The government did not vaccinate until epidemics broke out and then often forced individuals to receive vaccinations without adequate preparation or consultation with local medicine people.

The first well-documented epidemic occurred among the Menominee in 1861. The disease was so widespread and so severe that the Kiowa on the southern plains recorded it as the "smallpox winter." The disease spread quickly among Catholics because priests insisted they bring the dead to church for funerals. By June 1, one hundred cases had been reported. The county board of health ordered that people not be taken to church for funerals, and the agent ordered the priest to close the church. When the priest defied the ruling, the agent had the county sheriff arrest him, closed all the stores and schools, and employed a physician to vaccinate the remaining eight hundred people. Of the 150 cases that resulted from this epidemic, 79 deaths occurred, nearly all Catholics. Non-Christian Menominee employed their traditional method for prevention against the spread of communicable disease by scattering into the forest. In 1873 the Menominee experienced an epidemic of a milder form of smallpox. Outbreaks of other diseases also made life precarious. A measles epidemic in 1885 resulted in five deaths at the boarding school; on the reservation as a whole forty of one thousand Catholics died. At that rate, the resident priest wrote in concern to the bishop at Green Bay, "the tribe is doomed." The high death rate led the government to establish a hospital at Keshena with Catholic nuns in charge. The hospital, along with better food supplies through farming, helped reduce the death rate, and after 1900 the birth rate began to rise. Compulsory vaccination against smallpox for children in Indian schools in 1907 and compulsory vaccination of all not immune in 1909–11 practically put an end to the disease on reservations.[11]

Epidemics continued to decimate small bands that followed their older migratory lifestyle. In the 1880s and 1890s settlers reported that Native families camped around Perkinstown near Medford to gather ginseng lost half their numbers to smallpox. Around 1900, the disease nearly wiped out a Native village near Spirit Lake, southwest of Medford. Scattered cases surfaced among Native peoples living outside reservation communities and in isolation.[12]

Despite the availability of vaccinations, the rural settler population also suffered from periodic outbreaks of smallpox into the twentieth century. In the winter of 1873, the smallpox epidemic that visited the Menominee also wiped out the settler village of Humbird in Clark County. Around 1907, a Marathon health officer reported that the county had been "bothered a lot" with smallpox. The townships of Hull and Marathon had cases of smallpox in 1914 and 1916. These twentieth-century cases seem to have been the milder form, which could still be deadly. The government did not compel non-Native adults to be vaccinated, but it suggested that lumber employers urge their workers to get vaccinated and required children to have proof of vaccination to enter public schools. It also provided for quarantine. By 1912 smallpox had dropped to an insignificant number at the bottom of a list of the top thirty causes of death in Wisconsin. But a new, virulent disease was already abroad. Tuberculosis had entered the population in the nineteenth century, and there was no vaccination for it.[13]

TUBERCULOSIS, THE HOUSE DISEASE

In 1912, as part of their anti-tuberculosis campaign, the Wisconsin Lung Association created a poster they hoped would attract the attention of women to their risks of contracting TB. "Spend Every Available Moment In the Open," the poster advised, because "Women Suffer Too Much Indoors." The poster noted that the majority of deaths from TB occurred among women and depicted a mother with her small son walking on a tree-lined path. The poster conveyed what health-care workers of the time believed, that TB was a "house disease." Women were not only the majority of victims in this epidemic but also the primary health-care providers for prevention and treatment.

The professionals knew that curing Wisconsin women was far more complicated a task than a mere poster could convey. Tuberculosis was sometimes called the slow killer because infected people did not die quickly, as with smallpox. TB spread through households and held them in its grip for years. After German bacteriologist Robert Koch isolated the TB bacillus in 1882, the Wisconsin State Medical Society urged that infected patients be separated from families and, if possible, seek a warmer, dryer, higher-altitude climate. By 1905 Koch had developed a test to identify the disease in its early stages, a procedure that attracted worldwide attention when it earned him the Nobel Prize. Medical scientists concluded that the best time to treat the disease was in its early stages, when 75 percent of those infected could be healed. Experts were not sure how the highly communicable disease was spread but thought that home health care was inappropriate because TB spread so easily. The philosophy of the time was to give patients good care away from home in a sanatorium, educate them for self-care and prevention, and then send them home. During the nineteenth century Wisconsin people who could afford it often traveled with other midwesterners to the Southwest, where the U.S. government had already set up treatment centers for military men. Private sanatoria became common retreats for wealthy patients, where a combination of high altitude, dry air, sunshine, and healthy food were expected to either cure them or help them spend their last days in comfort. By 1905 doctors who had earlier considered Wisconsin too cold and too low in altitude for treating TB patients concluded that low humidity, equable temperature, and lots of sunshine in an institution with large grounds and a good water supply in a "sightly" location were the most important elements in the cure.

Those who could not afford to leave Wisconsin or seek institutional care usually had only home care. A few counties had "pest houses" in the nineteenth century, but these were used mainly for smallpox, scarlet fever, or diphtheria cases and normally housed only those who had no one to care for them at home. By the late nineteenth century local authorities simply lodged TB patients in various institutions for the mentally disabled, the poor, or the aged. Authorities often could not even diagnose TB, much less offer advice on home treatment. In their homes, women continued to diagnose, treat, and prevent with very little knowledge of how to do so.

Health-care reformers urged state officials to adopt policies to reduce the incidence of tuberculosis. Officials were aware that TB was a problem in Wisconsin, but no one knew how much of a problem. The first step, therefore, was to establish a Tuberculosis Commission to study the number and location of cases. The five-man commission reported in 1905 that during 1900, the first year for which any records existed, more than 2,000 had died. By 1905, with records still incomplete, the number had grown to 2,500 per year. That year the TB death rate in Wisconsin was 10.52 per 10,000 inhabitants. About one quarter of all cases came from Milwaukee, the greatest number from one area where the public almshouse, the house of correction, and many old homes were located, but TB was now everywhere, in rural as well as urban areas.

On the commission's recommendation, the legislature passed a bill to build a state tuberculosis sanatorium modeled on institutions in the eastern United States and Canada. The state chose a 210-acre site at Wales, and the 200-bed hospital began receiving newly diagnosed and relatively healthy patients in 1907. But most of the twenty thousand people infected, the most seriously ill and the most contagious, were still being cared for at home and in a variety of local institutions, usually asylums or poor farms. By 1908 TB was the number-one cause of death in Wisconsin; by 1910 more than twenty thousand people had the disease, and each year another several thousand were being infected.[14]

In 1910 Dr. C. A. Harper reviewed the problem before a conference of trustees and superintendents of county asylums for the insane in Green Bay. He pointed out that there were twenty-four different county institutions for the mentally disabled and poor now accepting TB patients, thus endangering all inmates. He recommended that counties build small "shacks" next to the main institutions to segregate TB patients. Advanced cases required little care: good food, fresh air, rest and exercise, a good nurse, and an occasional visit from the physician would cost counties very little extra. These smaller county facilities could keep patients close to friends and relatives. Harper left the problem where it had been before, with local authorities, who might or might not be able and willing to establish a new facility, and with families.

Between 1895 and 1910, TB became a dangerous epidemic among Native people as well as settlers. Because the government had doctors under contract

You Make Life What It Is!

IMPORTANT CAUSES OF DEATH IN WISCONSIN 1912

Cause	Number
HEART DISEASE	2443
TUBERCULOSIS	2362
PNEUMONIA	2066
STILL BIRTHS	1699
CANCER	1673
ACCIDENTS AT BIRTH	1582
APOPLEXY	1466
OLD AGE	1362
BRIGHTS DISEASE	1196
DIARRHEA	1145
VIOLENT ACCIDENTS	691
BRONCHITIS	524
STOMACH DISEASE	500
DISEASE OF ARTERIES	347
SUICIDES	310
TYPHOID	306
RHEUMATISM	287
SCARLET FEVER	285
MENINGITIS	285
DROWNING ACCIDENTS	280
DIPTHERIA	279
APPENDICITIS	265
INFLUENZA	255
WHOOPING COUGH	232
PARALYSIS	223
MEASLES	127
INSANITY	124
ERYSIPELAS	69
PERITONITIS	63
SMALL POX	3

STATISTICS PREPARED BY WISCONSIN STATE BOARD OF HEALTH

What will the Future bring You and Yours?

Causes of Death poster, 1912. By 1912 the Wisconsin Anti-Tuberculosis Association ranked tuberculosis the second-highest cause of death, killing 2,362 people that year. Note that maternal and infant mortalities are divided among several categories, such as stillbirths and accidents at birth, and that smallpox is last in the list of thirty causes of death.

or resident on reservations, it is possible to chart the spread of TB more precisely there than in settler communities. The government assumed responsibility for Native peoples' health care in the late nineteenth century when it decided to eradicate smallpox. That task was accomplished with vaccination, but no vaccine existed for tuberculosis, and even doctors had little knowledge about how it spread. The government did little to stem what was becoming known as the "white plague" among Native communities.

The swift spread among the Lac du Flambeau Chippewa can be followed through the monthly reports of diseases and injuries submitted by the La Pointe agency physician, who gathered data on all tribes within his agency. The physician reported in 1896 that general health was improving and was stable. In June he stated, "Health has been exceptionally good during past three months." In February he reported a few new tuberculosis cases; by September most deaths were due to the disease; and by October 1897 thirty-nine of forty-eight women examined had tuberculosis. In 1900 the adult cases seemed to level off generally, but conditions had deteriorated in schools, where children were not being isolated adequately. In 1903 the government made its first systematic health surveys.[15]

These first surveys by Washington health authorities indicated that TB was more pervasive in Native than in settler communities. The Indian inspector concluded, "Pulmonary tuberculosis is widespread. It is common. It is fatal. It is insidious. It is everywhere." Although physicians reported widespread TB in Indian schools, the government was still not certain how pervasive it was. The Indian Bureau chose Dr. Aleš Hrdlička, a trained medical doctor and self-taught physical anthropologist who was curator of the Smithsonian Institution's Division of Physical Anthropology, to conduct a more detailed survey of families in six tribes. The Menominee were one of the groups he visited.[16]

When Hrdlička arrived among the Menominee, he found the people friendly and willing to cooperate in the study. They even asked relatives to return home so the survey could be more complete. They were eager to know how to care for the ill and, if severely ill, how long they might live. Hrdlička examined one hundred Menominee families. It is not clear how he selected the families; probably they were Catholics who lived close to the agency and were eager to participate. His survey still exists in the National Anthropological Archives at the Smithsonian Institution. Of the one hundred families he visited, sixty had at least one person infected. In many cases the entire family was infected, a condition he noted by putting little crosses before their names. Similar conditions existed in other Native communities. Hrdlička's study resulted in the first centralized health program within the Indian Bureau. The new supervisor of schools, Elsie Newton, made Native children's health her primary concern. In the absence of a vaccine, the government tested for TB, removed the infected children from the schools, and sent them home. The government also built regional sanatoriums to care for infected children. By 1915 it had constructed four of these structures, including one at Fort Lapwai in Idaho, where Wisconsin Native children were sent. Like the state institutions, the federal sanatoriums took only the most recent cases, those who seemed the healthiest. The Menominee reservation matron was soon visiting homes, reporting infectious diseases to the agency physician, and sending the children to the hospital for TB tests. If the tests showed the children to be recently infected, they were sent to the Idaho sanatorium. Others were sent to local hospitals.[17]

What began as a policy of concern turned into yet another system of coercion. Previous coercive policies had left many Native women with great distrust of federal initiatives. Because they expected to care for their sick children at home, many resisted the new removal policy by simply refusing to take family members to the hospital for testing. Even the promise of recovery and the "good" of the patient did not make sending sick family members away to be cared for by non-Native strangers acceptable.

Sanatoriums could treat only a few of the less seriously ill children; thus, the government had to develop a program for treating the more seriously ill and for prevention. Officials decided to dispatch matrons to teach Native women to care for family members in the home. These field matrons, mostly white women and often the untrained wives of agents, were to instruct Native women on basic household health. Matrons and nurses provided information on the importance of sanitation, disposal of garbage, screening windows and doors, cooking and nursing, and cleanliness of person and house. The government had no systematic program to recruit and train Native women to become professional health-care practitioners, nor did it offer government support for training among Native women as a whole. One scholar who studied government health-care policies noted that tuberculosis rates did decline among Native people in the early twentieth century. Prevention in schools may have slowed the spread of the disease there. But he concluded that the increase in farming and stock raising improved nutrition, which reduced infection rates.[18]

Settler families could not be coerced as were Native families. State officials worked indirectly through local doctors and nongovernmental organizations to educate women about home prevention. The Wisconsin State Medical Society set up its first five-member committee to study TB in 1903, and while it urged a campaign to educate the public about the contagiousness of TB, the way it spread, and its curability, the committee found little support among physicians. Only the two committee members from Milwaukee signed their own 1904 report. Those two were also active in supporting a campaign in their city, which would soon become the center of Wisconsin's first public movement to eradicate the disease. In Milwaukee, doctors, state officials, and women reformers worked together to generate support for establishment of a Wisconsin Anti-Tuberculosis Association. Public exhibits in a downtown building, with lectures and stereopticon slide demonstrations twice a day, attracted more than fifty thousand people.

Women's groups in Milwaukee quickly threw their support behind the organizing effort for a Wisconsin branch of the Anti-Tuberculosis Association (WATA), and in 1907, for a Visiting Nurse Association, both national nongovernmental organizations. Gertrude Cushing, a Wisconsin Federation of Women's Clubs member known for her campaign to establish kindergartens, was at the WATA's first organizing meeting in Milwaukee. The group was to be a lay organization, modeled on the Consumers' League, in which women had been active. Their job would be to educate and mobilize the public. During the first two years, women participated in campaigns for legislation to exclude tubercular teachers and pupils from classrooms unless they tested TB-free, to replace the common drinking cup in public places with new bubbler drinking fountains, to survey Milwaukee to determine the extent of TB there, and to inspect schools.[19]

Lay members did not control the organization, however. While women remained on an advisory board, male doctors dominated the group after 1910, when thirty-one-year-old Dr. Hoyt E. Dearholt became executive director. Although the national group supported grassroots initiatives and mandated that one-half of all funds raised be returned to locals to support these initiatives, Dearholt created a highly centralized, self-contained organization run by a professional staff with local "paper" organizations that had no control over any portion of the income generated or any initiative in planning local programs. WATA did train a small cadre of public health nurses and establish TB screening clinics. Rural people flocked to these clinics, but the WATA steadfastly referred them to private physicians and refused to back state-sponsored public health programs.[20]

WATA officials knew that TB was a growing problem among rural families as evidenced by a 1911 Dunn County study. They selected Dunn County in northwestern Wisconsin for the survey because most farm families were native-born and because WATA expected TB rates there to be "average" or perhaps lower than other rural areas of Wisconsin with high numbers of immigrant families. By 1911, public health authorities thought they knew how TB spread: through infected sputum as well as through contaminated utensils, clothing, and houses. Dunn County farm households should have had relatively low rates of contagion because the farm women kept their houses "exceptionally clean." Wisconsin had passed a law in 1907 requiring that living TB cases be registered; the field worker had only to collect the names from the county clerk and interview the families to see which preventative methods they used. It seemed easy enough.[21]

Field worker Kathrene Gedney found that the Dunn County clerk had registered 265 deaths caused by TB, a fairly low rate of 8 per 10,000. But the clerk had no record of live TB cases in the county because doctors had refused to register them. Asking around, Gedney found plenty of infected people still living in households but few rural housewives who knew how to prevent TB from spreading among family members. There were no county public health nurses. County public health officials were supposed to oversee fumigation of houses after family members had contracted communicable disease, whether they recovered or died, with the standard TB disinfecting practice, using formaldehyde for more than six hours. In practice, public officials either did not know or ignored these standard fumigation procedures. They took no action at all or considered whitewash or a short treatment with sulfur sufficient, and they gave women no instructions on prevention. Many doctors did not even know how to diagnose TB correctly. Of those who did, one-third refused to tell women they had TB in their families. A number of the women, unsatisfied with the doctor's diagnosis, had sought second opinions (some consulted up to nine doctors); a quarter of these doctors also lied to them. Another third of the doctors correctly diagnosed the disease and informed patients but either gave no precautionary directions or offered incomplete instructions on prevention. Women continued to use common water dippers, wash food utensils together, and allow family members to sleep with infected kin.

The report offered the experience of one woman as an example of why doctors were unreliable. She consulted five physicians before one correctly diagnosed her disease. He advised rest, a good diet, outdoor living, and care in containing her sputum. He gave no instructions on personal contact or on treatment of utensils, clothing, or houses. When her condition continued to worsen, in desperation she tried a ten-dollar "consumption cure" patent medicine.

Gedney's report showed TB rates were increasing in rural Dunn County at the same time that city rates were dropping. Ten townships in Dunn County now had higher rates than Milwaukee and other cities that had active prevention programs. She found proof that prevention could make a difference. In Tiffany township, for example, she found very low rates because the physician who cared for most of the families gave women thorough instruction in preventive measures. Before the public could be educated, she concluded, doctors needed to appreciate and act on their responsibilities to patients and the community.

A decade of work probably lowered TB rates in the four northern settler counties. In 1924 a statewide survey showed that Clark had an infection rate of 3 per 10,000 and Taylor almost 4 per 10,000, rates far lower than overall for the white population, which remained slightly more than 6 per 10,000 for the entire state in 1928. Marathon had more than 7 per 10,000 and Lincoln almost 8 per 10,000, rates higher than the national average. Wisconsin's Native population remained most at risk. In 1928 the Ho-Chunk, who had no reservation and neither federal nor state health assistance, had a rate of almost 76 per 10,000. A study of infection rates in the 1930s found the Native population of Wisconsin as a whole still had a TB rate eight times greater than that of the general U.S. population.[22]

MATERNAL AND INFANT MORTALITY

For women of childbearing age, that is from fifteen to forty-five, maternity was a far greater health risk than TB. Despite advances in medicine, deaths from infection during pregnancy and childbirth seemed to be rising in the second decade of the twentieth century. Dr. Mendenhall estimated that the death rate from maternity in Wisconsin in 1913 might be twice as high as that from tuberculosis, then the major cause of death from disease. By this time health-care researchers had developed new ways to statistically describe maternal mortality rates, to compare different areas, and to measure the decline in rates as an indicator of successful health-care reforms. The Wisconsin maternal mortality rate would then be expressed as an MMR of 14 per 1,000, 14 maternal deaths for every 1,000 live births.[23]

Mendenhall's statewide statistics showed that while maternal deaths were relatively low in Clark, Taylor, and Lincoln counties, the rates for Marathon County were among the highest in the state. Among Wisconsin cities, Wausau had the second-highest rate. Infection-producing intervention, Mendenhall believed, was increasing as more doctors assisted at births. Sixty-four percent of maternal deaths in Wisconsin were due to infection, which was largely avoidable and seldom existed in hospitals. Puerperal sepsis, the technical name for infection during pregnancy, was simply wound infection, Mendenhall maintained, and could be prevented. She advocated that physicians specially trained in obstetrics replace the general practitioner so that the danger of infection would be removed for the pregnant woman. She also advocated the establishment of well-equipped hospitals and nursing visits in rural areas.[24]

Researchers looked at infant mortality as well. They used the number of deaths during the first year per 1,000 live births as a measure and called it the Infant Mortality Rate (IMR). By 1925 records showed almost 120,000 infants had died since 1900, but they also showed that the IMR had dropped from 120 per 1,000 in 1908 to 82 in 1914. More infants died in the country than in the cities, but those who survived had a healthier childhood than in the city. Rural women breast-fed children more often than city mothers, thus eliminating diarrheal diseases, and contagious diseases were less common than in the city. Mendenhall thought that perhaps overwork, lack of proper food and rest, and lack of education on general health were causes of poor health among women and children, along with lack of access to professional medical assistance.

Midwifery in rural areas did not seem to be a cause. In fact, some of the lowest infant mortality rates existed in counties with the highest numbers of midwives. Taylor County, for example, had a high percentage of midwives but one of the lowest maternal mortality rates. Some physicians thought that lowering maternal mortality was the key to lowering infant mortality as well. Most infants who died in the first months died at birth, or from being born prematurely, or from birth defects or birth injury.

The infant death rate remained shockingly and stubbornly high. Between 1914 and 1917 alone 20,000 infants died, about 20 percent of all deaths. The overall drop masked vast differences among communities. Some reduced their rate to 50 per 1,000; others still had rates of 175 per 1,000. The rural death rate declined very little during these years. Even if children survived to celebrate their first birthdays, thousands more died by age five.[25]

What struck me after I had reviewed local health care was how little help women had in protecting themselves and their families from life-threatening risks. How, I wondered, had they managed at all? The answers lie in a network of local, informally trained female healers who helped other women in their tasks of healing. Rural women relied on a group of trained care givers to assist them in keeping their families healthy. These care givers received training in a variety of ways—from experts within their communities, from formal institutions outside their communities, and from the experience of assisting neighbors in need. Together these health-care givers formed a system that functioned within neighborhoods with a minimum of assistance or control from outside authorities. Almost invisible to outsiders, frequently unsanctioned by public officials, these care givers were, nonetheless, the experts to whom women turned when unable to deal with medical emergencies on their own. The stories of these local assistants, often untold to outsiders, help explain how rural people survived harsh conditions in small, isolated communities. These stories begin with Isabella Wolfe St. Jermaine, who practiced within the Lac du Flambeau community for almost fifty years.

Care Givers
Isabella's Story [Wolfe, St. Jermaine, born in North Carolina, 1870–1957]

Chance played a big part in my discovery of Isabella's story. I had gone to Lac du Flambeau to research the development of tourism there. Just before leaving town, I was sitting in a local coffee house chatting with the owner when an elder came in, introduced as Dorothy Thoms. We briefly discussed my project on rural women's history, and Dorothy said: "My grandmother went all over on snowshoes delivering babies." I grabbed a paper napkin and jotted down her name with a note to talk to her again. I remembered the encounter, but

I lost the napkin and did not follow up the next year. I did work in the regional National Archives in Chicago that year. Looking at a list of government employees, I noticed Isabella Wolfe had been hired as a nurse in 1897. The mental image I had formed of Dorothy's grandmother trudging off on snowshoes to deliver a baby suddenly came back to me. The next summer I sat at a kitchen table with Dorothy and her daughter Anita and asked. The women *were* the same. Dorothy's grandmother was Isabella Wolfe St. Jermaine. Anita handed me a photograph of young Isabella in her nurse's uniform. Isabella's story began to take form.

In 1897, twenty-six-year-old Isabella Wolfe arrived at the Lac du Flambeau reservation to take up her health-care duties as the school nurse. Miss Wolfe, as she was called, was born in Cherokee, North Carolina, where she attended the Cherokee Indian School. Her father, Joseph, was Cherokee; her mother, Mahala Abernathy, was of European descent. According to family oral traditions, Isabella graduated from Carlisle Indian Industrial School in Pennsyl-

vania and received nurse's training nearby. Isabella was part of a small number of Native nurses being formally trained in health care during the late 1880s and early 1890s. She marked her graduation, probably in 1897, with a studio photograph. It shows the serious young woman in a striped, high-necked uniform and an apron with thermometers tucked into it, holding a book and standing by an ornately carved end table with a glass and vial—presumably of medicine—on it. Her pyramidal cap announced to all that she had received formal nurse's training.[26]

As soon as Isabella graduated she was hired as a nurse at the new government boarding school in Lac du Flambeau. The government at the time considered young women like Isabella to be the backbone of its new Native health-care system. They would come from Native communities, receive formal training, and then

Isabella Wolfe at graduation, 1890s. Combining skills gained in formal nurse's training with traditional Cherokee and Ojibwe remedies, Isabella served the Lac du Flambeau community as midwife and nurse from 1898 until her death in 1957. Sporadic U.S. government health-care assistance during that time was inadequate for the community's needs.

work among Native people. Their employment signaled that Native women might extend their important role in traditional healing into the new medical systems established by the government. By 1897 more than half of the assistant matrons/nurses in Native schools were Native women.[27]

It was a time of opportunity but of great challenges as well. The daughter of Margaret Runkel, who served as the first sewing instructor at the Lac du Flambeau boarding school, remembered that her mother often sat up with sick children and that she also lined caskets with soft fabric for those who died. Sometimes, when parents asked her to, she trimmed a silk pillow with ribbon and placed it under the child's head. Many Natives had tuberculosis, sore eyes, running ears, and scrofula (a swelling of the lymph nodes, especially in the neck, perhaps caused by tuberculosis). It must have been a great comfort to worried parents to have as competent a nurse as Miss Wolfe available to care for their children. Isabella worked for the government for almost two years. She married Jack St. Jermaine in 1898 and resigned from government employment at the end of June 1899.[28]

The government policy of hiring Native women in health care was short-lived. Before long, the government was hiring mostly white women for professional positions at its schools. Forty percent of the 653 women who served as nurses and assistant matrons between 1897 and 1905 were Native women. By 1905, while the number of Native nurses increased slightly, the overall percentage of Native women among matrons and nurses declined from 53 to 26 percent. Native women were being edged out as health-care providers during these years. Isabella, a success by all accounts, was not one of a long line of government Native women health-care providers at Lac du Flambeau. The government closed its nursing station at the school by 1912 and also discontinued the regular physician's position on the reservation, merely contracting for weekly visits from doctors in the nearby town of Minocqua. Instead the government relied on white matrons, who usually had no formal nurse's training. The first Lac du Flambeau matron, charged with enforcing health rules in the community in 1912, angered people with her arbitrary dictates and could not obtain their cooperation.[29]

If one looked only at governmental records, it would seem that the Lac du Flambeau community had no trained resident health-care worker. But they had Isabella. After her marriage, Isabella continued to use her nursing skills to help the people at Lac du Flambeau. Isabella birthed her own three children, a daughter, Ramona, born in 1899 and two sons born in 1900 and 1906. Ramona saw to it that her daughter Dorothy had a chance to learn from her grandmother. Dorothy remembered spending summers with Isabella near Buckskin Lake, learning how to rice, to sugar, and to bead, and she also remembered Isabella trekking to different homes on snowshoes to deliver babies. As the only trained nurse midwife on the reservation, Isabella was in great demand by birthing women. In her little black bag she carried both traditional medicine—such as leaves for poultices—and modern medicine. When people came to her home for care, she treated them, fed them, and sent them off with food. Isabella's husband was chief of police for many years, and he often took her on calls. Jack was more than six feet tall, a well-known guide, a great storyteller, and a respected member of the community. Over the years, Isabella became known simply as "Grandma Jack," the woman everyone recognized as the community healer and midwife.[30]

Isabella was also known for her farming and her fine handwork. In 1922 the matron at Lac du Flambeau visited the fifty-two-year-old Isabella, who by then had been married to Jack St. Jermaine for twenty-four years. She was living in a well-maintained six-room frame house with a large garden. The matron described Isabella as a "marvelous farmer" with "a wonderful aptitude for doing anything she undertakes well." The matron chronicled her skills:

> Expert bead worker and proud of the Cherokee beadwork tradition.
> Knits, makes moccasins, rag rugs, quilts.
> Cans and preserves large quantities of fruits and vegetables.
> Picks and cans wild berries every year, sometimes makes maple sugar
> and syrup. Raises 60 chickens and has a cow.
> Raises flowers and shrubs.
> Has an "extra good garden."
> Has a good painted six room house with a screened porch.[31]

The records of the fairs held in 1915 and 1916 bear out the evaluation. Isabella won prizes for the best Indian collection and for corn, tomatoes, cucumbers, pickles, butter, fruit and jelly, and home cooking. In 1918 the *Milwaukee Journal* featured Isabella as a "prize food producer." That year she won three first prizes at the state fair for canned fruits and vegetables. During the summer she had dried and stored the rest of her garden produce. She kept three cows, made butter, and raised a large flock of chickens. A photograph showed her displayng the fair entries at the side of her frame home, the bounty of garden, fresh and canned (including dried braided corn hanging from the side of the house), along with samples of sewing and beadwork.[32]

The women of Isabella's family are justifiably proud of her public record of growing and making things, but they also remember her unrecorded health-care work in the community. Anita told me to ask any of the elders about her. They did not recall a woman named Isabella, but when I mentioned that she was also known as "Grandma Jack," they smiled in remembrance.

There is another way in which Isabella is remembered. Before I left, Anita and Dorothy took me to see her land, where a huge lilac bush still stands. Isabella loved that bush, Anita explained, because her family always had lilacs growing in the yard. When she arrived in Lac du Flambeau from the south,

Isabella missed the lilacs. She had a relative send a cutting from the family lilac bush. Isabella planted and nurtured the cutting, and the bush flourished. Soon people were asking her for cuttings. She gave one to each person who asked, as freely as she gave her help to those who needed health care. Now every May, Isabella's lilacs still bloom all over Lac du Flambeau.[33]

Isabella was unusual in receiving such a high level of training in non-Native medical care, and she symbolizes what might have been had the government helped young women obtain training and had it recognized the value of their work as health-care providers. But her life also symbolizes the way in which the informal system of health care functioned during those years. Women were able to provide for their own needs independent of the government.

EARLY MEDICINE PEOPLE

Her full Native name was *Kitchi Che Mon Eke*, the Lady Who's the First Farmer, but most people referred to her simply as Chemon. We know about Chemon because in the 1990s descendants still remembered her as a healer who practiced medicine until she died in 1925. She was born into the Crane Clan at Keshena in 1854, a few years after the Menominee established a village there. At the time of the 1922 industrial survey, Chemon was sixty-eight and still practicing medicine. She had a comfortably furnished and very neatly kept three-room log and frame house on twenty-one acres of cleared land with twenty-six apple trees, a flock of chickens, a log stable where she kept a pig, a cow, and several calves, an attached hay barn, a wagon shed, and a well with a pump. She had all the necessary implements, outbuildings, and animals for farming. Her son lived with her, and each April the two made maple sugar together. At the annual fairs she won prizes for her beans, onions, squash, and garden products as well as for her moccasins, tanned buckskins, and women's traditional outfits. Chemon performed publicly in special dance outfits that displayed fine Menominee ribbon- and beadwork, and she appears in numerous photographs from the early twentieth century. She was known for her beadwork. In the 1990s her granddaughter Arlene Sipical Creapeau sometimes brought out Chemon's beaded bags to show the women who gathered weekly to sew, knit, crochet, and embroider.[34]

Chemon's reputation as a healer lived on among her descendants as well. Allan Caldwell, Chemon's grandson, remembered her to be well known and respected in the community as a medicine woman. She taught his father where to gather medicines. Granddaughter Arlene Sipical Creapeau recalled, as she showed Chemon's beaded work, that she knew a lot of Indian medicine. Creapeau said that other medicine women, such as Margaret Dixon, gathered roots and made medicine, too. Native and non-Native people alike went to Dixon for treatment.[35]

Chemon, Menominee medicine woman, 1915–16.
Known to the community for her healing skills,
Chemon also taught her children and great-
grandchildren how to gather and grow medicines.
In this photograph Chemon displays her dance
regalia for anthropologist Samuel Barrett. The
embroidery, ribbonwork, and beadwork were part
of efforts by Chemon and other non-Christian
Menominee women to preserve the tribe's material culture.

Almost all of the medicine women in the northern Wisconsin Native communities belonged to the Midewiwin, the Grand Medicine Society, which passed on knowledge of songs and herbs to its members. Men and women alike purchased membership in the society and, after a period of instruction that might last as long as four years, participated in an initiation ceremony that transferred power to the new member. Women who joined the society received preliminary instruction in the practice of medicine before or during initiation. As the women advanced through higher degrees, they received additional training and often became specialists in particular ailments. The society systematized and improved curative practices and kept a record of ceremonies and songs that were an essential part of treatment. The use of song while administering medicines joined the mental and physical remedies. Pictographic birch-bark records kept track of bodily diseases and herbal cures for each illness. Medicine pouches and other ritual objects contained medicinal materials. For these Native people, good health and morality were closely intertwined. Disease, members believed, resulted from unbalanced or incomplete relations between humans and the *manitos,* or spirits. Rituals re-established balance and completeness, and the manitos then cured the sick. The medicine person had to know which actions might have made the ill person susceptible to disease.[36]

Medicine people brought the experience of generations to the processes of healing. Frances Densmore, an anthropologist for the Smithsonian Institution's Bureau of Ethnology who talked to medicine women in Minnesota and

Wisconsin between 1910 and 1925, made a careful survey of the practices of this traditional science. Densmore described medicine women as poised, keen eyed, and self-confident. They practiced specific medical procedures, such as splinting fractures or cutting away gangrenous areas when surgery seemed necessary, and used many practices to prevent disease. They boiled water when uncertain of its purity, burned cedar boughs to purify the air in lodges, burned sage during contagious illness to fumigate, and smoked and aired bedding to rid it of insects and impurities. They bathed frequently, used sweat lodges year-round, burned refuse, made lye from hardwood ashes, and used it for washing dishes, clothing, and bedding. They were skilled herbalists. "It is a teaching of the Midewiwin that every tree, bush, and plant has a use," Chippewa women told Densmore. In preparing these specific herbal remedies, women could choose from 143 plants, almost half of which settlers also considered to have medicinal qualities and which could be found listed in published phar-macopoeias used by physicians and lay healers alike. The women gathered plants, usually the roots, in the late summer and early fall, taking journeys to areas where particular plants grew. They offered tobacco and thanked the plant. They dried, pulverized, and stored the medicine in bags, usually of buckskin, and boiled the medicines in maple syrup. Complex remedies might contain as many as twenty herbs. Women administered these remedies using general curative techniques such as sweating, steaming, enemas, poultices, and needle application beneath the skin.[37]

Densmore was not just documenting a dying tradition. When she visited Lac du Flambeau in 1910, Midewiwin ceremonies were still held regularly. Densmore saw medicine poles scattered around the community, erected by people who had received the power to cure the sick. And in the 1940s, when anthropologist Robert Ritzenthaler visited the Ojibwe in Minnesota and Wis-consin, he found people still intensely concerned about health and interested in herbal medicine. Ritzenthaler saw herbs drying on home rafters and noted a brisk trade in Native medicines. Menominee medicine women reported similar training and practice and recorded songs used in healing for Dens-more. The Menominee remembered grandmothers and great-grandmothers who gathered medicines and herbs. Because of the importance of plants for medicine as well as for food, during the early twentieth century women con-tinued to travel great distances to gather them but they also raised many of their medicines along with vegetables in their gardens.

Although Native people's system of medicine had been overwhelmed by the smallpox epidemics, it still efficiently served a broad range of maladies from which settlers as well as Native people suffered. Native healers were often the best-trained medical help available. Healers treated settlers, sold them herbs, and taught them to cultivate medicines indigenous to Wisconsin. Letitia Single Dunbar, for example, remembered settling around the middle of the nineteenth century at Little Rib, where she found Native people, probably Chippewa, living along the shores in wigwams. One day visiting Native women found a settler child sick. They immediately gathered and brewed herbs for the child to drink. The child recovered.[38]

Few professional health-care providers accompanied early settlers as they filtered into the Wisconsin woodlands. Most rural settlers doctored themselves, using what family remedies they or their neighbors knew or could find in medical self-help books. Historians of health care sometimes call this "domestic medicine." In practice, domestic medicine meant women diagnosed, prescribed, cared for, and tried to prevent disability and illness in their families without direct professional medical assistance. Herbal treatments formed the basis of this domestic medicine.

Settler families continued to buy medicinal herbs from Native peoples and to learn how to use them well into the twentieth century. They combined these local herbs with seeds and remedies brought from the eastern United States and from Europe. They grew large herbal gardens and used the products either in fresh or dried form, as poultices, teas, and enemas. Michael Lisz remembered his Polish grandmother, who lived near Stevens Point in 1869, having a huge herb garden—thirty rows of different herbs, each row forty to forty-five feet long. Lucille Boneske, who grew up near Athens, remembered her grandmother making her own remedies. Families pooled medical lore from kith and kin. One early settler had two grandmothers, one who had learned Native remedies in West Virginia, another who was a practical nurse. A mother-in-law contributed further information, and a German neighbor offered her medical expertise. George Rietz, the son of one of Athens's first settlers, recounted his grandmother's skills: "My grandmother was the doctor, and if anybody got a cold she rubbed him all over with goose grease, gave him a purge from all kinds of herbs, and put him to bed to sweat it out." A recipe from an 1870s medical record book is a bleak reminder of the efforts of settlers to defend themselves against serious contagious disease. It recorded ingredients to use for cholera: laudanum, camphor, ginger, peppermint, cayenne pepper, Hoffman's abelia.[39]

Of necessity, a great variety of women acquired and practiced general healing skills. The descendant of one family reported that both her parents, who ran a hotel, doctored people. Another remembered her grandmother sewing up injured loggers on her kitchen table. Harriet Gunderson's Indiana-born Swedish grandmother, who lived just east of Wausau, left shoes and clothes in a handy place so she could go out in a hurry, often alone, to care for the sick and dying in all kinds of illnesses and childbirth. If infants died, she baptized them, and whether infant or adult she laid out the deceased and prepared the body for burial. In addition to a general medical practice, this grandmother birthed about two hundred children although she never registered as a midwife. She asked no fee for services and never refused a call, practicing from the 1880s until 1919, when roads allowed patients to reach more distant, professionally trained doctors.[40]

Women supplemented their own healing skills and those of neighborhood midwives and healers with patent medicines, often purchased at medicine shows. In the early twentieth century, medicine shows met the demand for commercially produced remedies and instruction on how to administer them. Popular lectures on medicine, sales of patent medicine, and entertainment went hand in hand in the small rural towns of northern Wisconsin.

The availability of professionally trained doctors differed with location. Early Athens residents remembered that a Dr. Schultz, who had attended medical school in Germany, arrived in 1880. He sent difficult cases to Dorchester, which had its own town doctor in the 1880s. By 1902 outlying crossroads communities had doctors as well. My mother Theresa was birthed by a nearby Bruckerville doctor in 1902. Even after physicians settled in small towns and communities, however, most settler women called doctors only for prolonged illnesses or medical emergencies.[41]

Doctors usually mixed their own medicines and often ran pharmacies as well. In Athens, Dr. Schultz opened a combination tavern and pharmacy, asking drinkers to pay but offering free medical treatment, including home calls, to patients. Each small town soon acquired a general store or a drugstore that also carried patent medicines and herbs purchased from local growers. When domestic remedies failed, people consulted their local chemist. The pills that Rosa took in 1896 to abort her pregnancy probably came from the local drugstore Pratt and Company, which throughout that year advertised pills, potions, and cure-alls. Pratt's touted pills with this jingle: "A little ill, then a little pill. The ill is gone the pill has won." Pratt and Company was located next to the village doctor's office.[42]

Dr. Barber, who ran a pharmacy in Marathon City, was typical of the country doctors who still practiced in the early-twentieth-century rural north. Helen D. Hering wrote in her memoirs fifty years later of Dr. Barber: "A combination doctor, do-it-your-self druggist, zoologist, politician, and all-around good friend." Barber was formally trained in medicine at the University of Illinois and at Kansas City Medical College; he interned at the Kansas City hospital and in Niles, Michigan, and practiced at Winona in Minnesota and at Galesville, Chili, and Greenwood in Wisconsin before settling with his wife and daughter in Marathon City in 1906. His daughter, Mildred, who as a child often accompanied him on cases, remembered him taking chickens, rabbits, and eggs in payment and often giving flour to poorer patients.[43]

These country doctors provided much-needed medical care in the northern counties. Dr. Thomas G. Torpey and Dr. Huber worked in Minocqua, just east of Lac du Flambeau. Both began practicing in the 1890s and were known as "timberland doctors" who treated lumberjacks. Like Barber, they took what patients could offer in the way of payment—cordwood, meat, or garden vegetables—and transported patients to hospitals in Tomahawk or Rhinelander only when they could not achieve home cures. Kate Pelham Newcomb, herself a country doctor in the 1930s, eloquently described the hardships they faced as they went out in the severest weather to try to reach patients. She offered her respect for their skills despite their gruff demeanor and rough appearance. As one account said of Dr. Torpey, he served lumberjacks, settlers, tourists at resorts, and Native people and never charged unless they asked, then set a price he thought they could pay, and "never killed them."[44]

The number of doctors in Wisconsin gradually increased during the late nineteenth century, both in towns and in rural areas. After 1908, when state registration of physicians began, their numbers rose slowly, climbing from 1,681 to 2,896 over the next two decades. During that time the doctor-to-patient ratio in rural areas declined, from 1/1,051 to 1/1,235 between 1910 and 1920 alone. The percentage of rural villages with populations under 1,500 that had two physicians dropped from 32 to 17 percent. Doctors who treated rural patients tended to locate in larger towns.[45]

Rural people were not unusually healthy, just of necessity more self-sufficient in terms of health care because they had fewer physicians available to care for them. Death rates, disability days, and work days lost to illness seemed to be the same whether a person lived in city or country. Women tended to most farm accidents at home without the aid of trained doctors. They treated inquisitive children who, left unattended for a moment, suffered serious burns from boiling soups and water, doctored lacerations on the hands or feet of children and adults, cleansed wounds, splinted broken bones, and used home herbal and commercial remedies. They could not repair fractured skulls with herbs or splints. Nor could they mend internal injuries, especially blows to the stomach, which might perforate the digestive tube or colon, leading to peritonitis and swift death. There was no way Matilda could heal her husband after he received that kick to the stomach. It is amazing that she and other women did so well at healing their family members and neighbors with so few medicine people to help them.

THE MIDWIFE'S DOMAIN

"We have invaded the domain of the midwife in this pioneer land," Children's Bureau field worker Dr. Florence Sherbon wrote from Marathon County in July 1916. Sherbon was in this northern county because the state of Wisconsin had asked the U.S. Children's Bureau to help analyze maternal and infant mortality rates. Bureau officials decided to sample two counties: one in an established farming area in the southern part of the state where the predominantly native-born people employed only doctors for birthing; the second in north-central Wisconsin, in an area recently settled, where midwives attended a large number of births.[46]

The state medical society had lobbied for almost a decade for the law that required registration of Wisconsin midwives. The 1907 law mandated that all new midwives take an exam in English and offer evidence of practical training in a recognized school. A midwife could apply for an exemption certificate that allowed her to practice as long as she conducted herself "reputably." It was also lawful for anyone to provide free emergency service if a physician or registered midwife could not be secured, and in some cases these unregistered persons might even charge for services. Because the law was ambiguous and because it made no provision for the supervision of midwives, enforcement proved impossible. The state board of medical examiners, established under the medical practices law of 1897 to register physicians and charged with administering the new midwife registration act, did little more than keep registration files. Only three hundred had registered in the entire state by the end of 1910, most of them in Milwaukee. By 1917 the number of registered midwives in Wisconsin had declined to fewer than eighty. The attorney for the state board of medical examiners admitted that many more practiced midwifery than had registered.[47]

During the decade from 1907 to 1917, only sixteen midwives from four north-central counties registered with the state. Lincoln and Clark counties each had four, Taylor County had three, and Marathon County had five. In making their survey in Marathon County in 1916, the Children's Bureau agents concluded that there was no enforcement of midwife registration in rural areas and no supervision of midwives who were in practice. Most midwives were of foreign birth, in their fifties and sixties, and unable to pass a written examination in English. Hence, most had not even attempted to register with the state. Although professionally trained doctors recognized the need for these country midwives, they were often not supportive of their work. Physicians were engaged in a struggle to define themselves as professionals and to make their professions pay a living wage. Most opposed the training of midwives and any system that envisioned a permanent role for them. In some counties, physicians' opposition to midwives and insistence on registration undoubtedly accounted for the phasing out of all midwives.

Lincoln County is a case in point. During 1897–98, midwives birthed the majority of children in the county. By 1900 the numbers had dropped to fewer than 25 percent. Almost thirty midwives reported births in county records between 1903 and 1905. Ellen Stiefrater, who registered as a midwife in 1909, birthed more than seven hundred babies in her eighteen years at Merrill, almost a third of them between 1897 and 1907. She, along with three other midwives, registered between 1907 and 1910. By 1916, however, Stiefrater and the other midwives were gone, and they had not been replaced.[48]

Lincoln had a growing number of physicians during these years, many of whom had graduated from respected colleges in the United States and Europe. Concern about upholding the dignity of the medical profession and collecting fees brought them together to form the Lincoln County Medical Society in 1903. During the next decade, the society set fees the members should charge, listed patients who were delinquent in paying those fees, and began a campaign to stop midwives and other non-physicians from practicing medicine. Lumbering had furnished a large number of patients, single men with a variety of industry-related injuries, but as lumbering declined doctors turned to alternative sources, including obstetrics, to maintain their incomes. Country doctors continued to practice in Lincoln County and to receive whatever country people could pay, but in Lincoln as elsewhere, the search for higher incomes led many doctors to abandon rural areas at the same time that they opposed midwives practicing there.[49]

Taylor County had four midwives registered. One was Adelaine Guse, who registered in 1909 and reported her occupation as "midwife" to the 1910 census taker. Adelaine came from Germany to the United States in 1884 and two years later began birthing babies. In 1896 she registered the births of fifty-four babies, averaging about one a week. By 1904 she estimated she had birthed about five hundred infants. During the next five years she birthed another five hundred. Meanwhile, as her business grew, she took time to attend the Milwaukee School of Midwifery in 1898 and received her diploma. She returned to the school in 1907 for a second diploma and probably at that time interned for six months in a hospital. By 1909 she was competent, well trained, and experienced. But there were many other midwives in Taylor County who never registered at all. In fact, Children's Bureau field workers believed that Taylor County had the highest number of practicing midwives of any of the four counties.[50]

Clark County also had four midwives registered. Yet according to local reputation, the best-known midwife in this county was Louisa Braun Horn, who never registered. Louisa migrated to the United States in 1871 when she was sixteen and five years later married Frank Horn. She bore seven children of her own and helped birth uncounted others. The Colby Historical Society, which preserved her satchel in its collection, called her a renowned midwife who practiced in the 1890s and early 1900s. She is listed on the 1910 census not as a midwife but as a laborer on the family farm.[51]

Children's Bureau officials decided to analyze Marathon County as a midwife test case. Marathon did not have the highest number of midwives—a number of counties had more—but it had high rates of maternal and infant mortality and a large number of immigrant midwives concentrated in several distinct townships. It was much simpler to survey there than in other counties where midwives and families were more diverse. During 1914 and 1915, rural midwives had registered only 383 or 16 percent of the births in Marathon

County, but in two predominantly German townships the percentage was 36, and in two villages it was 79. In one Polish township, midwives reported 86 percent of the births. Sherbon and her coworker Elizabeth Moore knew that, although these midwives were well regarded in their communities, few were registered to practice. Only five midwives registered in Marathon County between 1907 and 1916.[52]

Whether registered or not, reporting of births was haphazard at best. By state law, all births were to be registered within seven days. Field agents found one midwife did not even have the necessary forms. Others said they did not fill out registration forms themselves because they were unable to read and write English. Even those country midwives registered and literate in English found it impractical to promptly register births, which came at unexpected intervals. Agents found one midwife who did make the effort to register births once a month, another who had her daughter-in-law fill out and file the forms, and a third who asked the local doctor to handle her registrations, though he seldom did. Most of the neighborhood midwives simply asked the father to fill in the forms and register the births. In one community the minister filed the birth certificates once a year.[53]

As pay, most midwives took whatever the families could give. What the families usually offered turned out to be from one to five dollars. This "donation" often covered staying with the mother for a full day, cleaning the house, and caring for the family. In this way, the family could avoid the costs of doctors and hired help while the mother was recovering. Most women worked right up to the time of labor and, despite the efforts of physicians and nurses to keep them in bed for nine days after delivering, usually resumed work after three days. With a midwife who stayed at least one day and cleaned up before and after the birth, a family might get by with only kin and neighborhood help. Agents found a number of foreign-born midwives exemplary in training and practice. Midwives told vivid stories in 1916 about their practice and about the incredibly hard work it took to survive on this northern frontier.[54]

Polish midwife Andred Podgorski, forty-three, had practiced for fourteen years. This small, gnarled woman who weighed less than one hundred pounds had birthed thirty babies in 1915. Andred recounted a harrowing story of her early life. Orphaned at eight, she had no education, never went to school, and could not read or write. "Has never known anything but the most grinding toil," the agent jotted on her interview sheet. Andred had worked with families for her room and board and then supported herself with full-time work. Her grandmother and mother-in-law were both midwives, and she learned from them. When she had arrived in Ohio from Poland fourteen years earlier, she helped a physician with obstetric cases. Flooded out of her Dayton home, she and her family moved to Chicago and then in 1912 purchased twenty acres of stump land for six hundred dollars. She had birthed her own thirteen children without help, delivering them, tying the cord, bathing them, and then, on principle, returning to bed. Twelve of the children were still alive and healthy, but times were hard for her. Her husband, who had to work in the paper mill on arriving in Marathon County, had been severely injured, received no compensation, and could not work. Andred now worked outside with animals, garden, and crops and birthed all the babies within five miles. The unfinished tarpapered house in which she lived was difficult to keep clean, but Andred was careful to wear a big apron, wash her hands with soap and a brush, and use carbolic acid. She reported no stillbirths and no mothers' deaths, and her four infant deaths were not related to obstetrics.

Andred Podgorski, Polish midwife, 1916. Field agent Dr. Florence Sherbon hired a professional to take this photograph of Andred in front of her pioneer home in Mosinee. Like other frontier midwives, Andred cared for her own children, worked outdoors, and birthed her neighbors' babies.

German midwife Anelie Kettle, sixty-five, had experienced much the same conditions. The interviewer reported her as stout and stocky, with a strong-featured, bronzed, weatherbeaten face, someone who "moved with wonderful celerity and efficiency, and surprising energy and dynamism." Anelie spoke no English but could read and write and had received some training in Germany from the midwife who had attended the births of her three children. The twenty-four-year-old Anelie came to the United States with only her experience and a German book on midwifery. Her family said she once had a license, but there was no record of any in Madison, and she was reluctant to talk to the agent because she feared she would be charged with unlawful practice. Her daughter explained that Anelie was careful to wash her hands in the family basin and that, while she carried only cloth tape to tie off the cord, she called the doctor if anything did not seem right. "For forty years this woman had been the main dependence and main stay of the women of this sturdy pioneer community," the agent wrote, with no infant or maternal deaths and only one stillbirth in the last two years. Anelie's ability to perform physical labor also impressed the agent. The family had chickens and cows, which she still helped tend. Each year she put up large quantities of wild raspberries, wild strawberries, plums, blueberries, blackberries, and gooseberries. The family seemed prosperous and had a good house and barn. Shrubbery and flowers flourished in the yard. Outside Anelie wore a clean cotton jacket, dark skirt, and sabots. Inside she went barefoot, in a light-colored waist, cut off at the elbows and open at the throat, with a short, full skirt. Anelie seemed to the agent an amazing woman, the model of the pioneer midwife.

Midwives such as these provided more than mutual aid. Local records and those of the Children's Bureau show that midwives continued to practice in large numbers well into the twentieth century in north-central Wisconsin. While few registered, many unregistered women practiced in isolated areas, most with assistance from doctors only in emergencies. Midwives who located in towns and developed professional practices had large numbers of rural patients and birthed hundreds of children.[55]

Doctors seemed convinced that rural people could afford to hire their services but were too miserly to do so. One doctor wrote to the Children's Bureau in 1918 that the farming community simply did not want to pay for the extra services of a visit by the doctor and a doctor would not make calls if he was not paid. Nor were settlers willing to employ a trained nurse; instead, they hired a practical nurse at the time of birthing. Agents learned from their research that doctors were charging $20 to $22 for a confinement visit, more cash than most families could afford. Moreover, most people lived twelve to fifteen miles from a doctor and five to eight miles from a telephone. Even in good weather, it could take two to three hours to reach a rural family after a doctor was contacted.

"What are we to do—the baby will not wait for the doctor to come," one woman told a Children's Bureau field agent. Some families did call doctors, knowing they would probably not arrive in time to offer assistance. One family called the doctor in desperation when a baby started bleeding: fifteen hours later the physician arrived, just in time to watch the child die.[56]

Agents found that most Marathon County doctors lived in the city of Wausau and that many townships and small towns had few or no doctors. Of the areas surveyed by agents in detail, three townships and one village had no physicians at all, although one Wausau doctor did make a five-mile trip to one of them twice a week to hold office hours. Two more townships and two villages had one doctor each. When the number of rural doctors declined after 1900, there simply were not enough to serve the rural population at any price.

Despite the absence of doctors in Marathon County, the infant and maternal mortality rates there were low compared to the county studied in southern Wisconsin, where, with an abundance of doctors, death rates for infants and mothers were much higher. The agents concluded that the availability of many experienced midwives in farming communities accounted for low mortality. Reformers hoped midwives might provide health care to rural women, at least temporarily. They lobbied hard for the Sheppard-Towner Act of 1921, which appropriated federal funds to promote welfare during maternity and infancy and to provide temporary training for midwives in rural areas. Congress refused to continue this work, however, and doctors, registered nurses, and hospitals would henceforth dominate the health-care system that provided for birthing women.[57]

THE NURSING SISTERHOODS

It was almost noon when I arrived in Broken Arrow, Oklahoma, and drove into the carefully tended grounds of the Sisters of the Sorrowful Mother convent. I had come in search of information on the nuns and the hospitals they staffed in north-central Wisconsin between 1890 and 1925. My mind was full of memories of my mother's last hours in 1953, when nurses in coifs and white aprons had crowded around to care for her final physical and spiritual needs. They prayed as her breath became more labored and finally ceased. Later, as I researched health care in northern Wisconsin, I was reminded of those last hours when I read a description, also from the 1950s, of the small Sacred Heart Hospital in Tomahawk, founded in 1893 by the Sisters of the Sorrowful Mother. The sisters moved deftly about in their starched white muslin wimples and coifs and long white hospital gowns, over floors waxed and polished to a mirrorlike gloss, through corridors of dark woodwork and scrupulously clean painted walls, amid the scents of beeswax and incense. This image sent me on a search for written records. The motherhouse had moved from Milwaukee to just outside Tulsa, a short detour on my annual research trip from New Mexico to Wisconsin.

The archivist welcomed me, introduced me to nuns as we ate lunch in the cafeteria, and then led me to their records to the basement. There I found oral accounts by the nuns collected in the 1930s; histories of the order and its founder, German-born Mother Frances Streitel; and photographs of its hospitals established in Tomahawk, Rhinelander, and Marshfield.

Sisters had been in the business of nursing and running hospitals in the United States for more than seventy years when they began opening care centers in northern Wisconsin. Before the Civil War, Catholic sisters opened approximately twenty-five hospitals. Despite strong anti-Catholic bias within the country and the military—Dorothy Dix, superintendent of Union Army female nurses, was resolutely anti-Catholic and anti-immigrant—the government called on 617 sisters from twenty-one different communities to help care for sick and injured soldiers. Eventually, Catholic nuns accounted for one-fifth of all Civil War women nurses. Many of these women had hospital nursing experience, and most of them were daughters of immigrants. Veteran nurses of the Sisters of the Holy Cross established nursing schools after the Civil War, while the Sisters of St. Joseph of Carondelet (CSJ) went west, establishing St. Joseph's Hospital in Denver in 1880. The CSJs cared for yellow fever victims in Memphis in 1879 and, during the 1880s, established a Menominee Hospital at Keshena in the wake of a measles epidemic. These early ventures eventually became part of ambitious plans by a number of Catholic sisterhoods to build and staff hospitals across the country. For thirty years, nursing orders engaged in almost constant hospital building, as first one town and then another vied for their services. By 1920 an estimated half of all patients in the United States were being treated by these sisterhoods in "sisters' hospitals." The sisterhoods were already running 40 percent of all hospitals in Wisconsin by 1900. In northern Wisconsin, settlers and Native peoples alike depended on the Sisters of St. Joseph and the Sisters of the Sorrowful Mother for care in a string of hospitals.[58]

Before the sisters established their facilities, few public or private hospitals existed in north-central Wisconsin. Physicians cared for patients at their home or in the doctor's own home-office. People in isolated areas depended upon whatever lay health care they could find locally. In the late nineteenth century, lumber companies established a privately funded system of health-care insurance, similar to later HMOs, to care for their employees. The system flourished in the late 1880s and early 1890s as competing hospital organizations attempted to attract physicians to northern cities to establish and staff these "ticket hospitals." The American Hospital Aid Association (AHAA) operated hospitals in

Eau Claire, where it was headquartered; in Rhinelander; and in several other cities, including Wausau.

In this system, lumber companies sold insurance tickets to timber workers for five to ten dollars a year and deducted that amount from their wages. The fees went to the AHAA, and the workers received a ticket. The AHAA reimbursed doctors for services rendered to the injured or sick worker. A ticket certificate from the Riverside Hospital in Wausau dated 1899 is preserved in the Marathon County Historical Society.[59]

The health insurance covered only the worker, of course, not his family. But the existence of these hospitals brought a number of well-trained doctors and nurses into northern towns. Most of these early hospitals were crude, merely boarding houses with a dozen beds or cots. Nuns at Rhinelander and Tomahawk operated their early hospitals in much the same way. At Tomahawk, nuns went into camps themselves the first year to solicit commitments from lumbermen and later depended upon agents to sell their health insurance. Until 1910, when lumbering declined in these areas, the majority of the nuns' patients were lumbermen.[60]

These early health-care systems might have evolved into more widespread managed care. Fraternal organizations, pioneers in life insurance, attempted to develop health insurance similar to loggers' health-care plans in Marathon County. Organizations there encountered vehement opposition from members of the newly formed county medical society. In 1905 its members agreed not to work for "any society, organization, or corporate body" and to work only on an individual fee-for-service basis. Later that year the society voiced its opposition to "a certain organization more or less permanent in our community" that had offered fixed-price service for entire families who agreed to use only the organization's physicians. The medical society damned such practice, which it called "Club Practice," as a European import below the dignity of any self-respecting physician. "To place himself at the beck and call of every member of an organization for a certain fixed price, regardless of the amount of service rendered," one resolution read, "[would] strike a blow at the future high standing of our profession." The society repeated the resolution in 1910, including municipalities, clubs, and lodges such as Eagles, Owls, or Moose. They threatened to bar from membership any doctors who provided such service and to refuse to recognize them professionally. They also opposed the establishment of a county hospital in 1904. In the 1890s the nuns managed to avoid opposition from doctors by allowing them to use the hospitals for their patients. Eventually the nuns established well-equipped operating rooms so doctors could perform procedures there rather than at home.[61]

The nuns literally built their hospitals from the ground up. The four nuns who arrived at Tomahawk in 1892 had twenty-five dollars in cash, just enough

Sacred Heart Hospital, Tomahawk. Established by the Sisters of the Sorrowful Mother in a small house in 1893, the hospital grew rapidly into an imposing three-story brick building by 1908. Sisters added a smaller two-story isolation unit in 1910. Their hospitals at Rhinelander and Marshfield underwent similar growth during these years.

to pay for a month's rent and to buy beds and blankets, toweling, and a red tablecloth. Their first rented house was an old saloon with two back rooms where snow filtered in over the beds of patients and bedbugs bedeviled them. After a few months the nuns were able to rent a better house, and they soon began to travel to the lumber camps, bringing cough medicine and quinine pills and soliciting subscriptions from the "woodboys." Sister M. Dhyonisia recalled how polite the men were, how the foreman gave them his separate quarters in which to spend the night, and how he urged the men to subscribe and to donate as well. Signing his name at the head of the pledge sheet, the foreman went to each man, asking, "How much for you?" In the spring the foreman withheld the sums from the men's paychecks and brought the money to the nuns. The nuns remembered how the men came infested with lice, which they battled with boiling water and disinfectant. A sister remembered being paid by one family with a fine young Jersey cow for her nursing in a private home. Tickets and donations enabled the nuns to build their first hospital in 1904. The women of Tomahawk donated food for a feast to celebrate the hospital's opening and helped raffle off a doll to raise cash.[62]

The nuns doubted the benefit of nurses' training at first, but the sisters' hospitals soon established their own training schools. Protestants, who sometimes refused to go to Catholic hospitals, found them the best run in the area, and gradually they became popular. Sometimes both patients and doctors complained about the restrictive Catholic ideals by which the nuns ran the hospitals, but there were few alternatives until 1916, when a movement to establish nonsectarian institutions began. It would herald the end of the sisters' hospitals' practical monopoly, but nuns continued to provide the best-available hospitals for many rural settler families.[63]

Many of the nuns who staffed these sisters' hospitals were foreign-born; their lack of English skills barred them from teaching. In Wausau, where the Sisters of St. Joseph built and staffed St. Mary's Hospital in 1908, we have a fairly good portrait of these women from the 1910 census and their declarations of intention to become citizens, made in 1917 before the circuit clerk. Only three of the twenty-four nuns were born in Wisconsin, and the parents of those three had been born in Europe. The foreign-born nuns, most from Bavaria, arrived in the United States between 1900 and 1909. Their average age in 1910 was thirty-one, although two were in their early forties and the youngest only twenty. Some had come directly from Germany; others via Rome and the motherhouse.[64]

The nuns' hospital remained the primary one in the region. In 1908 Marathon County opened a hospital next to the asylum and poorhouse, but it took only contagious cases and served as a maternity and general hospital for the poor. The privately supported Wausau Children's Infirmary, started in 1910, had only two beds and one nurse and was also used as a juvenile detention home for county cases. When the nurse had no patients at the infirmary, she worked outside among poor women. A number of doctors maintained small hospitals, primarily for their own patients.[65]

Nuns also staffed a number of government hospitals for Native communities. Among those for whom the government provided health care were the Menominee; missionaries and government collaborated on their care beginning in 1886. Missionaries reported an alarming death rate among the Menominee in 1885. Father Zephyrin wrote to Bishop Krardbauer in April of that year, "The death rate this spring in the Reserve is frightful." In the previous four months, in addition to five who had died at the mission school, thirty Catholic Natives died, three-fourths of the victims under twelve years old. During a ten-month period in 1885, out of a total population of one thousand Menominee Catholics, 39 babies were born while 74 people died, nearly eight percent of the entire Catholic population. The resident government agent was alarmed, too. He offered to build a hospital for the Native community and to pay the Sisters of St. Joseph six hundred dollars a year to staff and operate it. The health situation had not been this bad since the smallpox epidemics of the 1860s.[66]

The hospital was ready for patients in January 1886, when Sister Mary Clarissa Walsh, who had nursed the children during a previous measles epidemic, took over administration and became the hospital's main nurse. Born in Tipperary, Ireland, in 1848, Sister Clarissa entered the motherhouse from Peoria, Illinois, in 1869, took her vows in 1872, taught schools in Tennessee, and nursed in the West for eleven years before transferring to Keshena in October 1883. Sister Clarissa worked at the hospital for nine years, asking to be relieved of her nursing duties in 1892.[67]

That year the government completed a new hospital for the Menominee at Keshena and the Sisters of St. Joseph put German-born Sister Mary Augustine Meeman in charge. Sister Augustine remained administrator of the hospital for thirteen years, until her death in 1905 at age sixty-seven. The order reported simply that at Keshena Sister Augustine's "opportunities for self-renunciation and heroic charity were many." The hospital served as a multipurpose institution, admitting the sick, the seriously diseased, and elders unable to care for themselves. In 1910 it listed seven patients. During these years, health conditions stabilized and the population increased. The sisters themselves ended their work at Keshena in 1913, when the government, which had built and maintained the nuns' hospital, attempted to bring the sisters under its control.[68]

After the nuns left, the government expanded the Keshena hospital and built a second one at Neopit in 1920. Women preferred to birth their babies at the agency hospital at Keshena because it was, some said, free and better and because it had both a nurse and a physician. The Neopit hospital primarily served the lumber mill families; most of its patients had been injured in mill accidents. It was operated like the earlier "ticket" hospitals, with the government withholding seventy-five cents each month from employees' pay and charging patients $2.50 per day during use of the hospital. At Neopit the government hired a well-trained nurse and later appointed a physician as well. The Menominee now had better medical facilities and care than most settler communities.[69]

The ad-hoc combination of health-care practices in which formally and informally trained people assisted women and their families functioned in these communities well into the twentieth century, long after health-care reformers had discovered that the majority of the rural population might need something more. These reforms, a result of the Country Life and the urban Progressive movements, prescribed health-care policies for the rural population. The story of how public health reforms developed and were implemented begins with Florence Brown Sherbon, who left a detailed account of rural women's health care in a series of letters and reports from Marathon County in 1916.

Public Health Reforms
Florence's Story [Brown, Sherbon, born in Iowa, 1869–1944]

She signed her name Florence Brown Sherbon, MD, on the report for the Children's Bureau of the Department of Labor. Florence coauthored the rural child welfare study with Elizabeth Moore under the title *Maternity and Infant Care in Two Rural Counties in Wisconsin*. Unnamed in the report were the two rural counties: Iowa County, in the older, established southwestern part of the state, and Marathon County, in the more recently settled northern area. In 1916 Florence spent three months in Marathon County as a field agent, collecting information on health conditions for the study.

As I sat in the National Archives reading the letters Florence sent from Marathon County back to the Children's Bureau, she emerged as a reformer dedicated to women's health, learning from rural women and midwives how they lived and what they needed. Those letters, written while Florence was deciding how to transform her life into one dedicated to women's health needs, form the basis of the story that follows. The letters reminded me of my own reaction to farm women when I was living in a farming community in southern Colorado in the 1970s. I, too, was impressed by the physical and mental strength of these rural women, their endurance, their willingness to work through seemingly insurmountable tasks. Because of these encounters, I had chosen rural women as the main focus of my research, and I persisted in writing about them when it would have been much easier to write about urban women, many of whom left rich and full accounts of their lives.

Florence, I realized, had begun to see her own life through the eyes of the women she interviewed and watched during those three months in northern Wisconsin. The letters from 1916 bridged the two parts of her life, joining her birth on an Iowa farm to her death in Lawrence, Kansas, at the age of seventy-five, a respected professor who had taught and published on the health of the family.

Florence was born in Iowa in 1869, graduated from the University of Iowa, and received nurse's training at the Iowa State Hospital. She stayed on after graduating to supervise nurses before moving up to superintendent of the hospital. She returned to school and received her MD in 1904. Shortly after graduating, she married a classmate, and they owned and managed a sanatorium in Iowa for the next twelve years. During this time, Florence bore twin daughters and then her marriage dissolved, something neither she nor her biographers explain. By January 1916 she was working for the Children's Bureau as a field investigator. That summer she left her daughters with her mother in Chicago and traveled north to Marathon County to begin fieldwork. She was forty-seven.

While Florence was in Marathon County, Congress advised the Children's Bureau that there would be no increase in its appropriation for the next year. Florence could complete the project, but then her contract would terminate. At the end of summer Florence wrote up the notes for the Wisconsin study and began to look for another position. The following summer, she took a job

Florence Sherbon. After reporting on the health-care practices of women in Marathon County in 1916, Dr. Sherbon devoted the rest of her life to studying, teaching, and writing about ways to improve family and child care. She posed for this photograph with her cat at home, near the University of Kansas in Lawrence. She died in 1944 at seventy-five, five days after retiring from teaching.

in Kansas as temporary chief of child health for the Board of Health, but she stayed on for two years. Asked to teach a course on home nursing for the University of Kansas Home Economics Department, she soon became a full-time member of the department. Over the next twenty-five years she worked part-time for the state, taught and published articles and books on family health care, and became a well-known authority in the field. Meanwhile, she saw her daughters through the university, cared for her ailing mother, and retired at seventy-five, only five days before her death.[70]

Letters in the Children's Bureau explain the importance of the summer of 1916 to Florence and to our understanding of the health of Marathon County's farm women. Three agencies supported the study: the Wisconsin State Board of Health, the Wisconsin Agricultural Extension Service, and the newly formed Children's Bureau in the U.S. Department of Labor. After considerable discussion, officials from the three agencies chose Marathon County as one of the two counties to be studied and selected Dr. Sherbon to conduct the interviews.[71]

Florence was in Wisconsin by early July, and her most detailed letters to the Children's Bureau begin in mid-month. She was somewhere outside the city when she scrawled "Wausau" at the head of her July 14, 1916, letter. She sat on a log in the shade, swatting at clouds of mosquitoes. Across the road was a patch of virgin forest. She had just returned with her fellow field worker, Elizabeth Moore, from a trip out into the country, with "a big burly Irish mail carrier" as their chauffeur. Florence watched a young German couple putting away hay. She wrote:

The babies [2 and 3 years old] sit quietly and cheerfully by and watch while the stacker puts away the hay in the big mow. The woman, barefooted[,] manages the big farm team as it goes back and forth pulling up the huge fork-fulls of hay.... Since I started this letter they have gone into the house and hastily eaten something (4 P.M.). (I could hear that their mouths were full as they yelled at the team which became restless with the mosquitoes). Now they have driven off for another load, the woman sitting in the big hay rack, with both babies beside her each with a chunk of bread in his fist. They must have swallowed their own whole.... She grips the ground... [with her bare feet] when she walks and has a long, lithe, springy tread which would delight an athletic director. Her arms are lean and supple and some of her movements as she swings around the heavy double-tree and turns the big team make me think of the maneuvers of a woman in a cobra dance I once saw.

Florence went on to tell about another mother she visited. Although current health practices called for women to rest before giving birth and for at least a week after, this mother had washed in the morning, gone to the woods to boil maple syrup in the afternoon, and given birth that night. On the third day after giving birth, she set bread to rise; on the fourth, she swept the house. Florence wrote, "Mother says she feels perfectly well, and whole family seem happy.... It's awfully disconcerting to have ones preconceived ideas get such jolts. I am not nearly so sure about some things as I used to be!" Physical activity did not seem to harm the mothers.[72]

The next day Florence wrote to another bureau colleague about the roads. They were like a boulevard passing through stretches of magnificent woods for five or six miles, then became new and rough, then almost impassible. In fact, they proved impassible, and the ancient rented Ford gave out. When the chauffeur could not get it started, they hailed a farmer, who stopped haying to take them back to town. Florence was still mulling over the strength exhibited by the country women:

[I] believe we will find the balance in favor of the country woman. I am constantly surprised at the physical vigor and endurance they exhibit.... We find these families, many of them, living under conditions not dissimilar to 'summer cottage' life, which we all find so reconstructive when followed for even a few weeks. We will row, tramp, and work out generally under strenuous conditions and get a new lease on life. I see no logical reason why the same life the year round with substitution of the hay field and the potato patch for the row boat and the "hike" may not be a fine thing for the human stock.... The families feed their growing children with mighty little fuss about it and they do surprisingly well.[73]

The following month Florence went into midwives' homes (her interviews are the basis for the section "The Midwife's Domain"). By September she had

completed her interviews and was planning to go to her sister's apartment in
Iowa City, where her mother would join her with the twins and she would
write her report. She wrote, "Miss Moore and I have certainly had a glorious
summer together, it has been quite revolutionary for me physically and I seem
to have a new attitude toward life in general." Finally, she wrote from Iowa City
that she was glad to be back with her kiddies but missed her "pal" Elizabeth,
with whom she had shared the fieldwork in Marathon County.[74]

The highly urban professional health-care reformer expected to find demoralized, degraded rural women. Instead, she was struck by their vitality and
energy. And ever after she had the image of the rhythmic movements of women
at work haying and turning the wagon team to remind her of what women
were capable of physically. Because of Florence's enthusiastic work, we know
much about the health care of women in northern Wisconsin.

PUBLIC HEALTH OFFICIALS

When Sherbon and Moore arrived in Marathon County in 1916 to study the
health of women and children, the first thing they evaluated was the enforcement of public health rules. In 1916, Wisconsin's public health system was
barely forty years old. It consisted of a state supervisory board, local health
boards, and a sanitary code, established with the support of physicians. On
their recommendation, Wisconsin had followed the precedent of Minnesota
and Michigan, establishing in 1876 a state Council on Health to investigate disease, especially epidemics, advise local boards, and make general rules, known
as a sanitary code. The state council only recommended establishment of local
boards of health, which were to act as registrars of vital statistics and have
exclusive jurisdiction to remove the causes of filth and disease. In creating a
sanitary code the council depended primarily on precedent in Great Britain
and in eastern states, but state officials insisted that the council have very limited powers. Attorney general O. W. Wright wrote to the physician who prepared the sanitary code that the cornerstone of the whole structure was to be
Jefferson's republican limitation on personal liberty expressed in the phrase,
"To keep men from injuring one another."[75]

Local officials often believed public health measures unnecessary and state
policy an intrusion on local authority. The sanitary code recommended that
local boards establish rules to maintain public health. These regulations
included quarantine against smallpox, disposal of dead animals and human
excrement, control of diseased animals, and inspection for unclean food and
water and inadequate housing. Many towns ignored the recommendations.
Observers reported that the town of Marshfield, for example, had filthy privies
and streets in the early 1880s. In 1883 the state council ordered every town, village, and city to establish a board of health but left implementation of that

order to local officials. Urban death rates did decline in the last years of the nineteenth century, but rural public health varied depending on how well or poorly local officials applied the state board's suggestions.[76]

The so-called "Asiatic" cholera scare of 1892 brought increased support for a state authority to control public health. The disease never spread to Wisconsin, but lingering fear allowed the state board to expand its power over the spread of other infectious diseases, especially smallpox, to order compulsory vaccination for attendance in any school, and to recommend that employers order their employees to be vaccinated. Once the scare had passed, however, opponents of "state meddling" challenged these rulings in the state supreme court, which held them "unreasonable and extraordinary." The state board backed off, advising local boards to be sure of the menace to citizens before taking any radical action. When five Wausau physicians petitioned the board to remove a health officer for incompetence, it refused to intervene. Even after the turn of the century, public health policy hardly existed in north-central Wisconsin.[77]

Sherbon and Moore considered Marathon County's local boards totally inadequate to maintain public health. About half of the local health officials were physicians in the ten townships they studied, the usual proportion in the state. The county paid these men either a nominal fee of about ten dollars a year or by the job. But both farmer and physician conceived of their main job as posting and removing quarantine notices and fumigating homes after cases of scarlet fever, diphtheria, and smallpox but not after measles, whooping cough, or tuberculosis. Whooping cough and measles cases were never isolated although both killed infants, whooping cough eight times more frequently than diphtheria. Local health officers did not inspect the water and milk supply or food handling at camps and infirmaries. Only one board had ever investigated a complaint about unsanitary conditions, in a local dairy.[78]

Doctors did not report births, deaths, or the occurrence of disease. Marathon and Elderon townships, for example, kept no local records of births and deaths at all. In Kronenwetter the clerk's records were so disorderly that Sherbon and Moore could not tell anything about the health condition of the township. In Hull township the clerk admitted that reports on births and deaths were incomplete and that he did not try to get complete records. "If you press that kind of thing, you get in bad with your neighbors," he told the agent. Nor did doctors report to health officers occurrences that required placards and fumigation. Physicians seldom reported measles, whooping cough, or epidemics of scarlet fever and diphtheria. In some neighborhoods where physicians reported no cases of these diseases, mothers told agents that practically all the children had them at one time. Many families simply did not call doctors; therefore, no matter how contagious the illness, it was not reported.[79]

According to law, the boards of health were to meet every month to assess the condition of public health. Sherbon and Moore found that none met monthly, a few met once each fall after the election to appoint the health officer, and some never met, taking care of business through informal contacts, as was often done in rural areas. The two women concluded that town officials certainly could not be depended upon to reduce maternal and infant mortality rates.

SAVE THE BABIES

Sherbon and Moore's visit was the result of a focused campaign by Wisconsin reformers to reduce maternal and infant mortality rates. The Extension Division of the University of Wisconsin in Madison was the first agency to respond to the call to improve the health of women and children in rural areas. In 1915 it created three correspondence courses on the health of mothers and babies, conducted by a woman physician, and disseminated written material for women through the press, reaching an estimated 300,000 readers a week. The project was immensely successful in gaining the attention of urban women.[80]

The College of Agriculture soon joined in the project, using recently appropriated federal funds for improving rural life to send speakers into rural areas to discuss the health of mothers and babies. It dispatched Dr. Dorothy Mendenhall to speak in twenty small towns or villages. She followed her two-hour talks with informal discussions on care of mother, infant, and child and held free clinics for mothers and babies. Local clubwomen were then to sponsor follow-up weeklong clinics. Marathon County women organized their first Baby Week program in Wausau in 1915 and were planning a second in the spring of 1916.[81]

A Children's Bureau representative was in Madison arranging for a Marathon County survey at the time the 1916 Marathon Baby Week was being discussed. The local organizer, a "very energetic and able" woman according to the extension division, had already raised six hundred dollars for the clinic and expected the Baby Week to generate local support for the employment of two county nurses. The plan called for seven physicians, all specialists, to examine each child with an attending nurse. Sherbon, who planned to be in Wausau the week of the clinic, agreed to be one of the examining physicians.[82]

Sherbon took her place in the line of physicians and tried to be helpful, but at the end of the first day she wrote to the Children's Bureau of her frustration at the scene. Mothers were enthusiastic enough. They enrolled three hundred babies, but the local organizational structure was not capable of handling such a complicated and large program. The first morning only one elderly female physician, who seemed "arrogant," appeared, and in the afternoon only one male physician showed up. The second day several doctors arrived, but at

10:00 AM instead of the scheduled 9:00 AM. Some of the babies had to wait until afternoon without water. Sherbon called them "a mob of fretful tired babies," the whole scene "a disorderly mob." It was, she concluded, "too big an undertaking for the existing leadership." She thought it best if the Children's Bureau not become too closely identified with the Baby Week affair.[83]

After Sherbon and Moore completed their 1916 study, the Children's Bureau made one more attempt to improve the health of children in north-central Wisconsin. After the United States entered the European war in April 1917, the Children's Bureau reformulated arguments for child preservation. Children were a national resource, and activities on their behalf should be considered part of the patriotic war effort because a higher percentage of infants died each year on the home front than did young men fighting in the trenches. The bureau decided to hold a giant weigh-in throughout the country, mobilizing local groups of women to assemble corps of physicians and nurses to weigh and examine children. A poster sent out for the weighing campaign summed up the theory graphically. It showed a band of children of all nationalities trudging up a hill, their faces toward the sun. Overhead was the legend, "The Health of the Child is the Power of the Nation." The Woman's Division of the Wisconsin Council of National Defense folded the better babies program into its new wartime agenda, promising to mobilize the women it had organized in all parts of the state. From its headquarters in Madison, the Woman's Division began to organize local child welfare committees in north-central Wisconsin for the statewide weigh-in.[84]

The campaign started well in Lincoln County, which already had a public nurse, who helped the volunteers organize. In May 1918 physicians and nurses examined 2,246 children, about two-thirds of the 3,500 children under six years of age in the county. The volunteer committee completed the massive task at a cost of only $67.60 to the county.[85]

Work progressed more slowly in the other three counties. In Clark, where there were nearly five thousand children under six years of age, women managed to organize only a little more than half of the thirty-four townships. In Taylor County, where the men of the local Council of National Defense did not support the weigh-in, women weighed and measured only 1,330 children. Marathon County, the largest of the four, with the most children under six, did not even attempt to organize outside the major city of Wausau. Here, too, men of the county Council of National Defense did not support the initiative.[86]

Still, Wisconsin women, who mobilized with great enthusiasm, had a good deal of success. With 65 percent of all children under six weighed and measured, Wisconsin surpassed any other state. State organizers claimed that ten counties employed rural nurses as a result of the weigh-in, that some counties had even opened free baby clinics, and that many had launched campaigns for hot lunches in the schools.

The Health of the Child Is the Power of the Nation, 1918. Refusing to abandon their commitment to protect children's health despite U.S. entrance into the European war, reformers at the Children's Bureau and the Women's Committee of the Council of National Defense promoted the weighing and measurement of children nationwide in the spring and summer of 1918. Posters by well-known artists showed children as an important part of the nation's wealth.

POSTWAR PLANS

During World War I, the Wisconsin Women's Committee of the Council of National Defense developed an ambitious postwar plan to improve public health in all areas of Wisconsin. Leaders hoped to organize campaigns in every county to secure permanent agencies for the protection of the civilian population, especially ones that would reach out into rural districts. They envisioned not only county nurses but also full-time health officers, medical inspection of city and rural schools, clinics for cities and rural communities, TB sanatoriums with outpatient departments, and better cooperation in reporting and quarantining contagious diseases. The group supported an amendment to the 1913 nurse bill to make county public nurses mandatory as well as appropriation of funds to create a Bureau of Child Hygiene with a woman physician at its head. "Every county should have a County Nurse" became their rallying call. Meanwhile, women in the counties circulated petitions asking for county nurses. In La Crosse, they gathered six hundred signatures from rural women and, when the board voted down the request, publicly rebuked the men until they reconsidered and voted for the nurse. La Crosse women said they had worked for more than ten years to get this one nurse. Of the 140 public nurses employed in Wisconsin in 1917, more than half worked in Milwaukee and most of the rest in industries or schools or as general nurses. The Wisconsin Anti-Tuberculosis Association (WATA) funded three of the state's five county public nurses.

The influenza epidemic struck in fall 1918 with few public nurses in other counties. One public health officer called it "the greatest social and economic loss ever sustained in Wisconsin from a disease outbreak." More than 11,500 people in Wisconsin died from influenza during 1917–20. The only treatment was nursing care in the home. Everywhere, families were overwhelmed as, one after another, members came down with the virulent flu. Normally, family members nursed each other, but during the epidemic whole families were unable to supply that care and there were few public health providers to assist. Schools were closed, and some counties mobilized teachers to visit sick families, but elsewhere both settlers and Native people suffered because they simply lacked the care that trained visiting nurses might have provided.[87]

In 1919, following the influenza epidemic, Wisconsin revised its public nurse law and made county nurses mandatory. It also authorized a Bureau of Child Welfare and Public Health Nursing and appropriated five thousand dollars for its first year of operation. Dr. Mary P. Morgan, the bureau's first director, began with an ambitious program to follow up on the wartime children's year campaign. It emphasized improving and maintaining children's health by getting complete birth registration in the counties, promoting breast-feeding, establishing health study groups for mothers and young girls including nutrition classes to teach them how to care for underweight children, and encouraging communities to establish children's health centers. Dr. Morgan estimated that the appropriation for the first year was just enough to run the bureau and hire a field nurse to supervise the centers. Federal funds under the Sheppard-Towner Act would eventually be used to supplement the project. Under the new law, counties had to pay for their own nurses. Volunteer groups would have to raise money to run the centers.[88]

Morgan saw her primary task as reaching rural areas. A state survey of rural schoolchildren's health had revealed serious problems. Although conducted in a single county, officials expected that the survey represented rural areas as a whole. It showed more than half the schoolchildren had defective teeth, one-third had enlarged or diseased tonsils, and more than one-quarter had defective vision. Morgan's plan was to use the rural nurses to suggest ways in which the community could organize its health resources cooperatively. She planned to help community health councils establish health stations that could also be used as infant welfare clinics. Marathon and Clark were among the five counties designated to receive centers.[89]

Women's groups in the northern counties had not been very successful in their attempts to establish public health nursing in Taylor, Clark, and Marathon counties. There was considerable support among women's groups in Taylor County: the board appropriated money for a nurse in 1917 but offered so small a salary that the position stood vacant for several years. The board never really supported the program: it employed a nurse for only one year after it became mandatory in 1919 and discontinued the position when it became voluntary again in 1923. Women's groups used the war to argue for expanded public health in Clark County, managed to get the board to take up the question of hiring two county nurses, but failed to get its approval. Clark County also employed a nurse for only one year when it was mandatory. The women of the Marathon County Council of Defense worked out a plan to ask their board of supervisors to make a temporary appropriation for a demonstration of rural county nursing and then campaigned in November 1918 to make the appropriation permanent. WATA offered its support, issued a special report calling attention to rural conditions, and encouraged agitation for a county nurse. Marathon County employed two nurses from 1920 to 1923, but when the law became voluntary, it too cut the appropriation, reducing the number of nurses to one and then cutting her salary. Stationed in the town of Wausau, she could do little to help rural women.[90]

Lincoln County, meanwhile, had hired Theta Mead to be its first publicly funded nurse. Mead was exceptionally well trained. Born in 1878 near Grand Rapids, Michigan, she had graduated from Valparaiso University in Indiana and from St. Luke's Hospital Training School in Marquette, Michigan. She did postgraduate work in Boston and then took the eight-week WATA public health nursing course in Milwaukee. In addition, Mead had deep ties to the community. Her father was a planing mill operator who had moved to Minnesota in 1886 and from there to Lincoln County, where Mead joined the family in 1907 and worked as a private nurse. After taking the WATA nursing course, she returned to begin her job as Lincoln County nurse. Mead knew the people most concerned with community health and worked comfortably with them; likewise, the community gave her strong support. Mead kept a scrapbook of articles published by the *Merrill Daily Herald*, including one announcing her employment and explaining her duties. The article concluded, "She is ready to work for you and with you." The newspaper frequently reported her local talks, noted her trips to various areas in the county to help with epidemics, and published her advice to families on preventing the spread of disease. Other articles advised families to give their children milk instead of coffee for lunch, to get checkups by physicians before children began school, and to make sure their schoolrooms were safe. In 1917 Mead opened a First Aid and Rest Room at the county fair and exhibited her plans for winter work in Merrill and Tomahawk, gave a course on elementary hygiene and home care, and had consultation hours at the county supervisor's office each Saturday afternoon. The paper published her annual reports to the Lincoln County Board of Supervisors.

During her first year, Mead reported to the Lincoln County board that for her school work alone she traveled 1,460 miles by automobile and 710 miles by rail, examining 411 pupils and finding 607 physical defects. She had examined children in seventy-six rural schools and in all Merrill and Tomahawk city schools, both parochial and public. She then reported the defects to parents, gave medical attention to children when possible, and tried to help anyone who came to her because there were no public clinics or hospitals in Lincoln County. For a while there were so many calls she had to work at night. When the calls reached sixty a day, she decided to respond only to emergencies at night. The board was very satisfied with her work, noting that she had saved the county money and that such work could help in preventing "disease, death, and pauperism."[91]

After a few years Mead no longer considered children's health to be the most important public health issue. The biggest problem in Lincoln County, she thought, was the lack of prenatal and natal care and the large number of stillbirths and deaths to babies under one week of age. The women were much interested in the subject, she wrote to the Children's Bureau, but the county was so large that she simply could not cover the area. She hoped joint-district schools might employ their own full-time nurses so she could devote her time to maternal and infant health. Mead was still committed to public health nurses working in rural areas, but she had decided that she could best serve that need by training more nurses. Before she resigned in 1922 to accept a job training public health nurses in Minnesota, Mead urged the board to appropriate more money to hire a second nurse and to offer free care for those referred by the nurse, poor commissioner, or committee of the poor. The board did not hire a second nurse, but it did continue to hire a public health nurse to work in schools without nurses and to act as general health counselor throughout the county in preventing the spread of communicable diseases, investigating cases of child neglect and violations of child labor laws, and arranging for traveling clinics. The duties of a single nurse were an impossible burden, but the county appropriated money for her work and gave her its support. Of the four northern counties, Lincoln County was the most committed to public health nursing.[92]

The Wisconsin Bureau of Child Welfare organized energetically in the other three northern counties. It engineered large gatherings of state agencies and representatives of nongovernmental organizations, including many women's groups; sent its "Child Welfare Special" train into these counties; and set up children's health clinics. In some towns the clinics were warmly welcomed. At Loyal in Clark County, the school superintendent encouraged examinations of all schoolchildren and the community generally supported the clinics. In the small town of Milan, an active women's club helped collect children to be examined. Field workers reported the Colby baby clinic "a howling success." In other towns, bureau nurses and doctors encountered hostility from local communities, which perhaps considered the clinics an unnecessary state intrusion on local responsibility to provide health care. One nurse reported, "I have an idea the Marathon women would not be disappointed if we did not come back next winter." A doctor noted, "To do anything at Neillsville is considered impossible."[93]

The Marathon County Medical Society disapproved of the plan for a prenatal clinic from the beginning. In December 1920 society members voted unanimously to oppose establishment of the clinic. Representatives of the local support group, the Federated Charities of Wausau, visited with the doctors in February 1921 to try to gain their support and then went right ahead with the clinic plans. In April 1921, furious at the women and their supporters for proceeding with the clinic, the medical society passed a resolution formally opposing the clinic and urging physician members not to participate in its operation. The Marathon County doctors' boycott did not succeed. A number of physicians braved the condemnation of their colleagues to staff the clinics. By 1928 Marathon had two permanent centers financed by local funds with examinations being made by local physicians.[94]

Taylor, Clark, and Lincoln counties also opened clinics. Taylor County had one of the first five-year demonstration centers with state financing and staffing, but at the end of that time it lacked funds to continue the clinic. Clark had two local centers financed by local funds and staffed by bureau physicians who performed the examinations. Lincoln had two state-funded centers staffed by state physicians. Except for Taylor, the counties still had their clinics at the end of 1928. Matching funds also supported the "Child Welfare Special" and its two-person staff, a woman physician and a nurse. The train visited small towns in Marathon County for two weeks in 1923 and in Lincoln County for one week in 1924. Its purpose was to get people interested in health issues and possibilities. The real work had to be done on the ground, however, developing community support to provide permanent health care.[95]

It had taken two decades of work to develop a delivery system to assist rural women in caring for their children. Through every phase, state and federal officials had depended on groups of local women to support their efforts. While state and national reformers, local women, and the rural women whom they hoped to serve did not always agree, male officials of the area were often particularly unhelpful and some organized doctors vehemently opposed all public health proposals. Still, a system was finally devised that met the needs of at least some rural women in their quest to protect their families.

The fledgling system did not effectively integrate immigrant rural women into this plan. Almost all of the women's volunteer organizations, and WATA as well, were composed of native-born women. The Council of National Defense, organized during the war, drew its members from native-born women in small towns, not from farming communities. The state and federal bureaus totally ignored the traditional health-care workers so important in immigrant communities, made no effort to draw in immigrant midwives or to offer them training, and failed to recruit immigrant daughters or other bilingual women for nursing training. The Wisconsin Children's Bureau did no survey of midwives, compiled no list of organized midwifery training schools, and offered no instruction for those midwives who continued to practice. The bureau reached few mothers. Of 60,000 mothers who birthed babies each year, the bureau estimated that only about 3,000 received any prenatal instruction at all. Only 130 of almost 3,000 doctors in the state referred mothers to the bureau for prenatal literature.[96]

The campaign for improved public health did not extend to Native communities. The federal government had the primary responsibility for the health of the Lac du Flambeau and the Menominee communities. The Menominee had hospitals, doctors, and nurses but no public health nurse to work with the people on prevention. Lac du Flambeau had no hospital during this period. It had one field nurse, but her efforts to obtain a regular hospital and nurse were unsuccessful. The first state appropriations for public nurses to work with Native families came in 1928. At that time the Ho-Chunk, who were scattered through the settler communities, had no health care except what they could obtain from local doctors. Experts estimated that TB remained a staggering problem within the Ho-Chunk community, with rates of almost 76 per 10,000 compared to the Euro-American rate in Wisconsin of slightly more than 6 per 10,000. TB hospitals were totally inadequate for the Native population. Experts estimated that it would take at least $100,000 to care for TB cases alone.[97]

During the 1920s in rural northern Wisconsin the public health campaign also faltered among settler communities. Because the women who most needed the health programs were not involved in their delivery, the campaign had shallow roots, and when urban native-born middle-class women turned their attention away from health-care reform, the movement could not be sustained.

Reformers did help reduce infant and maternal mortality in settler communities by providing some state assistance for health care. They were also able to identify the basic cause of high mortality rates. Sherbon, Morgan, and Mead all realized that women's work was not the cause; it lay elsewhere, in the inadequate health care available to women as they attempted to preserve their own and their children's physical well-being. These and other reformers articulated fundamental rights for women that paralleled their responsibilities in maintaining family and community health. They had a right to participate in formulating public health policies, to organize in their support, and to demand that government implement them. Defending these rights would entail a major change in the relation of women to their government, a change that they would have to fight to obtain in the years to come.[98]

5

Caring

My grandmother Matilda raised eight children virtually alone after her first husband died and her second husband turned out to be a poor provider. An accident; a wrong choice in time of crisis. Her own family was of little help: her grandparents and mother had died in Bohemia. Matilda and Karl had brought her father and his mother to the United States, but both died before Karl's fatal accident in 1902. Matilda's two brothers came to the United States: one moved to California after serving in the military during the Spanish-American War; the other settled near her but died in 1907. Matilda's sister, who lived a few miles away, had little to spare from the struggle to feed her own family and to hold onto her mortgaged farm. When Matilda married a second time, her new husband, Leo, brought few kin to the union. His brother sent a barrel of apples from Door County in 1909. Matilda's kinship networks cracked and broke under the strain of immigration and the first generation of settlement. According to family accounts, when her youngest child, Emma, was born in 1909, Matilda was in despair about how to feed her eight children. She told the older children she wished Emma had never been born because there was so little to eat. The children did go hungry at times. Matilda cared for them with little support from kin and none from the government.

Although Matilda, following German custom, was pregnant when she married, she must have realized that in those hard times bridal pregnancy could be risky. The next generation of daughters abandoned the practice. Bridal pregnancy was replaced with an ideal of marriage before pregnancy. Although her youngest son fathered a child out of wedlock, none of the daughters bore out-of-wedlock children, as far as we can determine such intimate matters from marriage dates and birth dates of their first children. As young women moved out of their homes and worked at some distance until they married, often among people of different ethnic, religious, and economic groups, families and communities could not assure that young men would marry the women they impregnated. Society stressed control of young women's sexuality to limit the births of one-parent children, who could become dependent on family networks or the wider community. Most of the burden for sexual self-control—and opprobrium for lapses—fell on women.

Matilda's daughters all married and raised families of their own, apparently with relatively little external restraint over their sexual activities. As Matilda aged, she needed special care, and she turned to her children for assistance.

Like other elders who farmed, she continued work on her farm as long as possible and then was cared for by her children. Some elders moved into small nearby towns that serviced the agricultural community, towns where they had attended churches and purchased supplies, where they felt comfortable. Churches, which usually included people of all ages, often provided a close community to assist elders only as needed, letting them age with relative independence. Others began a migratory life that took them many miles from their home farm as they moved to the homes of different friends and kin, as Matilda did, in search of security in old age.

Dependent Children
Myrta and Catherine's Stories [Full names, birthplaces, and life dates unknown]

Myrta and Catherine were orphans, but they lived with farm families who treated them much as their own children. Their stories stand as proxies for those of many rural children. We know about their experiences because both were committed to the state school at Sparta, indentured out to foster homes on farms, and later interviewed by field agents of the Children's Bureau.

Myrta, her seven brothers, and her parents lived in a small house on a heavily mortgaged farm. Within a four-month period, her mother and father were taken to the hospital for the insane. The children stayed on in the little house. Myrta gathered wild berries to sell in order to get enough food for them to eat. Her older brothers were abusive and mean to Myrta and her three younger brothers. When the youngest became very ill with meningitis, the state committed Myrta and her three young brothers to the state school. Catherine, whose family background and history are less clear, was committed to the state school when she was seven. As was the practice, the school indentured both to foster homes on farms. Myrta was fortunate. In her home she received much kindness and lived comfortably. Her foster parents did not nag or make heavy demands upon her. When she turned eighteen, she asked to continue living there. They gave her five dollars a week for her work. Myrta hoped it would always be her home.[1]

Catherine's experience was different. In less than two weeks, she was back from one home, and two months later, after a second placement failed, she was back again. After these failures, the state kept her at the school for a year. Then one day Catherine and the other girls her age were called into the waiting room, where a tall man with a kindly expression was waiting. He wanted a little girl to take home as a companion for his daughter, who was just about Catherine's age. This visit was the man's second. Several years before, the officials had shown him all over the buildings and grounds and allowed him to watch the children at play before he picked a boy to come home with him. The boy was still with the family. This time, the reception seemed less cordial.

Officials told him nothing about the children's histories and simply ushered in the candidates to stand before him. He looked over the young girls and chose Catherine as the most promising. They left immediately to catch a train home. When they reached the home, Catherine found herself on a fair-sized farm with a large barn, dogs and cats, and a creek just across the field. The family lived in a roomy and attractive white frame house. Her capable and loveable foster mother wanted sincerely to give Catherine a good home and have her grow up as a sister to her own little girl. There were now five in the family: the foster son, about ten years older than Catherine, the daughter, the two parents, and Catherine.

At first Catherine was a disappointment to her new parents. She was stubborn and determined to have her own way, sometimes taking three hours to wash a few dishes just because something had gone wrong. She had a bad temper and would "fly at" the boy in the home, letting out a torrent of profane words. She was slovenly in her habits and careless of her appearance, and the foster mother was many times ready to give up, especially when Catherine went wading in the creek in a new pair of white shoes and ruined her dress. If the family went visiting, Catherine was a source of continual embarrassment to the foster parents, who described her conduct as coarse, forward, quarrelsome, "saucy." She was unable to get along with other children. At eleven, Catherine became "man crazy," following visitors around the house or sitting in dark corners with them at parties. Catherine was always respectful to her foster parents, however, and at times tried hard to behave well. She was several grades behind in school when she first came to her new home but quickly caught up. She became fond of church, and her behavior eventually improved. She studied for her confirmation and looked forward to membership in the church. After three years in her foster home, the hard times seemed over.

When Catherine turned thirteen, an agent of the Sparta school appeared suddenly. He said Catherine must go live with her sister Jeannette, who had married, was living in another part of Wisconsin, and had obtained a court order to have Catherine's custody transferred. The foster mother bitterly opposed the move and begged that Catherine be allowed to remain, at least until after her confirmation. Just when Catherine was making good, after they had both struggled so hard, it seemed unfair for her to leave. The meager report that accompanied the court order stated that Jeannette's home was satisfactory and that her husband was a mechanic who could provide for Catherine as well as their two small children. The sister thought it was her duty to take Catherine since they could afford to care for her and, besides, Catherine might help take care of the young children. There seemed nothing Catherine or her foster mother could do to change the order.

Catherine's new home was a four-room cottage, neat and clean. But the sister expected her to care for the two children, both of whom were under four years of age, and Catherine soon fell behind in her schoolwork. Her sister urged her to quit school, work in a factory during the day, and do housework every night. Finances were tight, as the husband's wages were only $25 per week and irregular, while rent alone cost $35 a month. The YWCA tried to interest Catherine in joining a club, but the other girls shunned her because her appearance was untidy and because her sister had a bad reputation in the community from staying out late at night. Within six months, the officials returned Catherine to Sparta. Later they learned that Catherine had been assaulted while with her sister.

The stories of Myrta and Catherine, taken from a series of stories told by foster children to visiting Children's Bureau investigator Anna Lundberg in 1923, illustrate the hazards and uncertainties that orphaned children faced. Sometimes foster homes were beneficial places for the girls, even better than what kin might provide, as the stories of Myrta and Catherine illustrate. For others, foster homes became nightmares of mistreatment and unremitting hard work. The procedure of indenture put children designated "orphans" at risk for abuse of all kinds, from sexual assault and physical abuse to simple neglect. Children in their own homes also sometimes suffered from these abusive living situations, and one cannot measure the occurrences in either these quasi-public foster homes or in private homes, but the accounts of the Sparta schoolchildren offer vivid details of the varied experiences children had when in the care of others, kin and nonkin, as they struggled toward adulthood and responsibility over their own lives.

THE SPARTA SCHOOL

The stories of Myrta and Catherine reveal the complexity of caring for needy children. During the nineteenth century, Wisconsin, like other states, tried to sort out its dependent citizens and arrange for appropriate institutions to care for them. Wisconsin separated the visually and hearing impaired during the 1850s. By the 1860s it had separated the mentally handicapped. In the 1880s officials turned to the problem of how to care for dependent children who were not mentally or physically disabled.

Most states adopted one of two options to care for able but dependent children aged three to fourteen. California, New York, and a few other states subsidized private institutions for the care of dependent children. Michigan placed children in state-operated boarding schools. The Wisconsin legislature opted for a third system, a form of home or foster care. In 1886 the state of Wisconsin established its State Public School (later known as the State School for Dependent Children) about 125 miles northwest of Madison at Sparta. The school provided a temporary home for children until they could be indentured out to foster families on farms. Children lived with the farm family, were assigned farm household chores, and attended local common schools. If the family wished, it might legally adopt the child or, when the child turned eighteen and the indenture ended, pay her fifty dollars. The money would help her live until she could find work and a place to stay. Physicians certified that the child had no contagious or chronic diseases and was sound of mind. At the time, the state was a pioneer, as a Children's Bureau agent later wrote, "in recognizing the provision by the state for its dependent and neglected children." In the next thirty-seven years the state cared for six thousand children under this system.

The system did not turn out quite as planned. The Sparta school, intended for able children, could not always return physically and mentally handicapped children to the counties, and these children accumulated at the school and were indentured out as well. By the twentieth century, most Sparta schoolchildren were urban, some of them hated farm work, and few had any use for farming skills when they returned to cities. Officials ignored these facts and continued to believe that farm work was healthy for children. According to the Children's Bureau study, children worked very hard and often were deprived of an education. Moreover, if the family in which the child was placed wanted to adopt the child, it could do so without notifying the birth family. Children were sometimes kept from communicating with members of their families.

Complete indenture records for the Sparta school no longer exist. Surviving records show that beginning in 1887 with 17 children, indentures grew to more than 200 by 1894, reached a peak of 321 in 1896, and then gradually declined to 200 to 300 a year until 1919. As of 1923, 52 percent of the children were boys and 48 percent girls, while 57 percent of those indentured were boys and 43 percent girls. Of the 827 indentured between 1913 and 1917, about one-third were adopted, one-third remained wards of the state, and one-third reached age eighteen and were released or returned to their parents.

Counties had different policies regarding schools. Lincoln County, for example, kept all dependent children in the local poorhouse until 1905, after which it sent almost all of them to Sparta. These children were not always orphans. Parents sometimes sought a place to have their children cared for while they dealt with temporary crises, and local officials told parents they could retrieve children when they were able to resume care. But the judicial transfer surrendered parental rights to the state, which could then allow foster parents to adopt the child without parental knowledge. The Sparta school was established as a temporary refuge for children of families in crisis, but it evolved into an institution that broke up poor families.

The practice of adopting out state school children without a separate adoption proceeding remained in full force until 1918, when parents brought a lawsuit to have their child returned. The court case made the Sparta school notorious. Governor John Blaine called it "a blot upon our civilization and a disgrace to the state" and launched reform efforts. In the next four years, amid public criticism of the system, the state reorganized the school and the number of remaining indentures dropped to 61. Meanwhile, in a 1920 decision, the state supreme court held that the state must obtain written consent from the natural parents and give them written notice before adopting out their children.[2]

During this period of reform, the Wisconsin Board of Control, which oversaw all agencies, asked the Children's Bureau to make a field study of the system. The bureau decided to investigate how the home had functioned from 1913 to 1917, interviewing children, officials, and farm foster parents. For months agents visited children and the people to whom they had been indentured. When the fieldwork was done and a draft report completed, Grace Abbott, director of the Children's Bureau, sent it to Governor Blaine for his review. Blaine blocked its publication, arguing that the system was now fixed and that Abbott's agents had gathered irrelevant information from years earlier. "I can scarcely see what benefit there is to be gained by broadcasting an unreliable report relating to matters over six years ago," he wrote angrily to Abbott. Social workers were often "people who have no children and who know nothing about children, but who have an inveterate desire to supervise other people's business. . . . [T]he less snooping there is done by the state the better it is for the child and for the foster parents." The indenture system might be imperfect, he concluded, but no better system was being suggested. Certainly Wisconsin did not need social workers to help rehabilitate children. He concluded, "It is community duty rather than the duty of any special group, self-constituted or otherwise constituted, to see that the parents of the neglected and dependent children are rehabilitated."[3]

The chief investigator and author, Anna Lundberg, defended her report, its conclusions, and the condition of the school. She argued that the state needed to do away with the indenture system entirely and encourage the counties to work with the children. Abbott felt that Wisconsin had been "especially neglectful" but that the bureau could not tell the state what to do; it could only point out the facts without condemnation and suggest options. The report was never published.[4]

While the state denied it and the Children's Bureau was unwilling to push the point, the system had been hard on most of the children. It was certainly right to ask them how they regarded the system. Some, like Myrta, found a true home and stayed on after indenture, but many homes could not provide the stability that the state, parents, and children all wanted. The report evidenced a change in attitude toward rural life. Social workers who had earlier considered the rural environment healthier than an urban environment because it lacked dance halls, movies, and theaters that might corrupt young people now seemed to feel that children were at risk in foster homes in rural areas as well. Rural areas were not necessarily the best place for all children; many from urban areas did not want the hard work that went with rural foster homes, even with kind and caring foster parents. There were real differences among children, parents, public officials, and social workers. The question of how to maintain the rights of children, without imposing new state control over both mothers and children, remained unsettled.[5]

GETTING HELP

Short of giving up one's child to the Sparta school for indenture or adoption, no uniform policy for family assistance existed in rural areas of Wisconsin before 1913. Kin and neighbors could offer emergency short-term help, during illness or temporary disability. A community could extend help to a couple of extra families, but neighbors were hard-pressed themselves and had little time and energy to spare. Exceptional gardening, livestock, or dairying skills might allow women to produce surplus for barter or cash, but they lacked access to most marketing groups. The "widow's cow" might keep the family in milk for part of the year (when the cow was fresh), but a woman needed to have more than one cow, be a skilled butter maker, and have a market for her butter to get a cash income. The isolation of early farms presented challenges. If the husband remained in the home and abused the family or refused to support the farm enterprise, women had little help from church or state. Usually a woman's main alternative was to work herself and her children harder at home and at paid work for neighbors. In summer and after school, perhaps at a younger age than the mother wished, she employed her children, who often dropped out of school even before age fourteen, when most were expected to begin working full-time.

Parents worried, should they be injured or die, what would become of their children. Insurance for parental health and life hardly existed for most of this period. A few fraternal orders promised compensation in return for fees from working families, but there was no government supervision or examination of insurance-related financial affairs. Insurance companies could run sloppy operations: unsecured loans were not paid, political in-fighting occurred, poor bookkeeping flourished, some paid out more than the return in interest could sustain, records mysteriously disappeared. Families had trouble collecting claims. As people aged, younger members were not recruited to sustain the payments. Premiums were the same whatever the insured's age. Fraternal organizations used funds collected as premiums for other purposes. There were too few members to spread the risk, and inadequate premiums were assessed. One 1916 examiner's report of the Patrons Mutual in Rhinelander, an outgrowth of the Grange, found no dates of issue or expiration for policies, notations on slips of paper scattered among other pages in a desk, and in lieu of cash premiums many promissory notes which were never collected. Most companies and fraternal orders refused to insure women at all and, when they did, offered little more dependability. A 1917 report on the Women's Woodmen Circle, an auxiliary of the Woodmen of the World, described that group as "rent with internal dissensions and quarrels." The executive council had mahogany paneling, desks, and chairs, a frescoed ceiling, bevel-edged mirrors, documents bound in full Morocco leather, liberal salaries with travel expenses. They had fancy titles for locals—"groves"—and for meetings—"Supreme Forest Conventions"—but knew nothing about members' mortality or selection of risks. The "Supreme Physician" allowed local medical examiners to enroll almost anyone regardless of health. While such practices may have made people feel good, the group could not fulfill its payment promises upon members' deaths.[6]

The Royal Neighbors and the Catholic Order of Foresters, both pioneers in insuring the lives of women, offered internal financial discipline and organizational integrity to back up their policies. The Royal Neighbors provided group support as well as death benefits and enlisted both Protestant and Catholic women in north-central Wisconsin after its formation in the 1890s. In 1905 the Catholic Church formed a women's auxiliary to the Catholic Order of Foresters, which had offered insurance only to men when it formed in Chicago in 1881. The insurance was accessible only through Catholic parishes, but rural parishes were slow to organize these units for women before the 1920s. When parishes did offer membership, women quickly joined. The Dorchester unit, formed in 1921, included many Catholic women of German ethnicity.[7]

Gradually, other groups offered life insurance for women, although they often capped women's policies far lower than those for men. The Bohemian Roman Catholic Central Union, for example, capped payments at $300 and $500 for women, while men could insure themselves up to $1,000. The Polish Association of America also capped women's policies. None of the groups paid large benefits, but even small amounts helped families deal with the death of an adult, whether male or female.

Almost no organizations or companies offered health benefit plans. The Lutheran Aid Association offered sick benefits in 1905. The United Order of Foresters gave some benefits for male members' permanent partial disability, and a few paid for total disability. Even labor unions did not support state disability insurance, worrying that such plans would be mismanaged or under the control of business interests. When a job disability law did pass the Wisconsin legislature, it did not apply to farm work.

Local officials coped as best they could with the problem of dependent children during the nineteenth century, usually simply paying mothers to care for their own children or paying other women in the community to care for orphans. Absence of the father, through death or abandonment, was the primary cause of children becoming dependent. When such dependence was combined with a mental or physical handicap or inadequate care by the remaining parent, local agencies mandated institutional care. The only public institution available for caring was the poorhouse, and most rural counties had no poorhouses until late in the nineteenth century. A mother and her young children might be sent to the poorhouse temporarily for custodial care. Handicapped, dependent, delinquent—all shared the same institution.

Wisconsin was one of the first states, in 1913, to pass a law providing county aid to dependent children in their homes. This law was not mandatory, however, until a second law in 1915 required counties to provide aid, established a minimum amount to be disbursed to families, committed the state to pay up to one-third reimbursement, and established uniform rules for assistance. Although mandatory, the law was not enforced. Both counties and the state refused to appropriate funds. Rural aid to dependent children continued to be uneven and sometimes absent until the 1920s, but it did allow many parents to care for children at home and reduced the number sent to the Sparta school. By 1919 Lincoln County was offering financial aid to about seven thousand "orphans."[8]

The first comprehensive state welfare law to cover all rural children was passed in 1929. This legislation urged—but did not require—counties to make provision for rural social welfare agents. Citizens' advisory boards were to take on the responsibility, but in the four rural counties of this study only one had been established by 1934. The Depression of the 1930s finally brought massive infusions of state and federal moneys to support a uniform system of child welfare in rural homes.

If public institutions offered little child care, private agencies offered almost none. Although welfare agencies had been established by various religious denominations, particularly Catholics and Lutherans, they were usually located in urban areas. A 1926 list of child-care institutions showed none for the north-central Wisconsin counties. The Children's Home and Aid Society of Wisconsin, based in Milwaukee, listed no boarding homes in these counties for 1920. Parish priests did not, apparently, accept family welfare as one of their charges. Churches, when they took care of families at all, helped only parish families deemed worthy of assistance. Since there were no public or private agencies, hardship families relied on kin and community networks—traditionally tended by women for the very reason that they, too, depended upon the networks in case of need. First-generation immigrants often had either no elder women to help with caring or diminished help because of the stress of establishing new farms and households.

The most needy children were those born to unwed mothers. Rural families and communities had developed their own codes against premarital sexual relations, but when community sanctions failed, when young people coupled and a pregnancy resulted, the traditional task of the family and the community was to arrange a marriage, with the biological father if possible or with another male willing to assume the social role of father. Normally these marriages took place three months into the pregnancy, once the woman was certain she was pregnant. A country saying, "the first child always comes early," signaled acceptance of these bridal pregnancies. A few communities retained the older custom of male elders forcing young men to marry the mothers of their children. In some Wisconsin Polish communities, the local priest acted as the community patriarch who arranged marriages. A Children's Bureau agent who visited one Polish community in 1916 reported, "Illegitimate children are rare for the simple reason that the priest forces a marriage in cases of indiscretion." Such may have been the local practice in the nineteenth-century communities, but if the young woman worked out in another ethnic or religious neighborhood, local patriarchal power had no effect.[9]

Occasionally the father might offer some temporary support, as did my uncle, who refused to marry the mother of his first child. When young men declined to care for their offspring or those of others, the young woman's family was left with the responsibility of supporting both mother and child. Daughters who for whatever reason could not keep these pregnancies and births a "family matter" sometimes found that their activities became a matter of public record and control. Women usually kept their babies, cared for them or had someone else step in while they worked, searched for a suitable surrogate father, and then married. When they could, families sent daughters away to the city or to live with an aunt or cousin during pregnancy. Young women often stayed on in the city, a perfectly acceptable route for a young rural woman to take since so many were already going to the cities to seek work. Or they returned months later to their home community and resumed their lives. Sometimes a child's grandmother would claim the child, asserting it was due to her own late, unexpected pregnancy. Regardless of strategies to deal with fatherless children, mothers and their families bore the primary burden for physical and psychic care of the child.

Obtaining court-mandated support from the father was extremely unlikely. Some counties expected the district attorney to prosecute the alleged father to obtain child support. Rural district attorneys seem to have been very reluctant to prosecute, however, particularly if the men came from wealthy and powerful families. Social workers complained in one report from the 1930s that district attorneys seemed to defend the alleged fathers rather than the young women when they went to court. This report went on to explain, "If she is courageous enough to continue to ask for action, the preliminary hearing and the trial become a veritable shambles to which the idle men and evil gossips of the county resort for amusement and material for subsequent morbid speculation and predatory activities."[10]

Social workers believed women were discouraged from seeking support by "gangs" of men and boys who swore to the mother's promiscuity. It is not clear how these "gangs" functioned. The social workers reported that older, "unprincipled" men recruited young boys who became their "tools" in preying upon certain women until they became community outcasts. The community ignored the young men's activities. One 1897 letter from Marinette County helps explain how this process might have worked. The district attorney, in responding to the governor about a complaint lodged by the mother of a young pregnant daughter, explained the case at length and sent the transcript of an interview he had with the young woman, Phoebe Swanson, and her mother, Mary. The mother had asked for prosecution of Anson Place, whom she said had pulled Phoebe "out of the house into the back yard and there had intercourse with her." Mary had already complained to Anson's father, who responded that he could do nothing with the young man. The district attorney asked why Mary had allowed Anson to do such a thing; she replied that he had threatened to "take the sides out of the house" if Phoebe said anything about him. According to the transcript, the district attorney charged Phoebe with having sexual relations with other young men. "No use of your crying and breaking down," he said to Phoebe, "I know that you are known as a bad girl and complaint had been made about you before." To her mother he said, "half a dozen boys are willing to swear that they have been with her and that you were in the house when they had intercourse with her.... [F]rom what I know in regard to your daughter... I don't feel that it is proper to issue a warrant... I don't think it is a case which will warrant the county going to the expense."[11]

Most communities were unwilling to accept responsibility for supporting children born out of wedlock. This attitude, and single women's need to work, may have resulted in larger numbers of unwed mothers offering their children for adoption. In a study of upstate New York, one researcher found that more than two-thirds of unwed mothers signed over their babies for adoption between 1890 and 1907 and that 80 percent of mothers under age sixteen did so. A similar pattern developed in northern Wisconsin as it became a settled rural area. One 1925 study showed that 43 percent of young women in Wisconsin who bore children outside of marriage were from rural communities and 54 percent from communities with populations under five thousand. A fifth were domestics, frequently from rural areas where custom had once dictated that marriage should follow pregnancy. Now, whether in towns or in the country, marriage did not automatically follow pregnancy. Young women cared for in state homes for girls were encouraged to give up their children, often before completing the six to eight weeks of maternal nursing that social workers felt was necessary for the child's health. Thus mortality rates of children born out of marriage were much higher than those born within, and evidence seemed to point to overly early adoption as the cause, as well as poor care for unwed pregnant young women because of hostility in their communities.[12]

If the county did offer aid, it was conditional: a second child might result in losing that support, as happened to one mother in Lincoln County. The board of supervisors stripped Carrie Nelson of the aid she had been receiving to raise her children. A terse note in the board minutes read, "Bore bastard child no more aid."[13]

MOTHERS' PENSIONS

The movement for mothers' pensions was the first effort to provide systematic support to women who needed help in caring for their children. Between 1911 and 1913, twenty states, including Wisconsin, passed acts providing aid to mothers. Women reformers supported legislation in Wisconsin for the same reasons they did in other states. There was growing sentiment among the middle class that motherhood was a condition that should keep both working-class women and their children out of the work place. Motherhood should be a time for mothers to focus on child care in the home. Childhood should be a time to learn and play, not to work. Mothers were the best people to raise children, reasoned the reformers, and children should not be institutionalized when a crisis disrupted family income.

Motherhood could be celebrated for any number of reasons, and the rationale for supporting mothers' pensions varied. Some argued that mothers had a right to pensions on the basis of social justice: they had a right to assistance from the community simply because the state had a duty to assist anyone in need. Others argued that the job of birthing and raising children gave mothers special social status and, like soldiers, they should receive assistance in return for their work. A few argued that it was simply cheaper than existing aid. Private welfare agencies, which traditionally provided for urban mothers only when family men were injured or otherwise unable to provide a family wage, seemed stingy and inadequate. Reformers favored the state as the delivery agent for support for all women who needed assistance in raising children.[14]

In Wisconsin, as elsewhere, women's clubs were among the strongest supporters of state rather than private welfare for mothers. By 1912 a broad network linked local, state, and national club members in support of legislation for mothers' pensions. Progressive Republicans in Wisconsin endorsed such legislation in their 1912 platform, and when elected they enacted that pledge into law in 1913. Wisconsin became one of the states with the highest percentage of families receiving aid, but the aid was meager. Like other reform bills, state mandates depended upon local officials to implement laws. Some counties delayed implementation for years.

Looking through the lens of Lincoln County, one can already see the outline of how traditional practices would affect the mothers' pension law when it was implemented in 1917. The commissioner of the poor reviewed aid requests, and much depended upon what he recommended to the board of supervisors. In 1915, for example, the Lincoln County Committee on the Poor urged the board to be careful in offering financial assistance: "There is a danger of encouraging professional pauperism," members reported, "Some persons seem to feel that the County 'owes them a living' and don't seem to make any serious effort to support themselves or families and we recommend that the Poor Commissioner be instructed to make as careful an investigation as possible in each case, before granting aid." Yet in 1920 a different commissioner of the poor wrote more humbly, "Why some people are poor and unable to provide for themselves God only knows, I don't." He went on to advise, "Public opinion in Lincoln County want the poor well cared for." Finally, he referred the men to the Bible passage where Christ said to sell everything, give the money to the poor, and follow Him.[15]

Women were about two-thirds of all people receiving "outside aid" in Lincoln County between 1911 and 1917. Of these, half were widows; the rest received aid because their husbands were either gone, alcoholic, in prison, or physically impaired in some way. Most of these women received aid under the Dependent Children Act, but beginning in 1917, when the county offered mothers' pensions, the statistics changed very little. The numbers rose slowly over the next seven years. The pension amount was never enough to support a woman and her children, only to supplement her income. The almost $14,000 that went to fifty-six eligible women in 1921–22 gave them an additional $250 a year or $21 a month toward the amount they needed to survive. It helped buy groceries and pay for rent, wood, some clothing, and medicines. Most rural women struggled to stay on the farm if they could, to run it with the help of children, kin, and neighbors. When the cost of living rose dramatically in the 1920s while farm prices declined, many had to move to town and take whatever off-farm jobs they could find.[16]

Delinquent Daughters
The Stories of Lotta, Karie, and Lottie [Fictional women in Edna Ferber's novel Come and Get It (1935)]

"It was a country of timber and ore," wrote novelist Edna Ferber, "a rich and wildly beautiful country, already seared and ravaged . . . the hills all about were bleeding from a thousand wounds." Loggers came from fifty miles away to spend their money in Iron Ridge. Iron Ridge, said one logger who had grown up at a logging camp thirty-five miles outside the town, was "fine and tough and gay... a man's town." Ferber's lumberjacks squandered their money there in spring after a winter working in the woods. Silver Street, a main street lined with wooden saloons, was paradise for the men who mined and logged. Ridge House, built by New England investors and decorated outside with scrolls, jig-saws, turrets, cupolas, pillars, and gables, had an arcade inside—gambling rooms and a saloon, a fine bar with a "ladies" room, and a handsome high-ceilinged dining room. Loggers and lumbermen could seldom afford the Ridge House, but they frequented Sid Le Marie's Alcazar Theater just down the street, where admission cost only a dollar. In rooms of red plush and gold paint, the "girls" sold beer for a dollar a bottle and room keys that fitted no doors.[17]

With this setting Ferber framed the three-generation story of Lotta, Karie, and Lottie Jr. Iron Ridge was a thinly disguised Hurley, Wisconsin. The fictional women's lives were based on Ferber's research into the lumbering culture and the experiences of women like Lotta Morgan, who was murdered there in 1890. Their lives serve here as a proxy for the women about whom families and communities seldom wrote. In Ferber's fictional account, Lotta Morgan was the featured dancer at the Alcazar Theater. Ferber introduced Lotta as she waited to go on stage. A brass band blared "I Can Dance the Can Can, Can You?" Orange, green, and scarlet posters with a cancan dancer, her full skirt lifted to show a calf, beckoned loggers in to see her act. The cancan, "the wicked dance from Pa-ris!" the owner shouted. The men "stamped and cat-called and whistled shrilly between their teeth" and smoked pipes or cigars while twenty women in tights and short spangled satin skirts performed a pirated form of the *Black Crook* against a backdrop of cotton flowers and paper trees. Dances, sketches, and playlets gave way to cancan girls in long flounced skirts, low-cut tops, black slippers, and stockings. Then the curtain went up, revealing Lotta sitting on a tree stump in a woodland scene, an ax on her shoulder and high-heeled boots laced over her calf. She sang a logger's drink-ing song, and the audience joined in. Lotta was a favorite with the loggers, but the miners began to yell insults. Fights broke out. Two young loggers, Swan and Barney, rescued her from the stage, where she cowered frightened before the brawling men.

In Ferber's novel, the Swede named Swan marries Lotta. Swan knew little about Lotta except that she had come from the stockades, a place at the end of town "where women were kept virtually prisoners. A high wooden fence sur-rounded the place. Bulldogs and bloodhounds made escape impossible." Lotta Morgan had escaped, breaking her leg scaling the high fence, crawling almost half a mile in the snow. Gossips said she was the daughter of a Portuguese and a Finn, that she had tattoos on her body, that she already had a husband when she married Swan. Ferber describes Lotta as a neat and excellent housekeeper, a good cook, "the professional prostitute turned house-wife, and content."

Two years later Lotta birthed a daughter with pale yellow hair and blue eyes. Swan and Lotta named her Karie. When Karie was ten, Lotta was brutally murdered, but she had been so well accepted by the town that a minister gave her eulogy.

Ferber skips to Karie's life twenty-eight years later, when she is head waitress at the Ridge House, where her daughter, Lottie, now eighteen, is also a waitress. We learn that Karie, after being orphaned at ten, grew up wild and ugly. She slept with Swedish lumberman Lars Lindbeck, married him, and bore Lottie Jr. When Lars died in a logging accident, Karie raised her only child alone by working as a waitress. Karie has become an exemplar of the perfect small-town waitress—spunky, independent, capable, casual, maternal, insolent, friendly, with "tremendous energy and a zest for life."

All of Ferber's waitresses walk regally—they have to keep the meals on the plates—but their carriage attracts male customers who "get fresh." Lottie Jr. does not like waiting on tables, hates the pawing of men, but is "aware" of the potential value of her good looks. Lottie is in revolt against her mother's "good" life.

> LOTTIE: I'll be good, but not the way you been good all your life, doing
> things for everybody and getting a kick behind for it.
> KARIE: What you getting at, Lottie? Tell your Ma.
> LOTTIE: Never you mind, Ma. I know where I'm heading in. You do like
> I say and we'll both wear diamonds."

Ferber's story is fiction, not fact, and her melodrama keeps it from becoming a believable tale of a sex worker turned performer, her waitress daughter, and her ambitious granddaughter. Lottie did not become a mistress to the lumber baron—instead she married the son—and the story focuses on her descent into frivolous consumption with Karie looking on from the sidelines. The story, by rights, should be Karie's, and Ferber fails in her attempt to create a female dynasty founded by a sex worker and a waitress. Ferber did provide a social and emotional account not available in the standard histories, but even in 1930s fiction such a story could not be told completely because authors could not yet portray a sex worker, waitress daughter, and would-be mistress granddaughter truthfully. Selling sex to both lumbermen and lumber barons was tolerated during the lumbering era but could not, even fictionalized, be discussed fully in print. It was, however, as close as anyone got to telling the story of these women.

Concern over sexuality in northern Wisconsin emerged sometime in the late nineteenth century. Rural industry and agriculture became intermixed as commercial farming replaced the earlier combination of lumbering and subsistence farming. Small towns in northern Wisconsin had served a number of different communities—the men who congregated around intensive work in the forests, settlers who farmed nearby, and small groups of Native peoples. The ethnically diverse communities tolerated a worker culture that often included drinking, gambling, and "whoring." As the economy changed, the middle classes increasingly attempted to impose their standards of conduct on working-class white and Native cultures.[18]

This middle-class response did not, at first, affect Native women. The federal government, despite its control over Native peoples, did not normally intervene in their domestic relations during the nineteenth century. Because there was no precedent for federal law that applied to marriage or sexual relations and because states had no jurisdiction on Indian lands, the government allowed Native peoples to develop their own codes by which each tribe controlled domestic relationships and used customary guidelines for marriage and divorce. The government eventually outlawed plural marriages and payments in exchange for marriage, but the codes themselves were administered by Native police and judges. The government relied primarily upon missionaries and the forced education of young people in boarding schools to change social customs. During most of this period, therefore, Native women's domestic relations and their sexuality did not come under the state's control unless they became citizens or chose to be married under state law. Hence there were no reformatories for young Native women as there were for white women.[19]

In the settler communities, however, the period from 1910 to 1920 was a great era of building reformatories for girls and World War I the peak of detention and incarceration of young women. Family, community, and church monitored and channeled sexuality into marriage, supervising by gossip and shaming. Young rural women were often the ostensible objects of reformers' concern because these country daughters migrated to cities and became potential urban victims. Reformers also suspected that country women developed into those incompetent urban mothers whose homes were a cause of delinquency in their daughters.[20]

Urban middle-class reformers urged surveillance of the sexual activities of working-class youth. They discovered houses of prostitution in rural areas, alerted state legislatures, and convinced them that unsuspecting country women were being lured into prostitution, a process popularly called "white slave traffic." By 1914 the Wisconsin legislature was investigating parlor houses, assignation houses, dance halls, and other places in small towns where rural men might find commercialized sex and country women their downfall.[21]

SELLING SEX

By the 1870s, brothels as well as farms dotted the northern Wisconsin frontier. The intermixing of industry and agriculture in north-central Wisconsin— where lumbering and mill towns concentrated large numbers of single men—

seems to have been the primary cause for the commercialization of sex. Whether seasonal or year-round work, these rural industries gave northern Wisconsin a character different from the more established southern farm areas, or so people seemed to think. Sex workers settled in small towns and outside of them, as they did on other frontiers in the West during the late nineteenth century. Reformers believed that prostitution was growing during these years, and, in truth, as industrialization provided more labor-intensive jobs for men and attracted more single men from Europe, women expanded their services, including sexual services, for them. Sex workers left evidence of their work in two places: small-town court records and letters of complaint that reached local officials. From these sources we have only a sketchy view of these women's lives but fairly specific evidence of how various people responded to the commercialization of sex.[22]

The best description of sex workers in the north-central Wisconsin lumbering areas comes from an 1887 letter written by the pastor of a Methodist church in Merrill, a small Wisconsin town located nineteen miles north of Wausau on the Wisconsin River. Merrill developed in the nineteenth century as a lumbering town tolerant of male workers' freedom to "whore, gamble, and drink." Such activities became part of the worker culture in the pineries of Lincoln County, where Merrill was located. Pastor J. T. Woodhead addressed his complaints to the state governor. Woodhead, concerned with what he called "slaughter pens in the Wisconsin woods," emphasized that young women were at risk there. One had hanged herself in the Merrill jail a few years earlier, and another had been "abused all night" in a local saloon.[23]

About a mile from the Merrill bridge, on the Wausau road, Woodhead had seen one of these "slaughter pens for Wisconsin girls." The minister described it in very precise detail:

> It is a roomy building with either 11 or 13 windows on the chambers, 6 I know on one side. There are rooms below, a wing, and then a long ground attachment, possibly a dance house, etc. The whole is enclosed with an upright plank or board fence from 8 to 10 feet high. The fence corners on the road but there is no entrance there, the gate is beyond. There are one or two little gates cut in the fence towards the woods. The plot contains near one acre: is situated where several lumber tracks enter the Wausau road. It is a lonely spot, not a house in sight, though only two rifle shots from the editorial sanctum that denies its existence. Over the hill, the flaunting sign near the chamber windows, seen from the main road, says—"Gold Dust Saloon.". . . The time the boys come out of the woods in spring is the most fearful. The saloon keepers will have the men's earnings at any risk.

Woodhead grumbled that "settler" ministers did not complain about such conditions because they were afraid of being "unsettled."[24]

Woodhead enclosed a clipping from the Merrill *Weekly Times* that recounted murders and abductions that had occurred in these "dens of vice" in the pineries of northern Wisconsin. Women, the newspaper editorialized, had been sold into bondage, then guarded by brutal proprietors, procurers, and "bulldogs." Wausau also had its den, in which "deplorable incidents" had occurred. Local politicians, the editor concluded, allowed men who operated such "dens" to buy protection.[25]

Whether kept against their will or not, adult women who regularly exchanged sex for money could be arrested because local governments had criminalized these activities in the nineteenth century. Usually, however, local officials controlled commercialized sex by refusing to issue licenses to businesses that provided space for sexual activities. If town boards issued licenses for the houses to do business, objections by local reformers seldom influenced the boards.

A German farmer named Andrew Hoffman, who lived just north of Wausau, explained what had happened when he and his neighbors attempted to influence the local board. Hoffman wrote to the governor in 1892, complaining that eighty-eight voters, a majority in the town of Maine, where a "house" was located, had signed a petition asking the board not to license it. Board members notified him to appear before them with witnesses to substantiate his charge. He did so. The next day the board issued the license anyway. Hoffman then had the owner arrested. But, Hoffman complained, the case "has been on the books for about two years without coming to trial and I cant go away from home or any where to do a days work or anything." He closed his letter to the governor with the plea, "If you could do anything to help me it would confer upon me an everlasting favor."[26]

Even when local district attorneys brought cases to trial, the all-male juries were reluctant to convict. It took three juries to finally render a guilty verdict on the woman who ran the "Cotton Farm," a brothel that operated near the Marathon County Poor Farm in the late 1880s. In most cases, complaints simply resulted in arrests, a fine, and the resumption of business. The criminal docket for Lincoln County Municipal Court for 1887–97 indicates that officials usually balanced the opposing interests of reformers and those engaged in commercialized sex by arresting and fining the women and men involved in offering sex for money and then letting them continue to operate. Between 1887 and 1897, fifty-two women and men appeared before the municipal judge in Lincoln County on charges of "keeping a house of ill fame" or for practicing prostitution. Most were fined from $10 to $35 and released. During these years, officials brought only one client before the judge. At the district attorney's request, the judge dismissed the case.[27]

Complaints about sex workers and the businessmen and -women who employed them continued to drift into the governor's office during the early twentieth century. Undoubtedly, complaints also led the legislature in 1914 to investigate "white slavery" in the countryside as well as in the cities. Most complainants singled out commercial sex as the main problem, but they also opposed drinking and gambling sites, which they saw as encouraging prostitution. Venereal disease became another reason to object to the commercialization of sex. Almost always complainants accused village or town boards of laxness in law enforcement and appealed to higher officials who might prove more responsive to their concerns.[28]

A few reformers endorsed community action to halt such activities. Georgia David wrote to the governor on November 27, 1903, complaining about a saloon keeper in Merrill who had sold whiskey to her underage son. When she had the keeper arrested, witnesses swore that the boys had not been drinking in the saloon and that the boys were lying. The saloon keeper, she wrote, was also keeping a "disorderly house" in Merrill. The district attorney told her it was impossible to convict a saloon keeper. "I wish Carrie Nation would visit these northern towns. She'd find plenty followers," David concluded.[29]

David was probably wrong about Carrie Nation getting Merrill women to ax their local saloons. It is unlikely that even Carrie would have been able to rouse the Merrill community. German settlers there were not supportive of temperance drives that so absorbed Protestant reformers and led them to condone temperance vigilantism. The Woman's Christian Temperance Union (wctu), once active in Wisconsin, had declined by the 1890s.

In the 1880s, the wctu campaign to raise the age of consent symbolized its determination to protect young women. Demands for state regulation of sexuality came first from middle-class reformers, who generally insisted that protection already exercised over young middle-class women be extended to working-class women. Under Frances Willard's guidance, the wctu in the second decade of its existence launched a "Home Protection" campaign. Willard returned to her home state of Wisconsin in 1884 to urge members to take up the crusade to raise the age of legal consent to sexual relations. The Wisconsin law, like that of most states, provided no penalty for males engaging in sexual activities with minors unless force could be proven. Willard and the wctu constructed a narrative of seduction by middle-class white men who, while outwardly respectable, secretly seduced innocent young women. The solution, Willard suggested, was a campaign to raise the Wisconsin age of consent to at least fourteen. Seduction of younger women would be defined as rape and punishable by life imprisonment. The wctu had spread through middle-class communities in small towns of north-central Wisconsin in the 1870s, and women rallied to Willard's call. In 1887 the Wisconsin legislature raised the age of "protection" to fourteen. This reform was short-lived, however, because in 1889 concerned senators reduced it to twelve and changed the punishment for rape from life imprisonment to as little as one year in prison if the child could be "proved" to be a "common prostitute." Wisconsin reformers were outraged, but the decline of the WCTU in Wisconsin by the 1890s meant further change would have to await a new secular-based campaign. By 1920 such campaigners had raised the age of consent to sixteen.[30]

CONTROLLING SETTLER DAUGHTERS

On July 22, 1901, Rose Wilcox, who lived in the central Wisconsin village of Pilot Knob, sat down to write a letter to Governor Robert M. La Follette. Rose informed the governor that her neighbor Cora was "leading a low and degraded life." There was strong talk, she warned, of "whitecapping"—hooded vigilante punishment—for Cora and the man with whom she was "carrying on." Rose went on: Cora's children were "contaminating" other children in school and her husband did not seem to care. Could the governor send a detective to get positive facts and arrest them? She signed the letter, "I remain yours for purity, Mrs. Rose Wilcox." There is no indication that Governor La Follette sent a detective or took any other action. He filed the letter where I found it more than ninety years later.[31]

Rose's letter tells us something about what one citizen sentinel considered inappropriate sexual activity by a married woman. Rose apparently felt she had a duty to report such conduct to the state authorities. She did not think that neighbors acting on their own to punish Cora and her lover was a good idea, but she offered their "talk" as evidence that there was community disapproval of Cora's activities. Moreover, Rose considered Cora's husband remiss in not restraining his wife's sexuality. Such unrestrained sexual activities would infect Cora's children, who could then "contaminate" other children, thus spreading the condition among the community through its youngest members.

Rose's letter does not tell us who talked about "whitecapping." Rural communities had sanctioned various forms of violence throughout the nineteenth century: destruction of property along with personal violence such as lynching, tarring and feathering, shivarees, and whitecapping were all means whereby communities had patrolled and controlled sexual activities. Jane Pedersen described one 1889 incident in Trempealeau County where Norwegian farmers lynched a neighbor, an alcoholic whom they had repeatedly warned to stop physically abusing his family. Apparently there were few such cases. In 1909 the sheriff of Taylor County reported that a man caught having sexual relations with his daughter narrowly escaped tarring and feathering by "skipping out." In this case the sheriff arrested the man on a charge of rape. He was tried, convicted, and sentenced to twelve years in prison.[32]

Such community action was a remnant of ritualized local control over sexual relations dating back to the Middle Ages and known as *charivari*. It usually began with the clamor of bells, pots, and pans outside the house of those who transgressed community standards through adultery or inappropriate marriage, frequently when very young women married older men or widows married too soon or too often. The practice spread to rural North America in the seventeenth century and continued into the nineteenth. Newspapers reported a La Crosse shivaree as late as 1904.[33]

After the late 1880s, however, whitecapping was more common than shivaree. Whitecapping usually involved nighttime attacks by people who often wore white caps to disguise their identity, hence the term. Whitecapping was a peculiarly North American form of extralegal justice, at times directed against radical dissidents, oppressed groups, or oppressive employers and property owners but also used to punish sexual activities considered inappropriate by various groups. The White Cross Movement of the 1880s campaigned against prostitution. In the Midwest in the 1920s, the Ku Klux Klan targeted inappropriate sexual activities.[34]

Whitecapping, like shivaree, was performed primarily by young white males. Saloons were sometimes the places where young men planned these extralegal activities, but any place where young men congregated informally might be the site. Rooted in community sanction, whitecapping existed with the acquiescence of local officials and sheriffs, who monitored and controlled the extent and type of vigilante justice and sometimes joined in themselves.[35]

The surveillance mechanism and decisions about whom to target are not easily discernable. Occasionally newspaper accounts reflected community disapproval. An 1893 account in the *Wood County Reporter* revealed a sympathetic attitude toward a sexually abused young woman but also reflected acceptance of the activities that occurred. The newspaper reported that Emma's mother had died when she was fourteen and her father had "ruined her." The article went on: "Sinking gradually to the lowest depths, she became the common plaything of the neighborhood. . . . A full understanding of the circumstances compels a pity[,] for this woman is but little better than a child in years and more helpless than an infant in determining right from wrong." While the newspaper proclaimed Emma innocent and blamed her father for ruining her and neighbors for making of her a "common plaything," it reported neither official nor unofficial punishment for her treatment.[36]

An account from one young woman's public trial clearly shows that neighbors were involved in seeking to stop violence toward young women as well as in controlling their actions. Fern's case went to trial in Lincoln County, and her story comes from the judge's notes. When Fern was two, her mother died. Following her death, Fern stayed with neighbors during winters while her father worked in the woods. She spent the summer with him. An older brother left home when he was sixteen; after Fern finished eighth grade in 1916 at age fourteen, she was often alone. Fern testified that a neighbor who lived a half-mile down the road stopped by while her father was gone. Fern clearly remembered that June day: it was a Tuesday, and the neighbor's wife was washing clothes; Fern could see her from the house. The judge jotted down Fern's account:

He came and put his arm around me and said I was a nice girl and fleshy. I tried to get away. He took me to chair and held me in lap. He put his hands on my lap & said I had fat legs. He put his hands under my dress & on my private parts and rubbed me. Said I was unwell & it would not hurt me & I would not get into trouble when unwell. I said he should leave me alone & I was scared of him and had heard of his getting others in trouble. Wanted me to have intercourse and carried me into bedroom. Put me on bed and had intercourse with me.

Fern said she was afraid to tell her father because the neighbor warned her that if she did the law would be after her. He gave her fifty cents, which she said she did not want and threw on the ground. He picked it up and kept it. In late July the same farmer found her picking blackberries, put her down, and had intercourse again. In August, when he came to the farmhouse, Fern locked him out, but later when she thought he had gone and she went to the well to get water, he followed her back in and carried her to bed again. During threshing season he grabbed her in the barn. In October, when neighbor women visited, Fern finally told them what had happened. The next day one of the women told Fern's father, and he swore out a complaint. A long, acrimonious trial followed.[37]

The father called in the law to deal with his neighbor's sexual transgressions, but the neighborhood farm women had been crucial in deciding that action was required. Fern's father, rather than a public institution, remained responsible for her care until she reached eighteen. Once young women reached that age, however, they were legally free from the control of parents and the state reformatory and relatively free to do as they wished. Some young women chose to commodify their bodies and exchange sex for money, an illegal activity for which they could be arrested. But the line between legal and illegal activities was not always clear. Nor was it clear what action should be taken by the community to control the activities of women under age eighteen. Family, community, and church had lost much of their power (and inclination) to monitor young couples and channel sexuality into marriage. Old methods of surveillance no longer were effective, but communities were reluctant to share knowledge about sexual activities publicly. Such details seldom appeared in the local press. In one court case where a neighbor was convicted of sexual assault, the local newspaper discreetly noted that he had been found guilty "of the crime for which he had been accused."[38]

Some people shared Rose's opinion that children could be a bad influence on their peers and believed that these small but dangerous contaminants should be removed from their homes and communities. In the same file as Rose's letter is one dated 1898, from the director of the Wisconsin Home for the Feeble Minded to a man who was attempting to get his nephew released from the home. The director categorically refused his permission. The boy, he wrote, "is vulgar in conversation, a confirmed masturbator, and is charged with, and has freely confessed, sexual crime on one of the animals on the place. I consider him unsafe to be at large, and have steadfastly refused my consent to even his temporary return to the community."[39]

While no similar document expresses the opinion that a young woman was a danger to the community through masturbation, there is some evidence that the practice—in the early twentieth century still being called "self-abuse"—could cause concern. In 1913 Mary Berry, superintendent of the Milwaukee Industrial School for Girls, warned matrons not to leave girls in rooms for too long. The superintendent considered that "too-long confinement" could lead to "self-abuse" and "other wrongs more damaging than the first committed," perhaps a veiled reference to lesbianism. Still, Berry concluded her warning with these words: "Let us never blame a girl for doing a thing we would do under like circumstances." That enlightened admonition might indicate changing attitudes toward masturbation, but these young women had already been locked up to isolate them from influencing others as well as from being influenced themselves.[40]

Young women cross-dressing, 1910s. These young women near Medford are probably playing at heterosexuality, but such role playing might have allowed them a type of homosocial couple intimacy as well. Parties where young women dressed as couples and even staged mock weddings were common at this time. Amateur photographers could preserve these informal moments with hand-held cameras.

More revealing are the records of the industrial school established to control the activities of young white women. In 1875, after the Wisconsin legislature outlawed the practice of committing young people under twenty-one to county poorhouses, private charities established the state's first two reformatories, one for males and one for females. In 1885 the state, which was already providing some financial support to these institutions, transferred all dependent boys and girls under fourteen to the newly established

Men in a bar, 1910s. Judging from their clothing, these young men were rural workers. At either end of the bar, older men wear hunting coats. All share a space reserved for men: during the early twentieth century many native-born middle-class Americans supported the exclusion of women from bars.

Sparta school, and in 1916 it took over financing and managing the industrial school. The school's mission was to "train and restore" young women ages fourteen to eighteen who were vagrants, who had violated criminal or civil laws, or who had "fallen into bad habits or have inherited vicious tendencies, or are in manifest danger of doing wrong." The reformatory board usually paroled young women between eighteen and twenty-one, along with younger women considered to be "rehabilitated," to work in private homes.[41]

During the forty-five years from 1875 to 1920, counties committed more than 1,700 young women to this industrial school for rehabilitation. Of these, more than 1,300—above 75 percent—were committed during the fourteen years from 1886 to 1900. Local courts decided which young women were in need of "rehabilitation," and rural sheriffs brought them to the school from all over the state. Between 1880 and 1920, sheriffs from the four predominantly rural north-central Wisconsin counties of Lincoln, Taylor, Clark, and Marathon brought 114 women to the school.[42]

Although showing on average only about three admissions per year, these records reveal which young women the communities considered at risk. According to industrial school records, almost ten percent of the admitted "delinquent" girls had been sexually abused by male relatives or neighbors; six percent were admitted after their fathers, foster fathers, or male relatives sexually abused them.

Attacks by neighbors and friends might lead to young women's commitment. Fourteen-year-old Viola, left alone by her parents, was abused by a sixteen-year-old neighbor. Kathi, originally admitted for theft and paroled to work, wrote to one of the matrons that she was ruined by the brother of the teacher at her place of employment. "I wish you had never let me out of the school," Kathi wrote, "I am ruined. . . . Something awful is going to happen to me."

Some young women who were victims of family violence were also committed. In the fall of 1891, fifteen-year-old Bertha D. swore out a complaint against her thirty-four-year-old father for compelling her to have sexual intercourse with him. He had first forced her into intercourse in July, she testified, and had continued to do so until she initiated the warrant. Though Bertha's assertiveness in seeking help from the courts may not have been common, her background seems quite ordinary. Her mother had died about two years earlier. Since that time, Bertha and her sister, Annie, age sixteen, had lived with their father. Bertha seldom attended school; Annie, disabled with polio, confirmed that she, too, had been abused. Arrested and jailed, the father maintained his innocence, insisting even to the local Lutheran pastor that he had not had intercourse. The case was held over to the April term, but in late March, just before his hearing, the father strangled himself with a towel suspended from the door of his jail cell. The sheriff took both daughters to the Industrial School for Girls, where they were committed until twenty-one years of age because they were "in manifest danger of becoming confirmed in vice."[43]

In another case, Clara reported that after her mother died she kept home on the farm for her father and brothers and that once her father "slung" her on the bed and did "wrong." Later, she had a child by another man. One young woman related that she was sexually abused by her grandfather and uncles. She eventually engaged in sexual activities with married men for money and gave her father part of her earnings. Two other women reported they were abused by foster parents. In 1909 twelve-year-old Allevina's father was convicted of rape. According to the commitment record, he had begun to engage his daughter in "play" even before his wife died and he remarried. Because Allevina later had intercourse with boys, local officials considered her "incorrigible" and committed her to the industrial school.[44]

There is no way to know how often such violence occurred or, as Linda Gordon has argued, if incest, especially man-child incest, was a regular form of family violence. Indeed, reported cases may only tell us that people were noticing it more, and indictments may only indicate that courts extended jurisdiction over an activity previously considered the responsibility of neighbors or families. Neighbors and kin knew about incest cases in their communities. They spoke of father-daughter and brother-sister babies, or "blood" babies.

These issues were not to be discussed publicly, for they concerned deeply held taboos, the violation of which called for serious social and legal penalties. Since denial was the only defense, it was difficult to sort out the true from the alleged. I could find no records of settler men convicted of incest in north-central Wisconsin. Court records indicate that a few local officials did arrest and attempt to prosecute men for incest, but incest was a capital offense for many years, and local officials usually charged men with the lesser penalty of rape. Eventually, incest was reduced from a capital crime to a lesser offense in Wisconsin and some men were convicted, but courts were always unsure of the proper way to determine evidence and punishment. Gordon concluded in her study that, overall, early-twentieth-century reformers failed to control sexual irregularities with young family members. They advocated expanded state power to protect children and held mothers responsible for the environment that allowed such misdeeds. Girls needed agency to protect themselves from early sexual irregularities, Gordon argued, but instead they were subjected to more control.[45]

A later study, conducted on incarcerated rural Wisconsin girls, showed that most young women came from the homes of the working poor, where one parent had died and the surviving parent had difficulty supervising the young girl, offering either no guidance or abusive treatment. These families, researcher Katharine Lumpkin noted, had failed in some respect to live up to "community standards and recognized norms," but the community also had provided no assistance to the parents. Local authorities offered the young women no alternatives to incarceration, such as supervised probation.[46]

Historian Mary E. Odem argues that the result of efforts by reformers to protect young women and extend female authority into the criminal system resulted in more surveillance, policing, and punishment of adolescent female sexuality than that of males. White middle-class women embraced state regulation to restrain the predatory behavior of male seducers but could not control the legal-judicial powers set in motion. The courts, reluctant to enforce the law against men unless they were nonwhite or immigrant, punished women with harsh treatment. In sum, the courts failed to protect women and targeted only the most vulnerable males for punishment.[47]

Young women who seemed to have been testing the limits of constraints on their sexuality might also end up in the industrial school. Keeping "bad company," staying out at night, being "on the streets," going to hotels with men, and frequenting dance halls all show up as reasons for commitment in the records of the Industrial School for Girls. She is a "perfect sport," wrote one matron of sixteen-year-old Gertrude in 1902.[48]

Houses of prostitution, saloons, and dance halls all appear to be locations where officials considered young women to be at risk. In the 1890s, a number of young women "in need of care and control" were admitted because their mothers were sex workers and kept their children with them in their places of business. Courts committed a number of other young women because they lived in "houses of ill fame."[49]

Two dance cultures existed in the late nineteenth century. One was a dance culture of family or neighborhood amusements held in a private environment controlled by local supervisors. The other, also private, was a commercial "sporting" dance culture where males of all classes went to purchase the physical services of working-class women—everything from dancing to sexual intercourse. After the turn of the century, a new, more public commercial dance culture emerged, offering entertainment to youth of both sexes, a place where they could dance and negotiate various types of relationships.[50]

Traditional dance continued, but social clubs and amusement societies, followed by regular commercial dance halls, enticed young women into this new space. Dance halls transformed the old "sporting" dance culture into one where working-class youth of both sexes could meet and mingle without community or parental supervision and without previous friendships. As the locale and clientele changed, so too did the dance styles. Public dancing reduced the pelvic motions of the "tough" dancing of the "sporting" culture and replaced it with a style that allowed for mild heterosexual intimacy in public. Dance halls also allowed young women to trade sexual favors for male treating and to experiment with unconventional sexual and social roles.[51]

The records of the Milwaukee Industrial School for Girls contain some intriguing notes about dance halls. I found the first specific reference to "going to dances" as a reason to incarcerate a young woman in an 1899 entry. Young Emma K., a sixteen-year-old farm daughter, a Lutheran German, was brought in by the Marathon County sheriff because she had gone to a house of prostitution, perhaps only to dance but presumably putting herself at risk for engaging in paid sexual activities as well.

References to dance halls became much more frequent in records after 1907. Fourteen-year-old Julia P.'s Catholic Belgian family, which objected to her running around with men and boys and going to dances, had her committed in 1908. The next year the sheriff of Clark County brought in Mildred V., a fourteen-year-old Methodist of German and Dutch ancestry whose parents were dead and who was working out. She was reportedly staying out nights and going to dances and theaters. In 1914 the Marathon sheriff brought in three Lutheran Germans who were also fourteen or fifteen. Frieda B. went to dances and shows, and Hattie B. went to saloon dance halls. Another young woman was put away for drinking between dances. Admissions records more generally complained about "bad company," but one of the symptoms seemed to be attending dances. Dance halls at saloons began to appear in records as locales where young women met young men with whom they later engaged in sexual activities.[52]

Your fingers "dance" the whole day long,
Let's fill to-night with dance and song!

"Your fingers 'dance' the whole day long. Let's fill to-night with dance and song!" 1910s. This printed card hints at new workplace invitations to dance as heterosexual couples on a date rather than at family and community dances where young people attended in groups. The woman's uplifted leg also signifies an exaggerated sexuality.

Controversies over dance provide an important window into changes in attitudes about sexuality held both by young women and among those monitoring family and community conduct. Rural dance was a venue for performance. The movement of the dances themselves, the special outfits worn, the erotic social and physical contact with young men—all contributed to the popularity of dance.

Once confined to red-light districts that males alone visited, the new dance halls drew same-sex and gender-mixed groups of friends. As dance halls moved out of red-light districts, rural areas offered sites of minimal control by reformers and officials. In the 1920s the rural roadhouse and dance hall became favored spots for evasion of prohibition and prostitution laws. The northern Wisconsin woods became a refuge for bootleggers as well.[53]

Women's responses to confinement in the school differed, ranging from grateful recognition of the help matrons gave, to successful efforts to escape. The records include many comments about young women's marriages and their return to proudly show infants. Records also indicate that a number of young women contrived elaborate escape plans; sheriffs pursued escapees and often returned them to the school.[54]

Despite some control by communities and officials, during the late nineteenth and early twentieth century a young woman had considerable freedom over her sexual behavior, especially if she was working out, as she usually was, on a neighboring farm, in a nearby village, or even at some distance from home and community. With whatever guidance she had from kin, church, peers, and community, she determined her own conduct.

Rural areas had always offered opportunities for daughters to move spatially through the landscape. Young people walked distances that seem immense to us today. During much of the year roads were impassible by any conveyance, and so they walked—to school, to run errands, to visit, to work for neighbors, to attend local dances. For longer trips, by the late 1880s trains were available and young women used them to reach city jobs.

Still, most young women had little or no access to personal transportation at home. Adults tended to reserve both horses and buggies for family outings or for important errands. When bicycles became available at low cost in the first decade of the twentieth century, young women had far less access to them than did their brothers. Joseph Jantsch, who lived across from the Schopper-Schopp farm, recalled that a family usually had as many bicycles as it had males. A bicycle was the fastest vehicle on the road, he noted, and a farm lad could pass a horse and buggy on the level. At five miles per hour—the speed farm boys expected of themselves and their bikes in this community—boys could go beyond the nearest town six miles away to as many as fifteen miles in a single outing. For celebrations such as the Fourth of July, boys might stay away all day, riding over in the morning and returning in the evening. Older youth used bicycles for courting and for business, such as fetching parts from town for broken threshing machines. After Jantsch finished high school and began teaching at a country school, his neighbor Frank Schopper (my uncle) would bicycle over to the schoolhouse for evening programs. A bicycle light helped him return after dark over the bumpy country roads. In 1914 young Schopper bought himself an Indian motorcycle, which gave him even more

Visiting by bicycle, 1910s. Rural families were able to purchase low-cost, easily available bicycles, but Joseph Jantsch later recalled that a family usually had only as many bicycles as it did males. Sons could venture up to fifteen miles in a single outing and stay away a whole day for celebrations such as the Fourth of July. Or they could visit neighbor girls—if only to share a pail of ice cream.

mobility. Certainly a few young women had bicycles. One photographed in 1909 pedaling along a country road with a lunch bucket over her handlebars was probably a teacher going to work. None of the Schopper-Schopp or Jantsch daughters had bicycles, while their brothers used them to roam quite far at young ages.[55]

Once of age to marry, young women had no legal constraints on whom they might choose for a marriage partner. Miscegenation statutes, which restricted White-Indian marriages in some states, did not exist in Wisconsin or Minnesota. Swedish immigrant Amanda Peterson lived with her Chippewa husband at Lac du Flambeau from their marriage in 1898 until her death in 1956. In 1899, when an Outagamie County clerk denied a marriage license to Mable Bennett, a white teacher who wished to marry an Oneida man, the district attorney intervened to see that the license was issued. My aunt married an Ojibwe man from White Earth in St. Paul, Minnesota, in 1920.[56]

By 1920 most young women seem to have been trying to avoid bridal pregnancy, something many of their immigrant mothers had practiced, both in Europe and in their new Wisconsin homes. Through abstinence, abortion, or adoption young women could avoid community disapproval. All of these alternatives were increasingly utilized as the ineffectiveness of community control and the inaction of the state to protect young women—except to incarcerate them—became evident in the early twentieth century. I suspect that high school education, where organized social supervision could be provided by school officials, was the favorite alternative for wealthier native-born young women, but in rural north-central Wisconsin most young women were immigrant daughters and high school enrollments remained low until 1920. Before 1920 young women were expected to work between age fourteen and marriage; after 1920 it increasingly became the norm that they also went to high school. High schools gave supervised access to members of the opposite sex, introducing the tradition of high school sweethearts and June marriages following graduation.[57]

Women who remained within the limits of permitted sexuality could still show their opposition to control through their dress. Changes in dress among rural women are clearly visible in photographs from about 1910 forward. Hemlines rise, clothing fits more loosely, women strike poses that emphasize their bodies in ways more suggestive of their sexuality. Little research has been done on changes in dress among rural women, but an article by Dorothy Behling offers some intriguing clues.[58]

Behling studied Ashland, a small isolated town in northern Wisconsin. Using advertisements in local newspapers and interviews to measure the movement

Rural working women, 1910s. Although their aprons identify them as women taking a break from work, the body language of these four young women indicates a sexualized presentation of self newly borrowed from popular culture. Hand-held, simple-to-use cameras allowed working women to replace the more formal poses of late-nineteenth-century studio photographs with informal snapshots.

of fashionable ready-to-wear into this rural area, she asked women how they obtained their clothing and what they wore to dances, to work, and for Sunday walks. Behling found that most dry-goods suppliers for small mining and lumbering towns in Minnesota, the Dakotas, and Wisconsin were based in Minneapolis. Around 1915 they shifted from peddling and providing company stores with yard goods and notions to offering ready wear. By 1918 salesmen of the Wyman-Partridge Company in Minneapolis were sending salesmen on the road with trunk shows of the latest fashionable apparel—suits, coats, blouses, and dresses. The salesmen spent a day displaying the apparel at company stores and taking orders. About the same time new apparel shops specializing in women's attire opened in small

Rural working women in the city, 1910s. Once in the city, young working women could wear elaborate hats and have studio photographs taken with friends. Here, too, women presented themselves in more consciously sexualized poses.

towns. Nineteenth-century rural women had always followed fashion closely, buying patterns and copying clothing from photographs. They often bartered, bought at discount, or remade clothing to approximate these fashions. Now, however, they needed, or at least often wanted, the cash to buy clothing ready made. Dress became both more commodified and more sexualized as urban ready-made clothing appeared in rural areas. Dress had once been an icon of eroticized sexuality that people depended upon as a way to identify the propensities of young women. Now, as one popular dance song went, everyone was doing it.[59]

Families and communities had removed much of their control over young men's sexuality, but they attempted to retain some command over young women. As they sought equality, many young women demanded sexual freedom as well and tested the limits of the constraints imposed upon them. Other, usually older, women saw the need for greater freedom but acknowledged the continuing importance of sexual restraint and often agreed that the state should assume the patriarchal duties formerly undertaken by families and local communities.

Historians have noted a drop in tolerance for premarital sexuality in the late nineteenth century. German immigrant women, who had regularly practiced bridal pregnancy after they arrived in the United States, usually delayed those pregnancies and marriage until ready to set up a new household. By the time their daughters came of age, the prohibitions against adolescent sexuality were much stronger. If they knew about their mothers' sexual practices, they also knew that times had changed: there were growing sanctions against premarital sex because marriage after pregnancy could not be guaranteed in newly settled and religiously and ethnically mixed communities.[60]

Within settler communities, some women reformers and social workers resented the subordination still required of young women in matters of sexuality. Young men were allowed great freedom in their activities while community authorities, previously responsible for constraining those activities or arranging for reparations should unrestrained sexuality result in injury to women, seemed shockingly inactive. Most of these women reformers did not want local patriarchal control of women's sexuality. They opted instead for expanded state support for women, envisioning an enlarged sphere for the officials of state and nation. Most of these progressive reformers eventually supported suffrage so that women could participate more directly in determining public policy, both in urban areas and in rural areas, where nearly half the female population still lived in 1920. Increasingly, however, large numbers of rural women were moving to the city, where discussions over their sexuality would continue.[61]

These examples of gendering and disciplining sexuality on a northern frontier give us only glimpses of how rural people shaped and reshaped their ideas about what was proper behavior. Words and deeds continually shifted as the economy, the family, and politics affected all the groups who shared this rural space. How different rural people defined and regulated their sexual lives and those of others is as essential a part of the story of rural life as it is of urban. Restoring sexuality to our picture of the rural past should help us better understand both those young women who flocked to the cities in the twentieth century and those who chose to stay behind to reshape rural institutions.

CONTROLLING NATIVE DAUGHTERS

Native women remained largely outside the system that evolved to control the activities of settler daughters. While missionaries and government officials had attempted to influence sexual activities, Native people usually refused to conform to non-Native practices. The federal government had no laws regarding "domestic relations," and state laws that attempted to regulate settler practices did not extend to reservations. Native people retained control of their domestic relations throughout the nineteenth century. Native parents continued to exercise customary control, whatever that may have been in each community. Usually they helped arrange marriages for daughters at a fairly young age, but young women were often quite independent in arranging a second or a third marriage and in controlling their sexuality. One goal of the boarding house system was to replace customary practices by indoctrinating young children with Anglo-American ways.

Regulation of Native women's sexuality was more complex than that of settler women because both customary and government law were changing in the late nineteenth and early twentieth centuries. Increased surveillance and a willingness to use force to control young women became a hallmark of the early twentieth-century Indian Bureau. Christian missionaries, secular reformers, government officials, and various Native communities all had visions of what was "good" for young women and what constituted "bad" conduct on their part. Add in the racism that shaped non-Native peoples' attitudes, and it becomes quite complicated to sort out the mix of demands young women faced.

Even changes in government policy are not clear because policies developed in Washington were applied differently in different localities. Pressure from reformers can be seen most clearly in the meetings of the Board of Indian Commissioners, whose members began to seriously discuss the regulation of Native marriage in 1900. Reformers believed there was danger to the Euro-American community from the growing popularity of Native cultures among whites who were imitating Native dress and ritual, learning to make handcrafts, and generally "playing Indian." Much of the concern was actually with the assimilation by whites of non-white cultures, but the result was to increase efforts to remake Indians into "Christian citizens."

The Women's Board of Domestic Missions, an arm of the Presbyterian Reformed Church of America, forcefully presented the case against Native dancing and customary marriage relations at its annual meeting in 1914. The government must take action against dances, record marriage relationships, and safeguard family life, the women argued. They asked for an increase in the number of field matrons, who, they thought, should be charged with moral surveillance. The commissioner of Indian Affairs was already concerned about the need for more inspectors and the danger posed by women elders who continued to teach customary practices to young women returning from boarding schools. These "bad standards" were endangering young girls, the commissioner thought.[62]

Because reformers could not control young girls' private lives, they often sought to restrain public activities, especially dances. Dance was an important feature in the lives of both settler and Native women, but it had a different place in each culture. For Native people, dance was central to the continuation of their cultures, for it embodied much of what was sacred to their lives. Native peoples' efforts to continue their dances—usually sacred in origin but also

increasingly social in powwows—varied by region and community. The controversy over dance at the Menominee Indian annual fair of 1915 shows how
complicated issues of dance could become.

At the Menominee reservation, most people had converted to the Catholic
religion and no longer sponsored Indian dances. Despite complaints from
the government and missionaries about ritual dancing—the government
feared it as a source of insubordination, the missionaries as evidence of sexual
"immorality"—small groups of non-Christian Menominee had continued
their private dance traditions and made them accessible to Catholic kin who
could no longer sponsor their own. In addition, the community was evolving
its own public dances, which would eventually become powwows, as a way to
combine public dance and Native outfits as emblems of identity in ways that
would be acceptable to the agent. Pictures from 1915 show a dance group that
regularly performed for both Indian and white visitors.[63]

After a particularly successful fair in 1915, the agent at Keshena sent the
commissioner of Indian Affairs in Washington a newspaper clipping that
noted the Menominee had performed gift dances, which the reporter
identified as "pagan" dances. Surely the agent regretted his mistake, for the
commissioner demanded an explanation since "old time" Indian dances were
supposed to be banned. Actually, there were three dances at the fair, the agent
explained. Indian dances were merely an impromptu response to visitors' requests for demonstrations of old dances; they were not formal exhibitions. A
few Menominee elders and their visitors had simply been entertaining themselves. Others had been either square dancing, the traditional settler dance in
which many Indian youths also participated, or doing more modern dances
such as the waltz, tango, and hesitation. The agent insisted to the commissioner that allowing these modern Indian dances was a way to attract the
older people to the fair and, likewise, allowing the popular dances was a way to
keep young people from going to town.[64]

Dance was not the only controversy that exhibits the government's growing
surveillance of Native women's sexuality. Government officials became convinced that, despite the work of missionaries and educators, young people
were not abandoning the older customs. When they returned to reservations,
older people, especially female elders, were influencing them to retain older
customs or at least to adapt what they had learned at school. Missionaries
bombarded the Board of Commissioners, a citizen group that advised the
Indian Bureau on policy, with complaints about the lack of regulation of marriages and cohabitation.

The government solution was to charge field matrons with surveillance
and warnings that Native couples must be married to live together and divorced when they decided to live apart. The customary pattern had been for a
mother to take the children if a marriage ended and for relatives to care for

them until she decided to marry again. Now the government wanted to force
Native people into compliance with settler domestic relations laws. The board
had already received various proposals urging the federal government to intervene in Indian domestic relations. In May 1915, the commissioner of Indian
Affairs dispatched Circular 992, which emphasized that the field matron
should be a force for "development of moral welfare of the Indians and the
reservation life." Her job was to be in touch with the moral conditions of each
family and to protect girl students who returned to the reservation, to urge the
importance of legal marriage and divorce, and to persuade them to "do away
with marriage by Indian custom."[65]

The result was predictable. When a matron went around making lists of
couples and instructing them to marry, they simply ignored her. Settler-style
marriage was restrictive and divorce costly. It turned out that it was also too
expensive for the state to prosecute. The agent at Keshena affirmed that it was
not possible to control marriage and divorce even among the predominantly
Catholic Menominee.[66]

The government persisted in its concern about the domestic relations of
Native youth. A 1916 circular sent out to all agents asked about the lifestyles
of youth after they returned from boarding school, giving superintendents a
chance to offer new arguments for control of Native families. Only one school
superintendent questioned the questionnaire: "I have no suggestions to make
about the Indians. I think they are doing very well indeed, everything considered. But I have a deep-seated grouch against an overwhelming large number
of Caucasians who are not living up to their opportunities. A Board should be
organized to investigate them." Most superintendents responded as expected,
offering suggestions about improving the post–boarding school lives of young
people. A large number commented about what they considered "lax marriage
relations" and "standards of morality."[67]

Matrons, meanwhile, had taken up their new tasks with enthusiasm. By
1916 the field matron at the Menominee reservation had already conducted
surveillance of each family and reported her objection to early marriages to a
member of the Board of Commissioners, Edward E. Ayer. She appeared that
year at the Lake Mohonk Conference, where reformers had gathered to debate
policy toward "Indian and other dependent peoples," to urge legislation for the
"proper detention of wayward women and girls as well as boys, to check child
marriages, wife and family desertion, and other domestic irregularities."

When voluntary compliance failed to bring change, the government
planned alternative methods to control family relations. The most extreme
proposals came during World War I, in March 1918, when an internal board
memorandum relating to returned Indian students suggested new controls. It
recommended that community centers be set up so that "social service workers" with "police powers" could deal with problems of "family morals." Reform

schools, one for boys and one for girls, were to be built for young people not conforming to social workers' standards. The desire to turn social workers into police, then, was the culmination of the shift from Indian to state control of Native sexual relations.[68]

Elders and Special People
Matilda's Story [Rauscher, Schopper, Schopp, born in Bohemia, 1870–1958]

Her friends called her Tilli. We youngsters never called her that, of course. Or even by her given name, Matilda. We always referred to her by the more formal kin term, Grandma Schopp. Grandma Schopp lived in our family during my teenage years. She came to us in 1947, after we had returned to California from a brief stay in New Mexico. I was thirteen; Matilda was seventy-seven. She had to leave in 1956 after my mother was diagnosed with incurable cancer. Matilda was then eighty-six. It was years before I reflected on this once common act: Grandma had come to live with her daughter and family.

One day—I no longer remember the occasion—my mother and grandma were talking in German. I was usually left out of these conversations because my mother never taught me to speak or understand German. It seemed normal

Matilda's birthday, 1950s. In later life Matilda sampled comfortable life in suburban southern California. She celebrated this birthday with daughter Theresa at her side and surrounded by family and friends.

for the two women to talk in German and not to share their stories. For some reason, that day they translated for me, Matilda saying something about the "poorhouse" and how she would not have liked to go there. It seemed like a fortunate escape for which she was grateful. The two laughed and the granddaughter always remembered the strange word *poorhouse*. I never asked questions when they talked. I just assumed it was a place where poor grandmothers went when they were not fortunate enough to have daughters to care for them.

Teenage granddaughters are likely to remember grandmothers with whom they live in a very special way. I remember Matilda as a quiet woman who did not want people to make a fuss over her. Both my parents treated Matilda well. At least I do not remember her ever being treated badly. I do remember mother and dad fussing over her, which is how I know that she did not relish that sort of attention. I suppose Matilda's children selected our home as the place for her to live because we were a relatively stable family, though we did have a tendency to move around. I remember Grandma Schopp in at least four houses over those years. My mother and father got along relatively well together. My mother did not work outside the home.

Matilda's major possession was a trunk brought with her from the farm. On the few occasions when I got to see inside this trunk, I was impressed with its abundance. There were always extra pairs of the beige cotton stockings that Matilda insisted on wearing, and several new aprons made up by the last dressmaker, and fabric for the next dress. There were dishtowels, and some linens, and extra elastic garters, the kind that looked like bracelets and fastened the rolled stockings right up under the knee. I wish now I had an inventory of each item in that trunk. My reaction I do remember. The trunk symbolized contradictory things for me. It conveyed a sense of plenty I did not have because I had to go to the store to buy each item I wanted. At the same time, I knew Matilda kept these things because she had learned she might not be able to get what she needed because of the insecurity of her life.

There was a quiet dignity in her determination to keep her life simple and close to what it had been during all those hard years on the farm. She would accept a small surplus for the sake of security and an occasional deviation to please us and stop our pestering, but she had very few material possessions in her life and she seemed to wish for little more. Her poverty had left her with the need not to accumulate but to keep her life simple and adequate, always insisting, "I ain't so baticular."

Matilda had once sewn her own clothes and those of her children, but she no longer sewed. She did darn socks with a beautiful straight weave. I do not remember her cooking, although she supervised my mother's occasional holiday *stollen*. She did not crochet those fancy chair doilies with the pineapple designs that my Italian grandmother turned out endlessly. When asked to produce a pair of knit stockings, however, she could do so in a day. Her thin

Matilda's sampler, 1883. In Bohemia Matilda learned her alphabet along with needlework, as had American women earlier in the nineteenth century. She brought her letter sampler with her to the United States, along with a second sampler of embroidery stitches.

metal needles flashed along, and I marveled that she needed no written directions. Matilda never took me aside to instruct me on how to live my life in accordance with her ideals, but I knew what they were: do not be so "baticular," be comfortable with what you are given, do not accumulate too much or anything too fancy.

Most of Matilda's conversations were with my mother in German. They spoke *Plattedeutsche,* not *Hochdeutsche,* my mother explained to me one day when their mention of the term somehow caught my attention, the language of the common people, not so fancy. Later, when I asked my German teacher, she said that Low German was spoken in one region of Germany and High German in another: it had nothing to do with class or status. Matilda was convinced it labeled her as coming from a lower social class, an indication that she had suffered discrimination for it. I thought she did not feel proud of her language. Nonetheless, Matilda always spoke German to her children and did not know English well. With World War II so close behind us, it is not surprising that I seldom heard either German dialect spoken outside our home.

Grandma's inability to speak English and my mother's determination never to teach me German kept me from learning about our family's past. I never asked; Matilda never offered. Nor did my mother offer to tell me about that history. The few of my mother's letters I have recovered from kin are seldom revelatory. The one card written by Matilda, to her brother-in-law who had an orchard in Door County, thanked him for sending a barrel of apples. She wrote it in 1909, when the family was desperately poor. But there are no diaries, no hoard of family letters, no letters exchanged with relatives in Bohemia. I knew only that Matilda had come from the village of Christianburg in Bohemia, then a part of the Austro-Hungarian Empire and now a small village called Kristanov in the Czech Republic.

In 1988, curious about Matilda's homeland, I found Kristanov on a Czech map and arranged a visit for July. I crossed the Austrian border in the north with a German graduate student whom I invited along to help with translation, and we drove through southern Bohemia, to Budweis and Krumlov. Incredibly green to someone from the American southwest, the farmland skirted the Šumava Mountains, in valleys where large dairy herds and lumbering operations coexisted. We arrived at the village of Kristanov. There had been a Rauscher family there until 1945, when, like other Germans, they were forced to leave. The Czechs deported these "Sudaten Germans" because the Nazis had used the pretense of wanting to reunite with them to invade Czechoslovakia. Most of these Sudaten Germans found refuge in East Germany. The Czech government established collective farms on the confiscated land and replaced the German landlords with Slovaks.

Only two German women were allowed to remain in the village of Kristanov because they had married Czechs. One, Maria Bartova, was still farming there. We visited Bartova's farmstead, a large structure that housed animals, storage, and living space under one roof. The countryside around her farm was especially beautiful—bright green meadows, purple thistles blooming in the fields, blossoming potato plants, small haystacks everywhere. I was struck by the similarity of this part of Bohemia to northern Wisconsin, also a hilly land with meadows and valleys separated by wooded hills.[69]

Grandma Schopp never talked to me about her home in Bohemia, never communicated with the more distant kin who lived there, never indicated any interest in visiting her homeland. Wisconsin became her home. But she was willing to leave Wisconsin, too, as did all her children except the oldest son and one daughter. Kin, not land, was home to her. Like many immigrants, Matilda and Karl left their elders behind when they struck out from their small villages, but they saved enough money to send for their two surviving parents. Both Matilda and Karl took care of their parents and expected, in turn, to be taken care of by their children.[70]

Although Matilda remarried after Karl died in 1902, she had little help from her second husband, Leo, in caring for her family. In 1909, when Matilda's oldest son, Frank, turned fourteen, he quit school and began to farm full-time with her. Matilda had inherited the farm from Karl when he died, and she kept the title in her name, continuing her round of chores with Frank, sending her other children to work on neighboring farms and then to the city as soon as they could find a place to stay and work. Matilda and Frank moved the old log house and built a new frame house in 1919. Frank used the old log house for his growing blacksmith business. According to family memories, Leo never lived in the new house; he was permanently gone by then. Matilda had no assistance from the state or county in raising her family and only occasional help from neighbors and kin. The family survived by hard work and Matilda's iron discipline as she organized her children's labor and her own. After Emma, the youngest, left for the city in 1923, Matilda must have felt her task nearly done, and on August 6 of that year she deeded the farm to Frank. In turn she asked Frank to sign a formal agreement, as was common in many German families, to allow her to stay on the farm as long as she lived. She planned to work while she was able and then to be cared for by her son and his wife, when he married, until her death.

Despite the written agreement, Matilda's life did not turn out as she planned. In 1927 Frank married Lucille, a wealthier Milwaukee woman of German heritage whom he had met while she was visiting friends in a nearby village. Frank had a nice car by then, and he had plans to open a garage and re-pair cars. However, there were not enough cars in the rural areas to support all the young men who wanted to become mechanics, and so Frank continued to be the neighborhood blacksmith and to farm. He supplemented their still-inadequate income by bootlegging liquor made in the basement in a retrofitted copper canning kettle. He mortgaged the farm to make ends meet. Matilda continued to milk the cows. Lucille kept house—and took out her disappointment by scrapping with Matilda.

No one remembers just when things went wrong. Frank got along with everyone. He could not understand the tensions that increased every year. One daughter, born in 1930, remembers her mother being mean to Matilda. The eldest daughter, born in 1928, remembers Matilda refusing to help her mother during childbirth, probably the birth of the third daughter, in 1935, when the family had no money for a doctor and had to find a neighbor midwife to assist at the birth. Lucille must have realized that there would never be enough money to care for their daughters easily, that she would have to struggle just to keep the farm, their only source of income. When the man who owned the mortgage came to foreclose, Frank seemed unable to fight. Lucille faced down the lender and saved the farm.

Afterward, Lucille managed the household and Matilda lived away from the farm for periods of time. Frank asked her to come back, and she lived in a small room just off the living room for a while, but it never lasted long. She tried staying with her sister, then a niece, then a daughter in St. Paul, then a son in Oregon. She left the farm for good in 1947, when she was seventy-seven, starting to go blind from cataracts, and no longer able to work. There must have been a family council—phone calls and letters—to decide which daughter would accept responsibility for Matilda. Some daughters were living a precarious life themselves: one on an unpromising farm in Canada, three others working full-time. My mother was not working outside the home, her two oldest children were grown, and I was the only child living at home. And so I had a chance to know Matilda. When she left our home, she lived for two years with a daughter in Milwaukee, where she died in 1958, only one year before her daughter Theresa, my mother, died.

Matilda had cared for and kept her children alive through hard times and still managed to hold onto the farm. She had fulfilled her obligation to care for her parents and in turn was cared for by her children.

I have told Matilda's story not only because it is my family story but also because it is so at odds with that ideal Wisconsin settler family of literature, Laura Ingalls Wilder's *Little House in the Big Woods*. In that book, not as well remembered as *Little House on the Prairie*, Pa builds a cozy log house in the woods and tends animals and gardens while Ma prepares the food, makes and repairs the clothing, manages the small household, and maintains the family's health. Yet most German immigrant women, like Matilda, did all a woman was supposed to do in the house and shared all the work of the men as well, clearing stumps and stones, working in the fields, and harvesting—and it was still not enough. She had to know how to survive if the male could not do his share to care for the family—through accident, poor health, abandonment, not bringing home the "family wage" he earned, or, like my grandfather Leo, refusing to perform farm work.[71]

The assumption seemed to be widespread that, as in Wilder's stories, if a family could not make it in the Big Woods, they should move farther west to the prairie or back home to their parents. A woman seldom had any sense of entitlement to the land, even if she held the deed as a widow, as did Matilda. Land belonged to those who could successfully work it, and doing so was difficult for one adult. In terms of practical skills, German women, accustomed to handling animals and performing field work, were probably in the best position to continue farming, but when combined with family duties and lack of a cash income, success did not come easily. And all these efforts did not insure they would be cared for by their children.

NATIVE ELDERS

Like elder settler women, Native women expected their families and communities to help care for them in old age. They also expected to remain productive members of their families and communities and developed varied strategies to provide for their old age. Some important differences between settler and Native existed, however. Traditionally, many Native communities maintained more than one residence. Though their migratory lifestyle was curtailed and their hunting areas shrank as they were confined on reservations, most families still maintained several places where they lived for a part of the year. Elder women continued to spend time ricing and sugaring at family encampments in spring and fall. Many families kept two houses, one in the woods or countryside and one in town.

Keeping two houses was the norm for Lac du Flambeau Chippewa. In 1917 agent D. H. Kipps wrote to the commissioner of Indian Affairs that most Native families still had two homes, one in the communal village of Lac du Flambeau and one on their private allotment to which they moved at planting time and remained through the harvests. Thus during the harshest part of the year, in winter, elder women lived in the village, convenient to kin and friends who could help them if needed. Most elder women managed to care for themselves with a minimum of help. In the late 1890s and early 1900s, the government sometimes bought supplies for elders unable to care for themselves—usually flour and pork. In 1916 an official estimated that only about three percent of the people at Lac du Flambeau were needy and that they were taken care of by friends or the government. Native families seldom called upon the government for extra stores from the warehouse. In 1922, when the government took the industrial survey at Lac du Flambeau, almost all elder women were caring for themselves, gathering and growing food, and making things to sell.[72]

Of the 135 households at Lac du Flambeau in 1922, almost one-third had people age seventy or older living in them. Two-thirds of these households had a woman seventy or older. Only one of these women lived alone, and only two had kin other than their husbands living with them. The rest lived with their elder male partners, kept house and gardened, gathered and processed. The older husbands often still hunted, trapped, and fished. Some still chopped wood. They lived together and got by with a little help. The government assisted only a few of the elders with extra rations.[73]

Most women remained productive and active despite their age. They put together several sources of subsistence to provide some security. Grandmother Burgess, eighty-eight and blind, lived with her daughter, sixty-six, and grandson. She had a Civil War widow's pension. She also sold braided rag rugs and woven bags. Her daughter made beadwork and moccasins as well as gathering berries and rice and making sugar. Her grandson farmed and supplied the women with meat and fish. The three lived on Main Street in town, in a well-kept two-room house. Sha ba ti go kwe, eighty-eight, lived with her son, fifty-two, a successful guide who trapped, hunted, and fished. She amazed people with her industriousness: she still sugared, making both sugar and syrup, gathered and canned berries, made and beaded moccasins, and quilted. Mother and son had a one-acre garden in back of their home on Pokegama Lake. Bashan na ni kwe, seventy-eight, lived alone in her two-room home on Main Street although she had two sons. She also made sugar and syrup, gathered wild rice and berries, tanned hides and made moccasins, and crafted birch-bark articles. The matron could not help but remark, "Mrs Catfish [her English name] is a great grandmother. She is a very active lady, a good housekeeper, and a good cook. She frequently visits son's farm and son and his wife stay at her house while in town."[74]

In household after household, the matron found these women in their seventies and eighties almost all still engaged in gathering, farming, processing, and manufacturing objects. Whether living alone, with elder partners, or with children or grandchildren, the women were able to care for themselves with a little help.

A second group of women, in fourteen households, should be mentioned here although they were younger than the group I call elders. These women were mostly in their fifties and sixties, but their household arrangements were different. They were all married to men from eight to twenty-four years older. The women were similarly industrious and engaged in most of the same activities as the older women. They had more children and grandchildren in their households. They are a different generation, perhaps indicating a period when there was high female mortality and men sought younger women as partners.

These younger women provided care for elder males. There was no similar group of younger men, except sons and grandsons, who helped care for the older women.

Assistance to elders is more difficult to trace among the Menominee. A request from the assistant superintendent to the commissioner of Indian Affairs in 1914 listed a group of 157 people who she felt needed government assistance: 57 percent were women. About 20 percent of these women were in their sixties.[75]

That period must have been unusually difficult, however, for by 1922 there were far fewer people needing assistance. The farmer rather than the matron conducted the survey in 1924–25, so we know less about the elder women here than at Lac du Flambeau. We do know that they were similarly independent of government aid: only three couples in their seventies are noted as having government rations furnished to them. Of 277 households, a smaller fraction than at Lac du Flambeau had elders age seventy or older living with them, only four percent. The farmer, like the matron at Lac du Flambeau, admired the efforts of the elders to care for themselves and of kin to help. These elder women had varied household arrangements. The families seemed more mixed than those at Lac du Flambeau. Some elder women lived with sons and daughters-in-law or daughters and sons-in-law. Some lived with grandchildren. Several lived with partners near their own age or lived alone. At least five lived with adopted children. One lived alone in the summer and moved in with her daughter in winter and received rations. Many lived in tidy houses built by the tribe.

There were no poorhouses in either community. Needed assistance came from kin, with a few supplements from the government. Most elders remained at least partly self-sufficient, and family members supplemented their work. Unlike my grandmother, Native elders did not have to fear the poorhouse.

POORHOUSE, ALMSHOUSE

Matilda's first husband died young. Her second husband, Leo, my grandfather, lived until 1947. It never occurred to me to ask my mother about her father. In 1947, when I was thirteen, my mother mentioned her father to me for the first time. When I walked into the room, she was holding a letter and crying. "What happened?" I asked. "My father died," she replied. That was all she said.

Many years later I learned Leo's story. He was a man who hated farming but loved playing music and was in demand for community dances. He worked winters in lumbering as a young man, as a husband, and then as a father, but he refused to farm. After Matilda asked him to leave her farm, he lived with different people in the community, helping neighbors with odd jobs. One neighbor remembered him helping to dig a well. Leo was, according to his nephew, difficult to live with, and as he aged he was passed around to different families. Finally, at one home he was responsible for the death of a valuable cow and was asked to leave. At that point, when no one else would take him, he applied for admission to the institution that Matilda feared so much, the poorhouse. He died there at age seventy-five.

Given Matilda's concern over the poorhouse, I was amazed to find how few women ended up there. The poorhouse was one of the oldest caring institutions. Established in the nineteenth century to provide for dependent poor and usually called almshouses, these rural poorhouses were dreaded places, a symbol of defeat for the working poor and a recognition that the family had failed to provide. Women did everything they could, including starve their children, to stay out of these places. Still, communities considered it their responsibility to care, however badly, for their dependent members. In the nineteenth century, whole families might be cared for at the poorhouse.

Marathon County purchased ninety acres of land in 1856 for its poor farm but abandoned it and then re-established it over the next fifteen years. Until 1902, when it was transferred to the county asylum, it had few "charges" or inmates. In 1906 the county moved all its charges into a new home on the asylum grounds. The "almshouse," as officials then called it, had a manager, Henry Kurtz, seventy; a matron, Ida Nelson, twenty-three; a cook; and a nurse—all of German heritage. Of the thirty charges, all but three were men. A seventy-eight-year-old German-born widower was the eldest. Fred Fantow, about whose circumstances the records are silent, at twenty-five was the youngest. We know little about the women. Two were of Russian Polish heritage: seventy-three-year-old Caroline Domhowsky and Maria Lepinski, for whom not even an age was recorded. A third was a ten-year-old girl of unknown ethnicity. Clearly, most women had managed to stay out of the poorhouse.

Lincoln County established its eight-acre "poor farm" in 1875, as soon as it was carved out of the northern part of Marathon County. The poor were to earn part of their keep by working the land, but by 1894 taking care of the poor was the largest single expense in the county budget. That year the county purchased an eighty-acre farm, and by 1901 a new building was in use. We have a list of inmates from 1902–5, when they were mostly males. The farm was producing butter, eggs, milk, fresh vegetables, and meat by 1909, but the county found that after selling the farm produce and receiving some money from the state it still cost $236 annually per inmate. By 1915 the sex ratio on the farm was seven men for every woman, with most women over sixty and a number in their seventies. Neither these women, nor the more numerous men, were able to run the farm. Aside from the inside staff at the home, the county paid a physician to care for the elders and hired young men to do most of the farm labor.

By 1923 Lincoln County supervisors were concerned about the rising cost of care, especially when they heard that other county farms were entirely

Marathon County poorhouse, about 1900. Inmates gather for meals, segregated by sex. In 1906 the county built a new "almshouse," as officials called it. Matilda's second husband, Leo Schopp, died in the Marathon County poorhouse in 1947 at seventy-five after kin and neighbors refused to care for him any longer.

self-supporting. The county struggled to make the farm pay for itself, but by the time elders arrived at the farm they were no longer able to do much work. "When a man or woman goes before the County Judge and asks to be committed to the home, he or she is pretty generally incapacitated beyond the stage where they can work. If they are able to perform manual labor, the probabilities are they would not ask to be committed to the home," wrote one trustee of the poor. The county had a 154-acre farm producing food and helping farmers by breeding and selling pure Holsteins, but the outbuildings were in deplorable condition, decayed and unsanitary, and it was costing the county $26,500 a year, $564 for each of the forty-seven people. The county felt it had a responsibility to take care of the "unfortunates," but it never worked out the financing for separate care of the mentally disabled or for a tuberculosis sanitarium. Instead it continued to make the poor farm available for the very old and infirm and to send people needing special care to other county institutions.[76]

By the early twentieth century, most young children or mentally ill inmates had been removed from local poorhouses. Protestant congregations, mostly native-born people, pulled their elderly from public poorhouses, leaving mainly poor immigrants, Catholics, the chronically ill, and the very old. The number of inmates remained about the same, probably no more than two percent of the population, but as more poorhouses were established their symbolic power to bring fear to the elderly increased. Most women stayed out of the poorhouse either by living with kin or friends or by receiving stipends from the county to remain on their own. Being sweet tempered and helpful made elders more welcome to those who cared for them, but the threat of putting even the "greedy and disagreeable" in the poorhouse was so distasteful to families that they tried to work out alternatives. Great-aunt Caroline was one of those "greedy and disagreeable" women, her niece wrote, but the family could not face the guilt of putting her in a home. Instead the family boarded Great-aunt Caroline around. There was a German saying repeated on such occasions: *Ein gutes Gewissen ist ein sanftes Ruhekissen* (A good conscience is a good pillow to rest on). My mother must have had a guilty conscience that her father ended his days in the poorhouse, but in our family he was never mentioned, while our sweet-tempered grandmother was kept by her children in old age.[77]

THE ASYLUM

Women needed and wanted assistance in caring for family members who had extended periods of dependence. The responsibility fell primarily on women, although all family members shared in the burden imposed by lengthy disability. The community shared these burdens by providing funds for care either in the home or at specialized institutions—homes, houses, farms, schools, hospitals, or asylums—financed and operated by state or local government. These institutions were meant to help, and they often did, but good institutionalized care was difficult to achieve, in part because funds were never ample, the staff not quite well trained, and the supervision almost always inadequate. Yet, as early experiments in community care for its dependent members and as assistance for women in their primary responsibility of caring for disabled kin, these early efforts deserve sympathetic and searching scrutiny.

The earliest institutions in Wisconsin—the School for the Blind (1849), the Institute for the Education of the Deaf and Dumb (1850), and the Wisconsin Hospital for the Insane (1860)—were all part of the nineteenth-century asylum movement. Each had an independent board of trustees appointed by the governor, and each had popular support. These institutions were not meant to replace the women of the family in their care-taking tasks but to offer places where the poor who had no kin might be given care. This system of caring for the few visually and hearing impaired people seemed to work fairly well.

When the new Wisconsin Hospital opened in Mendota in 1860, it gave priority to the mentally handicapped, who had previously been cared for in various ways at the local level. Usually these unfortunates had been left in jails or poorhouses, where observers found them at best neglected and at worst abused. The asylum was considered to be a humane reform. The buildings were new, the staff optimistic, the trustees committed. Asylums were never an ideal solution, for they took people far from their homes, housed them with others who had similar problems, and offered custodial care dependent upon vague and varying standards and specialized medical care that varied from place to place. Still, for most inmates the alternative was not a cozy family life cared for by loving kin but poorly supervised and unplanned local public care that seemed barbaric.

By 1871 the state had unified control of its six separate institutions under the Board of Charities and Reform (BCR). The BCR took a new look at the situation and found many people still in poorhouses and jails. Staffed by moral reformers, the BCR felt its imperative and sacred duty was to care for the mentally ill in a more humane way. On the advice of reformers, the state decided to decentralize the system, share costs with the counties, and encourage them to build asylums and care for people at the local level. In the next decade, the state abolished separate trustees and established a board of supervisors but kept the BCR, which would have responsibility for county asylums as well as supervision over the state board of supervisors.

As the northern part of the state was settled, the hospital for the mentally ill at Mendota struggled to care for its patients. The state measured the hospital's capacity by how many patients could be provided with beds. Officials watched the number of beds climb from the original 32 in 1860 to 48, then to 103, and then in 1870 to 362. By that time officials realized one hospital could not contain all those who needed care. In 1873 the state built a second hospital at Winnebago, just north of Oshkosh, and transferred 150 of the northern patients there. By 1880 the hospital at Oshkosh converted treatment rooms into wards and crowded in more patients. It now had five hundred beds. Mendota had converted the hospital chapel into wards, and it also had five hundred beds. The hospitals could take no more patients.

Caring for the mentally disabled at home was the most disruptive of family life. The hospitals were filling with chronic cases who could not be cured and who ended up being institutionalized year after year. Families were desperate for places. The BCR could recommend expanding the existing institutions or building in other locations. Reformers were reluctant to build, yet something had to be done. They developed a new alternative, based in part on the psychiatric theories of the time and in part on the realities of the problem. Experts thought the most recently insane were the most curable. Most stayed less than a full year. Central hospitals tried to choose those most likely to recover, and chronic cases were kept at the local level. Almost four hundred remained in poorhouses, jails, or other local institutions. Every place was overcrowded; patients were receiving custodial care, not treatment.[78]

In 1890 the federal government collected statistics on disabled or impaired people in the counties of Marathon, Clark, Taylor, and Lincoln. While probably not complete, these numbers give some idea of the crisis in caring for these patients. The total number of disabled people in these four counties was 228. About half were mentally handicapped—then classified as "feeble-minded" and "insane." Of these, approximately half were being cared for at the hospitals in Oshkosh or Mendota. Some counties sent their people to the northern hospital near Oshkosh; Marathon County was spending two thousand dollars yearly to send its patients to Mendota. In addition, it was caring for 103 locally. Marathon County decided in 1893 to establish a county asylum.[79]

In 1881 the state legislature had authorized counties to build their own asylums for the chronically disabled so that state hospitals could focus on treatment of those most likely to recover. The state partially funded these county asylums and supervised them through a state board. The board visited each facility and could order state funds withheld if the county asylums were not maintained appropriately. Neither the state nor the public looked on these as "charity institutions": all classes were to be cared for there in a homelike setting with married couples managing the units, the wife as matron, the husband as superintendent. In the next nine years, twenty-three counties built local-care facilities for chronic cases.[80]

Marathon County issued bonds, asked for state appropriations, and embarked on a system to provide care for the chronically ill at the local level. It purchased a farm at Easton, not far from the county seat of Wausau, and built a large building. The farm asylum opened in 1893 with 34 people: 24 from Marathon, 16 from neighboring counties. It filled rapidly.[81]

When we check the asylum in 1910, as the federal census takers did, we see a large institution that cared for 191 patients, mostly of German ethnicity, as was its staff. Joseph and Theresa Roehl, married for twenty years and both aged forty-two, shared supervision of the asylum. They lived on the grounds with their three grown children and had their own cook. Their staff consisted of male and female supervisors (of Danish heritage), both in their thirties, bosses for farm and barn (of Swiss heritage), a farmer, three male attendants, and five female attendants, one of whom was of Norwegian heritage. There was also a laundress, a cook (French Canadian), and a woman baker. All native-born staff members but one were born in Wisconsin. There was neither a resident physician nor a nurse.

Women were a minority in this community of patients: 82 shared the asylum with 109 men. Most of the women, 54 percent, were between the ages of forty and fifty-nine; almost 30 percent were in their forties. The youngest was seventeen. Only nine were seventy or older, thus making it unlikely that Alzheimer's or dementia was the reason that brought most of the women here. Rather, these were chronically mentally ill women of middle age, almost

Marathon County poorhouse nurse, about 1900. The nurse was key to maintaining the health of inmates, who were usually elderly and frail. Together with the man and wife who supervised the house, the cook, and the serving women, nurses cared for those whose families could or would not offer a home.

half of German ethnicity, 25 percent Yankee or immigrants from Great Britain, ten percent Scandinavian, and only two Polish, both foreign born.

The increase in the number of chronically ill patients in the next decade was enough for a second asylum farm to be built in Clark County in 1922. The county brought twelve of its patients back from Marathon County and several "custodial" patients back from the state hospital for long-term "humane care and kind treatment." It accepted patients from other counties as well. The matron and superintendent came from the Marathon asylum to direct the new facility in Clark County. When they retired in 1936, their son and daughter-in-law replaced them. Well-funded local care with stable long-term supervision seemed to be popular and to offer the best possible solution for women who could not be cared for by their family members at home.[82]

In a lifetime of caring, rural women had obligations that went beyond the duty to prevent or cure acute illnesses. The larger communities within which these women lived expected them to care for dependents who were particularly vulnerable because of young or old age, those chronically and physically or mentally disabled at any age, and girls aged fourteen to twenty-one, particularly at risk for abuse as they reached sexual maturity. Individual women provided most of the support to these people within the family. Local and state agencies offered at best small supplementary funds and assistance. Assistance of any kind came with some sort of oversight and control over how women would care for dependents. For each family, the fear was that they might have to depend on such state aid and manage the restrictions that came with it.

Community and state expected the family, primarily the women, to care for all dependents. During the nineteenth century, however, the state of Wisconsin, like states elsewhere, assumed greater responsibility for individuals who had no kin to care for them: orphans or elders, the poor and sick, the mentally disabled. It developed institutions for categories of individuals for whom the family could not or would not provide. Wisconsin townships opened institutions to assist in the care of some orphan children and for mothers who needed assistance with dependent children in their homes. The state gradually supplemented local assistance with a system of "mothers' pensions," small amounts of money to help women keep their families intact. Women continued to care for dependent elders, those who could no longer work effectively or for long periods of time. Elders varied in the type of assistance they needed. Some had chronic frailties but were in fair health. Others were in good health but suffered from confusion and disorientation. A good number had physical and cognitive needs—for assistance, oversight, nursing, cooking, and cleaning. All elders needed help, formal and informal, from family and community in what have been called "exit rituals," preparation for the end of life. Women cared for most of these elders in their homes. When they could not, the state provided poorhouses and asylums as substitutes for familial care.

State institutions cared for dependents of settler families only. Except in rare instances, Native care of dependents remained with their communities. The federal government gradually increased its dominance over Native peoples beginning in the late nineteenth century. By 1920 it was exercising considerable control and planning for even greater monitoring of women, thus replacing systems of customary support with those applied by outside agencies, which imposed their own world views.

6

Learning

My uncle took me up in the loft of the old log house where my mother grew up. He had used the downstairs as a blacksmith shop since the family moved into their new house in 1919, but he continued to store old stuff in the loft. He opened a dusty wooden chest. It was full of schoolbooks. He put into my hands a green book with a painted cover showing children. "This was your mother's," he said. The title read: *The Swiss Family Robinson; or, Adventures of a Father and Mother and Four Sons in a Desert Island.* I opened the cover and there was her penciled name, "Theresa Schopf." On the flyleaf were the words, "Given to Theresa Schopf for Good Work in Spelling With Kindest Regards, Your Teacher, Jos. Jantsch, 1914." I turned to the preface. It was dedicated to the "young inquirer after good," for whom, the authors hoped, "the accidents of life may be repaired by the efforts of his own thought, and the constancy of his own industry." It was the story of a Swiss pastor who planned to settle on a farm in the late eighteenth century but was marooned with his family in New Guinea.[1]

Sitting in that dusty loft, I remembered what my mother had said about her school days. She was an especially good speller, she told me. At the beginning of her eighth year, a family member was ill, and her mother kept her home from school to nurse the ailing person back to health. She never went back to finish the eighth grade. In fall of 1914, she would have been thirteen. Her mother, Matilda, had finished school at fourteen and gone to work. Theresa always wanted to finish her interrupted schoolwork. Forty years later she wrote to a friend about that desire. The reality was that at thirteen she was done with formal schooling. Theresa never forgot her joy in learning and the way her teacher had encouraged her that year.

In Europe, children's learning experiences differed from country to country depending on what group or nation controlled national politics. Germans had an excellent system of basic education, and Matilda would have learned to read and write in her village German school. But that same German educational system was oppressive when Germans occupied Poland and forced Poles to attend schools with no regard for local desires or customs. Still, most Europeans and Americans shared what could be called, broadly, a Western European education, and most adult immigrants from Europe were literate in their national languages. Settlers saw the common schools as a continuation of what they had learned in Europe or the eastern United States, but under local control and supported by local taxes. Protestant native-born settlers may have seen schools as a way of indoctrinating non-Protestant peoples, but they shared a European heritage despite ethnic and linguistic differences. Settler communities built one-room schoolhouses to provide common education and controlled them almost entirely. Catholic settlers and German immigrants supplemented these publicly financed and controlled schools with parochial and German-language schools. Few immigrant girls were able to complete common school; fewer still went on to high school.

The Native peoples, however, were in quite a different position in relation to learning. Native people had understood and used European language and customs in the fur trade, but they had adopted them voluntarily based on their own needs. They learned informally in daily interactions with Europeans. The settlers to Native lands, likewise, learned Native languages and customs for practical purposes, for trade and non-economic cultural exchanges. Alongside this language and culture of trade existed hundreds of tribal cultures kept in balance with changing conditions through a selective adaptation of skills, materials, and customs. Native/French, or Métis, existed as multicultural and multilingual people, sometimes choosing to live among settlers, sometimes among Native peoples. They formed bridges among cultures.

In Native communities, government day schools were voluntary for most of the nineteenth century. By the end of the century the government was forcing children into boarding schools, where they were taught a foreign culture intended to replace, even eradicate, their home schooling and culture. The government also licensed private religious boarding schools, which provided the only alternative for Native families. Finally, realizing the failure of its schools, the government attempted to integrate Native children into public schools.

Who taught in both settler and Native schools was important to parents. The locally controlled system composed of one-room schoolhouses led to problems of recruiting, paying, supervising, and training teachers. Schools competed for a small pool of trained teachers because the state did not provide adequate teacher training, while gender, ethnicity, and economics all determined which few would be recruited and trained as teachers. The federal government, after a brief experiment with training Native women to teach, refused to consider them at all for the federal educational system. Finally, even settler one-room common schools and teachers were eliminated through consolidation. In practice, access of all daughters to the profession of teaching was limited, and mothers had the task of teaching their children what they wished of their cultures to be carried on to the next generation. They expected their daughters to be the primary transmitters of culture.

Schooling Settler Daughters
Theresa's Story [Schopp, Tinucci, born in Wisconsin, 1902–59]

Theresa entered her one-room school in 1908 from a predominantly German-speaking family. Matilda could read and write as well as speak German, but at home she had taught Theresa only how to speak German, not to read or write it. Unlike other German immigrant children, Theresa never attended parochial school to learn German in preparation for her First Holy Communion. Theresa's family could not afford to pay tuition at the parochial school in Dorchester, five miles away. Her formal education was entirely in English at the local one-room public school.

When Theresa started grammar school at six, she brought many skills already learned at home. These skills included a sense of order from that crowded home, an eagerness to emulate her elder brothers and sisters and learn English, a desire to meet other children, to study. Time at school also gave her relief from the crowded home, a chance to read instead of doing chores, time to play, the privilege of wearing a clean dress and taking it off when she came back home, to keep it nice for another day. She was never as eager to put on shoes, for she seldom wore them indoors at home and had to wear whatever was available from older children, even if they pinched, as she remembered they did. In those ill-fitting shoes she walked the mile to the Eau Pleine School each morning. She was about ten when she posed for a picture with her twenty-seven schoolmates. Theresa stood in the front row, with the youngest children, in a plaid dress, the collar slightly askew, her hair pulled back in braids. Her older half-sister Betty stood farther back, next to their teacher and neighbor, Joseph Jantsch. Her brther Ed stood to the left of Jantsch.

Spelling bees were major events at the school and the place where Theresa first sensed her ability to learn. I have her *Modern Spelling Book: Lessons in the Orthography, Pronunciation, Derivation, Meaning and Use of Words.* When she had mastered the book's 209 lessons she could spell, pronounce, and define thousands of words. She knew, for example, that the name *Minneapolis* was formed "by affixing the Greek *polis,* meaning 'city,' to *minne,* the Indian word for 'water.'" She stayed in school through that wonderful seventh grade and her triumphs in spelling. Then her schooling ended.[2]

My mother felt her lack of schooling as a personal deprivation. In her family, only the youngest daughter, born in 1908, completed the eighth grade and received a graduation certificate. In her neighborhood it was uncommon for a child to finish, and those who did were the younger or the disabled, those who could be spared because of other siblings' full-time work.

A number of nostalgic memoirs exist of these schools, but the record of what went on within them is sketchy at best. Records were not collected by the state, for these were essentially local institutions. The curator at the Colby

Eau Pleine school, about 1913. Theresa is in the front row, fourth from the left; her sister Betty stands next to Joseph Jantsch, their teacher, while Ed stands to his left. Most settler women wanted their daughters to attend these one-room multi-grade classes but often kept them home to help with domestic and outside work. Theresa dropped out of school after the seventh grade to help care for a sick family member.

Rural Arts Museum has gathered hundreds of the red ledgers that tracked student attendance in the twentieth century. They give only a bare outline of what went on. Joe was there; Jane was absent. The name of the teacher. The name of the school. The date.

At the Rural Arts Museum a schoolhouse sits comfortably near the relocated log house in which Theresa grew up, to remind people of the importance of learning to these early settlers. Ironically, this schoolhouse that represents the common school was not a common school at all but the parish school of a Lutheran congregation thirty-five miles south in Granton. The 24-by-40-foot wooden school was built in 1886, at the beginning of the Lutheran parochial school movement. Still, old-timers find it a satisfactory representation, one that evokes memories of their childhood experiences. They remember carrying lunches in syrup pails to similar schools, teachers boarding at homes and arriving at school early to build fires in the heating stoves, outdoor toilets and kids who, when angry, swiped others' caps and threw them down the hole. Memoirs can tell us something about those cold walks to school each morning. One former student from Clark County recalled those long hikes as a time to enjoy the outdoors, unpaved roads as a time to reflect, and the first spring days as a time to notice the blooming mayflowers and cowslips and returning robins.[3]

SLANT SCRIPT

THE MODERN SPELLING BOOK

LESSONS IN THE ORTHOGRAPHY, PRONUNCIATION, DERIVATION, MEANING AND USE OF WORDS.

AMERICAN·BOOK·COMPANY
NEW.YORK·CINCINNATI·CHICAGO

The Modern Spelling Book, *1896. This book equipped Theresa for a lifetime of literacy. She took pride in her neat handwriting, properly spelled words, and correct grammar. During the 1940s she wrote hundreds of letters to her husband, who was overseas in the military. In one of her few surviving letters from the 1950s, she wrote regretfully of not being able to continue her education.*

Theresa had another reason for looking forward to school. She was the sixth-born of Matilda's children but the first-born from her union with Leo Schopp, the Bavarian immigrant Matilda had married in haste after the sudden death of her first husband. Probably Matilda's nephew brought Leo over to help with the harvest that fall. By January Matilda had decided Leo would do for the husband she badly needed to help raise her five young children. As with her first husband, and in accordance with German custom, Matilda made sure she was pregnant before marrying Leo in April 1902. Theresa was born five months later, in September. Leo was bringing home money from his work in the woods and as a musician. There was enough money to send for a nearby physician instead of a neighborhood midwife to help Matilda with childbirth.

In the census of 1910 the family seemed intact. The census taker listed Leo as a "farmer," with stepson Frank described as a "farm laborer" and Matilda as "home maker." A 1911 photograph shows Leo in front of the log house, holding his accordion, surrounded by children and neighbor youth. My mother, Theresa, sits on the wooden chair with bare feet in a print dress and white apron, arms folded firmly in front of her, proudly wearing a black cap that Leo had brought her. She remembered her father fondly for such impractical gifts. Theresa, who sits between her older sisters, would have been about nine. Theresa's younger brother and sister and mother Matilda were not in the photograph. Despite the shabby log house in back of the group, the family looks quite secure.

The photograph was not a real picture of the poverty of Theresa's first nine years. After the first few years of marriage, Leo ceased to be a good provider. He may have brought gifts for his daughter, but he brought little to help feed the family, and he refused to do routine farm work. The relationship with Matilda had soured after their third child was born in extreme poverty in 1908. Theresa was already old enough to understand the arguments between her parents, Matilda's growing bitterness. What good did a black cap do to help feed her eight children?

During the next few years, school would have provided a sanctuary for Theresa as the arguments between her parents increased. Leo continued to come home without contributing to the support of his three children and five stepchildren. Fortunately, the oldest daughters went to work on neighboring farms as they reached thirteen or fourteen and dropped out of school. Frank, the first-born son, liked farm work. At fourteen, he was already a full-time farm laborer at home. Leo and Frank got along well, but Leo watched Frank work rather than working with him.

Theresa did not like farm work either, although she had no choice but to do the chores Matilda assigned. As a younger daughter, she probably had fewer outside chores and did more housework than the others. Her older sisters and Frank were kind to her—she remained close to all of them as she grew up.

But the farm was a place she grew to hate. School offered a taste of another world. Theresa knew there was no hope that she could continue her education. Like her half-sisters, she would have to work on neighboring farms. But she could plan to leave as soon as she was old enough. Family records show Theresa still at home for her sixteenth birthday in 1918, but she departed for St. Paul sometime later that year. Leo disappears from the family about the same time. Without Leo and the other children and with the gradual development of a small dairy, the family did better. They built a new frame house and moved into it in 1919. No one remembers Leo living in the new house.

Theresa returned occasionally to visit her mother and brother Frank. Except for one year when she and her husband owned a nursery farm, Theresa refused to live again on a farm. She never had a garden or canned vegetables. To my memory, she never even raised a houseplant. Home for her was always where there was no farm. She saw her father very little after he left the farm and she moved to the city. Yet she seems to have shared his distaste for farm work and farm life. Her daughter, Theresa vowed, would not grow up on a farm and would never be forced to leave school. She would have the learning of which Theresa had been deprived.

BUILDING THE COMMON SCHOOLS

Local one-room schools, so little written about, were the central institutions of learning in each township. Different succeeding ethnic groups adopted the ideology and practice of free schooling as they moved into central Wisconsin townships. While many states offered no free public school until the late 1860s, Wisconsin copied northeastern states in mandating free elementary schooling in its 1848 school law. This law gave the responsibility of organizing school districts, and almost total authority for administering schools, to township boards of supervisors. Town boards examined and certified teachers. The state tried to enforce uniformity in textbooks, discouraged sectarian class materials and teaching, and mandated that certain classes be taught: reading, writing, arithmetic, geography, English grammar, and orthography. The local board could add whatever classes it wished. By mid-century, the state mandated a three-month school term. The sixteenth section of each township had been reserved by law to support schools. Proceeds from the sale of these federal lands, plus state, township, and district taxes, were to finance operation of the schools. When the state created for each county the position of school superintendent in 1861, it shifted to them the responsibility for certifying teachers, inspecting schools, and conducting teacher institutes.[4]

Until the 1890s, local communities were responsible for financing schools. As time went on, they received financial aid from both county and state. By 1897, for example, the Deer Creek school district estimated it received about two-thirds of its financing from its district levy and the other third about equally from county and state. In the early twentieth century, when rural people demanded improved transportation and local governments had to appropriate large sums to build bridges and pave roads, the state legislature increased financial aid to local schools somewhat. As the state increased its aid, however, it also expanded its requirements—more and longer school days for more years, more subjects, better buildings, more equipment—which further increased costs.

Few of the hundreds of common schools so painstakingly built by the early settlers in the 1870s and 1880s remain in northern Wisconsin. An old schoolhouse seldom stood empty when it had outgrown its use. School boards sold their old log or clapboard structures. As early as 1878, St. Kilian's Catholic church moved the old Colby schoolhouse and used it until the parishioners raised enough money to build a new church. In Taylor County in 1912, an old schoolhouse was cut in two when it was moved; one part became a restaurant and the other a private residence. In 1913 one Deer Creek school was toted away to become the Zastrow Cheese Factory. One by one the simple structures disappeared, either moved or expanded with new wings and plastered to become regenerated schools that lived on indistinguishable from their new appendages. These structures were not something to be nostalgic about, although the Medford School District did remodel the Pleasant Valley School during its 1974 centennial and taught the third and fourth grades there for the year. With its new siding, rows of tight windows, and new roof, it seemed like a completely new building, except for the cupola bell tower rising above it. Kreie School waved its flag daily as well after it became a fifth-grade schoolhouse in 1973.[5]

Many midwestern communities published centennial books to commemorate a century of existence, but most gave scant attention to the history of their community schools. The centennial committee at Stetsonville in Taylor County was different: it carefully collected the scattered record books of the early school boards and pieced together an account and then gathered photographs of early schools, standing solidly behind groups of schoolchildren and their teachers, some on winter days when the students wore boots, others on windy spring days, a few even showing interiors. A village or itinerant photographer visited each school near the end of the term so that students and teachers could have these images to remember their school days.[6]

We know from photographs of classes taken around 1910–14 that most schoolrooms were similar to the one in which Theresa learned her basics at Eau Pleine School. A photograph from an unidentified schoolroom about the same time and area shows twenty-three students and a teacher dressed in a black high-necked, long-skirted dress, her hair pulled up into a pompadour. The younger children sit at double desks, girls on one side, boys in the center, their textbooks open on their desks, other books on shelves below, just visible

Inside the one-room school, 1910s. Students sit at double desks, girls on one side of the room, boys on the other. Windows have blinds and there is a wastepaper basket, students have books, and the teacher has blackboards, but a flag is the only object on the walls. A 1902 state committee report on rural schools called country teachers "incompetent culls" in a "suicidal" small-district system and recommended school consolidation. Most settlers preferred to keep local one-room schools.

through the iron fretwork. The younger girls dress in checked, striped, or plain dresses and pinafores with long black stockings and shoes, their hair pulled back with large bows tied on either side or in back. The young boys wear dark shirts and pants; one wears bib overalls. The room has three blackboards with chalk writing on them, an American flag with forty-five stars, and no pictures on the wall.

School board record books remain our primary written memory of how communities built and managed their common schools. Small groups of men met in private homes, in stores, in whatever building could hold the ten to twenty of them to elect a president, treasurer, and clerk. Some of these officers held their posts for years. The treasurer of the Little Black Center School remembered serving for forty years after being elected in 1918, until the school consolidated in 1958. Records silently mark the ethnic changes as well. One began in English, continued in a half-Norwegian script, then switched to a mixed German-English summary as new immigrant groups inherited the school record book and struggled to find the right English word.[7]

Communities attempted to keep their schools within two miles of each home. For the first schools, families within the community donated land, logs for construction, and labor to construct the schoolhouses and desks. Once established, the district school board met each July. It set the tax levy, hired the teachers, bought books and supplies, arranged for repairs and maintenance, kept a census, and made reports. Although experiences varied by school, the chronology was similar to the following, excerpted from the records of Little Black Liberty School:

1876 On May 2, Peter Liberty chaired a meeting of fifteen residents who met at the Hoff home and elected officers. Raised $200 for teachers, $75 for incidentals. To have a three-month school, $80 to pay for school. Mary Vezey to be first teacher. Board to negotiate with the Wisconsin Central Railroad for land and commence building at once.

1885 Built new school at cost of $300. Classes to meet for five to eight months. "Wm. Fahrenbach was geben the right to cut all the hay on the school land provided he would take care of the school, clean same and black the stove."

1909 Sixty students, new school voted.

1910 New school completed at cost of $1,800. Amanda Pries hired as teacher.

1911 School divided into two rooms and two teachers hired, Mary Thornton and Crystal Begilow.

1920 Enrollment declined. Returned to one-room school with Alice Hoff as teacher.[8]

School records sometimes tracked the development from an ungraded rural school into a graded town school, as they did in the school district that became Stetsonville. From a small schoolhouse built in 1876, the school expanded to a graded school with an eight-month term in 1900, then to a two-story brick school in 1912.[9]

Generally, schools followed a similar routine. In the smaller districts the teacher and her students performed most of the chores. She arrived early to start the fire in the wood stove and swept the floor. Students volunteered or elected fellow students to perform the other chores: carry the wood (in 1885, one school district estimated it took eleven and one half cords of wood to heat its schoolhouse), heat water and clean up the wash stand (often simply a board fastened across one corner of the building with a common washbowl and towel), wash the blackboards and dust erasers, sweep the outdoor toilets. Older students sometimes constructed teeter-totters and swings in the school yards and helped water ice-skating rinks.[10]

Down the road from where Theresa lived in Marathon County was the Haltom School. Hattie Munkwitz, who taught in 1912 and 1913, received fifty-three dollars a month, not enough to keep her there for long. Young women came and went in a steady procession at the Haltom School. Haltom had an average of two teachers in every three years for the thirty-four years from 1879 to 1913, over 80 percent of them women. These teachers varied in age, from seventeen-year-old Pauline Kiehl in 1892 to fifty-six-year-old Charlotte Folsom in 1893. Wages steadily advanced during the early twentieth century but remained so low that there were always jobs available. By 1917 wages had increased substantially, yet there existed a shortage of trained teachers.[11]

Rules established for teachers do not seem extreme. Teachers were, however, not allowed to smoke or drink. One district warned them not to attend dances on weekdays, and one in 1927 decreed that there be no more dancing *in* the schoolroom. Teachers were often required to reside within the school district, at least during weekdays. Women in the community took the responsibility of boarding the teacher, making room in their crowded houses by bunching up their children even more to give her a private room, planning larger meals, and adding her clothing to the weekly wash. Teachers often joined in chores as they had done at their home farms. They sought local diversions. One teacher reported reading all three books in the town library while teaching there for a year.[12]

Far more girls than boys were in the rough seats of those one-room schoolhouses the young teachers presided over. Girls, especially those between ages ten and thirteen, were more likely to be enrolled than boys of that age. Yet, if they were more likely to be enrolled, they were also more likely to be absent than enrolled boys. At Haltom, for example, in 1898 thirty-three girls attended and only fourteen boys. Yet only those girls five to eight years of age attended more than 120 days. Girls absent more than one hundred days were almost all ten to sixteen years old. This irregular attendance reflected the flexibility of female work that they were growing into. Young boys were already regularly employed at appointed tasks; young girls were likely to be needed as tasks arose and then kept home to help, whether at planting time or when someone in the family needed nursing.[13]

Attendance was quite irregular. Local newspapers sometimes reported the grim statistics of absences and tardiness. In April 1886 the Schofield teacher, Mollie Hollis, told the newspaper that during the twenty days she taught in the previous month, only 14 of the 23 enrolled children had attended at all, and of these 8 had sometimes been absent or tardy. At Kelly, teacher Mary Brogran reported of her nineteen days taught the previous month: 36 of 41 enrolled attended, and of these 29 were sometimes absent or tardy.[14]

We know from Theresa's story why one young girl dropped out of school. There is one record, however, that tells us in greater detail how difficult it was

Table 1: Schools and Students in North-Central Wisconsin, 1881–1921, by County

Years or County	Number in County	Percent in School	Number in Private Schools	Number of Public Common Schools	Number of Public High Schools	Number of Private Schools
	Students			**Schools**		
1881–82 (age 7–15)						
Clark	1,678	89	59	81	2	1
Lincoln	596	100	0	15	0	0
Marathon	2,506	90	0	98	2	0
Taylor	443	75	15	23	0	1
1890–92 (age 7–14) (attended 12 or more weeks)						
Clark	3,282	88	86*	111	NA	4
Lincoln	826	96	0	36	NA	0
Marathon	4,395	77	103	141	NA	4
Taylor	1,226	85	NA	56	NA	3
1898–1900 (age 7–13) (attended 12 or more weeks)						
Clark	4,221	87	156	128	6	0
Lincoln	1,055	80	22	59	2	0
Marathon	5,915	84	276	173	2	15
Taylor	2,101	94	79	69	1	2
1910–12 (age 7–14) (rural only; attended 24 or more weeks)						
Clark	5,995	64	194	145	7	NA
Lincoln	1,399	75	132	68	0	NA
Marathon	6,319	73	687	194	5	NA
Taylor	2,943	62	80	74	0	NA

			(In high school)				
1920–21 (rural only)			Number	Percent			
Clark	4,393	62	910	21	138	10	NA
Lincoln	1,825	60	43	2	76	1	NA
Marathon	7,439	50	331	4	207	6	NA
Taylor	2,247	63	322	14	77	4	NA

*A separate table for Lutherans, 1891–92, reported
Clark   68 students in 2 schools
Lincoln   165 students in 2 schools
Marathon   338 students in 6 schools
Taylor   52 students in 2 schools

Sources: Wisconsin Department of Public Instruction, *Biennial Report,* 1881–82, 1890–92, 1898–1900, 1910–12, 1920–22

for farm girls to continue their schooling. In 1923 the Children's Bureau conducted almost 550 interviews with children who had been indentured out from the Sparta State School for Dependent Children between 1913 and 1917. Eighty percent of the children had been indentured to farms, and they attended schools all over the state, including in Marathon County, where Theresa had her brief schooling. The interviews with young girls give a sense of how difficult it could be to achieve even these precious few years of education. As a group they may have worked harder than other children, but their experience echoes Theresa's.[15]

Although most schools were meeting for 160 to 180 days by 1910, the state required indentured children to attend school for only 120 days each year. Ten percent of the foster parents failed to meet even this minimum attendance contract, 70 percent met the minimum, and fewer than 20 percent exceeded it. In an exchange of letters with the Children's Bureau in 1915, its field agent Ethel Hanks called the law requiring compulsory school attendance for children ages fourteen to sixteen who were not lawfully employed "disorganized and ambiguous" and a law to enforce attendance in continuing education by young people ages sixteen to seventeen "a talking law." Neither applied to children in agricultural work. The law still required town children ages seven to fourteen to attend only 120 days.[16]

The following excerpts from interview notes with farm girls explain why rural daughters had so little schooling.

> Bertha, indentured at 10, kept away from school two or three weeks at a time according to school record. Does a great deal of housework, helps care for three young children, prepares breakfast, milks five or six cows every evening, helps with other farm work. Received two whippings with a strap and has been cuffed. Dislikes school, she is older and larger than other 6th grade girls and ashamed to go.[17]

> Mamie, 10–13, Cleaned barns and milked four or five cows a day, sometimes drove the team on the hay ford and hay loader as well as ironing, washing, and baking. Forty-one absences one year. Mamie says, "I went to school quite regular, but not too regular. The first month they kept me out to work on the farm and sometimes on wash days."[18]

> Stella, 10–14, helped with farm work, including plowing. School authorities say had no chance to show what she could do in school, often kept home and when she did attend was too tired to study. One year attended only three days, another 29 days. At 15, was only in the 3rd grade.[19]

> Flora, 15, got up early, prepared breakfast, made lunch for boarder, at noon came home and prepared lunch for family. After school sewed and helped with housework, washed supper dishes. Also washed, ironed, or cleaned. Foster mother suggested if Flora got up earlier she would have time to make beds and

wash breakfast dishes. Said maybe if she attended vocational school, which met only three or four days a week, she would have more time. Flora does not like school, her foster mother explained, because she is large and feels awkward and ill at ease there.[20]

Christina, 16, liked to read but had no time, foster parents demand endless amount of work from her. School 2½ miles away from foster home. Averaged only 55 days a year for three years. Failed arithmetic exams but never went back to take exam. Doing much of the housework now because foster mother in poor health.[21]

For those young girls who could attend regularly, schools offered a variety of opportunities for social interaction. Community schools were geared to yearly rituals that united parents and kin with students. The annual Christmas pageant brought mothers to make costumes and to coach children on their spoken lines. Later in the year they sponsored fund-raising basket socials, raffling off prepared meals to men who enjoyed dinner and the company of the woman who made it. Usually remembered as an aid to rural romance, these socials had the practical goal of raising money to buy victrolas, organs, and playground equipment.

On the last day of the spring term, the school held its annual picnic for the entire community. Families brought lunches, and the schoolteacher organized games and competitions. At these times, with families riding in from all directions in their buggies—and later in their first automobiles—the district common school seemed to embody its highest goal, that of uniting the community in providing learning for the next generation.

The success of a school and its image depended on the homogeneity of the community and its teachers. As we shall see, many communities worked to replace early Irish teachers with bilingual teachers who could instruct in English and speak the settler community's language: Norwegian, German, Danish, or Polish. Communities composed of Catholics and Protestants had to deal with the religious instruction of children. Secularism grew in these communities, to offend neither and to make both welcome. Catholic parents often withdrew students for one or two terms to attend parochial school in Medford. It was all they could afford, but it allowed Catholic students to receive religious training and learning. Evangelical Lutherans offered the same opportunities, along with German-language summer schools. Protestant sects each established their Sunday schools, where children could be taught the church doctrines. Common schools lessened the tensions and brought children of different faiths together for one learning experience.

The school had also to accommodate students from different social classes. Economic differences were relatively unimportant among the early settlers because of their common struggles to build farms, communities, and villages, but as more families moved from subsistence to moderate income, the range of students widened. Wealthier farm families participated in setting school policy and were involved in the schools. They often encouraged daughters to graduate from grammar school, seek teacher training, and return to teach. They sent their children to school carefully dressed and provided them with full lunch pails. Poorer families, who sacrificed the much-needed labor of their children, frequently had to take them out of school to meet family crises and had to send them to school shabbily dressed with meager lunches. My aunt remembered lunching on little more than an apple. One Medford woman of German descent remembered that Bohemian children brought only popcorn in their lunch pails.[22]

The common school never approached its ideal as a unifier of community identity. Rather, it remained a bundle of contradictions, a pride and a burden, a conduit of status, a molder of equality and inequality, a conveyer of learning and a guardian of measured ignorance. Still, rural women sacrificed both labor and precious cash to fund the schooling of their children—to see that they were in attendance as often as possible, that they were conventionally dressed, that they valued their literacy and respected their young female teachers.

Schopper girls dressed for school, 1910s. Rose and Anna stopped at the neighbor's house across the road for this picture. Women worked hard to dress their daughters appropriately for school. Shoes handed down from older siblings were carefully polished, clothing remodeled and patched, ribbons ironed. Amanda Sebold remembered her mother staying up nights to wash and iron the children's school clothes for the next day. In 1916 state laws still required only 120 days of school for rural children seven to fourteen years old. Like Rose and Anna, many did not finish the eighth grade.

Through special fund raisers, sponsored school projects, boarding of teachers, and encouragement to husbands to involve themselves in school management, the women assured the place of public schools in their communities.[23]

Daughters knew that when asked to drop out of school and assume family responsibility they were sacrificing their one chance for learning. It must often have seemed unjust to them, as it does to us, that they were asked to stay out of school so frequently to help with work in house and field. It was this sentiment that eventually helped establish not just the right to schooling but also the right to have all the schooling available to them and to reach for more.

Farm daughters who left rural areas, if deprived of schooling, later worked hard to secure schooling for their urban daughters. Theresa, born in 1902 on a Wisconsin farm, was forced to drop out of school in 1914, when she was twelve years old. Her daughter, born in a Minnesota city in 1934, finished elementary school, high school, and college through the PhD. For children who remained on farms, the battle to balance chores with learning continued.

THE PRIVATE SCHOOLS

The public school ideal envisioned homogeneous communities controlling schools with a minimum of state regulation. Local school boards would decide on the amount and kind of religion in the schools, the language of instruction, and the faith and ethnicity of teachers. During the nineteenth century as the common school system took form in Wisconsin, this ideal gradually became more focused. Public education would be based on an English-language interdenominational Protestantism. In Wisconsin, an 1840 law allowed bilingual teaching, but a supplementary 1854 law mandated that the main subjects be taught in English and an 1885 law limited instruction in foreign languages to one hour per day. The 1885 law also mandated secular teachers and no religious instruction in the schools.

German-speaking immigrants had come from countries with mandatory but free state-controlled education. Each country had a state religion, and citizen taxes paid for both churches and schools. There is some evidence that a number of German immigrants became active in local politics to hire German-speaking teachers. In an address, unfortunately undated, the Medford *Deutschen Schulverein* (German School Association) of Taylor County welcomed the pioneers of Chelsea and Greenwood townships to form similar associations in their areas. It urged the pioneers to use the *Deutschen Schulverein* to elect men to local office who would employ teachers who could speak both German and English and, where the majority of students were German speaking, teach German in the schools. Such teachers, the Medford Germans argued, would be more likely to remain in the community. Teaching the German language would help maintain the German culture.[24]

State laws did not ban German entirely. School records from Marathon, the most densely German of the four counties, indicate that German was still being taught in the public schools through the 1880s. In 1867, Casper Fenhause and John Saemer both taught German. Saemer even taught Bible history and catechism in German. In the late 1870s, the town of Berlin regularly purchased both German and English primers.[25]

Until 1885 many school districts also offered German during a two-month summer school, while English remained the language of instruction during a three- to five-month winter school. Thereafter, English became the primary language at public schools throughout the year. The law that allowed only one hour per day to be taught in a foreign language reduced German to a minor part of the school curriculum. The curtailment of German in public schools led to a rapid expansion of the Lutheran school system in north-central Wisconsin. German Lutherans believed the German language was essential to their church services and to preserving cultural ties with Germany. By 1889, the Wisconsin and Missouri Lutheran synods each maintained more than one hundred schools in Wisconsin.

That year, the governor urged enactment of a law to control private schools. In response to the proposed Bennett Law, modeled on a Massachusetts bill passed the previous year to regulate Catholic schools, Lutherans became the principal defenders of parents' rights to control their children's education in Wisconsin. The Wisconsin Synod led the opposition, arguing that the bill would give local public school boards, or magistrates, the power to decide which parochial schools should be recognized, to fine parents if they neglected their children's attendance at private schools, to use the fines to fund public schools, and to dictate how many subjects had to be taught in English. The synod invoked the "natural rights of parents and the Constitution" in defense of its right to administer and conduct schools, rallied opponents of the bill, and forced the legislature to repeal it. In 1913, when the legislature considered another bill to regulate private schools, the Lutherans branded it a "Second Bennett Bill" and prevented its passage.[26]

During World War I, some Lutherans fought off a proposal that would have required English to be the only language taught in any school in Wisconsin. They argued that the state had no right to prescribe the language of religious instruction. "Our congregations," the Missouri Synod stated, "should not be coerced by legislative measures," especially since the churches had shared the burden of fighting a war for democratic principles. "The parents have the natural right to control the education of their children . . . [and] the right to say what medium shall be used for religious instruction." Most parishes became bilingual or all English during this time, and most schools already taught secular subjects in English. Still, many small schools were forced to close. Congregations had established them originally to preserve the German language, and when that function disappeared, they did, too.[27]

While they lasted, private Lutheran schools were an important alternative for students. They taught in the German language. Students attended English schools during the winter and supplemented their education at parish schools during the summer. Scattered accounts from the four north-central counties mention these German Lutheran schools. John Brunner, recalling his late-nineteenth-century school experiences near Medford in Taylor County, said that most Lutheran children attended two months of German school so they could speak, read, and write the language. Loretta Kuse also remembered that in the 1880s Lutheran children attended either a German school or German catechism classes in Medford. Erna Zimmerman of Marathon County recalled that her German school, around 1900, began one month after the public school closed and that she learned religion and German.[28]

Catholics did not expand their private school system in north-central Wisconsin to perpetuate a foreign language useful for religion or culture. Catholics came from many nations, and Latin was the language of the liturgy. Because the church considered public schools to be nondenominational Protestant schools, the Third Plenary Council, held in Baltimore in 1884, ordered each parish to establish a school and required Catholic parents to send their children to these schools. By 1900 almost-two thirds of all Catholic parishes had built schools. In homogeneous ethnic communities, religious instruction might be in a foreign language, but because of the mixed language communities, year-round parish schools were usually taught in English. By 1914, when my mother, Theresa, prepared for her first communion, her religious books were all in English.[29]

The Sisters of St. Francis at La Crosse staffed most of these new parish schools in Wisconsin. This order traced its origin to a group of German sisters from Bavaria who came to the United States in 1849 with a mission to promote education. Overcoming the bishop's opposition and with the support of Bavarian priests, the women established a teacher-training program in 1864 with seven sisters and postulates, women who had joined the order but had not taken their final vows. In October of that year the order opened its first two schools at Jefferson, a town of 1,500 about fifty miles west of Milwaukee. The order spread rapidly through southern Wisconsin in the 1870s. By the end of the decade, the sisters estimated they were teaching more than 2,500 children. All of these early sisters were bilingual in German and English. Some took examinations for credentials and also taught in rural public schools.[30]

In northern Wisconsin, few German Catholic communities had established schools by the 1870s. At La Crosse, however, there was a school for three hundred, and perhaps for this reason the Sisters of St. Francis relocated there in

1871 and built St. Rose Convent. From La Crosse, the sisters founded parish schools across the north. By 1882 they had established thirty-two schools and two orphanages. That year, thirty-seven-year-old Ohio-born Sister M. Ludovica Keller assumed leadership of the order as mother superior. Mother Ludovica had taught school for sixteen years and served as assistant mother superior for more than six years before being elected the order's leader. For the next thirty-five years, until 1928, she used her firm executive ability to propel the order into its great era of school expansion.

Mother Ludovica supervised establishment of most Catholic schools in the four north-central Wisconsin counties of this study. By 1910 there was a good supply of educated nuns to teach in the larger towns and villages. At Medford, for example, four American-born nuns taught while a German-born nun kept house for them. By 1921 the Franciscan sisters also staffed schools at Athens, Colby, Dorchester, Edgar, Greenwood, Humbird, Loyal, Marathon, Mosinee, Neillsville, Rozellville, Stanley, and Stratford. In many of these small towns Catholic women raised money to finance the schools, often by sponsoring bazaars. Some schools competed with public schools for students. When the Stratford school opened in September 1902, more than one hundred students abandoned the common school. The mayor sent his daughter to inspect the school, according to Franciscan accounts, and was impressed with the good order and discipline the sisters had established. In most communities the Catholic school did not seriously compete with the public schools because so few parents could afford to send their children to private schools. Whenever they could, parents enrolled their children in the Catholic schools at age twelve to take religious instruction for their first communion. The children then returned to the common schools to complete their education.[31]

HIGH SCHOOLING

Nearly all school-age children enrolled in public or private schools by 1910, but the percentage that went on to high school remained low. While 95 percent of the children aged seven to thirteen were in school in the four core counties by 1910, probably fewer than a third were in school by ages sixteen to seventeen, and only 11 percent by eighteen to twenty. The percentages remained virtually unchanged during the next decade.[32]

The number of high schools in the four-county area increased very slowly during the first decades of the twentieth century. In 1881 there were only five: two each in Clark and Marathon, one in Lincoln, and none at all in Taylor. By 1900 Taylor had added a high school and Clark and Marathon still had only two. By 1920 Clark had ten, Marathon six, and Taylor four, but Lincoln remained steady with one. An average of 12 percent of these counties' rural students attended high school: Clark had a quarter of its rural students enrolled; Taylor had 16 percent; Marathon, five percent; and Lincoln, three percent.

Theresa's teacher, Joseph Jantsch, left a detailed account of his difficulty in getting into and graduating from high school. His experiences, those of the first young person in his area to attend high school, are worth looking at closely for the reasons so few students went on to high schools from rural areas and almost no young women attended. In order to attend high school, there had to be a school one could enroll in, and a young person had to get there.[33]

Joe, as he was called by his family and friends, lived across the road from Theresa, on the far western edge of Marathon County. There were no high schools in that area in 1906 when, at thirteen, Joe decided, with the encouragement of his older sisters, to go on to school. The closest Taylor County high school was fourteen miles northwest at Medford. Luckily, Clark County had just built a new two-story brick high school at Colby, twelve miles south of the Jantsch farm. Joe could contemplate attending high school only because his older sisters had worked in nearby towns during the winter and returned to work on the farm in the summer, providing the family with farm labor so the middle son could attend school for four additional years.

Making the decision to go to high school was itself difficult. Joe planned to enroll when he graduated from his country school at thirteen, but as he worked at home over the summer he talked himself out of it. By September he had decided not to go. His neighbors and friends of his parents prodded him, continually asking why he had changed his mind. "They almost commanded me not to miss the opportunity," he wrote. Community support, then, was an important element.[34]

Joe also felt he was poorly prepared to undertake high school work. His father visited the common school teacher and arranged for Joe to receive additional instruction in physical geography and algebra. The additional semester of preparation and the teacher's assurance that he could handle high school work convinced Joe. Parental assistance, tutoring, and continued encouragement from a teacher who had gone to high school were essential.[35]

Parents and older siblings accompanied Joe to Colby to talk to the principal and to look for a place to board. Since his parents did not speak English, Joe's brothers and sisters made inquiries, trying to find a family interested in providing Joe with a room and board in exchange for chores he could perform. At the school, they found the principal was still gone for the summer, so they could not talk to him. Unsuccessful, the family turned its buggy homeward, and Joe remembered, "The world was already appearing too complicated for me and I wondered just how it would all work out for the best."[36]

But someone at the school gave Joe's name to the principal when he returned. The principal wrote to tell Joe the date he should appear for classes.

On that Monday, his mother and brother hitched up the work horses and drove the twelve miles to Colby to deliver Joe. While Joe attended class, his mother and brother again looked for a place for him to stay. Finally, his mother began chatting with Mrs. Haselbach, a German woman who tended the bar at a local tavern. She said that Joe could sleep in her parlor until he found a room. With this promise, his family left him. It was the first time Joe had been away from home, and he remembered the first month because he was so lonely. Colby seemed a city to him, for it had electric lights, which he had never seen before.[37]

The friendly Haselbach family welcomed Joe into their crowded home. One daughter even found him a part-time job picking onions and preparing them for winter. He studied in the barroom at night. On Saturday nights there were dances in the room over the bar. A country youth had so much to learn. On Sunday mornings Joe went to Mass at the huge Catholic church and found many high school students there as well. The students were kind to him, even, he later remembered, the lawyer's son. After looking in vain for a place where he could work for room and board, he found a group of boys rooming by themselves and willing to take him in. It cost a dollar a month for food and a dollar for rent. Joe studied hard and found he had done well when he received his first report card at the end of the month.[38]

That weekend Joe hiked the twelve miles home. He had walked to Dorchester previously, about ten miles round trip, for religious instruction, but this longer walk so exhausted him that his parents arranged to have him return by train— his first train trip—taking him to Dorchester to ride the six miles back to Colby with two suitcases full of food. He would walk home often after that first month, carrying a little suitcase, sometimes through harrowing weather, resting along the way at the home of family friends. They encouraged him to persevere. "The immigrant farmers could conceive nothing more honorable than to become educated," he wrote, "During those four years of my school life, it was still an occasion of awe and bewonderment."[39]

During the second year he found a farm where he could do chores in exchange for room and board, but the work was hard. His sisters taught him to milk, but he never mastered the skill and was relieved when he found he could board for six dollars a month with the family of a German butcher. His sisters sent money for the room and board. The butcher's wife fed him on dumplings and sausages, and her adopted son became Joe's pal. He did chores around the barn and house and tutored the son in exchange for organ lessons. During his third year at school, an older sister loaned him ten dollars to buy a 4×5 plate camera and developing outfit.[40]

In the spring of his third year, Joe took an examination for a certificate to teach and passed it. His teachers encouraged him to stay in school and earn his degree. Joe's brother Bill, who had started school during Joe's third year and was renting rooms with him, decided to drop out, much to the disappointment of their older sisters. During Joe's last year, he boarded with a septuagenarian Civil War widow, paying six dollars a month and chores, plus farm goods, for his room and board. In his senior year, Joe's peers elected him class president and valedictorian.[41]

Joe's older sisters attended his graduation. Joe's youngest sister, Hattie, who was fourteen the year Joe graduated, never went to high school in Colby. As a girl, would Hattie have had the support of parents or neighbors for such a difficult four years? Would any of the work arrangements Joe made have been considered appropriate, even for a country girl accustomed to hard work? Hattie chose instead to follow her older sisters into the city, to find a job. None of the Jantsch daughters had any high school education.[42]

Beyond high school, there was little hope for further education. The Country Life Movement spawned a vocational college experiment in 1902. Marathon County had one of the first two county vocational technical colleges designed for the "rural classes." Clark County eventually had one as well. These colleges offered a two-year course of study, including both traditional subjects and practical training. Practical training was differentiated by gender in a way similar to the emerging division in agricultural colleges—agriculture courses for young men, home economics for young women. These vocational colleges, reformers hoped, would not only involve college-age students but would offer twelve-week short courses in the winter for rural adults as well. The staff would advise farmers on practical issues, organize youth clubs, and hold local conferences on rural life. These colleges did not attract enough students from farm families to make them financially viable, however. The classes were too small to pay for the high costs of establishing separate facilities, and most of the colleges closed by 1917. Marathon County shuttered its college that year, the same year Congress passed the Smith-Hughes Act, appropriating funding for vocational-technical training in high schools. High schools in Wisconsin then became the prime locus of these courses.[43]

The common school thus provided the only learning most young women would receive in rural areas before 1920. Rural ungraded schools were neither as bad nor as good as reformers thought. They were child-centered; teachers used mixed age groups to cope with diverse student needs and encouraged a family-like atmosphere and a connection to daily life. But probably no more than 40 percent was child-centered teaching; the remainder was recitation and rote learning. Teachers were underpaid and textbooks inadequate. For rural parents, however, it seemed a good combination of learning methods. And many settler daughters, like Theresa, during their brief time in these one-room schools developed a love of learning and passed it on to their daughters.[44]

Schooling Native Daughters
The Dousman Story [Rosalie LaBorde Dousman, born in Michigan, 1796–1873; Jane Dousman, born in Wisconsin, 1812–88; Kate Dousman, born in Michigan, 1815–ca. 1867]

By all accounts—scanty though they are—Rosalie Dousman was a woman of great skill and influence. The Catholic priest Edward Deams later praised her as a "lady of great accomplishments." Nurse, physician, pastor, and friend of the Menominee, she was, most of all, a teacher. Rosalie began teaching the Menominee children in 1828 at Green Bay. She followed the Menominee as they moved, first south from Green Bay to Little Chute on the lower Fox River, then in 1837 southwest of what is now Appleton to Lake Poygan, where the Catholic Menominee established a school and farm. She moved with them to the new settlement on the Wolf River in 1852.

The decision by Rosalie and her daughters to remain with the Menominee community through all their moves, from Green Bay to Little Chute to Lake Poygan and finally into the forest, is understandable if one knows something of Rosalie's Métis heritage. Rosalie was born into the LaBorde family in 1796. Her father, Jean Baptiste LaBorde, was French; her mother, Marguerite Chevalier, was from a prominent Mackinac Menominee/French trading family. When Rosalie was twelve, the family moved to Green Bay, where she met and married the American John Dousman, a member of the Dousman trading family of Prairie du Chien. Early marriages were common among Métis families, and Rosalie would have been only twelve or thirteen years old when she married in 1808. She bore four children between 1812 and 1820. The couple moved southwest of Green Bay to the present-day site of De Pere, where they opened a gristmill and distillery. Shortly after the birth of their first child, Jane, in 1812, a party of Native warriors (either Ho-Chunk or Chippewa, the accounts do not agree) on their way to join the British to fight against the Americans attacked and burned the Dousman mill and distillery. Forewarned, John escaped to Mackinac, where he planned to join the American army. Certain she would not be harmed personally, Rosalie stayed behind, hid Jane in the basement, and convinced the attackers to leave. A neighbor accompanied Rosalie and Jane to Mackinac. They returned to Green Bay in 1824. Thérèse Baird later spoke of her joy when the Dousman family returned and she had the company of her former playmate. The two families shared the same house. The Dousmans were not well-off financially, however, and Rosalie was expecting her seventh child when John died in 1828.

Because Rosalie had to find outside resources to care for her seven young children, she started a school. Some accounts describe it as a "sewing school" for women and girls. It was probably modeled on the schools that French nuns had established in Canada and the Northwest to spread basic literacy and needlework skills along with piety. Perhaps Rosalie and her daughters had attended nuns' schools in Mackinac. Jane, now sixteen, and thirteen-year-old Catherine helped with the school.

In 1831 Rosalie and Jane began teaching at the free school prominent Catholic families had established for Indians at Green Bay. By treaty, the American government promised the Menominee an annual allotment of $2,100 for education, and the Menominee at Green Bay expected to decide how these educational funds were to be used. When the government chose to fund an Anglican school, the Menominee refused to send their children there and it soon closed. In 1831 Catholics at Green Bay managed to get an endorsement from the local Indian agent for a stipend to support their school; when the government refused the stipend, however, they began to subsidize Rosalie to teach Menominee children at her home school. Thirty-three Menominee and seventeen children of mixed heritage attended her school the first year, to learn "industry and Christian morality." From that time until she quit teaching in 1869, Rosalie was the main teacher to the Menominee for both material and spiritual matters. Jane and Catherine helped her with the teaching.[45]

When the Menominee people moved from Green Bay to Lake Poygan, Rosalie moved with them. By 1839 the Menominee Catholics had built their own school, where Rosalie taught the young children and older girls. Four different priests taught the older boys. As priests changed, Rosalie stayed on to teach. Sometime around 1847 the government subsidized the Poygan Catholic school, paying stipends to the current priest and to Rosalie, who taught the children English, arithmetic, and geography. Rosalie's daughter Jane, now in her twenties, opened a free sewing school for adult women. The Menominee women, skilled rug weavers, learned quickly. Any who wished could also learn how to make bread and soap at Jane's school.[46]

Rosalie spoke Menominee, French, and English fluently and probably Chippewa, the common language of the fur trade, as well. She was said to have the support of the chiefs, the government, and the Catholic priests. The degree of support varied depending on the priest, the chiefs, and government policy. When the French-speaking Catholic missionary Father Anthony Gachet visited Keshena in 1859, seven years after the Dousmans and the Menominee people had settled there, Rosalie stood near him at the altar in the little wooden church and translated his words into Menominee. She also translated the words of the Menominee women into French when they asked to confess to Gachet. Father Gachet later wrote that the Menominee regarded Dousman as "their mother."[47]

As government employees, Rosalie and Jane sent in regular reports about their progress. While government reports are almost always partial and one-sided, those filed by Rosalie and Jane do give some sense of what went on within the school. Rosalie reported the young students as embarking upon that "great and tedious" task of learning English. The Dousman school offered some advantages to these scholars. The classes were small and ungraded; children of different ages were together where the older who had already mastered some of the work could help the younger; the Dousmans spoke Menominee so that they could explain the subjects in the students' own language. And perhaps most important, the students returned to their own Menominee-speaking homes in the evenings. Mothers sometimes took young girls out of school to help with mat weaving, as Rosalie described in 1855, "an article of comfort to them and trade." In spring when parents and children normally left to harvest and process sugar, she closed the schools.[48]

Rosalie used a curriculum much like that offered the children in settler schools. She divided her students into four levels, with the youngest first learning the alphabet and simple words, then progressing to the second and third levels, where they learned to spell, read, and write on a slate, and finally to the fourth, where they continued reading and writing but also learned orthography, arithmetic, and geography. Like settler children, the Menominee children read *McGuffy's Eclectic Third Reader.*[49]

While learning new skills was an immense task for children, it gave them an important role in contributing to family and community. In her reports Rosalie always commented on the children's willingness to learn even the most difficult subjects. In 1856, even non-Christians were voluntarily attending, "particularly those of Oshkosh's band." During these first difficult years, the school seemed successful.[50]

The Dousmans' biggest success was in the training Rosalie and Jane offered in handcrafts. Along with reading, writing, and arithmetic, the Dousmans taught young girls knitting as well as plain and fancy sewing. Rosalie wrote in her 1855 report of the young students: "They take particular delight in all kinds of needlework." When Jane began teaching in the industrial school, she offered instruction not only to the girls but also to adult women. Jane reported, "They are very ingenious with the needle, and readily learn to make garments." She showed them how to knit mittens and socks and to sew coats, pants, shirts, and gowns. By 1856 mothers and their young daughters were attending together, non-Christians as well as Christians coming regularly and working industriously. The older girls were welcome to attend one day a week. While the sewing school was discontinued for a time in 1859, a period when food was scarce, it resumed in the early 1860s.[51]

In 1869 a controversy over claims by priests and traders deeply divided the community, and Rosalie was drawn into the conflict. The controversy resulted from the priest's and traders' insistence that their claims be settled first, before annuity money and seeds were distributed to the community. The proponents of immediate claim payment, including the government blacksmith, decided to refuse the seed and the annuity payment as a way to pressure the government into paying the claims. The Christian chief Keshena, backed by the priest Gachet, supported payment of claims. Rosalie apparently supported payment after the distribution of annuities and the delivery of seed to plant the next crop. According to stories, Gachet encouraged supporters to provoke her departure with threats and insults, and Chief Keshena introduced a resolution in the Menominee council to have Rosalie banished from the reservation.[52]

As the disagreement escalated into open rebellion against the agent's control, he moved to quell the conflict. He fired the blacksmith and warned that the American government, "the Strong Arm, that rules over this Country," would put the rebels in state prison if they did not take the annuities and the seed first and settle the claims later. A special investigating agent sent from Washington attributed the cause of the trouble to a local attorney who had taken the claims case for the priest and traders. He called Rosalie "a teacher, nurse, counselor, provider, priestess, [and] gratuitous interpreter to the missionaries," devoted to the temporal, intellectual, moral, and religious welfare of the Menominee. He said the Menominee called her "mother."[53]

The conflict cemented the Dousmans' place in the community and government support for their teaching. By 1861 and 1862 the government was officially paying Rosalie, Jane, and Catherine (Kate) each three hundred dollars per year. Rosalie taught the younger children, Kate instructed the older children, and Jane supervised the sewing school. In 1861 the government hired three more teachers. For the next decade Rosalie and her daughters taught with increased government support. Jane's yearly reports to the government showed great quantities of clothing being produced by her students: pants, shirts, skirts, gowns, dresses, and sunbonnets.[54]

The Catholic clergy continued to intervene in Rosalie's schools, however. In 1864 Rosalie reported that the current priest had ordered her to close the government schools and when she did not, entered her classroom "in a furious manner," insisting he should teach catechism in the school at a particular time. The priest also demanded payment of annuities for his religious services. Every priest for the last four years, the agent wrote wearily to his superiors, had disturbed the peace by demanding such payment.

The following year, in 1865, smallpox ravaged the settlement. The Dousmans closed their schools as the quarantine rules required. Most non-Christians left the community, scattering to live in the forests, but the new priest, the fourth since 1852, insisted the Christians stay, congregate for Mass, and bury their dead from the church. When the Christian death toll continued to mount and the priest still refused to enforce the quarantine rules or prohibit public gatherings, the government ordered him to leave. The remaining Catholics scattered to the forests. By 1867, after fifteen years in their new settlement on the Wolf River, the population had declined from more than 2,000 to 1,800.

Kate died sometime during this period, probably in 1868 or 1869, and her death discouraged Rosalie and Jane. There were natural disasters, too; great winds and fires swept through the standing timber in 1868. Doubtless tired from years of wrangling with the clergy and demoralized by disease and natural disasters they were helpless to prevent, Rosalie and Jane moved to the nearby village of Shawano in 1869. Rosalie died there four years later, and Jane returned to Green Bay, where she died in 1882. The government discontinued their school for many years, and no Catholic missionaries returned to the Menominee until the Franciscans established their mission in 1880.[55]

Menominee elders later spoke of Rosalie and her daughters with affection. But, like other Métis women, the Dousmans were hardly remembered by outsiders. Métis women, those of mixed French and Native heritage, as well as other Creole women occupied a crucial place between Native and European cultures during the nineteenth century. The women who intermarried with French traders found important ways to mediate between cultural groups, offering hospitality along with medical and educational services to Native and European alike. Lucy Murphy calls them "Public Mothers" because of their status in their communities and their work in welfare, diplomacy, and peace making. Métis created the first French-Native cultures and then, as the English and Americans arrived, added elements of these cultures. Like the Dousmans, they often spoke several Native languages, French, and English. They carried on the tradition of elite women who combined public and private, social and political roles in their cultures. These Métis women continued to be influential leaders in both worlds long after the fur trade declined. Dousman fashioned her life in the tradition of these Métis cultural brokers, as an intermediary between U.S. officials, missionaries, and the Menominee.[56]

It is significant that Rosalie and Jane did not choose to remain within the Menominee community after Kate died. Given the context, with most of the Menominee themselves fleeing the reservation, it is understandable that they should choose to leave as well. The first twenty years of reservation life seemed a failure, not just in terms of health and welfare but in education as well. Clearly, that assessment was not entirely true. Menominee women had learned many new skills as they continued to practice their older industrial and agricultural skills. But a new beginning would have to be made before the Menominee would be able to stay put in their community and flourish.

ST. JOSEPH'S BOARDING SCHOOL

While each Native culture had its own customs, usually learning was accomplished through stories. Embedded in both secular and sacred narrative, told in a group's own language, these stories taught about origins, migrations, and history as well as offered precepts on how to live one's life. Stories told about specific sites, relations with kin, and individual experiences. The stories might be told at special times—during rituals or specific seasons or interspersed with work or activities as they seemed appropriate. Elders, who often spent a great deal of time with grandchildren, did much of this teaching, continuing to be an important source for tribal history and tradition as children and youth grew to adulthood. Parents and neighbors added stories. Storytellers adapted each tale to present circumstances. The young were taught to listen attentively to these stories, to memorize them, and to remember their significance. The handing down of collective memory was a shared community task of teller and listener.

This method of learning predominated in north-central Wisconsin until the Indian Bureau introduced its boarding school system in the 1880s and 1890s. This American system of learning forcibly removed children from their homes, placed them in large institutions, and forbade the use of tribal customs and language. It imposed a Christian-based culture upon students in both government-controlled schools or, in areas where Catholic or Protestant missions had already converted Native people, in clergy-run schools. Whether government, Protestant, or Catholic, the schools attempted to replace parents as the source of teaching and control. Children and their parents either resisted or worked hard to preserve their customary methods of learning despite the new teaching methods. Much local knowledge was lost, but much also survived within families and communities.[57]

Another model existed. Sweden adopted a family-based system where specially trained teachers visited Native Sami homes to teach them basic sanitation and some skills. These teachers helped Native peoples adapt their arts to the tourist trade and develop reindeer culture. While still an imposed agenda, the Swedish system was minimally intrusive. The American system was at the other extreme. In the late nineteenth and early twentieth centuries, administrators and teachers in both public and private institutions assumed Native people should play little role in defining what they needed and wanted. In practice, parents and children did influence the system, its methods, and even its content, but they had no power to develop functional school programs that combined general knowledge with local knowledge and lore of the places they called home, nor did they develop formal training programs for their own teachers. Women handed on much of the customary and local knowledge by teaching children language and values at home despite state opposition.

In the fall of 1886 Mary Dodge entered St. Joseph's Indian School, the Franciscan boarding school at Keshena in the Menominee Nation. That summer, Mary had returned from three years in St. Louis at the Convent of the Sisters of St. Joseph of Carondelet. According to accounts by school officials, those years had been good for Mary. She was the only Native child at the convent, and the nuns treated her well. Mary was, after all, the embodiment of what they were trying to achieve in their mission school in far-away Wisconsin. A chronicler of the mission later wrote, disapprovingly, that Mary had become a "pet" among the nuns.[58]

Mary was the daughter of Catholic parents who wanted their children to learn to read and write English and to learn about the European-Catholic culture. Mary's father, Louis Dodge, was born in 1852, during that difficult first period of settlement on the Wolf River. The Keshena survey of 1925 listed Mary's mother but not her name. Mary was born in the 1870s, into a turbulent time when the Menominee were confronted by the competing interests of priests, agents, and traders. It is not surprising that the Dodges chose to send Mary away to school.

Mary would have had the Sisters of St. Joseph as her teachers at Keshena. They had been teaching at the mission school since 1883, and it was probably Mother Clarissa who arranged for Mary to be admitted to the motherhouse in St. Louis. Mary's father, like other parents, was unhappy with the new mission school, but not because he objected to his daughter getting an education. He obviously wanted her to be schooled. Most of the Menominee Catholics wanted their children to be educated, but they wanted influence over that education. At first the mission priest was sympathetic to the parents' wishes. He spoke the Menominee language fluently. The Native men built a large two-story building for the mission boarding school. Native parents asked that some sisters be brought in as teachers. Brothers had taught all the children; now sisters were to teach the younger children and the older girls while the brothers were to teach only the older boys. The sisters followed the common schools' curriculum, instructing in English. Before school began each day, the priest gave the students religious instruction in the Menominee language.

When Mary entered St. Joseph's in the 1880s, older Native methods of learning were still being used by most Menominee. Women of the non-Christian minority still told origin and migration stories, maintained the rituals within which the stories were embedded, and initiated their daughters into Midewiwin beliefs. Catholic Menominee women also taught their children language and history and their daughters what they needed to know of the traditional skills and their roles as women. Mary's mother had no formal schooling, although she may have attended the Dousmans' sewing school. Still, she would have begun Mary's training early, and Mary's grandmothers, if still alive, would also have contributed stories.

Catholic parents expected to continue teaching their children in this way, but they also wanted schools to teach them new skills. Many Menominee signed petitions requesting that Catholic schools be established. Menominee Catholics offered to build a mission school and asked that sisters be brought in to teach younger children. The Sisters of St. Joseph of Carondelet, a teaching order based in St. Louis and specializing in Native children, promised to send teachers. The government, which was contracting with churches to run schools on reservations in the 1880s, agreed that because of the large number of Catholic Menominee the mission school should be awarded a contract. The government also planned to build its own boarding school and to allow parents to choose between the two schools.

The result, however, was that the boarding schools vied for students. When the new mission boarding house was completed in 1883 and the Sisters of St. Joseph installed at Keshena, the priest told parents that they *must* send their children to the Catholic school rather than to the government boarding school. Catholic parents did send eighty of their children to the new mission school, but from the beginning a number of students ran away. Three months after the new school opened, a fire started in the early hours. The sisters saved all eighty students by hustling them out of the burning dormitory at 3:00 AM into the courtyard's deep snow. Mary's father volunteered his house as a day school while the priests raised money to rebuild. Native people constructed the school, and it was open again by fall of 1884.[59]

What followed we know primarily from a mission chronicle. That winter an epidemic of measles, a highly contagious viral childhood disease, broke out in the community. Children brought the disease to the mission school, where it swept through and left five dead. Other children died after being sent home. The death rate among Catholic adults and children was disastrously high: during the next four months forty died.[60]

Parents blamed the sisters and the priest for the deaths. "A movement like a revolution took hold of them and many demanded their children be taken home," the mission chronicler wrote later, "It required great circumspection and firmness on the part of the Fathers to quiet down the minds of the parents and meet the ugly talk heard everywhere." Parents sent their children to the mission school that fall with great reluctance, the chronicler continued, "prompted only by fear of refusal of the sacraments; the children though they came were filled with aversion and dislike towards the school and teachers." Mary's father was among those who lost confidence in the missionaries. From one of their strongest supporters, he became an outspoken critic. With great misgivings, Louis Dodge sent Mary to school in the fall of 1886.[61]

Mary refused to stay, but she did not leave alone. Instead she led a revolt. Nine other girls left with her, all insisting they would not return. Others followed them, also refusing to return. There was, the chronicler continued, "quite a revolution on the reservation." Parents refused to force their children back into the mission boarding school and began to send them to the new, overcrowded government school. "Whole crowds ran away again from [St. Joseph's] school," the mission chronicler concluded.[62]

Native parents quarreled with the missionaries, but many Catholics continued to send their children to the mission school. The sisters agreed to establish
a hospital at the school and to control contagious diseases. By 1888 enrollment
had reached 120.[63]

Generally, the Sisters of St. Joseph developed good relations with parents. It
was common for parents to camp near the school and visit their children frequently. The sisters included parents in special events and extended small
courtesies when they visited the school. In 1896 the newly arrived mother
superior admitted white people to the schoolroom before a celebration and
kept Native mothers waiting in the cold. When they complained to the order's
headquarters, she was promptly replaced. Menominee Catholics petitioned
the government to use tribal logging funds to support the school after it ended
subsidies for Catholic schools. The school survived a fire in 1893. When the
girls' school burned again in 1901, Native funds helped replace it with a new
brick building. By 1904 there were 225 children in the parochial school and only
50 in the government school. In 1905 two girls burned the government school
to the ground. The Catholic school survived, although records say a similar attempt was thwarted there. During the influenza epidemic of November 1918,
the school dismissed students and only one died that fall, an amazingly good
record considering the disease's virulence and high mortality. The school reopened three weeks later.[64]

The nuns had always taught skills valued by Native women. In addition to
the basic common school curriculum and instruction in English, the sisters
taught girls how to keep house and cows. After 1885 sisters specially trained in
handwork conducted regular courses in making lace, embroidering in silk
and cotton, making paper flowers, and fancy knitting. The young women also
made all the clothing for the Native children and Sunday dresses for themselves. They made aprons, skirts, undergarments, cloaks, and night dresses for
the girls; everyday suits, shirts, undershirts, and drawers for the boys; and
mittens for all. The sisters sent an exhibit of the young women's needlework to
the 1893 World's Columbian Exposition in Chicago, along with samples of
shoes made by the boys, crayon drawings, and regular class work. In the 1920s
sisters replaced art with instruction in beadwork for the girls. They made
beaded belts, headbands, wristbands, necklaces—anything that could be decorated with beads. During the summer, girls sold the beadwork to tourists.[65]

In the 1990s, female elders discussing their experiences at the Catholic
boarding school shared pleasant memories from the 1920s and 1930s. Native
women and Catholic nuns seemed to have reached a kind of understanding at
last. The elders remembered the beadwork they had created, the fun they had
had. After the Neopit day school opened in 1913, sisters taught there as well.
About 120 students attended, slightly fewer than half of them female.[66]

Catholic Menominee women sent their children to the nuns. The mothers demanded and eventually received respect for their children's needs. Students found classes to be helpful. Occasionally, they still ran away. On the whole, however, the parochial schools became more responsive and closer to the families than the government schools. Mary Dodge, with her resistance, had helped shape that collaboration. Sarah Shillinger, a Mohawk scholar who studied the St. Joseph's school, concluded that Menominee adopted passive resistance to the boarding school's assimilation attempts and that during subsequent conflict over land allotment the people remembered St. Joseph's favorably.[67]

The Catholic church was committed to promoting adherence to its religious precepts rather than simply replacing Native cultures with an American mode. Missionaries and nuns were products of an international religion that had to adapt to different cultures. As immigrants themselves, the sisters understood the desire to retain language and culture. The Church did punish Catholic Menominee to force compliance with its religious practices. The priests, for example, deprived some people of a High Mass at death, a ritual especially important to Menominee because they considered the ceremony to be protective of one's spirit. And priests sometimes threatened parents with excommunication for not sending children to Catholic schools.[68]

Father Engelhard Troesken, who administered the school from 1918 to 1942, did much to foster among Native parents positive attitudes toward the school. Father Engelhard visited their homes and was fluent enough in the Menominee language to write a prayer and instruction book. The school provided clothes and shoes for students. Josephine Daniels, who later recalled her experiences at the school, remembered that a kindly white man had spoken Menominee to her when she arrived in the early 1930s and had given the children candy and popcorn.[69]

Father Engelhard wisely left the disciplining of children to the sisters. Strict obedience was taught, Daniels remembered: "When you became a Catholic student you never ask[ed] why. If you asked why you got a slap in the mouth. If you were smart you would catch on right away and you got along with anybody." Sister Dorothy Agnes, Daniels recalled, was a tall muscular woman who used to paddle disobedient children. The nuns' role as disciplinarians helps explain why they might be remembered by young students in a less kindly light. The sisters' institutional role was to instill obedience, and Native children learned to temporarily submit to their control just like Catholic schoolchildren elsewhere.[70]

The missions' tolerance or encouragement of Native culture could not erase the underlying tension. The religious education was fashioned by colonials to ensure submission of Indigenous peoples, while Native traditions emphasized independent teaching and learning to preserve their own cultures. Still, it made the Native people's relationship to their mission schools somewhat different than that with government schools and offered some influence on the learning offered at the latter.

THE GOVERNMENT SCHOOLS

While mission schools were an option for Menominee parents and children, Native peoples elsewhere had no choice. Government boarding schools, with their rigid but changing policies, remained the norm and the educational institutions Native people most resented. In Wisconsin, as elsewhere, government schools became symbolic of cultural oppression. Ironically, the longer the government maintained the schools, the more authoritarian they became, in part because the government uniformly replaced day schools with boarding schools and in part because parents who refused to send children to school were dealt with more ruthlessly as large authoritarian boarding schools were built on each reservation.

Constitutional and civil rights issues are at the core of any discussion of government education. Settler parents claimed the right to make decisions for their children's education under the constitution. While state laws increasingly encroached on these rights—requiring school attendance, increasing lengths of time children must attend, mandating that they be taught in English—rural settlers did control their local schools, with a few important exceptions. The federal government, on the other hand, claimed authority over Native peoples and their children as a way to prepare them for citizenship. To achieve this goal it denied them the right to control their children's education. Officials not only forced attendance for all Native children but between 1896 and 1902 the government explicitly denied the right of parents to designate which school their children attended. When this rule was relaxed, parents had to petition the government in person to be able to send their children to alternative schools. After the government ended subsidies to Catholic mission schools, many closed, and parents then had to pay for any alternative education they wished for their children as well as obtain permission for it.[71]

We can trace the expansion of government control over the Lac du Flambeau community. From the 1850s to the 1870s the government was content to simply staff day schools, primarily with teachers of mixed Native heritage who taught in English but also in Native languages. These day schools were voluntary, allowed children to remain at home to receive customary teaching along with their school learning, and gave parents access to children and the school. In the 1880s the government evolved a much more restrictive view of education, requiring exclusive use of English in all schools receiving federal money. To enforce control over language and content, the government embarked upon a policy that required all Indian children to attend boarding schools away from their families and culture. Agents ordered Native police to forcibly take children away from their parents and grandparents, who were often entrusted with their care and education. They hid the children. Agents used open force and, when they could not find hidden children, retaliated by withholding rations. Starvation became their main weapon.[72]

A policy of training Native women to staff Native schools existed for only a short time. In the 1890s the Board of Indian Commissioners discussed providing higher education to Native students who showed "a special capacity to become teachers." Most teachers across the country were women by 1899, and the Indian Bureau could easily have expanded teacher training schools at Hampton and other off-reservation boarding schools, from which the government hired a number of well-trained Native women in the mid-1890s. Even though the government had a policy of not assigning Native employees to their home communities, many Native people shared attitudes in common, especially respect for community ties, and the policy of hiring these women as teachers and matrons could have been a positive one. By 1896 the superintendent of Indian schools reported that of 1,400 employees nearly 25 percent were Native, but only 27 were teachers and 27 assistant matrons. He advised that normal schools at Carlisle, Hampton, Haskell, and Santa Fe increase their training of teachers.[73]

It never happened. Estelle Reel, who served as superintendent of Indian schools from 1898 to 1910, reversed the policy of hiring trained Native employees. Reel hired male teachers in preference to white women and white women in preference to Native women, even when those hired were clearly unqualified. According to Patricia Carter, Anglo-American teachers who taught Native girls often displayed greater confidence in their intellectual abilities than Reel did. While some teachers must have encouraged young Native women to persist in their studies, most never knew the parents and students well enough to do so. Reel demanded "absolute unquestioning obedience to superior officers."[74]

During the 1890s, Washington's short-lived policy of partially staffing boarding schools with Native teachers and matrons had been implemented in the Lac du Flambeau Nation. After the turn of the century, however, the government discontinued hiring Native teachers and matrons under the guise of "professionalizing" the staff. As each Native woman left, she was replaced by a non-Native woman. By 1910 the entire teaching and administrative staff at Lac du Flambeau was non-Native.[75]

Lac du Flambeau had only a few Catholic families and thus no Catholic boarding school. A number of Catholics sent children to schools away from the community. Some parents sent their daughters to St. Catherine's Convent boarding school in St. Paul, others to St. Mary's at Odanah until the government closed it in 1915.[76]

Parents who had intermarried, either with non-Natives or with Natives of other communities, also contested the agents' right to force their children into schools. These sometimes powerful parents wished to have their children attend off-reservation schools, even universities, and to have funds released from tribal accounts for this purpose. Agents insisted that the children attend the government boarding school. By 1912 the agents had driven two quite different groups of Native parents together. Both wanted influence over their children's education: one group to continue customary teaching practices, the other to seek more education at schools they considered to be better than those on reservations.[77]

In response parents invoked their constitutional rights to control their children's education. In 1912 a group of parents obtained a writ of habeas corpus to gain their children's release from government schools. The agent appealed to Washington, which referred him to the district attorney at Milwaukee. The question was, "Can a parent at common law surrender custody of an infant so as to preclude recovery by habeas corpus?" Previously, replied the district attorney, the answer had been no, but now it was yes. If parents could withdraw their children, then the efforts of the government and the missions to "civilize" the Native people would be "abortive." The agent had an authority that superseded the U.S. Constitution in regard to Native parents and children.[78]

At Lac du Flambeau forced attendance angered many parents right from the beginning. If they objected to their children attending, school officials forcibly seized the children from their homes or even from other schools. In a number of cases, officials kidnapped children and took them to school. Parents attempted to use the courts to regain custody of their children, but the courts uniformly upheld the rights of government over the children. In one notorious case, the superintendent kidnapped children from St. Mary's school at Odanah and forced them to attend the government school. If children ran away from the government school, agents had them arrested and returned. Not all children hated school, and many parents wanted schooling for their children, but most parents and children resented and resisted the school officials' arbitrary authority.[79]

Children running away from the Lac du Flambeau boarding school indicated that conditions within the school were not good. Facing an environment where their language and culture were forbidden was a daunting task; facing the discipline and health hazards was another. Older girls resented being confined to their rooms and often left in the evening to meet friends, behavior that early staff simply ignored. As time went on, however, staff attempted to actively restrain the freedom of older girls and to keep them at the school for longer periods of time. In 1903 the superintendent began sending older girls out to work on farms. In 1904 he decided to keep all girls over thirteen at the school during vacations. Thus young women had a decreasing amount of

Lac du Flambeau boarding school, 1896. The U.S. government required Native children aged five through their early teens to board in the large dormitories built on the shores of Lake Pokegama. Parents were forced, occasionally at gunpoint, to relinquish their children. At school students were forbidden to speak Ojibwe, to wear traditional clothing, or to maintain Native customs. Young women studied half a day and worked the rest of the time in the kitchen and laundry as well as in the sewing room, where they created most of the clothing and linens required at the school.

freedom in their lives. Reports of girls running away increased in 1907 and 1908. In March 1908 eleven girls ran away. These reports probably reflected both increased restrictions and a greater number of young women who found the school intolerable.[80]

Beyond restriction, there was punishment for infractions of internal rules at the Lac du Flambeau school. While most Native parents did not use physical punishment to discipline their children, the government sanctioned it. Government rules did distinguish between what it considered too severe a punishment—with a strap—and that which was acceptable—with a switch. In September 1902, when the boys' disciplinarian used a strap, he himself was disciplined, but the superintendent excused his action by saying he was a new employee and asked that he be given another chance. Physical punishment was something most students tried to avoid by following the rules or eluding detection.[81]

Health hazards were not within students' control at the Lac du Flambeau school. A new building meant the physical plant was usually not the cause of bad health, but contagious disease was a constant danger because of the large number of children confined in dormitories, even when the rooms were not overcrowded or old. Smallpox, diphtheria, and tuberculosis were threats at various times. The school had its own hospital and nurse. Nurses were well trained and the main health-care providers. The agency doctor visited occasionally, but in the 1890s he was sometimes found drunk and unable to work. Nurses and staff dealt effectively with a group of students exposed to smallpox while off the reservation. On their return they were quarantined, as were any adults who became infected. In March 1901 the superintendent reported that twelve people had been isolated in the "pest house" but that the children were not very sick. Aside from this scare, the students seemed quite healthy during the early years of the Lac du Flambeau school. Some months there were no children in the school hospital. From 1904 to 1906, about twenty-six children were ill each year, only a few of them seriously. In April 1907 there was a critical case of diphtheria. Neither the agency doctor nor the nurse diagnosed the girl's disease correctly, and by the time a neighboring doctor was called in, identified the illness as diphtheria, and obtained antitoxins, the girl was too sick to be saved. The doctor immediately gave the antitoxin to the family and quarantined exposed children, and there were no further serious illnesses or deaths from diphtheria.[82]

The school did not do as well with tuberculosis. By February 1908 there were numerous tubercular students, and the following year four died. During the next twenty years tuberculosis spread, and the school did not address this serious health problem. As we have seen, tuberculosis among Indian tribes in Wisconsin was the major untreated disease for the next several decades.[83]

During the early boarding school years many of the staff at Lac du Flambeau, including supervisors, were Native people. Ho-Chunk Mary Ann Paquette was assistant and then matron from 1896 to 1908. Her brother Peter taught farming at the school from 1895 to 1903. During this time Isabella Wolfe, a Cherokee nurse, worked there. For several years a Native woman served as assistant teacher. Kate Eastman, the widow who taught sewing classes from 1895 to 1904, lived at the boarding house, and her daughter played with Native children. In the winter many families came into the village of Lac du Flambeau from their scattered farms and thus were close to the boarding house while the students were in residence.

The superintendent tried to arouse students' interest. Opening in 1895, the school offered new equipment and facilities. Heath was good, and parents could visit children each Friday afternoon and attend entertainment put on by the students. When parents complained about abuse by the first matron, the superintendent transferred her and soon made Mary Ann Paquette assistant and then chief matron. Much of the staff was Native and seemed genuinely interested in good care for the children. Peter and Mary Paquette were certainly not lenient with students, but they appeared to be concerned about their welfare. When Ruben Perry resigned in October 1902, Peter Paquette became acting superintendent. He had hopes of replacing Perry, but agency rules dictated that another white man become superintendent, and Paquette was passed over for promotion. Peter left in 1903; Mary in 1908. The early years must have seemed, to at least some parents, to offer advantages for their children.[84]

Henry Phillips, who began his term as second school superintendent in 1902, was dictatorial. By 1907 health conditions had deteriorated and government policies had become more restrictive. Students were running away; some were restless. The agent wrote, "The older boys have asked whether they were to live and die in the institution." By 1907 children at Lac du Flambeau endured many of the worst characteristics of boarding school life. The school became a symbol of colonial oppression that lingered long in the community. It taught industrial skills that Native people considered valueless because so few jobs were available for those who did not farm and did not wish to enter the tourism economy. In the early 1920s, as tourism became many women's mainstay, the matron encouraged women in their handwork and helped students market their work. She conducted the 1922 industrial survey and painstakingly indicated which schools the students attended and what kind of work the mothers did at home. Still, the government school became part of cultural loss as each succeeding generation of women learned fewer and fewer Native skills. The goal of the government boarding school remained the same: to eradicate Native culture. People resented the government's authority to impose such a policy even as they came to terms with its existence and struggled against it.[85]

By government standards the Lac du Flambeau boarding school had badly deteriorated by 1917. In a special report that year an official recommended discontinuing the boarding school and building a day school. Another report indicated that while the program to teach young girls to incubate and hatch chickens was practical and helpful, the academic program was totally inadequate. A carpenter's wife was substituting the day this official visited, and she was not teaching but entertaining the children. In a second room a teacher with no training was floundering. The students had no exercise, although the official could do little better than suggest marching them around and adding basket-ball and folk dancing. He recommended that adolescent children be sent to non-reservation schools for four to five years and not be permitted to return home for vacations.[86]

By 1917 the government was hiring Native women at the school only in sub-ordinate positions—as assistant cook, laundress, and seamstress. The assistant cook, for example, was seventeen-year-old Mable Gauthier, whose Swedish mother ran a boarding house and raised chickens and a cow while her father worked for the government as an interpreter. Her aunt was the very successful resort owner Margaret Gauthier, and her brother had ambitious plans to start a similar resort at Sand Lake. The family lived in a substantial eleven-room house. Mable had one of the few year-round jobs. The official praised her as neat and pleasant. In fact, he found all the employed Natives to be generally attractive and efficient. Still, he opposed employing them at the school. He worried about the "dangers" of hiring Natives, for they were "unduly sensitive to their racial feelings and suspect they are discriminated against."[87]

INTEGRATING THE PUBLIC SCHOOLS

If the government hoped to close down parochial boarding schools in Native communities in the 1890s, it soon envisioned shuttering its own boarding schools as well. In a movement parallel to the effort to divest Native commu-nities of their land and transfer it to individuals, the government began a pol-icy of removing Native children from government schools and transferring them into the common school system. It was the first massive school integra-tion attempted by the government, which estimated that more than half of all Native children had been integrated into the common school system by 1921. The other half remained in government boarding schools, parochial schools, and an increasing number of day schools on reservations.[88]

Those numbers masked great differences in the extent of integration by dif-ferent Native communities. During the early twentieth century the govern-ment had attempted to force the Wisconsin Ho-Chunk, who had no reserva-tion, into government schools. By 1920 the government had transferred most Ho-Chunk to public schools, but at Lac du Flambeau the number of Chippewa children in public school was barely one-third, and the Menominee had even fewer students in public schools. Integration thus remained fragmentary during this period, but it formed an important part of Native children's experience.[89]

In 1895 the superintendent of Indian schools reported from Washington, DC, that the time was ripe "for the full transfer of [the education of Native youth] to State control." The states must quit considering Indians as foreign-ers for whom the federal government supplied education. Some states were indifferent or hostile to this plan, but Wisconsin was among those willing to work for the transfer of control. The superintendent considered the Lac du Flambeau Chippewa, the Menominee, and the Ho-Chunk among those who were self-supporting and "fairly ready to live under the same laws with other citizens of the States." To achieve this transfer, however, the superintendent had to override parents' wishes. He asked for a congressional waiver of laws that required parental consent before agents could transfer Native students to public schools. He questioned the "propriety" of making education depend on the consent of "half-savage parents." Besides, it was "inconvenient." At times, the superintendent wrote, it was desirable to depend on the "prejudices of influential older Indians," but the officials had a "higher and deeper" necessity to protect youth against these prejudices. Presumably he received that waiver, for the government began transferring Indian children to common schools in the 1890s and the process continued slowly and unevenly during the first decades of the twentieth century. Native youth in Wisconsin were among the first in the nation to be integrated.[90]

The policy of integrating Native students into the common schools needs some explanation. Throughout the country at this time, segregation of non-whites in separate schools was increasing; indeed, educational segregation remained firmly in place until the civil rights movement of the 1950s challenged state and local policies. The government, which had instituted racialist policies toward Native peoples, was not concerned about the civil rights of Native parents: it was violating these rights by coercing their children into schools not of their choice, whether government- or county-run. Rather, it was part of the movement away from large institutions of incarceration at the end of the nineteenth century that inspired this change. Professionals were abandoning the policy of building large institutions for health care, for example, and urging counties to provide for that care locally. The government planned to maintain a few of the larger Indians schools, such as Hampton and Haskell, and boarding schools in isolated areas, such as the Navajo Nation in the Southwest, but it wished to close down as many of its troubled schools as possible. The boarding house experiment had clearly not succeeded: it was expensive and difficult to administer hundreds of those schools.

Overriding the rights of Native parents and elders did not set a good precedent for protecting children's rights once they reached the public schools. School integration began with attempts to safeguard treatment of Native children. Early contracts with school districts promised ten dollars for each Native child admitted. In return the districts promised to "protect the pupils included in this contract from ridicule, insult and other improper conduct at the hands of their fellow pupils, and to encourage them to perform their duties with the same degree of interest and industry as their fellow pupils, the children of white citizens." The bureau commissioner knew that settler sentiments, particularly in the West, were likely to make Native children unwelcome in their schools, but he felt attitudes were changing.[91]

Officials believed that racism toward Native people was ebbing, but in fact racism toward all people of color was growing in the United States. As schools became separate and unequal and southern black communities struggled to support their own schools, Native children were being asked to enter white schools by themselves. After 1906 bureau officials dropped the protective clauses from school contracts but increased pressure on agents to integrate children. As racism in the schools deepened, so too did the segregation of Native students into vocational training. By 1924 the courts in a number of states had held that local school officials could establish segregated schools. As Frederick Hoxie concluded in his study of Native education, most states tolerated a limited number of integrated schools. Wisconsin was one of those states. The common school, the quintessential symbol of freedom and democracy for settlers, became something very different for hundreds of Wisconsin Native children.[92]

In a 1919 report on schools in Wisconsin, Samuel A. Eliot wrote that many Native children were not attending any school. One reason was that many parents had to depend on migratory work in lumber camps, mines, and the fishing industry for their income. A more important reason, one Eliot noted, was that "white children do not treat their Indian comrades quite as they would white comrades. They are inclined to make fun of them or to ridicule their insufficient English, or their queer clothes." Teachers were not interfering with the harassment, and in many school districts parents were objecting to the attendance of Indian children at all. Eliot did not call these actions—or lack thereof—racism. Instead he noted that Indians were "curiously sensitive to ridicule." Students would attend a day or two, then disappear. He hoped the children would be more welcome and attendance would improve, but for now he advised that boarding schools be maintained.[93]

With good reason, then, Native parents were reluctant to send their children into these hostile settings. Enrollments in government boarding schools remained high despite official efforts to integrate Native children into local public schools. Small towns in northern Wisconsin, Ojibwe historian Brenda Child later noted, "have an unfortunate history of discrimination against Indians." Native parents and children preferred separate government boarding schools, even intertribal schools some distance from home, to the discrimination they faced in these small Wisconsin towns.[94]

Few Menominee parents attempted to use the public schools. Usually they sent older sons to public school but kept older girls and younger children in mission or government schools. By 1922 some Menominee parents were sending girls to a convent in Bayfield, a good distance from home, or to the government boarding school at Tomah. The government may have encouraged these transfers for older girls because it wanted to control their sexuality and to prevent parents from arranging early marriages for them. Most parents, however, kept girls in the community's boarding school. Fewer than a quarter of the daughters attended public schools.[95]

The Ho-Chunk, who were entirely integrated, suffered most from the integration policy. Ho-Chunk had been among the earliest Wisconsin Natives to seek education for their sons and daughters. They had sent children to German Lutheran day schools and to government boarding schools, such as the one at Tomah and one at Wittenberg, which the government controlled from 1895 to 1919. Mountain Wolf Woman, who later told her life story to anthropologist Nancy Lurie, attended the Tomah school and later the Wittenberg school. Mountain Wolf Woman especially enjoyed her time at Wittenberg, where she became friends with the matron, an Oneida woman. After the government turned the Wittenberg school back to the Lutherans in 1919, almost all Ho-Chunk children attended public school.[96]

In memoirs, settlers seldom reflected on the treatment accorded Ho-Chunk children in the public schools. One account remains; though it does not name the school at which the incident occurred, it does identify the children involved as Ho-Chunk. The storyteller remembered when schools had segregated drinking cups for Native and white. He also remembered how a new teacher got rid of the Native children who attended the school. Secretly calling on the non-Native students to collude with her, the teacher shouted and threatened Native children with physical punishment. The ruse was successful: it so terrified the Native students that they fled the school and never returned. At least one young Ho-Chunk woman, Helen Stacy, from a prosperous Christian Ho-Chunk family graduated from high school at Neillsville. She intended to teach in the schools, but no district would employ her.[97]

The Lac du Flambeau community had one advantage: a local public school. Because the government allowed whites to purchase land and settle on the reservation, there were already fifty to sixty children who needed a public school by 1896. Vilas County agreed to establish a school in 1902. From the beginning some Native children attended, and as the policy of integration expanded and conditions at the boarding school became more oppressive, fewer non-Indian and more Chippewa children enrolled. In 1922 thirty-six of the forty-four pupils were Chippewa and the county was planning to rebuild and enlarge the school. By that year, about half of all Lac du Flambeau children attended public school.[98]

There was no nearby high school, however. Those who wanted higher education had to travel to Minocqua, a nearby resort town. Minocqua merchants had hired Native guides and beadworkers and had cultivated a romanticized view of Native peoples to encourage tourism, but when it came to admitting Native children to high school, sentiments were far different. The non-Native students attempted to make Native students feel inferior. Young people had only their early training to fall back on in this hostile environment. Parents and grandparents prepared their children to survive the abuse they knew would greet them at school.

Grandma Bell was one of the grandmothers who prepared children for public school. A skilled craftsperson, Grandma Bell made moccasins, reed mats, and rag rugs; did beadwork and birch-bark work; tanned hides; sewed dance regalia; and dressed drums for ceremonial use. She still made maple sugar and syrup and gathered wild rice, but she also baked bread. She kept a five-acre garden and gathered herbal remedies to supplement those grown at home. Joe Chosa was only two when his mother died and Grandma Bell began to care for him. She showed Joe where to find and how to use medicines, always spoke to him in Ojibwe, and taught him to be proud of his culture and heritage. After her husband died, Grandma Bell decided to send Joe to the public high school in Minocqua rather than to the boarding school so he could continue to help her at home. Grandma Bell warned Joe that some people would not like Native people and would try to make him feel inferior. She told him he should be proud of his heritage, proud to be an Indian. And, she advised him, "Wherever you go, you try to treat other people as you would like to be treated."[99]

The teachings of elders like Grandma Bell were fundamental to Native children's ability to persist, whether in boarding or public schools. An absolute sense of self-worth and pride in Native culture reinforced and strengthened students' efforts to learn despite attempts by others to hinder and control them. Without that learning, Native students could not live successfully in two worlds.

The authoritarian treatment of parents and children within schools embittered Native peoples. Women continued to teach children to be independent and to preserve cultures, but the legacy of the government boarding houses persists today. On the Lac du Flambeau reservation there stands an old white two-story building, now empty and abandoned. It is all that remains of the large government boarding school complex, started in 1895 and composed of twenty-five buildings that occupied 780 acres of land along the shores of Pokegama Lake. Once a boys' dormitory, the remaining building somehow survived the gradual dismantling of the complex after it closed in 1928. A century after the boarding houses opened, the people of Lac du Flambeau had to decide how to treat this last remnant of a system created, as Cindi Stiles of the Tribal Historic Preservation Office said, "to remove all traces of tribal culture from the children." Should it be destroyed, allowed to disintegrate, or preserved?

It is not an easy decision. Stiles contended that, as a symbol, the building could continue to "loom as a reminder of the clash of two cultures, of contact, consequences and survival." Kelly Jackson, her colleague at the Tribal Historic Preservation Office, agreed. She saw the building as a symbol of efforts to wipe out the culture and language. "Let it stand and tell the story," she argued, "so they never forget. Let our children learn and know what they have survived in a place that can tell the story all by itself if you just listen." Jackson saw the old dormitory building as a way to tell her people's story, a story of cultural survival.[100]

These are living debates over history, and while settler communities may preserve examples of their one-room schoolhouses or mourn the buildings' demise in the consolidation movement, their conversations do not carry this anguish of cultural and linguistic loss. Even in my family, some members who do not visibly identify with their Chippewa heritage carry the bitterness of what they consider to be cultural destruction. Government boarding schools became sites of both cultural persistence and cultural loss. Should we, the descendants of settlers and Natives, tell the story emphasizing only that loss, or should we, as Jackson argues, listen to those Native peoples who want to carry the stories of survival, of struggle to live a better life and to learn their own languages, and "stand strong in front of the same government that tore the Indian spirit down and fight for balance between their way and ours"?[101]

Young people had many sites for learning. Customary learning at home, Catholic boarding schools, day schools, and public schools all offered alternatives to government boarding schools. The government attempted to replace Native ways of learning with day schools, then boarding schools, and finally integration into the public schools. At each site, students and parents clashed with government policy and assumed the right to control their learning. Native parents wished to have their children preserve tribal cultures and to equip themselves for a life in a country dominated by a culture not only at odds with those traditions but also intent on destroying them.

Teaching the Teachers
Amanda's Story [Sebold, Sister Theodine, born in Wisconsin, 1902–89]

It was raining that July day in 1917 when fifteen-year-old Amanda Sebold arrived at the Franciscan Sisters' house in Dorchester, two miles from her family farm. The nuns were waiting to accompany the young woman to the St. Rose Convent, their motherhouse at La Crosse, where Amanda would be officially received into the order as a novice.[102]

Amanda Sebold. Known as Sister Theodine for most of her teaching and administrative career, Amanda dressed in simple lay clothing during a 1988 interview at the St. Rose Convent in La Crosse. Born on a farm near Dorchester, a few miles from my mother Theresa's home, she became one of the region's most highly educated women.

Seventy-one years later, in July 1988, I sat in one of the commons rooms at the St. Rose Convent in La Crosse. Across from me, in a comfortable armchair, sat eighty-six-year-old Amanda, now known as Sister Theodine, who told me about her life before entering the convent. Amanda grew up on a hundred-acre farm about six miles from where Theresa did just east of Dorchester. Amanda was a year older than Theresa, the Sebold farm was larger, and the family better off, but not much. Like Theresa, Amanda began her education at six years of age, learning her basics in the common school a mile from home. Like Theresa, she also attended through the seventh grade. Amanda was the middle-born of eleven children. Her older sisters were already working in Oshkosh. The family expected her to do the same.

Then, in 1913, when Amanda was eleven, something happened to change her life. The Catholics wanted a parochial school for their children, and the Dominicans promised they would assign two nuns if the community would build a schoolhouse. After discussing the matter, the Sebold family decided it was doing well enough to donate one hundred dollars to help build the school. Amanda was one of the children who greeted the two Dominican nuns who came to teach that fall.

Amanda became much attached to the sisters that year and decided she, too, would like to do just what they were doing: become a nun and teach. She asked the nuns if she could join their convent, but when they inquired at the motherhouse in Racine the mother superior replied that Amanda was too young. To feed Amanda's ambition, however, the family decided she might start Dorchester High School the next fall. Meanwhile, Franciscan Sisters from La Crosse had replaced the Dominican sisters as teachers at the Dorchester parochial school. Amanda repeated her desire to become a nun and teach. In 1917, after Amanda turned fifteen, the sisters helped her apply for admission to their motherhouse. When Amanda took her final orders at the Franciscans' St. Rose Convent in La Crosse, she took the name of Sister Theodine.

After entering the convent, Amanda's life diverged radically from those of other country daughters. She was able to finish her high school education and receive teacher training at Viterbo College, the Catholic normal school in La Crosse. She taught in parochial schools and then attended college when she was in her forties, graduating from Catholic University in Washington, DC, with a doctorate. Returning to Viterbo College in La Crosse, she became academic dean and then president-dean.

Amanda's story is unusual because she was able to achieve high academic distinction, obtain her doctorate, and become a college president. Her achievement was due in part to being a very bright and determined young woman in a family that valued and could afford education as well as vocation and in part because she happened to live close to schools that could provide the opportunities she needed—both public and private. Amanda was able to become part of an all-female system that trained and promoted from within, that offered job security and a community of women for support, that gave her an opportunity unique to young women who chose to teach. A separate teaching order allowed Amanda to compete only with women and to achieve high rank and status within a closed community. Her professional life was compatible with the spiritual life to which young women like her committed themselves. Gender determined the position of women within the church hierarchy and the parochial schools created by the Catholic church but allowed them broad opportunities within that place. Teaching in the public schools offered young women few similar opportunities.

Catholic parochial schools flourished outside of the struggling public schools with the dedicated teaching of women just like Amanda. In Wisconsin Catholic sisters taught in some public schools in the nineteenth century, but as parochial schools were built the nuns taught there. The church and convents provided for their needs. Since Catholic hospitals developed at the same time as parochial schools, sisters had excellent free health care. They could return to the motherhouse in sickness and old age, as did Sister Theodine, allowing other sisters to care for her. Most rural daughters who joined the teaching orders—and a considerable number from this area did—continued to have supportive families and kin who monitored their needs. The status of teaching sisters was high within most communities where they taught, whether rural or urban. Church members who supported the establishment of parochial schools, especially women, developed additional community support systems for the nuns. Friendships, letters, small gifts, and personal services lessened the burden of work.[103]

For Amanda, and for a few other farm daughters, parochial schools offered not only a way out of farm life but also a way up into a scholarly life and a profession. Sister Theodine lived out her life surrounded in work and prayer by her Franciscan sisters. The year after she told me of her life, seventy-two years after she had entered as a young girl of fifteen, Sister Theodine died at St. Rose Convent.

TEACHER TRAINING

In that summer of 1917, the future Sister Theodine was heading toward one of the best teacher training institutions in Wisconsin. By 1890 Mother Ludovica had established a teacher training school in La Crosse called the St. Rose Normal Training School. Students had usually completed their elementary education when they entered the convent as novices. At the training school, they had a chance for a year or two of high school courses. In addition, they attended summer school for in-service training. The motherhouse established correspondence courses with home study guides, followed by exams and certification. In 1902 the convent issued a teachers' handbook containing 155 pages of methods, procedures, and inspirational hints. The convent regularly published articles on teaching methods and, from 1907 to 1919, a quarterly called *Maria Angelorum*. Beginning in 1907, the community also published individual textbooks for geography, history, and grammar.[104]

Sisters differed from public school teachers in a number of ways: they were older, they often stayed for long periods in one school, and they received support for continued training. Sisters returned to the motherhouse in La Crosse for summer courses, and after 1910 they also received support for attending the state normal schools at La Crosse and Superior. If the group was large enough, the normal school teachers came to the motherhouse to teach classes. In 1923 collegiate courses were added to the normal school summer sessions. In 1932 this program became the St. Rose Junior College, and in 1937, Viterbo College.[105]

Through this impressive educational system, large numbers of rural daughters were recruited and trained for teaching in northern Wisconsin. Each entering novice was asked to write a brief autobiography describing her youth and background; thus we know something of their lives before they entered the convent as well as after they joined. Seventy of the young women who entered from the four north-central counties left such sketches. Most were German immigrant farm family daughters who as children had alternated between public and private Catholic schools. Parents were usually unable to afford private school for their daughters' entire education; nor did they have resources to keep them in public high schools or to send them to normal schools for teacher training. Large clusters came from the German communities of Marathon and Athens, which had established early parochial schools. The families had to get by without the very important work of the daughters. For daughters of larger families with at least some resources, convent life offered an alternative to marriage: a respected profession with mobility and security.

Entering the convent required a written recommendation from the parish priest followed by a formal agreement between the young woman and the convent, certified by her parents to show that they were willing to give up her services. The convent agreed to care for the young woman as long as she stayed and followed the rules. She could leave any time she wished; the convent could expel her if she refused to abide by its rules.[106]

Only a few sisters wrote about their specific reasons for entering the convent or the circumstances surrounding their decision. Alodia Fastner was encouraged to join by her parents. Her mother had wanted to become a nun in Germany but to do so required a dowry; in America it was possible for her daughter to become a teacher even though the family was poor. Some parents opposed their daughter's wishes. Elizabeth Veit was warned by her mother that she would die of tuberculosis in the convent because she was sickly; she defied her mother and joined anyway. Rose Braun felt the call to enter the convent so strongly that she had unsuccessfully tried to "drown the thought." Celine Schumacher, who joined in 1907, thought the sisters seemed so happy and privileged that she wanted to be a part of their community. Martha Weiler joined because she found Catholic school religious instruction interesting. M. Austina Burger remembered, "for girls, my sisters and I thought they were only on this world to get married." Joining provided her freedom to choose an alternative.[107]

Lutheran women never had access to a teacher training system in Wisconsin. Early Lutheran schools depended on male pastors educated in German institutions to teach in their schools. When the supply of these foreign-trained pastors proved inadequate, the Wisconsin Synod established a college in Milwaukee, modeled on the German gymnasium, to prepare young men for educational as well as pastoral work. This system also failed to produce enough trained male teachers. As the synod expanded its parish schools, it hired more women. By 1893 women made up 14 percent of the teachers in the Wisconsin Synod's 141 schools. Because no Lutheran teacher training school existed for women in Wisconsin, schools often relied on the untrained daughters of ministerial families. Finally, the joint Wisconsin, Minnesota, and Michigan Synod established a General Teachers' Seminary at the new Dr. Martin Luther College in New Ulm, Minnesota, that admitted women. The college graduated its first woman teacher in 1898. While the number of trained women teachers increased steadily thereafter, Lutheran schools maintained a larger proportion of male teachers than public or Catholic schools and offered no teacher training in Wisconsin.[108]

Meanwhile, rural school districts struggled to find trained teachers willing to serve the settler schools at the salaries they offered. Short on funds, local schools hired whomever would work for the paltry wages—usually young women who had completed their own elementary education, worked at home for a few years, and had no teacher training. Local schools boards hired the best qualified or the best connected by kinship or community ties and issued them certificates to teach. Few of the young women found the wages enough remuneration to endure the isolation of boarding at farms and teaching in schools that may have had blackboards and a globe but little else.

Between 1880 and 1910, the state of Wisconsin collected statistics showing women's steady rise within the teaching profession and their low wages. Women had first moved into teaching in Wisconsin when the Civil War made it difficult to find male teachers. This shortage continued into the postwar era, when the westward movement and the boom of the 1870s opened other opportunities for young men but few to young women. In rural areas, the number of women teachers increased more rapidly than in urban areas, where wages for teaching were generally better. A few rural school boards tried to hire men in the 1890s and 1900s, even instructing directors specifically to look for male teachers and to pay higher wages than those offered to women, but they could not keep men in the classroom. The low pay and poor conditions of employment combined with the availability of training for higher-paying jobs made long-term employment as teachers unattractive to men. Young women remained the most available and the best buy for most school boards, which employed them in increasing numbers. Counties kept the better-paid positions of principal and superintendent for men, thus further removing chances for women to advance to more responsible and higher-paying jobs. In some cases, as school districts grew, school boards replaced women who had been principals during the formative years.[109]

The four north-central counties of this study reflect these general trends. By 1880 women already accounted for more than 75 percent of the teaching force, and by 1890, more than 80 percent. The percentage declined somewhat during the next decade, probably because depressions and unsettled economic conditions drove men back into low-paying positions, but by 1910 women held 90 percent of the teaching jobs. Wages continued to be low, on average rising from $29 to only $44 a month during these thirty years. Male wages, meanwhile, rose from $39 to $64 a month. Men were consistently chosen for the better-paying jobs: those in urban areas, in graded schools where they taught the higher grades, and in wealthier school districts.[110]

Teaching, whether public or private, was accompanied by low wages, but it continued to bring high status to women in rural areas. In these communities, teachers held special places of authority, just as schoolhouses held a special place as sites for community rituals. Women worked hard to obtain these jobs, and they were not available to all. Immigrant daughters of various ethnic groups found teaching to be an unreachable dream because it demanded special

Table 2: Teachers and Their Wages in North-Central Wisconsin, 1881–1912,
by County, by Sex

Years or County	Number of Teachers	Number of Female Teachers	Percent Female	Monthly Wages for Female Teachers (dollars)	Monthly Wages for Male Teachers (dollars)
1881–82					
Clark	144	119	83	28	40
Lincoln	27	20	74	31	48
Marathon	130	80	62	28	37
Taylor	34	29	85	27	30
1890–92					
Clark	215	181	84	30	45
Lincoln	46	38	83	33	36
Marathon	189	128	68	33	39
Taylor	74	63	85	31	44
1898–1900					
Clark	212	170	80	32	49
Lincoln	61	45	74	31	33
Marathon	211	159	75	35	35
Taylor	91	69	76	32	47
1910–12					
Clark	217	187	86	43	70
Lincoln	77	73	95	41	50
Marathon	245	222	91	36	58
Taylor	122	112	92	57	79

Sources: Wisconsin Department of Public Instruction, *Biennial Report*, 1881–82, 1890–92, 1898–1900, 1910–12

training and release from the obligation of helping to support their families. Competition for these jobs could be fierce.

Wealthy native-born parents tried to keep their daughters in school and, if possible, to arrange for them to teach. These English-speaking daughters dominated teaching in the ethnically mixed area of north-central Wisconsin during the nineteenth century. Immigrant women supported the one-room country schools that dotted the countryside, welcomed the schoolteachers into their communities, and often volunteered to board them. Women who spoke only German often boarded teachers who spoke only English.[111]

The chances of these immigrant women's daughters going on to high school—or even to the state normal school for the few weeks of summer school necessary to qualify for teaching—were very slim in the nineteenth century.

Thurine Oleson remembered proudly how one especially bright Norwegian named Martha Stromme, after attending the "common country school," went to the normal school at Oshkosh for a few weeks, took an examination, received a certificate, and began to teach.[112]

If young farm girls wanted to continue their learning and teachers were in such demand, it seems quite logical that the state would want to equip them to take up these careers. Yet there were no funds available for teacher training. Few families could afford to get along without young women's farm work and to spare the extra money it would take to train them as teachers. Of the almost two hundred teachers who held certificates in the four counties in 1880, almost 90 percent had only short institute training, eighteen had normal school training, three had a year of institute training, and one had a certificate based on university training. The figures had changed little by 1920, when for the first time the state required a high school diploma to teach.[113]

After the turn of the century, immigrant daughters increasingly joined this work force, but they could claim little additional training. A certificate of graduation from grammar school and a ten-week teacher training course would qualify them. A list of 202 names on teachers certificate stub books for Clark County for 1908 and 1909 show German surnames for almost 25 percent of the teachers, the same percentage that was foreign-born or had foreign-born parents in Clark County.[114]

Conflicts must have flared as women of the new ethnic groups worked their way into the teaching profession. Irish teachers in eastern and western cities had to fight for the right to teach in public schools. Norwegian and German daughters later worked to displace Irish and Yankee teachers in the Midwest, offering dual language skills and knowledge of ethnic communities as their special qualifications. Polish women, in turn, fought to establish themselves in areas where German teachers predominated, a story recounted in detail in the section on spirituality. Teaching was not a despised occupation. It brought high status among new immigrant groups anxious to succeed at the professions as well as at farming. It marked the rise of rural immigrant women from common to higher education, from farm hand to white collar. It was almost impossible for young people from northern Wisconsin to make their way to the University of Wisconsin at Madison. The superintendent of education's biennial report estimated in 1904 that only one percent of all young people in the state attended the university. Odds did not improve in the next two decades. Theresa's teacher, Joseph Jantsch, taught at the Eau Pleine School in Bruckerville after graduating from Colby High School in 1910. A few years later, he attended a normal school and then the university at Madison. Jantsch, with great effort, educated himself. He could inspire his students to learn, as he did Theresa, but he had no power to arrange for her or for other young students to obtain higher education for themselves.[115]

Realizing that few young people could get to the university at Madison for any type of education, the state of Wisconsin established normal schools with the goal of teaching young people how to teach. By 1900 there were normal schools at Oshkosh and at Stevens Point, but for rural youth traveling to these schools remained difficult and board expensive. Instead of training teachers, these schools mainly served as high schools for students in nearby villages and farms or as places where local residents could obtain two years of college while living at home, before transferring to the more expensive university in Madison. About three percent of young people were in high schools and normal schools by 1904. By 1910, as we have seen, only about ten percent of the young people in the north-central counties attended high school. A decade later the four counties had only twenty-one high schools, which did not train rural youth for teaching either. Mainly, only urban youth attended high school and then taught only in urban schools.[116]

Mary D. Bradford, a farm daughter who later became Kenosha County's superintendent of schools, was sympathetic to rural women's attempts to receive teacher training. In a memoir, Bradford explained why normal schools trained few teachers for rural schools. Most young women could not hope to enroll in these normal schools because entry requirements were high. In the 1870s, when Bradford entered Oshkosh Normal School, she had to have a formal nomination, signed by her city superintendent of schools, testifying to age, health, and moral character. After Bradford finished one year of the program, she was offered a job teaching in the Kenosha High School. Needing the money and eager to begin teaching, Bradford took the job without finishing her teacher's training.[117]

When the Stevens Point Central State Teachers College opened in 1894, Bradford joined its faculty as principal of the grammar grades model school. Of the 201 students attending that first year, Bradford counted 41 percent from the city of Stevens Point, another 30 percent from Portage County, and only a few from other counties. In other words, most were urban students. Almost half of these students had already taught and wished to use additional professional training to obtain jobs teaching in high school rather than in rural common schools. Realizing that normal schools were training almost no teachers for the common schools, the state appropriated funds for county teacher training institutes.[118]

Marathon established one of these early county training schools at Wausau in 1899. At that time, the county employed two hundred teachers outside the city of Wausau; more than one-quarter of them were inexperienced. During the first year, the school enrolled untrained youth to whom the county had refused to grant certificates because of low grades on their tests. Only one of twenty-three students had teaching experience. By 1902 enrollment was sixty-four, fifty women and fourteen men, fewer than half of whom graduated. The number of graduates declined over the next two years. The Marathon Training School's 1904 annual report showed a class of twenty-six; all but two were young women. By this time only about five percent of country teachers had attended any training school at all. The state extended the training time to two years and increased its support for additional training schools. In 1908 a new training school opened at Merrill in Lincoln County. Taylor County opened one at Medford in 1911. Clark County began to offer training courses at local high schools. Teachers residing in these counties could attend the training schools for free.[119]

These county schools remained the primary trainers of rural teachers until 1920. By 1918 almost 1,500 teachers had received training to teach in Wisconsin's rural schools. Of these, more than half (832) had graduated from county training schools, fewer than four hundred from high school, and only 273 from normal schools. Those who graduated from normal school could pick and choose from jobs available, including positions in urban schools or high schools at higher salaries than counties could pay their common school teachers.[120]

Between 1880 and 1920 most country teachers did not have access to any of these methods of training. Instead they received their training at county-sponsored teachers' summer institutes. Counties usually held these gatherings during July or August. The first institutes in the 1880s were usually for five days. By 1904 most lasted for ten days, although Lincoln County still required only five days. They became longer during the 1910s, increasing from days to weeks and then to months. Officials expected these institutes to prepare most of the teachers for rural schools. While employed at Stevens Point, Bradford also taught at these summer institutes. She liked the earnestness of the mostly rural teachers who attended and planned to return to rural schools to teach. The training sessions made a real difference, and teachers eagerly signed on, but they were an inadequate substitute for extensive teacher training. After 1920 the institutes were eliminated through the spread of high schools and county training schools.[121]

Rather than improving the training, certification—set up to eliminate poorly trained teachers—simply made it more difficult to become certified. Many underqualified teachers taught in rural schools because they had no access to teacher training. The Haltom school board, for example, was forced to hire a number of teachers with six-month teaching certificates and with grades of only 40 out of a possible 100 on the reading, grammar, and arithmetic certification tests. Bright students like Theresa could not compete: no scholarship system existed even if the family could have gotten by without her help. To forgo Theresa's daily farm work would have required a better family income and more widely available social services before the family could consider the long-term economic gains for this daughter. And teaching jobs would have had to pay better. Teachers eked out a living at twenty to thirty dollars a month on two- to four-month contracts signed just before the school term began. They had to take jobs where they were available, often far from family, in distant communities where transportation home was difficult. By the turn of the century, conditions were improving in rural schools, but the professionals at Madison were already losing patience. Their solution: consolidate the thousands of one-room schoolhouses into a smaller number of central schools.

TEACHERS AND SCHOOL CONSOLIDATION

The movement to consolidate rural schools was a major reform of the Progressive Era's Country Life Movement. Born of urban reformers' fervent belief that rural areas needed schools like those developed in cities, the consolidation movement took form in the early years of the twentieth century, flourished before World War I, and after fierce battles in many states gradually subsided in the economic hard times of the 1920s and 1930s. According to the most careful scholar of the movement in the Midwest, consolidation left a legacy primarily of more high schools rather than better ones and town rivalries based on athletic competitions.[122]

The consolidation movement swept through Wisconsin as it did other midwestern states. It pitted urban reformers against intractable, stubborn rural communities that for the most part ignored or fought school consolidation. It is difficult to know just what rural women in Wisconsin thought about school consolidation as a whole. In some areas of Iowa, women were among its staunchest supporters, but these seem to have been mainly Protestants who saw school consolidation as a part of rural church revitalization. In northern Wisconsin—an area with many predominantly Catholic communities, a thriving parochial school movement, and many scattered ethnic neighborhoods—it was likely that instructions from Madison reformers would have had a reluctant if not hostile reception. And since poorly trained women teachers were a main justification for consolidating the thousands of one-room schoolhouses into single facilities located in the largest nearby village, the movement was not likely to have widespread and wholehearted support.[123]

Young women hated many aspects of teaching in isolated one-room schools. They were lonely places to work and offered poor pay; further, no specialized training for that type of teaching was available. Urban school reformers assumed that the urban model offered an ideal learning environment. They seldom discussed alternatives for rural areas: better pay and training for women from the local communities, encouragement of women to teach for longer periods in local schools, improved local facilities, a system geared to making schools meet the needs of rural people. In any event, rural parents and potential teachers seem not to have been consulted about what they thought would be best for themselves or their children. Women could not vote even in school elections in Wisconsin during the period in which the drive for consolidation took form.[124]

In Wisconsin, advocates argued that consolidation offered the prospect of well-paid, better-trained teachers, each instructing more pupils at a lower cost per unit. Recently improved roads and vehicles would allow consolidated schools to transport students to these more distant schools. Traveling by horse and cart, kept warm by heaters, the students would arrive at school dry and fresh.[125]

Professionals buttressed their arguments and plans for consolidation with evidence gathered by the Committee of Six on Rural Schools, established in 1900. In its first report, in 1902, the committee emphasized that equal education for all children could not be achieved until rural teachers were better trained. "Poor teachers," the committee reported, "are the bane of the rural school. Country teachers are, in most cases, young, immature, half-trained, ineffective, and lacking in professional ideals and ambitions.... [T]hose who are found really successful in the work of teaching . . . are gradually gathered into the city schools of the land, through the greater watchfulness of city school officials and greater emoluments which they offer." Cities, continued the committee report, left the "culls to wreak their incompetency on the country children." The turnover of these so-called culls was frequent. One-third of the teachers dropped out each year. The committee called the small-district system "suicidal." School consolidation would allow better teachers to teach in fewer township schools.[126]

Inadequate rural teacher training was the main reason state educational officials supported consolidation of schools. They also believed the quality of teaching would be improved by employing "the brightest young men in the community" rather than young, inexperienced "girls." Young women taught because low wages attracted few men, but even for young women, teaching paid less than working out as "hired girls." The state superintendent's biennial report for 1902–4 lamented, "the sentiment in favor of consolidation grows very slowly"; his 1904–6 report concluded, "the country schools seem to have reached a stage of arrested development."[127]

Some north-central Wisconsin counties experimented in consolidation between 1903 and 1908. In Clark County, Hewett and Dewhurst towns joined to establish a consolidated school at Columbia, a district that covered thirty-six square miles. The main cost, boasted the superintendent, was thirty dollars for five wagons to transport children to school for nine months. Lincoln County followed in 1908, establishing two consolidated schools, one in Pine

River with 68 students and another in the town of King with 34 students. It furnished transportation for the first time.[128] After these first few consolidations, the movement stalled in north-central Wisconsin. When Owen, a community in north-central Clark County, consolidated before 1910, the change was not popular. Farm families could barely support the one-room schools, and the cost of consolidation proved to be much more than simply paying for transportation, although the state did contribute increasing amounts to rural schools after 1908. The consolidated school was supposed to combine all grammar schools and offer a few years of high school as well. No existing school buildings were large enough to accommodate so many students, and the cost of building a new, usually brick two-story building ran to thousands of dollars. Consolidation was not the money-saving proposition the reformers had promised. The new school districts had to raise funds through higher taxes, usually through a bond issue.

Professionals in Madison assumed that school boards would welcome the chance for better schools and teachers and could convince parents of the need for change. When school boards proved to be divided among themselves over the proposed educational reforms, state officials brought county superintendents together to discuss educational needs and to exchange ideas on how problems might be solved. The discussions convinced only a few to support consolidation.

Proponents of the spreading parochial school systems in rural Wisconsin also objected to consolidation. Catholics often saw the consolidation movement as Protestant inspired, especially where Protestant reformers took the initiative in promoting it. The wealthier Catholics were increasingly being asked by their churches to support parish schools for their children. Poorer Catholics depended upon the public school system. Where Catholics were a majority in the community, they could determine who taught school and often chose a Catholic woman. Where they were a minority, they tried to see that teachers did not turn the mandate to keep schools nondenominational into an overtly Protestant program.[129]

Ethnicity could also be an important element in retarding consolidation. Many immigrant communities used public schools to teach ethnic languages and to preserve ethnic culture. The small Danish community that had settled in 1893 near Withee in northeast Clark County refused to consolidate with nearby Owen. Instead it added its own high school in 1910. When a rural sociologist visited the Danish community in 1948, its members were still refusing to consolidate. It seems likely that Clark County had more high schools than other counties in the area because residents resisted consolidation earlier. A large number of high schools, then, was not necessarily a commitment to provide higher education for settler children but an indication that communities were resisting the consolidation movement by establishing small high schools that served only a few students.[130]

Agricultural extension experts also took up the consolidation cause. They argued that, since farm size was increasing through land purchases and the number of farm families decreasing, falling enrollment made one-room schools economically inefficient. They proposed expanding the size of school districts. Although both the rural population and the number of small farms were still increasing in the four north-central counties, many schools there had fewer than fifteen pupils. These agricultural experts also urged more graded schools and high schools and better transportation facilities.[131]

Professional educators blamed opposition to school consolidation on the system of electing county superintendents. There was too much democracy in education, according to some progressive reformers. The election of school superintendents seemed to result in officials who knew little about education even if they knew enough about local politics to get themselves voted into office. Superintendents found it difficult to make unpopular decisions when faced with coming elections, and lobbying by relatives and friends was hard to resist. Yet removing power from local hands and replacing local people with professionals was not an automatic improvement. Few women were directly involved in decisions relating to education: ethnic settler women could hardly influence school policy.

The issue of women in politics was intimately involved with educational matters. While women worked for and assumed they would be able to vote on educational issues, male politicians blocked full compliance with school voting rights until 1906 and often opposed full voting rights before World War I. When Mary Bradford was appointed as the Kenosha school superintendent in 1910, it was hailed as an example of Wisconsin's progressive school system, but hers was an exceptional case. Women with teaching experience could have made major contributions in a large number of jobs at the superintendent level, but they were denied entry, probably by men who wished to keep the better-paid superintendent jobs for themselves. There were ways to involve more women in educational policy. One was to politicize women, as women reformers wished, so that they could run for and be elected to school offices. The other was to depoliticize education and replace male politicians with female professionals. World War I halted most attempts to consolidate schools.

The war also brought a new tone to the Wisconsin superintendent of education's annual report, which in 1916–18 replaced its condescension when discussing rural schools and teachers with a new practicality. "The young teacher will go where she finds better social conditions, coupled with a good salary," the report concluded. As to management of the schools, the report admitted that people who controlled the schools were in the villages and cities and that they also controlled the localities' administrative and business affairs. They shaped educational matters and voted to offer better teacher salaries than the poor farmers could pay. The report declared, "The salary question is largely and almost entirely economic. To solve it in the rural communities we must see to it first that the farmer who supports the school system is paid for his labors, both mental and physical." Urban critics, continued the report, wanted rural communities to pay better wages to teachers but to sell produce cheaper. Then it concluded:

> When the rural communities receive just compensation for their mental and physical exertions, can market their produce without being preyed upon by unscrupulous middle men, they will be able to shorten their hours of labor, create better rural social conditions and have the ability to pay all laborers in their midst, including the teachers, a compensation equal to that of any other class of people.[132]

If the new superintendent of education and the reformers in Madison were correct, then consolidation had foundered not because of inattention to gender, ethnicity, or even a sense of place but on the hard bedrock of economics. Rural people simply could not afford to pay their teachers enough because they had not enough money. Such a conclusion was essentially correct: reforms in teaching and access to high school and fine schools could have followed from prosperity. But prosperity itself would not eliminate the crosscurrents that had made consolidation fail in rural areas. Communities and the women within them wanted, above all, to influence their children's learning experiences.[133]

After the war, settler communities would continue as they had, sustaining community and family life primarily through their own strategies. Native communities, which had resisted the reforms that took control out of their hands, would struggle separately alongside these settler communities in northern Wisconsin. Both communities had come to suspect the reforms of outsiders who stressed centralization and control at a distance. When it came to learning, they felt that they knew best.

7

Matters of the Spirit

Women seldom wrote or talked about spiritual matters to outsiders, and when they did so, it was with hesitation, unless it was their special profession, as it was for Catholic nuns or Native spiritual leaders. Nor did others write often about such matters. Thus, as historian I can only recreate a small part of this life of the spirit, awkwardly, with as much imprecision as the records left by the women themselves. Spiritual relations were intensely private for individual women and their communities, and I have tried to indicate here only the outlines of the most physical manifestations of these matters of the spirit. Even in the case of my grandmother Matilda, I could learn little about her spirituality. Her grandchildren remember her as "religious," and I know she read her breviary almost daily when she lived with our family in old age. She scrupulously followed the established Catholic rituals and regulations.

This much I could learn. In Wisconsin Matilda attended church as frequently as she could, limited by the irregular mission services in Dorchester and the often impassible roads. She practiced a type of domestic religion, hanging religious pictures on the walls of her log house, kneeling with her children in prayer before them. She had priests baptize her children as soon as possible after birth. Poor as Matilda was in 1909, she arranged for her first-born daughter, then twelve, to move to nearby Medford and live with her sister to receive two weeks of religious instruction. Out of meager earnings, she bought white fabric to make a special dress for her daughter's First Holy Communion ceremony and kept an elaborately printed certificate dated October 14, 1909, on the wall of her log house to commemorate the occasion.

My grandmother had moved to the United States from an area of Europe where most nations still maintained state religions. Here there was no state religion, and settlers were free to practice religion as they wished. Most north-central Wisconsin settlers were nominally Christian, but of two separate branches of Christianity, Catholic and Protestant, each divided into a variety of smaller groups. Despite their claims of unity, Catholics sometimes splintered into ethnically based congregations. Protestants were more splintered than Catholics: they divided into Lutheran, Congregational, Methodist, and other Protestant denominations. Early Lutheran churches were frequently ethnically based: German, Norwegian, and a Danish community of Grundtvigians. There existed no single Christian religion upon which to build a common culture. Religion remained a private part of settlers' lives.

Native women had far more constraints on the way in which they expressed their spirituality than did Euro-Americans. Despite government attempts to suppress the older Midewiwin ceremonies, they continued to be practiced into the twentieth century among some Chippewa, Menominee, and Ho-Chunk. Women played an important role in the Midewiwin, participating actively in the ceremonies' healing aspects and in the other ways in which the religion provided for the community's spiritual and social welfare.[1]

Three other religions, newly introduced, provided Native women with other spiritual paths. Christianity, brought to this area primarily by Catholic missionaries, found most converts within the Menominee. By the late nineteenth century, an estimated two-thirds of the Menominee had adopted Catholicism and adapted it to their needs. Beginning in the 1880s, a new religion, the Dream Dance, made its way east from the Dakota. Like its counterpart, the Ghost Dance, which flourished at the same time farther west, this new religion spread quickly to groups looking for spiritual renewal. During the 1910s, another religion, Peyotism, moved north from the Southwest. Whether Midewiwin, Christianity, Dream Dance, or Peyotism, women used religion as a way to resist cultural loss, to create new support systems, and to help protect themselves and their families. Each of these religious paths offered ways in which women could maintain their sense of the sacred, their cultural heritage, and their community ties. Sometimes a person practiced a number of religions. The family of Mountain Wolf Woman, a Ho-Chunk who died in 1960, held three rituals for her—Midewiwin, the Native American Church (Peyotism), and Christianity—to symbolize the importance of all three in her life.[2]

Native and settler women carried spirituality, matters of the spirit, with them everywhere. Rooted in individual prayer, meditation, a sense of the sacred, and community ritual, marked by sacred sites and houses of worship, spirituality was made a part of women's lives in different ways. For some, religion suffused all of life, their relationship to all beings and objects. For others, religion marked a way of joining their daily lives to other sacred worlds and beings. For yet others, it was less constant and less intense, a physical and psychic space held in reserve for times of need—death and illness, mistreatment by others, the misalignment of chance that caused misfortune. It offered solace and assistance, lifting the spirit when daily life failed to provide joy. It could offer, simply, a way to conform to community norms, when others felt that joint supplication to "higher beings" was necessary for the welfare of all. Finally, it offered to many rural women additional protection for themselves and their children, a way to enforce standards of conduct on others. For a few, the orders of Catholic nuns—the sisterhoods that taught and healed—provided a route for rural daughters out of their isolation within families into communities of women who shared a devotion to matters of the spirit.

Native

TAIL FEATHER WOMAN AND THE DREAM DANCE

In 1920 anthropologist Leonard Bloomfield arrived at Zoar on the Menominee reservation. Over the next few weeks, residents shared stories with Bloomfield as they hosted his visit. The Zoar community, sometimes also called Crow Settlement or It Forks, stood at the meeting of three rivers, deep in the woods, fifteen miles northwest of Keshena and about three miles from Neopit. Members of the old Thunder Clans had moved there in 1881, after the government agent had forbidden them to dance both their older Midewiwin medicine dance and the newer Dream Dance, which they called a peace dance. Here, out of the government officials' view, they continued to dance and to maintain their religions.[3]

A few members of the Zoar community were now farmers. They had cleared small fields and planted oats, corn, potatoes, and grass. Every year they also planted large gardens. They had teams and extra ponies; wagons, sleighs, plows, drags, and other tools; wells and pumps. In the winter many men logged while women tended the farms. In spring they made maple sugar together. By 1920 many families had new log houses, buildings with sleeping rooms above. Bloomfield probably slept in one of those rooms, under the eaves. Bloomfield's chief informants became close and parental friends. He wrote of one, "[she] became as a mother to me, guiding my speech as one does a child, for she has little English."[4]

That summer and the next, residents helped Bloomfield record and translate a series of texts. Their goal was to record, in the Menominee language, stories that were still remembered and told at Zoar but that had disappeared in the larger Christian community as children attended boarding schools and ceased to speak the language. Bloomfield eventually published a volume of the stories he collected. People told Bloomfield stories about animals and how most Zoar women gathered ginseng and berries, wove mats, baskets, and patchwork quilts, and did washing in Neopit while a few farmed. One woman described a mat she wove. It was six feet by three feet, woven from a weft of waykoop and a warp of weeds gathered in the summer, bleached, dried, and dyed. Woven into the rug were happiness bands of red. Above and below each happiness band were protection bands of red arrow points. Happiness and protection were the spiritual gifts she wove into her rugs.[5]

Among the stories told to Bloomfield in 1920 was one he called "The Origin of the Dream Dance." It was Tail Feather Woman's story:

> At the edge of a lake dwelt these people. When they were dwelling there some soldiers came to them to fight them. Then a certain woman took her child on her back and ran down to the lake to go lie in the water. When she had lain four days in the water, she began to starve.... When she had lain four days in the

water, a Spirit came to her. . . . She went out of that place. A wash-tub was lying outside. "Take it up; take it along where your people dwell," she was told by the Spirit. "You will tell your men-folk to go slay the creature [a deer] that you are to use on this drum, so that you may make a drum. Let them hurry about it. Then when they have completed the drum, they will dance together."

The women were to join the men in singing, give them food, and see that no one left the ceremony. The story continued:

> The reason the dream-drum exists is that this brown-skinned Indian was given it by the Great Spirit. The reason they all frequent this dream dance ceremony is that they may deal kindly with each other, that they may never fight each other, exchanging things by way of reciprocal gifts. That is why the brown-skinned man dances the dream dance, that the Indians may deal kindly with one another, and love one another.

Each time the Dream Dance was performed the story of how it began was to be repeated.

The woman who had the vision and originated the Dream Dance was Dakota (Sioux). One English-speaking contemporary to the event, Benjamin G. Armstrong, wrote in 1892 that her vision took place in May 1876, following the Battle of the Little Bighorn. Other dances of religious revival called Ghost Dances were being spread south across the Plains, but this one was different. It spread eastward through the woodlands. The woodlands tribes had formerly accompanied their dancing with a small hand-held drum, about fifteen inches in diameter. Tail Feather's drum was not held in the hand and was, as the story says, the size of a washtub. It was to sit near the ground, supported by a special frame. Armstrong observed ceremonies at a Chippewa gathering near Ashland, Wisconsin, in the spring of 1878 and interviewed Tail Feather Woman. She told him that the Spirit told her that the small drum was no longer large enough to keep away bad spirits and that they must give up all their other dances. She was heading west to teach the dance to the Crow and other tribes.[6]

One of Tail Feather Woman's instructions was that the tribes to which she gave the dance and the songs must construct a large drum and pass it on to another tribe. Thus the big drum was introduced from one community to another. Informants told one anthropologist that the first drum in the Zoar community arrived via the Potawatomi as early as the 1860s, but that detail calls into question the date of the battle during which Tail Feather Woman had her vision. If it was introduced this early, agents took little note of it. The first documented effort to suppress the Dream Dance was by the new agent, E. Stephens, who arrived in 1879.[7]

A Franciscan father, who had himself just arrived to establish a boarding school, left an account in what came to be called a "Chronicle." According to his version the Menominee had a "great addiction to dancing" and held a dance every year that lasted from a week before to a week after July 4. On these occasions Ho-Chunk, Potawatomi, and Chippewa came together to celebrate. Franciscans condemned the dances as "pagan," involving "gross violation of decency and chastity." They supported the agent's efforts to suppress the dances.[8]

When the agent banned the Dream Dance among the Menominee in the summer of 1880, the Franciscan father wrote, the people armed to resist the order: "Even the women had their hand knives in hand hidden under their clothes." The Indian Bureau in Washington authorized the agent to enlist forty soldiers from the Catholic Menominee to suppress the dance. This armed force arrested the leaders, chained them, and placed them in wagons to be locked up in jail. The other dancers dispersed but threatened to get help to fight the armed Catholics. Alarmed, the agent sent for U.S. troops from Chippewa Falls. Nothing happened, the account concludes, but there was no further dancing while Stephens remained agent. That was until October 1882, when community opposition forced his replacement. His successor allowed the dances to resume.

An account from Shawano gives a slightly different version. It agrees in describing the annual dances and Stephens's order to stop dancing. This account says that Stephens first ordered the Indian police to stop the dancing, and when that move failed he asked the interpreter, Joseph Gauthier, who operated a mercantile company in Keshena, to appeal to them to cease. During this confrontation a gun accidentally discharged, a woman attacked the agent, and he fled to nearby Shawano, where he called for troops from Fort Snelling in St. Paul. In this version, settlers stayed away from the reservation during the several weeks the soldiers were present. The troops fraternized with the Natives and nothing disturbed the peace. Then the soldiers left. "The Indians kept on dancing," this account concludes.[9]

Yet a third version adds that the agent told the census taker that local Catholics felt threatened by the new religious dances taking place in the forest. Perhaps. But later stories tell of Catholics being invited to the dances at the Zoar community. There, in July 1882, a large number of Indians, painted, wearing ribbons, beads, and feathers, came to dance. The Menominee continued the Dream Dance, always in fear of interference from the Catholic priests and the disfavor of agents. New drums arrived in the community during the early twentieth century.

In other communities, such as Lac du Flambeau, Native people encountered less opposition to the practice of the Dream Dance. The ritual was especially strong at Lac du Flambeau, where there were few Catholics to complain. In 1902 the agent at Lac du Flambeau reported that people there were taking a drum to Perkinstown and Willow Lake to give it away. He tried to persuade them not to go, but generally agents at Lac du Flambeau did not actively interfere with the dance. Musicologist Frances Densmore witnessed a drum being sent from Lac du Flambeau to the Menominee in 1910.[10]

One reason the Dream Dance spread so rapidly to all these communities was that before contact with Euro-Americans they had shared the Midewiwin, which emphasized physical and spiritual healing. The Dream Dance did not replace the Midewiwin, which continued to be practiced throughout this period, secretly on reservations after it was banned in 1883 and openly where groups of Native people lived in more isolated communities. Two Indian villages in Taylor and Menominee counties were composed of people from various tribes. Best known was the McCord village, near Perkinstown in central Taylor County, where people from the Midewiwin and Dream Dance societies often gathered to practice their religions freely well into the 1930s.[11]

The government remained opposed to all "traditional" dancing, whether it accompanied the Midewiwin or the Dream Dance. Regardless of orders from Washington about "traditional" dance, the Dream Dance was still being performed at Zoar when Bloomfield arrived in 1920. Secular public versions were performed at Lac du Flambeau in the late 1920s, and it was still being performed in the 1930s, when the government finally loosened its ban on dance and Native religious rituals.[12]

By 1950 the Dream Dance was still alive, but elders were concerned that it was "going dim." A group of Menominee asked anthropologist J. S. Slotkin to

Lac du Flambeau dancers, 1920s. Anthropologist Huron H. Smith documented the continued importance of dance in Ojibwe communities. The secularized, public dances reminded Native and settler families of the importance of gift-giving and community ritual.

make a written record of it. The elders held the rites weekly, but the dance's survival seemed doubtful because many young people did not know the practices. While some elders believed the dance could still be maintained, others wanted a written description in case it could not. The elders gave Slotkin the first detailed account of the Dream Dance.[13]

Elders explained to Slotkin how the drum was cared for and used. Once a drum had arrived in its new home, it became the possession of one family, usually a husband and wife. Together they were responsible for the drum's care and for organizing the dancers, feasts, and giveaways that accompanied the drum ceremony. Other community members belonged to one or another drum society. Women shared responsibility for the drum with the men, but the drum usually took the man's name, such as the "Pete Sam Drum." According to Julia Beaver, whose husband owned a drum, it was the symbol of the world: "In this Drum, that's the world . . . we each have a place in it." The drum, she explained, was like the earth, and the men who sat around it were the workers of the spirit. Julia described her husband's role as fatherlike and the members of his drum as her family. Her husband was the chief male warrior. Seven other men in the society also became male warriors, and each of the eight men had a male assistant.

Julia was the "chief woman"; there were three additional principal women, all called "warrior women." Each of the four represented a cardinal direction, and each had an assistant woman warrior. The women repaired and cleaned the drum paraphernalia, prepared the ritual meals, and originally sang along with the men. Although many women no longer sang by the 1950s, the men still considered them central to the ceremony. "Us fellows," one man told Slotkin, "we're just working for the women folks, they got the Drum from the Great Spirit. When that Sioux woman got the Drum from the Great Spirit . . . Great Spirit told her that she's not the only one, there's lots of different women. . . . It's just going to be like your sisters . . . all them women is all your sisters." Julia treated all the members as part of her family.[14]

Today the tradition of the big drum lives at community powwows. In August 1995, nineteen groups from across the United States and Canada brought their drums to the Menominee dance grounds. Hundreds came to dance, to renew friendships, to reinforce cultural identity, to show off their beaded and woven outfits. More than fifty years after Slotkin's visit, the big drums still beat among the Menominee.

PEYOTE WOMAN

Peyotism, now called the Native American Church, was the newest religion to be practiced among Wisconsin Native families and had the smallest number of adherents. According to tradition the peyote religion was started by a woman in the Southwest. In the 1870s and '80s it spread from Mexico to the Lipan Apache, to the Kiowa and the Comanche, and then north to the Ho-Chunk, who provided many converts.[15]

Various tellings of the origin story agreed that a woman or women started the original peyote practice, but versions differ. One has a sister looking for her lost brother when she herself becomes lost and is attacked by soldiers. Like other versions, this one tells of a deity sending a message directing the person to eat the small button cactus. In one variant, the woman awakes, eats the cactus, gains strength, and carries it back to her tribe. Some say it was an Apache woman, but Apaches may have simply been the main group that introduced the religion north. Known as Peyote Woman, she came to be symbolized in the peyote ceremony as the woman who brings morning water. The religion was confined to males in some tribes, while in others women and children accompanied men, entering into the ceremony only if they were physically ill and in need of special medicine. Gradually, however, all the tribes admitted women so that by 1925 the practice was not limited to men anywhere. From the beginning, Ho-Chunk and Menominee women took an active part in the rituals.[16]

This religion was usually referred to as "medicine." A number of men later testified to its especial effectiveness for respiratory illnesses, such as tuberculosis, but the medicine was considered to be general protection, physical and spiritual. Mountain Wolf Woman, perhaps the best-known woman practitioner, described it as better than other religions: "Peyote alone is the best. I learned very many things."

Most of the peyote came from southern Texas. Gatherers and growers enjoyed a flourishing business in the 1880s. Anna B. Nichols described her enterprise in Laredo, Texas, where she grew three thousand cacti in her garden in 1888; a photograph shows her standing proudly before her crop. During the 1890s the use of peyote in religious ceremonies spread northward. Late in the nineteenth century it reached the Ho-Chunk in Nebraska. In 1908 Mountain Wolf Woman and her husband learned of it in South Dakota, where peyote meetings were held every Saturday. A group of Ho-Chunk brought it to Black River Falls, Wisconsin, in 1909. It was introduced to the Menominee in 1914.[17]

We know most about the introduction of Peyotism into the Ho-Chunk culture from anthropologist Paul Radin. A graduate student at Columbia studying under Franz Boas, Radin was in Nebraska and Wisconsin in 1908 gathering information on the Ho-Chunk Midewiwin. When he arrived, the Ho-Chunk communities were being divided by the introduction of the new religion. Practitioners were not only proselytizing and competing for members but were also antagonistic toward the Midewiwin. The Dream Dance had not demanded any single allegiance, but like Christians some peyotists insisted new members abandon other religions. Many peyotists had been Midewiwin members but now had no allegiance to it and readily became informants about its practices. Radin was born into the family of a Russian Jewish rabbi, had grown up in Elmira, New York, and had studied history in Berlin and Prague, as well as at Columbia with James Harvey Robinson. He married the historian's daughter, Rose, in 1910. Radin was fascinated by the men who had left the old ways and were working to create a new religion. Over the next few years (1908–9 and 1911–12), Radin depended on these men to describe both the Midewiwin and the peyote religions.[18]

John Rave, also known as Little Redbird, described his conversion as occurring during a time of crisis, both cultural and personal. People were divided over the fundamental issue of how to survive as a distinct culture. His father was a chief in the Bear Clan, which traditionally had an important role in healing. Rave, who had been born in Wisconsin, had traveled a great deal, learned different languages, toured Europe with a circus, and in middle age, while living in Nebraska, grew discontented with the Midewiwin. He thought its members were practicing a formal religion devoid of a satisfactory relationship with the deity. While traveling in Oklahoma during 1893–94, he met peyote eaters. After eating his first peyote, he had fear-inspiring visions, and on the third night he saw God and the morning star and all things clearly. It is not certain if his wife went to Oklahoma or if he shared peyote with her after he returned. He said they were both cured of disease after eating the peyote. He brought back a supply from Oklahoma and asked people to bring their diseases and be cured. Within seventeen years he had converted half his community to the peyote faith.[19]

Radin was also able to pay Crashing Thunder to write his account of peyote's role in his life in the Ho-Chunk syllabary, which Radin had translated and published in 1920. Crashing Thunder was Mountain Wolf Woman's brother, but Radin got only the male view of religion. Twenty-five years later anthropologist Nancy Lurie met Mountain Wolf Woman while working in Black River Falls. In 1958 Lurie invited Mountain Wolf Woman to travel to Ann Arbor, Michigan, to tape her memoirs. Mountain Wolf Woman's niece, Frances Thunderland Wentz, helped Lurie translate the account.[20]

Mountain Wolf Woman told of her experiences with three religions. Her mother-in-law had her join the Midewiwin and told her she would be a leader. Later, Mountain Wolf Woman became a Christian. To ease the pains of childbirth, she ate her first peyote; finding it helpful, she began attending meetings. She explained, "when we went to Nebraska I ate peyote which is even a Christian way." Mountain Wolf Woman described the whole family—her parents, her husbands, her sisters and brothers—attending peyote meetings. From being medicine, it became a religion. One night, after eating twenty peyotes, she had a vision. She saw Jesus: "I never knew such pleasure as this. There was a sensation of great joyousness." Peyotism was an experiential religion. It did not just talk about God but allowed adherents to "see" God much as Christian mystics might experience Him. She had seen something holy. Later, she and her husband moved to South Dakota. There they ate peyote with the Dakota, who adopted her. She returned to Nebraska and then, with her brothers, to Black River Falls. Mountain Wolf Woman and her family became the center of the Black River Falls peyote group, holding meetings every Saturday night. Ostracized by the others, the peyote people lived together. It was to this group that a Nebraska delegation came in 1908. Mountain Wolf Woman remembered the occasion vividly almost fifty years later: "They filled two train coaches with Indians. They even had their drums and they sang in the train, drumming loudly. They got off at Black River Falls. We went there with our wagons. . . . Eventually, we were going to have a big peyote meeting. They came to us and brought a big teepee. . . . There were all kinds of Winnebago, Nebraskans and a lot of Wisconsin Indians. It was very pleasant."[21]

As Mountain Wolf Woman became older, she began attending a Christian church, but she remained a strong supporter of peyote, sponsoring a commemorative meeting in 1958 to celebrate the fiftieth anniversary of its introduction into Wisconsin. Symbolic of her participation in three spiritual traditions— the Midewiwin medicine lodge and the Christian and peyote religions—her family held rituals for all three at her death.[22]

By the time Mitchell Neck introduced peyote to the Menominee in 1914, the government was looking for ways to stop its spread. For many years, Christian missionaries had urged the government to treat peyote as an illegal substance rather than as part of a legitimate religion. U.S. marshals arrested Neck, arguing that peyote came under an 1897 law that barred liquor, "an intoxicating substance," from being introduced into the reservations. After the government argued its case in the U.S. District Court in Milwaukee, the federal judge held that the law clearly did not apply to peyote and ordered the prisoner released. Following this decision, anti-peyotists attempted unsuccessfully to obtain a federal law prohibiting its use. Meanwhile, non-Native and Native canvassed reservations, warning people not to use peyote.[23]

The conflict over peyote divided almost every group that had campaigned for Native rights. John Collier, head of the American Indian Defense Association and later commissioner of Indian Affairs within Roosevelt's New Deal administration, considered Peyotism an important Native religion that should be allowed to coexist with Christianity and other faiths. The Society of American Indians, which had campaigned for greater autonomy for Native people, split over the issue. Zitkala-Sa (Gertrude Bonnin), a popular lecturer and writer, was openly crusading against the new religion by 1915, speaking to groups of white reformers and to Native Americans about its danger. She linked liquor and peyote in a pamphlet published and circulated by the Woman's Christian Temperance Union in 1917.[24]

Peyotism survived to officially become the Native American Church in 1918, and members achieved the legal right to use peyote in their ceremonies. Some adherents referred to the religion as "medicine," but mainly it offered general protection. Women were most active among the Ho-Chunk. The practice never grew among the Chippewa at Lac du Flambeau. At Menominee, small numbers of families, usually those who had some Christian education, maintained a group where women took an active part. The majority of Menominee women, however, participated only in the Catholic religion.

THE CORPUS CHRISTI SOCIETY

Catholic Native women also influenced Christian practices. Menominee women found a way in their annual celebration of Corpus Christi. This Catholic feast was observed every June by Catholic priests, but it was the women's work and their enthusiasm for the event that made it, as the *Indian Sentinel* reported in 1905, the "National Holy-day of the Menominees."[25]

Christianity, especially Catholicism, offered attractive features to Indians. Most importantly it gave access to spiritual power and emphasized good works in ways similar to Native religions. It offered Jesus and saints as guardian spirits and protectors, ritual prayers and teaching, baptism to protect infants, key priestly support for opposing government removal policies, and a religion that through most of the nineteenth and into the early twentieth century depended upon Indians themselves to translate, interpret, and convince other Native people to join them. Among the Menominee, a community where women were attracted to Catholicism, Rosalie Dousman played an important role in interpreting the religion. The Corpus Christi ritual fit well with earlier Native practices.[26]

A women's society was responsible for fashioning the Catholic ritual into something particularly "Menominee." In 1881 the priest at Keshena mission started two groups, a Temperance Society for the men and an Altar Society for the women. During the first years the Temperance Society flourished: at one time sixty Native men belonged. But the society men and Father Oderic clashed in 1888, and he cancelled their temperance celebration that September. The celebrations were reinstated, but the group, now renamed the Total Abstinence Society, never recovered its former popularity. Membership numbered no more than twenty-two in the years between 1904 and 1920 and reached a low of eleven in 1907. Meanwhile, the Altar Society, called the Christian Mothers after 1898, continued to flourish. The Menominee observed the first feast of Corpus Christi in the 1840s, but it did not become an elaborate celebration until the 1880s. In 1889 there was a major procession with the bishop and fifteen priests. The Altar Society bought a new canopy and the Oneida band played.[27]

We have a good description of the 1904 procession. Preparations began several days before the feast, when Menominee families begin to gather,
pitching tents on the hills around Keshena. Women from each settlement—
Keshena, Kenepowa (West Branch), and Little Oconto—created chapels of tree
branches and boughs lined and decorated with flowers, laces, and other materials. Religious pictures adorned little altars inside the chapels. The circuit along
which the procession was to pass, about a mile, was lined with trees with flags
mounted at the top and interspersed with high posts covered with evergreen
boughs and flags, garlands, and floral wreaths. The mission buildings were
also decorated with boughs and garlands. Banners and flags of many sizes and
colors fluttered from the church steeple, windows, and housetops. Families
decorated their houses, erected little altars at the doors and windows, and
placed pictures, flowers, and candles there.

All was ready when the bishop of Green Bay arrived at the Shawano railway
depot. A leading merchant and one of the priests from Keshena escorted him

*Corpus Christi celebration, 1900s. Most years from the 1840s to 1960, Catholic Menominee
women garlanded their homes and outdoor chapels with flowers and pine boughs for this
spring ceremony. The Confraternity of Christian Mothers, organized in 1898, paraded as a
group. This holiday was a time for families to gather and to feast and for children to be ritually
received into the Catholic religion.*

to the mission, followed by vehicles full of people. At the reservation boundary men and youths on horseback joined the procession; before reaching the mission church schoolchildren fell in; then all children, horseback riders, and the bishop proceeded to the church for a reception. The next morning beginning at five the clergy celebrated masses. At nine the bishop celebrated a High Mass with choir and sermon, and then the procession started out amid clanging bells and firing guns. At the head of the parade men carried the American flag and the cross. Then followed the Keshena brass band, children from the mission and government schools, the bishop with the Blessed Sacrament under the canopy, the Temperance Society, the Christian Mothers, and schoolchildren carrying church banners. Catholics from Shawano and the surrounding countryside and other reservations joined the Menominee. Prayers were spoken in Latin, English, Menominee, Ojibwe, and German. After the procession, women served a feast. In the afternoon the bishop confirmed the children and gave the benediction, the choir sang the Te Deum, and the bishop and visiting clergy left.[28]

The ritual remained basically Catholic, but the altars, the chapels, the decorations, and the feast were reminiscent of the traditional Midewiwin. The women's groups, responsible for the altars, remind us how important are the sites of sacred ceremonies and their garnishing. Dance had been banished, but music and embellishment remained, and women were important in using them to make the new religion their own. Catholicism grew slowly among the Menominee, and the few non-Christians at Zoar always maintained Native religions, but there was also a link between the two groups. Non-Christians invited Catholic relatives to attend their rituals, much to the priests' dismay. One Menominee man I talked to remembered growing up in the 1950s, when those who practiced the old religions kept lookouts and performed rites in secret. Zoar had been founded so that people could practice their religion out of sight of government officials and priests at Keshena. But there is no doubt that women also saw the Catholic religion with its public affirmations and rituals as offering a way to protect themselves and their families from the calamities of life.

Feasting, the communal consumption of food and drink, was a public ritual for which women in all these Native religions shared a special responsibility. They stockpiled food, collected it from others, managed preparation and distribution. Women also scheduled ceremonies, advised on protocol, and participated in some or all parts of other religious ceremonies, but arranging feasts was their special responsibility. Feasts honored spirit guardians, ancestors, spirits of slain animals, or Catholic saints. In return for these ceremonies, guardian spirits assisted and protected humans. By organizing feasts, women empowered individuals and communities and made themselves exemplars of the ethical practice of gifting others.[29]

Catholic
Amalia's Story [Streitel, Sister Frances, born in Bavaria, 1844–1911]

Amalia lived only a short time in northern Wisconsin, but she left a long legacy in the ideals she shared with the women who joined her order and the hospitals she founded. Most nuns left stories only about their work, but Amalia's story tells us much about why she and others came to northern Wisconsin and what they hoped to accomplish. Thus her quest to find a path and the circumstances that brought her to Wisconsin are relevant to this story of women in the north-central counties. Her quest is neither secular nor modern but deeply spiritual and mystical.

Amalia Streitel, later known as Mother Frances Streitel, who founded the Sisters of the Sorrowful Mother and established a string of hospitals across northern Wisconsin, did not expect to leave an account of her struggle to find her spiritual path. In the two years before Sister Frances left Rome for Wisconsin, she wrote a series of letters to Father Francis Jordan, founder of the missionary order to which she then belonged, and asked him to burn them. Against her wishes, Father Jordan preserved her letters, and in 1976 the Sisters of the Sorrowful Mother translated them from German to English and published them.[30]

The letters began in 1883. Amalia had been struggling with her call to the religious life since youth. She was born into a Bavarian family in 1844, her father a government official, her mother from a family of brewers. An official biography describes Amalia's early exposure to the virtues of

Mother Streitel. Well educated, dedicated to poverty, prayer, and the sick, Mother Streitel established a string of hospitals in north-central Wisconsin. She and the Sisters of the Sorrowful Mother considered their work with the sick to be a form of prayer. Today the St. Joseph's Hospital they founded in Marshfield is the only major rural referral center in Wisconsin and the second-largest rural teaching hospital in the United States.

"charity, obedience, orderliness, and self-control." As the daughter of an upper-class family, Amalia received an extraordinary education: grammar school at a local convent, then enrollment in a Franciscan academy at Augsburg, where she studied language and the music of the elite. At seventeen, the year before she graduated, she wrote, "I was called to the religious life in a special manner." Her parents, especially her father, disdained her "religious whims" and insisted she join in the secular life expected of a young woman of her social station. If she were to embrace the religious life, her parents insisted, she must neither enter a strict order nor dedicate herself to service of the sick. These were the two things Amalia wanted most. In 1868 she began teaching language, needlework, and music to young girls at a convent near Munich. From this time on, her experience, education, and family status marked her for administrative work in the church.

Father Jordan was organizing a female branch of a new teaching order in Rome. Amalia traveled there to help create what she hoped would be an ascetic missionary order devoted to the poor. She was six years older than Father Jordan, articulate, and passionate in her conviction, clearly able to attract other women to her vision. This period was one of great spiritual ferment among young women in Bavaria. Thousands flocked to religious orders rather than accept their role in society. Mother Frances, as she was now known, asked postulants to spend a year in Rome, toiling in poverty as preparation for mission work. Mother Frances emphasized the egalitarian aspect of community life by caring for the young postulants who joined the order: she cooked dumplings and brown sauce for them, cleaned their rooms, and washed their simple clothing. As young women arrived in Rome, Mother Frances began her correspondence with Father Jordan. She wrote to him that nuns such as these were instruments of God who had a "buoyancy of soul," free souls able to find others with an ambition to serve the Lord, "tools that sharpen themselves on the keen edges of others."[31]

Sister Frances had earlier found these keen edges in the lives of saints. One model was St. Teresa of Avila, the sixteenth-century Spanish mystic who founded the Carmelites as an order dedicated to spiritual exercises. Attracted to a contemplative life, Sister Frances transferred to the Carmelites in 1882, but while there she became convinced that prayer was not enough. "I deeply loved the sick. . . . I loved the poor," she later wrote to her confessor. These loves led her to a second model, St. Francis of Assisi, the twelfth-century Italian who had committed himself to poverty and to ministering to the poor. Unable to choose between the two, Sister Frances realized her calling was to somehow combine an active Franciscan life that emphasized healing and teaching with the Carmelites' contemplative life. Her task, Sister Frances often told others after she left the Carmelite convent, was to reconcile the examples of St. Teresa of Avila and St. Francis of Assisi and with her followers to "strive to remedy the spiritual and social needs of mankind, teaching it again what it means to pray and work."[32]

Although the saints Francis and Teresa were the main spiritual models for Sister Frances, these twelfth- and sixteenth-century predecessors were not her only guides. She also saw herself and the women she gathered about her as similar to St. Clare of Montefalco, who founded the Order of the Poor Ladies to try to keep alive St. Francis's commitment to poverty and the poor. When she found a book about St. Clare in which the saint appeared without shoes, Sister Francis asked Father Jordan's permission to go about in only sandals. She thought walking barefoot would be even better, for it showed "complete contempt for the world," but she settled for wearing sandals only in the house and not on the street. She once called them "innocent sandals."[33]

Testing every decision against the Franciscan ideal of poverty, Sister Frances negotiated a way for the fledgling convent to compromise with the lax world. "Do you want us to have curtains," she queried her spiritual advisor in February 1883, "Do you think St. Francis would tolerate this?" The next month she asked, "Shall I dare to incur the expenses for a sewing machine?" It pleases God, she wrote, that "we love poverty in regard to food and other things." She wrote of having a head covering without starch or artistic drape, "nothing . . . except a simple capuche with a black veil which falls in natural folds." Her purpose was not just a personal asceticism but one that by its example might turn the tide of a world in which religious life was shallow. To accomplish her goal, she was prepared to forgo "all right to possessions, even the smallest items," to completely eliminate "inordinate sensual nature" and "one's own judgments." Undivided surrender to the will of superiors as the executors of God's will to accomplish the practice of perfect obedience was her proclaimed goal.[34]

Despite her reluctance to assume authority, in 1885 Father Jordan appointed Frances spiritual director of the Sisters of Charity of the Sorrowful Mother. In many ways, northern Wisconsin was the best place for her to be. Mother Frances and her nuns came to the United States with nothing. They begged for food and money to start their hospitals. They lived in cold, uncomfortable houses. They worked barefoot in the gardens in the summer and patched— and sometimes shared—stockings and shoes in the winter. The sisters often wore the simplest of capuchins and ragged habits as they worked the soil of their gardens, raising food for themselves and their patients. It was perhaps as close to twelfth-century Italy and the lives of the early Franciscans as they could get. A nun arriving fresh from Rome at the motherhouse in Marshfield found a sister in her ragged habit and night capuchin, working barefoot in the garden. Seeing her surprise, the sister warned, "We do things differently than in Rome."

Thus Sister Frances reconciled her mystical experiences of hearing the word of God with becoming one of God's earthly supervisors, of being "superior" to the other "sisters." She felt it was a mistake to be made "superior to others," yet that was what God had called her to do, and she would counter her position as "superior" by practicing self-denial. "The Lord gave me talent for teaching and training, but the fear of being talented or becoming vain and self-complacent in the position of teacher, prompted me already years ago to put aside all signs of higher education and choose housework instead," she wrote. The office of superior, like that of teacher, was full of dangers for her, but she would remain in charge until the Lord sent a more suitable person. Meanwhile, she practiced self-denial by managing the kitchen and taking the most uncomfortable room in the house. She knew her preferences were not acceptable, that a superior should not humiliate herself before "her subjects," but, she told Father Jordan, "the Lord requires of me nevertheless that I practice this virtue, which has become so rare, practice it in order to teach others." Being an authority was a "terrible moment" that she had to endure: "The Lord will find me and guide me to that place where I do not wish to be."[35]

Despite her obvious success in Wisconsin, Rome grew less satisfied with Mother Frances by 1896. Authorities removed her as superior after eleven years, recalled her to Rome, and did not allow her to return to Wisconsin. Rome appointed as the new mother superior Sister Johanna, one of the early sisters in the order and a close advisor to Sister Frances. The sisters at Tomahawk, Rhinelander, and Menominee wished to contest her dismissal and appealed to the motherhouse at Marshfield to follow them. Sister Frances counseled acceptance of Rome's decision, and the nuns remained loyal to her wishes. No secession occurred. Sister Johanna accepted the burden of authority from Mother Frances, and the nuns continued her path of poverty, ministering to the sick and dedicating their lives to expanding the hospitals she had founded. Relieved of that burden, Sister Frances lived her last fifteen years in Italy, where she helped care for neglected children and spent much time in prayer. She died in 1911.[36]

THE NURSING SISTERS

The European nuns who came from Germany to nurse the ill on the Wisconsin frontier did not write about their spiritual journeys as did Amalia. But they did talk about the hard work of establishing hospitals on the northern frontier and caring for the physical needs of the sick. Between 1937 and 1939 Sister Beda interviewed many of the Sisters of the Sorrowful Mother about their work. No other source comes closer to revealing the nuns' spiritual life than this series of oral histories told to a sister nun. Most of the nuns were young and healthy, able to withstand the harsh climate, poverty, and hard work. They looked back with a sweet nostalgia on the hard times and how they had combined work and ritual. One story that a number of them related was about building the chapel at Marshfield in 1901–2. Sister Melania called it "A Sweet Remembrance of My Life."

In 1901, early in the spring, the sisters decided to build a new chapel separate from the hospital. The first chapel, a room in the hospital, was too small, and the sisters' prayers disturbed the patients. The mother superior assigned four of the strongest novices—one was Sister Melania—to dig out stones for the foundation. "We accepted with great pleasure," Sister Melania recalled, and "started out with pickaxe, shovels, iron bars across our shoulders. . . . Did we ever have fun out there in God's nature." A neighbor dynamited the largest boulders. The novices loaded the stones on the wagon, and Sister Basilia, who had charge of the horse, hauled the stones. Other neighbors helped, but the young novices "did our share of it; the greater our piles were, the greater our joy." The sisters laid the piles of rock against the foundation for reinforcement. "It will be a difficult thing to tear that chapel down," Sister Agnes said.[37]

Sister Ferreria continued the story. The chicken coop was in the way of the site for the new chapel, so a laborer nailed handles to the corners and the young women carried it to a new place. They cleared away all the woodpiles, which had logs five to six feet long, used for heating the house. The sisters also removed all the waste lumber while workers erected the building. They rose at 3:00 AM to do this work.[38]

The sisters had no money to build the chapel, so two men in the community put up security. These two met with the sisters to discuss the plans. Mr. Steinmetz thought the chapel should have a tower; Mother Johanna thought a tower was against "holy poverty." Steinmetz insisted—they were all speaking in German, of course—a chapel without a steeple was like a bride without a veil, with only a *kopftuchlein*, a head cloth on. Finally Johanna gave in. And so, said Sister Annunciata, "the cozy little chapel received its cozy little tower." The project also included adding rooms to the hospital building.[39]

Holy poverty and toil for the glory of God fit well with the German work ethic and the difficult conditions the early founders faced. The work connected with the building of the chapel was a perfect example of that ideal and how the women valued the joining of two vows. Holy poverty embraced and valued poverty as a form of worship that could provide a place for reflection.

The wash water story also illustrates the practice of holy poverty. This event took place between 1895 and 1897. Sister Clotildis entered the convent at Vienna in 1895 and began washing clothes in Rome as a candidate for the order. Nuns did not glorify hard work, although it fit well with prayer. While still in Rome, they washed church linens entirely by hand in cold water, but they welcomed the washboards a priest brought them from the United States. "All day long we prayed while washing, in strict silence, no small sacrifice coming fresh from the world," related Sister Clotildis.[40]

After five months in Rome, Sister Clotildis sailed for America from Genoa on the *Kaiser Wilhelm*. After being invested in September 1895, she worked in the laundry that winter. There was always a lack of water, she said, for the pump could fill only a few pails at a time. The hospital was just north of the city, but there was not enough pressure to supply water. Washing was a complicated affair, requiring a Saturday soaking and large quantities of wood to heat the water on Monday. Sister Clotildis went to the mother superior, who offered no suggestions, only affirmed that the wash must be soaked. In tears, Sister Clotildis told Sister Leocadia her troubles and that she had prayed to the Lord to give her light but none had come. Suddenly, as they were talking, "the Holy Ghost came." She solved the problem. Together, the sisters took the washtub outside, filled it with snow, and lugged it back to the wash kitchen. Refilling the washtub and melting the snow gave them a big wash kettle of water. Then they went into the woods, pulled off rotten branches broken by the wind and hauled them back to feed the fire. Thus the sisters brought God into their most daily and mundane tasks and enlisted His help in such humble assignments as washing clothes. They kept alive the tradition of poverty, work, and prayer.[41]

Nuns worked so hard for such long hours that they could barely say prayers when they finished, exhausted, at midnight. The priest urged them to shorten their prayers, assuring them that "God would take their prolonged hard work as prayer."[42]

BUILDING THE CHURCH, ORGANIZING THE LAITY

As large groups of Catholics arrived in the 1870s, they organized congregations and built churches. With time, the communities replaced small wood churches with brick, established rectories, and moved from missionary to parish status. At Dorchester in 1876, for example, parishioners built St. Louis Catholic Church—the oldest parish between Stevens Point and Ashland, they claimed—but it remained a mission church until the 1890s. Then they built a brick church, established a Christian Mothers' Society, and obtained their first resident pastor. Although pastors stayed on average three years during the period from 1897 to 1921, the laity built a rectory and school-convent and opened a Catholic school.[43]

Smaller villages had no churches at all. In Stetsonville in 1883, "A desire for a house of worship was strong," wrote the village chronicler, "yet there weren't enough people for each denomination to build churches." Finally, in 1885 a Catholic donated an acre of land and Catholics built the first church. Ministers came from nearby churches to preach on Sundays. Colby Catholics began to meet in a school building in 1879 and then in a new church in 1889. At Medford, Athens, and other towns, Catholics went through a similar process of parish building.

The Catholic Slovenians at Willard left a detailed record of their progression from wilderness laity to organized, visible parish. When Catholic Slovenian families settled in large numbers at Willard in 1908, they first attended church in Greenwood, eight miles away over rutted roads. Visiting Slovenian priests listened to their stories of hard times and, occasionally, Greenwood had a priest who could give sermons in Slovenian as well as in German. In 1910 a group of Catholic families incorporated as the Holy Family parish, using the schoolhouse for their first Mass, said by a visiting priest. In 1912 the parish built its first church, crowding into the still-unfinished building, using planks laid across nail kegs for their first pews, to hear Mass

Die Regeln und Vortheile, der Grzbruderschaft der christlichen Mütter der St. Ludwig's Gemeinde *(Rules and Benefits, Organization of Christian Mothers for St. Ludwig's Parish), Dorchester, 1898.* Matilda kept this pamphlet and her badge as mementos of the one women's group to which she belonged. Like members of Protestant women's groups, Catholics cleaned and garnished church buildings, organized fund raisers, and enjoyed the company of the "sisterhood."

on Christmas. Although priests could say Mass in a new church, they seldom stayed long, for they had to board with families. In the first six years after the church was finished, three pastors came and left; the congregation received its first permanent pastor only after promising to build a rectory in 1918. Slovenian-speaking Father John Novak arrived with his suitcase that year, and the parish industriously started building.[44]

Women joined men in the woods cutting trees. They also raised money to buy new pews for the church and to help build new altars. They roused their families on winter Sundays and dressed them warmly for the cold walk to the small church at Willard, for some a distance of three miles. They sent their children for religious instruction. The Willard history records that the first church society, chartered in 1910 to help male members with medical care and mortuary expenses, did not admit women and that they had to wait until 1923 to get their own "Mary Help Society," which allowed them to get insurance. To join, women needed a statement by the priest that they had "performed their Easter duty," that is, gone to confession and communion during the year ending on Easter Sunday.

Women expressed their spirituality through many aspects of their lives. Religion was often their only comfort and protection in hard times, and they offered this solace to their children. Like health care, religious education remained primarily the task of women. While parishes were struggling into

existence, rural women taught children prayers and the basics of their Christian beliefs. Like Matilda, Catholic women often hung pictures of Jesus and Mary on the walls of their log houses and knelt their children before them. Mothers made sure their children were baptized, received at least some formal religious instruction, took first communion. When there were no churches nearby, mothers arranged for a few weeks of religious education at nearby parishes with resident priests.

First Holy Communion was an important ritual for Catholic mothers. My grandmother Matilda was able to mark my mother's special day with a formal portrait taken in 1914. Although poor, Matilda managed to arrange for religious instruction and to make a dress that symbolized Theresa's coming of age and her acceptance into the Catholic Church. Theresa sits poised in her white dress at

Theresa Schopp first communion, 1916. Matilda scrimped to outfit Theresa appropriately for her First Holy Communion. She edged the white cotton dress and slip with lace and trimmed the tulle veil with flowers. Perhaps Leo paid for the studio photograph in nearby Medford, an unusual expense for a young woman.

this threshold to young womanhood and to a life to be lived within the Catholic Church. Matilda hoped Theresa's faith would offer comfort and protection, as her own had.

POLISH SECESSION

During the early nineteenth century, when the Catholic Church had its base among Irish immigrants in the eastern part of the United States, it was dominated by Irish clergy. As German immigration increased in the Midwest in the later nineteenth century, German clergy challenged the Irish for control. In this area of north-central Wisconsin, however, German parishioners and German clergy already dominated the Catholic churches, and only the ideology of church governance caused parishioners to fight among themselves. German immigrants divided over two philosophies of church governance: those who believed that clergy should dominate and those who believed that the Catholic church should move toward a more congregational model, with parish control over administrative matters, sometimes including the right to decide on who would be assigned as parish priests. In practice, of course, parish members could force unwanted priests to leave by withholding their support, a tactic often used. They could appeal to higher clergy for a new priest, or they could simply assume that the parish had the authority to control at the local level. Such an anti-clerical philosophy posed grave dangers to the church hierarchy, for it could be transferred to other aspects of the religion. A similar movement had once led to the Protestant reformation and eventually to religions in which the parishioners exercised much greater control over the clergy. With the arrival of new immigrants, ethnic conflict could be the entering wedge for such anti-clerical thought.

At the turn of the century, with a surge in Polish immigration, the German clergy faced a new challenge. Scholars have sometimes described the Polish Catholic church as a national church. At first, the American clergy attempted to integrate Polish immigrants into pre-existing German parishes. As more Poles arrived, conflicts occurred. In describing German-Polish clashes at Stevens Point, Michael Goc attributed them to earlier conflict in Germany, where Germans had suppressed the Polish language and the Polish Catholic church; to a national feeling; to class division; and to the arrival of Poles after German American culture had already taken form. All these factors affected women as well as men.[45]

Catholic churches, attempting to establish multinational parishes in Stevens Point, soon became rent with divisions. Feuds broke out among Irish, Germans, and Poles. Although most of these ethnic conflicts have not been well documented, we can get some sense of the level of disagreement over teaching in the records of the Sisters of St. Joseph, an order that spread into northeastern Wisconsin where both German and Polish communities existed. Most of these schools were in the eastern part of Marathon and Portage counties. By the early 1900s Portage County was about one-third Polish. Many Polish communities spread northwest into Marathon County but looked to Stevens Point for professional services by Polish immigrants and for Polish-owned businesses. The public market at Stevens Point was a gathering place for farmers from the surrounding countryside to buy hay, firewood, livestock, and surplus produce. By 1900 the market had what was called a "Polish Corner," where Polish shops and saloons lined the streets and Polish was the language of trade.

These Polish immigrants had come from a country occupied by Russian, Austrian, and Prussian states. Their landholding had been curtailed and their language suppressed. In Poland they had formed underground schools to maintain the Polish language and customs. Not only the Poles' desire to preserve their customs and language but also the issue of what status the Poles would have within the American Catholic churches provoked German-Polish conflict. Germans, especially in town, were well-established middle-class merchant families. The Poles were mainly urban working class. Although middle-class Polish merchants quickly established businesses to meet the demands of Polish town and country people, prosperity was no guarantee that their hard work would yield acceptance within the comfortably situated second- and third-generation German communities. To quiet dissension, in 1876 the archbishop at Milwaukee sent a Polish priest to found a new Polish parish, called St. Peter's Church, on the north side of Stevens Point.[46]

Politics reflected the divisions as well. Republican Germans and Democratic Poles had divided over the Bennett Law of 1889 because of its compulsory attendance provision, which mandated that children remain in school until age fourteen. Farm families opposed state regulations that would keep children away from home when they were needed to work on the farms just being carved out of the sandy soils around Stevens Point.[47]

Young women from the German communities had been successful in opening teacher education to immigrant daughters. They staffed countless country and Catholic parochial schools. Young Polish women had to face these newly entrenched German teachers. Poles who got through the public schools and were able to get their credentials had little trouble finding jobs because Polish parish schools were growing rapidly and both common and parochial schools looked for Polish teachers. The problem was within the religious orders, which were dominated by German women. Conflict began at St. Peter's when the Polish priest requested that the Milwaukee order supply Polish sisters. The Milwaukee convent, like the convent in La Crosse, was predominantly German, with a mother superior of German ethnicity. The Milwaukee convent staffed several schools, and the young Polish women who entered the convent expected to teach in parishes where priests were requesting Polish-speaking teachers. One sister, looking back at the conflict that developed between the German and Polish sisters, called it the "battle of two languages."[48]

Young Polish women from the Stevens Point parishes began to enter the convent at Milwaukee in the late nineteenth century. The large Polish parishes encouraged young women to join the teaching orders so that they could, in turn, staff smaller parish schools. As the Polish sisters recounted in their history, there seemed to be among the German and the Irish nuns—those in charge of the Milwaukee convent—a growing "fear, envy, and hatred of everything that was Polish." As the number of Polish postulants increased—to Polish women it seemed that vocations among Poles exceeded those among other nationalities—they found themselves relegated to a separate and lower status. According to their chronicles, Polish postulants came seeking freedom and "a new way of earning a living" in teaching. Instead of teaching, one was sent to a German parish in Wilmette, where her duties included pasturing the cow. Several other Polish women found themselves doing housework in German missions or working in sanatoria rather than teaching. Six young postulants, sent from St. Peter's parish, joined because they wanted to teach. They demanded Polish-speaking confessors and training to teach Polish youth in Catholic schools. When the Milwaukee convent seemed unresponsive, five of the six returned home and complained. Sister Oswalda Wisniewski, who had returned to St. Peter's to work under a German mother superior, later told the story tersely: "The five returned home and the talk of the parish against such injustice grew steadily stronger. Unfavorable comments were made about the [Milwaukee] community." With their priests' help they contacted Polish parishes in Detroit and Chicago and asked for sisters willing to join them in a new convent that would train Polish women to teach.[49]

The chronicler continued: "The news about the sisters spread like fire and the reaction in the parish created troubled confusion." To withdraw individually from an order because of incompatibility was one thing; to organize a secession, a revolt, was another. The older Polish sisters were distressed. At the Milwaukee motherhouse, Mother Alfons met with the Polish mother superiors to work out a compromise. She proposed a special province exclusively for the Polish sisters but under the administration of German superiors. The Polish sisters rejected the proposal, believing the German superiors were the source of the problems. Separation under these terms would still mean inequality.

The "Sisters' Separation" ignited German-Polish tensions from Detroit to Chicago. Sister Siegfried, the superior at St. Peter's, asked to be removed. In spring Sister Alfons notified the parish priest, Reverend L. Pescinski, who had taken the part of his five parishioners, that none of the teachers would be allowed to return to staff his parish school in September. The case was debated and criticized at the market square in Stevens Point. Father Pescinski went to the bishop in Milwaukee and asked that Mother Alfons assign Polish administrators. She refused: there were no Polish sisters competent enough to manage the new province, she insisted.

To quiet the growing conflict, the bishop decided to ask two Polish sisters from Chicago to assume leadership of the new province, and they presented themselves to Mother Alfons. Chicago was already on its way to becoming the center for Polish education. St. Stanislaus would have almost four thousand students and sixty-five teachers by 1910, all teaching with Polish textbooks. The matter now became one of male authority over female authority. Mother Alfons defended her right to control decisions within her convent. The sisters would have to choose, she told them. The rebels notified Mother Alfons of their intention to form a new community in July 1901. They had bought fifteen acres, a house, and barn at Hull, just north of Stevens Point, and planned to make it their new motherhouse. Sister Siegfried packed her trunk and returned to Milwaukee. Sister Felicia, who would head the new community, said each sister could choose where she wanted to go. Eighteen from Chicago and twelve from Detroit decided to join the new Stevens Point convent. Stanslaus Singer later recalled how Sister Clara had stood firm when Mother Alfons rejected the compromise, telling her, "We are Polish. I am joining the Poles." The seceding sisters took the name Sisters of St. Joseph. By the fall of 1903, sisters were staffing schools in Chicago, Detroit, and Green Bay as well as at Stevens Point, Hull, and several other Wisconsin parishes. In 1910 they counted 151 sisters teaching 8,503 students in 22 schools.[50]

A 1902 photograph of the ground-breaking ceremonies for the convent shows nine sisters in their habits of St. Francis flanked by another five postulants in black habits with black capes and a number of novices dressed in black. On one side are a throng of Polish women in their summer finery, with middy blouses, long skirts, and flowered hats. Children line the other side and behind them stand the male priests and Polish leaders. The community had won an important victory.

The founders' proper attire for the ground-breaking ceremonies belied the very hard work of establishing the new convent. Not only did the sisters staff the schools, they also did all the work at their farm convent: pulling stumps, milking cows, laying a brick road, chopping wood. One sister even became their cobbler. Like other Polish mother superiors, Mother Clara helped with the farm work, even spreading manure around the corn plants, the chroniclers boasted. The sisters ate simple meals of bread, butter, syrup, and coffee for breakfast and lunch and potato casseroles for supper. They sang Polish songs during their "peeling parties." They had meager meals, recalled Mary Veronica

Convent dedication, 1902. The Polish Catholics of Stevens Point assembled to break ground for the new motherhouse for the Sisters of St. Joseph. The bishop ascended the dais with priests who had supported the nuns in their secession from a German-dominated order; the sisters gathered below. To the right were novices in flat hats and dark dresses, on the left stood lay women in their fine hats.

Wolashek, but they had a rich spiritual life. Added Sister Rita Glowacki, "We prayed much and worked hard."[51]

Protestants
Mary's Story [Wicker, Pitcher, probably born in New York, 1832–87]

This story explains how Mary, and then other women, helped establish the Methodist Episcopal Church in north-central Wisconsin. In 1873, when Mary Wicker Pitcher arrived in the Colby area from Ithaca, New York, with her family, there was no Methodist church. Undeterred, she went from place to place expounding the scriptures. Soon she was holding Sunday services in the schoolhouse, asking visiting ministers to preach. She found a preacher who promised to settle in Colby, but there was no church. Together with other parish women, Mary helped raise money to buy land and build a church. Lumbermen contributed logs, mill men sawed them, and the church went up slowly. It took a decade, but by 1883 the congregation had a wooden church on the corner of Clark and Second streets, its spire rising high above the row of newly planted trees that crisply marked the edges of the lot. The women went on to raise enough money to pay off the debt and to buy a four-hundred-pound bell for the church. By 1885 the women had organized themselves into a Ladies' Aid Society, which held quilting bees and served suppers to raise money for their church.[52]

Women preachers were welcomed in the northern woods, with its dearth of churches. Settlers listened to whomever would preach the divine word. We know little about the spread of Methodism through the north woods. It was probably Mary who conducted the first Methodist service in Medford in 1875 at a local sawmill. And the sparse records show that Methodist women, both English and German speaking, were active in organizing Ladies' Aid Societies and Foreign and Home Missionary societies. Their fund-raising abilities were legendary, and their story is a part of Mary's story. She probably died in 1887, but her family stayed on to become long-term members of the Colby Methodist congregation, and other women took up her work.

Accounts mention that the women of the German Methodist Evangelical Church of Wausau, founded in 1883, had a *Frauenverein* (Women's Association) by the next year. The group kept its minutes in German, and most of the congregation's women belonged. A photograph from 1897 shows twenty-four women crowded into the living room of the Stuhlfauth home, clustered around Mrs. Stuhlfauth. The women all look comfortably fed and clothed, clearly middle class. The Methodist churches' Ladies' Aid Societies were ubiquitous in small towns, to which rural folk came on Sunday mornings: many rural women belonged. In a few parishes, men objected to their organizing, arguing that they were not voting members of the church and thus not entitled to

Lutheran church, Athens, late 1800s. Settlers' churches rose from forest clearings amid stumps and slash brush. Sundays brought women to the rough pews in their best clothes to pray for their family's protection.

official recognition, but the women persisted. The men who preached in the early churches often served several congregations at mission churches, but where lists of early members are preserved women were prominent and sometimes predominant.[53]

The Methodist Church encouraged women to take an active role in church maintenance, even if most paid ministers were male. Money the women earned often helped build the first churches and parsonages, pay the salary of the first full-time ministers, and maintain church buildings. In 1898 the Ladies' Aid Society of the English Methodist church in Wausau had three committees that took care of the church kitchen, looked out for church members, and called on newcomers to the city, all in addition to providing financial assistance to the church through their fund-raising activities.[54]

Difficult times made financial support precarious in the 1880s and 1890s. Women's work kept the churches going. Great fires regularly swept many of the small towns in the 1880s, destroying the first wooden churches and homes. Churches were seldom insured and often mortgaged. Male ministers went where parishes were wealthy enough to support them and their families. As one Methodist presiding elder tersely reported after a fire destroyed the church at Spencer in 1886, the minister had "heard a call from a Presbyterian congregation in Fort Howard, and was not disobedient unto the heavenly vision." The next year the presiding elders reported "another year of calamity... in Spencer and Marshfield, the church barely escaped but entire business portion of Marshfield swept away." The preacher who served both communities left, the report continued, because he "did not seem to meet with that cordial cooperation without which but little can be accomplished." Colby and Unity also suffered from emigration and death, although they were able to pay off the last installment due on extension work in 1888.[55]

Despite fires and hard times, Methodist membership managed to keep pace with the increase in state population during the 1880s. Methodists debated vigorously in the late 1880s and early 1890s as to whether women should be eligible equally with men for membership in the Lay Electoral Conference and in the general conferences. They settled the issue in the affirmative, at least in principle, by 1896. Wisconsin Methodists were strong supporters of women's suffrage and the Woman's Christian Temperance Union. Barely out of the mission era themselves, Methodist women of Wisconsin joined in creating societies to support missions elsewhere. Wherever ten ladies gathered and donated one dollar a year, they could form a Foreign Missionary Society and receive *The Heathen Woman's Friend*. Missionary work was not new to the women of the Methodist Church. One of the first missionaries among the Ojibwe Indians on Lake Superior, Rebecca Jewel Francis, was appointed by the Methodist Board of Foreign Missions in the 1860s and taught in a small village on Keweenaw Bay at L'Anse.[56]

By the new century, however, Methodist women's missionary work was overshadowed by their interest in secular reforms. Methodism was transmitted within the family, through hymns at home and in the church, and by the "sisterhood" of women who became the backbone of each parish. More than any other church women, Methodists were poised to go "secular" with their beliefs about women's public role. By the 1880s, Methodists in Wausau were organizing a Lyceum Association that brought in female public speakers. They also sponsored hundreds of local Woman's Christian Temperance Unions. Methodism trained women to organize, and when they turned their attention to secular reform, they were ready to assume leadership and to train their daughters to participate. They joined the progressive reform movements in great numbers. The church became a place from which to launch social reforms as well as the religious revival that Mary Wicker Pitcher had inspired when she arrived in Colby in 1873.[57]

BUILDING LUTHERAN CONGREGATIONS

Although the Methodists arrived early and, with the help of women like Mary Wicker, founded thriving congregations, Lutherans formed the largest Protestant denomination in north-central Wisconsin. The building of Lutheran churches and parsonages flourished with the influx of German settlers in the 1880s. Larger towns with full-time clergy acted as mission bases from which ministers made their rounds to outlying settlements. Small groups of families then formed congregations, usually meeting in a house, a school, or a local business until they had time and money to build their own church. Each of these, in turn, became mission bases for congregations in surrounding communities. Dorchester families formed the *St. Petri Stift Gemeinde* (St. Peter Lutheran Church) in 1879; they built a church in 1883 and a parsonage in 1884. Stetsonville families formed their *Evangelisch Lutherischen Zion's Gemeinde* (Zion Evangelical Lutheran Church) in 1885 and built their first church in 1889. Colby had three Lutheran churches by the 1890s.[58]

A few of these early churches wrote centennial histories detailing the difficult first years of building congregations. Trinity Lutheran Church in Athens published its centennial history in 1982. Athens had no resident pastor before 1891. Until that time congregants depended on a missionary from nearby Dorchester. The missionary also served nine other neighboring towns, where he preached for a week at four- to six-week intervals. Black Creek was his "largest preaching place" in the early 1880s; about thirty German families gathered there to hear him. At Athens, where a smaller group of Lutherans had formed the *Evangelish Lutherische Dreieinigkeits Gemeinde* (Trinity Evangelical Lutheran Church), the secretary read services at the public school on the Sundays when the Dorchester minister could not come. Finally, in 1885 a local lumberman donated land and lumber, and members built their first 30-by-50-foot church. For the next two years, they shared a minister with Dorchester. In 1892 a new resident pastor confirmed twenty-five children. The church went through several years of conflict over whether or not to allow members to join fraternal lodges and whether or not to build a day school. Women formed a Ladies' Aid Society as soon as the pastor arrived; it became a symbol of unity as it put seventy-three charter members to work raising funds with bazaars and potluck dinners. It initiated a Missionary League and paid for church projects. Young people formed their own society and lobbied for a school. By 1913 the school had been built and employed two teachers.[59]

Day-to-day accounts of relationships between Lutheran women and their pastors are less common than these institutional histories. Fortunately, Bernhard Ungrodt, pastor of the Lutheran church in Medford and its outlying missions, left a diary that allows us to chart his interactions with the women of rural congregations. Pastor Ungrodt was born in Thuringia, Germany, in 1827 and after theological school spent twelve years as a missionary in South Africa. In 1858 he married Johanna Schroder, a young woman who had grown up in South Africa, the adopted child of another missionary. With their four children, Bernhard and Johanna moved to Wisconsin in 1867 and served several ministries before settling in Medford in 1881. Bernhard was pastor at the Lutheran church for nineteen years, and after he died in 1900, Johanna remained active in the church until she died in 1918. Their three daughters, Maria, Julia, and Sophia, taught at the church school and the Sunday school.[60]

Settlers had formed their congregation at Medford in 1876, but until the Ungrodts arrived in 1881 a regular Lutheran minister visited only every six weeks and elders preached sermons at funerals. The women of the parish organized their first Ladies' Aid Society that year and were no doubt active in raising money to build the large two-story wooden house that was still unfinished when the Ungrodts moved in with their children, who numbered eight by this time, in fall of 1881. A photograph shows them in front of the first parsonage, surrounded by farm animals and cords of carefully stacked stove wood. With the help of the Ladies' Aid Society, a new church was finished in 1885. Pastor Ungrodt kept his diary during the almost two decades that he served his congregations. He mentions his wife, Johanna, many times, notes the special services of the Ladies' Aid Societies, and comments on the importance of women in the churches.

As the wife of a Lutheran pastor, Johanna was crucial to Bernhard's success. She performed the historic task of model mother and wife, especially important since Luther had first instituted the practice of a married clergy. Lutheran ministers' wives were often expected to be choir directors and organists, thus keeping the extensive Lutheran liturgical music tradition alive. They were expected to be leaders in the Ladies' Aid Societies but also models of rectitude and subordination to their husbands. Johanna accompanied Bernhard on visits to parishioners in Medford, on missions to Stetsonville, Rib Lake, and Chelsea, and to synod meetings in Milwaukee. She was insubordinate only in regard to the garden, which Bernhard considered worthy of note in his diary. He commented on his birthday, "The wife and children have given me much happiness and companionship." Johanna's granddaughter Irene Ungrodt Leverenz later wrote, "I remember her as a gentle, kindly soul whose large family and stern preacher husband must have demanded a great deal of fortitude."[61]

Ungrodt also described the activities of the Ladies' Aid Society as playing a central role in sustaining the church. The ladies paid off the last two hundred dollars of the church's mortgage in July 1895 and in October of the next year gave a supper that netted the congregation seventy dollars. In March 1900 they purchased the Methodist church building and moved it to their church grounds to serve as a schoolhouse.

Women were the church's most active members. They attended weekly services more often than men, played the organ when the Ungrodt women did not, and sang in the choir. When their church attendance was low, it was usually due to bad weather or roads. The roads were often "smeary" in spring and nearly impassible in fall until the snow was deep enough for sleighs. Summers were short, busy times for farm families, so attending church at all was a sacrifice. Ungrodt commented on the rare notable occasions when there was good attendance of men or more men than women. At one confirmation, he noted, the church was filled and "the ladies' side didn't have a vacant place."

In return for their regular attendance and financial support, women demanded much of their pastor. In addition to expecting church service and Holy Communion for spiritual nourishment, women often called Ungrodt for emergency baptisms when newborns seemed in danger of early death and they asked him to officiate at baptisms after Sunday services. They expected him to instruct children—and themselves if necessary—for Holy Communion and to give them the sacrament at home when they were ill and unable to go to church. They expected his visits even when not ill. They wanted him to perform marriage ceremonies for their children, to pray over their husbands, their children, and themselves when they passed on, and to bury them even during the week.

Women also expected Ungrodt to listen to their complaints about men's activities. He wrote in 1891 that Pechstein's daughter was "molested by 2 scamps" as she returned from singing school and was afraid to come to church. Mrs. Zeit sent him "a long page about the inhuman treatment from her husband and then a long, long epistle about it." He noted family abuse by men who drank.[62]

Women left to parish men the issue of pay for their pastor. The men squabbled over pay when it was hard for the congregation to raise money, especially at the smaller churches in Stetsonville and Rib Lake. Women provided social services themselves, informally. Being active in a congregation, being seen weekly in church, exchanging information and gossip insured that women would have coreligionists to help them in time of need. Struggling to get to services, even in bad weather, probably seemed well worth it to women.

One especially popular event, the mission festival, took place annually at each parish church. Every August and September beginning in the 1890s the Lutheran parishes in Medford, Stetsonville, Dorchester, Menominee, and Neillsville held a festival to collect money for foreign missions. These gatherings were always special affairs for the Lutheran communities. Loretta Keach, reminiscing in 1997, remembered vividly the joy of attending the festivals as a child in the early 1920s. People dragged out the organ, cook stoves, and benches to a wooded lot on her uncle's farm. There ministers preached morning and afternoon. The organ booming through the woods, the smell of chicken cooking on the wood stove, the taste of ice cream after dinner, all came back to her. Pastor Ungrodt preached at many of these mission festivals in the 1890s. The money collected was not large. At Medford the collections usually brought in

$35 to $60, but the festivals organized by women brought their families together and made church members into a community.[63]

Mainstream Lutheran congregations were not the only ones to thrive in northern Wisconsin. A small community of Grundtvigians, a variant of Danish Lutheranism, settled near the village of Withee in Clark County. For more than twenty years this Danish community practiced its own brand of Lutheranism based on the teachings of Bishop Nikolai Grundtvig, a nineteenth-century educator and minister who founded the Danish Folk School movement and incorporated it into the Danish Lutheran Church. Grundtvigianism folded agrarian, cooperative, and nationalistic teachings into religion. It flourished in rural Denmark in the late nineteenth century.[64]

In 1892 pastor A. S. Nielsen arrived in Withee with three Danish families. Nielsen, a follower of Grundtvig, together with the families—the Jorgensens, the Frosts, the Stockholms—formally organized a congregation and invited other Danes to join them. They planned to build a church, and by July 1896, when the Nazareth Danish Evangelical Church was dedicated, there were eighty paying members and a congregation of 350 persons, most born in Denmark. Today the cemetery remains, proclaiming the presence of these early parishioners: Hansens, Nielsens, Jensens, Jorgensons. The old church was torn down in the 1960s and replaced by a new one.

Members of the Nazareth Danish Evangelical Church formed a Danish Brotherhood Society and a Danish Sisterhood Society, a Ladies' Aid Society, and a Young People's Society. By 1909 the congregation had built a community hall, established a Sunday school, and instituted a Danish language school that ran for six to eight weeks each summer. The community had a library of Danish books and a reading circle, a dramatic society, and an assembly hall used for all church and nonchurch functions. In 1909, when the community began to have Saturday night card games and frequent public dances, the church built a separate assembly hall closer to town. Until then, however, there was no separation between the secular and religious communities.

This division—the establishment of separate halls—signified the first crack in a philosophy that had emphasized an unbreakable bond—a "national spirit," Grundtvig called it—that represented a conscious fellowship of a people united around its historical and spiritual values. A flourishing national life demanded interaction among generations and social classes, a spiritual and social fellowship that transcended all differences. The uniting bonds were to be the group's Danish language, its national history, and its fellowship. The community assembly hall served as a folk high school for young adults, offering lectures and group recreation programs. The church societies fostered producer and consumer cooperatives of the type that prospered in Denmark. The core group tried hard to attract more Danish settlers of similar persuasion. They feared settlement by non-Danes, who would change the community's character. In a booklet published in 1908 by the Danish Colonization Association, its organizers stressed the need for "a spiritual fellowship between peoples of the same descent, the same way of thought, the same purpose in life, the bond of the mother tongue." Recruitment in Denmark proved unsuccessful, however, and after 1920 Danish national restrictions on emigration doomed the hopes of the original group. The settlers were unable to keep their children on the farm and could not replace or expand their numbers.

Social patterns contributed to the decline. Danish women worked out as domestic servants before marriage, married late, and had small families. Their daughters continued the tradition, taking jobs as servants on local farms or in neighboring towns. The *Dansk Sëstersamfunds* (Danish Sisterhood) was dominated by older settler women who spoke Danish at meetings, but younger women formed a Lutheran Guild and used English as their main language. The older generation wanted daughters, especially, to marry within the community and opposed unions with Catholics. Although the young English-speaking women who left presumably married Protestants, perhaps Lutherans, the daughters were marrying non-Danish men from outside the community. Even young American-born men who stayed on the farms began to marry out. Thus within two generations the attempt to link spiritual and social communities based on exclusive criteria of nationality and language had to be abandoned. We do not know what the younger generation kept of church teachings about cooperation and the importance of community. It is difficult to know what else the Grundtvigians might have done to maintain their community.[65]

Today one finds German Amish communities thriving in some of the same areas of northern Wisconsin. Amish women sell bread and noodles at Saturday morning street fairs in small towns. They wear the same types of dresses and sunbonnets their mothers did, although the cloth may be patterned polyester rather than cotton. The last organized religious group to arrive in this area, the Amish left Pennsylvania in the early 1920s and some settled near Medford in Taylor County. They still plow with horses and plant without pesticides. Popular as renters of land, young Amish families farm in the style of the non-Amish owners—and live in houses with whatever modern conveniences the owners provide—before they buy land and return to traditional ways. Women are expert with the horses and buggies they use for transportation. They still meet for religious services in homes. The Amish established the practice of selling processed food to neighbors: apple butter, sausage, and maple syrup were early favorites. In those days Amish women were already making quilts and selling them as well. Strong-willed Amish women and their daughters sometimes leave the religion and the community, but for many the lifestyle is satisfying. Their numbers are constantly replenished from

Pennsylvania, where land prices are higher than in northern Wisconsin. The women also do not work out or delay marriage, so birth rates remain high. Most people of German heritage welcomed these new German ethnic settlers whose religion dictated a lifestyle that seemed similar to that of ancestors who had settled in north-central Wisconsin.

CROSSING RELIGIOUS BORDERS

We have a story in our family about Catholic and Lutheran religious borders. One day Matilda hitched up her wagon and, after giving her children strict instructions about the work they must complete while she was away, drove the five miles into town to buy supplies. There she met a woman, also alone in her wagon, also shopping for her family. I imagine them stopped in the middle of the street for some reason, each with the reins in her hand, chatting amiably in German a few minutes before flapping the reins and urging their horses toward home. The woman asked Matilda to visit. When she arrived home, Matilda told her children about the invitation. "Are you going to visit?" one eagerly asked. "No," Grandma replied, "She is Lutheran."

That story gives me pause to think about the willingness of Christians to cross the boundaries of religious communities. These border crossings or their absence are worth examining in greater detail, even if they are hard to find. The Catholic Church discouraged social contact with Protestants. While the Royal Neighbors admitted Catholic women and some joined, the Catholic Foresters organized through parishes and remained an exclusively Catholic group. Catholic priests on the Menominee reservation tried to limit Catholic parishioners' contact with non-Catholics, particularly at dances. The Catholics obeyed the injunction against sponsorship of Native rites themselves, but some always insisted on attending the ceremonies organized by kin. They found ways to avoid the church's sanctions and to cross religious borders in their daily lives. In practice, large numbers of people ignored the injunctions of the Catholic Church and married across religious affiliations.

Intermarriage was of concern to both Catholic and Protestant churches in the nineteenth century. The Catholic Church refused to recognize marriage between baptized Catholics and unbaptized persons or to recognize children of these marriages as legitimate. During the 1830s to 1880s, however, the church allowed dispensations because the laity was tolerant of intermarriage. By the turn of the century, interfaith marriage was increasingly accepted by Catholics as well as by Protestants. The Catholic Church officially recognized intermarriages as legitimate in 1917. Still, among some ethnic groups concern about marrying Protestants lingered into the 1920s and 1930s. I remember my Italian grandfather refused to speak to his daughter for ten years after she married a divorced Protestant man.[66]

The Catholic Church gave its youth considerable latitude in marrying out ethnically. It was a universal church: in theory, at least, ethnicity could safely be ignored by young people as long as they married Catholics. It was up to the family to enforce ethnic conformity. We know from one study of 1880 marriage practices in Wisconsin that young people tended to choose partners from their own ethnic as well as religious groups. At that time, first- and second-generation immigrant Germans and Norwegians married within ethnic groups more than 80 percent of the time and even Britons married in more than 50 percent of the time. By 1910, however, most Western European immigrants were marrying out. European Poles were still likely to remain endogamous, but almost half of German immigrants were marrying out. Western Europeans were now being accepted by the socially and politically dominant Anglo-Protestant groups. As this new, ethnically mixed "white" majority was taking form, racial divisions hardened.[67]

The dominance of German ethnic groups in northern Wisconsin ensured that many young people who remained there would still be able to find partners of their own ethnicity. But religion remains an important boundary. Matilda would not visit with a Lutheran woman despite their similarities, the obvious affinity, and the opportunity to become friends. Only one of her five daughters was married by a Lutheran minister. While no family is "average," my family seems typical.

At times communities could cross religious boundaries to help each other, but as communities grew and public facilities became more readily available the potential for greater separation increased, too. Catholic sisters furnished health care to Tomahawk, a small rural community in need of health care in 1894. The sisters also visited Lac du Flambeau, but language and culture made communication with Native women far more difficult. Earlier settlers had crossed religious borders out of necessity, but even then settlers tried to surround themselves with coreligionists. Isolation on the frontier reinforced marrying within ethnic groups, but the congregation of different groups in urban areas during the early twentieth century encouraged exogamy. Only one of Matilda's daughters, the eldest, married a man of German heritage. Others married men of British, Italian, and Native American heritage.

Health care was one of the most frequent avenues to interfaith appreciation, if not permanent alliance. Protestants supported the small hospitals established by the nuns and sought their services. The Catholic nursing sisters welcomed and frequently reported amicable encounters with Protestants. Nuns often begged for food with which to feed themselves and their patients, and although they usually visited Catholic families, Protestants donated supplies as well. One day while begging around Marshfield, the young nuns visited a home where the woman lectured them, saying they should be working for wages instead of begging. Then she cut a loaf of bread in half and gave it to them. They found out later it was the home of a Protestant minister. Lutheran men, usually single, often loggers, came to the nuns at Tomahawk hospital for care, and some donated money or volunteered help to the sisters.[68]

An elaborate example of cooperation was a public supper the Tomahawk women planned in the 1890s to celebrate the opening of the hospital and to raise funds for its operation. Tomahawk residents wanted the nuns there, helped them build the first hospital, and gave them whatever food they could spare. The entire community contributed something toward the public dinner, everybody came to eat, and everybody paid. The nuns cooked and the town women served.[69]

Sister M. Agnes remembered Sister Clementia as the organizing force behind the public meal: "She knew how to go around with people and besides this she knew how to draw and paint, in which arts she even gave lessons to the children of several families; that's how she came in contact with the ladies." Tomahawk, Sister Agnes added, "like the rest of our Missions, was poor, almost as poor as Nazareth." Sister Dyonisia described the dedication vividly to Sister Beda forty-five years later. Community women sold tickets for the public supper and organized a play and music. Someone donated a doll for a raffle. The women brought layer cakes, scones, pies, and meat—whatever was needed. The sisters cooked, the novices brought out the food, and the town women served it. The nuns even made ice cream. "That day brought nice financial help to the Sacred Heart Hospital," Sister Dyonisia remembered with satisfaction. People donated two hundred dollars during the event.[70]

Despite the success of the public meal, the nuns did not circulate with the group that day. They stayed in the convent cooking while novices brought out the food. While mingling with secular Catholics and Protestants was necessary in hospital work, the nuns normally did not socialize. Yet remembrance of the Tomahawk women's kindness lingered in the nuns' memories.[71]

The hospital at Stevens Point became a similar site for the collaboration of sisters and community women. Like Tomahawk, Stevens Point had difficulty in obtaining a hospital. Two private hospitals had already failed, and patients were being taken by train to Oshkosh, about seventy miles away, to be treated. The Women's Club and local doctors decided in 1912 to form the City Hospital Association, with two separate boards of directors, one made up of doctors and local male leaders, the other entirely of clubwomen. The women held offices of vice president and secretary while the men served as president and treasurer. The secretary, Mrs. C. B. Baker, managed much of the day-to-day business of running the association. Clubwomen combed the city for donors, urging them to contribute funds for building and furnishing the hospital. One wealthy widow, for example, donated furnishings for the reception room as a memorial for her husband. The group raised ten thousand dollars, built the hospital, and agreed to donate the new building to the sisters if they would manage and staff the hospital. The sisters drove a hard bargain, insisting that they also receive free and clear title to the hospital. The agreement settled, the Women's Club exultantly reported in the local paper, "Every detail of hospital work, from the janitor service and scrub women to cooks, nurses and finances will be scrupulously accomplished by those who have renounced the world and are devoting their lives to the care of the sick and afflicted, without money and without prize."[72]

The community's women gratefully welcomed administrator Sister Cornelia and the first two sisters when they arrived late in December 1912. Sister Cornelia was born on a Kansas farm and into a family that had helped the sisters sustain their Wichita enterprise—her parents mortgaged their farm and provided produce for the hospital. Sister Cornelia had become a novice at Marshfield in 1893, had taken nursing courses, had nursed at the order's St. Mary's Hospital in Oshkosh, and had been an administrator there for four years before moving to Stevens Point. She brought an understanding and a model of how the community and those dedicated to caring could cooperate. She was already known for her work of feeding the needy in Oshkosh, and she continued the practice after she arrived in Stevens Point. Other nuns carried on the tradition when Sister Cornelia left. As her biographer wrote of the sisters, "They made love visible by showing their community and nation how to care for its people." Through these means they broke down barriers among people of various religions. All could participate in supporting the community's health care.[73]

The Catholic nuns had to mingle with Protestants to a certain extent in their hospital work. For the most part, however, rural Catholic women in the late nineteenth century sat tightly within their religious communities. Protestant women developed more extensive interdenominational relations through secular activities, but those activities were akin to missionary pursuits. Daughters were left with the task of developing relationships across religious borders.

A PRESBYTERIAN WOMAN PRAISES HER LORD

But how did rural Protestant women regard their relations with the deity? For that I turn to a Presbyterian's account. Presbyterian women also organized in the 1870s. They held "sociables," with oyster suppers a favorite. They even organized an archery club in Wausau. Like other church women, they were more likely to write about the weather in their journals than about their spiritual journeys. An exception was Maria Morton Merrill, who lived near Black River Falls and who, upon reaching age fifty-eight in 1890 and being in "good health for a person of my age," determined to "praise the Lord" in her diary. Maria had traveled from her birthplace in Maine to work in textile mills, which financed her education. She taught at a female seminary in New York before marrying her brother-in-law after her sister's death. They moved to Wisconsin to farm. After he died in 1882, she ran the farm. Her diary opens with praise to God for sparing the lives of her family for the past eight years and surrounding its members "with many comforts and blessings of which we are not deserving.... May God make us thankful for the mercies of the past and help us to do better the coming year." Later that "cold and backward" spring—it was May, and for more than six weeks she had been too overwhelmed by work to write in her journal—she felt lonely after a visit from her newly wed daughter and husband and began to write again. Care and work would soon drive away the loneliness, she predicted: "Providence has wisely ordered that most people shall work for a living and work is a good tonic for a wounded spirit." So was religion.[74]

During the next five years, Maria lost her good health; she moved off the farm, lived with her stepdaughter, and then moved to Winona, Minnesota, to live with her son, who was studying at the normal school there. Now sixty-three, she felt her age. It was a life too short "to fit the soul for its future career," she wrote. Maria summed up her spiritual goal this way: "A life of usefulness is the only life worth living. To overcome the selfishness of the heart and strive day by day to live for the good of others and trusting in the Lord's power to help us, repenting of all our sins and serving Him faithfully[,] praying for guidance in the smallest concerns of life, these are but the duties of all Christian people." She missed the farm and wanted to return, but she had already resigned herself to approaching death. "I can't say that I have enjoyed life much since I have been here," she wrote, but "[my time] cannot be very long at best and in the far away future of the next world it will make no difference whether I die in Wisconsin or Minnesota." She was now using religion as an aid to give her "grace and patience and courage," to take her "through to the end." Still missing her farm, she followed her son to a teaching job in Eyota, Minnesota. Then, at sixty-five, she and her son moved back to the farm. He had not liked Eyota or teaching there. Being home did not make her happier, nor was her son pleased about returning to a run-down farm. At sixty-seven, which she believed would be her last year, she praised God again for his goodness. Her final entry in the diary was about the cold March weather: "I long for the spring sunshine and the warm breezes, but I suppose they will come in their own good time." While the diary ends on that cold day in March 1899, Maria lived for another five years. She died at seventy-two.

Maria's diary is a reminder that historians often underestimate the importance of ordinary women's spiritual lives. Like many women, Maria used religion as a way to reconcile herself to the hardships she endured. In religion she found strength to persevere, to accept hard work and old age, and to live out her life with quiet dignity.

8

Political Landscapes

I remember that Matilda was living with us in the late 1940s when the question of her citizenship came up. It was shortly after World War II, my father was recently home from overseas, and he asked whether or not she had registered as an "enemy alien." That term swims uneasily in my memory. My father was probably very conscious of her status because he had narrowly escaped being classified that way as well. They shared foreign birth: she as a German, he as an Italian. He was made a citizen formally when his National Guard unit was nationalized in 1940. Checking the records, the army found that many young men who had immigrated as children and whose parents had not been naturalized were technically aliens, or in the case of my grandmother and father, enemy aliens. My mother and I were citizens by birth. In 1948 I was thirteen and aware for the first time of her voting. For some unknown reason, I pestered her to vote for Harry Truman although she was a Republican. She told me she had.

Such skimpy introduction to formal politics—the knowledge that Matilda never became a citizen and could not vote, and that my mother was and did—satisfied me for a long time. Later I realized that politics was much more complicated, a matter not just of formal or electoral politics but also of informal political activities, and how private power could affect women's place in society. While writing this book, I realized that my grandmother was certainly a powerful woman in many ways but that she had very little public, formal power. And so I left this question of politics until the end, hoping I would somehow come to understand how rural women faced questions of power in their lives with so little officially allotted to them.

I found more public political activity than I expected to in those north-central counties of Wisconsin. Rural settler women were active in groups like the Royal Neighbors and the American Society of Equity, in women's clubs, and in the suffrage movement. I learned much about the role of Native women in their communities' politics. I have contented myself with telling mostly the story of the public formal role of women in politics.

Most settler women did not claim political power outside their separate sphere as women or as mothers; rather, they exercised power from within. Yet women continued to talk about change in their status, about joining together in promoting change, and about claiming new rights for their daughters as well. Few women were as visible as those who wrote advocating rural reform; their voices stand out as evidence of reformers attempting to understand those settler women who did not voice their concerns in public but who were gradually making their way into clubs and public life.

Nowhere is the difference between settler women and Native women clearer than in the area of politics. Many of the demands for "Progressive reforms" were "Unprogressive" when applied to Native people, scholar Peggy Lowe has argued. While settler women worked to expand their role in politics, the U.S. government acted to restrict that role for Native women, who lived within nations that had been occupied and increasingly deprived of their sovereignty. They joined with Native men in an effort to retain the treaty rights their nations had negotiated with the U.S. government and to hinder that government's attempts to control all aspects of their lives. Native women and men worked against efforts by the Indian Bureau to withhold from Native peoples the economic, religious, social, and parental rights settlers claimed. In addition, women resisted the government's attempts to replace the Native practice of codependent but separate gender spheres with the Euro-American theory and practice of separate but subordinate spheres for women.

Settler women sought to move out of their subordinate spheres in many ways. Merely parading in the streets or speaking at public gatherings could constitute a bold statement. In the late nineteenth century, when few rural women were visible at all in public affairs, they joined groups advocating that formal political rights be extended to them. This chapter begins with a farm daughter who achieved political visibility and reconciled her public role with the expectation of most men that she remain subordinate and invisible as a woman.

Claiming Public Space
Mary's Story [Davison, Bradford, born in Wisconsin, 1856–1943]

In the fall of 1894 a group of teachers, recently arrived at the new Stevens Point Normal School, hired a buggy to see the surrounding countryside. Thirty-eight-year-old Mary Bradford was one of the teachers. They drove out to Plover, a flat sandy area just south of Stevens Point, past farmhouses that looked, as Mary later recalled, "terribly down-at-the-heels."[1]

Mary's Yankee parents had pioneered a farm south of Kenosha in the 1850s and 1860s. The fifth of seven children, she grew up on the small dairy farm where her mother was an expert cheese maker. After her father was injured in a wagon accident in 1861, mother and children took over all the farm work. Women, Mary remembered, did all the work in the hay and grain fields—mowing, raking, piling, pitching, loading and unloading, reaping, binding sheaves, and shocking—with only the help of a hired neighbor girl and male threshers. Their work brought enough profits to send Mary to Latin school and high school in Kenosha. A teacher at sixteen, wife at twenty-two, and widowed mother at twenty-five, Mary was left with a ten-month-old son and a ten-year-old stepson to support. While her mother cared for the children, Mary went back to work. She taught high school for twelve years in Kenosha County, beginning a career that would lead her deeply into politics.

Coming from Wisconsin's prosperous and fertile southern farmlands, Mary was depressed by the land south of Stevens Point. It looked like a desert. Another teacher, from New England, was equally dismayed. She remembered tidy eastern farms and country villages with well-painted houses on orderly tree-bordered streets. It was a poor choice for an excursion, Mary mused. Later trips north from Stevens Point changed her mind about the landscape. She saw magnificent stands of pine and picturesque roads that wound through the countryside. She was impressed by the great paper mills that lined the Wisconsin River.

During the next twelve years, from 1894 to 1906, Mary became a prominent person in Marathon County as a master teacher who held summer institutes to prepare poorly educated young women to teach in one-room country schools. She moved comfortably among county superintendents as she planned institutes, and she became active in the Wisconsin Teachers' Association, sitting on a committee to study the need for teachers' pensions. She wrote pamphlets on methods for teaching arithmetic. Mary was still at Stevens Point when she had her first encounter with the politics of education, one that would propel her into the political arena. In February 1906 Theran B. Pray, president of the normal school, interrupted his meeting with the board of education to return to Michigan for his mother's funeral. During his absence, the board voted to dismiss him. Many local people and teachers were dismayed at the abrupt and unexplained action, but the regents warned teachers not to criticize. Mary and three others resigned in protest.

Mary took over the kindergarten training school at the state institute in Menominee. She also wrote a column in *The Wisconsin Journal of Education* titled "In the Classroom," which offered practical help for elementary teachers. It was a chance, she said, to "write myself clear" on subjects of importance. With friends' help she filled five to ten pages a month for a year; then she left to teach at a normal school in Pennsylvania. In 1910 the school board of Kenosha asked Mary, now fifty-four, to return home to become city school superintendent. In 1910, that was big news. The *New York Times* reported it this way: "New Woman School Head—Kenosha, Wisconsin follows Chicago's Example, and Elects [the school board actually appointed her] Female Superintendent." An old friend wrote to warn her to be careful of politics and to "appoint the policeman's daughter."[2]

Mary Bradford now held one of the state's most important political offices. Nationwide, reformers saw her appointment as part of a trend to place capable women in charge of large city school systems and to bring women into public prominence. Unavoidably, the position of school superintendent took Mary, and other early women superintendents, into local politics. Women could not yet vote, but through their school work they were allowed to hold these important political offices.

Bradford said later that of the many Wisconsin school superintendents holding office at that time only those at Wausau and Oshkosh wrote to congratulate her. The others did not

write, she wryly noted, because almost every superintendent in the state probably thought Kenosha more desirable than the position he occupied. Her responsibility was heavy—to make the appointment of a woman to the superintendency of a major city school system a success. Her first test came when she faced the sixteen-man school board, composed of businessmen, lawyers, a dentist, and workmen from various factories, including a teamster. The board awarded her a three-year contract with only two negative votes: one by the board president, the other, she said, by a German opposed on principle to a woman being put in a man's place.[3]

Mary Bradford, 1892. Born on a farm in Kenosha County, Bradford dropped out of the normal school at Stevens Point to teach but went on to supervise summer institutes in Marathon County from 1894 to 1906 and to serve as the first woman superintendent of Kenosha schools from 1910 to 1921. Bradford developed subtle political strategies to guide her educational reforms. She wrote, "I could never have accomplished what I did had I acted obtrusively the role of leader."

For the next eleven years, from 1910 to 1921, Mary carried that responsibility, honing her political skills and refining the political philosophy she felt necessary to succeed as a woman holding public office in Wisconsin. She expanded her power in different directions, as president of the Wisconsin Teachers' Association, as head of the Education Committee of the Wisconsin Federation of Women's Clubs, and as public advocate for school reform. She backed kindergartens, home economics and industrial arts classes, summer schools, and special facilities for handicapped children. She insisted that laws prohibiting sales of tobacco and liquor to youth be enforced. Tobacconists, who had been fined for selling cigarettes to minors, and what she called "the saloon element," which dominated Kenosha politics, denounced her.[4]

Political strategies kept her in office. She developed the habit of courting "the voting fathers" to garner public funding of her school proposal. Then she mobilized public opinion, suggesting that all superintendents pay attention to using publicity to loosen the "stumps," as she called citizens indifferent to school issues. In the end, she offered this tactical advice to women in politics, advice that spelled out in detail practices developed by many women who sought or held political office in the early twentieth century:

> [Men,] at least a large majority of those I had to deal with, do not like to be dictated to by a woman. Subordination of self was best, and I resolved to practice it in all matters that did not involve principle. The advisability of this policy may be more readily seen when it is known that the members of the [city] council twitted the school board with being "tied to a woman's apron strings" and some of the men were sensitive about it. I therefore early adopted the policy of concealing the "apron strings" and not allowing them to appear in my relationships with these men. In those round-the-table conferences, measures that I believed in and that I hoped might be brought about sometime, would be suggested and discussed as to purpose and probable cost, as tried out in other cities. Then the matter was allowed to rest. It often happened that at some future meeting, some one would propose the consideration of the measure that had been discussed in the privacy of the committee room, and he had the pleasure of having done something of a constructive sort. I could never have accomplished what I did had I acted obtrusively the role of leader.[5]

It was not possible for a woman to act openly as a leader. She had to operate with circumspection or become the target of every male who thought he should have her job simply because he was a man. This reality gave women a double task in politics.

And that double task was exhausting and discouraging. In 1921 Mary retired from politics, refusing to run for state superintendent, an elective office. Despite the encouragement of suffragists, she felt she had done her part in politics. She spent her last twenty years traveling and nourishing her private life. But she had left her mark on women's politics in Wisconsin.

ROYAL NEIGHBORS OF AMERICA

On the morning of June 10, 1899, Jennie Philpott arose early to get ready for the Modern Woodmen of America picnic at Greenwood in Clark County. There would be all the usual tasks: preparing food, dressing the children (eleven-year-old Ralph; Dacy, now eight; and little Alpha, who was three), seeing that her husband, Thomas, had his best clothing clean and ready. Thomas was a blacksmith, but today he would wear the shirt she had carefully ironed, the suit she had brushed. Today was a special day for thirty-five-year-old Jennie as well. Today she would not be on the sidewalks watching the picnic parade but in the streets with other women, performing the intricate drill maneuvers they had been practicing for weeks. Jennie's name appears on the first list of Royal Neighbors of America (RNA) members in the town of Loyal in 1898 and on the Loyal census for 1900, and it is from these sources that we know about her participation in the RNA and about her family. We do not know for certain that she drilled in the streets of Greenwood that day, but at least fourteen of the early members did. Jennie, an RNA officer, was very likely among them.

When the rest of the family was ready and the other preparations finished, Jennie would have dressed in her freshly laundered, starched, and ironed white shirtwaist and long white skirt. Next came the identifying markers that the Royal Neighbors of America had sent her from its headquarters. She probably had one of the official RNA badges pinned in just the right place, about four inches below her left shoulder. Like the other Loyal members, she would have worn a white hat with "RNA" across the front. When she lifted the white hat and placed it precisely on her head, she was ready for the crowds that would line the streets of Greenwood to watch.[6]

A photographer was there that day as the women went through their drill, their long white dresses swinging over the dirt street of Greenwood village. In the photograph, later made into a postcard, the women are shown in the distance. Onlookers fill the curbs, and behind the women is a brass band with a tuba and two trombones. Parked buggies line the street in the foreground. Across the front of the postcard are the words "R.N.A. Drill M.W.A. – Picnic June 10, Greenwood, in Clark County." The women are too far away to identify, but Jennie was one of the first to sign up for the RNA in nearby Loyal. It would have taken sickness or an unusual event to keep her from performing with the other women of the Loyal "Camp Hope."

The women that day were occupying very public space with the Modern Woodmen of America (MWA). To belong to the RNA, a woman had to be a "lady relative" of an MWA member and between the ages of seventeen and forty-five. The MWA, a national fraternal organization popular in northern Wisconsin, provided important benefits to its male membership. It offered camaraderie and support that could bridge ethnic differences; more importantly, it offered life insurance, which was difficult for workers in the lumber industry to obtain any other way. Through the organization, men insured their lives and also received financial support when sick or injured on the job. The MWA encouraged men to form women's auxiliaries to help organize social events, but it did not offer insurance to women. Women founded the RNA to provide that insurance.

The official history of the RNA begins this way:

In November, 1888, Marie L. Kirkland put a notice in her local paper, the Council Bluffs, Iowa, *Daily Nonpareil*, to call a meeting of the wives of Modern Woodmen of America members to arrange a social. Nine women, including Marie Kirkland met and formed a "ladies auxiliary" to Modern Woodmen Camp 171. Within a year the group reorganized as a secret social organization with a constitution, rituals and articles of incorporation, and renamed itself Royal Neighbors of America. . . . Between 1892 and 1894, the idea of forming a fraternal benefit society was much discussed.[7]

Forming their own benefit society was "much discussed" because the women had no way to purchase life insurance. Although fraternal organizations were being formed throughout the country in the 1870s and 1880s to offer affordable insurance protection for male members, both commercial insurers and fraternal organizations excluded women from coverage. In 1894, after learning that they could incorporate as a fraternal benefit society in Illinois and offer insurance to members, the RNA organization signed a charter with 4,100 members. The RNA was soon adding one thousand members each month. Four years later, early in 1898, twenty-four Loyal women and three men petitioned for admission and became Camp 819, named "Hope." Women from this camp performed as the drill team in the streets of Greenwood in the summer of 1899.[8]

Groups like Loyal's Camp Hope ritually publicized women's new organizing. It spread rapidly because of the many ways in which the camps helped members: by giving cash payments for illness and other emergencies, by visiting the sick, by furnishing a physician's care, by offering a special camaraderie and the opportunity to mix with social groups from other villages and towns. They also gave women a public presence through drill displays and floats entered in Fourth of July parades. Husbands cheered on the organizing of the first camps and often lent their MWA halls for events. Camp Hope held its first meeting on January 26, 1898, at an oyster supper sponsored by the local MWA. The nearby Neillsville RNA camp sent a woman speaker who helped install the first officers at that meeting.[9]

Enthusiastic locals, such as Camp Hope, fed the national organization. Membership climbed to 49,000 by 1900, then jumped again after 1903, when the RNA removed the requirement that women be related to MWA members. By 1909 membership had grown to almost 250,000 in more than 5,800 camps, 80 percent of whom carried insurance. During these years the RNA spread through the four north-central Wisconsin counties: fifteen camps with 480 charter members formed between 1898 and 1910. As the RNA expanded, its membership attracted diverse groups, as evidenced by the women who joined at Loyal and at Colby.

Jennie Philpott was typical of most Loyal members. They were over thirty years of age; born in Wisconsin of native-born parents, frequently from New

PETITION FOR CHARTER

To the Supreme Oracle, Officers and Members of the Head Camp,
Royal Neighbors of America:

We, the undersigned, being of lawful age and meeting the requirements of the By-Laws for membership of the Order, do hereby respectfully petition the Head Camp, of

ROYAL NEIGHBORS OF AMERICA

Situated in Peoria, Illinois, to establish a Local Camp in _____*Loyal*_____, County of
_____*Clark*_____, and State of _____*Wisconsin*_____, and to grant a
Charter and confer full power to operate as a Fraternal Organization.

Dated at _____*Loyal*_____ this _____*26*_____ day of _____*Jan*_____ 189*8*

SIGNATURES

Signature	Beneficiary	Fraternal	Signature	Beneficiary	Fraternal
Mrs. Iddie R. Albright		1	Mary Bowman		23
Mary Alta Thomas		2	J. Richmond. M. D.		24
J. Alice Philpott		3	Mrs. J. Wiric		25
Pearl M. Holmes		4	Mrs. Anna Van Camp		26
Eva Edmond		5	Jennie Philpott		27
Dollie Grans		6			
Cornelia Whitney		7			
Annie Mengel		8			
Florence E. Barton		9			
Josiah Frasier		10			
Ida Filber		11			
Fannie Smith		12			
Mary Boyer		13			
Eliza Snyder		14			
Emerett C. Barker		15			
M. M. Grans		16			
Olga F. Barton		17			
Mary E. Welsh		18			
Minnie Church		19			
Lettie Mulroy		20			
J. H. Welsh		21			
Maggie Richmond		22			

Royal Neighbors of America petition, 1898. Members of the Loyal chapter, including Jennie Philpott (number twenty-seven), were mainly married women who signed up to obtain insurance. Membership also meant appearing in public displaying the purple sashes, caps, and pins of the RNA.

York or Pennsylvania; from middling families working in rural areas. Their husbands were self-employed artisans, like Thomas Philpott; worked in mills as supervisors or laborers; or owned small businesses, either farms or shops. Their families were small, from one to four children.[10]

Colby women organized their RNA camp in 1901, three years after the Loyal group. The Colby camp traced its origins directly to Emma Fuller, who moved to Colby with her husband and sons in 1897. Fuller had belonged to the RNA in Illinois, and she canvassed town and countryside to find the first twenty members. Colby members differed from those in Loyal. Typical was Anna Chase, age twenty-eight, newly married the previous year with no children. She was born in Wisconsin but her parents and those of her husband, Frank, were German immigrants. Anna and Frank owned a farm. Like Anna, thirteen of the other twenty original Colby members were married, almost all were under thirty, and most had no children. Only a quarter of them had parents from New York or Pennsylvania, while more than a quarter had foreign-born parents. More than a third were farm women. While none of the Loyal women were single, six of the Colby women were unmarried, three of them teachers. The Colby RNA members displayed their organization in the 1905 Fourth of July parade with a large decorated float carrying fifteen members, including Anna Chase and organizer Emma Fuller. In the July 4, 1910, parade the Colby women put themselves in a model canoe with RNA on its prow and the motto "We Paddle Our Own Canoe" on the side.[11]

The first step toward organizing came out of women's desire to care for themselves and their families. But these steps were important as women began to move into the public sphere in order to obtain what they needed and wanted as a group: the life insurance coverage the traditional fraternal organizations could not furnish. While a private group, the RNA offered members a new

Royal Neighbors float, 1910. Joining the Royal Neighbors allowed women not only to buy life insurance for their families but also to claim public space in community parades. Colby members created a float with the slogan "We Paddle Our Own Canoe" for the July 4 parade in Clark County. The Colby camp, formed in 1901, was still meeting in 2005.

public presence and organizational structure that few women had outside their churches. RNA women met to provide for common needs, in this case life insurance and supplementary medical assistance. The RNA drill teams and floats were public displays in which both married and unmarried women occupied the political landscape in new ways. These ritual displays indicated that white middle-class rural women were organizing themselves into groups similar to the male lodges, not yet quite free from the male groups but developing separate agendas to meet separate needs. This initial organizing also drew them deeper into the demands for women's suffrage and toward contemporary economic issues that women's suffrage might be able to affect. In 1911 state and local representatives at the national RNA gathering voted to support the Susan B. Anthony Suffrage Amendment. As one suffrage play written for members warned, "We have rocked the baby's cradle long enough—let us take our turn at rocking the trust to sleep." Such distrust of large economic conglomerates was similarly affecting the groups of women who were being swept into the largest farm organization in Wisconsin, the American Society of Equity.[12]

AMERICAN SOCIETY OF EQUITY

In December 1917 the American Society of Equity (ASE) met for its annual convention in Wausau. Adelaide Junger, state president of the Minnesota Women's Auxiliary of the ASE, came by train across Wisconsin to represent the Minnesota women who had flooded into the auxiliary during the previous four years. She planned to speak for all of the women of the Women's Auxiliary, the WA as they referred to themselves. Junger, too, had something to say about the hand that rocked the cradle as she rose to address the assembled men and women. "You are always telling us that the hand that rocks the cradle rules the world," she began, "Now, how do you account for the fact that if we are rocking the cradle and ruling the world we have nothing to say?" Junger then launched into a twenty-minute talk defining the status of women in the ASE and summarizing their experiences in the nine years since male members began forming women's auxiliaries.[13]

The ASE, organized in Illinois in 1902 by J. A. Everitt, originally had a single economic purpose: to set farm prices. In his book *The Third Power,* Everitt described American society as composed of three powers: money, labor, and farmer. Farmers, the "soil owners and workers," were a "third power" whom he wanted to become discontented with their condition, investigate the cause, and take action to change it. He had harsh words for the "money power," especially boards of trade that middlemen had formed to control market prices. He called them "sapsucking, unholy, godless things," a "devilish power" that speculated in farm products to make profits for the "non-producing class."

Farmers must organize to control prices, to achieve an "equitable distribution" of the wealth, to stabilize remunerative prices for their products.[14]

Equity spread rapidly through midwestern states, especially Wisconsin, Iowa, and Minnesota, attracting new members who chafed at Everitt's limited vision of only setting farm prices. They advocated direct marketing as well and after ousting Everitt in 1907, installed new leadership. The following year, when members decided that women should be admitted into the group in separate auxiliaries, membership had reached ten thousand in Wisconsin alone. The ASE organized its Women's Auxiliary, in part at least, to further its new goal of developing a cooperative union for producers and consumers, thus minimizing the middleman's role. Women were in charge of family consumption on most farms, and so it seemed logical that they also be involved in the ASE cooperative movement. The new cooperatives were to buy as well as to sell. Members envisioned cooperative creameries, cheese factories, warehouses, grain elevators, sales agencies, cold storage plants, and packing plants. In some locals members even talked of cooperative laundries and bakeries. Local WA units could be formed only if male members wanted an auxiliary, admitted only wives and daughters over sixteen years of age, and gave members no vote in the ASE or official representation at ASE meetings and conventions. Women did have a column in the society newspaper, Equity News, their own ASE auxiliary badge, and a separate women's convention held at the same time and place the male members met for their annual conventions.[15]

The ASE and its auxiliary took root among farm families who were developing commercial farming in areas still underserved by marketing mechanisms. It was especially strong in the northwestern part of the state but also in Marathon and Clark counties and in the southern tier of townships in Lincoln and Taylor counties, where dairying was developing in advance of a market infrastructure. These areas became centers for organizational activities of both the ASE and the WA. At its peak in 1920, ASE claimed 90,000 members in 900 locals in 44 counties, most in Wisconsin. ASE leaders believed the WA was so important that it even subsidized paid organizers to increase membership. By 1919 about ten percent of the locals in Wisconsin had an active WA, totaling perhaps a thousand members overall. Although only a small part of ASE membership, the WA was an important example of farm women organizing publicly and engaging in the discussion of farm policy.[16]

The 1908 ASE conference at Knapp in Dunn County was the first attended by the new WA members. Mrs. Ole Samuelson of Stanley humorously recalled that gathering. They were looked upon, she remembered, as "a bunch of idealistic dreamers by nearly all of our farmer sisters; yes, and even by some of our farmer brothers." It seemed impossible that women would take part in solving farm problems, wrote Samuelson.

But the first women members pinned on their official white and gold wa badges and went to the conference. Samuelson traveled by train with another woman delegate, both "continually rubbernecking out of the car window at every station expecting other delegations from other locals to appear with flying banners," and marched up the plank sidewalks of Knapp to inquire about the national convention. Someone told them a bunch of farmers were meeting at the town hall, but the women found the doors locked and no one there. Bravely, they went on to the hotel, where two other women wearing wa badges appeared, perhaps the local arrangements committee, Samuelson and her companion thought. It turned out the four were the only women members at the conference. Finally, two officers arrived and the six women held the first wa national convention. Their business completed, the women walked over to the men's meeting, where, as Samuelson recalled, "the encouragement received by the beginners of our work was not spent too freely." They stood in a corner until one of the male officials finally welcomed them and seated them in the front of the room.[17]

From that hesitant beginning the women gathered numbers and the courage to develop their own agendas, to speak up about political issues, and to raise the question of their place in the male-dominated group. The men had envisioned their women's auxiliary primarily as a "helpmeet" group, to assist the men "in every way possible" and to "promote the moral, intellectual and social sides of farm life." As an Adam's-rib type of group, the women were to have little autonomy. By 1919, however, when the men added auxiliary members to committees such as those on chautauqua and education, some women shared in decision making in the larger male group. They were also speaking on general political issues, as in their opposition to a postwar proposal to settle veterans on marginal land, which would have increased production at a time when farmers were being plagued by overproduction. By then, women were also questioning their place in the organization itself.[18]

ase had not offered the women equity, but it did present a path out of the kitchen. A woman's place was not only in the kitchen, according to ase policy, but, at least for one afternoon a month, at a wa meeting. Carry Miller described the meetings in brief: first a business meeting, then a program furnished by the hostess, assisted by her children and friends, then lunch, conversation, and new ideas. Farm women were busy, said Miller, but they could arrange their work to have at least one afternoon for a club meeting like the city people. wa did not offer farm women much, but it was more than they had before. Organizers wrote of the possibility of affiliating with the Federation of Women's Clubs. Friendly notes from suffrage associations appeared periodically in the wa columns of the Wisconsin state and national ase newspapers.[19]

From the *Equity News* we can glean a sense of how the locals organized. Just east of Clark County's western border were two small villages, Thorp and

Worden, which formed a local in July 1907. It began with eighteen members and soon added fourteen more. Until 1913 it was the only WA in the four north-central counties. Occasionally the Thorp-Worden local sent reports to the women's column of the *Equity News*.

If the Thorp-Worden local is any indication of women's organizational activities, they used methods women had long employed to raise funds for their church groups. They sold quilts, aprons, and rugs as well as suppers, lunches, and ice cream. Like the RNA, they publicized their group by entering a float in the Stanley Fourth of July parade. The Thorp-Worden WA float, bearing the goddess of liberty surrounded by women dressed in national costumes, won the first prize. They used funds raised by food and craft sales, along with their prize money, to send Samuelson and her companion to the 1908 ASE convention and to buy shares in the nearby Stanley Dairy and Warehouse Company, an early and successful cooperative to which many families belonged. The local reported in 1917 that fifty people shared Thanksgiving dinner with its leader Samuelson, whose husband, Ole, was president of the ASE local. Following Thorp-Worden's lead, the WA spread its locals through the north-central counties, from villages as small as Stanley to cities as large as Marshfield, which drew in farm women from the surrounding countryside.

About five miles east of Colby, just over the Marathon County line in Hull township, women formed an auxiliary in 1912. Within two years it had eighty members. More than half the men in the Hull ASE had a woman from their family in the WA. The Hull WA owed its success in great part to the work of Katharina Hunkel Brehm. Like other women active in the WA, Katharina (known to her friends as Kate) was a mature farm woman with years of experience. She was born in Wisconsin; in 1887 she married Edward Brehm, who had just arrived in Hull township from Sheboygan. The parents of both Kate and Edward were born in Germany; both also had brothers farming nearby. By 1912 Kate had birthed six children; the eldest was twenty-two and the youngest nine. A younger neighbor, Hulda Heintz, became the local's first president, but Kate was one of eighteen charter members who formed the first WA, and she served as vice president. Most other early members, who included Kate's new daughter-in-law, were also younger, but Kate would become the best known of the group. Along with her husband, she helped start the Hull cheese factory. In 1915 the couple worked to bring five ASE locals together to form the Harmony Cooperative at Colby to purchase feed and to ship livestock. Kate attended state and national meetings as a Hull representative. Eventually she became a paid organizer for ASE, traveling throughout Wisconsin and Minnesota, urging other farm women to join. The Hull WA increased rapidly. Both the women's group and the cooperative lasted into the 1960s: the WA under the name of the Homemakers Club, the Harmony Cooperative a familiar symbol rising near the railroad.[20]

In those heady first days of organizing, women talked about farm women's rights. Caroline Emmerton of Bloomer, a farm woman who lived north of Stanley in Chippewa County, wrote to *Equity News* in 1912: "Women who share in burdens of producing wealth upon the farms, should be admitted to full fellowship in the co-operative movement." Caroline's parents, Sarah and Thomas, were English-born; her father was president of the local ASE and cofounder of the successful Farmers' Store Company. Caroline, the sixth of nine children, had stayed home with a brother to help run the farm. At forty-one she was an experienced farm woman with a clear vision of women's importance to family farm operations. Four years later, as national secretary, she welcomed WA sisters to the 1917 convention at Fond du Lac by posing this rhetorical question: "Can we hope the power of suffrage will elevate the thoughts and broaden the minds of womankind?" Clearly she thought so, for she went on to hope a better time was coming for "the farm women of our land." She urged farm women to study business methods, to understand what cooperation meant and how it could help farmers keep the profits from their labor. ASE women needed to become strong in their clubs so they could be recognized by women in city clubs as well.[21]

At the state convention in 1916, the women displayed a broad concern with the conditions they faced. Discussions were followed by resolutions on the topics of unjust banking laws that allowed husbands to take women's earnings deposited in joint accounts and the 1907 federal law that stripped native-born women of their citizenship if they married an alien.[22]

Women had seldom discussed the politics of gender publicly in ASE, but they were beginning to talk about women's political needs at their national conventions—to men as well as to women. ASE was one of the Wisconsin groups to endorse women's suffrage as the campaign for voting rights intensified in the state. At the 1917 state conference, national Women's Auxiliary president Alice Sparks spoke about the first nine years of the WA, how its delegates had taken a small place in a corner at the front of the hall, how the president had insisted they take a better place and told them they were "never again to take a back seat." She spoke of the importance of farm women leaving their never-ending work routines to meet and discuss the "welfare of the home and the nation," of the need for farm women, the sisters of equity, to demand equity for themselves. Sparks hoped the WA sisters would encourage and help the ASE brothers "till the many unjust conditions of farm life are done away with." That same year Mrs. W. Rich, editorial manager of *Equity Papers*, encouraged the "farmer and his wife" to contribute to the evolution of an "industrial democracy," with political education and improved country life, recommending that women serve on commissions in rural areas and study the science of politics because it affected their lives and homes as much as the lives of men.

She predicted suffrage would come: "This man-made rule of government will needs be reversed and men and women will walk the broad path of equality."[23]

Still, nothing had quite prepared the national delegates for Adelaide Junger's 1917 open demand for democracy within the ASE. Junger was speaking in Wisconsin as president of the Minnesota WA. Paid organizers from Wisconsin had been very successful in helping women form locals in Minnesota: Katharina Brehm of Colby found women to be receptive, and the organizing went quickly. In the three years between 1915 and 1917, 220 Minnesota women organized themselves into eighteen locals. By September they had more than a sufficient number of locals to organize a state branch, and Brehm traveled to St. Paul to help them form their organization. Adelaide Junger was probably already active in the group: she was soon listed as a state organizer and the president of the Minnesota WA.[24]

Junger was a German immigrant from Sandstone, Minnesota, who had arrived with her parents from Prussia as a ten-year-old in the 1870s. She married John Junger, a New York native of Luxemburg heritage, in 1881, and by 1900 the couple had settled in Delano in Wright County, Minnesota, where Adelaide bore several children. When she gave her talk to the Wisconsin ASE in Wausau, Adelaide was a confident and successful farmer in her mid-fifties. Her husband was president of the local ASE in Pine County, Minnesota, which was formed in 1913.[25]

During that chilly trip across Wisconsin in bitterly cold December 1917, Adelaide caught cold. She felt wretched and had just about decided not to speak. When no other woman stepped forward, Junger made her way to the podium and excused herself as not feeling well and probably able to say only a few words. She was willing to speak, however, because "the women have not much to say and are very seldom represented." Her twenty-minute talk was the strongest political statement about farm women to emerge from the ASE, and we have it only because at that meeting a stenographer recorded her speech.

Junger had started out with the old metaphor about the hand that rocked the cradle, but she went on to deliver a different message. Equity had preached cooperation to the women until, Junger said, the women thought they could do wonders. She went on:

> You men got together and decided that you wanted to teach us to cooperate. You made your constitution and By-Laws and you just included yourselves. The women were not in it. Now, it does look strange, doesn't it? And then you want to blind us the same as they do with our horses; you want to blind us and make us feel good and make us feel big and that we are ruling the world.

It must have startled some of the men when Junger went on to lecture them. Equity had preached cooperation to the women, said Junger, but it had not given them the tools to implement the practice. One leader had told her, "Now, you ladies don't want to get too radical. Go slow, because I tell you the Government is doing quite a lot for us just now." But, Junger continued, country women must get together with city women and work against government interference. To go slow and not get involved in politics was bad advice, for the whole system was run by politics, with "Big Business . . . galloping along and taking everything away from us that we have." That statement inspired applause. Later in the talk, her indictment of big business for arranging things so that the poor in the United States could not get the food they needed also brought applause. "We ought to be with [the male ASE members] all the time right along," she argued, "Give us a chance to help you, and we will do it and be glad to do it." Women were helping to feed the world; "Why, then can't we have something to say when it comes to voting? Aren't we entitled to it? I do not see why you men think that it is for you only. Let us get right in and help you all we can, and I am sure we can change all that needs to be changed." The bankers were getting hold of the land instead of the farmers, and farmers—men and women—should join with city brothers and sisters to oppose their power. Junger spoke for women members who wanted to be part of the main ASE organization, to have a place there to influence the agenda with the men, not just to shape a separate women's agenda.[26]

For the women involved, the WA opened new ways to discuss and participate in issues relating to farm politics and to women's inequities. For those who assumed leadership roles, it offered public practice of new skills—speaking, organizing, and negotiating joint programs with male leaders. There were discussions of community laundries and bakeries, of farm management, production, and marketing. At its peak from 1917 to 1919, the ASE provided a place where women could raise questions of equality within the organization and express brave wishful statements about equity. None, however, spoke as directly as did Adelaide Junger at that December 1917 meeting in Wausau, when as state president of the Minnesota WA she spoke to male and female delegates.[27]

The ASE was soon distracted by a major financial and political crisis that divided the group into two factions, both battling over control of the national organization. Wisconsin members, for the most part, remained within the ASE. In Minnesota, many members left the ASE and joined the Nonpartisan League, a group that favored more government control over the economy. The Wisconsin ASE board minutes concluded bitterly, "The [Minnesota] Society was utterly wrecked." The ASE survived, but the squabble left the Wisconsin ASE weakened, in control of a national ASE that was composed mainly of Wisconsin members.[28]

The ASE declined in the 1920s. In the 1930s small locals continued to exist throughout its core membership area in northern Wisconsin: Marathon and

Lincoln counties still had active units; Clark County had only eight members in a single local at Dorchester; Taylor County had no members at all. By that time the women's auxiliaries were also gone. Some moved into homemakers groups that the agricultural extension agents began to organize in 1918. The Colby WA finally dropped its ASE affiliation in 1928 to become the Homemakers Association. Others simply disintegrated along with the male locals.[29]

TO VOTE AND HOLD OFFICE

In 1904 Charlotte M. Hughes wrote in her Merrill High School *School Bell Echoes,* "In the last twenty-five years we have seen women rise from very obscure positions to those on an equal footing with men. They now are nearly equal in all industries. In the next twenty-five years we will no doubt see women as man's equal in all things." Hughes was pleased with women's progress to a "nearly equal" position with men in the years between 1879 and 1904 and confident that the years from 1904 to 1929 would see equality "in all things." Flossie Kingsley, a classmate of Hughes, seemed equally optimistic. She created fictional future lives for alumni in the same 1904 *School Bell Echoes* to show that women would achieve impressive status: head of the Wisconsin university, a brilliant lawyer, a leading physician, scientists (including an astronomer who discovered a new planet), businesswomen, administrators, prominent educators. There was no high political office yet, but one former classmate had been there "preaching òn Women's Rights."[30]

Twenty-four young women and only five young men were graduating in 1904 from Merrill High School. At that moment of scholarly triumph, it perhaps seemed as though women could indeed achieve almost anything. Looking at the suffrage movement in Wisconsin, however, it is difficult to see what made young Hughes so absolutely certain that women's progress to a "nearly equal" position with men had been achieved and why Kingsley projected such an optimistic future. The suffrage movement in Wisconsin was at its lowest ebb in 1904. The activist grandmothers and mothers of young women like Hughes and Kingsley had worn themselves thin campaigning and seemed to have little to show in the way of formal legal rights. Yet it was this younger generation that would, in the next two decades, continue the campaign for suffrage and eventually guide the national suffrage amendment through the legislature, making Wisconsin the second state to ratify it.

The Royal Neighbors of America and the American Society of Equity both supported the suffrage movement in Wisconsin. This support brought the issue of suffrage closer to rural women like those who lived in and around the small town of Merrill. It did not, however, bring suffragists themselves much closer to rural women. Nor did it, for all its local endorsements, become a broad mass movement in the countryside. Suffrage had a difficult time making head-way in Wisconsin because, unlike the RNA and the ASE, it did not draw as directly on the grassroots traditions of rural women.

A realistic look at politics gave no cause for the young women's optimism. Wisconsin, including northern Wisconsin, had been the site of an active suf-frage movement in the late 1870s and 1880s. Women had organized in both Wausau and Merrill, the two largest towns in the four north-central counties. Organizers brought Susan B. Anthony and other suffragists north to speak. In March 1878, when the Liberal League of Wausau booked Elizabeth Cady Stan-ton to lecture for their ladies' course at the music hall, the *River Pilot* provided very favorable publicity for the sixty-two-year-old suffragist. "A ready speaker, brilliant conversationalist, and in argument has never been equaled," the paper promised readers for the twenty-five-cent lecture fee. When a booking error brought Stanton to town two days early, she gave a private lecture for the ladies and then the promised public lecture on Sunday evening to a full house. As vice president of the Liberal League, speaking on the "objects of the Liberal League," Stanton dwelled at length on the unequal "condition of women." The next year Susan B. Anthony arrived in Wausau to deliver her famous "Women Want Bread not Ballots" lecture. Actually, she told the crowd, women wanted both.[31]

Many people agreed with Stanton and Anthony that women should have the vote. Supporters formed the Marathon County Woman Suffrage organiza-tion, which flourished. Two years later, in February 1880, six hundred residents of Marathon and Lincoln counties signed the suffragists' petition endorsing women's suffrage. These activities did not result in passage of universal suf-frage, but they helped push through a referendum on school and municipal suffrage for women, approved by male voters in 1886.[32]

In northern Wisconsin and in other areas, suffragists went to the school and municipal election polls in the spring of 1887 to exercise their new though limited voting rights. The Wausau *River Pilot* reported that women voted there as well as in Oshkosh, Ripon, and other parts of the north. State suffragists estimated that more than two thousand women had voted or tried to vote in that election. At many of the larger polling places, however, officials turned women away because the attorney general had issued orders not to accept women's votes. Denied their electoral voice, the women challenged the state in court. The lower courts upheld the women's right to vote, but the state supreme court held that the referendum had only established the "principle" of woman suffrage: women could not vote until legislation implemented the principle. The hugely expensive costs borne by the Wisconsin Woman Suffrage Associa-tion in these unsuccessful appeals not only devastated the Wisconsin suffragists but also moved the national suffrage movement to abandon state campaigns for partial suffrage and to support instead a national amendment granting full suffrage.[33]

A few Wisconsin women still voted in rural municipal and school elections, but allowing women to vote was a local custom rather than an enforced right. Presumably women did vote on school issues in some places in north-central Wisconsin, but little evidence of political activity is available. An 1895 voter list for the school district of Loyal in Clark County, for example, named only males.[34]

After 1901, when the legislature finally passed a school law providing for separate ballots for women to vote on school matters, a few references to their activities do appear. A 1903 appeal against building a schoolhouse in Longwood, Clark County, mentions that "men and women, assembled at a school district meeting properly called, to designate a school house site." The year before, Clark County women joined men in petitioning against change in school boundaries in the townships of Dewhurst and Levis. Opposition to a graded school provoked this petition, and the discussion revealed that men had asked women to sign the petition only after two groups of men had argued themselves to a stalemate. Still, women's names do appear, the first I have found on any document of school matters: Maggie Alsenbach, Emma Wright, Eliza Haeuel, Mary Tykac, Martha Varney, Emma Iverson, Nettie Primmer, Anna Waller. By 1904, after almost twenty years of working to confirm limited school voting rights, women were finally exercising them. The right to school suffrage came only after constant court and polling place challenges. In 1906 the Wisconsin Supreme Court in *Hall vs. The City of Madison* finally settled the issue. Women could not be denied the right to vote on school issues. Over the next decade, it became common for school reformers to urge women to take up issues relating to schools, to discuss them thoroughly, and to rally support for their children.[35]

Although the courts clearly had affirmed women's right to hold offices relating to school matters in 1875, men continued to question this right as late as 1888, when one who lost his bid for county school superintendent challenged the victorious female candidate in court as ineligible for office as a woman. The highest political position to which a woman could aspire in the late nineteenth and early twentieth centuries was county superintendent of education. The job was an arduous one: the superintendent administered the public school system, condemned unfit schoolhouses, ordered new schools to be built, examined teachers and granted certificates, visited and directed all activities in the schools, instructed teachers in their duties, and encouraged the public to take an interest in education. The county superintendents reported directly to the state superintendent and to their county board of education.[36]

The first Wisconsin county to appoint a woman as superintendent of schools

was Price, just north of Taylor County. Phillips, the county seat, was a booming lumber town full of entrepreneurs from the eastern United States, European
immigrant workers, and a group of exceptionally well-trained schoolteachers.
Between 1887 and 1925, nine women held the position of school superintendent, a string interrupted by a single male appointed for only a short period
during World War I. The duties increased each year as the school system grew.
In the 1890s Janette MacDonald supervised fifty-one school districts, three
graded schools, and one high school. May McNely, who served as superintendent from 1903 to 1916, supervised eighty-three school buildings in seventy-nine
school districts and organized two teachers institutes and two teachers' conventions yearly. She managed a $70,000 budget.

   None of the women who achieved these highly political positions of responsibility discussed how they obtained them. Thousands of lumber workers,
many foreign born, were resident during the November elections but gone by
spring when the school elections usually took place. These women perhaps
served as a bulwark for the permanent settlers who struggled to control
county politics. Despite the tradition of women holding the position of superintendent in Price County, it was still big news when Mary Bradford was
appointed to the superintendency of Kenosha in 1910. By that time, women
were also slowly moving on to school boards. Statewide, twenty-eight women
served in that capacity in 1914.[37]

   For Hughes and Kingsley, young women graduates of 1904, there was not
yet much evidence of women's formal political rights. Their grandmothers
and mothers had ignited the dream of equality, however, and young women
expected their rights to be granted in the near future because they had grown
up during the activism of the 1870s and 1880s. They had imbibed the words
of Susan B. Anthony: "failure is impossible." They were soon joining the campaign the older women had launched, undaunted by their failures.

Organizing for Change
Nellie's Story [Kedzie Jones, born in Kansas, 1858–1954]

In spring of 1911, Nellie Kedzie Jones and her husband Howard Murray, with
their daughter Eleanor, moved to a farm near the Little Eau Pleine River in
southwestern Marathon County. It was a large farm, more than 1,600 acres
covering about 1,000 acres of marshland and part of what had been Rice Lake
before its 23,000 acres had been drained for farmland. Native people had once
called the area Smokey Hill because of the mist or haze from the lake. Even
though the lake and the mist were now gone, Nellie and Howard decided to
call their new home "Smokey Hill Farm." Fire had run through the region the
year before, and much of the land was marsh; it must have been an exception-

ally good price that brought the couple to this cut-over land with its huge stumps. They bought it with a five-year mortgage.

Nellie and Howard had come to this part of Wisconsin from Minneapolis. They were not typical farm people. She was a robust fifty-three; he forty-five but in ill health. Daughter Eleanor was five years old, recovering from infantile paralysis and not able to walk. Their two years in Minneapolis had not been good. Howard had accepted the ministry of the Lyndale Congregational Church in 1909, and Nellie taught Sunday school there as she had at a Congregational church in Kalamazoo, Michigan, where Howard previously pastored for seven years. Theirs had been a late marriage, in July 1901, while Howard was still a professor of history at Berea College in Kentucky. They probably chose Wisconsin because of its reputation for being a healthy place to live. Other middle-class professional people, similarly caught up in a back-to-the-land craze, were also moving to farms.

Nellie knew all about farm life. Born on a Kansas farm in 1858, she lived there until she went to Kansas State Agricultural College in Topeka in the 1870s. After graduation she moved back to Kansas and taught in country schools until her family sold its farm in 1877. Like Mary Bradford, Nellie's career resulted from the early death of a husband. After teaching for several years, Nellie married Robert Kedzie, a professor at Mississippi Agricultural College. Who knows what she might have achieved in Mississippi, but seven weeks into the marriage her husband died and she returned to her family in Topeka. According to Nellie's version, the president of the local college called on her simply because she was a graduate of that school. Sometime in 1882 the family asked him to supper. After finishing an excellent meal that Nellie had helped prepare, the president asked her, "Do you think you can teach Kansas girls to make such biscuits as these we have just been eating?" Nellie replied, "I could try."[38]

Nellie became an early pioneer in home economics during her fifteen-year stay at the University of Kansas. She launched her program with one hundred dollars to buy equipment, in three small rooms and a large one, with a table, a dozen wooden chairs, and an "elderly" wood range. When she left fifteen years later, a large new home economics building bore her name. It is sometimes difficult to imagine how innovative and progressive early home economics pioneers believed themselves to be. Nellie did not consider home economics to be training for marriage but for life. As a widow and working woman herself, Nellie assumed that all women would have a home. Whether or not she married, a woman would have to care for herself and her dependents. She needed knowledge of hygiene and foods for good health and sewing skills to make clothing in a day when there were still few ready-made garments available and seamstresses were expensive. Nellie conceived of home economics as an underpinning for self-sufficiency, a program built on the regular rigorous academic classes. For example, Nellie taught beginning cooking to young women only after they had successfully completed a standard chemistry class.[39]

Hygiene was a new subject when Nellie—the only woman teacher at her Topeka college—introduced it to women students. The college soon hired a professor of physiology to teach both men and women. During this time, Nellie honed her speaking skills and shaped her attitudes toward the role of farm women. She taught butter and cheese making in her cooking classes but opposed teaching young women to milk because she thought it was "not a woman's work." Graduates from her program fanned out across the country to start home economics programs in agricultural colleges, taking with them Nellie's ideas of just where a rural woman's work should end. She left Kansas State in 1897, at a time when the split between home economics and political economics was being codified into a strict division between public and private. Political economics was public; home economics private.[40]

After leaving Kansas State, Nellie continued to teach, in Peoria, Illinois, at Bradley Polytechnic University, and to lecture, even after marrying Howard. She spoke at farmers' institutes in Illinois, Indiana, Iowa, Michigan, and Wisconsin. Earnings from her speaking always formed an important part of the couple's income. Now that Howard's meager ministerial pay was gone, her off-farm lecturing and writing continued to offer a stable source of income as they built up their Marathon farm.

Nellie was a farm daughter, but it is not clear how much farming experience Howard had, although he grew up in a lush agricultural area in Santa Clara, California. He received his education at Oberlin and at a theological seminary in Chicago. Howard seemed happy as a minister until his bout of ill health in Minneapolis, but he was delighted with the new farm and wrote to his sister Ada in May 1911 of its beauty—apple trees blooming, woods full of trillium and other flowers. The season was late, he wrote the next month, but with a hired man's help he had already planted 30 acres of grass, 25 acres of oats, 4 acres each of barley and sugar beets, and a little garden. Nellie, meanwhile, took up the normal farm woman's chores, without city amenities like piped gas, running water, or sewer. She was maintaining the six-room country house, cooking for the family and three hired men, caring for milk and butter. By June Howard had a fine hay crop, both he and Eleanor were feeling better, but he was worried about "poor Nellie." Howard wrote to his sister, "I do a great deal of house-work and save her all I can." He described Nellie as "a wonder" but overworked.[41]

Howard was not the only person to consider Nellie a wonder. The home economics building at Kansas University, where she taught from 1882 to 1897, bore her name. She had lectured at farm institutes in Springfield, Illinois, for the last six years and had booked again for the fall of 1911. This farm woman already had a successful career in home economics behind her and planned to continue it from her farmhouse in Marathon. Less than two miles from Smokey Hill Farm was a spur of the Northwestern train line, which could take her to the Soo Line, which, in turn, took her to the trading village of Auburndale. From Auburndale there was a fine road to the Twin Cities and Chicago. Her farm was close enough to allow her to continue lecturing, and she did. She also wrote articles for the *Country Gentleman.* If Nellie was not working on the farm she was writing and lecturing, until 1918, when they left the farm. Howard, a hired girl, and a hired man all helped her keep house and career going for the seven years she lived at Smokey Hill.

Nellie Kedzie Jones visits a home economics exhibit, 1910s. From 1912 to 1918 Nellie farmed in Marathon County with her husband, lectured for farm institutes, and published advice for rural women in the Country Gentleman. She conceived of home economics as an underpinning for self-sufficiency and urged farm women to demand status as economic partners. "Speak up and the husband will 'divide up,'" she predicted. She became state leader for the University of Wisconsin Home Economics Extension in 1916.

Nellie's career can be traced through letters her husband wrote as he worked to provide better conditions for her home and professional life. Howard did well at farming. By August he was receiving regular checks from the creamery, like "a real farmer and dairyman," he wrote proudly to his sister. Howard had a regular hired hand and extra summer help from college students, but when Nellie was home she handled all the housework until she had earned enough money to hire a woman to help her. When Nellie left in fall of 1911, Howard was, as he put it, nurse, cook, chambermaid, and farmer. When Nellie left for a second time, he had to hire a second woman to help do the sewing. Howard wrote in November 1911 that Nellie slept ten hours a night when she could and mused, "Probably why she can stand up under so much heavy work." In December she was off again to give a talk for seventy-five dollars. She did not want to speak full-time, but when "hunted up" and paid well, she went. Nellie stepped in as a six-week replacement when the head of domestic science at the University of Wisconsin in Madison had a break-down; then she accepted an appointment as "lecturer at large" from the university. By May Nellie was working so hard that Howard turned over the out-side work to hired help and took over management of the house.[42]

At the same time that Nellie was "lecturer at large," she was also writing a regular column for *Country Gentleman*. Nellie had sent nine articles off to the magazine by October 1912, "a quick and easy $500," Howard noted. With the extra income, they hired a German couple to help, and by June 1913 they were holding their own financially and raising ducks, pigs, and steers as well as cows. Nellie had to prepare for her ten-day institute tour in Illinois and Minnesota in January 1914, but Howard was now regularly helping her with the articles and ghostwriting some of her speeches.[43]

Each summer Nellie worked on the farm. In winter she spoke at institutes—including a circuit to Wyoming and Utah in 1915—while hired neighbor women took charge of the house. The winter of 1915 she was gone for seven weeks. She booked lectures to bankers' conventions in Tennessee for the following August. That year was record-breaking for cold and wet—the coldest August on record killed all the corn and potatoes. "Nellie's earnings have been good and the price of land hereabouts is rising all the time," Howard wrote in August. Although the family had a phone, they still could not afford indoor plumbing.[44]

By the end of 1915, Nellie and Howard had become more ambivalent about staying on the farm. Nellie was traveling so much that when she was home she was too tired to do her farm work. They hired a maid so Nellie had more rest when she was not on the road. During January 1916 she spoke in Utah, Mon-tana, and South Dakota. The following winter Nellie and Eleanor accepted the offer of a house in Chicago for five months. Howard soon joined them, hiring help to run the farm. By May 1917 the family had decided not to stay full-time on the farm, but the money from Nellie and Howard's writing allowed them to keep the farm while they lingered in Chicago. Then, in April 1918 the *Country Gentleman* fired the woman who headed the women's department and the new department head decided not to publish Nellie's articles any longer, thus ending the farm subsidy from writing. Nellie was forced to look for full-time work. When the University of Wisconsin offered her a permanent part-time position traveling the state as an extension leader, she accepted. The job, which paid $250 a month, allowed Nellie and Howard to sell the farm and move to Madison permanently. Eleanor was already in school there, and they had hopes that Howard could find a job, too. "She lives to travel," Howard wrote of Nellie in February 1920.[45]

For Nellie, the dream of farming into old age had ended, but during the almost eight years on the farm she left a legacy in the *Country Gentleman*. In her monthly articles, Nellie offered a practical political economy for her audience of rural women. Her advice focused on work, self-improvement, domestic economic relations, and leadership in the community.

COUNTRY WOMEN'S CLUBS

Nellie's theories about farm home management eventually became the foundation of the rural women's club movement. Assuming a gendered division of labor on the farm, Nellie suggested that farm women consider themselves executives, even generals or campaigners, who had the right to delegate work to husband or hired help. They should requisition help from their husbands for the hardest work whether outside or in—for example, the washing. If he had a hired hand to help him outside, she should have a hired woman to help her inside. If she had no hired woman and her husband had a hired man, she had a part-time right to the hired man's help for her hardest housework if her husband did not help. As for outdoor work, some was lighter than domestic work, she noted. Riding a mower was easier than washing, and a woman could well trade such outdoor work for more arduous tasks. Nellie did not discuss children's work on the farm, a telling absence that indicates she probably believed adults were responsible for all farm work and children should not even be required to do much work around the house. They simply should put away their own things, she suggested. Presumably they would concentrate on learning trades: boys studying agriculture; girls, domestic science.

Having delegated the heaviest work, farm women nevertheless faced an endless round of chores. Just do less, Nellie counseled: "Eliminate, eliminate, eliminate." Do not iron; do little sewing and remodeling. What was left the farm wife should measure and value, then add a margin for safety, and simplify her life as much as possible. She must be sparing of her labor and take care of herself. Both she (and her hired woman, if she had one) should take short rest periods each day, with a nap in the afternoon. She should take off an afternoon one day a week, refuse to work on Sundays, and take at least a week each year to go away.

With this additional time for herself, a farm woman should engage in activities of self-improvement. With only forty minutes a day, she could finish a chautauqua certificate in four years and get a reading diploma. On her half-day off she could go to farmers' fairs or read. She could follow a fad, collect something, have some fun, even engage in a little nonsense. Nellie suggested women attend week-long short courses sponsored by the university extension and the farmers' institutes, which would take them away from their work for several days to concentrate on larger issues concerning rural life.

Underpinning this ability to organize her own time was the need for a farm wife to have a clear business relationship with her husband and the farm. While the woman could concede to the husband the "big picture" of the business and reserve the "details" for herself, she should nevertheless consider herself a partner in the domestic firm. She must know her rights, such as the right to have her husband not sell or trade the farm without her consent and the right not to be forced to leave the farm if she did not want to sell it. She had the right to veto his decisions, although she should do so sparingly and in private. The wife should not depend on money kept back from her own enterprise, as had been the custom. Instead she should demand the status of a partner, with a bank account, joint or her own, for access to the farm business income. Her wedding ring, Nellie suggested, meant that it was her business, too, and she should take from the purse what she needed. "Speak up and the husband will 'divide up,'" she predicted. The husband should represent the farm enterprise publicly and be in charge of sales, but she should do the buying and keep the books. And she should never underestimate her business ability and by implication overestimate his, as was often the case.

Women also had an important role in public politics, at least those aspects that affected domestic conditions. Like other domestic feminists of the time, Nellie allotted public power to women sparingly, using her role in the household to argue for a community presence in political issues that affected children, schools, asylums, and anything related to protection of the home. Sidestepping the issue of whether or not farm women should want the vote, she urged women to use it if they had the chance. They should participate in school and town meetings, sit on boards relating to these "domestic" political issues, "push out [their] mental horizon on every side," merge family and country life. Still, they should follow a middle-of-the road course, advocating evolution and not revolution, and use the "feminine traits" of moderation, cooperation, mediation, and tact to foster reconciliation among the classes, to "cultivate sanity," to help make complicated lives easier.

Rural women would probably not be office seekers, Nellie concluded, but women elders should be considered "treasures" for their wisdom and experience, attributes that would make them valuable in some public offices. There was a role for women as leaders, especially in developing cooperative buying and selling clubs and cultural activities that would bring people together and keep them from leaving rural areas for cities. She saw the movements for consolidated schools and hospitals, rural nurses, and hot lunches as important issues about which rural women could become active community leaders. These causes were all popular among progressives, and Nellie hoped women would follow the lead of reformers such as herself in lending public support for changes that would improve country women's lives.

Conspicuously absent from the activities Nellie listed were those she did not feel would benefit rural women or help develop the bonds of community she envisioned. On the whole, she saw religions as community dividers and did not linger over encouragement of spiritual development. Nor did she see visual or literary arts as particularly helpful for rural women. Hers was a blueprint modeled on the Country Life Movement and the initiatives of progressive reformers who believed that their brand of domestic and community political change would preserve the family farm. She offered to rural women the best the reformers had to offer.

In all her organizing, Nellie Kedzie Jones emphasized the need for country women to form clubs parallel to and in contact with those radiating through cities and towns. In Wisconsin, as elsewhere, this movement drew thousands of women into formal organizations in the late nineteenth century. Most began as self-improvement clubs where women met to study and read in the fields of literature, art, history, philosophy—any subject the assembled dozen women wanted to pursue. In urban areas, larger groups divided their members into departments to study and then adopt civic projects. Developing and improving municipal services, facilities, and amenities occupied these women as they scanned existing schools, parks, and health and social services, noting the need for their establishment or improvement. Clubwomen greatly expanded the theory of municipal responsibility and public power. In the 1890s, when local groups began to affiliate into regional, state, and national federations, the potential for unified mass action increased dramatically. From the founding of the national General Federation of Women's Clubs (GFWC) in 1890, membership grew to more than 1 million by 1914. The tendrils of organization reached deep into the urban middle classes throughout the country. By the 1896 GFWC national convention, it had a committee for "social economics"; by 1898, industrial and civic committees. By 1910 the federation was compiling lists of women's legal rights in each state and supporting legislation to improve conditions. In 1898 the group had noted the presence of new territory for the "kingdom of women." The Wisconsin Federation of Women's Clubs, known as the WFWC, emphasized not just what was wrong but what was getting better and how not only women but the entire community could benefit. It supported professional careers, but it also stressed that women could gain public power as mothers.

The WFWC members who backed this "kingdom of women" were solidly middle class. The majority of the leaders were married and over forty-five, and half had live-in domestic servants. Their husbands had businesses or professional occupations, and the overwhelming majority, almost 70 percent, were members of Congregational or Presbyterian churches. A third were college women; many had been educators in public schools. The group was predominantly pro-suffrage, but its leadership had strong ties to church work and to hereditary organizations, such as the Daughters of the American Revolution. Although the WFWC always urged women to vote whenever and wherever they could, early leaders refused to support total suffrage, in their view a radical concept. Instead they urged involvement in children's education, which seemed to them "normal and rational." By 1906 leaders had changed their tone, now arguing that the vote was necessary not just to protect children but also to defend working women. Members lobbied the legislature in 1909 for protective legislation for working women. Attention to this matter led in 1911 to a closer study of suffrage, and the 1912 convention voted more than two to one to endorse general suffrage. The club urged its members to study political economy and governmental finances and politics; it created a political science committee, which evolved into the women's suffrage committee. The committee concluded that school suffrage could not give women what they needed politically, for they could not vote on constitutional questions. Members now focused on perfecting techniques to channel public opinion to support suffrage and on legislation that would help protect their children and working daughters. Leaders told the clubwomen that women's "special power lies in their organization." They had the power at hand, in their organizations and in their ability to mobilize others to support their causes. The WFWC expanded rapidly along with its support for political power. From 70 clubs and just over 3,000 members in 1896, it grew to 259 clubs with 13,500 members in 1917. Committees provided training for women in fields of civics, industrial and social conditions, home economics, public health, and women's suffrage. In two decades, self-education had moved from an evening study of literary classics to a strategy to obtain full participation in the political process.[46]

In 1917, as the United States entered the Great War, the WFWC committed itself to war work. Two-thirds of the women served as heads of countywide women's committees, where clubwomen performed "civilian war work." They folded this work into their long-term goals, however, arguing that in order to defend the home front the protection of children and female workers must continue throughout the war. The leaders maintained and expanded their organization by forming districts of several counties that could oversee war work, mobilize clubwomen, and increase membership. They had in mind to expand into the countryside to reach their "sister-women."[47]

Nellie was the agent of the expansion of women's clubs to country women. Her gift to Marathon from her new office as extension leader in Madison was Mary Brady, the state's first home demonstration agent. Brady arrived in Wausau in the spring of 1918 and immediately began organizing rural versions of women's clubs. Brady urged each new club to join the Federation of Women's Clubs. She reported them as Home Demonstration Clubs to the county's extension agents, but many simply called themselves "women's clubs." By the end of the first year and a half she had organized fourteen clubs in the countryside. "It is such pure joy to get to the women and get their enthusiasm and happiness over their clubs and meetings," Brady wrote, "I only wish I might be able to organize and have a successful club in every town in this county." She moved slowly at first, guiding each group with careful support until it was established firmly.[48]

Brady joined the editorial staff of the *Marathon County Farm Bureau Journal* as soon as it was formed in June 1919. The farm bureau, the Wausau Chamber of Commerce, and the Marathon County Bankers Association sponsored the monthly publication. Brady urged that women's groups organized during the war for Red Cross work not disband at war's end: "The life of the woman on the farm is apt to be so filled with home duties that she finds little time for outside activities. But at the same time, it is a duty she owes to herself and to her family to get in touch with her neighbors in some kind of social activity. She will be better for it." Brady suggested that Home Demonstration Clubs be open to all community women who wished to join.[49]

In May 1920 the *Journal* reported on eleven of the fourteen clubs formed between 1918 and 1919. The first clubs were established at Ringle, Holton, Athens, Texas, Harrison, Milan, Four Corners, Edgar, Corinth, and Rib Falls. Soon after, clubs formed at Elderon, Maine, Johnson, and Wausau townships. The Ringle Club, which women had organized to do Red Cross war work, invited Brady to give a demon-

The New Woman, 1900s. This young unidentified woman from Merrill, Lincoln County, exemplified the necessary confidence of those who faced the task of changing the laws that kept women from full citizenship. High school graduates in 1904 identified their status as a "nearly equal position" with men and predicted "equality in all things" by the end of the 1920s.

stration immediately upon her arrival in the county. At her suggestion, it reorganized in June 1919 as a Home Demonstration Club. The club at Athens had similarly organized a Red Cross society in the fall of 1917, meeting in the village hall each Friday to knit for the soldiers. By spring 1919 the group had nothing to do and had dwindled to seven or eight members. Brady helped the women organize a community club to meet every two weeks at the homes of different members. By summer 1919 membership was up to twenty and the group was organizing a picnic to raise funds for community projects. It had joined the wfwc and was calling itself the Women's Club of Athens.

By June 1919 Brady had organized the clubwomen into a group called the Marathon County Women, who gathered that month for their first county-wide meeting. She urged the women to work to provide hot lunches in the schools. During four months of the year, children's lunches froze while they walked to school and barely thawed by noon. For fifty dollars, clubwomen could buy a stove, dishpan, kettle and cover, and 18-inch-square oilcloths for each desk and then provide cocoa or soup. Brady urged affiliation of these locals and the county organization with the Wisconsin Federation of Women's Clubs, and like the Athens club, many signed on. In this way, she expected them to work in concert with urban women. Progressive reforms had reached the countryside.[50]

Outside of Marathon County, however, there was little organization of women's clubs in north-central Wisconsin until 1922. During the war, home

Rural clubwomen, Marathon County, 1923. When Mary Brady arrived in Wausau as the first home demonstration agent for Marathon County in 1918, she told reporters, "I only wish I might be able to organize and have a successful club in every town in this county." By 1923 almost two hundred of these rural clubwomen showed up for a get-together in Wausau.

demonstration agents came north from Madison to showcase canning tech-niques and women attended special outings, helped organize boys' and girls' clubs, involved teachers in various programs, and worked for the Red Cross. They did not, however, create clubs to work on peacetime projects. Not until 1925 did the Clark County extension agent report organizing four groups, at Neillsville, Globe, Levis, and Granton. The Taylor County agent helped organize the first women's club at Stetsonville in 1925. The Lincoln County agent men-tioned none at all.[51]

Despite the lack of women's clubs in other counties, thirty-two existed in Marathon by 1923, enough to form a county federation. These women were from small towns and townships as well as from the city of Wausau. Clubs were especially important in supporting public health programs, establishing TB clinics, attracting children's specials (trains from Madison that displayed health-care information); in setting up travel camps, bathhouses, county ceme-teries, rest rooms in towns for country women, playground equipment, and hot lunches; and in sponsoring boys' and girls' shows. A photograph taken at Marathon Park in Wausau in August 1923 shows two hundred women repre-senting county women's clubs. Country women now had a visible presence in the club movement.[52]

CAMPAIGNS AT HOME

Nellie Kedzie Jones had sidestepped women's major political battle of the day by simply saying women should use the vote if they had it. While she urged women to reform their farm work and to organize into country women's clubs, others campaigned actively for full political equality. During the nine-teenth century, the suffrage movement in Wisconsin had been dominated by native-born, Protestant, middle-class, and middle-aged women. One of this number, German-born Mathilde Franziska Anneke, who was active in Mil-waukee in the 1860s, was an exceptional woman in many ways. She inspired suffragists with her commitment to improvements for women and her insis-tence that women's causes be linked to the "honorable course of history," a connection that she had developed during the German revolution of 1848. She believed the liberation of women was inevitable and only needed reformers' help to make it a reality. She was part of a small group of liberal German men and women who had made common cause with the native-born Wisconsin suffragists, but most German immigrant women were untouched by women's politics during the nineteenth century. Organizations of German men, such as the German-American Alliance and the Brewer's Association, actively opposed women's suffrage. German women mostly worked quietly for suffrage, some from within the Socialist Party. Meta Berger declined the presidency of the

Wisconsin Woman Suffrage Association in 1915; she felt that her presidency would have given German American women a visible suffrage model but that her socialist activities might hurt the cause more than help it.[53]

Suffragists knew they had to have support from the large German American population in order to gain the vote for women in Wisconsin. The first test came in a state suffrage referendum scheduled for 1912. A new suffrage organization, the Political Equality League (PEL), tackled the challenge of attracting German Americans to the cause in support of the referendum. A young generation of women moved into leadership and adopted the strategy of building active local units across the state and recruiting German-speaking women to campaign. PEL emphasized outdoor soapbox oratory and motor tours. In places where autos were still rare, cars festooned with yellow suffrage bunting would bump over bad roads into rural towns and come to a halt on a dusty village street. Then a woman, still in her traveling attire of duster and tied-down hat, would stand up in the car and begin, as one suffragist put it, "to plead for her political freedom."[54]

Sophie Gudden of Oshkosh was often at the wheel for these "motor tours." Eleanor Flexnor once praised Gudden as "a quiet hero" of the suffrage campaign. Yet Gudden was anything but quiet, despite being a Bavarian immigrant who suffered from physical disabilities. Active in the Consumers League and concerned about the circumstances working women faced, Gudden was a skilled speaker and organizer who believed being a good woman citizen meant studying the conditions of women and children and putting the ballot into women's hands. She supervised successful efforts to translate news releases, placing them in German, Polish, and Scandinavian publications. She worked to convince her German countrymen of the need for suffrage, giving 150 speeches in the state during the campaign. When discouraged, she referred to her countrymen as "ignorant" and "hardhearted," but she convinced many of these men that their daughters needed the vote even if they thought their wives did not.[55]

Ada James and Katherine McCullough were also active in the summer 1912 motorcade campaign. In one photograph, James addresses a group of men while a cluster of young women looks on intently from the sidelines, some smiling encouragingly. The men stand before James, a few of the younger ones gazing attentively at her but others looking away in apparent boredom. Those averted glances seem to symbolize men's refusal to listen to her pleas for political freedom.

While motorcades and riverboats carried relatively unknown suffragists to hundreds of small northern towns, prominent women organized as well. Belle La Follette, wife of senator Robert La Follette, made the front pages when she returned to the state from Washington after the Senate adjourned in July 1912.

Audience for suffragist Ada James, 1912. Suffragists faced hostile or indifferent groups of men as they campaigned across rural north-central Wisconsin demanding political freedom for women. Here men look mildly bored as women eagerly listen from the sidelines. James urged men to consider the needs of their daughters even if they thought their wives ought not vote.

She and other suffragists wrote, persuaded, and spoke publicly until the November referendum. The state and national suffrage offices raised thousands of dollars for the Wisconsin referendum campaign.

Despite the efforts of Gudden, James, and others, the 1912 campaign failed. New York lawyer Crystal Eastman Benedict, who had arrived in Milwaukee just in time to plunge into the campaign, regretfully noted that it was a "heavy defeat." Eastman Benedict summed it up this way: campaigners had overestimated support from Scandinavians, Progressive Republicans, and Socialists while underestimating the hostility of the organized brewing industry. Eastman Benedict was one of the optimistic younger generation, members of which, although discouraged, were determined to continue the battle. The brewers could win only when allied with ignorance and prejudice, she predicted, "and it is our business to cut off these allies."[56]

The war, which the United States entered in April 1917, divided the women who had united in favor of suffrage. Some opposed the war or insisted on continuing suffrage campaigns despite it. Others used support for the war to expand the structures that women had developed to obtain suffrage and other rights, hoping to employ these networks to continue the suffrage campaign after the war.

As the national administration prepared for war, women in Wisconsin were already mobilizing. First into the field was the National League for Women's Service (NLWS), based in Milwaukee under the leadership of Mary Mariner. Similar to organizations being formed by men to support entrance into and preparedness for the war, the NLWS offered its services to the mayor of Milwaukee in February 1917. By the end of 1917 the league numbered 250,000 members in thirty-nine states. By the fall of 1918 Wisconsin had seven branches with more than 16,000 members: 15,000 women from 160 clubs in Milwaukee and 1,000 in Burlington (southwest of Milwaukee), but fewer than 200 in each of the other locals and none in northern Wisconsin. In the early days of the war, the state governor as well as the Milwaukee mayor endorsed this volunteer group and the mass meetings it held for women beginning in Milwaukee on April 20, 1917. The women described their job as helping to make "the people of our country think right and act right about the war." As the head of the Wisconsin NLWS explained, "Women cannot fight in the trenches, but they can give very valuable service in the second line of defense." Women flocked to these second lines. The Wisconsin branch of the NLWS promised to mobilize women on the home front for war work, and it did. It organized dances and recreation for military men, patrolled camp areas to prevent women from "loitering about," helped the families of military men, supplied women workers for factories, and enrolled women in canning and knitting projects.[57]

In addition to the NLWS, Wisconsin women worked through the Wisconsin Council of National Defense (WCND). Like other state councils, the WCND was composed primarily of male members, but a Woman's Committee under H. H. Morgan of Madison coordinated work with women's clubs—pro-suffrage and anti-suffrage, service and religious. Where few or no women's groups existed, the Woman's Committee formed new town and village groups. Thus, in northern Wisconsin, the WCND and not the NLWS recruited women into war work. One can imagine the incredible challenge of coordinating this effort. Old rivalries between Milwaukee and Madison emerged. Mariner complained, "How can a small group of Madison women prohibit forming a branch of NLWS in Wisconsin or any other organization[?]" The national group's policy, wisely, was not to interfere.[58]

Despite turf battles, the women were united in their intention to maintain an important role in the home front war. They quarreled with the male-dominated WCND locals over the national requirement that the boards appoint a woman to their councils, that women be allowed to participate in Liberty Loan fund-raising, and that they maintain a separate identity. Eventually the Woman's Committee of the WCND had 2,500 members, mainly in northern Wisconsin.[59]

The Woman's Committee also clashed with men over the formation of a Woman's Land Army. The government drafted fifty thousand Wisconsin farm men out of agricultural work into the military during 1917–18. Like their counterparts in Europe, Canada, and in some parts of the United States, Wisconsin women were prepared to replace male labor in the fields. However, the Council of Defense let each state decide whether or not to organize a Woman's Land Army for this purpose. The men of the WCND controlled this deployment decision, and it was clear they did not support such a group. When the WCND drew up a list of options to replace men in the fields, women were at the bottom, along with Asian immigrant labor. A Boys' Working Reserve was the first choice.[60]

The Woman's Committee was far more enthusiastic about forming a land army. In addition to its potential for organizing women, many middle-class reformers felt field work was healthy for young women. These women were already sending their young daughters to camp to experience the outdoor life they felt necessary for good health. They also knew that housework was the least desirable work to young women and that thousands had turned down wage work on farms to seek jobs in the city. When the men proposed that young farm women return from the city and stay on their farms to work there, one member of the Woman's Committee protested that they would receive no wages if they worked on the home farm. If they replaced men in the city or worked on some other family's farm, they would at least be paid, no matter how little.[61]

Nellie Kedzie Jones accepted chairmanship of the Woman's Land Army in April 1918, and news releases from the Woman's Committee announced that recruiting and training would follow. Women would mainly help in farm kitchens and aid farm women, and although some relocated city women might be trained to harvest wild raspberries in northern Wisconsin, they would not go to work on farms. Kedzie Jones held a home school for teachers at the state fair in September, assembling eighty young women for five days of camping and cooking, lectures on raising cattle, hogs, and cows, and learning how to run tractors. "If women are to be trained to go out upon the land next year," Kedzie Jones reported, "these women can be called upon to assist in recruiting the [Woman's Land Army], and some of them will be competent as leaders." She predicted that farm women would lessen their housework to labor more out of doors, do tasks considered "men's work," use more machinery to make work easier, arrange more convenient barns. "On some farms," she noted, "women will be the only help to be had."[62]

The men prevailed in blocking recruitment of city women to work in the fields, however, and Wisconsin formed no Woman's Land Army. Kedzie Jones and the Woman's Committee did manage to promote home demonstrations and the appointment of agents to present them. When the federal government made special wartime appropriations available, Kedzie Jones became the state demonstration leader, paid by the federal government, and county and state governments shared financing with the federal government to employ county demonstration agents. It was less than Woman's Committee leaders wanted, but more than they had before. They hoped the agents would be permanently funded.[63]

Just as the wartime network was being completed in northern Wisconsin, the armistice was signed and women began to debate what to do with the Woman's Committee and its local units. After the men disbanded the state and local CND committees, all funding stopped. A few women suggested asking the state legislature for money to continue organizing. Others hoped to use the organization to obtain legislation supporting better pay for women workers. Most of the women were exhausted by their efforts, however, and wanted no more than to return to their regular, already overworked lives. An exchange at the December 13, 1918, meeting in Madison summed up women's feelings at the thought of demobilizing. One of the country women said, "I cannot endure the thought of all these women going back to their inactivity and indifference." But, she concluded, "My personal feeling is that I myself wish to go back to my farming and take a rest. I am in favor of demobilizing." Another woman replied, "When I think what it has meant to the country woman to express her views and be part of the community life, it breaks me up to think of telling [her] to go back to pitching hay and scrubbing floors." Another concluded, "The women will never go back. In each county, there must be some women to go on."[64]

Some women did go on. Suffragists returned to their campaign to gain the vote. Wisconsin activists were in the House galleries in Washington to see passage of the Susan B. Anthony amendment. Back in Madison, they lobbied it through the state legislature. Wisconsin was one of the first states to ratify the Nineteenth Amendment in 1919. Wisconsin suffragists sent a thank-you note accompanied by a basket of flowers to each house of the state legislature; then they turned to the tasks of mobilizing women voters, forming a nonpartisan League of Women Voters from the remnants of the suffrage organizations, and supporting candidates who favored reform legislation for women. Wisconsin women now had the vote, but there was little time before the 1920 election to develop a strategy for deploying their new electoral power. Nellie Kedzie Jones planned a two-day short course in Wausau for country women but scheduled it for the day after the election.[65]

In Wausau, on the eve of the first national election with women as full voting citizens, Edith K. Moriarity wrote in the *Record Herald* that women were not likely to punish men for their previous opposition to suffrage. It was amusing, she reflected, to watch the candidates flopping around on the suffrage question. Nearly all the men had been anti-suffragist for the last decade. "Now [that] the women have the vote they can sit back and be amused by the antics of these men who are angling for their support," Moriarity wrote. Women would not be fooled because their organizations had kept records of politicians' actions on suffrage issues. Still, Moriarity gave men some credit for changing their views, even though the shift was "practically forced on them." She felt that women would probably not vote against these "floppers" if they took the right stand on the "live issues of the day."[66]

In order for women to vote in large numbers, they had to be mobilized. Marathon County is the best place to view the complexity of that process. This county had a consistently high voter turnout from 1900 to 1912: 75 percent compared to a national average of 64 percent. In 1916 Republicans strengthened their control over the party by convincing the German majority to abandon Woodrow Wilson for the more isolationist Charles Evans Hughes. By 1918 progressive Republicans were wooing Marathon voters. Socialists also made inroads in the county, garnering a considerable vote among some Germans in 1916 and even more in 1918 when the party opposed the war. While German Catholics generally disagreed with Socialists, German Lutherans were much more supportive of them. Many Germans in Marathon County voted for the jailed Socialist candidate Eugene V. Debs, and they even elected a Socialist to the state assembly. After 1918, Socialist support gradually declined, but in its place Republicanism gained ground. Women's suffrage greatly expanded the number of eligible voters in Marathon County. Democrats, while interested in the women as voters, were not as active in their recruiting efforts as were the Socialists and Republicans. Progressive Republicans, many of them supporters of Senator La Follette and committed to women's suffrage, hoped women would support their reforms.[67]

"Wausau Voters Flock to Polls.... Many Women Voting," the Wausau *Daily Record Herald* announced the day after the election. It is difficult to know how many women voted in Marathon County, but it had the highest total voter turnout of the four north-central counties, indicating that more women voted there than elsewhere. In the city of Wausau women turned out in force, some already waiting in line when the polls opened at 6:00 AM. In some wards women were a majority of the voters; in others they equaled men. One ward reported women were better prepared than men to vote, having less difficulty in marking their ballots. Almost two-thirds of all eligible voters turned out, about the same percentage as with an all-male electorate. The decline of the Democrats' fortunes, already falling in 1916, was impressive. The war had not been popular among German Americans, and Wilson Democrats lost badly. Together, Republican Warren G. Harding and Socialist Eugene Debs won 87 percent of the vote.[68]

About sixty women assembled in Wausau the next day to hear Jessie Hooper, president of the new League of Women Voters, speak at the short course organized by Nellie Kedzie Jones. Most were not from the city but from rural townships. Hooper had emerged into reform politics from a middle-class

Oshkosh family. Her husband was an attorney. She had vigorously supported the establishment of kindergartens and visiting nurse programs, important progressive reforms of the time, before becoming active in women's suffrage organizations. A Democrat by persuasion, she had supported the war and had toured rural areas to rally others, putting her suffrage activism on hold until the end of the war. She returned as a lobbyist during the campaign to gain ratification of the Nineteenth Amendment in the Wisconsin legislature in 1919 and accepted the invitation to serve as head of the nonpartisan Wisconsin League of Women Voters. Hooper advised her listeners to avoid party politics but to endorse legislation that would help women—equal pay, child welfare, education, federal aid to reduce infant and maternal mortality, better health-care facilities in rural areas. Women could not vote directly on these issues, she admitted, but they could vote for candidates who supported them.[69]

Historians have concluded that the nonpartisan political strategy was probably a mistake. Without strong pressure from within parties, candidates soon lost their fear that women would retaliate against unsupportive politicians. Men recruited women into their parties, but only for their votes, not for their advice on issues of concern to women. For a while clubs attempted to enlist women candidates to promote their causes, but for the most part these women found it difficult to gain the support of their male colleagues.

Women's participation in formal political offices in north-central Wisconsin remained meager throughout the 1920s. Their movement into positions as county superintendents of schools continued, as it probably would have without formal suffrage. Emma Lupinsky Miller became the first woman superintendent of schools in Taylor County in 1921. Clark County got its first woman superintendent in 1924, when the state superintendent of schools appointed Margaret van Natta of Neillsville. When she ran for election five years later, she defeated another women for the office. In Withee township, Clark County, Kathryn Handen and Anna Beilfuss Walter ran for trustee on the all-male village board in 1914 and both won, but Withee had a history of supporting women's suffrage in the 1880s, and its Danish immigrant population had a strong tradition of defending equal rights for women. Women were increasingly elected as county clerks, positions previously held only by men. In 1924 Ann Severt handily defeated incumbent August Rusch in the primary and went on to become the first woman county clerk in Lincoln County. Movement into clerkships, like school superintendencies, seemed to occur mainly because women demonstrated their abilities to excel at these jobs and did not threaten traditional male control of political parties.[70]

Women did challenge men for a variety of other elected offices. Local newspapers considered May Pitzke's 1922 candidacy for sheriff of Taylor County a joke, but she campaigned seriously and received a third of the vote. May and

MRS. CHARLES (MAY) PITZKE

MRS. CHAS. PITZKE
CANDIDATE ON INDEPENDENT TICKET
FOR
Sheriff of Taylor County

—

I Believe in Thorough Enforcement of Law
THE COUNTY PAYS ABOUT SO MUCH
FOR LAW ENFORCEMENT. IT COSTS NO
MORE TO GET IT.

—

AUTHORIZED AND PUBLISHED BY
MRS. CHAS. PITZKE

Moonshine   Must   be   Stopped

BEHIND A CAR WHEEL IT IS
A MENACE TO THE PUBLIC.

—

AT THE COUNTRY DANCE
HALLS IT THREATENS THE
MORALS OF OUR YOUNG
PEOPLE

AUTHORIZED AND PUBLISHED BY
MRS. CHAS. PITZKE

Star-News Printers

*Will Have
A Competent Man
Big as Myself
To Act as My
Undersheriff*

Pitzke for sheriff, 1922. This forty-year-old, six-foot-tall Taylor County farm woman promised to "Have a Competent Man Big as Myself to Act as My Undersheriff." Voters did not elect her to the position, but other women established a tradition of holding the office of sheriff in Wisconsin.

Charles Pitzke had farmed since the 1890s and were known for their prize Holstein bulls. May was born in Wisconsin, had raised six children, and was forty years old when she ran as an independent for sheriff. She was six feet tall and weighed more than 250 pounds; she was certainly strong enough to perform a sheriff's duties. She promised to "Have a Competent Man Big as Myself to Act as My Undersheriff." More women were voting, but even in the Medford ward with the highest number of women's votes in 1922, she garnered only 35 percent of the total vote.[71]

Winning public office depended on a complicated maze of local ties, as exemplified by Mildred Barber's successful election from Marathon County to the state legislature in 1925 at age twenty-three. Barber came from an old political family: her grandfather was active in county politics; her father was a popular country doctor and a member of the Wisconsin senate; her mother was a postmistress. Both Mildred and her father were progressive Republicans who had opposed entry into World War I and supported Robert La Follette. There was no Democratic opponent. The county had voted overwhelmingly for La Follette in 1924. Victory made her one of the first three women in the state assembly. The other two were much older, one an Independent.[72]

Barber's tenure was short-lived. She did not run for re-election. As progressivism waned, so too did support for women in public office and for reforms that would give women full political and economic equality. Public, formal power depended on private, informal power, which women were still seeking in their everyday lives.

One alternative existed for women who wished to become active concerning economic issues: joining the breeders' clubs sponsored by extension agents. As dairying grew in Clark and Marathon counties, so too did membership in these clubs. Photographs of members at meetings show that clubs continued the older tradition of mixed groups. Women and children attended meetings and picnics. Groups specialized, becoming buying and marketing clubs or supporters of youth calf clubs or of social events. A 1924 Cherokee Marathon Holstein club photograph shows both men and women, one even holding a baby. About one-quarter of the members of some one hundred breeders' clubs in Marathon County were women. These members helped establish women's presence in a central public organization. Further, women had a chance to hone their leadership abilities in these mixed groups.[73]

Gendering in agricultural groups coexisted with mixed membership in breeders' clubs. Institutes held in 1917 demonstrate how rural organizers mixed and separated women's activities. In the morning men and women listened to talks about agriculture. In the afternoon the groups divided: the men to visit hog pens and discuss manure and pea crop experiments, the women to view a modern equipped house. Nothing could better symbolize women's dual cultures—and their determination to participate in both.[74]

Neither women's nor breeders' clubs were independent and able to shape their own political landscapes. Extension agents had personal agendas, and women were not free to create their own. The extension service expected its agents to keep homemakers' clubs to a practical format that ignored most political issues, whether framed by women's organizations or by radical farm groups. Still, like the Royal Neighbors of America and the American Society of Equity, the women's clubs and breeders' clubs gave women a place to organize

Holstein club, 1924. Women of the Cherokee Holstein Club near Colby worked to eliminate bovine tuberculosis from herds. They sponsored dairy days in Marathon County, symbolizing the importance of dairy cows to the economy and attracting thousands of people.

and to learn organizational skills. Few alternatives were available as the Wisconsin countryside silenced more radical calls for political change.

GIRLS' CLUBS

During the fall and winter of 1923–24, high school principals asked young women in Taylor and Lincoln county high schools if they would like to make their future life on the farm. These students were only a small percentage of the young people between ages fourteen and eighteen and likely to be from wealthier families, for according to the 1920 school census for these counties only ten percent of young people were in high school. Less than 46 percent of the Taylor County group replied that they would like to make their future home on a farm. Of the Lincoln County group, less than 26 percent said yes. The difference reflected the old division between the north and south cutover. The lower tier, to which Taylor County belonged, had made a successful transition to farming. Only a slightly higher percentage of young men than women, 49 compared to 46 percent, saw a farm in their future in Taylor County. In Lincoln County a lower percentage of young men than women, 20 compared to 26 percent, said they envisioned themselves on a farm. While these students wanted to live on farms, far fewer had immediate plans to do so. More than two-thirds wanted to continue their education. Of these, 53 percent planned to take teacher training. Fewer than one percent planned to study agriculture.

Agricultural experts had hoped the future farmers would have specialized education, going on from high school to the university. Yet these high school students were the young people least likely to become farmers: they and their parents considered high school training a path away from farming rather than a preparation for it. Future farmers would come, then, not from this talented tenth that had the possibility of going on to college but from the 90 percent who had attended common school with no plans for more formal education.[75]

Administrators at the agricultural college in Madison knew they would reach only a few of these common-school educated young people through special training programs. Hundreds of young men and a few young women would take short courses in Madison, but most young people would have their main contact through the extension service and the boys' and girls' clubs the agents were organizing with federal funds from the Smith-Lever Act of 1914. By 1920, 87 percent of the nation's three thousand counties had extension agents organizing clubs. By 1925 an estimated five percent of all young country women belonged to these clubs. The ultimate goal of the early clubs, established first in southern states, was to reach adults who had not adopted scientific farming methods, introducing new crops and methods through their children. A second goal was to encourage youth to stay in farming. The girls' clubs, established across the country by agricultural agents during these years, hoped to make rural life more attractive to young women who, in turn, would create the comfortable homes that would keep boys down on the farm. Most programs began with training in such traditional homemaking skills as food preparation, health maintenance, and clothing construction.

As with women's clubs, however, girls' clubs could do more. They could give young women new skills, greater control over their daily lives, and a presence in the public sphere. Same-sex groups could foster gender solidarity and cooperation as well as autonomy, the use of new skills beyond the home, and a way to earn money and to achieve public status through individual prizes. In practice, competition was often with boys as well. Agents usually did not encourage girls to raise calves and pigs, plant corn, and garden crops. Still, some girls gradually moved into livestock clubs as well as specialized clubs for canning and sewing. By all accounts the clubs were popular with young girls and they did well at these tasks, often winning prizes at local and state fairs.[76]

Wisconsin was among the first northern states to organize girls' and boys' clubs. Extension agents claimed that the 43,000 youths participating in club projects ranked the state fifth highest in the country in membership by 1919. What boys and girls did in these clubs was vague in reports. The "Boys' and Girls' Page" of the first issue of the *Marathon County Farm Bureau Journal* bragged about the clubs and mentioned "Girls' Club Work" as canning fruit, canning vegetables, and sewing but did not list calf, corn, pea, and soybeans as particularly for boys. In practice, it seemed to depend on the agent, local farm families, and the persistence of girls and parents to be admitted to other than "girls' clubs." In the four counties, these clubs reached about three thousand youth each year, 25 to 50 percent of them girls, depending on how the male agent organized the groups.[77]

County agents gave varying amounts of time to these youth clubs, but agricultural officials asserted that the clubs were crucial to the country's agricultural health. Ralph V. Brown, agricultural agent for Clark County, put it this way in his annual report to the county supervisors: "The purpose of this work is to interest the children in agriculture and farm life, a vital need when young people are drifting to the city." The overburdened agents tended to turn club organizing over to others, usually to rural women. There was little uniformity in organizing, even within the four counties of this study. In each county, the approach was different.[78]

In Taylor County, agent R. A. Kolb went about the task of organizing youth systematically. At the Taylor County Training School, he instructed teachers that the goal was to have all children develop "a rural mind"—to grasp rural problems and become rural leaders—and that they should enroll every child. After teachers had enrolled the children, he distributed seeds. Youth work had established the potato industry in Taylor County, Kolb later boasted, because he was able to easily introduce new varieties to each family through the children. Young girls also enrolled in gardening, poultry, pig, and canning clubs.[79]

By contrast, in Lincoln County the agent established town agricultural committees and a community office and then hired Florence Dunn as a demonstration agent to coordinate the youth program. Dunn organized some young girls in the more agricultural townships into canning, potato, livestock, and poultry clubs. In the northernmost townships, where agriculture was not well established, she organized hot lunch clubs, which served in twenty-seven of the thirty-six area schools.[80]

"A dairy county covered with silos and silage" was the way agent Ralph V. Brown described Clark when he arrived in the spring of 1918. In Clark County young girls had more involvement in livestock projects. Like some agents in other parts of the country, Brown seems to have segregated boys and girls at first. He mentioned organizing a "Pure Bred Swine Club" for the boys and a "Boys' Livestock Judging Contest." By 1920, however, the new agent, H. M. Knipfel, was organizing calf clubs for both girls and boys. The impetus came from adult Holstein clubs, whose membership included women. While girls remained a minority in these livestock clubs, they are visible in the many calf club photographs where girls proudly lined up with the boys to display their calves. The agent also organized an encampment for club members at the county fair. The county board of supervisors soon appropriated three thousand dollars for the budding farmers, building a barn and dormitory with a kitchen and dining room and separate sleeping quarters for boys and girls. Almost two hundred youth attended these encampments, two-thirds of them girls. Overall, young women comprised 43 percent of the club membership by 1925.[81]

In Marathon County, the first of the four counties to have its own home demonstration agent and homemakers clubs, young girls were less visible in the livestock clubs. About one-quarter of members were in calf clubs—at Cherokee almost a third—but in most townships there was a heavy emphasis on sewing, canning, and hot lunch clubs for girls. Almost half of all clubs were devoted to these projects, and sewing and canning clubs were particularly successful. Girls were also active and excelled in the gardening clubs.

There was no assurance, of course, that club work would keep girls wanting to farm, but it could be a boost to their interest, skills, and involvement in farming. Purebred cattle and certified seed allowed young women as well as young men to introduce parents to new types of livestock and crops. Special projects gave them a sense of shared interest with neighbors and an opportunity for interaction with peers outside the classroom. Club activities gave young women a sense of what it might be like to succeed at farming.

Champion heifer, 1924. This unidentified young woman at the Clark County Fair displayed her heifer and ribbons. By the 1920s adult women numbered a third of the members of livestock clubs and young women 43 percent of the membership of the county's boys and girls clubs.

Awards offered not only community recognition—especially when young women won them at the state as well as at the local and county levels—but also a chance to make money and to take trips. Some girls made $35 to $50 with their garden produce, far more if they sold their award-winning calves. It is difficult not to feel the pride of Hulda Henze of Clark County, for example, as she showed her champion calf at the county fair roundup in 1924 or the delight of the unnamed young woman from Neillsville, her dress beribboned with prizes, showing her grand champion heifer in 1922. Or to wonder how Mildred Frieke, sixteen, felt when she won best club member for Wisconsin for her four projects. Her Montgomery Ward prize paid for a trip to Chicago to attend the International Live Stock Show. Or to smile at the image of Lucy Becker in her cornfield, the stalks towering above, the year she won a trip for being the best garden club girl in the state. Already a veteran gardener and prize winner, she took twelve first prizes at the 1919 county fair when she was in the seventh grade.[82]

We cannot know if the clubs succeeded in keeping young women down on the farm. Surely competitions, praise, tangible rewards in money and travel, the experience of organizing clubs and events made life more interesting for rural girls. And all these activities are known to help make women into leaders in their communities, whether they stay or move on to the city.

Native Women in Two Worlds
Mary Ann's Story [Paquette Barnes, born in Wisconsin, 1870–1929]

In September 1896, Mary Ann Paquette, twenty-five and single, began her first day as assistant matron at the Lac du Flambeau boarding school. All her life, people had emphasized to Mary Ann that her Indian background was a disability. Now, perhaps for the first time, it would be an advantage: the Indian Bureau was hiring Native American women for higher positions of responsibility.

Except for Native policemen, the Office of Indian Affairs had hired Euro-Americans almost exclusively in the 1870s and 1880s. Native police handled ordinary law enforcement while the regular army acted as a back-up force in case the police could not, or would not, deal with resistance to government policies. Native police served as intermediaries between the alien system and Native ways of enforcing conformity to community norms. They often depended on traditional ways of mediating conflict, and in a number of places they were drawn from Bear Clans, traditional keepers of the peace. Employing Native women, except as teachers in small day schools or as laundry women, was new. Hiring Native women as field matrons, boarding school matrons, and teachers was part of an attempt to "Indianize" the bureaucracy. By 1895 at least twenty-eight women of Native heritage were assistant matrons and twenty-eight were teachers on reservations.[83]

The superintendent of Indian schools enthusiastically supported this policy, even establishing teacher training courses at Carlisle, Hampton, Haskell, and Santa Fe. He felt a responsibility to introduce Native young people to "a corps of responsible workers," to offer them a chance at "full self-emancipation." He even objected to discrimination in salaries, something he termed a "serious error." Like Mary Ann, these new employees were often of mixed or Métis heritage.[84]

The process of hiring Native women and men was well under way at Lac du Flambeau when Mary Ann arrived. By 1895 one-quarter of the school employees were Indian. The agent hired Native women in 1896 as assistant teacher, assistant matron, and nurse. The agency had already engaged Mary's brother Peter Paquette as an industrial teacher, and he was now farmer for the school. He would later serve as acting superintendent of the Lac du Flambeau boarding school. Brother and sister seemed well qualified for their respective tasks. For the next twelve years, Mary Ann worked at Lac du Flambeau, beginning as assistant matron and after two years achieving the rank of matron. When Mary Ann became matron, she was one of seven Native Americans who served at the reservation. By 1900, matron, assistant matron, nurse, and girls' teachers were all Native women. Almost half of all employees, twenty-five of fifty-eight, were now Native people. For the next decade Mary Ann looked after her charges "like a mother hen," as one commentator said. Mary Ann was not only an excellent matron by Indian Bureau standards but also much loved by the Chippewa children in her care.

Mary Ann was from a well-known Ho-Chunk/French Metís family. Her lineage was impressive, leading back to Ho A Me No Kau, daughter of Chief White Crow of the Rock River band, who had married into the Paquette Catholic French trader family. According to historical accounts, Ho A Me No Kau was more than six feet tall, handsome, hospitable, generous, and kind—in short, a model Ho-Chunk woman. Therese Crelie, a Ho-Chunk/French woman, had married Ho A Me No Kau's son Pierre Paquette. Pierre was successively a fur trader, an agent of the American Fur Company in Portage, and an interpreter for both government officials and missionaries who visited the Ho-Chunk. Their son, Moses Paquette, also served as a government interpreter for many years. Mary Ann and Peter were Therese and Pierre's grandchildren. Their parents, Madeleine Lariviere and Moses Paquette, moved to Jackson County in 1879. Mary Ann was nine when she arrived in Portage and attended public school there.[85]

Mary Ann's older brother preceded her in government employ and may have helped her get the Lac du Flambeau job. But her family name would have been well known to the government official who did the hiring: Mary Ann and Peter would be the third generation of Paquettes to work for the American government.[86]

What seemed like promising careers for Mary Ann and Peter soon faltered. By the turn of the century, the Indian Bureau had reversed its policy of recruiting able Native women to be head teachers, nurses, and matrons and was refusing to appoint Native men as supervisors of schools. Scholars believe the change in policy came with the appointment of Estelle Reel as superintendent of Indian schools. She encouraged the hiring of white women as teachers and white men as superintendents. At Lac du Flambeau the list of Native employees shortened. Mary Ann held on to her job as matron, but by 1903 only an assistant cook and a woman who taught beading and basket making were also of Native heritage. The teacher was soon fired. In 1908 Mary Ann was still matron, but she had a white assistant. By 1912 the only Native employees were policemen and a woman interpreter.

While both Mary Ann and Peter retained their jobs, they were as anxious to move up in the bureaucratic ladder as were competent white employees. Peter excelled as farmer and teacher. He was responsible for developing successful agricultural training during the late nineteenth and early twentieth century, at a crucial time—the transition from lumbering to farming. He served as acting superintendent during a particularly bad period when the white superintendent was replaced for incompetence. He received $1,200 a year and ran the school as effectively as he had managed the agricultural educational program and the school farm. He consistently received excellent ratings. Instead of appointing him permanent superintendent, however, the Indian Bureau brought in a new white superintendent and reassigned Peter as farmer. Peter continued to be ranked as excellent by his supervisors, who even noted in his file that he would make a good superintendent. Finally, in 1903 the government offered him a position as principal of Navajo schools at Fort Defiance in Arizona, an isolated southwestern area not popular with white employees. Peter took the job. When he left for the distant Navajo Nation in New Mexico Territory in 1903, he was replaced by a white farmer. By 1908 Mary Ann was the only Native in a supervisory position at Lac du Flambeau.

Mary Ann, too, became discouraged with the changing policies in Wisconsin. After twelve years, her brother as well as all of the other Native employees formerly in supervisory and teaching positions were gone. Despite her success with the Chippewa, she must have felt alone. In 1908 she applied for transfer to the Ho-Chunk agency, explaining to the agent that she wanted "to work with my people." The agent, in turn, said he would not appoint her because it was the practice *not* to send people to work with their own tribes. The Indian Bureau would not allow her to transfer to the Ho-Chunk reservation, but it did offer to send her to the Navajo Nation to work with her brother. Mary Ann resigned her position as matron at Lac du Flambeau in June 1908 and assumed her duties as matron of the Fort Defiance Navajo Indian School in Arizona. The following month, the new commissioner of Indian affairs, Francis Leupp, named Peter as commissioner to the southwestern Navajo people. Mary Ann married trader Burris Barnes in 1913 but had no children and continued to serve as matron at Fort Defiance school until her death in 1929. Peter stayed on as commissioner for another ten years, until his death in 1939.[87]

Mary Ann's tenure in Wisconsin marked the retreat of the government from policies that might have given Native people more control over their own communities. She was allowed to work with Native people, but not her own Ho-Chunk. She chose to operate within the system, however imperfect, and to find a permanent place to use her skills. Her obituary described her as "kindly, and sympathetic, bright of mind and ambitious for the advancement of her youthful wards." As much as she could, she helped the children of other Native peoples work for academic achievement. She was one of a very small group of Native women working within the system, pushing at it where she could to give Native children room to grow and flourish there. That was no small accomplishment.[88]

WORKING AGAINST THE INDIAN BUREAU

For Native people, to work for the Indian Bureau meant to compromise, to enforce rules upon a community that opposed and often resisted them. From the outside, it is easy to see how rights reserved for settlers were routinely and flagrantly denied to Native peoples by the Indian Bureau and how Native peoples resisted these infringements. The Indian Bureau routinely, and increasingly, violated parental, economic, religious, and social rights. Parents resisted these violations at every level, from a Menominee grandmother brandishing an iron skillet against police who came to take her grandchildren, to the demands of Menominee mothers that a particular Catholic nun be removed for not treating them with courtesy and humanity, to the insistence that an Indian Bureau employee be removed at Lac du Flambeau for using excessive violence in punishing children. No representative of the government, secular or religious, went unchallenged when insisting on absolute control over children.

Women also maintained their right to use skills as they saw fit. They continued to expand their gardens and to retain a role in farming, although the government increasingly insisted that they relinquish field crops to men and confine their work to the household. They insisted on their right to gather, using whatever access they could obtain to sugaring and ricing areas as well as to berries, ginseng, and other seasonal products. Wherever they could, they arranged with settler families for access to older gathering areas. They also created and traded handcrafts despite lack of interest and support by the government. By continuing to support a subsistence economy, they ensured that some measure of economic independence was maintained for most of the people. Through their role in preserving, processing, and distributing food, they reinforced this subsistence economy.

Native women expanded the religions they practiced and taught their children. Whatever form they embraced, women adapted it to resist the imposition of foreign culture, to protect families, and to reinforce community cooperation in caring for each family. Feasts were the most visible way in which they fostered this sense of community, but through many less obvious means they encouraged women and men to perpetuate communal values, often at odds with the government's teachings that individuals should look after only themselves and their families.

Meanwhile, women continued to claim the right to control social relations within reservation communities. Despite government efforts to enforce lifetime monogamy, women made their own choices of husbands and domestic partners. The practice of young Ojibwe women climbing out of dormitory windows to meet male friends may not have persisted, but young women claimed the right to be assertive in sexual matters and to make their own domestic arrangements. Priests noted that Catholics seemed most interested in the sacrament of baptism and the practice of choosing godparents, which converts believed would help protect their children, and often ignored regulations the church had established to control the private activities of adults. Whether by direct action, petition, or mobilizing family, kin, and community opinion, women brought their influence to bear on public policy within the reserva-

tions. Women's determination to live in two worlds, to maintain and transform their cultures, can be found in photographs. Women at Lac du Flambeau
arranged public secular dances in which gifting continued to be practiced.
Menominee women organized during World War I to display support for
their men who served in the U.S. military.

Underlying the women's activities were beliefs in the sovereignty of Native
land and culture. Sovereignty, the right to collective control of a community,
resided in the people. Many tribes use the term *nation* to indicate that they
exist as separate entities and not as creations of the U.S. government. These
nations signed a variety of treaties granting certain concessions of land or law
to the United States while retaining particular rights and privileges for themselves. Thus, a citizen of a Native nation had certain rights that Euro-American
settlers did not. Native nations always defended these treaty rights. As members of Native communities, women had certain rights guaranteed by their
treaties. Not only did they have an individual right to land and to annuities,
many also claimed that treaties gave them gathering rights on traditional
lands. Women both were a part of this collective community and held a separate role within it.

The U.S. government often discriminated against women. For example,
when the government allotted land under the Dawes Act, it frequently assigned
married women half as much as married men. Native women often insisted
on their rights as women and as mothers. Tampering with tribal customs

*Menominee women, 1917. Women organized formally as a relief corps in support of World
War I. Menominee men volunteered for this war as they had in previous conflicts; their Civil
War Veterans Post was still active in the late nineteenth century.*

without working out a new system that treated women fairly led to endless disputes among complex families. Tribes differed in their internal gender relations. Customs within Euro-American communities also varied depending on state laws and changes in the national laws as women influenced them to protect their rights. One can understand why it was so difficult to negotiate power in these many political worlds. Most Menominee women clearly opposed allotment of land, as did most of the men. They wanted the land to be passed on to their children collectively. At Lac du Flambeau, where the tribe was unsuccessful in retaining its land intact, women and men increased their efforts to maintain gathering rights, especially to rice beds. Some protested when the government insisted that a woman who married a white man be deprived of her right and the right of her children to annuities.[89]

Among the Ho-Chunk, who had no guaranteed reservation land in Wisconsin, single women and married women who headed households filed for homesteads. In 1882 and 1883, individual women homesteaded 54 to 160 acres of land, most of it isolated and scattered, swampy and stony, insufficient for making a living. Because it took eighty acres and twenty milk cows to sustain a family of five and because the government refused to fund farm enterprises, Ho-Chunk women depended heavily on their handwork to support their families. Some mothers also insisted that the Indian Bureau help them obtain money from men who received annuities or money from land sales as married men but failed to share in support of their children.[90]

PLACES OF MEMORY AND POWER

Most sites of Native women's cultural preservation remain marked by memory alone. Family homes were significant places for preserving Native cultures often banned from public display. Large, permanent homes had more space for cultural gatherings and for storage of cultural artifacts. There women transmitted culture orally and through practice. They maintained and arranged kinship networks out of their homes, reinforcing them with material and spiritual gifts of support. They created their art work, especially beadwork and weaving, to transmit messages about their cultures. In these ways the women translated, taught, and made visible their cultures. They helped maintain small secluded areas for communal dances, both sacred and secular, even when banned by the Indian Bureau. These dances, the circles within which they took place, and the food shared there in feasts knit people together into communities.

A few places of memory have been preserved outside the reservation. Villages in Marathon and Taylor counties and on the border of Lincoln County are the best-known examples. There women and men from different tribes joined in new communities where they claimed the right to live as free citizens but to maintain their Native cultures. These villages were important because they were rare examples of what might have been: the coming together of people from many Native cultures to create a new community. A few families continued to inhabit McCord village in Oneida County until it was abandoned in the 1940s, but it lived on in the memories of those who had cherished that heritage. Today it is designated by the U.S. government as a "historic site" of special importance to American and Wisconsin history.[91]

Earlier, Métis had been able to live within communities like Green Bay and command respect from a mixed population. Many of the old families, such as the Dousmans and the Paquettes, continued to retain a singular place in local cultures, but the pressure to "pass" as people without a special heritage and place became so strong in the late nineteenth and early twentieth centuries that some Native people simply severed all visible public relationship to their communities, even if they maintained enrollment in a particular tribe. As time went on, some of their children also hid that connection, choosing to keep quiet about their heritage, to emulate settlers, to be defined simply as "citizens." Native women would have shared white women's limited rights and suffered the additional restrictions often imposed on those who appeared not to be of Euro-American heritage. Some of these women live among us still—sometimes even as relatives—fearing the prejudice toward Indigenous people that continues to exist in many communities in Wisconsin and Minnesota.[92]

In urban areas traditions persisted of old Métis families whose children had moved to the cities and prospered after the end of the fur trade. The William Borup family is one example. When Charles Borup, a Danish immigrant who was successively fur trader, lumberman, and banker, died in St. Paul in 1859, he was reputedly the wealthiest man in town. That made his wife, Elizabeth Borup Beaulieu, descendant of a Chippewa woman and a French Canadian fur trapper, the city's wealthiest woman. The Borups had founded their fortune by furnishing supplies to the Chippewa. Their children, including Virginia Borup, who married Irish immigrant Richards Gordon the year after her father died, helped continue the dynasty. Gordon started in the Borup firm and then founded his own successful hat and fur company in 1871. He landed a government contract for buffalo coats soon after and then popularized mink coats for civilian men. In 1886 Gordon took Paul D. Ferguson as a partner but remained in control of the company until the day he died in January 1911. His mixed-heritage son Charles took over and Gordon and Ferguson made another fortune manufacturing uniforms for the French, English, and American governments during World War I. While the family may have treasured its heritage privately, it made no public mention of it. Like a number of other mixed-heritage families, its members simply became one part of the ethnic mix in midwestern cities.[93]

Important Indian rights organizations did have a public presence in the Twin Cities. These groups brought together activists to work on various issues.

Although a photograph from the 1920s shows only male Indians demonstrating before St. Paul's city hall in traditional dress, we know that women belonged to branches of the Society of American Indians, which campaigned to eliminate the Indian Bureau's control over Native people's lives. Tracing these urban Native people is difficult. Social service agencies and the federal government counted them, but they counted so poorly that numbers depend on the time of year and how the counting was done. Estimates of the number of Native people in the Twin Cities vary. Possibly six hundred lived in the Twin Cities by the late 1920s. Social workers reported in that decade that Native people fared well and that they adapted well to urban life. We know that rights activist Alice Mary Peake Beaulieu, for example, was born in Minneapolis in 1920.[94]

Formal legal authorization of women's rights came slowly. About half of all Indians were citizens by 1917, and all received formal national citizenship by 1924. Even men were often denied their political rights by state and local governments, however, and not all tribal governments recognized women's civil rights and liberties. Like Euro-American women, Indian women continued to work publicly and privately for full formal citizenship rights. Indian women, however, had to negotiate these rights as citizens both of the United States and of their respective Indian nations.[95]

Regardless of formal structures, women maintained their political involvement in the lives of their communities. Tribal sovereignty, cultural preservation, and control of Native lands and natural resources were all a part of their political concerns. Resistance to policies of federal domination was supported by women, most visibly by elders who insisted that communities had an obligation to preserve these rights for future generations. Women also firmly believed in their essential role in domestic politics. In a study of contemporary Native women leaders, Diane-Michele Prindeville noted that they practiced politics in a way that offered important examples of how women worked for full participation in society. They did so not only by claiming the same rights as men in resisting infringements on their national sovereignty but also by supporting a broad concept of political activity. They worked for a more inclusive political identity that made care giving a political virtue and expanded the notion of civic service. This dual focus gave strength to the politics of settler women as well. Such strategies for power over political landscapes left an important heritage for women and for the men who supported their community ideals.

III

Making a New Home

9

Migration Stories

Matilda's experience during the years she scrimped to raise her children convinced her that there was no future for most of them in farming. The farm would go to the oldest son, Frank. The forty-acre farm was too small to divide; nearby farmland too expensive to buy. Even with a small dairy, the farm would provide Frank with a bare subsistence. He developed a blacksmith business on the side and would later bootleg liquor during Prohibition to feed his family. The youngest son would have to fend for himself. He tried working in Chicago one summer, came home and served as a day laborer on others' farms, and then was employed as a farmer for the state-run asylum in Owen. He moved west to Oregon, where he worked as a fisherman.

Perhaps the most important lesson Matilda passed on to her six daughters was the expectation of migration. Matilda taught them they would have to go elsewhere to find a new life. They grew up knowing that they would move away because there was no way for them to be supported by the land. Matilda did not demand financial help from her daughters once they left. She expected to stay on the farm for the rest of her life, but her daughters would have to support themselves. Matilda's oldest daughter, who had gone to Canada to farm, brought home stories of a similarly hard life there. The remaining five daughters looked to the cities for employment.

From talking to my relatives, I found that going to the city was a common event in the lives of many farm daughters. The daughters of the nearby Jantsch family had similar migration patterns: they, too, lived and worked in the Twin Cities between 1905 and 1925. The farms of Maria Jantsch and Matilda stood on opposite sides of the country road—dusty in summer, mucky in spring, deep with snow in winter. Between 1879 and 1908, Matilda and Maria birthed seventeen children, ten of them daughters. Maria, the elder of the two, was a midwife who helped Matilda, not only in childbirth but also as she raised her eight children. Their husbands frequently worked away from the farms to bring in cash. All but the two oldest daughters eventually left for the city.

From north-central Wisconsin, these farm daughters could strike out for either of two metropolitan areas, Milwaukee to the southeast or the Twin Cities of St. Paul and Minneapolis to the west. Both urban areas expanded rapidly in the first three decades of the century. Milwaukee grew in population from 285,000 in 1900 to almost 374,000 by 1910. By 1920 it would reach 457,000. The city boasted a burgeoning industrial base, everything from its already

NOTICE
TO YOUNG WOMEN AND GIRLS

Do not go to the large cities for work unless you are compelled to. If you must go, write at least two weeks in advance to the Woman's Department, Bureau of Labor, St. Paul, or to the Young Women's Christian Association in the city where you want to work.

They will obtain for you such a position as you ask; tell you about wages, boarding places and whatever you want to know.

Two days before you leave home, write again and tell the day and hour when your train will arrive and a responsible woman will meet you at the station and take you safely to your destination.

Do not ask questions of strangers nor take advice from them.

Ask a uniformed railway official or a policeman.

This advice is issued by the State Bureau of Labor and posted through the courtesy of the Railway Officials of this road.

Mrs. Perry Starkweather,
Assistant Commissioner
Woman's Dept.

W. E. McEWEN,
Commissioner of Labor,
STATE CAPITOL, ST. PAUL

"Do not go to the large cities . . ." 1910. The Minnesota Bureau of Labor warned young women not to come to the Twin Cities to work. Thousands left rural Wisconsin anyway, claimed responsibility for their lives at and outside of work, and remembered the good times they had as working women.

famous brewing industry to smaller factories specializing in food processing. In 1916 one of my aunts quickly found a job in a Milwaukee candy factory. Within a few years she had a white-collar job working for the telephone company. Two other sisters followed her there to work. Most of the daughters, however, chose the Twin Cities, helping to swell their population, which grew from almost 366,000 in 1900 to 519,000 in 1910 and 615,000 in 1920. The Jantsch daughters worked in Minneapolis, which had a substantial industrial base. My mother and her sister went to St. Paul, the smaller of the Twin Cities, which had a thriving commercial sector.[1]

The Twin Cities were a logical choice for the daughters of both families, as they were for many daughters on neighboring farms in north-central Wisconsin. While Milwaukee offered assorted industrial opportunities, the Twin Cities were closer geographically and had a booming mercantile sector as well as industry. Northern Wisconsin was part of a huge rural hinterland that supplied labor, mining and agricultural products, and markets for the Twin Cities. That hinterland spread north into Canada and west to the Pacific. No other large urban areas existed between the Twin Cities and Seattle. Dorchester was

The Jantsch sisters: left to right, Hattie, Mary, Emma, Anna, Rose, 1920. Women from the Jantsch family, who lived across the road from the Schopper-Schopp sisters, led the neighborhood exodus to obtain city work.

fewer than 150 miles from the Twin Cities, and trains ran regularly between the two places. The inexpensive rail trip, which allowed for visits home, seemed simple compared to the long voyages their parents had made across the Atlantic Ocean from Europe. Migration was what a daughter did to find new opportunities.

The Twin Cities did not always welcome or encourage these country daughters. "Do not go to the large cities for work unless you are compelled to" read one "Notice to Young Women and Girls" published by Minnesota's Department of Labor and Industry. In 1910 Mary L. Starkweather, head of the agency's woman's department, asked stationmasters to post these notices in every train depot in Minnesota. Of course, the Dorchester daughters ignored her warnings. Like other young people, they felt compelled to seek work in the cities. They poured into the Twin Cities from Minnesota's small towns. They came out of Wisconsin.[2]

Single country women were the majority of workers migrating to cities by 1910. There was a direct relationship between the closing of settlement opportunities in northern Wisconsin's woodlands and farmlands and the migration by daughters to cities. Yet these daughters remain almost invisible in historical accounts. Often portrayed as victims of the city, as indeed Starkweather expected them to be, they were instead resourceful young women who carved out new lives based on the choice to leave rural places and the determination to live independently.[3]

The Schopper-Schopp sisters and friends, 1910. Despite their poverty, evidenced by the log house, daughters learned to sew attire appropriate for young working women, including hats. In the front row, Mary Schopper is third from the left and Theresa Schopper is fourth from the right.

The stories of the Jantsch daughters frame the experiences of thousands of other young women, many of them from Wisconsin, who flooded into the Twin Cities in the early twentieth century, primarily to find work but also to enjoy the city itself and the fun it offered young women released from hard labor on farms into the independent life of wage work.

Moving On
The Stories of Anna, Rose, Emma, and Hattie [Jantsch, born in Wisconsin, 1887–1982; Jantsch Kumhera, born in Wisconsin, 1891–1983; Jantsch Gustafson, born in Wisconsin, 1889–1988; Jantsch Pilgrim, born in Wisconsin, 1877–1985]

Anna was the most sociable and the most adventuresome of the Jantsch daughters. She never married or had children but worked her entire life, even shaving a few of those many years off her employment records to continue to work longer. Anna was remembered in family histories not only for a lively personality but also for gifts to younger siblings and the care she took of her parents. After her parents moved into the town of Dorchester in 1920, Anna took turns with the youngest daughter, Hattie, caring for them when they became ill and in the last years of their lives. She developed close relationships with nephews and nieces and visited as families scattered to North Dakota and Washington. Brother Joseph Jantsch wrote of Anna and her sisters with great respect and appreciation, calling them "The Five Fold Blessings," who proved their worth over and over again through the years. In the Jantsch family, he wrote, "it was the girls who brought the greatest blessings to their parents and to their brothers."[4]

Anna worked in Minneapolis from at least 1910 until 1920. During most of these years, she lived with one or another of her younger sisters, Rose and Emma, who followed her to the Twin Cities. Rose and Emma were remembered by their family as being very close—they were only two years apart in age—but very different in temperament. Rose was a "hustler," always finishing her chores before taking up a book to read. Emma also loved to read and recited long poems, but she was calm, controlled, optimistic, philosophical. While their eldest sister Mary led the exodus from the farm, she ventured no farther than Chippewa Falls. Anna, Rose, and Emma were more daring. They continued to move westward.

Anna was the first to search for work in the Twin Cities. Once established, she offered each sister a place to live, helped her find a job, and introduced her to city adventures as she made the transition to the big city. Usually Anna lived with one or more of her sisters and when jobs were not satisfactory assured them it was all right to exaggerate their experience to find something better. In short, she looked after her younger sisters.

Finding a place to live was one of the Dorchester sisters' first concerns. Almost every year that the Jantsches are listed in the city directory, they resided at a different address. In 1910 Anna and Emma were at 1120 Chestnut; in 1911 and 1912 Anna, Emma, and Rose stayed at 212 Ninth Street; the following year they were at 1305 Second Avenue South. In 1914 only Rose is listed at 103 East Fifteenth Street, but in 1915 Anna, Emma, and Rose are all living there as well. Except for the 1910 and 1918 addresses, which were flats, all of these dwellings were single-family homes. In 1916 Anna, Emma, Rose, and their brother William moved into a large house at 1605 Second Avenue South. William, a younger brother, had just joined them and found a job as a helper at Dayton's Department Store. The four siblings pooled their incomes and rented a large house in a relatively affluent neighborhood. The *Minneapolis Blue Book*, which claimed to contain "the best families," listed neighbors at 1600 and 1610 Second Avenue. The house sat solidly on an ample lot on a tree-shaded street. It was situated close to a neighboring house on the left and had a large yard on the right with tall shade trees. Its two stories would have allowed the Jantsches to occupy the downstairs while boarders lived upstairs. It had comfortable front porches, high bay windows on both stories, four gables with a garret. The boarding house scheme did not work out, and Anna, her sisters, and brother moved in

1917, but for that one year we have a clear image of where they lived. Family snapshots also show Anna and her sisters together, as they often were in their time away from work.

Moving continued the next year when their younger sister Hattie joined them in another rented house at 510 Northeast Second. The *Blue Book* listed no families near this house. That summer the Jantsches broke up housekeeping and scattered. Hattie kept her clerking job at Mary Morris grocery store, and Rose stayed in the city because she planned to marry soon. Anna, Emma, and William went off on an adventure. The three pooled their savings to buy a Kissel Kar for $550 and made a harrowing trip to Dorchester in early June.

Dorchester was still home for Anna and the other Jantsch sisters. When they talked of going home it was to Dorchester, where the family gathered in summer and where they relaxed, going to the neighborhood dance hall, renewing acquaintances with schoolmates and neighbors. That summer William left for the army. When Anna returned to the city in fall she was listed living alone at a flat on Fifteenth Street. Hattie soon joined her there and later that year they moved to 1410 Stevens Avenue. In January 1920 when the census was taken Anna, Emma, and Hattie were all listed as boarders, renting along with two others, a married couple.

As a seamstress, Anna had the best-paid and most stable job of all the Jantsch women who worked in Minneapolis. She had learned her trade while in Chippewa Falls and always found sewing skills to be in demand. Seamstresses usually did not make a great deal of money. The industrial survey of 1918 in studying 521 seamstresses and sewers found that 61 percent received a "mere subsistence wage," between ten and fourteen dollars a week. Yet that classification placed seamstresses in the third-highest wage-earning group of women in Minneapolis, after professional and clerical workers.

Being a seamstress had been a profitable middle-class occupation for many women in the nineteenth century. While it is also true that thousands of sewing women slaved in tenement sweatshops, a middle-class woman with skill in constructing fashionable garments could support herself and her family decently. It was a favorite occupation for widows who were able to develop the skills to perform it well. The hours were long and the work usually seasonal, but once established in a community a seamstress could live comfortably and respectably. Nineteenth-century department stores paid less well but offered employment to thousands of women because many of their products were manufactured on their upper floors. After the turn of the century, the market for hand-crafted garments narrowed as women's ready-made clothing became more available. Clothing factories still hired hand finishers—usually older women, often widowed—but paid them less than power-machine operators.[5]

By 1910 many Twin Cities sewing women worked in large department stores doing alterations. Such employment could be very difficult because of busy seasons and Saturday work. When the Minnesota Department of Labor began to enforce shorter Saturday work hours in department stores in 1911, the most grateful workers were the women in alterations. One of the field inspectors reported that women might have as many as fifteen rushed pinnings and fittings on a Saturday and then be asked to stay that night to help with sewing or sales without extra pay. These conditions, the inspector reported, existed at nearly all the tailoring establishments and men's clothing stores. The busy season played havoc with legislation that attempted to limit women's workweek to fifty-four hours. So, too, did the classification of work. Making garments in factories or tailor shops clearly came under the law, but alterations did not. When fitting, sewing, and sales mixed, the work during busy seasons was exhausting. Wages for these sewing women remained low. In 1915 Donaldson's paid three women $6, $7, and $9 per week for cloak alterations and four women $8 to $10 for regular alterations, among the store's lowest wages. One woman, probably head of the alterations department, made $12 a week.[6]

Dressmakers, 1910s. Apprenticing to a town dressmaker, as country daughter Anna Jantsch did, could ensure better wages in cities as well. All small towns needed dressmakers, even after ready-made clothing became available. Special-order wedding gowns and alterations as well as upholstering provided continuing demand for women with expert sewing skills. The work was tedious, sometimes boring, and always hard on the eyes.

Anna avoided these harried department-store jobs. She tried to find positions in such places as retail furniture stores, where sewing skills were still needed for custom work. The 1918 industrial survey found her working for Moore & Scriver, a retail furniture and rug store on Nicollet Avenue, along with eight other women and twenty-one men. The women worked 8.5 hours a day, 50.5 hours a week in the winter and 46.5 in the summer, at weekly pay ranging from $30 for forty-two-year-old Variluah Starr, who kept the books, to $10 for Mary Addison, "colored," who dusted. Twenty-four-year-old Norwegian-born Anna Hove made $15 a week as forewoman. All the seamstresses—Anna Jantsch and the thirty-year-old upholsterer Jessie Keith, each paid $13 a week, and three others who made between $12.00 and $12.50—received wages that placed them in the "mere subsistence" category. Yet seamstresses still considered themselves well-off. Anna did. Her skills allowed her to obtain work easily in Minneapolis and later in San Francisco.[7]

Rose and Emma found jobs at a number of places while in Minneapolis, but they spoke most often to their children about working at Donaldson's department store as clerks, a common occupation for women who sought city work. Rose worked at Donaldson's in 1912 and 1914 and perhaps other years as well. Emma worked there in 1914, 1915, and 1917. Looking at Donaldson's during the years from 1912 to 1920 is a good way to understand what work was like not only for Rose and Emma but also for other country daughters employed at a large number of retail mercantile stores during this time.

When the Jantsch sisters arrived in Minneapolis, Donaldson's was a department store known for the spectacular building it occupied, the Glass Block. The Donaldsons had at first rented the original Glass Block, built in 1880, but they enjoyed such success that they bought the entire building and in 1884 replaced it with a six-story domed structure. Rose and Emma, who had grown up in a log house and had known mainly small, two-story mercantile stores, would have been impressed with the Glass Block. When they told others where they worked, all would have had an image of the huge windowed store on the corner of Sixth and Nicollet; it dominated the city's retail mercantile area.[8]

Donaldson's was organized in 1882 by two Scottish immigrants, brothers William T. and Lawrence S. Donaldson. After William died in 1899, Lawrence changed the store's name to L. S. Donaldson Company and shaped the treatment of his predominantly female work force until he died in 1924. Donaldson's became known for its paternalistic policies. The store provided inexpensive housing for single women at Donaldson Hall, hired a social worker to advise on workers' welfare, sponsored dinners for employees, assembled a marching band that played regular concerts at the store, and opened a voluntary training school. Donaldson even toyed with the idea of awarding company stock to long-term employees. But he also hired an undercover detective to watch women in the vicinity of the washroom to see if they were stealing display items. The company also delayed for three years implementing a 1911 state law limiting women's work to nine hours per day, six days per week, and led the fight to repeal the minimum-wage law passed in 1913.[9]

In 1914, when Donaldson finally complied with the maximum-hour law for women, Rose Jantsch was among the employees who presented the company a leather-embossed book of signatures in appreciation for its action. The shorter hours, they said, were an innovation that would "conduce so materially to the comfort and happiness of the people who are employed in the large stores of our city." Other stores followed suit the next year.[10]

Department-store jobs were steady, readily available, and easy compared to farm work, even if the hours were long. They offered opportunities to transfer to other departments if work in one place was not satisfactory. Rose sold handkerchiefs and then worked behind a lunch counter and, later, in the bakery. Selling and serving in these large stores allowed young women to observe urban middle-class attire and manners and yet enjoy the camaraderie of working with country women just like themselves.[11]

On the other hand, employees complained about low wages. Though the pay was better than for domestic and other service work and many manufacturing jobs, it remained too low to live on, even by working-class standards. While Donaldson grudgingly implemented the 1911 maximum-hour law, he flatly refused to obey the 1913 state minimum-wage law. He did, however, ask 131 of his employees living apart from their parents, including Emma Jantsch, if they were "earning enough to have anything over after paying ordinary expenses . . . to lay away anything by for emergencies."

About one-fourth of the women said they could save; among them was Emma, who was making only $7 a week but keeping house with her sisters. Other women who also answered "yes" had jobs paying $12 to $18 per week. Their words hint at how hard it was: "a little," "occasionally," "a little, sometimes," "a small amount," "very little if not living with a sister." A few explained how they were able to save: with steady employment, with residence at the company's hall, and by strict economy. One was able to buy insurance, another to buy a building.

More than 75 percent, however, answered emphatically that they could save nothing. Louise, who made $8 a week, retorted, "No, not a cent." Some explained why. A few were supporting children or parents. Others wrote, "Takes it all to pay expenses" and "All goes for the upkeep of the house." Evelyn, who made only $7, wrote, "Not at present as I have a doctor bill to pay." Many of these women had no chance to obtain alternative, better-paying work. Rose and Emma did not work permanently at Donaldson's. Like others who could, they moved on to better jobs in better places, whether in their own homes or

EMPLOYEES WHO ARE NOT LIVING AT HOME WITH PARENTS WILL
PLEASE ANSWER THE FOLLOWING QUESTIONS, AND RETURN THIS
SLIP TO MR. L. S. DONALDSON'S OFFICE.

L. S. DONALDSON COMPANY

1. Where are your parents living? *Canada*

2. Are you living with relatives? *No.*

3. Are you boarding? *No, doing light housekeeping*

4. Are you rooming alone? *No*

5. Are you earning enough to have anything over after paying ordinary expenses—
that is to say, are you able to lay away anything by for emergencies?

No it takes all I make to live and dress plain.

6. What salary are you being paid? *13 00 per wk*

Name *Violet M Lennox*

Millinery   Address *1623 3rd Ave S.*

May *17* 1915. *I have had seven years experience in Millinery*

Donaldson's department store, wage survey sheet, 1915. In reply to the question about saving for emergencies, Violet Lennox scrawled, "no it takes all I make to live and dress plain."
With seven years experience in millinery and earning $13 weekly, she could still barely meet
expenses. More than half of the respondents made less than $9 a week; Emma Jantsch
made $7.

in other waged labor. Although Rose and Emma married, raised families, and
lived into their nineties, their time in the city, working in the Glass Block, was
fondly remembered.

In 1912 the sisters had met Frank Kumhera, an electrician who lived in
Minneapolis part of the year and worked in Superior part of the year. Frank

was born on a Minnesota farm, but his family had sold it and he had grown up in a small town. Rose's daughter remembers that Frank lived down the street from the boarding house the Jantsch siblings ran. Rose managed the house, but none of the family seemed to have a taste or skill for renting rooms. While there, however, the friendship between Rose and Frank turned into a romance. When Frank enlisted in the navy in 1917 the couple decided to marry. When he returned, they moved to Superior, where he had a full-time job, and later with their two daughters moved west to Tacoma and then Seattle. Rose never returned to the Midwest. She died in Seattle.

Emma married in 1920. Always adventurous and ready to travel, she answered an ad in the *Minneapolis Journal:* "wanted, young lady to work as clerk in small town grocery. Write for details." She did and she went, spending three years working at a mercantile store in Timmer, North Dakota, waiting on Native people from Standing Rock reservation and Scandinavian settlers from ranches and farms. She developed a fondness for one of her young Swedish customers, Frank Gustafson, and took him home to visit her Dorchester family in the summer of 1919. After marrying in 1920, they returned to North Dakota to farm and ranch until Frank died in 1953. Their four children scattered to parts of California and Minnesota, some settling in Minneapolis.[12]

During the years from 1910 to 1930, Anna traveled to other places to work and live. She went west with Emma to Great Falls, Montana, where they worked at Glacier Park during part of two years. They also found employment in Seattle. After Rose and Emma married, Anna found a companion in their younger sister, Hattie, who joined her in Seattle. Hattie married in 1946 and lived in Watertown, Minnesota, until her husband died in 1964; then she lived in Minneapolis with Anna, who never married. Emma also returned to the city to be with her children and near Anna and Hattie. All three died in Minneapolis: Anna in 1982 at ninety-five; Emma in 1988 at ninety-nine; and Hattie three years later at eighty-eight.

WORKING OUT, MOVING OUT

Working out like the Jantsch sisters was not new for immigrant women. The type of work they did mirrored a major change for immigrant daughters, from domestic to white-collar work. The work history of the women in my German Bohemian immigrant family underwent a similar transformation: four of the six daughters completed the transition from domestic to white-collar work in a single generation. My grandmother began working out on neighboring farms in Bohemia at fourteen years of age in the early 1890s. After arriving in the United States she worked in a boarding house as a domestic before marrying in 1893. She bore eight children in the next seventeen years.

The eldest son, born in 1894, remained at home to farm. The eldest daughter, born in 1895, moved to Canada to farm. Five daughters and one son born between 1897 and 1905 all left farming. They began working out on local farms at fourteen like their mother, but they soon went to work in cities. By 1920 two daughters were in Milwaukee and two in St. Paul. The youngest was still at home, but she would follow their lead and eventually live in Chicago and then New York. Although the eldest daughter worked as a domestic in St. Paul for one year and the youngest also became a domestic worker, the other four daughters worked at clerical, factory, or sales jobs. These second-generation immigrants who fled their rural lives for booming cities were what might be called "the new immigrant daughters." They fit comfortably into the urban economy and were part of a new social class, between the middle and the working class, who no longer had to work as housekeepers in other women's homes. They could afford to live with one of the many working-class families who welcomed boarders for a few dollars a week, and they could take jobs in the expanding economy that allowed them surplus money for clothes and entertainment after they paid for necessities.[13]

Migration to larger and more distant cities signaled an important break with birthplace for these women. They tended to marry city men and to return to the farms only for visits. Although these daughters maintained ties to kin and to community, they apparently sent little money home from the city. Recent studies in developing countries show that large amounts of money flow from migrating children, both men and women, back to extended families, enabling them to remain in rural areas. This practice may have happened less frequently in the United States. Of the six children in my family who went to the city, only my mother is reported to have helped with small sums of money and a few gifts of furniture. Her mother and older brother struggled on, hoping to make their forty-acre farm support the two of them and the youngest daughter in the early 1920s without the help of city-bound family migrants. When I asked my uncle how they survived, he grinned: he had distilled and bootlegged liquor in neighboring towns for a cash income.[14]

A few accounts document earlier work patterns. According to a second-generation Norwegian, Thurine Oleson, who was born in central Wisconsin in 1866, two work patterns for young women existed when she was growing up in the 1870s. She explained the difference simply: "All the Yankees looked down on the girls who worked out. No Yankee girl ever did it . . . all immigrant girls did." By "working out" she meant housework, either on nearby farms or in local villages.[15]

Not all immigrant daughters worked out. Erna Oleson explained that in the wealthiest Norwegian families the parents refused to let their daughters work away from home. We know from other accounts that poorer Euro-American families did send their daughters out to work. However, some of these families did not consider such work acceptable and tried to hide their daughters' hard physical labor. Most immigrant families, on the other hand, considered it normal and a source of pride that their daughters were able to earn an income. For Norwegian, German, and Polish daughters, working out began at age fourteen, after completing seven or eight grades of grammar school. It continued until they married, usually between ages nineteen and twenty-five.[16]

The traditional work for immigrant daughters remained low-paying housework. Experiences varied with the household and the individual. Some who went into what they called "Yankee" or native-born Euro-American households in the 1880s found the work to be highly satisfactory. Thurine Oleson said about her experiences, "It was not the worst thing for a girl to go out and learn to do housework nicely, and it made good housekeepers out of us. . . . No one ever abused me. I was like a member of the family wherever I went." Working out was hardest for first-generation immigrant women, like Oleson's mother-in-law, who spoke no English. Native-born second-generation immigrant women, who had learned English in schools, gained mobility and status as wage earners by working out and lessened the burden on the family for space and food.[17]

Most young farm women who worked out apparently did so only in winter. Like their brothers and fathers who worked in Wisconsin lumber camps, young women returned home for the summer. Such seasonal migration was common for immigrant daughters who moved to small towns in winter to work for wealthy families or in hotels and boarding houses and then spent the summer working on the home place. Because central Wisconsin had few towns, winter jobs might be some distance from the farm, but young women regularly rode trains many miles away from home to work.[18]

By the 1890s immigrant daughters were doing much of the waged work on farms as well. An 1894 Bureau of Labor report queried more than five hundred farmers whether they had increased wages for female labor that year and, if so, why. Almost three-fourths replied that they had and explained their answers in one of two ways. Some gave negative accounts: "American girls won't work . . . too high toned to work on a farm . . . want to get along without work . . . all girls want to be ladies." The others were more precise: "Foreign girls will work out. American not. . . . Many girls think it degrading to be hired girl . . . rather not work in the kitchen . . . farm work too hard," these farmers said. More than 60 percent simply indicated that women preferred to work in village, town, or city. Another 20 percent said young women were drawn to teaching. The rest of the farmers, another 13 percent, said the women preferred jobs in offices and stores or factories. The other categories, each two percent or less, were marriage, dressmaking, or summer resorts.[19]

The survey told in broader statistical terms what the individual accounts showed. As daughters of native-born Euro-Americans left farm work, immigrant daughters took over many of these jobs. Even then the scarcity of immigrant daughters was driving up wages. They, too, found the work hard and disliked working in the kitchen. Family accounts mentioned similar complaints. Around the turn of the century, a transition away from farm work occurred.

Thurine Oleson's work life exemplified this transition. In her memoir, she defended the benefits of her experience working out in the 1870s. Many wealthy families looked down on her and others for working out, but "It was not until we were married and settled down that the working girls reaped their reward." She continued, "Whereas the well-to-do, proud Norwegian girls, who had thought it a disgrace to be a servant, now kept house in the same old-fashioned ways, we others had learned all the nice, up-to-date American ways, and American cooking, and were not a bit sorry." Oleson bore six daughters and two sons, but she did not want her daughters to work out. "Believe me," she recounted, "when my own girls were growing up, I worked my fingers to the bone to get them a good education so that they would have it easier than I did." Several "went away" to high school, and one attended college in South Dakota.[20]

Who stayed in rural areas and who went to the city? We have no systematic studies, but it probably varied by economic status. In wealthier families, younger sons might have family assistance in acquiring their own farms or a large acreage might be divided. Daughters might marry local farmers with their own land or even bring land with them into marriage. Or they might work at the few available middle-class occupations in small towns and in rural areas. My family was very poor after my grandmother's first husband died and her second did not provide enough cash earnings to supplement farm income. The eldest son, who inherited the farm, stayed in the small community of his birth. The six daughters and second son left for the city, dispersed by poverty and the lack of nearby off-farm jobs.

The economic infrastructure of these areas provided few jobs for these poor farm daughters. Town populations did not grow during the first two decades of the century. Marathon County, where the Schopper-Schopp children and their neighbors the Jantsches grew up, increased slowly in population after the turn of the century. In the first decade, it grew by fewer than 12,000 persons; in the second decade, by just over 10,000. Two-thirds of the villages and towns grew little, often through consolidation; the other third declined in numbers. Wausau, the largest city in the county, grew by only about 6,000 in these two decades—not nearly enough to provide work for discontented rural youth, who would have to compete with small-town youth who had access to high school education and social contacts that could give them an advantage in obtaining jobs.[21]

Young Native women did not have the same migration experiences as settler daughters. Seasonal migration had been an important part of their lives before moving on to reservations. Daughters traveled in family groups—to hunt, to fish, to gather rice and process maple sugar. Much of that migration continued into the twentieth century. The emphasis on schooling by government officials and by many Native parents increasingly interrupted these traditional patterns for young women. In fact, government agents built schools specifically to interrupt those seasonal patterns, to keep daughters and sons on the reservation. Native mothers had no choice but to send their daughters to boarding school, and because Native women married at a younger age than most settler daughters they often went directly from school into their own family life. The Lac du Flambeau boarding school placed some students in summer domestic jobs with white families, but employers treated them so badly that few wished to continue working there.[22]

Like settler men, Native men migrated to the Twin Cities, Milwaukee, and Chicago to find employment, especially when they were skilled artisans such as carpenters. They also took jobs closer to home whenever available. Truman Beane came with his father and twin brother to the Twin Cities from the White Earth reservation in Minnesota in early 1900, but he did not marry a Native woman or return to the reservation, although he remained enrolled at White Earth. Instead he married my German American aunt and raised his family in the city. Such experiences must have been quite common. Enrolled men and women could continue to receive annuity checks in the city, but young women went to cities less frequently than Native men or settler daughters. Native women exploited rural resources more intensively, selling products gathered or raised and marketing their handwork. North-woods tourism offered work to some young Native women. Work was strictly gendered: women did the cleaning, laundry, cooking, and serving while men did the guide work, maintenance, and outdoor work. These jobs offered important sources of cash and some job experience, but they did not provide year-round, well-paid jobs that employed the skills young people were learning in school, even homemaking skills, to say nothing of academic training.[23]

Some daughters did work farther from home. A few women from Lac du Flambeau worked in Chicago for part of the year, combining incomes from winter city jobs with summer employment at resorts, living at home and enjoying the companionship of family and friends. Because of the mixed-tribe Native schools, a few young women obtained full-time work teaching on other reservations. Thus a number of young women moved to Utah, to the Dakotas, or to other states. A few Menominee women also worked in Chicago or Milwaukee. It was difficult enough to obtain satisfactory work in the city but doubly difficult to find work that would allow them to return home to maintain their community ties. From the perspective of Native mothers, working away from home posed the danger that daughters might marry and leave the community permanently. Young Indian women left their homelands reluctantly because of their attachment to them.[24]

FINDING WORK, LEARNING IT

Before leaving home, settler daughters like those from the Dorchester families prepared themselves for work in the city. Exit skills—those things that would ensure a successful transition to city life, work, and culture—were essential. Being successful meant getting a job, a place to live, and a life of one's own on one's own. Home, school, and community all provided skills that helped the sisters migrate to the city.

The sisters grew up caring for younger family members—helping, sharing, and enjoying their company. Joseph Jantsch commented that his five sisters were so close that they seemed more like friends than relatives. The Schopper-Schopp girls, although half-sisters, exhibited the same type of sibling loyalty, concern, and enjoyment of each other's company. Sisters and neighbors offered advice to young women preparing to venture away, helped each other get to the city, provided temporary living space, and assisted in finding jobs. Parents expected daughters to leave for work at about age sixteen and to help their younger siblings leave.

Surviving on a family farm taught women to manage details. Chores gave daughters responsibility in the house, yard, and field at an early age. German immigrant families valued hard, sustained, efficient work, and daughters learned this ethic from their mothers. Serving their families at many tasks prepared them to handle easily the physical aspects of long hours of labor in the city with energy left to socialize after ten- to twelve-hour workdays. Most young women worked for neighbors after leaving school at the end of the seventh or eighth grade. Neighborhood farms paid poorly or in kind, but experience as a hired girl also taught that hard work was the norm. Prospective city work, free of both household and outdoor chores, seemed light and comparatively easy.

Personal tidiness was another essential skill for urban success. From older sisters, girls learned how to dress appropriately in clean shirtwaists and dark skirts, hats, and neat shoes. Family photographs show the young country women in attire that would be perfectly acceptable in the city. Anna Jantsch spent many hours helping sisters select fabric and patterns and then fitting clothing that allowed them to pass as urban women. The Schopper sisters had no family seamstress, but Matilda owned a treadle sewing machine. School photographs always show her daughters carefully attired, even if younger ones wore hand-me-downs. A taste for stylish clothing—and more of it—made city work doubly attractive.

Rural one-room common schools provided the sisters with communication skills. Although books were scarce, the young women developed a lifelong love of reading. They prided themselves on careful penmanship. All spoke German at home, but school and friends gave them an English-speaking culture as well. The older children learned to read basic German when they received religious instruction. Their mothers were literate in German and read regularly, probably German-language newspapers among other materials. Daughters, certainly Theresa, also took pride in their ability to spell English well. At the Bruckerville and Barry schools that the seven girls attended, the spelling bee was a major event. Theresa regularly spelled down her classmates, winning a prize in 1914, when she was twelve. The sisters frequently sent letters and postcards to family and friends.

While the census does not show how many country daughters moved to the Twin Cities, a 1915 Donaldson's survey offers one glimpse of them. The Minneapolis department store asked women employees to give their parents' place of residence. Farm women listed the town nearest home. Almost 40 percent of living parents were in small towns; in addition, some had come from these towns to live with children in the city, just as young immigrants often brought parents from Germany after they were established on farms in Wisconsin.[25]

The Minnesota Department of Labor tried to stem the tide of rural migrants. The bureau particularly discouraged young women with children from migrating to the city and, failing that, counseled that they increase their skills before they came. Industrial work or well-paid employment of any kind was impossible to find for a woman lacking experience, and the cost of living was high in the Twin Cities unless one could stay with friends or relatives. Of course, the Dorchester women planned to room with family immediately upon arrival.[26]

Although she never worked in the Twin Cities, the eldest Jantsch daughter, Mary, was the first of the Dorchester women to head west. Sometime in the 1890s, when Mary was in her teens, a girlfriend who was doing housework about fifty miles west of Dorchester in Chippewa Falls arranged a job for her. The next three daughters—Anna, Emma, and Rose—joined Mary in Chippewa Falls, each at about age sixteen. Most did housework, but Anna hired on with a seamstress. All followed the same cycle, leaving home in September and returning in June to work on the farm.[27]

Finding work was the first task. As with the Jantsch and Schopper-Schopp daughters, kin or friends often helped women find their first jobs. They read the "help wanted female" ads and changed jobs frequently in a constant effort to find higher wages, better working conditions, a more convenient location, more congenial coworkers. Women like the Jantsch sisters, who went home in the summer to help with farm work, searched for new city jobs each fall.[28]

Women often sought professional help to augment informal networks. Sometimes they wrote ahead to state or private placement agencies. As the population grew, employment services expanded. Mrs. Frieda Groecher had one of the earliest agencies: the Minneapolis city directory listed her home office on Twelfth Avenue North from 1884 to 1910. By then, seven other women advertised employment bureaus in that city. Private charitable agencies, including the Swedish Tabernacle Young Women's Employment Office and the Young Women's Christian Association, also offered their services. The Associated Charities Employment Bureau operated out of the Ramsey County courthouse, as did the Minnesota State Free Employment Bureau.[29]

Unions had long operated hiring halls for out-of-work members. Because most women were not organized and because union halls often had the atmosphere of working men's club rooms, women were not likely to use them. In 1917, when all of the Dorchester daughters but Theresa Schopp were in the cities, the World War I labor shortage pushed the Minnesota Department of Labor and the Minnesota Council of National Defense to expand job-placement services for women to meet national, state, and local needs. Farm labor was particularly scarce, but farm men in Minnesota and Wisconsin opposed sending city women to work in agricultural areas except to perform housework; they preferred to have experienced farm women in the fields. Many dutiful farm daughters returned home or delayed leaving for the Twin Cities until the war ended in November 1918. With two of their brothers in the military, the Jantsch sisters' help at home was essential.[30]

Learning specialized city work skills was not easy. Few high schools offered job training, and the new vocational schools primarily recruited boys wishing to go into factory work. Minneapolis had a Girls Vocational High School, but St. Paul's Mechanic Arts High School offered only art training for young women. Union apprentice programs were closely controlled and intended for young men.[31]

Most workers learned on the job. After beginning at low-paid temporary work, women received small raises and more permanent status. Companies sometimes hired experienced workers at low wages for a few days to confirm that they had the needed skills. Owners, managers, and coworkers trained new workers. Large clothing factories regularly employed instructors to teach on the job, and some department stores had in-house training programs. Mostly, however, young women learned by watching, asking questions, and gradually developing new skills through experience.

Only two of the Dorchester women, both younger sisters, attended nighttime business school to improve their clerical skills. Business school offered an opportunity to move into much better paying jobs. Hattie Jantsch's training in Minneapolis enabled her to get bank positions. In St. Paul Theresa Schopp attended Globe Business College.[32]

Globe Business College, St. Paul, 1920. Advertising claimed Globe was the largest and best-equipped business college in the Northwest, training students for a "bustling, hustling, success-making business life, in the great city of opportunity and progress—St. Paul." Young women who could afford business college might work as well-paid secretaries in the clerical boom of the early twentieth century, when women replaced most men in these positions. Theresa Schopp took a few typing classes at this college but did not learn enough to hold a clerical job.

Established in 1885, Globe College had expanded rapidly during the early decades of the twentieth century, when it actively recruited country migrants. But Globe did not come cheap. It took six months to complete the shorthand-and-typing class at a cost of $65 plus $5 for books. Or students could pay $5 for each night session and hope they were fast learners. Theresa, who considered herself a good speller, was encouraged to try, perhaps with just a textbook or a few classes. She left behind sheets of typed words in a Globe book but no evidence that she achieved enough proficiency to get a clerical job.[33]

Serving, sewing, and selling jobs were all held by the Dorchester daughters. Only Rose Jantsch and Mary Schopper ever worked as maids: Rose as a live-in companion and maid for one year, probably 1911, and Mary as a maid in 1914. In the mid-nineteenth century German immigrant daughters had flocked into domestic work in the cities. By 1910, however, the Swedes, 60 percent of whom were foreign-born or had foreign-born parents, dominated in the city's domestic work.[34]

Low pay—almost 70 percent of domestics earned less than ten dollars a week—deterred many women from housework, even if they did usually receive room and board in addition to their wages. Kitchen helpers and servers in restaurants and hotels earned even less, although they received supplemental meals and sometimes lodging. Eighty-one percent of these workers made less than ten dollars a week in 1918. Rose and Emma Jantsch occasionally worked as waitresses, but the Dorchester women avoided these jobs unless absolutely necessary. Fortunately, they found alternatives to be plentiful.[35]

Newer Swedish immigrants, who often spoke little English, had to take the low-paid domestic work that German ethnic country women could avoid. In Minneapolis 60 percent of the Swedish population was foreign born or had foreign-born parents. Domestic work was the predominant job available in Sweden, but conditions in the Twin Cities were a marked improvement over such work there, and experienced Swedes had little trouble finding jobs. They used these jobs as places to learn the English language and American ways between the 1880s and the 1910s, at the same time providing middle-class Twin Cities women with valued household workers. Housekeeping was not a job for women without skills, however. Louise Klapp, who worked for the labor department in 1911 and once tried for an entire day to place a country girl in housework, reported, "Housework is not any too plentiful." Housework, with no washing, was paying only six dollars a week but was still hard to find.[36]

Evelina Johansdotter left a memoir of her work experience in Minneapolis from 1901 to 1907. She arrived from Sweden in 1901 and through the Swedish employment agency found a job cleaning at a boarding house and then as a housekeeper for an old Swedish couple. Fed up with "haughty mistresses and suspicious old ladies," Johansdotter left her position and, after trying several others, took a job cleaning buildings where the other workers were also of Swedish descent. She earned enough to return to Sweden but made her way back to Minneapolis in 1905 and began cleaning again. She liked the friendship of her Swedish coworkers, free time in the middle of the day (she cleaned in the early morning and late afternoon), and the stable income. Finally, she left cleaning for a job in a factory where she could make more money. Domestic jobs were still available in the elite areas of Kenwood in Minneapolis or Summit Avenue in St. Paul. Yet many women who worked at cleaning preferred to live out rather than in, and cleaning in the expanding mercantile sector was an appealing alternative. One was not on call every hour of the day or night. A more attractive job was working as clerk or saleswoman in a department, grocery, or confection store.[37]

As we have seen, at least two of the Jantsch daughters worked as clerks in major department stores. Emma probably worked at Donaldson's in 1914, 1915, and 1917, and Rose worked there in 1914. Anna Schopper worked at the Golden Rule in 1919. These department stores were part of a vast retail mercantile sector.[38]

Anna Schopper and Theresa Schopp worked at confection stores, which offered a small but significant niche in the retail food chain. In 1923 St. Paul listed 217 firms under retail confections. Some were located in restaurants like the Parrot, a soda fountain on Wabasha Street. Fallon and Herges, where Theresa Schopp worked in 1923, was on University Avenue. In 1916 Anna Schopper worked in Smiths' Confection Store, located at Sixth and Robert streets and famous for their "Dollar Chocolate Dreams." Despite the possible delights of working in a confection store, neither woman stayed more than a year.

Emma, Hattie, and Anna Schopper worked at some of the largest grocery stores in the Twin Cities: Morris and Company in Minneapolis and Andrew Schoch Grocery Company and Michaud Brothers in St. Paul. Michaud, located on East Fourth and where Anna Schopper worked in 1917 and 1918, was one of the city's best-known retail grocery stores. In 1918 it employed fifty-four men and thirty women. All but nine women were clerks: five were cashiers, two telephone operators, and two billers. Anna was twenty-one, worked as a clerk for $10 a week, boarded, and did not contribute to the support of her family. She was not average in this regard: twenty-four of the women lived at home, and fourteen contributed to their family's support. Five were married—four of them to men in the army—and one was widowed with a five-year-old daughter. One cashier and one biller, at $15 and $20 per week, were the highest paid; the rest made $8 to $13 per week. The oldest was thirty-seven and the youngest

Andrew Schoch Grocery, 1925. Typical of retail grocery stores, Schoch required women to wear white aprons. Although Schoch Grocery was a well-known St. Paul store, its bushel baskets full of produce gave it the look of a corner grocery. Anna Schopper worked at the larger Michaud Brothers, which employed thirty women and featured departments with elaborate displays of expensive foodstuffs.

eighteen, but four were in their thirties, eighteen in their twenties, and two in their teens. They worked a nine-hour day, fifty-four hours per week. It was relatively stable, poorly paid work. Michaud's interior in 1918 probably looked much as it did in a 1920 photograph that shows counters brimming over with everything from wedding cakes to specialty cheeses and meats. The men are carefully attired in dark suits, starched high collars, and black shoes. The women are all covered with white aprons or dresses. Neatness and cleanliness were at a premium.[39]

SETTLING IN, MOVING AROUND

Settling in and moving around preoccupied working women almost as much as finding and keeping jobs that paid a living wage. Young working women, always seeking better and cheaper accommodations, commonly relocated every year. They did not have to live near work: trolleys took them comfortably all over town. They rented lodgings by the month and moved as they wished. Almost every year that the Jantsch sisters are listed in the city directory, they live at a different address.

Census records for 1910 and 1920 show that the solidly working-class neighborhoods in which these country women lived were ethnically diverse, populated mainly by the first American-born generation of families, with a sprinkling of foreign born. Most married women did not work outside the home. Instead, they worked at home, taking in boarders or running flats where lodgers lived individually, in shared rooms, or as couples. In 1910 Anna and Emma Jantsch lived in a flat at 1120 Chestnut Street, a Minneapolis neighborhood of boarding houses and single-family dwellings. Wisconsin-born Cora and Mathew Hickey, forty and forty-one, who had four grown children not living at home, ran the flat where the Jantsch sisters and twelve other workers lodged. Around them lived workers of English, Norwegian, Swedish, or American descent, mostly born in Minnesota or Wisconsin but some from New York, New Jersey, Canada, or Norway. On one side was a house with several families, including a policeman with his Norwegian wife, a family in the restaurant business, and several lodgers.

The 1920 census reports Anna Schopper boarding in St. Paul at 637 Mississippi Street and working as a saleswoman, probably at Schoch Grocery. Many vacant lots show that this neighborhood of mostly single-family dwellings, not far from the city street department and the railway yards, was a relatively new residential area. Few people took in boarders. In the neighborhood lived mostly people born in Minnesota or Wisconsin but also from Iowa, North Dakota, Canada, Sweden, Finland, Poland, and Russia. Many men worked for the railway. Two black families from Georgia and Alabama, the Davises and the Allens, who probably came north as railroad workers initially, lived amid white neighbors. The men worked as waiters, one son was a bellboy, and both women took in male boarders.

These places where the Dorchester women took up residence provided inexpensive, safe, and clean living arrangements. A broader survey taken in 1915 by Donaldson's department store showed that 75 percent of its workers boarded with relatives or others, probably in houses similar to those of the Jantsches and the Schopper-Schopps. More than two-thirds of these women roomed with someone other than relatives.[40]

The advantage of pooling wages as the Dorchester sisters often did was borne out by surveys done during 1914 and 1915 by the Minimum Wage Commission. The commission interviewed nearly six hundred working women in the Twin Cities and had them fill out forms showing the cost of living. After investigating 774 rooms where working women lived or that advertised low prices, the commission judged almost one-fourth of rooms renting for under $6 per month to be dirty, unsafe, or located in dangerous neighborhoods. For $8 a month, however, more than 90 percent of the available rental rooms were satisfactory. If single women pooled their wages, like the Jantsch sisters did, they could easily find double rooms at $12 a month. Even then, with two meals a day, the cost for a single woman increased to more than $16 per month. Combined with other costs and an average taken, $8 a week was the minimum wage on which one could live. At Donaldson's, 44 percent—more than two-fifths—of the women employed earned $8 or less per week. Because Emma roomed with her sisters, she could still live on the $7 she made each week. The sisters could live in solidly working-class neighborhoods in good houses.[41]

A LITTLE HELP FROM THE STATE

The 1910 notice by the Minnesota Bureau of Women and Children had warned women not to come to the city. As it became clear that thousands of young women would ignore the warning, the bureau refocused its energies on controlling the conditions women workers found there. Minnesota's concern for women workers was part of a larger national debate in the early twentieth century over whether these young working women needed special help to survive until they were safely married and at home raising families. While the working women devised their own survival strategies, middle-class reformers' concerns over working conditions had a basis in fact. Some reformers hoped to control the private social and sexual activities of these working women; others sought to develop legislation to improve work-place environments that included poor health and safety conditions, long hours, and low wages. Working-class males generally supported this legislation for women but not for men because they preferred union membership or assumed they could take care of themselves. Middle-class men, those who owned the businesses that employed women workers, assumed women needed protecting but were not always sure such protection should come from the state. Once allowed to intervene, the state might expand its power to protect all workers. Between 1910 and 1913 coalitions composed of Republicans and Democrats usually calling themselves "progressives" pushed through a series of laws aimed at protecting women workers: controlling hours of work, requiring adequate toilet facilities and rest rooms, and mandating minimum wages.

The Bureau of Women and Children in the Minnesota Department of Labor and Industries was responsible for enforcing these new laws. The first three bureau chiefs, all from reform backgrounds, interpreted their mandate broadly, taking violators to court and mobilizing local clubwomen to support enforcement of the laws. The new laws demanded a nine-hour working day, separate and adequate toilets, and a minimum wage to be determined by a Minimum Wage Commission. The commission was to survey the wages paid to working women, establish a "living wage," and set a minimum wage if one-sixth of the working women earned less than that amount. The commission was composed of the commissioner of labor and representatives from businesses, employees, and the public.

This protective legislation was designed to help women workers like the Jantsch and Schopper-Schopp sisters, who arrived in the Twin Cities at just this time. Their hours of work were among those regulated, their toilets and rest rooms inspected, their wages and cost of living surveyed. The bureau no longer warned these farm daughters to stay away from the city but held meetings to explain the new laws, publicized them in local papers, and employed trained field workers as well as women volunteers to assist with condition surveys. For the first few years, the bureau performed some individual services for women workers—helping them find work or collect back wages—but from 1912 to 1918, under the leadership of Agnes Peterson, it embraced self-help for the women workers it was charged with protecting.

Peterson had close ties to organized clubwomen in Minnesota. A graduate of Gustavus Adolphus College in St. Peter, she had been a volunteer with Associated Charities of St. Paul, a member of the social and industrial conditions committee of the Minnesota Federation of Women's Clubs, and a member of the National Women's Trade Union League. She was a strong supporter of women's suffrage and women's protective legislation. Peterson tried to avoid any publicity that would define the bureau as a welfare agency or one that dealt patronizingly with young women workers.[42]

Discussing a self-help leaflet planned by the bureau, Peterson wrote in January 1914, "We must not let these girls feel that we are in any doubt as to their capability of caring for themselves. Most of them are, and those that are not, must be won before we can influence their lives in any way.... After we get a large enough number to have confidence in us, we can reach the few who need special attention through these fellow workers." She insisted on using the term "wage earning women" instead of "factory, store, or working girls." When the local organizer for one of Peterson's self-help meetings allowed the phrase "homeless and underpaid girl problem" to be used in media releases, Peterson wrote to her sharply: "We both can agree that we can best serve the wage earning woman by never doing or saying anything which will hurt her pride, or will make her feel that we are exploiting her and her problems in order to advertise ourselves. . . . The woman wage earner particularly resents being heralded in the newspapers as a homeless girl. . . . We will under no conditions permit any outsider to connect the need of 'moral protection' with our meetings." Young women workers needed good food and a good place to live at a reasonable price, Peterson concluded; they did not need to have their morals protected.[43]

Like other states, Minnesota passed laws limiting women's work at night, but such legislation affected few directly. More important for the majority of women was legislation that mandated separate and equal toilet facilities. In a later era separate toilets became a rallying cry for opponents of the Equal Rights Amendment, but in the 1910s finding clean and safe toilets was a problem for many working women. Women's toilets were not just a middle-class concern: safe, clean toilets were a necessity for all workers equally. In fact, the lack of toilet facilities still remains particularly troublesome to women workers entering new jobs in urban areas in many developing countries. The women who flooded into the Twin Cities to work at the end of the nineteenth and the beginning of the twentieth centuries were no different. Legislation was prompted by a number of issues: the absence of separate facilities for women who desired them; exposure to assault if unlocked, open, and unsupervised; and, often, deplorable sanitary conditions. Larger department stores and factories usually provided adequate facilities without much prompting, but smaller businesses, often employing only a few women workers, were much less likely to agree that adequate facilities were necessary. Bureau inspectors worked hard to explain minimum standards to employers: an adequate number of toilets, located conveniently to the work place, wherever possible separate facilities for women situated away from areas where men slept, maintained in clean and sanitary condition. The bureau was satisfied with clean outdoor toilets if indoor ones were not available, although the expectation and hope was that women would have toilets within the buildings in which they worked. The bureau circulated photographs of model restrooms. An ideal large facility employing many women would include an adequate number of well-flushing toilets and toilet paper, plenty of sinks with hot and cold water for washing hands, clean towels, and a place to hang their hats.[44]

Appropriate recreational areas were also a concern of the bureau: it encouraged large employers to set aside areas in which women could relax and engage in seasonal outdoor activities. It circulated photographs of model factories and their facilities. It also urged factory owners to establish lunchrooms separate from machines, places where women would not have to eat amid the clutter, noise, and workday dirt of industrial equipment.

Better toilets and cleaner work areas were reforms compatible with the older doctrine of industry paternalism; maximum hours of work and minimum wages were not. Controversies over these issues eventually pulled the bureau into open conflict with Twin Cities business interests and into bitter political debates. Donaldson's eventually complied with the law regulating hours of work, but it organized and orchestrated a legal challenge to the minimum-wage law. The Minnesota Supreme Court upheld the law in 1918 only to have it, like similar state laws, declared unconstitutional by the U.S. Supreme Court in 1923. Subsequently, of course, minimum-wage laws for both women and men came to be a cornerstone of national labor policy.

Despite the formation of craft unions in the nineteenth century, most workers, especially women, were responsible for individually negotiating hours

Employee's recreation room lounge, 1916. The sign at West Publishing Company in St. Paul warns that eating is "positively forbidden," and one imagines that young women were encouraged to limit their recreation to quiet activities such as reading. Reformers considered comfortable recreation rooms—along with clean eating spaces and single-sex lavatories—essential to women workers' welfare.

and times of work with their employers. In rural areas, employees and employers, often neighbors, bargained for wages face to face. When seeking employment in smaller firms, women encountered similar bargaining conditions. The difference was that they had far more job options in the expanding Twin Cities. They could, and did, go elsewhere if they did not like their current position. Young women changed jobs yearly. The Jantsch women went home each summer, but even those who did not kept an eye out for the better chance and moved from job to job. They learned about available jobs from friends, siblings, and coworkers. Among the working class, talk about jobs, wages, and conditions of labor was a common language that all spoke.

Prospective workers would have quickly gathered information on the city's work climate, supplemented by reading general and labor newspapers. These country daughters avoided manufacturing and service work and sought employment in the retail mercantile industry, but that preference was fed by knowledge of factory working conditions. Even when factory jobs paid more, these native-born sisters sought out the less dangerous, less stressful, quieter, but usually also poorer-paid clerking jobs. I remember my father in the 1950s talking about factory women in a sympathetic if condescending way. His older brother and sister-in-law had both been machine operators in garment factories, so he certainly knew about factory conditions. He hoped I would never have to work in a factory. Wisconsin women would have known factory women and about factory jobs, but they had skills that allowed them to accept alternative jobs and head into the middle class. Because these jobs did not take them directly into industries where labor and capital collided did not mean they had no understanding of workers' struggles to better their conditions or of how different pasts shaped labor conditions in each of the Twin Cities.

By the time the Jantsch sisters arrived in Minneapolis, the first round of labor conflict over working conditions had ended with an uneasy peace. Between 1900 and 1902, hundreds of unions had developed—28,000 members joined three hundred unions and twenty-four strikes occurred during those years according to historian William Millikan. Between 1905 and 1914, the union movement slowed to a crawl as Minneapolis businessmen organized to keep factory shops free from union control. The Schopper-Schopp women were encountering a different labor history in St. Paul. The forces of business and labor were less polarized there, partly because the city did not have as dramatic an industrial growth nor as many powerful industrialists. A smaller number of women worked in St. Paul than in Minneapolis: in 1918 St. Paul had fewer than 4,500 women workers while Minneapolis had 19,000. For a combination of reasons, St. Paul was becoming a closed-shop city while Minneapolis was becoming an open-shop city, at least in some trades. St. Paul businessmen did not push anti-unionism to a point of confrontation, and many union leaders preferred negotiation over striking to obtain better working conditions.

A sort of gentlemen's agreement allowed unions to operate, even in such volatile industries as the needlework trades.[45]

Not all labor-management relations were so cozy. Still, the fact remained that St. Paul workers expected to unionize and to not be opposed at every turn by owners' hostile overreaction. Right through the war, more radical unions such as the Amalgamated Clothing Workers of America (ACWA) organized with impressive success in St. Paul. As ACWA organizer Sander Genis later wrote, the ACWA had to unionize Minneapolis because open-shop policies were threatening their successful work in St. Paul.[46]

At the same time, progressive legislators expanded the state's ability to protect not only women but all workers. A workers' compensation bill, passed in 1913, covered both women and men. Employers feared a future with either more state control of private industry or state ownership of industry and welfare services. State labor laws could not keep pace with workers' demands for greater control over work-place conditions. During the next few years union membership continued to increase as workers became politically energized and businesses signed agreements to increase wages. Alarmed by the growing specter of union influence on state policies, businesses regarded the extension of women's protective legislation into the area of wages as particularly dangerous. Minnesota was only one of almost a dozen states that passed minimum-wage laws for women between 1912 and 1913 and only one place where opponents battled their implementation.[47]

In 1914 the Minnesota Minimum Wage Commission conducted its first survey of women's wages. Of the 14,317 women workers aged sixteen and older in Minnesota, 6,500 were employed in the Twin Cities, somewhat more than two thousand in the mercantile sector and about 750 at retail mercantile jobs. The survey found that within this retail mercantile sector, in which most of the Dorchester daughters were employed, more than 61 percent of the women earned under nine dollars a week.

After determining women's wages, the commission conducted interviews to see what workers actually needed to live reasonably. It determined that a single woman on average would have to pay $4.80 for room and board, $1.81 a week for additional expenses (including five cents a week for insurance and ten cents a week for vacations), and $2.00 for clothing. These figures did not include items such as soap, the committee noted. Statistics showed that well over one-sixth of the women were making less than a living wage.[48]

The commission was particularly concerned about women it identified as "living adrift." These women, who were under twenty-five years of age, not living with relatives, and earning less than $12.50 per week, accounted for almost 70 percent of all wage-earning women. They were often able to cover only board, room, and clothing. Only eight percent of those earning under $12.50 could even afford carfare. Nor could they pay bills for doctors, dentists, and opticians; insurance, lodge, and club dues; or church giving. Women in mercantile jobs felt they had to spend more on clothing, but if they paid out even a small amount for all categories, the wages they needed increased from $8.38 to $9.26 a week. "I cannot afford it," the women often told investigators in response to questions on each category. The commission concluded, "Poverty, struggle and economy cannot be shown by any table." It recommended that the minimum wage be set at $8.65 a week.[49]

At the Donaldson Company, executives were already discussing ways to subvert the expected minimum-wage law. One plan was to announce to employees that when the act became operative all women making under $9 would be classified as apprentices, thus exempting them from the law. Another proposal called for forcing anyone receiving less than $9 to increase her selling power and to pass competency exams and anyone being paid more than $10 to have her wages reduced to offset increased costs. Company officials also hired an attorney, who advised them to seek a court injunction to stop the law's implementation, and recruited other department store executives to help finance the legal challenge.[50]

Solicitations for the legal challenge were successful: Northwestern Knitting Company gave the largest donation with $800, followed by Donaldson's with $500, and others for lesser amounts. The day the law was to go into effect, Minnesota district court judge Frederick N. Catlin granted an injunction halting its enforcement.

Judge Catlin agreed with the two main arguments made by the employers' attorney. First, the minimum-wage law was not a valid police regulation because the legislature had made the commission a "sort of independent supervisor *pater familias* of women workers and their employers" and allowed for unequal application of the law in determining different wages for different types of industry. Second, the law violated the Fourteenth Amendment by interfering with the right of contract between employee and employer. Police powers were not necessary to protect the safety, health, or morals of working women, said the judge. In fact, he opined, they would just as likely increase the distress and immorality if morals were dependent on wages. Eventually, the case made its way to the Minnesota Supreme Court, where Felix Frankfurter, representing the National Consumers' League, and Minnesota's attorney general defended the law. Minnesota women reformers organized in support of their arguments.[51]

On December 21, 1917, the Minnesota Supreme Court upheld the constitutionality of the minimum-wage law. The justices found it perfectly legitimate to grant the commission administrative powers to establish rules. Furthermore, the law was proper because "women in the trades are underpaid . . . [that is,] not paid so well as men are paid for the same service." The judges concluded that, "in the strife of employer and employee to secure a just share of the profits of their joint effort . . . women as a class are not on an equality with men." Do these conditions exist, is legislation necessary to remedy them, do such laws promote health, peace, morals, education, or good order, and are they necessary to the public welfare? The Minnesota Supreme Court thought so.[52]

Soon after the supreme court upheld the minimum-wage law, the Woman's Committee of the Commission of Public Safety decided to conduct an industrial survey to discover if employers were complying with the new minimum-wage standards established by the state and federal governments in war contract regulations. The department of labor agreed to gather the information, provide observations, interview selected employers and employees, and compile its findings in a final report. The survey left a snapshot of women workers and the middle-class women who worked to protect them.[53]

The survey revealed the extent of women's poor wages. Of the 51,361 women workers studied, close to three-fifths earned "a bare existence" or less. More than one-third received less. The survey estimated that, with wartime inflation of 50 percent, a $9 weekly wage purchased only $6 in prewar wages; a $14 wage, only $9.33. The compilers noted grimly the federal government's estimate that food costs, which comprised a large proportion of the poor workers' budgets, had increased 62 percent. Wartime inflation had caused the cost of living to far outpace the $10 subsistence level that the survey assumed. Statistics showed that 25 percent of the seamstresses and sewers, 27 percent of the machine operators, 39 percent of the saleswomen, 69 percent of domestic workers, and 89 percent of "unskilled workers" made less than $10 a week. Once the survey was published in 1920, the Minimum Wage Commission raised the minimum wage to $11.[54]

By this time, however, many reformers had already abandoned the idea that a minimum wage for women could solve the problem of low wages. National reformers were advocating equal pay for equal work, especially since employers who had hired women as replacements for men during the war wanted to retain them after 1918 to offset higher costs of doing business. The Council of National Defense (CND) sent a circular, dated December 19, 1918, urging all state units to insist "on the principle of equal pay for equal work, lest women be used to break down the hard-won industrial standards established by men." The CND warned that employing women at lower wages than men had been paid for the same jobs could become a pretext "for forcing women into lower paid and less desirable work."[55]

In 1920 the Minimum Wage Commission raised the wage base to $12, effective in January 1921. In its biennial report, the commission argued that women's wages were lower than expected from normal supply and demand economics. In June 1920 the demand for labor far exceeded supply, supposedly forcing wages up, but, the commission reported, violations of minimum-wage rates "would lead one to wonder whether wages paid to women are regulated by supply and demand to the extent that economists have in the past led us to

Industrial Survey of Women Employed Outside the Home

COMMITTEE ON WOMEN IN INDUSTRY IN CO-OPERATION WITH BUREAU OF
WOMEN AND CHILDREN DEPARTMENT OF LABOR

COUNCIL OF NATIONAL DEFENSE
WOMAN'S COMMITTEE-MINNESOTA DIVISION

MINNESOTA COMMISSION OF PUBLIC SAFETY
WOMAN'S AUXILIARY COMMITTEE

City or Town _Mpls_   County _Hennepin_ Date _10/2/18_ Name of Investigator _O. V. Laughead_

Name of Firm _Moore & Scriver_ 809 Nicollet Kind of Establishment _Retail Furniture Carpets_

Total No. of Employees _29_   No. of Men _varies 21_   No. of Women _8_   No. of Children under 16 _/_

HOURS OF WORK FOR WOMEN AND CHILDREN

Women:

No. hours per day _8 1/2_

No. hours per week _{ 46 1/2 summer / 50 1/2 winter }_

No. women working after 9 P. M. _/_

No. women working 7 days per week _/_

Children:

No. working over 8 hours per day

Length of day, if over 8 hours

No. working over 48 hours per week _/_

No. working after 7 P. M. _/_

SANITATION

Toilets: provided   No. _____ Separate for women _yes_ Condition _Good_ Location _each floor_

Drinking water _Spring_ Common drinking cup _indiv_ Public towel _Roller Daily_

Ventilation _good_   Light _good_   Cleanliness _good_

SPECIAL SURVEY OF WOMEN WHO HAVE REPLACED MEN IN ADDITION TO DATA
REQUIRED ON OTHER SIDE OF PAPER (Page 2)

	If man is in war service, give branch	Present wage per week of woman	Wages paid man replaced	Total hours per week of woman	Total hours per week of man replaced	Kind of work
1. On line one write name and address of woman replacing man						
2. On line two write name and address of man replaced						
1.						
2. _None_						
1.						
2.						
1.						
2.						
1.						
2.						
1.						
2.						
1.						
2.						
1.						
2.						
1.						
2.						
1.						
2.						
1.						
2.						
1.						

Industrial survey form, 1918. The detailed survey by the Woman's Committee of the Minnesota Commission of Public Safety offers a snapshot of the hours, wages, and working conditions at companies like Moore & Scriver, the furniture store where Anna Jantsch and seven other women sewed. Note the attention to toilets, drinking water, ventilation, and light.

believe ... and indicates that the law of supply and demand does not operate freely where the wages of women are concerned." The cost of living far exceeded the minimum wage, although "the commission lived on the hope that the cost of living would come down." It was difficult to compare men and women because of variations in wages and different industries, but in businesses where both men and women worked, males under twenty-one—unlikely to be heads of families and on average working a shorter length of time than women—still made more than women, according to labor department statistics. In response to the commission's arguments and actions, employers again applied for and obtained an injunction. The Minnesota Supreme Court again upheld the law.[56]

By this time, a case challenging minimum wage was making its way up to the U.S. Supreme Court. In *Adkins v. Children's Hospital,* a case opposing a District of Columbia minimum-wage law, opponents argued that adult women were "legally as capable of contracting for themselves as men" and that minimum wages were tantamount to price fixing. The Supreme Court agreed. The long legal battle against minimum wages had at last been won by business interests. The progressive coalition's disintegration in Minnesota and the United States in 1919–20 insured that the decision would not be reversed, or at least that progressive reformers would never again find it easy to unite across party lines. Progressives retreated back to their parties for security. Women's rights advocates split over the issue of protective legislation, many supporting the retention of protections for women, others advocating "equal rights."

Dorchester women had to be aware of the ongoing battles about their wages. And they must have known that better working conditions and higher wages ensured that as single women they would be able to support themselves, to take advantage of what the city had to offer, and to decide freely whether or not to marry.

Finding Partners

Theresa's Story, Again [Schopp, Tinucci, born in Wisconsin, 1902–59]

I grew up knowing that my mother, Theresa Schopp, had fled the farm for the Twin Cities, where I was born, and that she hated farm life. Born in 1902, the sixth of Matilda's eight children, Theresa went without shoes or wore hand-me-downs that pinched and crippled her feet. She quit school after seventh grade to care for sick family members. Theresa loved city life. She died in 1959, a southern California suburban housewife whose veteran husband sold real estate and whose only daughter was in graduate school studying history.

Theresa spent seven years working in St. Paul before she chose a permanent partner. Sometime around 1924, she met Charles Tinucci. The match was typical of those made by country women who had no intention of returning to

the farms from which they had escaped. They looked for suitable urban partners. Like Theresa, Charles came from a poor immigrant family. His parents
had married in 1899 in Italy. Charles, the youngest of three boys, was born in
1903, but there was little to offer three sons in rural Tuscany. His father left for
the United States in 1909; his mother remained, taking in washing to make
ends meet. By 1913 the family could afford to send the oldest son to be with his
father, and in 1915 the rest of the family joined them.[57]

Charles and Theresa had both grown up poor. His father, Oreste, rented a
house in a downtown St. Paul neighborhood that was crowded, dirty, and
tough. Charles remembered being chased by kids who threw coal at him and
his brothers. The boys gathered the coal to help heat their house. They soon
moved from that first home on East Ninth Street to nearby DeSoto, to a better
house but one still located in the tough downtown neighborhood. By 1920 all
but the youngest, a daughter born in the United States in 1916, were out of
school and working. The family could afford to move out and up.

When Theresa met Charles, his family was already living at 320 Fuller Street,
near the state capitol. Theresa would have been impressed with the Fuller
Street house. Wealthy families had once built these spacious homes to display
their good fortune. Later, the millionaires abandoned the area for grander
mansions on Summit Avenue. Working families like the Tinuccis were able to
obtain mortgages to buy these large houses. They subdivided the upper-floor
rooms into apartment rentals and partitioned the large, high-ceilinged downstairs rooms for family use. The area was ethnically mixed. Many Jewish families had moved there in the 1890s—one family still lived across from the Fuller
Street house—and nearby was the predominantly black community of Rondo.[58]

Charles recalled having black friends as a child. Evelyn Fairbanks would
later write warmly of growing up in her African American family about three
blocks from the Tinuccis. The families were working poor. Charles's father had
been a skilled terrazzo artisan in Italy and sometimes worked at that trade but
more often as a day laborer or janitor. When Theresa met Oreste, he was probably employed as a janitor at the *St. Paul Dispatch* building.[59]

The Fuller Street home was impressive. The front door opened into a hall-
way that had a beautiful mirror with two shelves, each with a marble top. The
dining room had a marble fireplace, a brass chandelier with prisms, and a
pump organ that the children were forbidden to play. There was a large bay
window through which a cousin remembered watching the lamplighter make
his rounds. The Tinucci family could afford such grandeur because the entire
family was working hard, as revealed by the 1920 census. Charles's mother,
Francesca, was keeping house, cooking for the four men, and caring for her
four-year-old daughter; Oreste was working as a laborer at a packing house; one
brother was a shirt cutter at the Guitermann Brothers factory and also worked
part-time as an elevator operator; another was a yard man at the Tri-State

Telephone and Telegraph Company. Charles was working as a delivery boy for the Schoch Grocery Company.

The family remembered Charles as a "hustler," always eager to better himself. Theresa would have been favorably impressed by such qualities. By the time she met him, sometime in 1924, he had moved on from delivery boy to messenger, then to clerk, then to manager of the Parrot Café. Motivated and hardworking, Charles had job opportunities not available to his black friends. Italian and Jewish children were often barred from college and higher white-collar jobs, but there were plenty of lower middle-class jobs available for young men. Theresa had a redheaded beau at the time she met Charles, but he was persistent and ambitious. Within a year he had a new job at the motor company and, no doubt, his first automobile. With his dark good looks, he resembled Rudolph Valentino, idol of the silent screen.

I try to imagine what it was like for Theresa, who had grown up in that small, cramped log house on the farm, to enter the grand Fuller Street house with Charles. Francesca, with Charles translating her Italian into English, would have made Theresa welcome in her home and at her table, heaping her plate with the fine Italian cooking for which she was known—spaghetti with tomato sauce, meat, and vegetables from the garden; the wild mushrooms she gathered and pickled; fruit and nuts; a fine chocolate torte or perhaps her newest achievement, a lemon pie she had learned to make from the baker who lived next door. There was always homemade red wine from the cellar, where Oreste stood guard against his sons' attempts to taste it before it was well aged. It would have seemed like a family of plenty, quite unlike the struggling one she had left.

Later, when Theresa had agreed to marry Charles, Francesca would pass on her recipe for spaghetti sauce. She would show Theresa how to brown the meat in olive oil over a high flame on the gas stove—either neck bones, spareribs, pork, or ground beef—then remove the meat to a large heavy iron kettle and add diced celery, onion, garlic, and green peppers browned in pan drippings. She would add two quarts of home-canned tomatoes that Oreste had grown in the back yard along with salt, basil, and oregano, bring everything to a boil, and simmer half-covered for hours until the sauce was thick. Finally, Francesca would add some of her canned wild mushrooms, taste the sauce with her big wooden spoon, and add a bit of sugar if it was too sour or some water or red wine if it was too thick. Theresa made this spaghetti sauce for Charles every week after they married.

LIVING IT UP

Street life and outings were an important part of the city experience for Theresa and other young working women. Walking in parks, eating at ice-cream parlors, window-shopping, going to movies, dances, and amusement parks—the

Twin Cities were full of things to do besides work. Young women without responsibilities for parents and children found many ways to amuse themselves at little cost. They visited St. Paul's Como Park on evenings and weekends to look at the gardens or to ice-skate. Parks were popular with country girls accustomed to being outdoors. My mother always enjoyed them; she also liked walking city streets to window-shop.

The Twin Cities were famous for their department stores. In Minneapolis, Donaldson's had its Glass Block with massed windows at Sixth and Nicollet. At Seventh and Nicollet, Dayton's Dry Goods offered twenty departments on its ground floor, all faced with huge windows. The Palace Clothing Store was at Fourth and Nicollet; Quinlan's women's ready-to-wear at 513 Nicollet. Many stores, like Dayton's, appealed to working-class women with sales, basement specials, and full-page ads in the Minneapolis newspapers. St. Paul had its own street of dreams by 1914, centered on Seventh and Wabasha and anchored by the Emporium and the Golden Rule department stores, their expansive glass windows facing each other across Seventh Street. The department stores provided jobs for young women while their contents fed the longings of all.[60]

Movies were an all-year delight within young working women's reach. The Wisconsin countryside offered few picture shows, although the Jantsch sisters probably saw some early movies in Dorchester and Chippewa Falls. By the time the women reached the Twin Cities around 1910, elaborate movie houses were being built downtown. During the next decade, Twin Cities entrepreneurs rushed to meet growing demand for these "moving pictures."[61]

In St. Paul, Wabasha and Seventh streets became a mecca for movie houses. The *Pioneer Press* featured the column "Chat of St. Paul Filmland," with summaries of movies showing at places named the Starland, the Blue Mouse, New Liberty, New Princess, and New Astor. By June 1920 one could choose from a great variety of films: tragedies such as *Behind the Door,* the story of a sea captain whose wife is captured by a U-boat submarine crew; thrillers like *The Dark Mirror,* in which a society girl, mistaken as a belle of the underworld, is captured and experiences frightening adventures; comedies such as *Dollar for Dollar,* where a charming woman blackmails a financier, or *The Deadlier Sex,* in which the heroine captures the hero and carries him off to the woods of Maine, where he learns to love nature; or a romance like *The Virgin of Stamboul,* where an American soldier of fortune and a beautiful beggar girl meet amid elegant mosques, camel caravans, and Turkish cavalry troops. In 1921 theaters would vie to show *The Sheik,* starring Rudolph Valentino as the desert chieftain and Agnes Ayres as the "civilized" woman who found romance with him.

Another pastime, dancing, had been a particular favorite in the country. The Dorchester sisters grew up moving to accordion music at dances held in barns with splintery floors; Theresa's father frequently played at these country dances. Later, young people walked three miles to Jerkwater, a neighborhood bar that had a second-floor dance hall with a smooth wooden floor. In the cities the young women found that labor union, ethnic, and religious groups sponsored dozens of dances. Union halls charged twenty-five to fifty cents, often admitting women free if they had escorts.

My mother loved to dance, although she seldom had the chance when I was growing up. I never asked her about her early dancing, but some years ago, sitting with one of my aunts drinking coffee, I asked her what she did in the city. She said she had first worked in a candy factory and roomed with a young friend's family. The year was 1916. "What did you do after work?" I persisted. "We went dancing," she replied, "every night except Monday." "Why not on Monday?" I asked. "Because," she responded with a smile, "the dance hall was closed on Monday."

Recreational opportunities, in addition to the need for more and easier jobs at better pay, influenced rural women's decisions to migrate to urban areas. City dance halls offered far more opportunities for socializing with peer groups, more frequently, with better facilities and music, and with less community supervision than country dance halls. Rural areas had always provided occasion for daughters to move spatially through the landscape. Young women walked what seem like immense distances today—to school, to run errands, to visit, to work for neighbors, to attend local dances. They had less access than their brothers to the new bicycles that became available in the first decade of the twentieth century, however. Urban areas offered inexpensive public transportation for young women to use as they wished. Early twentieth-century cities had centralized commercial areas with convenient sidewalks and streetcars. While young working women often lived near their job and walked there each day, they could afford occasional outings by public transportation. They also had increased amounts of leisure time and energy available for activities other than work.

City dance hall cultures flourished across the country during the early decades of the century. In the 1910s urban youth "danced like mad," wrote historian Tera Hunter. Ballroom dancing reached deep into neighborhoods in all regions and all racial and ethnic groups. Many young working-class women and men lived in crowded tenements or rented rooms with no places to work off their confined energies. Commercial dance halls provided, for a small cost, sites where young people could hang out, meet each other, and exercise. Dressing up and dancing reinvigorated workers, enabling them to persevere. Hunter argues that members of the middle class, whether white or black, claimed the right to control and direct this use of their bodies. This passion to dance was a pattern repeated elsewhere during these years. Mary Neth has argued that new forms of recreation, such as dance halls, may have increased dissatisfaction with farm incomes while better economic opportunities in the cities—not to mention more occasions to dance—pulled youth there.[62]

When rural women went to the city they had access to these new dances. Popular songs caught glimpses of those introduced during the early decades of the twentieth century. "Meet Me in St. Louis" promised, "We will dance the Hoochee Koochee. I will be your tootsie wootsie." The "Hoochee Koochee" referred to the Middle Eastern belly dance introduced at the 1893 World's Columbian Exhibition in Chicago; by the St. Louis Fair of 1904 it had already evolved into a popular couples' dance. Irving Berlin's 1911 song "Everybody's Doin' It Now" tracked the arrival of black dance into northern dance halls. The "Grizzly Bear" was one of many dances that incorporated supposed animal movements. These dances were as popular in middle-sized cities such as Milwaukee and Minneapolis, to which most Wisconsin farm daughters migrated, as in New York, Chicago, or Atlanta.[63]

While city and country girls danced, urban reformers worried about their morals. The line between the stylistic erotic dancing of the late nineteenth century "sporting" life meant for male audiences and the new couples' dances of youth seemed indistinct to urban reformers. The dancing craze engulfed urban areas after the turn of the century, bringing new dances with the movement of far more body parts to replace older, more upright body movement. According to one account, after a period of about seventy years during which dances remained almost the same, enthusiasts introduced some two hundred new dances between 1912 and 1914. As dancing became a favorite pastime, adversaries organized to counter the perceived moral threat. Even Jane Addams, then just beginning her social reforms in Chicago, became concerned about the dangerous influence dance halls might have on young girls. Reformers sympathized with working youth who, they agreed, relieved tired nerves and overstrained attention with dance, but they did not like the proximity of saloons to dance halls. Young people did not care. Second-generation immigrants could have danced at immigrant society halls, but they considered the commercial dance halls more American, according to some experts.[64]

Milwaukee reformers, concerned by the attraction of commercial dance halls, commissioned a study in 1912. Rowland Hayes, field secretary for the Playground and Recreation Association, began to collect statistics. On one Saturday evening in November, Hayes reported, of 9,300 dancers on Milwaukee dance floors, two-thirds were youths between eighteen and twenty-five, about 14 percent of their age group. They danced in public halls, in club halls, in fraternal halls, and in dance academy halls. At immigrant society halls, young people mingled with families and elders in relative safety, Hayes thought, but commercial dance halls encouraged drinking. He and others suggested that urban schools offer more recreation, including mixed couple dancing. When my aunt arrived in Milwaukee in 1916, public dancing was as popular as ever. She recounted that she did not dance at mixed-age immigrant halls but in commercial halls that young people attended in groups unaccompanied by adults.[65]

Urban jobs gave young women access to streetcars and to private cars and to dance halls open six nights a week. Some farm daughters even bought automobiles. Emma Jantsch left an account of her first car and how it related to her dancing. Emma, her older sister Anna, and their younger brother William were all working in Minneapolis by 1917. William found a car that he wanted to buy, but he could not afford the price. Thus the three siblings bought their first car in partnership. In June 1917 they brought it home from Minneapolis, on a harrowing two-day trip through a rainstorm, with William at the wheel. Emma recalled how wonderful it was to have the car at the farm that summer for the weekly dance: "No longer was it necessary to walk the two miles to the Jerkwater dance hall and retrace the same distance at 2 A.M. after the dance. Now we were able to extend our dancing limits to Dorchester [six miles away] and to more distant neighborhoods. No longer did we come home with a headache after the bumpy six miles in summer heat, or with half frozen feet in the winter cold." The car did not keep Emma on the farm even though it extended the range of her dancing. She returned to Minneapolis to work. Without city work, of course, she would never have been able to buy a car. In the city, young women could get by without a car—the car was a luxury. Public transportation allowed them to move around the city easily. Dance halls were within walking distance from most working-class communities. Young working-class men were buying cars and using them in courting or, as it soon became known, dating.[66]

Improved transportation in rural areas did not keep farm daughters "down on the farm." Instead it facilitated migration to cities, where the women eagerly participated in the new dance cultures as well as in new forms of employment. For these young women, migration, work, and dance all formed part of a transition out of rural into urban culture. Despite reformers' dire predictions, most probably settled into urban life without major problems, even if they "danced like mad."[67]

Minneapolis was also rich in commercial amusement parks. Between 1905 and 1914 the city's Wonderland Park, with its artificial lagoon, spectacular rides, and twenty-three buildings, could be reached by the local street railway. From 1906 to 1911 Lake Minnetonka's Big Island was a popular bathing and picnicking destination that also boasted one of the Midwest's largest dance pavilions. In 1916 the pavilion was moved to Excelsior, and a new amusement park opened there in 1925.[68]

Before World War I, outings and dates were made by streetcar or by walking. Most reminiscences testify to the safety of city streets for young women. Although by 1920 automobiles were beginning to fill the city, they were not a necessity; public transportation took families, groups of young people, and couples to all special recreational spots at low cost. Anna and Emma left their car at the family farm after spending the summer of 1917 there.

For most young women, finding male partners seemed a natural part of social activities. All places were possible venues to meet young men. One version of my parents' first encounter has them walking in Como Park. Dance halls were popular destinations, too, but women usually went to these large establishments with men they had met elsewhere. Catholic daughters met young Catholic men at the smaller, more tightly controlled Knights of Columbus dances. Another likely place to find a prospective suitor was at work. A second version of my parents' meeting places them at the Parrot Café, which my father managed and where Theresa probably clerked. Anna Schopper may have met her husband, Truman Beane, in the neighborhood where both lived. Rose Jantsch met her future husband, Frank Kumhera, when he rented a room a block away from the sisters. He worked in Superior for months at a time; while he was gone, Rose had other beaux. She and Emma would double date on afternoon trips to Lake Minnetonka.

Several photographs of my parents taken around the time of their marriage show the couple in various locations and tell us something about favorite places to go and what young women wore. These family photographs reveal the young farm woman indulging herself with clothing, wearing a recreational outfit including jodhpurs and boots, one of the popular short street dresses of the 1920s, and more formal attire. One photograph was taken with a hand-held camera, probably by Charles's brother, in Chicago in 1925. Theresa and Charles stand close together in a park, she carrying a fox fur and wearing a close-fitting cloche hat and a fur-trimmed satin dress she later said cost seventy-five dollars.

Although my mother did not talk much about city life, when she spoke of this time before her marriage it was to hint at freedom: to choose a partner, to buy expensive clothing, to have someplace to wear the clothes in public. Indulging herself with fashionable

Theresa and Charles, Chicago, 1925. Posed before their shiny roadster convertible, the couple displays a new public intimacy and a willingness to proclaim their affection as they gaze at each other. Theresa wears a fashionable middy-style two-piece print dress and has bobbed her hair.

clothing, studying and buying outfits, she must have tried to forget the deprivation of the farm. Clothing signified material success. She dressed for the pleasure it gave her, for the young man she courted, for the cameras that recorded their new life together. She was playing, at least a bit, the role of the vamp, while her partner, the handsome young manager of the Parrot Café, played the role of the sheik.

Automobiles were an important part of my parents' courtship. For the first time Theresa had access to private transportation when journeying to the public places in which she would be seen and photographed. Like the clothes and the photographs, the cars promised a comfortable and mobile life together. Automobiles show up in the photographs: shiny black or gray, hardtop or convertible roadsters. They form a backdrop, in the streets where she looks fondly down at him on a summer day, in the woods where they lounged on a camping trip. He spent his money on cars; she on clothes. He took her places. She posed for the camera, conscious of her appearance, the way she held her body. Their life together would always carry with it this public face of the family record. Charles had his own camera, the folding reflex type, which attached in a small leather case to his belt. Although neither of my parents shared much of their life with me verbally, they constantly documented their lives together and kept the photographs.

TYING THE KNOT OR NOT

Weddings remind us that the city was where country women founded new families. Six of the seven Dorchester sisters—three from each family—married in the Twin Cities. All but one had Catholic priests officiate. As witnesses the women usually chose sisters.

For all but Theresa, city ceremonies were simple and without fuss, only a few kin and friends present. When I married, I chose to have a simple ceremony as well; my father's argument in favor of a larger, more public wedding was that my mother had done the right thing for their marriage in agreeing to a big, Italian wedding. I suspect she would have preferred the simple postwar weddings that the other women had, but she was joining her life to a family that had its own traditions. A big wedding with a feast and dancing was one of them.

I have the portrait taken that fourth day of May in 1925. They were married in St. Mark's Church and then went to the photography studio. Theresa's dress is embossed satin, a straight sheath with capped sleeves and a long frill down the center front. The skirt and frill cover her knees and extend several inches beyond, revealing her white stockinged legs and two-inch white pumps. Her hair is bobbed and, perhaps, marcelled. Her body is surrounded by a mist of tulle, the full veil fastened with a headband. She holds a large spray of roses

Studio marriage photograph, 1925. Theresa Schopp and Charles Tinucci had a large Italian wedding that included a formal studio photograph. Years later Theresa described her wedding dress as a straight sheath of embossed satin with a long frill down the center front.

and ferns in her arms. Her wedding was a performance as well as family and religious ritual. After the photographer's studio would have come the elaborate reception.

For Francesca and the women in the family, weddings were times of great preparation: they usually cooked most of the food at home. The day before the wedding they roasted heaps of chicken. Francesca made spaghetti sauce from the garden tomatoes she had canned the summer before. She had prepared biscotti weeks earlier. There was plenty of Oreste's red wine, made from grapes grown outside their home. Because Charles's older brother belonged to the Knights of Columbus band, it probably played for the dance. All the relatives were invited, in part to repay the weddings the family had attended, in part to keep the extended family together. Italian cousins, uncles, aunts, nieces, and nephews would have outnumbered the relatives Theresa had there. Sister Anna and her husband and children who lived in St. Paul would have attended.

Her brother Frank might have traveled from Dorchester. Would her mother have come? Probably not: someone had to stay home to milk the cows.

After the wedding Theresa and Charles moved to Minneapolis, where he started a nursery business. Two sons were born in Minneapolis. Later the family moved to St. Paul, where I was born in 1934. Just before leaving for California in 1940, she lived again on a nursery farm. Theresa still hated farm life and never wanted to return to the Twin Cities, where she had lived for more than twenty years. She died in southern California in 1959 at only fifty-seven. She had the shortest life of any of the Dorchester women.

Theresa's sister Anna Schopper, who had married in 1920, raised five children and worked for the Northwest Railway for many years. I remember the wonderful fresh bread we always had on visits to her house on Mound Street in the 1930s. Her children, in turn, longed for the store-bought bread my mother served us. Like the four Jantsch sisters, Anna died in the Twin Cities, but she never left to work or raise her family elsewhere. Other young working women, like Theresa and Rose, called the Twin Cities home for a period of years and then moved on. For some, their working days were a brief interlude in their lives. But for all, their city experience was important, an essential part of their young womanhood, the days they had come out of Wisconsin to the city and flourished there.[69]

Perhaps it was normal for Matilda's daughters to depart the farm for elsewhere. Later, even Matilda stayed in California for a decade and then moved to the city of Milwaukee. Thinking of those who came and those who moved on, I realize how foreign it seemed to me to remain in one place, to belong, to form long-term relationships outside a nuclear family. I must have attended twenty different schools and lived in as many houses by the time I was Matilda's age when she arrived in Wisconsin. Matilda came at a time of declining opportunities, especially for young women. Perhaps it was normal to move, to live on borrowed land. They called this place home, and yet how different that feeling was from those of women who wrote about the land and their desire to stay or return. Matilda never wanted to go back to her Bohemian homeland; my mother never wanted to return to her Wisconsin homeland. Home meant not a place outside but a place inside, to be carried with you.

EPILOGUE

Remembering

In 1982 I drove my red Mazda subcompact with its New Mexico license plates into the yard of my uncle's Wisconsin farm. I had lost contact with my mother's family after she died in 1959. I was in graduate school then, and the loss seemed purely private. There was my dissertation to finish at UCLA, teaching in San Diego, a separation from my first husband, then the antiwar movement. By 1970 a back-to-the-land craze had swept me onto a small communal farm in southern Colorado. That brief but intense experience changed the way I looked at history. We had struggled on the farm to establish a small island where men and women shared work and decision making equally. I returned to teaching after two years, but I brought with me a commitment to continue that quest for equality through my work as a historian. I had met many resourceful and competent women on other farms while living in that southern Colorado community. Other historians were already writing about women's experiences, but mainly about urban women. As I re-entered academic life I hoped to bring some of the joy and strength I experienced as a farm woman to my study of the past. I dedicated my first book on rural women to my mother and her escape from a Wisconsin farm at sixteen. I crossed the country several times to do research on Pennsylvania farm women. Then one day, on a whim, I turned off Interstate 80 and drove north through Wisconsin. Remembering only the place name "Medford," I decided to look for my mother's home.

My mother had always given Medford as her birthplace because it was the largest town near her family's farm. It looked like every other small midwestern town I had seen: streets lined with tidy two-story clapboard houses, each with its carefully manicured yard. Too urban, I finally realized—my mother's family would have been outside of town on a farm. My mother's maiden name was Schopp, but there were no Schopps in the phone book. My grandmother had talked about living "by Dorchester." South from Medford on Highway 13 I saw a sign to Dorchester and turned off. The town "felt" somehow closer to home. The streets were short; many ended in cornfields. Men with tractor caps were entering and leaving the village stores; women were in their gardens. There was a Frank Schopper in the phone book, but no Schopp. I gave up and drove west toward the interstate that would take me home to New Mexico. From there I called my brother to see if he knew. No, but he did have an aunt's phone number. Frank Schopper, she confirmed, was my mother's half-brother, and, yes, he still lived on the old home farm, a few miles outside Dorchester.

The next summer I turned north off the interstate again. This time I drove directly to the post office in Dorchester. I explained to the postal clerk that my uncle Frank Schopper lived somewhere nearby and asked for directions to his farm. Two miles east on Highway A, then north one mile, then another half-mile east would bring me to the Schopper place. Highway A cut through high cornfields. Occasionally farmhouse yards, barns, and high blue enameled steel silos marked a crossroad. The Schopper place was on a dirt road; the small two-story frame house sat beside a gravel driveway lined with linden and poplar trees. I turned in and drove toward the house, then around it as the driveway led me into the back yard. I pulled to a stop near a slightly bent man who was chopping wood. I got out and introduced myself. "I'm Theresa's daughter, Joan," I said. "Oh," he replied, "We were wondering what happened to you." I suddenly understood what it meant to "claim kin." And how it felt. I was home.

The original log house in which my mother had been born and grew up was still there. Uncle Frank had covered it with clapboards, and it now served as his blacksmith shop. My uncle was thrifty and never threw anything away. In the loft of the old house I discovered schoolbooks, some with my mother's name in them. We talked about what life was like, growing up in that small log house: how the eight children all crowded into the loft, shivering in winter, sweltering in summer; how they spent most of their summers barefoot outside, working or down by the creek. I met his daughter, Mary Ann Reynolds, a woman almost my age who still lived nearby.

My mother never talked much about her early life on the farm. They were poor. She often had to wear shoes that were too small for her feet; she had to quit school after the seventh grade; she did housework for a neighbor one summer; then she left for St. Paul and worked there until she married. She told no stories about the farm. She said enough for me to know that times were very hard. It was the way she raised me that gave me clues. For example, one day when I answered the door of our very comfortable suburban home barefoot, she took me aside later for a mild reprimand. "You should not answer the door without shoes on," she said. When I asked why, she replied, "The person might think you have none." My mother never shared with me the story of her life or her feelings. Nor with my father. She died of pancreatic cancer in 1959 after a three-year illness. Shortly after, I returned to visit my father, who looked haggard and dispirited. He had been searching for a letter. He said, "You know, mother never talked much. I thought she might have left a letter." There were no letters. No stories.

My mother never saved mementos of her farm life, either. No photographs, no letters, no precious objects. She left everything behind. I tended to do the same: I kept none of my childhood photographs or letters from her. Some years later a friend sent me a letter my mother had written; it is the only letter of hers that I have. It is dated 1950, and in it she writes about wishing to return to school. I knew even less about her mother. For years I thought my German grandmother could not read or write because we received no letters from her and because when she received letters written to her in English others read them to her. A few years ago a cousin gave me a postcard written by my grandmother in beautiful German script; it is the only example of her writing that I have.

It took me several years to decide to use north-central Wisconsin as the locale for this book. The pain of my mother's impoverished childhood, the experiences she kept from me must have remained an unconscious risk. I decided to combine the impersonal distant past I had been recreating with this closer personal history. My mother's family seemed to have a tradition of moving away—my grandmother from her small Bohemian village; my mother from her Wisconsin farm; I from my suburban middle-class California home. We were not women who stayed in one place. We were not rooted, not one of us. It took me years to decide how to tell the story of my grandmother and my mother. I chose to root it in the land they left, to begin it with the lives of other women who lived in north-central Wisconsin and to end it when my mother married in St. Paul in 1925, nine years before my birth.

Without the help of my cousin Mary Ann Reynolds, this book could not have been written. She carries on the family tradition of saving and telling stories, a tradition nurtured and strengthened by her father. She has told me stories and shared pictures, both those she received from her father and those gathered from others. Uncle Frank died in 1984, and the farm had to be sold. Mary Ann helped raise money and organized volunteer labor to move the family's log house. Her nephew Doug Elliott did most of the work moving and fixing the house, which stands now in the Colby Rural Arts Museum. Mary Ann and her family restored it, using all the things her father had saved. Before he died, Uncle Frank told her where everything was kept in the house. Mary Ann often gives guided tours to schoolchildren as well as to adults. Her sense of history is nurtured by experience, story, and artifact, rooted in the Wisconsin landscape. She remembers.

My sense of history is rooted in imagination, archive, and written word. I tried to expand this sense of history, to make it the history of the women of a place that deeply touched my grandmother and mother and made their lives and mine a part of it. Because I was raised differently, in a different place, my relation to this land remains an uneasy one. I grew up with a mother who never gardened, worked outdoors, or, as I remember, even had a houseplant. My father, a former landscape architect and nursery man, designed our home gardens and looked after them; he did not pass on these skills to me. I read books and dusted furniture and joined the southern California car and beach cultures as soon as I could. As a result, I told this story differently than others would. My need to have a story and an understanding of the rural frontier women of my family kept me coming back to Wisconsin over the years.

During the writing of this book, and somewhat uneasily, I began to re-evaluate the ways in which my early life in Minnesota had been affected by the manipulation and use of Native cultures by settlers for their own purposes. The lines from Longfellow's *The Song of Hiawatha* are imprisoned permanently in my memory:

> *By the shores of Gitche Gumee*
> *By the shining Big-Sea-Water*
> *Stood the Wigwam of Nokomis*
> *Daughter of the Moon, Nokomis.*

That is all I remember.[1]

I know now that the story belonged to Woman of the Green Prairie, better known by her English name, Susan Johnston. She inherited her skills from her father, Waubajeeg, a great poet and storyteller. Susan grew up in an Ojibwe village along the Great Lakes, working in the gardens in summer, hunting in winter. In youth she was "accounted the surest eye and fleetest foot among the women of her tribe." She married Scotch-Irish trader John Johnston in 1792, after a fast during which she dreamed of a white stranger. The family encouraged the union with gifts and then with threats when she tried to leave Johnston. After the couple settled in Sault Ste. Marie, Michigan, Susan lived successfully in two worlds, an important person in both settler and Native communities. She was tall, according to visitors, uncommonly active and cheerful, a diplomat, healer, and poet. Her dress—she wore beaded leggings and moccasins along with a short gown of calico and a blue cloth petticoat—marked her as a woman of two cultures. Susan carried on the family's trading business but continued to dry fish and make maple sugar—in some years two tons of it. The only writing Susan left was the account books she kept for the family business from 1818 to 1828.[2]

Susan's stories, in altered form, became part of American culture through the writings of Henry Rowe Schoolcraft. Susan took charge of the twenty-one-year-old Schoolcraft when he arrived as Indian agent at Sault Ste. Marie in 1822 and began wooing her fashionably dressed and well-educated eldest daughter, Jane. Susan taught young Henry the rudiments of the Ojibwe language and began to tell him the stories of her people through her daughter, who translated them for Henry to write down. Schoolcraft published his first Ojibwe stories two years after his marriage to Jane. He stressed Native Americans' humanity and their basic similarity with white readers: Natives were not sentimentalized victims but intensely capable, like his mother-in-law. Later, after converting to Christian fundamentalism, Schoolcraft became a tyrannical husband and father and criticized Native religions because they helped the people retain their old ways. But the early stories, told by Susan to Henry through Jane and then read by Longfellow, became lodged in American culture. I do not know how *Hiawatha* got into my memory. By my reckoning, I only had six months of schooling in Minnesota before leaving for California at age six. But there it is.

Just before that departure from the Midwest and the severing of my ties with Minnesota and Wisconsin, another memory became imbedded. My father was a scoutmaster for a while, and my two older brothers scouts. Like other Boy Scouts in the 1930s, they learned woodlands crafts. In my brothers' bedroom on the second floor of our farmhouse were glass vials of seed beads that they strung on wire to make rings. One day when my brothers were gone, I invaded their space to appropriate the wondrous, brightly colored beads. The result of my attraction was a broken vial, a deep gash, and a traumatic doctor's visit for six stitches in my right index finger. The scar is still there as a reminder. In compensation, my father gave me the first doll I remember, a felt maple leaf of red and gold containing the head of a Native child, with long black hair, brown skin, and a leather headband. In these ways, Native women's stories and culture were appropriated, commercialized, and passed on to settlers' children.

Such appropriations and distortions of Native culture were common, and thus Native peoples became an abstract part of my culture. My aunt married an Ojibwe man from White Earth, but I do not remember him spending much time with our family. We never talked about my uncle's culture or visited his community, although I found out recently that his son spent a good deal of time with my family while I was young. A photograph from a 1936 visit to my grandmother in Wisconsin shows him a shy boy standing to one side of my father, me in my father's arms. Clearly, incorporating family history into this account of northern Wisconsin meant including Native women as well. Native history had always been there in some form but had not been acknowledged.

The taking of Native stories was never quite so clear as in Susan Johnston's case. Settler women also had their stories appropriated and distorted. Sometimes the stories were lost simply because they were not retold. I tried in this book to recover these stories and to identify the women to whom they belong. Although I am not a member of any of the many cultures I discussed, I tried to look into their history with an eye for what seemed to be important experiences to them. In reclaiming my own heritage I tried to value theirs as well.

Accounts of these women, Native and settler, are most easily found through family history. But finding and writing about family stories—our own and others'—is not easy. Often family members do not want that history written down and made public. Poverty, usually defined as economic failure, is not an acceptable family history, nor is it an acknowledged community or national history. Such privation is, to most families, personal and not to be talked about, even within the family. It was not, and often is still not, acceptable for neighbors to intervene directly in family quarrels, even assault or physical abuse, unless those neighbors are kin. Sometimes, in extreme cases, intervention is risked to protect children and young girls. Informal systems of mediation traditionally existed in ethnic communities, but they were difficult to maintain as groups scattered across the landscape and in any event are seldom described in writing. A few city agencies existed—settlement houses, churches, relief agencies—but few extended into rural areas. Poverty is simply not part of the remembered story.

One fairy tale is relevant here. My mother told it to me with evident pleasure, and I believe it sustained her through a difficult childhood and into later life, when she felt she could not speak about her past. The story is "The Princess and the Pea." The young woman, although a princess, is unable to reveal her station for certain reasons. To test her, hosts place a pea under her mattress, thinking that a princess, being very sensitive, will feel it. In the morning the princess complains of bruising and a difficult rest, thus proving that she is, in fact, better than others. I believe that my mother throughout her life attempted to erase her earlier poverty by believing that she was somehow better than her childhood circumstances. She had closed the door on her early life.

Opening doors is the historian's task. Doors to the past are closed—and opened—all the time. When I visited my grandmother's birthplace in Bohemia, there were only two German Bohemians left in the village, women who had married Czechs and were allowed to remain with their mixed-heritage children. There had been Rauschers, I was told, but like the other Germans they had been asked to leave at the end of World War II. Most went to eastern Germany. There had been relatively little bloodshed in that separation, but the people had to leave that place. I did not search for distant relatives in East Germany. I left that door closed, as had my grandmother when she left Bohemia.

I chose to open the door of my mother's childhood poverty only after years of telling my students they should open the doors of their own family's past. Each year of the nearly two decades that I taught women's history, I asked my students to go to the oldest woman in their family and ask her to open the door of her past and share her experiences. Students returned with the burden of that knowledge. Often those pasts had been full of unmentioned pain; of course, they also were often filled with strength, courage, and joy. The students did not know what would be in those rooms they entered, but they returned strengthened with the knowledge of their family history. I remember one Diné student who talked about her distress because she could not speak Navajo and her grandmother could not speak English. Her father had to act as translator. She realized then what she had lost by not speaking her native language.

My grandmother died in the 1950s, long before I even thought to open the door on her life and the lives of women around her. My link was through her first-born son, who had stayed on the land and shared her hard life, and through his daughter, to whom he told the family stories. Over the years she has shared those stories, as have other children of that generation. Those family stories, along with scattered written records, are what remain of the everyday experiences—local, social, private—that shape the more visible public and national history. These were women in a particular place they called home, the experiences of which they passed on to their families through the ways they lived their lives. Building economies, protecting families and communities, and making the choices that caused people to stay put in rural areas or move on to cities and beyond, these women shaped the landscapes, mental and material, we now travel through.

Notes

Abbreviations Used in Notes

AE   Agricultural Extension
ASE   American Society of Equity
BE   Bureau of Ethnology, National Anthropological Archives, National Museum of Natural History, Washington, DC
BIA   Bureau of Indian Affairs
BWC   Minnesota Department of Labor and Industries, Bureau of Women and Children
CA   College of Agriculture
CB   Children's Bureau
CCF   Central Classified Files
CIA   Commissioner of Indian Affairs
CSJ   Sisters of St. Joseph of Carondelet, St. Louis, MO
FSLC   Franciscan Sisters of La Crosse, WI
IMR   Indian Mission Records
LdF   Lac du Flambeau
MHS   Minnesota Historical Society, St. Paul, MN
MLID   Minnesota Labor and Industrial Department
MPSC   Minnesota Public Safety Commission
MUL   Marquette University Library, Milwaukee, WI
NA   National Archives, Washington, DC

NAB   National Archives Building, Washington, DC
NACP   National Archives, College Park, MD
NAGLR   National Archives, Great Lakes Region, Chicago, IL
NL   Newberry Library, Chicago, IL
NLWS   National League for Woman's Service
SCD   State Council of Defense
SCDWC   State Council of Defense, Woman's Committee
SHSW   State Historical Society of Wisconsin, Madison, WI
SSM   Sisters of the Sorrowful Mother, Our Lady of Sorrow Convent, Broken Arrow, OK
UW   University of Wisconsin
UWAES   University of Wisconsin Agricultural Experiment Station
UWMA   University of Wisconsin–Madison, Archives
UWMI   University of Wisconsin–Milwaukee
UWO   University of Wisconsin–Oshkosh
UWSP   University of Wisconsin–Stevens Point
WHSAD   Wisconsin Historical Society Archives Division, Madison, WI
WHSP   Wisconsin Historical Society Press, Madison, WI

Note to Introduction

1. For an extended discussion of nomenclature for Indigenous peoples, see Michael Yellow Bird, "What We Want to Be Called," *American Indian Quarterly* 23.2 (Spring 1999): 1–21.

Notes to Chapter 1

1. "Autobiography of Anna Leona Lansworth Stanley," Dorchester (WI) Public Library, dated "received 1993." I have added biographical details from an accompanying note on her life.

2. *The Wayland Greetings* (Mar. 1957): 47 and (Aug. 1894); letter from Weyland Academy (Beaver Dam, WI) archivist Amy Kuenzi to author, 28 Jan. 2004.

3. *The Wayland Greetings* (Mar. 1955): 9–10.

4. Robert C. Ostergren, "The Euro-

American Settlement of Wisconsin, 1830–1920," in *Wisconsin Land and Life*, ed. Robert C. Ostergren and Thomas R. Vale (Madison: University of Wisconsin [hereafter, uw] Press, 1997), 137–62, quotes on 143–44.

5. Ethel Alice Hurn, *Wisconsin Women in the War Between the States*, Wisconsin History Commission, Original Papers, 6 (Madison: State Printer, 1911), 81–82, 144–49.

6. Ingolf Vogeler, "The Cultural Landscape of Wisconsin Dairy Farming," in *Wisconsin Land and Life*, ed. Ostergren and Vale, 410–11, describes the many outbuildings and the migration of farmers from the south.

7. My thanks to Colleen O'Neill for help with analyzing the 1910 manuscript census.

8. George Hill, "The People of Wisconsin: The German Immigration to Wisconsin," Nationality Study, 5–22, box 7, Series 9/21/3, Rural Sociology Papers, uw–Madison, Archives (hereafter, uwma). By 1910 Marathon had over 54 percent Germans, Clark almost 20 percent, Lincoln 15, and Taylor 12. Ken Meter and Robert Paulson, *Border People: The Böhmisch (German-Bohemians) in America* (Minneapolis and New Ulm, MN: Crossroads Research Center and German-Bohemian Heritage Center, 1993), 22.

9. Herman Hërtel to Governor Leonard Farwell, undated, probably 1853, box 1, Series 34, Wisconsin Historical Society Archives Division, Madison, WI (hereafter, whsad).

10. Wisconsin Central Railway Co., mimeographed letter, Jan. 29, 1900; Kate Asaphine Everest, "How Wisconsin Came By Its Large German Element," State Historical Society of Wisconsin (hereafter, shsw), *Collections* 12 (1892): 332; Report from State Board of Immigration to Henry Casson, Secretary of State, 1899, box 1, Series 34, whsad.

11. Everest, "How Wisconsin," 310n2, 333.

12. S. C. Miles to Roeseler, 28 Oct. 1888, John S. Roeseler Papers, whsad.

13. S. C. Miles to Roeseler, 28 Oct. 1888, Roeseler Papers, whsad.

14. Addie Neff, County School Superintendent, to Roeseler, 23 Nov. 1888, Roeseler Papers, whsad.

15. Joseph Jantsch, "The Jantsch Saga" (1948, mimeographed), copy in author's possession, 7–8.

16. Jantsch, "The Jantsch Saga," 9–10.

17. Jantsch, "The Second American Jantsch Generation at Eventide" (1962, mimeographed), copy in author's possession, 10–21.

18. John A. Kurbs, "Hamlet of Browning," 76–80, and Marguerite Heidinger, "The Roman Catholic Church in Lampman," 137–41, in *Poets' Corner: A History of Lampman and District and the RM of Browning* (Lampman, SK: Lampman & District History Book Committee, 1981).

19. For Frank Sr. and Elizabeth, see *Poets' Corner*, 869.

20. For another view of farm life in Saskatchewan, see Christine Georgina Bye, "'Times Are Hard': A Saskatchewan Farm Woman's Experience of the Great Depression" (MA thesis, University of Calgary, 2001).

21. For Browning and oil, see *Poets' Corner*, 110.

22. The best overview of Poles is Michael J. Goc, *Native Realm: The Polish-American Community of Portage County, 1857–1992* (Stevens Point, WI: Worzalla, 1992).

23. Swedish information from sampling of the 1910 census by Colleen O'Neill; Frederick Hale, *Swedes in Wisconsin* (Madison: Wisconsin Historical Society Press [hereafter, whsp], rev. and exp. ed., 2002), map of density from ca. 1900; birth records from Clark County (WI) Courthouse.

24. "People of Wisconsin," George Hill, Nationality Study, 7–8, Series 9/21/3, Rural Sociology Papers, uwma.

25. Richard Hill, the rural sociologist, was of Finnish descent, and there was a Richard Hill still farming near Owen in the 1940s. See George W. Hill to Matt Maki, 24 Oct. 1941, Hill to George Halonen, 14 Oct. 1941, and Herman Crego translation from his letter, Saxon, WI, Nov. 1941, box 6, Series 9/21/3, D4-Finns, George Hill, Nationality Study, Rural Sociology Papers, uwma. Of the 96 families, 38 lived in the township of Hoard, 26 in Longwood, and 16 in Hixon. See also Glen Taggers, "The Nationality Project: With Reference to the Czechs," 1943, box 7, Series 9/21/3, Rural Sociology Papers, uwma.

26. Anne Lato Zajack, "A Brief History of Early Years," manuscript (n.d.), Thorp (WI) Historical Society Museum.

27. Zajack, "Brief History," for land agents; Linda Osowski Daines, "Ancestors and Descendants," typescript family history (n.d.), Thorp (WI) Public Library.

28. Typescript notes at the Thorp Historical Society Museum identify it as St. Hedwig of Silesia-Swieta. There is also a St. Hedwig of Anjou, but local opinion seems to favor the former.

29. Notes and clippings from *Thorp (WI) Courier* (19 Mar. 1891), and notes from Lorraine Sitter, Thorp Historical Society president, 12 July 2003.

30. Harald A. Pedersen, "Acculturation Among Danish & Polish Ethnic Groups in Wisconsin," typescript copy, 99 for the drop in farming among native-born daughters, 124 for city work, 135 for elders, 105 for education, box 1, Harald A. Pedersen Papers, Series 9/21/5, Rural Sociology Papers, UWMA. See also his PhD thesis, University of Wisconsin–Madison, 1949.

31. Harald A. Pedersen, "Acculturation," 34 for early settlement, 33 and 73 for U.S. and Danish cooperatives, 33 for immigrants, 141 for Danish, 44 and 82 for women working out, 57 for education of immigrant women.

32. Alfred Frost, oral history, 2 Aug. 1980; Louise Oshefski and Laura Olsen, oral history, 15 Oct. 1980, both Withee (WI) Public Library.

33. Keskimeki Scrapbook, Book A, clipping 8 Oct. 1983, Withee (WI) Public Library; businesses from *Withee Memories "From Logging Trails to Super Highways"* (Withee, WI: Centennial Book Committee, 2001).

34. Harald A. Pedersen, Family Schedules, box 1, Harald Pedersen Papers, Series 9/21/5, Rural Sociology Papers, UWMA.

35. I could not locate her on either the 1900 or the 1910 census.

36. For overviews of these nations, see Patty Loew, *Indian Nations of Wisconsin: Histories of Endurance and Renewal* (Madison: WHSP, 2001), and Nancy Oestreich Lurie, *Wisconsin Indians* (Madison: WHSP, rev. and exp. ed., 2002). The Menominee

Nation has published two volumes on its history: *Menominee Tribal History Guide: Commemorating Wisconsin Sesquicentennial, 1848–1998* (Keshena: Menominee Indian Tribe of Wisconsin, 1998), and *Menominee Indian Reservation Historical Review: Commemorating the Reservation Sesquicentennial, 1854–2004* (Keshena: Menominee Indian Tribe of Wisconsin, 2004). For the Lac du Flambeau Chippewa Band, see Leon Valliere, Jr., "Waaswaaganing Ojibweg Lac du Flambeau Chippewa Indians Gaa-izhiwebakishkweyaang," in Elizabeth M. Tornes, *Memories of Lac du Flambeau Elders* (Madison, WI: Center for the Study of Upper Midwestern Cultures, 2004), 9–76. "The Ho-Chunk Nation—A Brief History," at http://www.ho-chunknation.com, provides a good introduction to this group.

37. Axel Jacobson, Wittenberg, to A. E. Jenks, 6 Mar. 1902, and Publius V. Lawson, Menasha, to A. E. Jenks, 6 Feb. 1902, Series 1781, Bureau of Ethnology, National Anthropological Archives, National Museum of Natural History, Washington, DC (hereafter, BE); Paul Radin, an anthropologist who visited Ho-Chunk communities from 1908–13, mentioned these items especially in his book *The Winnebago* (Washington, DC: Smithsonian, Bureau of Ethnology, 1923; reprint, Lincoln: University of Nebraska Press, 1990), 61; Nancy Oestreich Lurie, "Winnebago History and Culture," lecture presented at Black River Falls, Seminar in Winnebago Culture and Acculturation for Community Leaders, typescript (n.d.), Black River Falls (WI) Public Library.

38. References are in reply to a standard query letter to postmasters from A. E. Jenks dated 16 Jan. 1902; Gaus to Jenks, 18 Jan. 1902; F. M. Griswold, Lake Mills, to Jenks, 10 Jan. 1902; E. P. Spragg to Jenks, 25 Feb. 1902; T. S. Chittendon to Jenks, 21 Jan. 1902; C. S. Blair to Jenks, n.d.; Maud Dodge to Jenks, 28 Jan. 1902; D. H. George to Jenks, 28 Jan. 1902, Series 1781, BE, all Series 1371, Bureau of Indian Affairs (hereafter BIA), Record Group 75, National Archives, Washington, DC (hereafter, NA). The National Archives also contains records of conditions for Ho-Chunk people around 1910.

39. Lance Tallmadge discusses Yellow Thunder and dancing in *Thunder in the Dells*, videocassette, produced by Dave Erickson and Lance Tallmadge (Lone Rock, WI: Ootek Productions, 1991); Bennett to Chas. A. J. Marsh, 4 Oct. 1894, box 11, H. H. Bennett Papers, WHSAD.

40. Louise Spindler, *Menomini Women and Culture Change*, American Anthropological Association, 64.1, Pt. 2 (Feb. 1962), Memoir 91, describes handwork on 117 and estimates for 1820 and 1857 on 708. The 1857 census estimated 914 children, 426 women, and 368 men. Alfred Cope, "A Visit to the Menominee," described the women's clothes; a copy of his memoir, published originally by *The Friend*, is in Menominee Indian Papers, 1817–56, 1857, 1861, Wisconsin Manuscripts BU, WHSAD.

41. Felix M. Keesing, *The Menominee Indians of Wisconsin: A Study of Three Centuries of Contact and Change* (Madison: UW Press, 1987), esp. 137–52; Cope, "Visit," also mentions about four hundred Métis at Lake Poygan asked to join the community; for Bonduel, see James A. Mehan, "Dousman Women, Catholic Teachers Among the Menominees" (MA thesis, St. Francis Seminary, Milwaukee, WI, 1939), 46–55; Oshkosh letter to John Sydam, 30 Jan. 1854, is in Ayer Manuscript 666.667, Newberry Library, Chicago, IL (hereafter, NL); David R. M. Beck, *Siege and Survival: History of the Menominee Indians, 1634–1856* (Lincoln: University of Nebraska Press, 2002), is an excellent introduction to early Menominee history.

42. Patricia K. Ourada, *The Menominee Indians: A History* (Norman: University of Oklahoma Press, 1979), 122–23; A. D. Bonsteel to A. B. Greenwood, Commissioner of Indian Affairs (hereafter, CIA), 23 Mar. and 28 July 1860, and report by Kintzing Pritchettel, 2 Aug. 1860, frame 1835, 1064–65, roll 323, M234, Letters Received by the Office of Indian Affairs, 1824–81, BIA, RG 55, NA Microfilm.

43. "Statistics of Employees in Green Bay Agency," frame 0512, roll 324, M234, Letters Received by the Office of Indian Affairs, 1824–81, BIA, RG 55, NA Microfilm; Phebe Jewell Nichols, "Brief Biography of Angus F.

Lookaround," mss BG, box 1, folder 1, Angus and Phebe Lookaround Papers, University of Wisconsin–Oshkosh (hereafter, UWO), describes his father joining at fourteen and later marrying Mary Weso, a Métis of Scotch-English and Menominee heritage.

44. Nichols, "Brief Biography."

45. Walter Hoffman, *The Menominee Indians*, 14th Annual Report, Bureau of American Ethnology (Washington: GPO, 1892–93): see plate 16 and description of houses 253, mats 248, and feast 286.

46. Ronald N. Satz, "Chippewa Treaty Rights: The Reserved Rights of Wisconsin's Chippewa Indians in Historical Perspective," *Wisconsin Academy of Sciences, Arts and Letters, Transactions*, 79.1 (1991): 53–55; Patricia Loew, "Newspapers and the Lake Superior Chippewa in the 'unProgressive' Era" (PhD diss., UW–Madison, 1998), 121–22, discusses insistence by some Ojibwe that they had the right to control resources on reservation land sold to whites.

47. Danziger, "They Would Not Be Moved," 183. Letters reporting yearly rounds are Clara Allen to James F. Gregory, 2 and 31 Dec. 1886 and 12 Apr. 1888, Letters Received by the Agent at Ashland, WI, from Lac du Flambeau Reserve, 1885–95, box 1, RG 75, BIA, La Pointe Agency, National Archives, Great Lakes Region, Chicago, IL (hereafter, NAGLR).

48. Satz, "Chippewa Treaty Rights," 73, 83–85.

49. Steven E. Silvern, "The Geography of Ojibwe Treaty Rights in Northern Wisconsin," in *Wisconsin Land and Life*, ed. Ostergren and Vale, 494–95.

50. Robert A. Birmingham, "The Rozellville Indian Community: Historical Background" and "Stray Bands and Dream Dancers: Indian Farms and Potawatomi Settlement in Central Wisconsin During the Late 19th and Early 20th Century," and Mark E. Bruhy, "Big Indian Farm Site (FS Site Number 09–02–03–001) and Little Indian Farm Sites (FS Site Number 09–02–03–002): Cultural Resource Site Inspection," Chequamegon and Nicolet National Forests, Forest Service, U.S. Department of Agriculture, copies on file, Office of the State Archaeologist, Preservation Division–

Public History Division, Wisconsin Historical Society, Madison.

Notes to Chapter 2

1. Fred Sheppard, "The Peshtigo Fire," Van Antwerp Wisconsin Folklore Collection, box 1, Disasters and Unusual Events, WHSAD. Sheppard uses the name Amanda in this account, but Emina is listed as the servant in the 1880 census, U.S. Bureau of the Census, Federal Population Census, Tenth Census of the United States, 1880, T9, Marinette County (WI), Peshtigo, Enumeration District 99, Sheet 7, Household 60, reel 1435, RG 29, NA Microfilm. The Sheppard family does not appear on the 1870 census.

2. The literature on the Peshtigo fire is voluminous. I have relied primarily on unpublished first-person accounts. The best secondary account is Robert W. Wells, *Fire at Peshtigo* (Englewood Cliffs, NJ: Prentice-Hall, 1968). The most widely available primary account is by the Catholic priest Reverend Peter Pernin, "The Great Peshtigo Fire: An Eyewitness Account," *Wisconsin Magazine of History* (Summer 1971): 246–72, reprinted with an introduction and footnotes in pamphlet form for the Wisconsin Stories series in 1971. Another contemporary account, compiled by Green Bay journalist Frank Tilton to raise funds for the survivors, is *Sketch of the Great Fires at Peshtigo, the Sugar Bush, Menekaune, Williamsville, and Generally on the Shores of Green Bay; with Thrilling and Truthful Incidents by Eye Witnesses* (Green Bay, WI: Robinson and Kustermann, 1871). *History of Northern Wisconsin* (2 vols., Chicago: Western Historical Company, 1881), also has a detailed account of fire in the area, 2: 579–83. The most recent account is Denise Gess and William Lutz, *Firestorm at Peshtigo: A Town, Its People, and the Deadliest Fire in American History* (New York: Holt, 2002).

3. Pernin, "Great Peshtigo Fire," unpaged.

4. The Chicago part of the lumber story is told in William Cronin, *Nature's Metropolis: Chicago and the Great West* (New York: Norton, 1991), especially ch. 4, 149–206.

5. Penciled sheets titled "A Terrible Reminiscence," in Josephine Ingalls Sawyer, "A

Personal Reminiscence of the Big Fire," as told to her by Mrs. Isaac Stephenson, who was living with her parents at Peshtigo, SC 908, WHSAD.

6. Sawyer, "Personal Reminiscence."

7. Sawyer, "Personal Reminiscence."

8. Sawyer, "Personal Reminiscence."

9. Mary Morris to Dr. Schafer, 5 May 1917, Mary Fairfield Morris Papers, WHSAD; Wells, *Fire at Peshtigo*, 166, 180–81, notes the telegram was sent Monday evening but not opened until Tuesday morning.

10. Women's extensive Civil War work is described in Hurn, *Wisconsin Women in the War Between the States,* especially 9–25, 47, 58, 63.

11. Relief Committee activities are in Mss. 218, Milwaukee Grain Exchange Records, 1854–1940, UW–Milwaukee: see especially "Ladies Union Relief Society of Westfield, New Jersey, 18 October 1871," and M. Brodish, Decorah, IA, 23 Oct. 1871 in Folder 1–23 Oct. 1871 and committee activities in Folders 24–31 Oct. 1871 and 11–30 Nov. 1871; for McDole, see M. T. Bailey to Conductor, 1 Mar. 1872, Folder Jan.-Mar. 1872, and letters from F. J. Bartels regarding King and from Lydia Russell to Superintendent Langworthy, 11 Oct. 1872, Folder Apr.-Dec. 1872.

12. Philadelphia to Mrs. Baird, Christmas 1871, and Nellie Rice and Annie R. Rice to Baird, 16 Mar. 1872, correspondence, box 2, folder 6, 1870–75, Henry S. and Elizabeth Baird Papers, WHSAD.

13. Sister Beda, interview with Sister M. Alphonsa, 19 June 1939, vol. 3, Sisters of the Sorrowful Mother, Our Lady of Sorrow Convent, Broken Arrow, OK (hereafter, SSM).

14. Margaret Gruener, interview by the author, 30 June 1997, Medford, WI.

15. Pernin, "Great Peshtigo Fire," editor's epilogue.

16. S. A. Barrett, "Material Culture of the Menominee Indians as Seen from August 1, to Sept. 3, 1910, Upon the Occasion of Collecting Ethnological Material for the Public Museum of the City of Milwaukee," Milwaukee (WI) Public Museum, Anthropology Collections, 122. This is probably the 1810 blowdown and fire mentioned in James G. Newman, "The Menominee Forest of

Wisconsin: A Case History in American Forest Management" (Phd diss., Michigan State University, 1967), 24.

17. Wells, *Fire at Peshtigo*, recounts a number of these stories, 41, 90–92.

18. Keesing, *Menominee Indians*, 168, 170.

19. Swankle discussed in journal, 49, reel 1, and Rouleau, 603–5, reel 3, George R. Gilkey Papers, University of Wisconsin–Stevens Point (hereafter, UWSP); Robert F. Fries, *Empire in Pine: The Story of Lumbering in Wisconsin, 1830–1900* (Madison, WI: State Historical Society, 1951; reprint, Evanston, IL: Caxton, 1989), 27 for floating office, 126, 205–6, 234.

20. Lucille Boneske, "The Athens Story," in Wausau Writers Club, *Rib Mountain Echoes*, vol. 3 (Stevens Point, WI: Worzalla, 1976), 91, 96, and Howard R. Klueter and James J. Lorence, *Woodlot and Ballot Box: Marathon County in the Twentieth Century* (Stevens Point, WI: Worzalla, 1977), 34, 40 describe Rietbrock enterprise; Centennial Book Committee, *Athens, Wisconsin Centennial, 1890–1990* (Tomahawk, Schofield, and Athens, WI: O.K. Printing, 1990), 8–14.

21. Kellogg's account of Phillips is in box 27, Louise Kellogg Papers, WHSAD.

22. For mill closures, see Daniel C. Scrobell, "Minocqua: A Confluence of Water, Timber and Rails," in *Forest History's Impact on the Growth of Tourism in North Central Wisconsin: Proceedings of the Twenty-Second Annual Meeting of the Forest History Association of Wisconsin* 22 (3–4 Oct. 1997): 10–23.

23. Scrobell, "A Confluence," 10–23.

24. Scrobell, "A Confluence," 35; Timothy Bawden, "Reinventing the Frontier: Tourism, Nature, and Environmental Change in Northern Wisconsin, 1880–1930," (Phd diss., UW–Madison, 2001), 121.

25. Bawden, "Reinventing," 114–15, 121, 129, 132, 139. Most camps tightly controlled their clientele; a number openly noted in their promotional literature that they welcomed "gentiles only."

26. Aliza Fleischer and Daniel Felsenstein, "Support for Rural Tourism: Does It Make a Difference?" *Annals of Tourism Research* 27.4 (2000): 1007–24; Edith Szivas and Michael Riley, "Tourism Employment During Eco-nomic Transition," *Annals of Tourism Research* 26.4 (1999): 747–71; Ruth Dickerson Gardner, *Lunch at Boney's Mound* (n.p.: privately printed, n.d.).

27. Joyce Laabs, *A Collection of Northwoods Nostalgia: From the Pages of the Lakeland Times* (Sun Prairie, WI: Royle Publishing Company, 1978, 1980), "Early Resorts of the Area," 1:83, "Resorts of the North," 2:103–10; Bawden, "Reinventing," 142, 144, 148, 200–201, 205, 207.

28. Bawden, "Reinventing," 7, 9; "Witt Family History," manuscript (n.d.), Minocqua (WI) Museum, discusses work of Emma Witt for Mrs. Wagner, probably before 1920.

29. Bawden, "Reinventing," 79; Laabs, *Northwoods Nostalgia*, 2:113 for lily pad pickers, 2:62 for fishing, 1:32 for hikers.

30. Laabs, *Northwoods Nostalgia*, 2:129; 2:136–43 for Camp Minocqua.

31. Bawden, "Reinventing," 251–53, 261, discusses influence of Camp Fire Girls and Seton.

32. Laabs, *Northwoods Nostalgia*, 2:129–39 describes Camp Minne-WaWa; Bawden, "Reinventing," 274, 279, 284, 287, 289, 306n39 for costs. The camp was sold in 1924 to the American Legion.

33. For early fish management, see George Becker, *Fishes of Wisconsin* (Madison: UW Press, 1983), 18–21; similar problems and restocking efforts occurred in Minnesota according to Steven R. Hoffbeck, "'Without Careful Consideration': Why Carp Swim in Minnesota's Waters," *Minnesota History* 57.6 (Summer 2001): 305–20.

34. Laabs, *Northwoods Nostalgia*, 2:95; Paul Brenner, "The Transition from Logging Camp to Resort," in *Forest History's Impact on the Growth of Tourism in North Central Wisconsin*, 33–43; Bawden, "Reinventing," 75; Arthur A. Oehmcke, *The Woodruff Hatchery Story* ([Wisconsin]: The Author, 1989), 1–7, 14–20.

35. Bawden, "Reinventing," 461–65.

36. Margaret E. Runkel, "My Life at the Lac du Flambeau Government School for Indian Children," manuscript (n.d.), UWSP.

37. Runkel, "My Life"; for employment information, see Perry to Agent Campbell regarding date she entered service, 28 Jan.

1899, and Perry to Agent, 18 and 28 Jan. 1901, Letters received from Lac du Flambeau Reservation and School, 1885–1914, BIA, La Pointe Agency, RG 75, NAGLR.

38. Runkel, "My Life"; Cordelia Sullivan list, 30 June 1894, and machines mentioned in Vine to Acting Indian Agent, 3 Dec. 1897, Letters Received from Lac du Flambeau Reservation and School, 1885–1914, BIA, La Pointe Agency, RG 75, NAGLR.

39. Perry to Acting Indian Agent, 17 Mar. 1898 and 4 May 1897, Letters Received by the Agent at Ashland, BIA, La Pointe Agency, RG 75, NAGLR.

40. Runkel, "My Life."

41. Runkel, "My Life."

42. Edmund J. Danziger, Jr., "They Would Not Be Moved: The Chippewa Treaty of 1854," *Minnesota History* 43 (Spring 1973): 180.

43. Fred J. Vine to Acting Indian Agent, 30 July 1897, Letters Received by the Agent at Ashland, Dec. 1895–Sept. 1897, BIA, La Pointe Agency, RG 75, NAGLR.

44. Fred J. Vine to S. W. Campbell, Indian Agent, 17 Oct. 1898; Fred R. Tripp, letter 24 Dec. 1900; W. S. Wright to S. W. Campbell, 3 Jan. 1901, all in Letters Received by the Agent at Ashland, Sept. 1899–3 Dec. 1901, BIA, La Pointe Agency, RG 75, NAGLR; Bawden, "Reinventing," 76, discusses hunting regulations.

45. "Report of H. B. Peairs, Supervisor in the Lac du Flambeau, Wisconsin Indian School, May 22–25, 1915," Lac du Flambeau (hereafter, LdF) 61866–15–916, BIA, RG 75, Central Classified Files 1907–39 (hereafter, CCF), National Archives Building (hereafter NAB), Washington, DC; Matthew M. Thomas, Kelly S. Jackson, and Marcus Guthrie, "An Archaeological Overview of Native American Maple Sugaring and Historic Sugarbushes of the Lac du Flambeau Band of Lake Superior Chippewa Indians" (Lac du Flambeau, WI: Lac du Flambeau Tribal Historic Preservation Office and the George W. Brown Jr. Ojibwe Museum and Cultural Center, 1999), 36.

46. Fred J. Vine to S. W. Campbell, 17 Oct. 1898, Oct. 1897–Aug. 1899; W. S. Wright to S. W. Campbell, 17 Aug. 1901, Sept. 1899–Dec. 1901, both in Letters Received by the Agent

at Ashland, BIA, La Pointe Agency, RG 75, NAGLR.

47. William J. Egbert to S. W. Campbell, 27 June and 26 Aug. 1907, 21 Apr. 1908, Letters Received by the Agent at Ashland, 19 May 1907–24 Jan. 1914, BIA, La Pointe Agency, RG 75, NAGLR.

48. Egbert to Campbell, 27 June and 25 July 1907, Letters Received by the Agent at Ashland, 19 May 1907–24 Jan. 1914, BIA, La Pointe Agency, RG 75, NAGLR.

49. L. F. Michael to CIA, 30 May 1914, LdF 60756–14–916, RG 75, CCF, NAB.

50. Oscar H. Lipps to CIA, 23 Oct. 1912, and "Status of Agriculture and Other Industries on the Lac du Flambeau Reservation," LdF 35198–12–916; W. N. Sickles to CIA, 18 June 1914, LdF 35198–14–916, RG 74, CCF, NAB.

51. Oscar H. Lipps to CIA, 23 Oct. 1912, LdF 35198–12–916, RG 75, CCF, NAB; Chief Education Division, "Memorandum Regarding Conditions at Lac du Flambeau Reservation," 23 Jan. 1914, LdF 79039–13–910, RG 75, CCF, NAB. See also L. F. Michael, "Report Lac du Flambeau School and Reservation," 12 Dec. 1913, LdF 152810–13–910, RG 75, CCF, NAB.

52. W. N. Sickles to CIA, 23 Sept. 1913, LdF 79039–13–910, RG 75, CCF, NAB; Michael, "Report Lac du Flambeau."

53. Report of Council Proceedings, 26 Mar. 1914, LdF 79039–13–910, RG 75, CCF, NAB.

54. Petition in L. W. White to CIA, 17 Feb. 1915, and Report on Council Proceedings, 25 Mar. 1915, LdF 20862–15–059, RG 75, CCF, NAB.

55. Assistant Commissioner E. B. Merritt to Reverend Philip Gordon, 7 May 1920, LdF 83367–16–300, RG 75, CCF, NAB.

56. Council regulations and copies of letters discussing enforcement, Mrs. Ben Gauthier to James Balmer, Government School, 24 June 1918, and Balmer to Gauthier, 25 June 1918, provided by Gregg Guthrie to the author. The Gauthier lodge was handled as an "exceptional" case to avoid establishing a precedent: in January 1924 the government granted the Gauthiers title to six acres of land under special legislation introduced into the U.S. Congress.

57. Report of H. M. Creel, Inspector, 26 Feb. 1923, LdF 17688–23–900, RG 75, CCF, NAB.

58. Alanson Skinner, "Recollections of an Ethnologist Among the Menomini Indians," *Wisconsin Archeologist* 20.2 (Apr. 1921): 41–74.

59. Newman, "Menominee Forest of Wisconsin," 10–32 for development of management, 35 for judgment about wealth. The tribe later successfully sued the government for bad management, but because members kept their land, they were able to insist on reforms within the system. A. Nicholson to Edward Ayer, 22 Dec. 1913, box 1, correspondence, Board of Indian Commissioners reports on history of policy, Ayer Manuscripts, NL. For later development of the lumber policy, see Thomas Davis, *Sustaining the Forest, the People, and the Spirit* (Albany: State University of New York, 2000), especially 132–35. The La Follette Act of 1908 confirmed Menominee property rights and their right to harvest the timber resources and also provided for selective cutting.

60. See letter from Reginald Oshkosh, Peter Lockaround, and others to Edward Ayer, 10 Feb. 1915, box 1, correspondence, Board of Indian Commissioners, Ayer Manuscripts, NL.

61. See Ourada, *Menominee Indians,* 175–76, for the New York appearance and quote; Keshena Minutes of Meeting, 10 Sept. 1915, box 2, Ayer Manuscripts, NL; Brian Hosmer, "Reflections on Indian 'Cultural Brokers': Reginald Oshkosh," *Ethnohistory* 44.3 (Summer 1997): 493–509.

62. Brian Hosmer, "Creating Indian Entrepreneurs: Menominees, Neopit Mills, and Timber Exploitation, 1890–1915," *American Indian Culture & Research Journal* 15 (1991): 1–28; Keesing, *Menominee Indians,* 230–33.

63. H. H. Bennett to Emma Pettibone, 11 Jan. 1904, box 12, and Cashbook 1904–5, box 18, Bennett Papers, MSS 935, WHSAD.

64. Steven Hoelscher, "A Pretty Strange Place: Nineteenth-Century Scenic Tourism in the Dells," in *Wisconsin Land and Life,* ed. Ostergren and Vale, 424–49.

65. Cashbook, 1904–5, box 18, Bennett Papers, WHSAD.

66. Hoelscher, "Pretty Strange Place," 432, 442; Bennett to George C. Sussenden, 3 Jan. 1899, box 11; to Brother Don, 27 Aug. 1901, box 12; to Friend Taylor, 3 Jan. 1882, box 9; to R. N. Burn, 13 Apr. 1905, box 13, all Bennett Papers, WHSAD; see also Sarah Rath, *Pioneer Photographer: Wisconsin's H. H. Bennett* (Madison, WI: Tamarack Press, 1979), 38.

67. Bennett to Brother John, 28 July 1902, and to J. D. Allen, 18 Aug. and 23 Nov. 1902, box 12, Bennett Papers, WHSAD.

68. Bennett to Brother Charlie and Ella, 6 Dec. 1902; to G. A. Willard, 18 Dec. 1902; and to C. B. Griggs, 27 Jan. 1903; Bennett to Mrs. W. L. O'Neil, 7 Jan. 1903, and to Miss Esther Crawford, 7 Jan. 1903, mention reasons he had to raise his prices; Bennett to Brother Edd, 4 and 18 Feb. 1903 request help in buying and complain about raising prices, all box 12, Bennett Papers, WHSAD.

69. Letters from Bennett to Mrs. J. H. Patterson, 27 Feb. and 1 and 13 Mar. 1903, box 12, Bennett Papers, WHSAD.

70. Bennett to Brother Edd, 12 Apr. 1903, and to Somers & Co., St. Paul, MN, 6 May 1903, box 12, Bennett Papers, WHSAD; see Michael S. Simons, "Aboriginal Heritage Art and Moral Rights," *Annals of Tourism Research* 27.2 (2000): 412–31, for a discussion of the issues of control and dissemination of culture in tourism.

71. Bennett to Brother Edd, 12 Apr. 1903, box 12, Bennett Papers, WHSAD.

72. Bennett to Gimbel Brothers, 29 Apr. 1903, and to Ely Moore, NY, 18 May 1903, box 12, Bennett Papers, WHSAD.

73. Bennett to Ely Moore, Jr., NY, 22 May 1903; to Yountz, 24 May 1903; to I. E. McCourt, MI, 31 May 1903, all box 12, Bennett Papers, WHSAD.

74. Bennett to Moore & Gibson, NH, 9 July and 2 Sept. 1903, box 12, Bennett Papers, WHSAD.

75. Bennett to Geo. Allanson, Milwaukee, 3 Feb. 1904, and to Fred Harvey, 1 Feb. 1904, box 12, Bennett Papers, WHSAD.

76. Bennett to Moore & Gibson, 5 and 17 Jan. 1904, and to Pella and Sons, 5 Mar. 1904, box 12, WHSAD.

77. Bennett to Emil Bercher, 12 Dec. 1904, and to Sommers, 5 Jan. 1904, box 12, Bennett Papers, WHSAD.

78. Bennett to Phoebe S. Acheson, 28 Aug. and 10 Sept. 1906, box 12, Bennett Papers, WHSAD. The author thanks Melanie Sainz for her help in describing the *pajgae*.

79. Jocelyn Riley, *Her Mother Before Her: Winnebago Women's Stories of Their Mothers and Grandmothers: A Resource Guide* (Madison, WI: Her Own Words, 1995), 3–4, 9; Jocelyn Riley, *Winnebago Songs and Stories* (Madison, WI: Her Own Words, 1995), 74, 81, 86–87.

80. Bennett to Choonahkakah, James Standing Water, 21 Mar. 1905; to Kettelson, 26 June 1905; to J. D. Allen, 6 Aug. 1905; to W. E. Holly, 26 Mar. 1906, all box 13, Bennett Papers, WHSAD.

81. On the general appeal of tourist art, see Nelson H. H. Braburn, "The Evolution of Tourist Arts," *Annals of Tourism Research* 11 (1984): 393–419, and Soyoung Kim and Mary A. Littrell, "Souvenir Buying Intentions for Self Versus Others," *Annals of Tourism Research* 28.3 (2001): 638–57. For Navajo tourist parallels in the early twentieth century, see Laura Jane Moore, "Elle Meets the President: Weaving Navajo Culture and Commerce in the Southwest Tourist Industry," *Frontiers* 22.1 (2001): 21–44. For another beadwork distributor, in North Dakota, see Kren V. Hansen, "Historical Sociology and the Prism of Biography: Lillian Wineman and the Trade in Dakota Beadwork, 1893–1929," *Qualitative Sociology* 22.4 (1999): 353–68.

82. On the issue of women's independence, see Patricia Albers, "Autonomy and Dependency in the Lives of Dakota Women: A Study in Historical Change," *Review of Radical Political Economics* 17 (1985): 109–24, and M. J. Schneider, "Women's Work: An Examination of Women's Roles in Plains Indian Arts and Crafts," in *The Hidden Half: Studies of Plains Indian Women*, ed. Patricia Albers and Beatrice Medicine (New York: University Press of America, 1983), 101–22.

83. Beverly Gordon, "The Whimsey and Its Contexts: A Multi-Cultural Model of Material Culture Study," *Journal of American Culture* 9:1 (Spring 1986): 62–63. Tourism promoted beadwork in the woodlands as it did pottery and weaving in the Southwest: Beverly Gordon and Melanie Herzog, *American Indian Art: The Collecting Experience* (Madison: Elvehjem Museum of Art, UW, 1988), 6–7; for the wider trade in the woodlands area, see Ruth B. Phillips, *Trading Identities: The Souvenir in Native North American Art from the Northeast, 1700–1900* (Seattle: University of Washington Press, 1998), especially 3–48; Erik Trump, "'The Idea of Help': White Women Reformers and the Commercialization of Native American Women's Arts," in *Selling the Indian: Commercializing and Appropriating American Indian Cultures*, ed. Carter Jones Meyer and Diana Roger (Tucson: University of Arizona Press, 2001), 159–89, argues that women reformers were also important in redefining the significance and encouraging the purchase of Native women's arts.

84. Terry R. Reynolds, "Women, Pottery, and Economics at Acoma Pueblo," in *New Mexico Women: Intercultural Perspectives*, ed. Joan M. Jensen and Darlis A. Miller (Albuquerque: University of New Mexico Press, 1986), 279–300.

85. Jolene Rickard, "Cew ete Haw I TIH: The bird that Carries Language Back to Another," in *Partial Recall: With Essays on Photographs of Native North Americans*, ed. Lucy R. Lippard (New York: New Press, 1992), 108, 110.

86. Keesing, *Menominee Indians*, 198, 203–6.

87. T. B. Wilson to CIA, 21 Oct. 1909, Keshena 85022–09–047, RG 75, NAB.

88. H. P. Marble, Assistant Superintendent to CIA, 23 Dec. 1913, Keshena 115736–12–047, RG 75, NAB.

89. Nicholson to CIA, 14 Feb. 1914, Keshena 9054–13–915; H. P. Marble to CIA, 7 Apr. 1914, Keshena 38782–14–915; H. P. Marble to L. S. Drake, Keshena 125315–15–913; *Shawano County (WI) Journal* (29 Sept. 1921), clipping in Keshena 79604–21–047, all in RG 75, NAB.

90. H. P. Marble to CIA, 24 Sept. 1914; Nicholson to CIA, 26 Sept. 1914; article by Wallace Meyer, 19 Sept. 1914, clipping from unknown newspaper, all in Keshena 100165–14–047, RG 75, NAB.

91. Clyde Ellis, "'There Is No Doubt... the Dances Should Be Curtailed': Indian Dances and Federal Policy on the Southern

Plains, 1880–1930," *Pacific Historical Review* 70.4 (Nov. 2001): 543–69; Clyde Ellis, "Five Dollars a Week to Be 'Regular Indians': Shows, Exhibitions, and the Economics of Indian Dancing, 1880–1930," in *Native Pathways: American Indian Culture and Economic Development in the Twentieth Century*, ed. Brian Hosmer and Colleen O'Neill (Boulder: University Press of Colorado, 2004), 184–208.

92. Undated letter from Agent A. Nicholson to Edward Ayer, received 11 July 1914, box 1, correspondence, Board of Indian Commissioners, Ayer Manuscripts, NL.

93. Joan M. Jensen, "Sexuality on a Northern Frontier: The Gendering and Disciplining of Rural Wisconsin Women, 1850–1920," *Agricultural History* 73.2 (Spring 1999): 163–64.

94. Department of the Interior, Office of Indian Affairs, Circular No. 884, "Promotion of Native Industries," 22 July 1914, RG 75, NAB.

95. Myrtle Marble to A. S. Nicholson, 5 Sept. 1914, Keshena, 38782–14–915, RG 75, NAB.

96. A. A. Jones to John H. Stephens, 25 May 1914, LdF 79039–13–910, NAB; Michael, "Report Lac du Flambeau."

97. Reports on fairs are in L. W. White to CA, 8 Oct. 1915 and 5 Feb. 1916, LdF 83106–15–047; L. W. White to CIA, 26 Sept. 1916, LdF 101939–16–047; James W. Balmer to CIA, 10 Sept. 1917, LdF 46171–18–047; Balmer to CIA, 14 Oct. 1919, LdF 89073–19–047, all in RG 75, NAB.

98. James W. Balmer to CIA, 14 Oct. 1919, LdF 89073–19–047, RG 75, NAB.

99. W. S. Coleman, Inspector, "Report on Industries," 10 Oct. 1919, LdF 88855–19–910, RG 75, NAB.

100. Mary E. Spinney, Exhibit D, attached to Coleman report, LdF 88855–19–910; Balmer to CIA, 16 Sept. 1920, LdF 78296–20–04, both in RG 75, NAB. Spinney mentioned braided and crocheted rugs, but the women were known for their finger-woven rugs especially, and many photographs show them weaving rather than crocheting or braiding.

101. James W. Balmer to CIA, 3 Apr. 1922, Records of the Education Division, Records of the Industries Section, Reports of the In-

dustrial Surveys, 1922–29, box 23, PI-163, Entry 762, RG 75, NAB (hereafter, Lac du Flambeau Industrial Survey, 1922); "Survey of Home Conditions of the Lac du Flambeau Reservation of Chippewa Indians," General Superintendent's Circular No. 5, LdF 1927–27–800, RG 75, NAB.

102. Interview with Reva Chapman, conducted by Marilyn Conto, *Lac du Flambeau News* (Feb. 1996); interview with Joe Chosa, conducted by Marilyn Conto, *Lac du Flambeau News* (Mar. 1996).

103. Records of the Board of Indian Commissioners, Reference Material, ca. 1875–1933; American Indian Defense Association Bulletins, box 2, PI-163, entry 1395, titled Office of Indian Affairs, *Bulletin 4* (1922): Indian Art and Industries, NL.

Notes to Chapter 3

1. Unless otherwise noted, all information on the women and their community is from Slovenska Druzba Committee, *Spominska Zgodovina: Historical Memoirs, Willard, Wisconsin* (Withee, WI: Isaacs, 1982), see Lunka, 84–85; Lazar, 81–82; Champa, 33–34; Francel, 39–40; and the priest, 156.

2. Slovenska Druzba Committee, *Spominska Zgodovina*, 31–33; numbers are from Rev. J. M. Trunk, *History of Slovene Communities*, pt. 8, translated by the Slovenian Genealogy Society and posted online in 1996: http://feefhs.org/slovenia/sidb1/trunk-wi.html (accessed 23 June 2003).

3. Slovenska Druzba Committee, *Spominska Zgodovina*, 81.

4. Slovenska Druzba Committee, *Spominska Zgodovina*, 155 for wood and pickles.

5. A letter from Agnes Lesar to the author, 2 Sept. 1997, described picking and excursions.

6. John Westimeier, Stetsonville, WI, store records, Colby (WI) Historical Society, Colby Rural Arts Museum; Mary Ann Reynolds identified these records as being from the Jensen store, originally located in Dorchester, WI.

7. Jantsch, "The Jantsch Saga."

8. Richard T. Ely, B. H. Hibbard, and Alonzo B. Cox, *Credit Needs of Settlers in Upper Wisconsin* (Madison: UW Agricul-

tural Experiment Station [hereafter, UWAES], Bulletin 318, 1920), 9–11.

9. For an overview of gardening, see Vera K. Niñez, "Household Gardens: Theoretical and Policy Considerations," *Agricultural Systems* 23 (1987): 170–71, 176–78, 178–79. Women's role in gardening is still an understudied field: see Patricia Howard-Borjas, *Women in the Plant World: The Significance of Women and Gender Bias for Botany and for Biodiversity Conservation* (Wageningen, Netherlands: Wageningen University, 2001), and special issue, "Jungfern im Grunen," *Ariadne* 39 (May 2001).

10. For the condition of agriculture in Bohemia, see Catherine Albrecht, "Rural Banks and Czech Nationalism in Bohemia, 1848–1914," *Agricultural History* 78.3 (Summer 2004): 317–45. For Germans, see Walter D. Kamphoefner, Wolfgang Helbich, and Ulrike Sommer, eds., *News from the Land of Freedom: German Immigrants Write Home* (Ithaca, NY: Cornell University Press, 1991), 304–15; R. R. Lee, "The Impact of Agrarian Change on Women's Work and Child Care in Early-Nineteenth-Century Prussia," in *German Women in the Nineteenth-Century*, ed. John C. Fout (New York: Holmes & Meier, 1984), 234–55; and Kathleen Neils Conzen, "Peasant Pioneers: Generational Succession Among German Farmers in Frontier Minnesota," in *The Countryside in the Age of Capitalist Transformation*, ed. Steven Hahn and Jonathan Prude (Chapel Hill: University of North Carolina, 1985), 259–92.

11. Leopold quoted in "Wisconsin Stories: Passenger Pigeons, Some Documents Relating to the Passenger Pigeon," *Wisconsin Magazine of History* 59 (Summer 1976): 259–81; the last flock was sighted in Marathon County in 1923. Jerry Condon, "The Last Passenger," 126–28, and Anastasia Furman, "From Clam Shells to Blue Collar Buttons," 44–48, both in Wausau Writers Club, *Rib Mountain Echoes*, vol. 3 (Stevens Point, WI: Worzalla, 1976). Pressure cookers replaced open-kettle canning only in the 1920s, when home extension agents began to publish bulletins explaining how pressure cookers could greatly reduce time to process vegetables and make the product

safer. Pressure cookers sold for $18 in 1921, but extension agents sometimes bought them cooperatively in quantities for as little as $13. Local stores carried canning supplies, and families used their precious cash or begged credit to buy the cookers along with the hundreds of Ball jars, caps, and rubber sealing rings that canning required. See Joan M. Jensen, "Canning Comes to New Mexico: Women and the Agricultural Extension, 1914–1919," *New Mexico Historical Review* 57 (Oct. 1982): 361–86.

12. Ida Hewitt, "Homesteading Memoirs," typescript (1981), copy provided by Bunny Marotta. The 160-acre farm of Josephine and Gustave Gauthier Robert was at the fork of the Chippewa and Fisher rivers, just west of the Taylor County line in Chippewa County.

13. Sister Theodine [Amanda Sebold], interview by the author, 6 Aug. 1989, St. Rose Convent, La Crosse, WI.

14. Arthur J. Latton, *Reminiscences and Anecdotes of Early Taylor County* (reprint, La Crosse, WI: Brookhaven Press, 2001), mentions Lublin.

15. Malcolm Rosholt taped interviews with Martha Liebe, 24 Apr. 1956; Paul Laska, n.d.; and Michael Lisz, 29 Nov. 1974, UWSP; see also Malcolm Rosholt, *Pioneers of the Pinery* (Rosholt, WI: Rosholt House, 1979).

16. Malcolm Rosholt taped interviews with Frances Scuoniewicz and Theodora Koziczkowski, 27 Nov. 1974, UWSP.

17. Goc, *Native Realm*, 95–96.

18. James W. Balmer to CIA, 3 Apr. 1922, Records of the Education Division, Records of the Industries Section, Reports of the Industrial Surveys, 1922–29, box 23, PI-163, Entry 762, RG 75, NAB (hereafter, Menominee Industrial Survey, 1922–25), 63.

19. Keesing, *Menominee Indians*, 139, referencing Henry Schoolcraft in 1847 uses the number 300 with cattle and farms; Schoolcraft, Henry Rowe, *Historical and Statistical Information Respecting the History, Condition and Prospects of the Indian Tribes of the United States* (Philadelphia, PA: Lippincott, Grambo, 1851–57), vi, 691–92; Peter Leo Johnson, *Crosier on the Frontier: The Life of John Martin Henni, Archbishop of Milwaukee* (Madison: SHSW, 1959), 146 mentions

the importance of farming and claims the Menominee had 1,000 acres under cultivation at Lake Poygan; estimates of land acres under cultivation at Lake Poygan vary from 10,000 to several hundred. Richard N. Current, *The History of Wisconsin: The Civil War Era, 1848–1873* (Madison: SHSW, 1976), 51, quotes an 1857 agent estimate of 150 farm families five years after the relocation. For Michigan farming, see Susan Sleeper-Smith, *Indian Women and French Men: Rethinking Cultural Encounter in the Western Great Lakes* (Amherst: University of Massachusetts Press, 2001), 73–84.

20. Menominee Industrial Survey, 1922–25, 63. Records vary between 1,017 and 1,070 for the number of Native people living on the reservation at the time: Chas. H. Burke, CIA, to Edwin E. White, 6 Nov. 1923, estimated 1,838, Keshena 84305–23–034, BIA, RG 75, NAB.

21. Frank Robitaille, Expert Farmer, to CIA, 14 Nov. 1912, Keshena 34968–12–916, BIA, RG 75, NAB.

22. Frances Densmore, *How Indians Use Wild Plants for Food, Medicine and Crafts* (Washington, DC: GPO, 1928; reprint, New York: Dover, 1974), 306.

23. Adapted from Frances Densmore, *Chippewa Customs* (Washington, DC: GPO, 1929; reprint, St. Paul: Minnesota Historical Society [hereafter, MHS] Press, 1979), 119–30.

24. Thomas R. Berger, *Village Journey: The Report of the Alaska Native Review Commission* (1985; rev. ed., New York: Hill and Wang, 1995), especially 48–72.

25. U.S. Commissioner of Indian Affairs, *Annual Report to the Secretary of the Interior* (Washington, DC: GPO, 1881), 173, and (1889), 304–5. For similar circumstances, see Joan Champ, "'Difficult to Make Hay': Early Attempts at Agriculture on the Montreal Lake Indian Reserve," *Saskatchewan History* 47 (Spring 1995): 27–35, and Patricia A. Shifferd, "A Study of Economic Change: The Chippewa of Northern Wisconsin, 1854–1900," *Western Canada Journal of Anthropology* 6 (1976): 16–41.

26. U.S. Commissioner of Indian Affairs, *Annual Report* (1890), 237.

27. Lac du Flambeau Industrial Survey, 1922, 126, 127, 128; photo from cover of the Lac du Flambeau Historical and Cultural

Society newsletter *Messinger* (Feb. 1999) identifies the family.

28. D. Sullivan to Leahy, 29 Oct. 1891, to Mercer, 7 Mar. 1893; Fred J. Vine to Mercer, 25 Feb. 1895, Letters Received by the Agent at Ashland, BIA, La Pointe Agency, RG 75, NAGLR.

29. L. F. Michael, Supervisor, "Report Keshena Indian School," 28 Apr. 1913, sect. 2, Industries, Keshena 57409–13–910, BIA, RG 75, NAB.

30. A. S. Nicholson to CIA, 7 June 1915, Keshena 60416–15–916, and 30 Mar. 1916, Keshena 8400–16–916, BIA, RG 75, NAB.

31. F. H. Abbott, Acting Commissioner, to A. S. Nicholson, 18 Feb. 1913, Keshena 22295–13–044, for Washington, DC, trip; A. S. Nicholson to CIA, 15 Mar. 1913, Keshena 25885–13–281, for loans; A. S. Nicholson to CIA, 18 Dec. 1914, Keshena 68556–14–16, for enthusiasm for farming, all BIA, RG 75, NAB.

32. Inspector Linnenam, Keshena superintendent, report (extract copy), 12 Oct. 1915, Keshena 8400–16–916, BIA, RG 75, NAB; other documents indicate his manipulation of councils to get his policies accepted.

33. *The Wisconsin Farmer* (20 Apr. 1916): 16, and *The Wisconsin Agriculturalist* (27 Apr. 1916): 8–9 and (31 July 1916), attached to "Report on Keshena Agency and School," 31 July 1916, Keshena 82203–16–910; Edgar A. Allen to CIA, 12 Feb. 1920, Keshena 137–20–916, all in BIA, RG 75, NAB; report on Menominee in Series 9/4/13, box 4, and Series 9/4/2, box 3, Emergency Demonstration Work, 1918–19, Agriculture Extension, College of Agriculture, UWMA.

34. W. H. Gibbes, Inspector, "Report," 31 July 1916, section 3, Industries, Keshena 82203–16–910; Edgar A. Allen to CIA, 31 Oct. 1918, Keshena 40876–18–916, BIA, RG 75, NAB.

35. Edgar A. Allen to CIA, 12 Feb. 1920, Keshena 13797–20–916, BIA, RG 75, NAB.

36. If the farm was rented to another I counted only the tenant, and sometimes when farming was for kin I omitted it because it was not clear who owned the land. Heber M. Creel, 10 Mar. 1923, Keshena 21059–23–910, BIA, RG 75, NAB.

37. Edna [Meier] Kelly, interview by Jean Saul Rannells, 16 Feb. 1985, Darlington, WI, box 1, folder 3, Rural Women's Oral History

Project, WHSAD; other family information is from Edna's obituary in the Darlington (WI) *Republican Journal* (30 Dec. 1999), 2: 2–5. Peggy Lee Beedle, "Silos in the Landscape: Technology and Silo Construction in Wisconsin" (MA thesis, UW–Madison, 1997), 2, 116, 119.

38. For Taylor statistics, see box 120, Series 9/4/3, Taylor County (WI), Extension Agents, Annual Reports, College of Agriculture, UWMA. C. E. Lee and Henry C. Taylor, *The Progress of the Dairy Industry in Wisconsin* (Madison: UWAES, Bulletin 210, 1911), shows various maps of Taylor County. County Clerk, "Certified Report of Dairy Statistics for Taylor County," 18 Sept. 1916, Annual Statement of Farm Products, 1888–1918, Dairy Processing Companies and Related Statistics, Series 323, Secretary of State, Elections and Records, WHSAD.

39. H. L. Russell, *Dairy Industry in Wisconsin* (Madison: UWAES, Bulletin 88, 1901), 5.

40. Russell, *Dairy Industry in Wisconsin*, 9.

41. *Mangel-wurzel*, from the German, "root of scarcity"; a variety of beet, it was an easily stored root vegetable used for fodder in Europe. N. S. Fish, "The History of the Silo in Wisconsin," *Wisconsin Magazine of History* 8.1 (Sept. 1924): 166.

42. Beedle, "Silos in the Landscape," 29–46 for early history; Fish, "History of the Silo"; Taylor County (WI) Extension Agent, box 120, College of Agriculture, UWMA.

43. G. N. Knapp, *Silo Construction* (Madison: UWAES, Bulletin 125, 1905), 83; figures from F. H. King, *The Construction of Silos* (Madison: UWAES, Bulletin 28, 1891), and C. A. Ocock and F. M. White, *Concrete Silo Construction* (Madison: UWAES, Bulletin 214, 1911).

44. Edward H. Beardsley, *Harry L. Russell and Agricultural Science in Wisconsin* (Madison: UW Press, 1969), 32–34. See also H. L. Russell, *A History of a Tuberculous Herd of Cows* (Madison: UWAES, Bulletin 78, 1899); H. L. Russell and E. G. Hastings, *Bovine Tuberculosis in Wisconsin* (Madison: UWAES, Bulletin 84, 1901), 84; H. L. Russell, *Dairy Industry in Wisconsin* (Madison: UWAES, Bulletin 88, 1901); H. L. Russell and Conrad Hoffman, *A Three Year Campaign Against Bovine Tuberculosis in Wisconsin* (Madison: UWAES, Bulletin 75, 1909).

45. Beardsley, *Harry L. Russell*, 25–31.

46. Lincoln County (WI) Agricultural Agent, Reports, 1915–22, box 64, Series 9/4/3, College of Agriculture, Agricultural Extension (hereafter, CA, AE), UWMA.

47. Taylor County (WI) Agricultural Agent, Reports, 1915–25, box 120, Series 9/4/3, CA, AE, UWMA.

48. Clark County (WI) Agricultural Agent, Reports, 1918–28, box 19, and Marathon County (WI) Agricultural Agent, Reports, 1919–29, box 69, both Series 9/4/3, CA, AE, UWMA.

49. Her etched image is in Wisconsin Dairymen's Association, *Ninth Annual Report, 1881* (Fort Atkinson, WI: The Association).

50. Mrs. L. E. Haws, "Butter Making," Wisconsin Dairymen's Association, *Sixth Annual Report, 1878* (Fort Atkinson, WI: The Association), 65–66.

51. Fannie Morley, "The Dignity of Butter Making, from a Woman's Standpoint," Wisconsin Dairymen's Association, *Tenth Annual Report, 1882* (Fort Atkinson, WI: The Association). Morley does not appear in reports again, and there is no indication that she ever joined the association.

52. F. C. Curtis, "Shall We Patronize the Creamery or Make Up the Milk at Home?" Wisconsin Dairymen's Association, *Twenty-Third Annual Report, 1895* (Fort Atkinson, WI: The Association), 157–69.

53. H. B. J. Andrus, "Some Ideas on Establishing and Operating a Whole-Milk Creamery," Wisconsin Buttermakers' Association, *Annual Report, 1902* (Madison, WI: Democrat Printing Company, 1902), 66–75; see also Joan M. Jensen, "Dairying and Changing Patterns of Family Labor in New Mexico," *New Mexico Historical Review* 75.2 (Apr. 2000): 162. Lincoln County (WI) Agricultural Agent, "Annual Report" (1915), Reports, 1915–22, box 64, Series 9/4/3, CA, AE, UWMA.

54. Figures from *List of Creameries and Cheese Factories in Wisconsin, 1895* (Madison: Dairy and Food Commissioner, 1896), 20, 39.

55. J. C. Chapin, "Troubles with the Hand Separator System," Wisconsin Buttermakers' Association, *Fifth Annual Meeting, 1906* (Madison, WI: Democrat Printing Company), 74–113; Jensen, "Dairying," 162.

56. C. T. Bragg, "The Relation of the Creamery to the Patron," Wisconsin Buttermakers' Association, *Third Annual Meeting, 1904* (Madison, WI: Democrat Printing Company), 282; L. P. Holgerson, "How I Interest My Patrons in Bringing Better Milk," Wisconsin Buttermakers' Association, *Seventh Annual Meeting, 1908* (Madison, WI: Democrat Printing Company), 56–58; W. P. Roseman, "The Creamery as an Educational and Social Center," Wisconsin Buttermakers' Association, *Fourteenth Annual Meeting, 1915* (Madison, WI: Democrat Printing Company), 43.

57. G. H. Benkendorf, "Handling of Hand Separators," Wisconsin Buttermakers' Association, *Sixth Annual Meeting, 1907* (Madison, WI: Democrat Printing Company), 136.

58. Chapin, "Troubles," 74–77.

59. Lee and Taylor, *Progress of the Dairy Industry*, 27–28; Roseman, "The Creamery," 52; H. L. Russell and U. S. Baer, "Development of Factory Dairying in Wisconsin" (Madison, WI: UWAES, 1906), 6; Benkendorf, "Handling of Hand Separators," 131–32, 134–36.

60. Alma Parge Lineaweaver, telephone interview by the author, 31 July 1998, Dorchester, WI.

61. Franklyn Curtiss-Wedge, comp., *History of Clark County, Wisconsin* (Chicago: Cooper, 1918), 696, account by Mrs. John Shanks. Clark County organized an Agricultural Society in 1873, but none of the three brothers appear among the names of the first officers.

62. U.S. Bureau of the Census, Agricultural Census, 1880, Wisconsin, Schedule 2, Clark County, Pine Valley Town, Enumeration District 168, 1–13, WHSAD.

63. History from J. Q. Emery, *The Wonderful Story of Wisconsin's Dairy Industry* (from *Butter, Cheese & Egg Journal;* reprint, Milwaukee, WI: Olsen, 1923), 4–5; Jefferson County (WI) *Union* (23 Feb. 1872); Wisconsin Dairymen's Association, *Second Annual Report, 1894* (Fort Atkinson, WI: The Association), 13, 15, 22 for the first planning meeting; Wisconsin Dairymen's Association, *Third Annual Meeting, 1875* (Fort Atkinson, WI: The Association), 11–13.

64. Emery, *Wonderful Story*, 12; Mrs. O. Dix, "Managing a Cooperative Cheese Factory," Wisconsin Cheesemakers' Association, *Proceedings, 1915* (Monroe, WI: Times Printing Company), 92–93.

65. Recollection by Mary Jantsch Gierl in Jantsch, "The Jantsch Saga," 14.

66. Jerry Reynolds, interview by the author, 2 July 1997, Dorchester, WI.

67. For Marshfield, see Don Schnitzler and Jeff Kleiman, eds., *The Marshfield Story, 1872–1997: Piecing Together Our Past* (Marshfield, WI: Marshfield History Project, 1997), 12–13.

68. M. A. Raeder, "Women as Cheese Factory Managers and Cheese Makers," 148–50; comments by W. A. Henry, 113, Wisconsin Cheesemakers' Association, *Eleventh Annual Report, 1903*.

69. The figures for 1887 are from "Dairy Map of Wisconsin," Wisconsin Dairymen's Association, *Fifteenth Annual Report, 1887* (Fort Atkinson, WI: The Association), and for 1915 are from George J. Weigle, *Butter Factories and Cheese Factories Operated in 1916: Dairy Statistics for 1915* (Madison, WI: Dairy and Food Commissioner, 1917).

Notes to Chapter 4

1. All references are from Eugene Caves to William H. Mybrea, State Attorney, 21 Nov. 1896, Wisconsin, Governor: Investigations, 1851–1959, Minor Charges and Complaints, 1880–1914, series 81, WHSAD. A different version of this story appeared as Joan M. Jensen, "The Death of Rosa: Sexuality in Rural America," *Agricultural History* 67.4 (Fall 1993): 1–12.

2. Two articles suggested methods for textual analysis: John D. Wrathall, "Provenance as Text: Reading the Silences Around Sexuality in Manuscript Collections," *Journal of American History* 79.1 (June 1992): 165–78, and Ranajit Guha, "Chandra's Death," *Subaltern Studies* 5 (1987): 135–65.

3. These conclusions are based on an examination of the 1880 and 1900 federal censuses for Plainfield and adjoining areas and the 1895 and 1905 Wisconsin censuses, as well as of the Plainfield, WI, *Sun* from Apr. to Dec. 1896; Malcolm Rosholt, *Our Country, Our Story: Portage County Wisconsin*

(Stevens Point, WI: Portage County Board of Supervisors, 1959), 128–29, describes the small Slovakian community.

4. James Mohr, *Abortion in America: The Origins and Evolution of National Policy, 1800–1900* (New York: Oxford University Press, 1979), 132–33, 139–40, 240, 242; Linda G. Gordon, *Women's Bodies, Women's Right: Birth Control in America*, rev. ed. (New York: Penguin, 1990), 69.

5. Dorothy Reed Mendenhall, "Prenatal and Natal Conditions in Wisconsin," *Wisconsin Medical Journal* 15.10 (Mar. 1917): 353–69; Florence Sherbon and Elizabeth Moore, *Maternity and Infant Care in Two Rural Counties in Wisconsin* (Washington: GPO, 1919); *Kloths v. Hess*, 126 Wis. 587 (1906).

6. See clipping and second letter, 19 Nov. 1896, G. Gray, Coloma, to Gov. William H. Upham, Wisconsin, Governor: Investigations, 1851–1959, Minor Charges and Complaints, 1880–1914, series 81, WHSAD.

7. Mendenhall, "Prenatal," 354n.

8. Details are from Record of Deaths, vol. 2, 1863–96, Marathon County (WI) Courthouse; Deaths, 1877–96, Taylor County (WI) Courthouse; Deaths Index and Registration of Deaths, 1870–79, Clark County (WI) Courthouse.

9. Jan Coombs, "The Health of Central Wisconsin Residents in 1800: A New View of Midwestern Rural Life," *Wisconsin Magazine of History* 68.4 (1985): 301; Mendenhall, "Prenatal," 354–55; for rates, see also Cornelius A. Harper, "History of the Board of Health," Wisconsin, State Board of Health, Histories of the State Board of Health, 1901–45, series 872, WHSAD.

10. Peter T. Harstad, "Disease and Sickness on the Wisconsin Frontier: Malaria, 1820–1850," *Wisconsin Magazine of History* 43 (Summer 1960): 83–95; Jack W. Hopkins, *The Eradication of Smallpox: Organizational Learning and Innovation in International Health* (Boulder, CO: Westview, 1989), 1, 14–15, 24. As late as 1921, more than 100,000 persons in the United States contracted smallpox. The following year, due to vigorous eradication programs, the number of cases dropped to 23,000; still, more than 600 persons died from smallpox that year.

11. E. Wagner Stern and Allen E. Stern, *The Affect of Smallpox on the Destiny of the Amerindian* (Boston: Bruce Humphries, 1945), 43, 65, 103, 117, 123–24, 131; Zephyrin to Rev. F. H. Krandbaauer, 24 Apr. 1885, reel 12, and "Chronicle of the Menominee Mission, Keshena, Wisconsin," reel 13, Sacred Heart Franciscans, Indian Mission Records (hereafter, IMR), Marquette University Library (hereafter, MUL); Annual Report, Lac du Flambeau Indian Boarding School, 1 July 1907, Administrative Files, Lac du Flambeau 1883–1914, BIA, La Pointe, RG 75, NAGLR.

12. Latton, *Reminiscences; Medford Historical Album*, Medford (WI) Public Library.

13. "Smallpox in Wisconsin—1925," Histories of the State Board of Health, 1901–45, Wisconsin State Board of Health, series 872, WHSAD; see also Children's Bureau agent reports, File 4–11–3-7, 1907 and 1916, Central Files, 1914–20, General Records, 1912–69, Records of the Children's Bureau (hereafter, CB), RG 102.2.1, National Archives, College Park (hereafter, NACP); Judith Walzer Leavitt, *The Healthiest City: Milwaukee and the Politics of Health Reform* (Princeton, NJ: Princeton University Press, 1982), 98, notes that parents rioted over forced vaccination of children in one Milwaukee ward.

14. "A Short Summary of the Background Pertaining to the Tuberculosis Program in the State of Wisconsin, June 25, 1943" and "Summary of Report of Wisconsin State Tuberculosis Commission, 1905," Tuberculosis History in Wisconsin Folder, Wisconsin State Board of Health, Histories of the State Board of Health, 1901–45, series 872, WHSAD.

15. "Monthly Sanitary Report of Diseases and Injuries (1896–1901)," Administrative Records, BIA, La Pointe, RG 75, NAGLR.

16. Quote is from Diane Therese Putney, *Fighting the Scourge: American Indian Morbidity and Federal Policy, 1897–1928* (Milwaukee, WI: Marquette University, 1980), 52.

17. Putney, *Fighting the Scourge*, 85–86; for Hrdlička, see "My Journey," box 181, and Menominee Study, box 170, in Aleš Hrdlička Papers, National Anthropological Archives, Smithsonian Institution, Smithsonian Museum Support Center, Suitland, Maryland.

18. Putney, *Fighting the Scourge*, 82, 90, 113, 140; Robert E. Ritzenthaler, "Chippewa Preoccupation with Health: Change in a Traditional Attitude Resulting from Modern Health Problems," *Bulletin of the Public Museum of the City of Milwaukee* 19 (1953): 175–258; see also U.S. Board of Indian Commissioners, "Report on Menominee Indian Reservation," 100, personal correspondence, 1847–1927, Ayer Manuscripts, NL.

19. Genevieve G. Mcbride, *On Wisconsin Women: Working for Their Rights from Settlement to Suffrage* (Madison: UW Press, 1993), 180–84.

20. Dearholt, a young orthopedic surgeon who had graduated from Rush Medical College in Chicago, was part of the original group of Milwaukee doctors concerned about TB. He served on the staff of the Milwaukee Children's Hospital and headed the education and publicity committee of the new WATA before becoming the full-time director.

21. The Dunn Survey is in Wisconsin Lung Association, records, 1907–78, box 9, folder 8, WHSAD.

22. "An Answer to the Questions Regarding the Menominee Indians, Residing on Their Reservation in Shawano County, Wisconsin, 1924," roll 17, IML, MUL; see also "Conference on Indian Problems," Madison, WI, 22 Mar. 1929, conference materials, 1929–62, Public Health Nursing Section, Indian Records, 1926–62, series 2207, box 1, folder 4, WHSAD.

23. Mendenhall, "Prenatal," 361.

24. Mendenhall, "Prenatal," 362–64. During the next decade, as specialized doctors took over childbirth, the maternal death rate did not decline. A study at the end of 1927, when better causes of death were available, showed that more than a third of the deaths from infection—puerperal sepsis—followed septic abortions: Charlotte J. Calvert, "Wisconsin Maternal Mortality, 1917–28: A Study," *Wisconsin Medical Journal* 29.2 (Feb. 1930): 65, 67.

25. "Report of the State Board of Health, WI, 1916–1918," Wisconsin Bureau of Maternal and Child Health, General Records, 1916–79, series 2708, box 3, folder 41, WHSAD.

In settler communities, children by this time were seldom felled by cholera, smallpox, typhoid, scarlet fever, or diphtheria, but measles and whooping cough remained serious and sometimes fatal diseases.

26. Biographical information is in Record of Employment, 1883–1927, and in Egbert to Agent Campbell, 12 Dec. 1907, Letters Received by the Agent at Ashland, General Records, Letters Received from Lac du Flambeau Reservation and School, 1885–1914, BIA, La Pointe Agency, RG 75, NAGLR. Nancy Cornelius, a member of the Wisconsin Odanah tribe, graduated from the Hartford, CT, Hospital School of Nursing in 1890: Signe Cooper, "Nancy Cornelius Skenadore, 1861–1908," *Nursing Matters* (12 Mar. 1991). Cornelius served as superintendent of the Oneida Mission Hospital near Ashland from 1899 to 1904. In a letter to the author, 14 May 2004, Cooper listed one Dakota woman as an 1886 graduate of the University of Pennsylvania Hospital School of Nursing. Carlisle's *The Indian Helper* 12.34 (4 June 1897) and 14.36 (30 June 1899) listed a number of graduates training at the Medico-Chirurgical Hospital in Philadelphia; half a dozen nurses were trained by 1899.

27. Wilber H. Ahern, "An Experiment Aborted: Returned Indian Students in the Indian School Service, 1881–1908," *Ethnohistory* 44.2 (Spring 1997): 282, Table 4.

28. Runkel, "My Life."

29. Ahern, "An Experiment," 282, Table 4, 301n58. See also LdF 18015–13–917 and LdF 21103–19–917.1, CCF, BIA, RG 75, NAB.

30. *Milwaukee Journal* (16 July 1970); Gordon MacQuarrie, "Tall Pines, Tall Guides, Taller Stories," unidentified clipping, 31 May 1936; Elizabeth Thoms and daughter Anita Koser provided clippings and family oral histories to the author at Lac du Flambeau, 10 July 2003.

31. Lac du Flambeau Industrial Survey, 1922, 97.

32. *Milwaukee Journal* (n.d., but probably the summer of 1918, at the height of government efforts to have women produce and can more food); for prizes, see Superintendent L. W. White to CIA, for Sept. 1915, 5

Feb. 1916, LdF 83106–15–047, and White to CIA, 26 Sept. 1916, LdF 10139–16–047, CCF, BIA, RG 75, NAB.

33. The lilac story is from Isabella's great-granddaughter Anita Koser, interview with author, 10 July 2003, Lac du Flambeau Nation.

34. The *Oshkosh Daily Northwestern* identified Chemon in a 1903 photograph as one of a delegation of sixty-five Menominee who participated in a ceremony marking the founding of the city of Oshkosh. A postcard labeled "Menominee Dancers, 1910," showed her with Neopit Oshkosh and other dancers. Anthropologist Samuel Alfred Barrett photographed her in 1915–16 with other dancers and in single portraits in dance regalia. *Menominee Indian Centennial, 1854–1954* (Neopit, WI, n.d.) reproduced the 1903 photograph; for the Barrett photographs, see numbers 2748, 6821, and 6820, Milwaukee (WI) Public Museum.

35. Allan Caldwell, interview by the author, 13 June 1997, Madison, WI; "Senior Women's Sewing Circle," taped interview of Arlene Creapeau, by Rebecca Alegria and Melanie White, 1 Feb. 1995, Catherine Wawkechon's home (n.p.), Menominee Tribal Offices, Neopit, Menominee Nation. Chemon married several times: the Franks, Sipicals, and Caldwells all trace their maternal lineage to her. Densmore spoke to a Louisa Martin, but she did not identify any woman by the name "Chemon."

36. Christopher Vecsey, *Traditional Ojibwa Religion and Its Historical Changes* (Philadelphia, PA: American Philosophical Society, 1983), 184–86; for the Ho-Chunk, see Paul Radin, "The Ritual and Significance of the Winnebago Medicine Dance," *Journal of American Folk-Lore* 24.92 (Apr.–June 1911): 149–208; artist Gerald Hawpetoss, Grand Forks, ND, 12 July 1994, notes from Jim Leary, tape index, Woodland Indian Project, Wisconsin Folk Museum, Madison, WI; Mosgokaodokwe (Blue Sky Woman), Menominee/Potawatomi, said her grandmother Natnoke told her women used to record their medicines in their beadwork.

37. Densmore, *Chippewa Customs*, 46–47, 127.

38. Letitia Single Dunbar, *Reminiscences* (Wausau, WI, 1930), 2–3.

39. Michael Lisz, interview by Malcolm Rosholt, 29 Nov. 1974, UWSP; Boneske, "The Athens Story," 93; Viola Stout, Edgerton, "Medical Lore," box 6, Fidelia Van Antwerp Papers, 1945–58, Wisconsin Manuscripts QW, WHSAD; unidentified medical record books, 1870–80, SC 46, Chippewa Valley Museum, Eau Claire, WI; Guenter B. Risse, Ronald L. Numbers, and Judith Walzer Leavitt, eds., *Medicine Without Doctors: Home Health Care in American History* (New York: Science History Publications, 1977), 2–9, discusses the various traditions.

40. Lucille Boneske, "Grandmother Schlais," Wausau Writers Club, *Rib Mountain Echoes*, vol. 2 (Stevens Point, WI: Worzalla, 1967), 128–29; "Mrs. Harriet Gunderson Tells of Early Days," Biographical Files, Marathon Historical Society Library, Wausau, WI.

41. Boneske, "The Athens Story," 93–94.

42. Plainfield, WI, *Sun* 26 (8 May 1896).

43. Helen D. Hering, "Country Doctor," Wausau Writers Club, *Rib Mountain Echoes*, vol. 3 (Stevens Point, WI: Worzalla, 1976), 52–61. After many years in practice, Barber turned his attention to politics, and in 1923, when local people elected him to the state senate, he left medical practice to younger doctors.

44. Adele Comandini, *Doctor Kate: Angel on Snowshoes, the Story of Kate Pelham Newcomb, M.D.* (New York: Rinehart, 1956; reprint, Woodruff, WI: Dr. Kate Historical Society, 1997), 174. Most of these early country doctors were men. The few women doctors practiced in towns but no doubt served rural women who lived close by. Dr. Margaret T. Trevitt, who practiced medicine with her husband in Wausau between 1886 and 1925, would have had country patients. She had trained at the Eciectte Medical College in Canada. As Wausau grew, she became primarily a city doctor.

45. Gordon L. Bultena, *The Changing Distribution and Adequacy of Medical, Dental and Hospital Services in Rural and Urban Communities in Wisconsin, 1910–1960* (Madison: UW, Department of Rural Sociology, 1966), 9–10.

46. Florence Sherbon to Miss Paradise, 14 July 1916, 4–11–3-5, Central Files, 1914–20, GR 1912–69, CB, RG 102.2.1, NACP.

47. Work of the State Board of Medical Examiners, 4–11–3-12; "Mr. A. C. Umbrent, Summary of Consultation, Milwaukee, 13 December 1917," 4–11–3-7, both Central Files, 1914–20, GR 1912–69, CB, RG 102.2.1, NACP.

48. Records of Births, Lincoln County (WI) Courthouse; midwives registration, Wisconsin State Board of Medical Examiners, Applications for Midwifery Licenses, 1909–34, series 1611, WHSAD.

49. Lincoln County Medical Society, Minutes, 1903–38, Wisconsin Manuscripts 14PB/6, WHSAD; see entries for 1903–4.

50. U.S. Bureau of the Census, Federal Population Census, Thirteenth Census of the United States (1910), Taylor County, Medford City, Enumeration District 173, Sheet 13B, series T624, reel 1737, RG 29, NA Microfilm; Birth Registration, Midwives and Physicians Report, 1892–97, Taylor County (WI) Courthouse; Registrations of Taylor County midwives Guse, Johnson, and Novak, Wisconsin State Board of Medical Examiners, Applications for Midwifery Licenses, 1909–34, series 1611, WHSAD.

51. U.S. Bureau of the Census, Federal Population Census, Thirteenth Census of the United States (1910), Clark County, Warner Town, Enumeration District 33, Sheet 7A, series T624, reel 1704, RG 29, NA Microfilm.

52. The report, later published as *Maternity and Infant Care*, did not identify Marathon as the northern county. Material for this section is taken primarily from field notes: see Florence Sherbon to Paradise, 14 July 1916; Elizabeth Moore to Meigs, 24 May and 12 June 1916; and Moore to Paradise, 20 May 1916, 4–11–3-5, Central Files, 1914–20, GR 1912–69, CB, RG 102.2.1, NACP.

53. Work of the State Board of Medical Examiners, 4–11–3-12, Central Files, 1914–20, GR 1912–69, CB, RG 102.2.1, NACP.

54. The interview schedules are in 4–11–3-12, Central Files, 1914–20, GR 1912–69, CB, RG 102.2.1, NACP.

55. I disagree with Charlotte G. Borst, *Catching Babies: The Professionalization of Childbirth, 1870–1920* (Cambridge, MA:

Harvard University Press, 1995), 5, 18, 66, and 200n29, that midwives did not have large practices. In this area, at least, some clearly did.

56. Sherbon to Paradise, 14 July 1916, 4–11–3-5, Central Files, 1914–20, GR 1912–69, CB, RG 102.2.1, NACP.

57. See Molly Ladd-Taylor, "Federal Help for Mothers: The Rise and Fall of the Sheppard-Towner Act in the 1920s," in *Gendered Domains: Rethinking Public and Private in Women's History*, ed. Dorothy O. Helly and Susan M. Reverby (Ithaca, NY: Cornell University Press, 1992), 217–27.

58. Estimate of patients in the hospitals of Catholic nuns from speech by Dr. Edwin Evans, "The Catholic Hospitals and Social Service," Edward E. Evans Papers, Speeches and Editorials, undated, WHSAD; John Morris Dodd, *Autobiography of a Surgeon* (New York: Walter Neale, 1928), 236, 244; Barbara Mann Wall, "Called to Mission of Charity: The Sisters of St. Joseph in the Civil War," *Nursing History Review* 6 (1998): 86, 89, and "Grace Under Pressure: The Nursing Sisters of the Holy Cross, 1861–1865," *Nursing History Review* 1 (Jan. 1993): 71, 82, and "Courage to Care: The Sisters of the Holy Cross in the Spanish American War," *Nursing History Review* 3 (Jan. 1995): 56–58; Carol K. Coburn and Martha Smith, "'Pray for Your Wanderers': Women Religious on the Colorado Mining Frontier, 1877–1917," *Frontiers* 15.3 (1995): 35–36. The 40 percent figure is from Philip Shoemaker and Mary Van Hulle Jones, "From Infirmaries to Intensive Care: Hospitals in Wisconsin," in *Wisconsin Medicine: Historical Perspectives*, ed. Judith Walzer and Ronald L. Numbers (Madison: UW Press, 1981), 110.

59. Dodd, *Autobiography*, 72.

60. Dodd, *Autobiography*, 72; Sister M. Kiliana, ed., *History of the Community of the Sisters of the Sorrowful Mother* (Milwaukee, WI: Convent of the Sorrowful Mother, 1960), 237–46.

61. Marathon County Medical Society, Minutes, 1903–34, Wisconsin Manuscripts 14PB/2, WHSAD; see especially entries for 17 Nov. 1905 and 20 Sept. 1910 and for hospital, 3 June 1904 and 30 Apr. 1906; Bultena, *Changing Distribution*, 9–10, 18.

62. See vol. 3, Sister Beda Oral History Project, SSM.

63. Dodd, *Autobiography*, 90–92.

64. Wisconsin Circuit Court (Marathon County), Naturalization Records, 1851–1991, vol. 3, Marathon Series 5, WHSAD; U.S. Bureau of the Census, Federal Population Census, Thirteenth Census of the United States (1910), Marathon County, City of Wausau, Enumeration District 9, Sheet 21, series T624, reel 1720, RG 29, NA Microfilm.

65. "Mrs. Celia Dame," 15 Dec. 1917, 4–11-3-7, Central Files, 1914–20, GR 1912–69, CB, RG 102.2.1, NACP.

66. D. P. Andrews, Keshena Agent, to CIA, 26 Mar. 1885, 512; Fr. Zephyrin to Rev. F. H. Krardbauer, 24 Apr. 1885; Fr. Oderic Derenthal to Provincial, 7 Oct. 1885; Derenthal to Provincial, 27 Nov. 1885, 518, 624, 683, reel 12, IMR, MUL.

67. "Chronicle of the Menominee Mission," 85.

68. Hospitals in Nicholson to CIA, 17 Oct. 1910, 83512–10–032, CCF, BIA, RG 75, NAB; Fr. Simon to Mother Agnes Gonzaga, 9 and 18 Jan. 1912, and Fr. Blase to Rev. Mother Agnes Agatha, 14 and 24 Feb. 1911, Sisters of St. Joseph of Carondelet, St. Louis, MO (hereafter, CSJ). Where the government did attempt to implement aspects of the "Save the Baby" campaigns, it claimed some progress, but it made no commitment to Native health and reduced funding after World War I: see Lisa E. Emmerich, "'Save the Babies!': American Indian Women, Assimilation Policy, and Scientific Motherhood, 1912–1918," in *Writing the Range: Race, Class, and Culture in the Women's West*, ed. Elizabeth Jameson and Susan Armitage (Norman: University of Oklahoma Press, 1997), 239–409.

69. L. L. Culp, Special Physician, to CIA, 24 June 1920, 53822–20–032; Robert E. L. Needberne, Medical Supervisor, "Report on Keshena Agency," 9 Apr. 1920, 314–20–032, both CCF, BIA, RG 75, NAB.

70. Mary Hawkins, librarian at the University of Kansas, kindly supplied material on Florence's later career. See Viola J. Anderson, *The Department of Home Economics: The First 50 Years, 1910–1960* (Lawrence: University of Kansas, 1964), 22–27; Florence

Brown sheets on file, archives, Spencer Research Library, University of Kansas, Lawrence, KS.

71. Grace L. Meigs to Dr. Florence Brown Sherbon, 30 Mar. 1916, with attached memo; Meigs, Memorandum for Miss Lathrop, Plan of Investigation in Wisconsin, 10 and 20 Mar. 1916; Lathrop to Sherbon, 17 June 1916, all 4–11–3, Central Files, 1914–20, GR 1912–69, CB, RG 102.2.1, NACP.

72. Sherbon to Paradise, 14 July 1916, 4–11-3-5, Central Files, 1914–20, GR 1912–69, CB, RG 102.2.1, NACP.

73. Sherbon to Mrs. West, 15 July 1916, 4–11-3-5, Central Files, 1914–20, GR 1912–69, CB, RG 102.2.1, NACP.

74. The resulting report did not please the Children's Bureau, which considered it simply "material" to be "worked over" by the office. Sherbon's name was on the report, but the final writing was the work of the Washington staff. Sherbon to Miegs, 3 Aug. and 10 Sept. 1916, and M. D. to Sherbon, 14 May 1917, 4–11-3-5; Sherbon to Paradise, 10 Nov. 1916, 5–11-3-5, all Central Files, 1914–20, GR 1912–69, CB, RG 102.2.1, NACP.

75. Attorney General to J. L. Reeve, 18 Sept. 1878, O. W. Wright to Dr. J. L. Reeve, 1879, and discussion of 5 Nov. 1879, (WI) Council on Health, Proceedings, 1876–1975, series 1796, reel 1, WHSAD.

76. Coombs, "Health," 307–11.

77. "To Gentlemen of the Board of Health, 8 June 1892" and discussion of "Public Education" in History of Board of Health prepared by State Historical Library, May 1949, Wisconsin State Board of Health, Histories of the State Board of Health, 1901–45, series 872, reel 1, WHSAD.

78. Sherbon and Moore, *Maternity and Infant Care*, 75–76; Harper, "History of the Board of Health," 117; Comandini, *Doctor Kate*, 205. The commitment to public health in the country was generally uneven: the U.S. public health service first advised that county health departments be subsidized in 1911, but the Rockefeller Foundation did not begin its rural health care work until 1916 and 1917.

79. Texas township, 4–11-3-7, Central Files, 1914–20, GR 1912–69, CB, RG 102.2.1, NACP; the following generalizations are

taken from the reports in that file of Texas, Pike, Kronenwetter, Hull, Elderon, Brokaw, and Marathon townships and Colby and Marathon City villages.

80. "Work of the State University," 4–11–12, Central Files, 1914–20, GR 1912–69, CB, RG 102.2.1, NACP.

81. Dr. Gillan, Extension Division, UW, interview, 28 Dec. 1915; Dorothy Mendenhall to Meigs, 4 Sept. 1917, 4–11–3-12, both Central Files, 1914–20, GR 1912–69, RG 102.2.1, NACP.

82. Meigs to Lathrop, received 25 Apr. 1916, 4–11–3-5; Grace Meigs interview with Dr. Bearholt and others, 21 Apr. 1916; W. K. Mitchell, Secretary, Wausau Baby Week, to Sherbon, 17 May 1916, 4–11–3-12, all Central Files, 1914–20, GR 1912–69, CB, RG 102.2.1, NACP.

83. Sherbon to Meigs, 24 May 1916; Sherbon to Paradise, 25 May 1916, both 4–11–3-5, Central Files, 1914–20, GR 1912–69, CB, RG 102.2.1, NACP.

84. Minutes of Statewide Conference of the Woman's Committee, State Council of Defense, 4–5 Feb. 1919, Women's Building, Madison, WI; Child Welfare Report, Report of the Work of the Woman's Committee, Apr. 1917–Mar. 1919, Wisconsin State Council of Defense, World War I, Records of the Women's Committee, 1917–19, series 1649, box 3, WHSAD.

85. Belott to Morgan, 10 and 30 June 1918; report of Nellie Evjue, all Wisconsin State Council of Defense, World War I, Records of the Women's Committee, 1917–19, series 1649, box 9, WHSAD.

86. Margaret Ryan to Morgan, 9 Dec. 1917; Stone to Morgan, 14 Mar. 1918; Morgan to Ryan, 7 June 1918; Ryan to Morgan, 9 June 1918; Morgan to Mr. J. E. Phillips, June 25, 1918; Report of Verna Phillips, Chair, Child Welfare Committee, box 11; Mrs. G. D. Jones to Mrs. Edith E. Hoyt, 27 May 1918, Hoyt to Jones, 5 June 1918, box 17, all Wisconsin State Council of Defense, World War I, Records of the Women's Committee, 1917–19, series 1649, WHSAD.

87. "Report Written for Mrs. E. F. Bickel, Chairman of Department of Health and Recreation Women's Committee, State Council of Defense, To Be Presented at State Conference of County Chairmen and County Child Welfare Committee Chairman at Madison, Mar. 17 and 28, 1918," 4–11–3-7, Central Files, 1914–20, GR 1912–69, CB, RG 102.2.1, NACP; Minutes of 13 Dec. 1918 Meeting, Wisconsin State Council of Defense, World War I, Records of the Women's Committee, 1917–19, series 1649, box 3, WHSAD; see also Harper, "History of the Board of Health"; Victor S. Falk, "The Influenza Epidemic of 1918," *Wisconsin Medical Journal* 75 (Aug. 1976): 31–32.

88. "Report of the State Board of Health, 1918–20," Wisconsin Bureau of Child Welfare and Public Health Nursing, Maternal and Child Health, Bureau of Community Health, General Records, 1916–79, series 2708, box 3, folder 41, WHSAD.

89. Mary P. Morgan, Director, Report on Prenatal Work, 1 Nov. 1922, 11–53–8; Estelle B. Hunter to Julia Lathrop, 9 Dec. 1919, 20–28–6; Tentative Outline of Health Centers in Rural Districts, Zoe La Farge, undated, 20–28–5, and accompanying correspondence of Nov. and Dec. 1919, all in Central Files, 1914–20, GR 1912–69, CB, RG 102.2.1, NACP; Wisconsin Bureau of Maternal and Child Health, box 3, has plans, Wisconsin Bureau of Community Health, General Records, 1916–79, series 2708, WHSAD; for the rural survey, see Ruth Estella Church, "A Survey of County Public Health Nursing in Wisconsin" (MA thesis, UW–Madison, 1935), 11, 13.

90. Howard to Morgan, 3 Sept. 1918, Mrs. L. H. Howard to Morgan, 23 Sept. 1918, Kennedy to Mrs. Mary Morgan, 19 Oct. 1918, all Wisconsin State Council of Defense, World War I, Records of the Women's Committee, 1917–19, series 1649, WHSAD; E. F. Bickel, 3 Apr. 1918, 4–11–3-7, Special Agent EM to Lathrop, 4 Apr. 1918, 4–11–3-7, both Central Files, 1914–20, GR 1912–69, CB, RG 102.2.1, NACP.

91. Undated articles in scrapbook from the *Merrill (WI) Daily Herald*, in Mead Photograph Album, Wisconsin Division of Health, box 2, series 2207, WHSAD; Signe Cooper, *Wisconsin Nursing Pioneers* (Madison: UW, Department of Nursing, 1958), 15–16; Signe Cooper, "Theta Mead, 1878–1922," *Nursing Matters*, 2 July 1991; Lincoln County

(WI), Board of Supervisors, Annual Meeting, 14 Nov. 1917, Proceedings of the County Board, 1874–1934, vol. 6: 1912–21, Lincoln Series 1, WHSAD.

92. See Lincoln County (WI), Board of Supervisors, meeting 20 Nov. 1924, Proceedings of the County Board, 1874–1925, vol. 7: 1921–25, Lincoln Series 1, WHSAD; see Sherbon and Moore, *Maternity and Infant Care*, 79–81.

93. Reports for Clark County (WI) are in box 6, folder 12; for Marathon County (WI), box 8, folder 4, Wisconsin Bureau of Maternal and Child Health, Programs and Demonstrations, 1922–61, series 2253, WHSAD.

94. Marathon County Medical Society, Minutes, 1903–34, Wisconsin Manuscripts 14PB/2, WHSAD, see particularly 9 Dec. 1920 and 11 Feb. and 8 Apr. 1921.

95. For the early stages of the plan see also Zoe La Farge, Field Nurse, "Reports on Work Done During Month of December 1919 and January 1920," 19 Dec. 1919 and 30 Jan. 1920, 20–28–8, Central Files, 1914–20, GR 1912–69, CB, RG 102.2.1, NACP.

96. Mary P. Morgan to Ethel Watters, 4 Apr. 1923, folder 8; S. Josephine Baker to Cora S. Allen, 12 Oct. 1926, Blanch M. Haines to Allen, 9 Nov. 1926, and Allen to Baker, 12 Nov. 1926, folder 9, all in Bureau of Maternal and Child Health, Children's Bureau Files, 1920–75, Wisconsin Bureau of Community Health, General Records, 1916–79, series 2708, WHSAD.

97. "Conference on Indian Problems," Madison, WI, 22 Mar. 1927; "Report of the First Year of Public Health Nursing, Done Among Wisconsin Indians" (1926), Public Health Nursing Section, Indian Records, 1926–62, series 2207, box 1, folder 4, WHSAD.

98. Jane Jenson, "Representation of Gender: Policies to 'Protect' Women Workers and Infants in France and the United States before 1914," in *Women, the State and Welfare*, ed. Linda Gordon (Madison: UW Press, 1990), 152–77.

Notes to Chapter 5

1. These stories are taken from the typescript draft of U.S. Department of Labor, Children's Bureau, Anna O. Lundberg, *Dependent Wards of the State of Wisconsin: A Study of Children Indentured into Family Homes by the State Public School* (Washington, DC: GPO, 1924), for Myrta, 429, for Catherine, 350–53, copy in Department of Public Welfare, Children and Youth Division, series 1401, box 7, WHSAD; this study was never published. For a more detailed discussion of the Sparta school, see Pamela Riney-Kehrberg, *Childhood on the Farm: Work, Play, and Coming of Age in the Midwest* (Lawrence: University Press of Kansas, 2005), 158–81.

2. Gov. John Blaine to Grace Abbott, 24 Feb. 1924, RG 102, 20–67–6, NAB.

3. John Blaine to Grace Abbott, 5 Mar. 1924, RG 102, 20–67–8, NAB.

4. See memos for Miss Abbott from Anna Lundberg, 8 Mar., 21 Aug., and 19 Nov. 1924 and 8 Apr. 1925, and Memorandum for Miss Lundberg and Miss Hopkins, 23 July 1924, all RG 102, 20–67–8, NAB.

5. Lundberg, *Dependent Wards*, 68; also see Linda G. Gordon, *Heroes of Their Own Lives: The Politics and History of Family Violence: Boston, 1880–1960* (New York: Viking, 1988), 59–77, on these issues.

6. Wisconsin Insurance Department, Examination Reports of Domestic Companies, 1903–65, Report on Joint Examination of the Woodmen Circle, 12 July 1917, box 8, 1916–17, and Report of Examinations of the Patrons Mutual Town Insurance Company, Rhinelander, WI, box 7, 1916, 163, both series 1049, WHSAD.

7. The Catholic Order of Foresters from Haltom township, Clark County (WI), later reprinted its original 1921 roster.

8. Lincoln County (WI), Board of Supervisors, Proceedings, Special Meeting, 13 June 1919, volume 6, 1912–21, series 1, WHSAD.

9. Joan Jacobs Brumberg, "'Ruined Girls': Changing Responses to Illegitimacy in Upstate New York, 1890–1920," *Journal of Social History* 18 (Winter 1984): 249, 263.

10. "The Children's Code in Wisconsin, 1929–1935," Wisconsin Conference of Social Work, Pub. No. 167, tentative draft, State Department of Public Welfare, Division for Children and Youth, Director's Subject File, 1913–unknown, WHSAD.

11. E. Eastman, District Attorney, to Governor Edward Scofield, 29 July 1897, box 1, series 81, Governor: Investigations, 1851–1959, Minor Charges and Complaints, 1880–1914, WHSAD.

12. Brumberg, "Ruined Girls," 260, gives adoption figures.

13. Lincoln County (WI), Board of Supervisors, Proceedings, Annual Meeting, 1916, Report of Commissioner of the Poor, volume 6, 1912–21, series 1, WHSAD.

14. Joanne Goodwin, "An American Experiment in Paid Motherhood: The Implementation of Mothers' Pensions in Early Twentieth Century Chicago," *Gender and History* 4 (Fall 1992): 323–42; Theda Skocpal, *Protecting Soldiers and Mothers: Political Origins of Social Policy in the United States* (Cambridge, MA: Belknap Press of Harvard University Press, 1992), 373–423; Jane Lewis "Women's Agency, Maternalism and Welfare," *Gender and History* 6.1 (Apr. 1994): 117–23.

15. Lincoln County (WI), Board of Supervisors, Proceedings, Annual Meetings, 12 Nov. 1915 and 9 Nov. 1920, vol. 6, 1912–21, series 1, WHSAD.

16. Lincoln County (WI), Board of Supervisors, Proceedings, Annual Meetings, 12 Nov. 1918, vol. 6, 1912–21, and 13 Nov. 1923, vol. 7, 1921–24; see also Special Meeting, 13 June 1919, vol. 6, 1918–19, and Annual Meeting, 20 Nov. 1924, vol. 7, 1921–24, series J, WHSAD.

17. All references to Edna Ferber, *Come and Get It* (1935; reprint, Madison, WI: Prairie Oak Press, 1991), particularly 108–78. Ferber's fictional Lotta was based on a real person, Lotta Morgan (1861–90), who was murdered in Hurley in 1890. Lotta never married Johnny Sullivan, the hotel owner/bartender with whom she lived, and had no children. She was known locally as a dancer, not a sex worker. Her murderer was never apprehended. Joe Carlson, Ironwood (MI) Carnegie Library, supplied information on the historical Lotta: Carlson to author, 23 May 2005.

18. See Karen Dubinsky, *Improper Advances: Rape and Heterosexual Conflict in Ontario, 1880–1929* (Chicago and London: University of Chicago Press, 1993), 3–4.

19. For a discussion of this issue, see Katherine M. B. Osburn, "'Dear Friend and Ex-husband': Marriage, Divorce, and Women's Property Rights on the Southern Ute Reservation, 1887–1930," in *Negotiators of Change: Historical Perspectives on Native American Women,* ed. Nancy Shoemaker (New York, London: Routledge, 1995), 157–75.

20. Mary E. Odem, *Delinquent Daughters: Protecting and Policing Adolescent Female Sexuality in the United States, 1885–1920* (Chapel Hill: University of North Carolina Press, 1995), 2.

21. John D'Emilio and Estelle B. Freedman, *Intimate Matters: A History of Sexuality in America* (New York: Harper and Row, 1988), 2.

22. Dubinsky, *Improper Advances*, 118, 143–62, explores this perception of north-south differences for Ontario, Canada, which had the same type of northern frontier as did Wisconsin.

23. J. T. Woodhead to Governor Rusk, 22 Nov. 1887, box 5, series 81, Governor, Investigation of Charges, Surveys, Relief, Disasters, and Social Unrest, 1851–1930, WHSAD.

24. J. T. Woodhead to Governor Rusk, 22 Nov. 1887, box 5, series 81, Governor, Investigation of Charges, Surveys, Relief, Disasters, and Social Unrest, 1851–1930, WHSAD.

25. J. T. Woodhead to Governor Rusk, 22 Nov. 1887, box 5, series 81, Governor, Investigation of Charges, Surveys, Relief, Disasters, and Social Unrest, 1851–1930, WHSAD, contains the clipping from the Merrill (WI) *Weekly Times.*

26. Andrew Hoffman to Governor G. W. Peck, 31 May 1892, box 1, series 81, Governor: Investigations, 1851–1959, Minor Charges and Complaints, 1880–1914, WHSAD.

27. Lincoln County (WI), Municipal Court, Clerk of Court, Criminal Docket, 1887–97, series 22, WHSAD; for the "Cotton Farm," see *Wisconsin Pilot and Review* (8 Nov. 1887): 3:6.

28. G. B. Johnston to Governor La Follette, 18 Mar. 1905, mentions concern with venereal disease, Governor: Investigations, 1851–1959, Minor Charges and Complaints, 1880–1914, box 1, series 81, WHSAD.

29. Mrs. Georgia David to State Governor, Governor: Investigations, 1851–1959, Minor

Charges and Complaints, 1880–1914, box 1, series 81, WHSAD.

30. The WCTU age of consent reform is discussed in Odum, *Delinquent Daughters,* 8–16, and in McBride, *On Wisconsin Women,* 108–12, 131–32.

31. Mrs. Rose Wilcox to Governor La Follette, 22 July 1901, series 81, Governor: Investigations, 1851–1959, Minor Charges and Complaints, 1880–1914, WHSAD.

32. Jane M. Pedersen, "Gender, Justice, and a Wisconsin Lynching, 1889," *Agricultural History* 67:2 (1993): 65–82.

33. "The Chivari of 1893," Pioneer Reminiscences Folder, Van Antwerp Wisconsin Folklore Collection, box 6, WHSAD; for the history of British "rough music," see E. P. Thompson, *Customs in Common* (New York: New Press, 1993), 467–531; Bryan D. Palmer, "Discordant Music: Charivaris and White-capping in Nineteenth-Century North America," *Labour/Le Travail* 3 (1978): 39.

34. Palmer, "Discordant Music," 39–62.

35. Palmer, "Discordant Music," 49–62.

36. *Wood County (WI) Reporter,* 39.49 (3 Dec. 1893).

37. Lincoln County (WI), County Court, Clerk of Court, Judges Minutes, 1917–19, box 1, folder 2, WHSAD.

38. Wisconsin School for Girls, Inmate Case History Books, 1875–1926, series 1381, WHSAD: case number for Viola, 2908, for Kathi, 1326. The case reported so obliquely is discussed later in this chapter. Odem, *Delinquent Daughters,* 2; the urban thesis is not convincing for this first stage of reform.

39. A. W. Wilmarth, 16 July 1898, series 81, Governor: Investigations, 1851–1959, Minor Charges and Complaints, 1880–1914, WHSAD.

40. Mary J. Berry, 31 May 1913, folder 1, series 1386, Corrections, Wisconsin School for Girls, Miscellaneous Institution Records, 1877–1927, WHSAD.

41. "Petition and Memorial of the Milwaukee Industrial School to the Legislature of the State of Wisconsin, 1878," Wisconsin School for Girls, Miscellaneous Institution Records, 1877–1927, series 1386, WHSAD; for the Sparta State School for Dependent Children, see especially the investigation of 1923 in File 20–67–6, CB, RG 102, NAB.

42. Wisconsin School for Girls, Inmate Case History Books, 1875–1926, series 1381, WHSAD.

43. Case 1085, Wisconsin School for Girls, Inmate Case History Books, 1875–1926, series 1381, WHSAD; see also Taylor County (WI) Courthouse Criminal Docket, 2:131.

44. Gordon, *Heroes,* especially ch. 7, 204–49.

45. Gordon, *Heroes,* 59–77.

46. Katharine DuPre Lumpkin, "Factors in the Commitment of Correctional School Girls in Wisconsin," *American Journal of Sociology* 37 (1931–32): 222–28, and "Parental Conditions of Wisconsin Girl Delinquents," *American Journal of Sociology* 38 (1932): 239.

47. Odem, *Delinquent Daughters,* 11.

48. Case 1949, Wisconsin School for Girls, Inmate Case History Books, 1875–1926, series 1381, WHSAD; see also case numbers 858, 1146, 2039.

49. Case numbers 1852 and 1861, Wisconsin School for Girls, Inmate Case History Books, 1875–1926, series 1381, WHSAD. After the turn of the century, health officials diagnosed an increasing number of women as having venereal disease or being pregnant. Matrons called in doctors to cure infected women and sent those who were pregnant either home or to a separate home for unwed mothers to birth their children.

50. Kathy Peiss, *Cheap Amusements: Working Women and Leisure in Turn-of-the-Century New York* (Philadelphia, PA: Temple University Press, 1986), 90–91.

51. Peiss, *Cheap Amusements,* 90–91.

52. All references are from Board of Industrial School for Girls, 1875–1926, Inmate Case History Books, series 1381, WHSAD.

53. Joan M. Jensen, "'I'd Rather Be Dancing': Wisconsin Women Moving On," *Frontiers* 22.1 (2001): 1–20.

54. Case number 2071, who later graduated from the Columbia School of Music in Chicago, Wisconsin School for Girls, Inmate Case History Books, 1875–1926, series 1381, WHSAD; see case number 1757 for escapees.

55. Jantsch, "Second American Jantsch Generation," 18–19.

56. Clark County (WI) *Republican and Press* 33.31 (1 June 1899): 3–4, reported the

Outagamie case. For discussion of cross-racial marriages, see Margaret D. Jacobs, "The Eastmans and the Luhans: Interracial Marriage Between White Women and Native American Men, 1875–1935," *Frontiers* 23.3 (2003): 29–54. Fourteen states and territories prohibited White-Indian marriages, mainly in the South and far West, but none between Massachusetts and Idaho in the North. See also Peggy Pascoe, "Race, Gender, and Intercultural Relations: The Case of Interracial Marriage," *Frontiers* 12:1 (1991): 5–18, for a 1921 case where the court held void the thirty-year marriage of an Oregon Indian woman.

57. Joan M. Jensen, *Promise to the Land: Essays on Rural Women* (Albuquerque: University of New Mexico Press, 1991), 38–49, discusses bridal pregnancy briefly.

58. Dorothy Behling, "Fashion Change in a Northwoods Lumbering Town, 1915–1925," *Dress* 9 (1983): 32–40.

59. Joan Severa, *Dressed for the Photographer: Ordinary Americans & Fashion, 1840–1900* (Kent, OH, and London: Kent University Press, 1995).

60. Wisconsin School for Girls, Inmate Case History Books, 1875–1926, 211–30, series 1381, WHSAD.

61. For an overview, see Joan Sangster, *Regulating Girls and Women: Sexuality, Family, and the Law in Ontario, 1920–1960* (Ontario: Oxford University Press Canada, 2001), 168–92; see also Regina G. Kunzel, *Fallen Women, Problem Girls: Unmarried Mothers and the Professionalization of Social Work, 1890–1945* (New Haven, CT: Yale University Press, 1993).

62. Letter from Edith H. Allen to the Board, Annual Meeting, 1914, 419; commissioner's view, 18 Oct. 1910 Annual Meeting, both in Ayer Manuscripts, NL.

63. The photographs are in the Milwaukee (WI) Public Museum.

64. For the dance controversy, see Bureau of Indian Affairs file 100165–14–047, RG 75, NAB.

65. Cato Sells, Indian Commissioner, Circular No. 992, 29 May 1915, box 1, correspondence, Ayer Manuscripts, NL.

66. Ayer Report 11, Aug. 1915, and for Menominee, see Nicholson to E. B. Linnen,

box 2, 15 Sept 1915, both Correspondence, Board of Indian Commissioners, Ayer Manuscripts, NL.

67. Bulletin 59, 7 May 1918, "Comments upon the digest of the opinions of 87 Indian Superintendents on returned student question," 4:418, Board of Indian Commissioners, Returned Student Survey, 1916–18, typescript by Frank A. Virtue, Superintendent of Tule River Agency, Porterville, CA, Ayer Manuscripts, NL; for marital relations and morals, see Bulletin 24, 19 Jan. 1917, 14, pt. 8 (p159 of bound volume), Superintendent Lindlay M. Compton, Tomah (WI) Indian School, NL.

68. Report of the Thirty-Fourth Annual Conference, 18–20 Oct. 1916, Lake Mohonk Conference on the Indian and Other Dependent Peoples, 1916; memoranda relating to returned students, Mar. 1918, box 1, correspondence, Ayer Manuscripts, NL.

69. I described this visit in a holiday letter to relatives dated 12 Dec. 1988.

70. The neighboring Jantsch family also brought mother Jantsch from Germany to live with them in 1883.

71. Laura Ingalls Wilder, *Little House in the Big Woods*, rev. ed. (1923; New York: HarperCollins, 1953); see Kathleen Hilton, "Growing Up Female," (PhD diss, Carnegie Mellon University, 1987), 209, for 1920 circular.

72. For Lac du Flambeau, see A. C. Tonner to Agent, 3 Feb. and 28 June 1899, and W. A. Jones, Commissioner, La Pointe statement, 9 Aug. 1899, La Pointe Agency, Administrative Records of the Lac du Flambeau Agency, 1888–1914, RG 75, NAGLR. For the Menominee, see A. S. Nicholson to Edward E. Ayer, 8 Dec. 1913 and 3 Jan. 1914, Keshena Menominee Agency, 1908–56, Miscellaneous Correspondence of Superintendent, RG 75, NAGLR.

73. D. H. Lipps to CIA, 20 June 1917, LdF 53692–17–910, and W. H. Gibbs, Inspector, Report, 1916, LdF 83362–16–916, both RG 75, NAB; Lac du Flambeau Industrial Survey, 1922.

74. Lac du Flambeau Industrial Survey, 1922. When the woman's name is not listed, I have referred to her by "Grandmother" plus the name of the eldest male listed.

75. H. P. Marble, Assistant Superintendent to CIA, 7 Jan. 1914, Keshena 1403–14–916, RG 65, NAB.

76. Lincoln County (WI), Board of Supervisors, Report of Trustees for Home, Hospital, and Farm, Proceedings, Annual Meeting, 13 Nov. 1923, vol. 7, series 1, WHSAD.

77. Carole Haber and Brian Gratton, eds., *Old Age and the Search for Security: An American Social History* (Bloomington: Indiana University Press, 1994), 116–17, 130–31, 179, 214n3; Esther Bloch, "Great Aunt Caroline," in Wausau Writers Club, *Rib Mountain Echoes*, vol. 3 (Stevens Point, WI: Worzalla, 1976), 163.

78. Lincoln County (WI), County Court, Clerk of Court, Judges Minutes, 1877–95, series 16, WHSAD; Council on Health, Memorial to Senate and Assembly from Northern Hospital for the Insane, estimating four hundred chronic cases at the local level, 19 Dec. 1877, Proceedings, 1876–1975, Mf. Reel 1: 1876–1926, vol. 1, series 1796, WHSAD; see also Charles Bardeen, "Hospitals in Wisconsin: A Historical Survey, 1816–1925," *Wisconsin Medical Journal* 24 (June 1926): 26.

79. I have found no account of caring for mentally disabled at home in this area, but for an earlier case of rural home care, see Joan M. Jensen, *Loosening the Bonds: Mid-Atlantic Farm Women, 1750–1850* (New Haven, CT: Yale University Press, 1986), 132–33.

80. Bardeen, "Hospitals in Wisconsin," 28.

81. Dale Wendell Robinson, *Wisconsin and the Mentally Ill: A History of the Wisconsin Plan of State and County Care, 1860–1915* (reprint, New York: Arno, 1980), 213, argued that people were better treated at the local level, but he did not investigate conditions there.

82. Clark County (WI) Hospital and Home, *50 Years of Progress, 1922–1972* (n.p.: publisher unknown, 1972), 9, 12; for claims, see box 7, 1924 for county asylums, series 278, WHSAD. By 1922 Clark County cared for eighty-two people from that county and sixty from other counties.

Notes to Chapter 6

1. Isabelle de Montolieu and Johann Wyss, *The Swiss Family Robinson; or, Adventures of a Father and Mother and Four Sons in a Desert Island* (Chicago: Donohue, n.d.).

2. J. N. Hunt and H. I. Gourley, *Modern Spelling Book: Lessons in the Orthography, Pronunciation, Derivation, Meaning and Use of Words* (New York: American Book, 1896).

3. *Wausau (WI) Sunday Herald* (5 Feb. 1898), 5C; Vieno Keskimaki in Jerry Apps, *One-Room Country Schools: History and Recollections* (Amherst, MA: Amherst Press, 1996; reprint, Madison: UW Press, 2004), 136.

4. Apps, *One-Room*, 51, 109.

5. Centennial Committee, *100 Year Anniversary, 1874–1974: Stetsonville, Little Black, Deer Creek* (Park Falls, WI: Weber & Sons, 1974), 158, 166–67, 171.

6. "Stetsonville Area Schools," in Centennial Committee, *100 Year Anniversary*, 152–71.

7. Clark County (WI), Yaeger School Records, 1892–1931, Small Series 3, WHSAD.

8. Centennial Committee, *100 Year Anniversary*, 160–61.

9. Centennial Committee, *100 Year Anniversary*, 155–56.

10. Centennial Committee, *100 Year Anniversary*, 153.

11. Haltom School Records, Colby (WI) Historical Society.

12. "History of Dill Creek School," typescript, Rural Arts Museum, Colby, WI.

13. Haltom School Records, Colby (WI) Historical Society.

14. *Wisconsin Pilot and Review* (20 Apr. 1886): 2:2.

15. Lundberg, *Dependent Wards*, 231–32, 422.

16. Lundberg, *Dependent Wards*, 287–88, 482–83; Ethel Hanks to Helen L. Sumner, 13 Feb. and 26 Nov. 1915, J. D. Beck to Hanks, 30 Dec. 1915, and C. P. Cary, State Superintendent, Wisconsin Department of Public Instruction, 18 Feb. 1916, all in File 10.211.53, Wisconsin Field Work, Central File, 1914–20, box 115, Records of the Children's Bureau, RG 102, NAB.

17. Lundberg, *Dependent Wards*, 310.

18. Lundberg, *Dependent Wards*, 315.

19. Lundberg, *Dependent Wards*, 316.

20. Lundberg, *Dependent Wards*, 317.

21. Lundberg, *Dependent Wards*, 306–7.

22. Loretta Keach, interview by the author, 1 July 1997, Medford, WI.

23. *Clark County (WI) Historical Society Newsletter* 15 (June 1998): 11.

24. Taylor County (WI), Medford Deutschen Schuleverein, "An Address to the Pioneers of Chelsea and Greenwood Townships," Wisconsin Manuscripts HO, box 4, folder 1, WHSAD.

25. Monthly Report, 1867, Reports of Public Schools of Marathon County (WI), County Superintendent Records; Report and Account Book for the School District Treasurer of School District 8, Town of Berlin, 1878, both Marathon County Historical Society.

26. Juliane Jacobi-Dittrich, *"Deutsch" Schulen in den Vereinigten Staaten von Amerika: Historisch-vergieichende Studie zum Unterrichtswesen im Mittleren Westen (Wisconsin 1840–1900)* ["German" Schools in the United States of America: A Historical Overview of Public Instruction in the Midwest (Wisconsin 1840–1900)] (Munich: Minerva Publikation, 1988), 112; Walter H. Beck, *Lutheran Elementary Schools in the U.S.* (St. Louis, MO: Concordia, 1939), 203–43, 319–20. In 1913 the legislature passed a bill that ended the practice of local officials allowing students to be absent from the public schools one or two afternoons a week to attend catechism classes, after which those classes could be attended only outside of school hours.

27. Beck, *Lutheran*, 329, 337.

28. John Brunner, *The Brunner Road: A Swiss-American Family's History* (Medford, WI, 1979), 20; Hildegard Kuse and Loretta Kuse, "Christoph David Kuse: Family History," typescript (1983), Medford (WI) Public Library; Erna Zimmerman, interview by Harriet Copeland, 3 May 1975, Wausau, WI, Oral Histories, Marathon County Public Library, Wausau, WI.

29. J. A. Burns, *The Growth and Development of the Catholic School System in the United States* (New York: Benziger Brothers, 1912), 300–302.

30. Sister M. Mileta Ludwig, *A Chapter of Franciscan History* (New York: Bookman Associates, 1950), 113, 120–22, 140–41, 143, 144.

31. Sister M. B. Bonaventuri Schoeberle, "Our Missions from 1864–1934," Franciscan Sisters of La Crosse (WI) (hereafter, FSLC).

32. For the state, the highest percentage attended between ages seven and thirteen in 1920: Frank Alexander Ross, *School Attendance in 1920* (Washington, DC: GPO, 1924), 249.

33. Joseph Jantsch, *My High School Days During the Horse and Buggy Era, 1907–1911,* typescript (1975), copy in author's possession. Jantsch kept a detailed journal from 1908 through 1911; this memoir is based on the journal as well as on his recollections.

34. Jantsch, *High School Days,* 1.

35. Jantsch, *High School Days,* 1.

36. Jantsch, *High School Days,* 2.

37. Jantsch, *High School Days,* 2.

38. Jantsch, *High School Days,* 2–6, 10.

39. Jantsch, *High School Days,* 9.

40. Jantsch, *High School Days,* 14–18, 24.

41. Jantsch, *High School Days,* 26.

42. Jantsch, *High School Days,* 25, 28.

43. Brian William Beltman, "Rural Renaissance in an Urban Age, The Country Life Movement in Wisconsin: 1895–1918," (PhD diss., UW–Madison, 1974), 157–63.

44. Larry Cuban, *How Teachers Taught: Constancy and Change in American Classrooms, 1890–1990* (New York: Teachers College, Columbia University, 1993), especially 129–30, 134.

45. Jeanne Rentmeester, *Wisconsin Creoles* (Melbourne, FL: privately published, 1989), 282, 238; my thanks to Lucy Murphy for supplying this genealogical reference. Joseph Ducharme, "An Episode of the War of 1812," in Wisconsin Historical Society, *Proceedings* (Madison: The Society, 1910), 149; Thérèse Baird, "Reminiscences of Life in Territorial Wisconsin," *Collections of the State Historical Society of Wisconsin,* ed. Ruben Gold Thwaites (Madison: SHSW, 1900), 15:211.

46. Mehan, "Dousman Women," 36–40.

47. Anthony M. Gachet, "Five Years in America: A Journal of a Missionary Among the Redskins—Journal, 1859," *Wisconsin Magazine of History* 18 (Sept. 1934): 75. Probably the youngest daughter, Elizabeth, then twenty-five, joined her mother and sisters in the move. That same year, she married John Wiley, a Shawano doctor who was under government contract to serve the Menominee. It is not clear whether the

young couple lived at Shawano or at Keshena during this time. For Elizabeth, see Sharon S. Thatcher, *The History of Merrill, Wisconsin: The Jenny Years, 1847–1881* (Merrill, WI: Merrill Historical Society, 2000), 149–50.

48. U.S. Congress, House of Representatives, Doc. 1855–56, 1:1, 356.

49. Mehan, "Dousman Women," 56–57.

50. Mehan, "Dousman Women," 57.

51. Mehan, "Dousman Women," 58.

52. Ourada, *Menominee Indians*, 122–23, 136, blames the new missionary, Gachet, for encouraging the Christian Menominee to burn Rosalie's house and insult her, thus provoking the threat to leave; see also Mehan, "Dousman Women," 57, 65–66.

53. A. D. Bonesteel to A. B. Greenwood, CIA, 23 Mar. and 28 July 1860, and report by Kintzing Pritchettel, 8 June 1860, frames 1577, 1835, 1064–65, Roll 323, M234, Letters Received by the Office of Indian Affairs, 1824–81, BIA, RG 55, NA Microfilm.

54. Hiring dates for Dousman daughters, "Statistics of Employees in Green Bay Agency," frame 0512, included in M. M. Davis to W. P. Dale, 30 May 1863, reel 324, M234, Letters Received by the Office of Indian Affairs, 1824–81, Green Bay Agency, 1824–80, 1856–60, BIA, RG 75, NA Microfilm.

55. U.S. Congress, House of Representatives, Agent Davis Report, 1864, Doc. 1864–65, vol. 3, 582–83; Davis Report, 1865, Doc. 1865–66, vol. 2, 621–22; Rosalie's report, 1855, 365; and Kate's report, reel 324, M234, Letters Received by the Office of Indian Affairs, 1824–81, Green Bay Agency, 1824–80, 1856–60, BIA, RG 75, NA Microfilm; Keesing, *Menominee Indians*, 160, 163–68; Nichols, "Brief Biography"; Ourada, *Menominee Indians*, 141.

56. Lucy Eldersveld Murphy, "Public Mothers: Native Americans and Métis Women as Creole Mediators in the Nineteenth-Century Midwest," *Journal of Women's History* 14.4 (Winter 2003): 141–66; Mehan, "Dousman Women," appendices.

57. For a discussion of Native methods of learning, see Madhu Suri Prakesh and Gustavo Estwa, *Escaping Education: Living as Learning Within Grassroots Cultures* (New York: Peter Lang, 1998), 3–9, 41–48. See also

Henry Goddard Leach to Mary Austin, 9 Aug. 1928, box 77, Austin Papers, Huntington Library, San Marino, CA; he was especially interested in Navajo transmission of local knowledge.

58. For Mary Dodge, see "Chronicle of the Menominee Mission," 90.

59. Ourada, *Menominee Indians*, 151–52.

60. "Keshena," undated transcript, CSJ.

61. Quotes from "Chronicle of the Menominee Mission," 80, 90.

62. "Chronicle of the Menominee Mission," 90, 101.

63. "Chronicle of the Menominee Mission," 891. After opening schools among the Dakota and Ho-Chunk in 1850, the Sisters of St. Joseph of Carondelet spread out to all parts of the United States: by 1910 they were operating 126 schools and teaching 41,000 students.

64. "Chronicle of the Menominee Mission," 163, 211.

65. "Chronicle of the Menominee Mission," Report of 1893; *The Catholic Educational Exhibit at the World's Columbian Exposition* (Chicago: Hyland, 1896), 20–21; typescript history, CSJ.

66. Josephine Daniels, interview, n.d., St. Joseph's Indian School Oral History Records, 1991–95, series 1, box 2, Interviews, MUL.

67. Sarah Shillinger, " 'They Never Told Us They Wanted to Help Us': An Oral History of Saint Joseph's Indian Industrial School," (PhD diss., University of Pennsylvania, 1995), xxi; for another fairly favorable assessment of the nun's schools, see Loew, "Newspapers," 135. By 1883, the Catholics had established eighteen boarding schools and were receiving almost $400,000 yearly in U.S. government contracts.

68. Shillinger, "They Never Told Us," 17.

69. Daniels interview.

70. Daniels interview.

71. Loew, "Newspapers," 158–60.

72. Retaliatory policies in Shepard Freeman, Superintendent of School, to CIA, 18 Feb. 1908, and Rev. Blaise Krake, St. Joseph's School, to F. E. Leupp, CIA, 11 Sept. 1907, Keshena 8904–08–820 and 77102–07–820, RG 75, NAB; withholding of rations as

punishment was allowed under the Act of 3 March 1893, Nicholson to CIA, 20 Feb. 1912, Keshena 18680–12–820, RG 75, NAB; for the practice, see E. B. Merrett to Nicholson, 3 Nov. 1917, Keshena 85240–17–820, RG 75, NAB; Congress banned the withholding of rations in 1904: see Francis Paul Prucha, *The Churches and the Indian Schools, 1888–1912* (Lincoln: University of Nebraska Press, 1979), 69.

73. U.S. Board of Indian Commissioners, Minutes, 1869–1917, 1 Oct. 1889, 237, Ayer Manuscripts, NL; U.S. Congress, House of Representatives, *Report of the Secretary of the Interior*, 54th Congress, 1st Session, 1896, Doc. 5, vol. 2, 352. Dorothy W. Hewes, "Those First Good Years of Indian Education: 1894–1898," *American Indian Culture and Research Journal* 5 (1981): 63–82, argues that the during these years the Indian schools superintendent, Swiss immigrant William N. Hailmann, supported Froebelian education theories that promoted volunteer enrollment, day schools, emphasis on family and community, the importance of nature, and Native crafts; his replacement did not support these theories.

74. Patricia A. Carter, "'Completely Discouraged': Women Teachers' Resistance in the Bureau of Indian Affairs Schools, 1900–1910," *Frontiers* 15.3 (1995): 71, 77; see also Mary Ann Paquette's story in Ch. 8.

75. U.S. Congress, House of Representatives, *Report of the Secretary of the Interior*, 54th Congress, 2nd Session, 1897, Doc. 5, vol. 2, 587.

76. Gail Guthrie Valaskakis, "The Chippewa and the Other: Living the Heritage of Lac du Flambeau," *Cultural Studies* 2.3 (Oct. 1988): 267–93.

77. A. S. Nicholson to CIA, 20 Feb. 1912, F. H. Abbott to Nicholson, 25 May 1912, Nicholson to CIA, 16 Mar. 1912, Elizabeth Charles to Secretary W. Fisher, 4 Mar. 1912, all Keshena 18680–12–820, RG 75, NAB.

78. A. S. Nicholson to CIA, 15 Nov. 1912 and 3 Mar. 1913, and memorandum, 26 Nov. 1912, Keshena 115738–12–820, RG 75, NAB.

79. For kidnapping, see John Flinn to Major S. W. Campbell, 4 Oct. 1906, La Pointe Agency, Administrative Records of the Lac du Flambeau Agency, 1888–1914, BIA, RG 75,

NAGLR; for the St. Mary's case, see Loew, "Newspapers," 146.

80. Discussion of young women leaving in the evening is in Superintendent Ruben Perry to Acting Indian Agent, 4 May 1897; placing young women in jobs is in Phillips to Indian Agent, 23 Oct. 1903; vacation policy is in Phillips to Campbell, 14 June 1904; runaways is in Egbert to Campbell, 23 Aug. 1907, and Wright to Campbell, 11 May 1908, when eleven girls were reported gone, all in Letters Received from the Lac du Flambeau Reservation and School, 1885–1914, BIA, La Pointe Agency, RG 75, NAGLR.

81. A matron was removed in January 1896, Perry to Mercer, 28 Jan. 1896; the disciplinarian was reprimanded in Perry to Indian Agent, 26 Sept. 2002, both in Letters Received from the Lac du Flambeau Reservation and School, 1885–1914, BIA, La Pointe Agency, RG 75, NAGLR.

82. Health reports are in Wright to Campbell, 1 Mar. 1901, Phillips to Indian Agent, 25 Apr. 1904, and Flinn to Campbell, 22 Apr. 1907, Letters Received from the Lac du Flambeau Reservation and School, 1885–1914, BIA, La Pointe Agency, RG 75, NAGLR.

83. See especially Flinn to Campbell, 24 Feb. 1908, Letters Received from the Lac du Flambeau Reservation and School, 1885–1914, BIA, La Pointe Agency, RG 75, NAGLR; see also Loew, "Newspapers," 138, for health problems.

84. Report of the Superintendent of Lac du Flambeau School, 13 Aug. 1896, in U.S. Congress, House of Representatives, 54th Congress, 2d Session, Doc. No. 5, *Report of the Secretary of the Interior*, 1897, 333.

85. Lac du Flambeau Industrial Survey, 1922.

86. Elsie E. Newton, Supervisor, "Report of Training and Activities of Girls," 18 Feb. 1920, LdF 24773–20–032, RG 75, NAB; E. B. Meritt to O. H. Lipps, 16 July 1917, Lipps to CIA, 20 June 1917, James W. Balmer to CIA, 26 June 1917, and W. W. Coon, Assistant Supervisor of Indian Schools, "Report of Supervision on the Lac du Flambeau School," 12–19 May 1917, all File 810, LdF 53692–17–810, RG 75, NAB.

87. Information on Gauthier from Lac du Flambeau Industrial Survey, 1922, 51.

88. Estimates vary: David Wallace Adams, *Education for Extinction: American Indians and the Boarding School Experience, 1875–1928* (Lawrence: University Press of Kansas, 1995), 319, says that from three hundred students in 1896 the number increased to one-half the students in public schools by 1915; Frederick E. Hoxie, *A Final Promise: The Campaign to Assimilate the Indians, 1880–1920* (Lincoln: University of Nebraska Press, 1984), 26, puts the number at 50 percent by 1921. Clyde Ellis, *To Change Them Forever: Indian Education at the Rainy Mountain Boarding School, 1893–1920* (Norman: University of Oklahoma Press, 1996), 144–93, describes the policy as applied to the Kiowa students.

89. See the Industrial Surveys for Menominee and Lac du Flambeau, BIA, RG 75, NAB.

90. U.S. Congress, House of Representatives, *Report of the Secretary of the Interior*, 1896, 4, 338, 343.

91. U.S. Congress, House of Representatives, *Report of the Secretary of the Interior*, 1896, 4, 338, 343.

92. Hoxie, *Final Promise*, 66–67, 234.

93. Report to George Vaux, Jr., chairman, Board of Indian Commissioners, Reports, 1915–19, 2 vols., 2–14, Ayer Manuscripts, NL.

94. Brenda J. Child, *Boarding School Seasons: American Indian Families, 1900–1940* (Lincoln: University of Nebraska Press, 1998), 22–23, discusses continuing racism.

95. Menominee Industrial Survey, 1922–25.

96. Nancy Lurie, *Mountain Wolf Woman, Sister of Crashing Thunder: The Autobiography of a Winnebago Woman* (1963; reprint, Ann Arbor: University of Michigan Press, 1966), 27–29. Some Ho-Chunk students stayed on when the government turned the Wittenberg boarding house back to the Lutherans: see Beck, *Lutheran*, 305–6.

97. "School Yarn," Van Antwerp Wisconsin Folklore Collection, box 1, WHSAD; the Stacy story comes from Arthur V. Casselman, *The Winnebago Finds a Friend* (Philadelphia, PA: Heidelberg Press, 1932), 120.

98. H. C. Cooper, Jr., comp., *History of Lincoln, Oneida and Vilas Counties* (Minneapolis, MN: Cooper, 1924), 192; Diana Anderson at the Walter E. Olson Memorial Library in Eagle River (WI) supplied information on this early public school: Anderson to the author, 23 May 2005.

99. Chosa interview, *Lac du Flambeau News*, 4.3 and 4.4 (Mar. and Apr. 1996); Chosa did not drop out of school when the students harassed him. For more recent attitudes in the area, see Rick Whaley with Walter Bresette, *Walleye Warriors: An Effective Alliance Against Racism and for the Earth* (Philadelphia, PA: New Society, 1994), 165–66.

100. Cindi Stiles, "Contact and Consequences: The BIA Boarding School in Lac du Flambeau," *Lac du Flambeau News* 9:3 (Mar. 2002): 7, 14; Kelly Jackson, "Remembering an Era?" *Lac du Flambeau News* 9:3 (Mar. 2002): 6, 12.

101. Jackson, "Remembering an Era?" 6; June Davis reviews a number of studies in "American Indian Boarding School Experiences: Recent Studies from Native Experience," *OAH Magazine of History* 15.2 (Winter 2001): 20–22.

102. Sister Theodine [Amanda Sebold], interview by the author, July 1988, St. Rose Convent, La Crosse, WI.

103. Florence Jean Deacon, "Handmaids or Autonomous Women: The Charitable Activities, Institution Building, and Community Relationships of Catholic Sisters in Nineteenth Century Wisconsin" (PhD diss., UW–Madison, 1989), 173–217.

104. Ludwig, *Chapter of Franciscan History*, 296–98.

105. Ludwig, *Chapter of Franciscan History*, 301–2, 317–18.

106. Account 229, Sister M. Ludmilla Kubat, 1899, and account 482, Alodia Fastner, who entered in 1907, FSLC; Deacon, "Handmaids or Autonomous Women."

107. Account 605, Elizabeth Veit; account 836, Celine Schumacher; account 500, Rose Braun; account 779, Martha Weiler; and account 676, M. Austina Burger, FSLC.

108. Beck, *Lutheran*, 193–94, 272–73, 455; Jacobi-Dittrich, *"Deutsch" Schulen*, 201, 207, 210.

109. For an overview of changes, see Wisconsin Department of Public Instruction, State Superintendent, *Biennial Report*, 1888–90, 1890–92, 1900–2, 1910–12, and 1920–22 (Madison, WI: The State).

110. Wisconsin Department of Public Instruction, State Superintendent, *Biennial Report*, 1890–92, 1910–12.

111. Bessie McDonald Fenelon, "A Teacher's Experience in the Pioneer Days," in Committee for Research on Price County Rural Schools, *Country School Reflections: Price County One Room Rural Schools: 1879 to Consolidation* (Phillips, WI: Price County Fair Centennial Celebration, 1985), 60–62.

112. Erna Oleson Xan, *Wisconsin: My Home* (Madison: UW Press, 1950), 107.

113. Wisconsin Department of Public Instruction, State Superintendent, *Annual Report*, 1880–81 (Madison, WI: The State, 1881), 317–19.

114. Clark County (WI), Teachers Certificate Stub Books (1909–30), series 8, WHSAD.

115. Wisconsin Department of Public Instruction, State Superintendent, *11th Biennial Report, July 1, 1902–June 30, 1904* (Madison, WI: The State, 1904), 21.

116. Jeff Wasserman, "Wisconsin Normal Schools and the Educational Hierarchy, 1860–1890," *Journal of the Midwest History of Education Society* 7 (1979): 2–3; Wisconsin Department of Public Instruction, State Superintendent, *11th Biennial Report,* 22.

117. Mary D. Bradford, "Memoirs," *Wisconsin Magazine of History* 15.1 (Sept. 1931): 48, 68.

118. Mary D. Bradford, "Memoirs," *Wisconsin Magazine of History* 15.3 (Mar. 1932): 318.

119. Wisconsin Department of Public Instruction, State Superintendent, *13th Biennial Report, 1906–1908* (Madison, WI: The State) 74, 76; "First Annual Report of the Marathon County Training School Board," 30 June 1900, "Report of Principal of Marathon County Training School," 5 July 1900, 49–53, and "Third Annual Report of the Marathon County Training School for District School Teachers," 1 July 1902, 30, all in Wisconsin Department of Public Instruction, State Superintendent, *Biennial Report, 1900–1902* (Madison, WI: The State); "Fifth Annual Report of the Marathon County Training School," 1 July 1904, 32, in Wisconsin Department of Public Instruction, State Superintendent, *11th Biennial Report.*

120. Wisconsin Department of Public Instruction, *18th Biennial Report, 1916–1918* (Madison, WI: The State), 54, and *Biennial Report, 1920–22* (Madison, WI: The State) 206–7.

121. Bradford, "Memoirs," *Wisconsin Magazine of History* 15.3 (Mar. 1932): 327.

122. David R. Reynolds, *There Goes the Neighborhood: Rural School Consolidation at the Grass Roots in Early Twentieth Century Iowa* (Iowa City: University of Iowa Press, 1999), especially the introduction, 1–16.

123. Reynolds, *Neighborhood*, 85–92, 104, 119–21.

124. See Ch. 8 for the battle over school suffrage.

125. Wisconsin Department of Public Instruction, State Superintendent, *11th Biennial Report*, 15.

126. Wisconsin Department of Public Instruction, State Superintendent, Committee of Six on Rural Schools, *Biennial Report, 1900–1902,* 26, 29, 32, 71.

127. Wisconsin Department of Public Instruction, State Superintendent, Committee of Six on Rural Schools, 42; *11th Biennial Report,* 68; *Biennial Report, 1904–1906* (Madison, WI: The State), 11. The comment about "hired girls" making as much as teachers is in *11th Biennial Report,* 20.

128. Wisconsin Department of Public Instruction, State Superintendent, Committee of Six on Rural Schools, *Biennial Report 1906–1908* (Madison, WI: The State, 1908), 18.

129. Reynolds, *Neighborhood,* 178–79, 213–14, 230–34.

130. Harald A. Pedersen, "Acculturation," 55.

131. Agricultural Extension, "Some Economic Factors Which Influence Rural Education in Wisconsin," *Research Bulletin* 40 (Oct. 1916): figs. 8, 10, 13 on pp. 9, 12, 21 and 1–2 on 32.

132. Quotes are from Wisconsin Department of Public Instruction, State Superintendent, *Biennial Report, 1916–1918* (Madison, WI: The State, 1918), 62–63.

133. Attacked by most professional educators as inadequate, the ungraded classroom impressed a few as flexible and adaptable to the needs of students of different abilities and to smaller groups. Helen Parkhurst, who taught in a rural ungraded school in Dalton, MA, used it as a model to liberate students

from the graded school system that forced them into a lock-step curriculum where all were considered equal in ability and interests. Parkhurst retained the traditional curriculum and textbook instruction but urged teachers to adapt the ungraded classroom to the larger urban graded system. This system survived in Special Education classes, where students unable or unwilling to learn in graded classrooms were put into smaller groups and teachers tailored learning to individual needs. See David Tyack and Larry Cuban, *Tinkering Toward Utopia: A Century of Public School Reform* (Cambridge, MA: Harvard University Press, 1995), 94–97, and Ron Brooks, "In a World Set Apart: The Dalton Dynasty at King Alfred School, 1920–62," *History of Education* 27.4 (1998): 421–40.

Notes to Chapter 7

1. Michael Angel, *Preserving the Sacred: Historical Perspectives on the Ojibwa Midewiwin* (Winnipeg: University of Manitoba Press, 2002), 13–14, 72, 144.

2. Karren Baird-Olson and Carol Ward, "Recovery and Resistance: The Renewal of Traditional Spirituality Among American Indian Women," *American Indian Culture and Research Journal* 24.4 (2000): 1–35.

3. Leonard Bloomfield, *Menomini Texts* (New York: G. E. Stechert, 1928), xi–xii, 18–19.

4. Description of farms is from Menominee Industrial Survey, 1922.

5. Description of weaving is from Phebe Jewell Nichols, "Weavers of Grasses: Indian Women of the Woodlands," *Wisconsin Magazine of History* 36.2 (Winter 1952–53): 130–36.

6. Benjamin G. Armstrong, *Life Among the Indians: Reminiscences* (Ashland, WI: Wentworth, 1892), 156–59.

7. The anthropologists' dispute is in Thomas Vennum, Jr., *The Ojibwa Dance Drum: Its History and Construction* (Washington, DC: Smithsonian Institution, 1982), 47.

8. "Chronicle of the Menominee Mission," series 1, 41, roll 13, IMR, gives the 1880 date.

9. Ila Hill Moede, *Grandma's Footprints: A History of Shawano, Wisconsin, 1843–1918* (Shawano, WI: The Author, 1991), 79–89.

10. Agent Wright to Campbell, 9 June and 10 Oct. 1902, Letters Received from Lac du Flambeau Reservation and School, 1883–1914, BIA, La Pointe Agency, RG 75, NAGLR.

11. Loew, "Newspapers," 148.

12. Moede, *Grandma's Footprints*, 72; Densmore Diary, 1910, Densmore Papers, box 1, Smithsonian Institution National Anthropological Archives; Frances Densmore, *Chippewa Music* (Washington, DC: GPO, 1910–13), 2:147. For the 1915 dance controversy, see file 100165–14–047, BIA, RG 75, NAB. The photographs are in the Milwaukee (WI) Public Museum. The drums were still traveling in the 1920s: see account of introduction into one Minnesota community in Maureen Matthews and Roger Roulette, "Fair Wind's Dream: Naamiwan Obawaajigewin," in *Reading Beyond Words: Context for Native History*, eds. Jennifer S. H. Brown and Elizabeth Vibert (Peterborough, ON: Broadview Press, 1996), 330–59.

13. J. S. Slotkin, *The Menomini Powwow: A Study in Cultural Decay* (Milwaukee, WI: Milwaukee Public Museum Publications in Anthropology 4, 1957), 9, 15, 18.

14. Quotes are from Vennum, *Ojibwa Dance Drum*, 83; Slotkin, *The Menomini Powwow*, 38, 56, 65 in the 1980s; Michael A. Rynkiewich, "Chippewa Powwows," in *Anishinabe: 6 Studies of Modern Chippewa*, ed. J. A. Parades (Tallahassee: University Press of Florida, 1980), 38.

15. Benjamin R. Kracht, "Kiowa Religion in Historical Perspective," in *Native American Spirituality: A Critical Reader*, ed. Lee Irwin (Lincoln: University of Nebraska Press, 2000), 242–46, traces it north to the Kiowa.

16. Mary Fast Wolf described in Paul Radin Papers, folder 13, series 4, box 1, MUL.

17. Omer C. Stewart, *Peyote Religion: A History* (Norman: University of Oklahoma Press, 1987), 215.

18. Paul Radin to Franz Boas, 28 May 1908, series 1, box 1, Correspondence, folder 1, Paul Radin Papers, MUL; Paul Radin, "The Culture of the Winnebago: As Described by Themselves," Memoir 2, *International Journal of American Linguistics*, Indiana University Publications in Anthropology and Linguistics (1949), 1–9; for Radin biography, see Mary Fast Wolf, "Paul Radin: New

Perspectives in Ethnology" (MA thesis, San Francisco State University, 1989), especially 2–11.

19. Paul Radin, *The Religious Experiences of an American Indian* (Zurich: Rheinverlag, 1950), 249–90; see also Paul Radin, "The Social Organization of the Winnebago Indians, An Interpretation," Canada Department of Mines *Museum Bulletin No. 10*, Anthropological Series 5 (Ottawa, ON: Government Printing Bureau, 16 May 1915).

20. Although Radin visited Lurie while Mountain Wolf Woman was there, he remained uninterested in her experiences.

21. Lurie, *Mountain Wolf Woman*, 47–48.

22. Lurie, *Mountain Wolf Woman*, 40, 45, 90–91, 107, 129; according to Mountain Wolf Woman, Thomas Roddy, a native-born white in Black River Falls who took troupes of Indian dancers about the country, also supported the introduction of the new religion, 129n10. The names *Crashing Thunder* and *Mountain Wolf Woman* were aliases: her English name was Stella Stacy: see letter to Radin signed "your Indian Sister," 1 Mar. 1958, series 6, box 2, folder 1, Paul Radin Papers, MUL.

23. For the Mitchell Neck peyote case, see Stewart, *Peyote Religion*, 215–25.

24. For Collier, see Kenneth R. Philip, *John Collier's Crusade for Indian Reform, 1920–1954* (Tucson: University of Arizona Press, 1977), 132–34; for Zitkala-Sa, see Karen Lerner, "Mother's Little Helper No More: Zitkala-Sa and Maternalism in Indian Reform, 1887–1938," (MA thesis, New Mexico State University–Las Cruces, 2002), 57–62.

25. "The Menominees," *The Indian Sentinel* (1904–5): 13.

26. Sleeper-Smith, *Indian Women*, 96–113; Lee Irwin, "Freedom, Law, and Prophecy: A Brief History of Native American Religious Resistance," in *Native American Spirituality*, 295–98.

27. Figures from statistics in IMR, series 1, MF, reel 13, reports beginning frame 0816, MUL.

28. "The Menominees," *The Indian Sentinel* (1904–5): 23.

29. Jennifer S. H. Brown and Robert Brightman, eds., *"The Orders of the Dreamed": George Nelson on Cree and Northern Ojibwa*

Religion and Myth, 1823 (St. Paul: MHS Press, 1988), 100–101, 143–44; Tressa Berman, "'All We Needed Was Our Gardens': Women's Work and Welfare Reform in the Preservation Economy," in *Native Pathways*, 143–46; Melissa A. Pflüg, "Pimadaziwin: Contemporary Rituals in Odawa Community," in *Native American Spirituality*, especially 124–25.

30. Sister Frances to Father Francis Jordan, 18 Feb., 16 July, and 11 Dec. 1883, *Letters of Mother Frances Streitel to Father Francis Jordan, 1883–1885* (Reproduced from *The Ave Mater Dolorosa*, Supplement 5, [Feb. 1976], translated from the original German, Broken Arrow, OK: Sisters of the Sorrowful Mother, 1998).

31. Kiliana, *History*, 1–13; Sister Frances to Father Francis Jordan, Apr., Nov., and 11 Dec. 1883, *Letters of Mother Frances Streitel*.

32. Sister Frances to Father Francis Jordan, 16? July and 11 Dec. 1883, *Letters of Mother Frances Streitel*.

33. Sister Frances to Father Francis Jordan, Feb./Mar. and 18 and 25 Mar. 1883, *Letters of Mother Frances Streitel*.

34. Sister Frances to Father Francis Jordan, 20 Feb. and 16 and 25 Mar. 1883 and 6? Jan. 1884, *Letters of Mother Frances Streitel*.

35. Sister Frances to Father Francis Jordan, 18 and 21 Feb., 27 and 31 Mar., 16 Apr., 12 July, and 25–26 Oct. 1883 and Jan. 1884, *Letters of Mother Frances Streitel*.

36. Sister Lela Mae Fenton, *Destroy Not the Wheat* (n.p.: publisher unknown, 1939), and Sister M. Carmeline Koller, *Walk in Love: Mother Mary Frances Streitel, Foundress of the Sisters of the Sorrowful Mother* (Chicago: Franciscan Herald Press, 1981), trace her life.

37. Sister Agnes, 30 June 1932, vol. 2, Sister Beda Oral History Project, SSM.

38. Sister Annunciata, 8 Dec. 1938, vol. 2, Sister Beda Oral History Project, SSM.

39. Sister M. Melania, 9 Apr. 1938, and Sister Ferreria, 30 Nov. 1938, vol. 2, Sister Beda Oral History Project, SSM.

40. Sister M. Salesia Rebhan, 10 Sept. 1937, vol. 1, Sister Beda Oral History Project, SSM.

41. Sister M. Clotildis Paul, 10 Sept. 1937, vol. 1, Sister Beda Oral History Project, SSM; see also "Sister M. Clotildis Paul," *The Ave Mater Dolorosa* 363 (Sept. 1957): 107–10.

42. Sister Sabastiana, 21 Feb. 1938, vol. 1, Sister Beda Oral History Project, ssm. The Benedictines also considered work as prayer: time was holy and they must use it well.

43. *Dorchester (WI) Highlights* 1.9 (Oct. 1960), discusses the first log church and mission priests; see also Beaulah Fischer, *Historical Sketches of Dorchester, Wisconsin, 1873–1973* (Dorchester, WI: Centennial Booklet Committee, 1973), 25.

44. Father Novak's account of the community was first published in Slovenian in 1923 and translated into English for Slovenska Druzba Committee, *Spominska Zgodovina,* 8–9, 179.

45. Goc, *Native Realm,* 72, 75.

46. Goc, *Native Realm,* 69–70.

47. Goc, *Native Realm,* 78.

48. See Josephine Marie Peplinski, *A Fitting Response: A History of the Sisters of St. Joseph of the Third Order of St. Francis* (South Bend, IN: The Sisters, The Order, 1982), 105–50, and "Early History of Congregation [Sisters of Saint Joseph] by Pioneer Sisters," 2, csj.

49. "Early History," 1–2 for Sister Oswalda Wisniewski quote, csj.

50. "Early History," Wisniewski account, csj.

51. Undated clipping, Sister Veronica Wolashek and Sister Rita Glowacki, and dittoed questionnaire of work of early convent life, csj.

52. Account from *Colby, Wisconsin, Centennial, 1873–1973* (Withee, WI: Centennial Committee, n.d.), 5, and Ruth B. Pilgrim, ed., *We Will Go Forth* (n.p.: publisher unknown, 1984), 137.

53. *Frauenverein* mentioned in Pilgrim, *We Will Go Forth,* 156, and in clipping of the Wausau (WI) *Daily Record-Herald* (13 Mar. 1931), Marathon County Historical Society. For opposition, see Centennial Committee, *Unmeasurable Grace–Measurable Growth: Trinity Lutheran Church, Phillips, Wisconsin, 1885–1985,* 25, Phillips (WI) Public Library.

54. Pilgrim, *We Will Go Forth,* 137, 156.

55. Presiding Elder's Report, Portage District, 1886, and Presiding Elder's Reports, 1887, 1888, Methodist Conference Archives, Sun Prairie, WI.

56. George W. White, "History of Wisconsin Methodism," handwritten manuscript, Methodist Conference Archives, Sun Prairie, WI; Pilgrim, *We Will Go Forth,* 11, 14, 43; J. Raleigh Nelson, *Lady Unafraid* (Caldwell, Idaho: Caxton Printers, 1951), 10.

57. *Wisconsin River Pilot* (27 Apr. 1886): 3:4, discusses the Methodist women and the lyceum movement.

58. *Colby, Wisconsin, Centennial,* 91–96.

59. "Trinity Lutheran Church, Athens, WI, 1882–1982," pamphlet (n.d.), 9, 15, 21, 23, Athens (WI) Public Library.

60. Obituaries, *Taylor County (WI) Star & News* (10 Apr. 1918) 4:3 for Joanna and (28 Nov. 1957) 1:6–7 for Sophia, who also served as town librarian from 1918 to 1943; they are also mentioned in *Lutheran Centennial Booklet,* 23, Medford (WI) Public Library.

61. Irene Ungrodt Leverenz, ed., *The Ungrodts: 1800–1984* (n.p.: privately published, 1984), 8 Feb. 1891, 16.

62. Leverenz, ed., *The Ungrodts* (4 Sept. 1891): 10 and (26 Oct. 1891): 12.

63. Keach interview; Fr. Blasins to Provincial, 9 Feb. 1888, reel 12, frame 891, imr, mul. Other Lutheran churches seemed to have a similar history: see "Trinity Lutheran Church, Athens, Wisconsin, 1882–1892," a congregation that went through the same mission era and then hired its first resident pastor and organized the Ladies' Aid Society with seventy-three charter members who supported the Missionary League with bazaars and potluck dinners.

64. Harald A. Pedersen, "Acculturation."

65. A similar Scandinavian Lutheran Church in Dorchester probably merged into a larger English-speaking Lutheran church: records at the Dorchester (WI) Public Library.

66. Anne C. Rose, *Beloved Strangers: Interfaith Families in Nineteenth-Century America* (Cambridge, MA: Harvard University Press, 2001), 49–66, 80, 101, 103, 119–28.

67. Richard M. Bernard, *The Melting Pot and the Altar: Marital Assimilation in Wisconsin, 1850–1920* (Minneapolis: University of Minnesota Press, 1980).

68. Sister M. Alphonsa, 19 June 1939, vol. 2, Sister Beda Oral History Project, ssm.

69. Mrs. Jacob Nick, interview, 30 July 1939, Sacred Heart Hospital, Tomahawk, WI, and Sister M. Dyonisia, interview, 4 July 1939,

Marshfield, WI, vol. 3, Sister Beda Oral History Project, ssm.

70. Sister M. Ferreria, 1 Dec. 1938, and Sister Mauritia, 12 Dec. 1938, vol. 2, Sister Beda Oral History Project, ssm; *The Story of Saint Joseph's Hospital: A Century of Caring, 1890–1990* (n.p.: publisher unknown, n.d.), 11.

71. Sister M. Agnes, 6–11 July 1939, vol. 2, Sister Beda Oral History Project, ssm.

72. Mrs. C. B. Baker to Sister Superior, 28 Nov. 1912, ssm; see also C. Jacquemin to Dr. C. Von Newpert, President of the Association, 6 Dec. 1912, ssm; quoted in Sister Mary Lu Slowey, "Sister Cornelia Springob, 1873–1954," in *Women of Vision: Reflections on Notable Women of Portage County* (Stevens Point, WI: Epitaph Press, 1999), 32.

73. Slowey, "Sister Cornelia Springob," 33 and 35 for biography, 36 for quote.

74. Maria Morton Merrill, Diary (1890–1899), SC 7, University of Wisconsin–La Crosse.

Notes to Chapter 8

1. Bradford, "Memoirs," *Wisconsin Magazine of History* 15.3 (Mar. 1932): 307.

2. Mary D. Bradford, "Memoirs," *Wisconsin Magazine of History* 16.1 (Sept. 1932): 48.

3. Bradford, "Memoirs," *Wisconsin Magazine of History* 16.1 (Sept. 1932): 50, 55, 59.

4. Bradford, "Memoirs," *Wisconsin Magazine of History* 16.1 (Sept. 1932): 63–64; see Janice Steinschneider, "'Not A New Woman, But an Improved Woman': The Wisconsin Federation of Women's Clubs, 1895–1920" (MA thesis, uw–Madison, 1983), 138–39, for her wfwc work.

5. Bradford, "Memoirs," *Wisconsin Magazine of History* 16.1 (Sept. 1932): 67, 82.

6. Close-up of the regalia can be seen in Selia Evans, *Royal Neighbors of America: 100 Years of Helping Hands* (n.p.: Royal Neighbors of America, 1995), 17, 23; Schnitzler and Kleiman, eds., *The Marshfield Story,* 234, shows women in regalia that includes the colored sashes.

7. Early history is from http://www.royalneighbors.org (accessed 14 May 2001); see also Evans, *Royal Neighbors,* 4–11.

8. Evans, *Royal Neighbors,* 14.

9. Loyal supper in *Loyal Centennial, 1870–1970* (Loyal, WI: Loyal Tribune, 1970), 61; see also *Withee Memories,* 82.

10. Thirteen of the twenty-seven charter members were listed on the 1900 or 1910 census: 77 percent were thirty or older; 77 percent non-farmers; 70 percent born in Wisconsin; 62 percent of parents from New York or Pennsylvania. One woman had no children; the rest had one to four. The original Loyal Petition is in the Royal Neighbors of America Archives, Rock Island, IL.

11. Three-quarters of the twenty Colby charter members were listed on the 1900 or 1910 census: 92 percent were under thirty; 27 percent farmers; 60 percent born in Wisconsin—27 percent of foreign parentage and 27 percent of parents from New York or Pennsylvania. The original Colby Petition is in the Royal Neighbors of America Archives, Rock Island, IL. For the 1910 parade, see *Colby, Wisconsin, Centennial,* 84.

12. Vote and play mentioned in Evans, *Royal Neighbors,* 24.

13. American Society of Equity (hereafter, ase), National Union, Fifteenth Annual Convention, Wausau, WI, 11–14 Dec. 1917, 166, whsad.

14. James Andrew Everitt, *The Third Power: Farmers to the Front,* 4th ed. (Indianapolis, IN: The Author, 1907; reprint, New York: Arno Press, 1975), vii–viii, 38, 41, 272–73, 276.

15. Lethe Viola Metcalf, "History of the Equity Society in Wisconsin" (BA thesis, uw, 1920), 2–7.

16. Metcalf, "History of Equity Society," 5; Carry Miller, ase, Wisconsin State Union, Proceedings, State Convention, Madison, WI, 18–22 Dec. 1919, 82, whsad. The number of Wisconsin's auxiliaries doubled between 1917 and 1919: twenty-eight locals had 533 members in 1917, and there were fifty-two locals by 1919. In the absence of membership lists, I have assumed that membership also doubled, since a minimum number of members was required to form a branch. See ase, National Union, Fifteenth Annual Convention, 177, and ase, Wisconsin State Union, Proceedings, State Convention, 1919, 82.

17. *Equity News* 6.8 (25 Aug. 1913): 117 refers to early badges; *National Equity News* 1.5 (16 May 1918): 3–4, copies at the mhs. Samuelson was state treasurer in 1916–17,

national treasurer from 1916 to 1918, and national secretary in 1918.

18. Carry Miller and Mrs. C. E. Merling, ASE, Wisconsin State Union, Proceedings, State Convention, 1919, 81, 85.

19. Carry Miller, ASE, Wisconsin State Union, Proceedings, State Convention, 1919, 81.

20. For Stanley, see *Equity News* 6.1 (10 May 1913): 7; 6.18 (25 Jan. 1914): 282; 9.20 (15 Feb. 1917): 700. Children's Bureau field workers commented on the Hull WA and the Colby cooperative in 1916 while surveying maternal and infant mortality in Marathon County (WI), File 4–11–3-7, RG 103, NA. See also the *Colby, Wisconsin, Centennial*, 97, 99. A note from Raymond Brehm to the author, July 2003, also added family material.

21. *Equity News* 6.5 (10 July 1913): 85 and 9.17 (1 Jan. 1917): 655; information on Caroline Emmerton (1871–1955) from Dolores Elliott and Pat Hebert; obituary from the *(Chippewa Falls, WI) Herald-Telegram* (11 May 1955); *Bloomer Centennial, 1855–1955* (n.p.: publisher unknown, n.d); *Chippewa County Wisconsin Past and Present*, 2 vols. (Chicago: Clarke, 1918).

22. *Equity News* 9:16 (15 Dec. 1916): 638; for the 1907 law, see Linda K. Kerber, *No Constitutional Right to Be Ladies: Women and the Obligation of Citizenship* (New York: Hill and Wang, 1998), 41–42.

23. ASE, National Union, Fifteenth Annual Convention, 152–53, 161–62.

24. *Equity News* 9.21 (7 Mar. 1917): 716; *National Equity News* 1.7 (21 Mar. 1918): 8:3.

25. *Pine County (WI) Courier* (23 July 1936) and (6 Mar. 1941) obituaries. My thanks to Sylvia and Ray Marcotte for this information on the Jungers.

26. ASE, National Union, Fifteenth Annual Convention, 167, 170, 172, 179–80; ASE, Wisconsin State Union, Proceedings, State Convention, 1919, 64.

27. ASE, Wisconsin State Union, Proceedings, State Convention, 1919, 64, 65.

28. *The Wausau (WI) Pilot* (21 Sept. 1920): 1:4 discussed the split and 1:3 announced that Kate O'Hare would speak locally for the Socialist campaign, with speeches directed particularly at women; ASE, Minutes of the Board Meeting, 13 Jan. 1920, box 1,

WHSAD; Edward Paul Halline, "Embattled Farmers" (BA thesis, UW, 1921), follows the disintegration during 1920, which, he concludes, was due primarily to selfish factionalism disrupting the organization, 117. The ASE lost its more radical agrarians in the split: by 1920 the Minnesota NPL had 65,000 members; the Wisconsin NPL only 20,000. Karen Starr, "Fighting for a Future: Farm Women of the Nonpartisan League," *Minnesota History* 48.6 (Summer 1983): 257, describes the NPL women's auxiliary, which had fifty clubs by 1921.

29. *Colby, Wisconsin, Centennial*, 109; Steven J. Keillor, *Cooperative Commonwealth: Co-ops in Rural Minnesota, 1859–1939* (St. Paul: MHS Press, 2000), 169–89, describes the decline of the cooperative movement in Minnesota.

30. *School Bell Echoes*, Merrill High School (1904), 8, 20, Lincoln County Historical Society, Merrill, WI.

31. Wausau, WI, *River Pilot* (9 Mar. 1878): 3:3 and (16 Mar. 1878): 3:3; Anthony's talk described in unidentified clipping, 8 Apr. 1879, Prohibition File, Marathon Historical Society, Wausau, WI.

32. Lawrence Graves, "The Wisconsin Woman Suffrage Movement (PhD diss., UW, 1954), 38, 45, 51.

33. Wausau, WI, *River Pilot* (12 Apr. 1887): 3:6.

34. McBride, *On Wisconsin Women*, 123, 183–84 for continued voting; Graves, "Wisconsin Woman," 65–80, 102; Clark County (WI), Town and Village of Loyal, Misc. Records, 1869–1903, Small Series 4, WHSAD.

35. Remonstrance, 2 Sept. 1902, Towns of Dewhurst and Levis, Clerk, Miscellaneous Town Records, 1884–1956, box 1, folder 5, Clark Series 12; Appeal, 19 Dec. 1903, Clark County (WI), Town of Longwood, Department of Public Instruction, 1850–1906, vol. 3, Series 630, both WHSAD; for support of women voters, see the *Merrill (WI) Daily Herald* (14 Apr. 1917), 1.

36. Committee for Research on Price County Rural Schools, *Country School Recollections*, 4.

37. Agnes O'Brien Kelleher, "Schools in the Early History of Price County," 54–56; Georgia Beaver Soulen, "Reminiscent School

History, Southern Price County," 56–59; Bessie McDonald Fenelon, "A Teacher's Experience in the Pioneer Days," 60–62; Janette MacDonald Cole, "Pioneer School Days at the Prentice and Spirit Districts," 63–64; and May McNely, "Conclusion of School History," 65–66, all in F. W. Sackett, comp., *A Glimpse at the Early History of the State of Wisconsin Relating to Price County* (n.p.: The Compiler, ca. 1906; reprint, n.p.: Price County Genealogical Society, 2003); see also Committee for Research on Price County Rural Schools, *Country School Recollections*, 4, for list of superintendents and duties; McBride, *On Wisconsin Women*, 87, 250; Taylor County (WI) got its first woman superintendent in 1921: Centennial Committee, *100 Year Anniversary*, 153.

38. Mrs. Nellie Kedzie Jones, "Pioneering in Home Economics," *The K-Stater* 4.1 (Oct. 1954): 6.

39. Kedzie Jones, "Pioneering," 8.

40. Kedzie Jones, "Pioneering," 8.

41. Howard to Ada, 14 May and 24 June 1911, box 1, Howard Murray Jones Papers, WHSAD.

42. Howard to Ada, 7 and 25 Aug. and 11 Dec. 1911, 17 Mar. and 19 May 1912, Howard Murray Jones Papers, WHSAD.

43. Howard to brothers and sisters, 25 Jan. 1914, Howard Murray Jones Papers, WHSAD.

44. Howard excerpts of letters, 17 Aug., 1 Sept., and 28 Oct. 1915, Howard Murray Jones Papers, WHSAD.

45. Howard letters, 27 Apr. 1918 and 3 Feb. 1920, Howard Murray Jones Papers, WHSAD.

46. The above is all from Steinschneider, "Not a New Woman," especially 63–66, 99, 117–27, 159, 163. As the WFWC extended into the largest cities of the northland, three leaders emerged: Emma Conley, Mary Howe Shelton, and Dr. Margaret Trevitt. Conley, a suffragist who taught home economics in college and in the University Extension Department, was on the WFWC Home Economics Committee in 1908–12 and 1918–19. Shelton, WFWC corresponding secretary from 1914 to 1916, had been secretary of the Rhinelander Business and Loan Association and superintendent of Oneida County schools. Trevitt, a well-known Wausau physician, was a vice president from 1906–8.

These women were largely responsible for spreading suffrage support in the northern counties.

47. Steinschneider, "Not a New Woman," 50, 55.

48. Home Demonstration Agent, Marathon, WI, Annual Reports, 1 Dec. 1918 and 11 Dec. 1919, box 69, Series 9/4/3, CA, AE, UWMA.

49. Household Hints column, *Marathon County (WI) Farm Bureau Journal* 1.1 (June 1919): 10. Brady was soon reporting monthly on club activities in "The Marathon County Woman's Page."

50. *Marathon County (WI) Farm Bureau Journal* 1.2 (1919): 1, 6; 1.5 (Oct. 1919): 6; and 1.12 (May 1920): 1, 6; *The Wausau (WI) Pilot* (28 Sept. 1920): 1.4, gave additional names of township groups.

51. Hale organizations mentioned in Narrative Report, 1 Dec. 1921–Dec. 1922, Clark County (WI), box 19, and Annual Report, 7 Apr. 1923–15 Nov. 1925, Taylor County (WI), box 120, both Series 9/4/3, CA, AE, UWMA.

52. Narrative Report, Home Demonstration Work in Marathon County, 1 Nov. 1923, box 69, Series 9/4/3, CA, AE, UWMA.

53. McBride, *On Wisconsin Women*, 16, 19, 46; for Anneke, see John D. Buenker, "The Politics of Mutual Frustration: Socialists and Suffragists in New York and Wisconsin," in *Failed Liberation: Socialism and Feminism*, ed. Sally M. Miller (Westport, CT: Greenwood, 1981), 128–29, 134.

54. McBride *On Wisconsin Women*, 133, 199, 209–13.

55. McBride, *On Wisconsin Women*, 204, 220, 223.

56. Crystal Eastman, "Political Equality League," in *Crystal Eastman on Women and Revolution*, ed. Blanche Wiesen Cook (New York: Oxford University Press, 1978), 66–70.

57. History of the NLWS from Mariner to Louise Pfeiffer, 21 Oct. 1918, box 5; Daniel Hoan to Women's Club, 15 Feb. 1917, and Grace Parker, national NLWS leader, to Mariner, spring 1917, box 4, all in National League for Woman's Service (hereafter, NLWS), Correspondence, 1917–19, Mariner Family Papers, Manuscripts D, University of Wisconsin–Milwaukee (hereafter, UWMI).

58. Coordination in Mariner to Maude

Wetmore, 17 May 1917; Florence G. Buckstaff to Mrs. John W. Mariner, no date; Mariner to Grace Parker, 4 May 1917 and 31 Jan. 1918, to H. H. Morgan 1 June 1917, to Wetmore, 20 Apr. 1918 (quote); Anna Shaw to Wetmore, 30 Apr. 1918, all in NLWS, Correspondence, 1917–19, box 4, Mariner Family Papers, Manuscripts D, UWMI.

59. Mariner to Wetmore, 23 Sept. 1918, NLWS, Correspondence, 1917–19, box 4, Mariner Family Papers, Manuscripts D, UWMI.

60. For other countries and places, see "What Has Been Done in Other States to Meet the Farm Labor Shortage" and "Farm Work of Women in War Time," State Council of Defense (hereafter, SCD), World War I, box 23, Series 1647, WHSAD. Generally, midwestern men were not enthusiastic about recruiting women for field work, perhaps because of their own central role in producing food products and the lack of alternative jobs for men: Minutes, 23 Oct., 6 and 21 Nov., and 4 Dec. 1917, in Minutes of the Agricultural Committee, 1917–18, SCD, World War I, Series 1647, WHSAD.

61. Minutes of Woman's Advisory and Executive Committee Meeting, 3 May 1917, box 3, State Council of Defense, Woman's Committee (hereafter, SCDWC), World War I, Series 1649, WHSAD.

62. News releases, Apr. and 13 Aug. 1918, Publicity Committee, box 21; for state fair camp, see Minutes, Executive Committee Meeting, Woman's Committee, 25 May and 12 July 1918, and Final Report, Department Chairmen, box 3; comments about short courses and predictions of future needs are in 6 Nov. 1918 Form Letter to County and Local Chairman of Woman's Committee, box 6, all in SCDWC, Series 1649, WHSAD.

63. For home demonstration agent plans, see Minutes of the Statewide Conference of the Woman's Committee, 4–5 Feb. 1918, box 3, SCDWC, Series 1649, WHSAD.

64. Questionnaires on demobilization in box 23; discussion in Meeting Minutes, Woman's Advisory Committee of the SCD, 13 Dec. 1918, box 3, SCDWC, both Series 1649, WHSAD; for the NLWS's decline, see folder 9, 1919, NLWS, Correspondence, 1917–19, box 4, Mariner Family Papers, Manuscripts D, UWMI.

65. McBride, *On Wisconsin Women*, 290–91.

66. *Wausau (WI) Record Herald* (1 Nov. 1920): 4:6–7.

67. For the complicated local politics, see David L. Brye, *Wisconsin Voting Patterns in the Twentieth Century, 1900 to 1950* (New York: Garland, 1979), 83, 105, 300–301; James J. Lorence, "Socialism in Northern Wisconsin, 1910–1920: An Ethno-cultural Analysis," *Mid-America* 64 (Oct. 1982): 31; and James J. Lorence, "The Ethnic Impact of Wilson's War: The German-American in Marathon County, 1912–1916," *Wisconsin Academy of Sciences, Arts and Letters* 66 (1978): 113.

68. *Wausau (WI) Daily Record Herald* (2 Nov. 1920): 1:1.

69. James Howell Smith, "Mrs. Ben Hooper of Oshkosh: Peace Worker and Politician," *Wisconsin Magazine of History* 46 (Winter 1962–63): 124–35; *Wausau (WI) Daily Record Herald* (2 Nov. 1920): 1:5 and (4 Nov. 1920): 1:7, 2:1.

70. *Withee Memories*, 11; "Early Frenchtown History," mimeograph (1948), and Keskimeki Scrapbook, Book C, both Withee (WI) Public Library.

71. Centennial Committee, *100 Year Anniversary*, 139.

72. Klueter and Lorence, *Woodlot and Ballot Box*, 314–15, 317; Hering, "Country Doctor," 59–61.

73. Annual Report Narrative, 30 Nov. 1925, Taylor County (WI), box 120, Series 9/4/3, CA, AE, UWMA.

74. Annual Report, 30 Nov. 1920–30 Nov. 1921, Lincoln County (WI), box 60, Series 9/4/3, CA, AE, UWMA.

75. J. H. Kolb, *Service Institutions for Town and Country*, Research Bulletin 66 (Madison, WI: Agricultural Extension Station of the UW and U.S. Department of Agriculture Co-operating, 1925), 26.

76. Hilton, "Growing Up," 191, 193 for numbers; the overall percentage was five, and I am assuming at least half were young women. See also Joan M. Jensen, "Crossing Ethnic Barriers in the Southwest: Women's Agricultural Extension Education, 1914–1940, *Agricultural History* 60 (Spring 1986): 168–80. Most members were white, native born, and relatively well-off.

77. *Marathon County (WI) Farm Bureau Journal* 1:1 (June 1919): 18.

78. Ralph V. Brown, Annual Report, 1 Apr.–1 Dec. 1918, and copy of report "To the Honorable County Board of Supervisors of Clark County," undated, Clark County (WI), 1918–28, box 19, Series 9/4/3, CA, AE, UWMA.

79. R. A. Kolb, Annual Report, Dec. 1920–5 Dec. 1921, Taylor County (WI), box 120, Series 9/4/3, CA, AE, UWMA.

80. A. H. Cole, Annual Report, 1920, and Annual Report, 30 Nov. 1920–30 Nov. 1921, Lincoln County (WI), box 60, Series 9/4/3, CA, AE, UWMA.

81. In some townships, such as Colby and Granton, about one-third were young women; there were never as many girls as boys in the calf clubs. Brown, Annual Reports, 1 Apr.–1 Dec. 1918, 30 Nov. 1918–30 Nov. 1919, and H. M. Knipfel, Annual Narrative Report, 1 Dec. 1923–1 Dec. 1924, all Clark County (WI), box 19, Series 9/4/3, CA, AE, UWMA.

82. Photographs for Clark County (WI), Hulda Henze in Narrative Report, 1 Dec. 1922–1 Dec. 1923, box 19; numbers in Narrative Report, 1 Dec. 1923–1 Dec. 1924, Lucy Becker in Annual Report, 30 Nov. 1925, and Mildred Frieke in Annual Report, 30 Nov. 1925, Eau Claire Dells, Club Picnic, Marathon County (WI), all box 69, Series 9/4/3, CA, AE, UWMA; see also the *Marathon County (WI) Farm Bureau Journal* 1.5 (Oct. 1919): 10.

83. In 1896 the government hired two Indian women as field matrons: see Lisa E. Emmerich, "Marguerite LaFlesche Diddock, Office of Indian Affairs Field Matron," *Great Plains Quarterly* 18.3 (1993): 162–71, and Lisa E. Emmerich, "'Right in the Midst of My Own People': Native American Women and the Field Matron Program," *American Indian Quarterly* 15 (Spring 1991): 201–16; for a later teacher (1920s and 1930s), see Esther Burnett Horne and Sally McBeth, *Essie's Story: The Life and Legacy of a Shoshone Teacher* (Lincoln: University of Nebraska Press, 1998).

84. U.S. Congress, House of Representatives, *Report of the Secretary of the Interior*, Report of the Superintendent of Indian Schools, 54th Congress, 2nd Session, 1896, Doc. 5, vol. 2, 352–53.

85. Black River Falls, WI, *Banner-Journal* (3 July 1929): 1; for the Missionary Mazzuchelli, see "Documents Relating to the Catholic Church in Green Bay, and the Mission at Little Chute, 1825–40," in *Wisconsin Historical Collections* 14 (Madison, WI: The Society, 1898): 159.

86. Family background is from Black River Falls, WI, *Banner-Journal* 28 (3 July 1929): 1.

87. La Pointe Agency, Payroll Reports, 1874–1912, and Administrative Records of Employees, 1883–1927, both BIA, La Pointe, RG 75, NAGLR; Black River Falls, WI, *Banner-Journal* (20 Sept. 1939): 2.

88. Black River Falls, WI, *Banner-Journal* 28 (3 July 1929): 1; sometimes agents' specific requests to hire Native women were turned down by the bureau: see Rebecca J. Herring, "The Creation of Indian Farm Women: Field Matrons and Acculturation on the Kiowa-Comanche Reservation, 1895–1906," in *At Home on the Range: Essays on the History of Western Social and Domestic Life*, ed. John R. Wunder (Westport, CT: Greenwood, 1985), 47.

89. See Wendy Wall, "Gender and the 'Citizen Indian,'" in *Writing the Range*, 208, for the example of Round Valley reservation in California; I have found no equivalent study of the Wisconsin situation. Loew, "Newspapers," especially 1–3, discusses concepts of sovereignty and rights as citizens of Native nations; for the loss of annuities and the right to enroll children, see E. J. Bost to Emelie Rousseau, 26 Feb. 1910, Letters Sent, Wittenberg, 10 Nov. 1909–7 Mar. 1910, Series 349, RG 75, NAB; men normally retained these rights when marrying Euro-American women.

90. For homesteading and annuity claims, see E. J. Bost to Judge F. A. Jaeckel, 23 Apr. 1910, and list of homestead entries; for farming conditions on homesteaded land, see Bost to CIA, 10 Nov. 1909; for claim to men's annuity, see Bost to Kate Blackdeer, 22 Jan. 1910; for profits from land sales, see Bost to Allen L. Hall, 28 Jan. 1910, all in Letters Sent, Wittenberg, 10 Nov. 1909–7 Mar. 1910, Series 349, RG 75, NAB.

91. George Amour, "My Birthplace: The McCord Indian Village" (1992), and Harry Talbot, "Indian Village," both manuscripts in Wisconsin State Archeologist Office, Wisconsin Historical Society.

92. Sleeper-Smith, *Indian Women*, 118, 140 for becoming "invisible" in other parts of the Midwest.

93. The Borup-Beaulieu-Gordon dynasty can be traced in Nancy L. Woolworth, "Charles Borup, Fur Trader, Banker, Lumberman," 13–17, Biography Files, MHS; "Charles W. Gordon," *St. Paul Dispatch* (27 Nov. 1939): 1:4; and "Richards Gordon," in *Minnesota Biographies, 1655–1912*, ed. Warren Upham and Rose Barteau Dunlap (St. Paul: MHS, 1912), 266; various family histories are in the Charles W. Gordon Family Papers, MHS.

94. Pauline Brunette, "The Minneapolis Urban Indian Community," *Hennepin County (MN) History* 49.1 (Winter 1989–90): 5; see also Nancy Shoemaker, "Urban Indians and Ethnic Choices: American Indian Organizations in Minneapolis, 1920–1950," *Western Historical Quarterly* 19 (Nov. 1988): 431–47; Gerald Vizenor, *Interior Landscapes: Autobiographical Myths and Metaphors* (Minneapolis: University of Minnesota Press, 1990), 16; and Priscilla Buffalohead, "Emily Peake: A Biographical Sketch," in Pauline Brunette, et al., *Ojibway Family Life in Minnesota: 20th Century Sketches* (Coon Rapids, MN: Indian Education Program, Anoka-Hennepin School District, No. 11, 1989), 42–43. Peake's mother probably was Emily Robitaille: see Daniel F. Littlefield, Jr., and James W. Parins, *A Bibliography of Native American Writers, 1772–1924* (Metuchen, NJ: Scarecrow Press, 1981), 279.

95. M. Annette Jaimes with Theresa Halsey, "American Indian Women: At the Center of Indigenous Resistance in Contemporary North America," in Annette M. Jaimes, ed., *The State of Native America: Genocide, Colonization, and Resistance* (Boston, MA: South End Press, 1992), 311–44; Laura F. Klein and Lillian A. Ackerman, *Women and Power in Native North America* (Norman: University of Oklahoma Press, 1995), 12–15; Diane-Michele Prindeville, "Promoting a Feminist Policy Agenda: Indigenous Women Leaders and Closet Feminism," *Social Science Journal* 37.4 (2000): 637–45; Diane-Michele Prindeville, "Feminist Nations? A Study of Native American Women in Southwestern Tribal Politics," *Political Research Quarterly* 57.1 (Mar. 2004): 101–12.

Notes to Chapter 9

1. Census material for Milwaukee and Twin Cities from the U.S. Department of Commerce, Bureau of the Census, *Fourteenth Census of the United States Taken in the Year 1920*, vol. 1 (Washington, DC: GPO, 1921), Hennepin County, MN, 473; Ramsey County, MN, 480; Milwaukee County, WI, 672; and U. S. Department of Commerce, Bureau of the Census, *Fifteenth Census of the United States: 1930*, Population, vol. III, pt. 1 (Washington, DC: GPO, 1932), Minnesota, 1187; Wisconsin, 1305.

2. Minnesota Bureau of Labor, Notice to Young Women and Girls, 1910, negative 32677, Visual Resources Database, MHS.

3. Elizabeth Faue, *Community of Suffering and Struggle: Women, Men, and the Labor Movement in Minneapolis, 1915–1945* (Chapel Hill: University of North Carolina Press, 1991), 24–27, deals briefly with the period before the Depression; Meridel Le Sueur, *The Girl* (Albuquerque, NM: West End Press, 1978; rev. ed., 1990), based on 1930s accounts, is the most powerful depiction of a young woman who did not fare well in the Twin Cities.

4. Jantsch, "The Jantsch Saga," 15, 26.

5. Minnesota Department of Labor and Industries, Bureau of Women and Children (hereafter, BWC), *Women in Industry in Minnesota in 1918* (St. Paul, MN: The Bureau, 1920), 17–18; for examples of these women, see 1918 Women in Industry Survey, Guiterman Brothers, 327 and 371, Microfilm SAM 222, Reel 13, MHS.

6. Louise Klapp to Mary Starkweather, 20 May 1911, and Ericson to Peterson, 1 and 17 Nov. 1913, BWC, Correspondence, box 1, MHS; see also "Survey of Female Employees Who Do Not Live at Home With Parents, May 22, 1915," box 3, Donaldson Company Records, MHS.

7. *Women in Industry*, 18; Hennepin County (MN) Survey Sheet, 10/12/18, #1557, Microfilm SAM 222, Reel 5, MHS.

8. Joel Thoreson, "Palaces of Dreams: Minneapolis Department Stores," *Hennepin County (MN) History* 49.2 (Spring 1990): 15–17.

9. For other welfare policies of the time, see Susan Porter Benson, *Counter Cultures: Saleswomen, Managers, and Customers in American Department Stores, 1890–1940* (Urbana: University of Illinois Press, 1986), 142–46.

10. R. L. Haw, treasurer, to L. S. Donaldson, 26 Aug. 1911, box 3, 14.372, folder 3; clubwomen reformers pressured department stores to maintain early closing, 5 Mar. 1914, box 3, 14.372, folder 3, both in Donaldson Company Records, MHS.

11. Sect. Chas. R. Lane, Memo, Department Store Group of Minneapolis Retailers Association, box 3, 14.372, folder 3, Donaldson Company Records, MHS.

12. Bob Gustafson, "Memories of Timmer," in "The American Jantsch Family Saga, Third Edition" (computer printout, 1998), 47–53.

13. I tracked the residences of my aunt and mother and their future husbands through manuscript census and city registers. The continued importance of income from boarders for urban married working-class women is traced in Joan M. Jensen, "Cloth, Butter, and Boarders: Women's Household Production for the Market," *The Review of Radical Political Economics* 12 (Summer 1980): 14–24.

14. For remittances from children, see Oded Stark, *Economic-Demographic Interactions in Agricultural Development: The Case of Rural-to-Urban Migration* (Rome, Italy: Food and Agriculture Organizations of the United Nations, 1978), 35–41; Bridget Hillk, "Rural-Urban Migration of Women and Their Employment in Towns," *Rural History* 5.2 (Oct. 1994): 191; Jantsch, "The Jantsch Saga," recounts gifts but no regular contributions to the family economy; Schopper-Schopp family history supplied by Mary Ann Schopper Reynolds.

15. Xan, *Wisconsin: My Home*, 150; the pattern was already clear in the 1850s: see Laurence A. Glasco, "The Life Cycles and Household Structure of American Ethnic Groups: Irish, Germans, and Native-born Whites in Buffalo, New York, 1855," *Journal of Urban History* 1 (May 1975): 339–64.

16. Xan, *Wisconsin: My Home*, 150.

17. Xan, *Wisconsin: My Home*, 149, 118.

18. My grandmother and many other immigrant women worked at boarding houses located near lumber camps and towns; Mary Ann Schopper Reynolds helped supply this family history.

19. Wisconsin, Bureau of Labor, Census, and Industrial Statistics, *7th Biennial Report* (Madison, WI: The State, 1894–96.

20. Xan, *Wisconsin: My Home*, 150.

21. In 1861 Marathon County stretched northward from Wood County to the Canadian border; Lincoln County was carved out of it in 1874. Statistics for Marathon County (WI) are from U.S. Department of Commerce, Bureau of the Census, *Fourteenth Census*, Population, vol. 1, 672.

22. Lac du Flambeau Industrial Survey, 1922; Menominee Industrial Survey, 1922–25.

23. Melissa L. Meyer, *The White Earth Tragedy: Ethnicity and Dispossession at a Minnesota Anishinaabe Reservation, 1889–1920* (Lincoln: University of Nebraska Press, 1994), 205, discusses women's preference to remain on the land.

24. Lac du Flambeau Industrial Survey, 1922.

25. Donaldson's 1915 survey, box 3, Donaldson Company Records, MHS.

26. Peterson to Mrs. Amanda Bollie, 27 Feb. 1914, Peterson to Miss Pearl Orand, folder July–Dec. 1915, BWC, Correspondence, box 1, MHS.

27. Jantsch, "The Jantsch Saga," 26.

28. Bettie Smith, letter to the author, 30 Oct. 2001.

29. For the work of welfare agencies, see Beverly Ann Stadum, "'Maybe They Will Appreciate What I Done and Struggled': Poor Women and Their Families: Charity Cases in Minneapolis, 1900–1930." (PhD thesis, University of Minnesota, 1987); welfare agencies tried to get work for poor women when they could.

30. Alice H. Wood to Mrs. Thomas Winter, 3 Aug. 1917, Minnesota Public Safety Commission (hereafter, MPSC), Woman's Committee, Committee on Women in Industry, Correspondence and Subject Files, 103.K.7.13B, MHS; see Stephanie A. Carpenter, *On the Farm Front: The Women's Land Army in World War II* (De Kalb: Northern Illinois University Press, 2003), 15–19, for attitudes towards women's labor during World War I.

31. For Dunwoody's Institute, see William Millikan, *A Union Against Unions: The Minneapolis Citizens Alliance and Its Fight Against Organized Labor, 1903–1947* (St. Paul: MHS Press, 2001), 65–72; see also John W. Larson "'The Best School in the City,' 1896–1916, Mechanic Arts High School: Its First Twenty Years," *Ramsey County (MN) History* 37.1 (Spring 2002): 4–9.

32. Jantsch, "The Jantsch Saga," 28.

33. Globe Business College, St. Paul, MN, undated pamphlet showing twenty-five in the class of 1913, 13, 36, 38; Albert H. Briest, Student Materials from Globe Business College, 1915; Printed Course Materials, folder 2, Globe Business College, Manuscripts Notebooks, P2070, all MHS.

34. Linda Mack Schloff, *'And Prairie Dogs Weren't Kosher': Jewish Women in the Upper Midwest Since 1855* (St. Paul: MHS Press, 1996), 129.

35. David Mauk, e-mail to author, 19 Dec. 2000, estimated that in 1900 only about 14 percent of foreign born and women with foreign-born Norwegian parents were servants; this figure dropped to ten percent in the next decade; few black women who lived in the Twin Cities worked as maids either: Faue, *Community of Suffering,* 196; Era Bell Thompson, *American Daughter* (St. Paul: MHS Press, 1986), 213.

36. Joy Kathleen Lintelman, "'More Freedom, Better Pay': Single Swedish Women in the United States, 1880–1920" (PhD thesis, University of Minnesota, 1991); Louise Klapp to Mary E. Starkweather, 25 Feb. and 3 Mar. 1911, Correspondence, BWC, 115.H.19.2F, MHS.

37. Lars Olsson, "Evelina Johansdotter, Textile Workers and the Munsinger Family: Class, Gender, and Ethnicity in the Political Economy of Minnesota at the End of World War I," in *Swedes in the Twin Cities: Immigrant Life and Minnesota's Urban Frontier,* ed. Philip J. Anderson and Dag Blanck (St. Paul: MHS Press, 2000), 77–90.

38. 1918 Women in Industry Survey, Golden Rule, 222, Microfilm SAM 222, Reel 14, MHS; *Golden Rule Store News,* 1919–1920, MHS, discusses work and play.

39. 1918 Women in Industry Survey, Michaud Brothers, 831, Microfilm SAM 222, Reel 13, MHS.

40. See Joanne J. Meyerowitz, *Women Adrift: Independent Wage Earners in Chicago, 1880–1930* (Chicago: University of Chicago Press, 1988), 64–68, 118–20.

41. Minnesota Labor and Industrial Department (hereafter, MLID), Biennial Reports, Minimum Wage Commission, *First Biennial Report, August 1, 1914 to December 3, 1914* (St. Paul, MN: The Department, 1914), 4, 24, 30, 37, MHS.

42. Biography in Mary Dillon Foster, comp., *Who's Who Among Minnesota Women* (St. Paul, MN: The Compiler, 1924), 250; obituary, *St. Paul Dispatch* (20 Apr. 1939): 10.

43. Agnes L. Peterson to J. W. Hamilton, 22 Jan. 1914, and Peterson to Mrs. Agnes L. Atwood, Duluth, 24 Feb. 1914, box 1, BWC, Correspondence, MHS.

44. Agnes L. Peterson to Mrs. H. S. Webster, 22 Aug. 1918, and reply from Webster on back of letter, box 2, Records of the Committee on Women in Industry, 1918–19, Correspondence, MPSC, Woman's Committee, MHS. I have not tabulated these responses, but the conditions of some toilets seemed truly abysmal.

45. Report, Sept.-Oct. 1919, Main Files, MPSC, MHS.

46. Sander D. Genis Oral History, interview by James Dooley, 6 Nov. 1974, 10–11, 16, Sander Genis Papers, MHS.

47. Minnesota Labor and Industrial Department, Trade Union Reports, Local 171, MHS, describes an all-female union (it had one male member) whose members received a 25 percent increase in wages during these two years; Carl H. Chrislock, *Watchdog of Loyalty: The Minnesota Commission of Public Safety During World War I* (St. Paul: MHS

Press, 1991), 236–37, 246–47, says Peterson did not advocate for women's wage increases but for child conservation; he does not analyze what she did for women.

48. MLID, Biennial Reports, Minnesota Minimum Wage Commission, *First Biennial Report*, 24–28, 37, 41.

49. MLID, Biennial Reports, Minnesota Minimum Wage Commission, *First Biennial Report*, 21, 22, 32, 37; *St. Paul Pioneer Press* (16 July 1914) and the Minneapolis *Labor Review*, which reported the divisive meeting on 17 July 1914, asked workers to support a "living wage" for women and pronounced the working woman the "wage slave of Minnesota," both clippings in box 3, folder 2, Donaldson Company Records, MHS.

50. Letters and notes relating to this campaign are in Employees: Minimum Wage, 1915, 1918, folder 5, 14.372, Donaldson Company Records, MHS.

51. The Catlin decision was reprinted in MLID, Biennial Reports, Minnesota Minimum Wage Commission, *Second Biennial Report, April 1, 1918 to January 15, 1921* (St. Paul, MN: The Department, 1921), 61–64, MHS.

52. MLID, Biennial Reports, Minnesota Minimum Wage Commission, *Second Biennial Report*, 65–71; *Williams v. Evans*, et al., *A. M. Ramer Co. v. Same*, 165 N.W. 495 (21 Dec. 1917).

53. Florence H. Harriman to Mrs. T. G. Winter, 2 Nov. 1917, MPSC, Women's Committee; Peterson to Winter, 31 June 1917, 103.K.7.13B, Report May-June 1918, 103.L.7.6; and Peterson to Winter, 31 July 1917, Women in Industry, Correspondence and Reports, MPSC, Women's Committee, all MHS.

54. MLID, Biennial Reports, Minimum Wage Commission, *Second Biennial Report*, 13–15.

55. Circular 35, MPSC, Women's Committee, MHS.

56. *Women in Industry*, 6–8; see also MLID, Biennial Reports, Minimum Wage Commission, *Second Biennial Report*, 14, 25; Carl H. Chrislock, *The Progressive Era in Minnesota, 1899–1918* (St. Paul: MHS Press, 1971), 181, 188; Barbara Stuhler, *Gentle Warriors: Clara Ueland and the Minnesota Struggle for*

Woman Suffrage (St. Paul: MHS Press, 1995), 194–95.

57. All information on the Tinucci family is from their family archives; my thanks to Fran Tinucci Belford, who assembled the collection.

58. Schloff, '*Prairie Dogs*,' 125.

59. Evelyn Fairbanks, *Days of Rondo* (St. Paul: MHS Press, 1990), 56.

60. O. E. (Ole Edvart) Rölvaag, *The Boat of Longing* (New York: Harper, 1933), 89–92.

61. Jantsch, "The Jantsch Saga," 3–4, describes Adam and Eve and the Colby shorts.

62. Tera W. Hunter, *To 'Joy My Freedom: Southern Black Women's Lives and Labors after the Civil War* (Cambridge, MA: Harvard University Press, 1997), 168, 180.

63. Robert C. Allen, *Horrible Prettiness: Burlesque and American Culture* (Chapel Hill: University of North Carolina Press, 1991), 225–32, discusses the introduction of the cooch in 1893; the lines from "Meet Me in St. Louis," are from Theodore Raph, *The Songs We Sang: A Treasury of American Popular Music* (New York: Castle Books, 1964), 296–99.

64. Ann Wagner, *Adversaries of Dance* (Urbana: University of Illinois Press, 1997), 241, 255–56, 303.

65. Wagner, *Adversaries of Dance*, 296–301.

66. Jantsch, "Second American Jantsch Generation," 19.

67. A good summary of this research on women's work is in Faue, *Community of Suffering*, 1–20; George W. Hill and Ronald A. Smith, *Rural Relief Trends in Wisconsin from 1934 to 1937* (Madison: UW Press, 1939).

68. See photographs in *The Excelsior Amusement Park from Rise to Demise, 1924–1974* (Excelsior, MN: Excelsior–Lake Minnetonka Historical Society, 1991), 18; and Karal Ann Marling, "Thrills and Nostalgia: The Amusement Parks of Hennepin County," *Hennepin History* 49.4 (Fall 1990): 13–32.

69. Anna Schopper died in St. Paul in 1974 at seventy-seven. Three other Schopper-Schopp sisters went to Milwaukee and Chicago: Rose died in New Jersey in 1977 at seventy-eight; Bertha in Milwaukee in 1999 at ninety-nine; and Emma in New York in 2001 at ninety-three.

Notes to Epilogue

1. The memory is mine, the spelling from Chase S. Osborn and Stellanova Osborn, *Schoolcraft—Longfellow—Hiawatha* (Lancaster, PA: Jacques Cattell Press, 1942), 129.

2. Osborn and Osborn, *Schoolcraft,* especially 75–98 for Susan's life; for School-craft, see Richard G. Bremer, *Indian Agent and Wilderness Scholar: The Life of Henry Rowe Schoolcraft* (Mount Pleasant, MI: Clark Historical Library, Central Michigan University, 1987); Susan's account books are listed as Item 327 in RG 75, National Archives and Records Administration, Chicago, IL.

Note on Sources

The women who populated north-central Wisconsin mostly did not leave their own accounts. By using a variety of research sources and methods, I have tried to give them a collective part in telling their stories. For a few, enough biographical information exists to create stories of their lives. Others make cameo appearances. Yet others form a background ensemble, adding voices and actions at various points in the larger story.

Three types of literary sources are included in this study. As I searched for history of the women in my own family, personal and familial sources accumulated. Other families shared their memories and collections with me. Archives offered many sources. Official government documents generated at the federal, state, and county levels and the private collections of individuals and institutions such as the Catholic nuns gave me their views but also a great deal of information on women with whom they came in contact. In addition, I have used photographs extensively in this research to elaborate on subjects mentioned in written documents and to suggest topics not mentioned in writings. The written sources range from major collections of documents and letters in the National Archives and National Anthropological Archives in Washington, DC, to regional collections at the National Archives Great Lakes Region in Chicago, the Wisconsin Historical Society, and the Minnesota Historical Society. I consulted more than one hundred individual series and manuscript collections at the Wisconsin Historical Society alone. I also found important material in out-of-the-way places, such as the Sisters of the Sorrowful Mother convent in Broken Arrow, Oklahoma, which preserved accounts by the nuns who started the first hospitals in northern Wisconsin. I looked for relevant archival sources in Germany and Czechos-

lovakia while on a Fulbright Fellowship and learned much in general about German emigration. I chose to focus on the experiences of immigrants after they arrived in north-central Wisconsin because there was little scholarly research on German immigrant women, especially on late-nineteenth-century migration from the Austro-Hungarian Empire.

The published material I used is cited in the endnotes. Much of it is older, well known, and available in libraries. Here I single out a few of the most recent publications for their importance in introducing readers to new research questions and methods.

Native American history is flourishing. The most recent overviews of Wisconsin Native nations are Patty Loew, *Indian Nations of Wisconsin: Histories of Endurance and Renewal* (Madison: Wisconsin Historical Society Press, 2001), and Nancy Oestreich Lurie, *Wisconsin Indians* (Madison: Wisconsin Historical Society Press, 2002). The Menominee Nation has published two volumes on its own history: *Menominee Tribal History Guide: Commemoration Wisconsin Sesquicentennial, 1848–1998* (Keshena: Menominee Indian Tribe of Wisconsin, 1998) and *Menominee Indian Reservation Historical Review: Commemorating the Reservation Sesquicentennial, 1854–2004* (Keshena: Menominee Indian Tribe of Wisconsin, 2004). Elizabeth M. Tornes, *Memories of Lac du Flambeau Elders* (Madison, WI: Center for the Study of Upper Midwestern Cultures, 2004), contains a history of the Lac du Flambeau Chippewa Indians along with elders' comments. The Ho-Chunk, Menominee, and Lac du Flambeau Chippewa web pages also provide a great deal of tribal history. Brian Hosmer and Colleen O'Neill, eds., *Native Pathways: American Indian Culture and Economic Development in the Twentieth Century* (Boulder: University

Press of Colorado, 2004), collects some of the most recent scholarly research on Native economies, including that of the Menominee Nation. Native education is an especially critical aspect of Indian history: Margaret L. Archuleta, ed., *Away From Home: American Indian Boarding School Experiences, 1879–2000* (Phoenix, AZ: The Heard Museum, 2000), contains several illuminating essays by Brenda J. Child and others. See also the overview by Jon Reyhner and Jeanne Eder, *American Indian Education: A History* (Norman: University of Oklahoma Press, 2004). Carter Jones Meyer and Diana Royer, eds., *Selling the Indian: Commercializing and Appropriating American Indian Cultures* (Tucson: University of Arizona Press, 2001), introduces many of the issues in which tourism and Native arts intersect. Lucy Eldersveld Murphy, "Public Mothers: Native American and Métis Women as Creole Mediators in the Nineteenth-Century Midwest," *Journal of Women's History* 14.4 (Winter 2003): 141–66, and Susan Sleeper-Smith, *Indian Women and French Men: Rethinking Cultural Encounter in the Western Great Lakes* (Amherst: University of Massachusetts Press, 2001), suggest new ways to look at women of Métis cultures.

Several recent works define new ways of studying rural women's lives. The special issue on rural women's history, *Frontiers* 22.1 (2001), is the best introduction to recent work in the field. For midwestern rural women, Mary Neth, *Preserving the Family Farm: Women, Community, and the Foundations of Agribusiness in the Midwest, 1900–1940* (Baltimore, MD: Johns Hopkins University Press, 1995), remains the most important analysis of government policies and settler resistance to them.

Specialized works offer detailed examinations of specific topics. Pamela Riney-Kehrberg, *Childhood on the Farm: Work, Play, and Coming of Age in the Midwest* (Lawrence: University Press of Kansas, 2005), 158–81, takes a close look at children's importance in the rural Midwest. Jane Pederson, *Between Memory and Reality: Family and Community in Rural Wisconsin, 1870–1970* (Madison: University of Wisconsin Press,

1992), describes rural Wisconsin families in an area with a large Norwegian immigrant population. Linda Pickle, *Contented Among Strangers: Rural German-Speaking Women and Their Families in the Nineteenth-Century Midwest* (Urbana: University of Illinois Press, 1996), and Barbara Handy-Marchello, *Women of the Northern Plains: Gender and Settlement on the Homestead Frontier, 1870–1930* (St. Paul: Minnesota Historical Society Press, 2005), offer important insights into women's lives on other midwestern frontiers. David R. Reynolds, *There Goes the Neighborhood: Rural School Consolidation at the Grass Roots in Early Twentieth Century Iowa* (Iowa City: University of Iowa Press, 1999), suggests issues that may have caused rural communities to resist this particular Progressive reform. Elizabeth Faue, *Community of Suffering and Struggle: Women, Men, and the Labor Movement in Minneapolis, 1915–1945* (Chapel Hill: University of North Carolina Press, 1991), remains the best source for women's urban labor although it is skimpy on the period before the 1930s. And, at last, there is an excellent collection of writings on Wisconsin women edited by Genevieve G. Mcbride, *Women's Wisconsin: From Native Matriarchies to the New Millennium* (Madison: Wisconsin Historical Society Press, 2005).

Robert C. Ostergren and Thomas R. Vale, eds., *Wisconsin Land and Life* (Madison: University of Wisconsin Press, 1997), introduces a wide range of approaches to the cultural geography of Wisconsin. Far too little research has followed up on these issues. For the intersection of science and culture see especially Steven R. Hoffbeck, "'Without Careful Consideration': Why Carp Swim in Minnesota's Waters," *Minnesota History* 57.6 (Summer 2001): 305–20, which brings together the history of tourism, environment, and government policy relevant for Wisconsin's waters. Alan L. Olmstead and Paul W. Rhode, "An Impossible Undertaking: The Eradication of Bovine Tuberculosis in the United States," *Journal of Economic History* 64 (September 2004): 734–72, underscores the importance of that campaign. For learning to "read" the

Wisconsin landscape, there is still no better book than Margaret Beattie Bogue's *Around the Shores of Lake Michigan: A Guide to Historic Sites* (Madison: University of Wisconsin Press, 1985).

For the European background of rural Irish, German, Swedish, and Polish women, see Christiane Harzig, ed., *Peasant Maids—City Women: From the European Countryside to Urban America* (Ithaca, NY: Cornell University Press, 1997). Catherine Albrecht, "Rural Banks and Czech Nationalism in Bohemia, 1848–1914," *Agricultural History* 78.3 (Summer 2004): 317–45, elaborates on the rural economic conditions in Bohemia.

Index

Page numbers in *italic* refer to illustrations

Illustration Credits

Calling This Place Home was designed at Minnesota Historical Society Press by Will Powers, and composed into pages by Allan Johnson at Phoenix Type, Milan, Minnesota. Printed by Thomson-Shore, Dexter, Michigan.